THE COMPLETE BOOK OF THE WORLD RALLY CHAMPIONSHIP

First published in 2004 by Motorbooks International, an imprint of MBI Publishing Company,
Galtier Plaza, Suite 200, 380 Jackson Street, St. Paul, MN 55101-3885 USA

Motorbooks International titles are also available at discounts in bulk quantity for industrial or sales-promotional use.
For details write to Special Sales Manager at Motorbooks International Wholesalers & Distributors, Galtier Plaza, Suite 200, 380 Jackson Street, St. Paul, MN 55101-3885 USA.

ISBN 0-7603-1954-5
Printed in China

HENRY HOPE-FROST
& JOHN DAVENPORT

MOTORBOOKS
INTERNATIONAL

THE COMPLETE BOOK OF THE WORLD RALLY CHAMPIONSHIP

CONTENTS

champeau
SUBARU
DATSUN
Castrol
DUNLOP
ENKEI
9

FOREWORD: CARLOS SAINZ

DOUBLE WORLD RALLY CHAMPION AND WINNER OF 25 WORLD CHAMPIONSHIP RALLIES

I am very pleased to have been invited to introduce you to The Complete Book of The World Rally Championship – a celebration of 30 years of the World Rally Championship. For me, the World Rally Championship has meant so many good things over the years.

My first WRC win was on the Acropolis Rally in Greece in 1990 and that was quite a big moment for me. Winning the famous rallies like Monte Carlo, Safari, 1000 Lakes (Finland) and RAC (Great Britain) gives you a special sense of achievement, even if you may sometimes have to fight much harder to win one of the other rallies.

I remember when I won my first drivers' title back in 1990. I was proud to have done something so positive for our sport in Spain. The following year we had our first Spanish contribution to the WRC, the Rally of Catalunya, which has proved to be an enormous hit and is very popular with both spectators and drivers.

I would not say that I have a favourite kind of rally. I like them all, especially if I have a good car. In that respect I have been fortunate in that I have always had the most fantastic support from the teams with whom I have driven – Ford, Toyota, Lancia, Subaru and now Citroën. The support from the spectators round the world has been amazing too. They all seem to think El Matador is fighting for them!

I have been driving in the World Rally Championship now for 18 years and it is a marvellous environment in which to work. The TV and media coverage is now the best it has ever been and with new rallies coming in, it is becoming a true World Championship. I am very happy to be a part of it and I hope that you will enjoy reading this book and discovering for yourself more about this great sport.

Carlos Sainz Madrid, February 2004

carlos-sainz.com
SPORT

INTRODUCTION

As a small boy I would often walk round corners in my parents' house, pulling on an imaginery handbrake and deftly crossing my arms and twisting my shoulders as I applied 'opposite lock'. I guess it was my way of appreciating – understanding, even – the heroic exploits of men with then unpronouncable names doing insane things in motor cars.

I was hooked on rallying at about the same time I got to grips with solid food and my imagination would work overtime. I well knew what was happening when a Ford Escort appeared to swap ends each time it went round a corner and I well knew why Lancia's Stratos sounded as wonderful as it did. With a former BMC engineer and amateur racer/rallier for a father, I could hardly be blamed!

When I reached double figures and had firmly made-up my mind that one of those Escorts would, one day, have my name on it, the end of November became my favourite time of year. Trips to the RAC – my 'local' World Championship rally – were life-changing events. School could go hang, as long as I could stand somewhere in the fog, the rain, the cold and the wind with the Old Man and see my heroes pulling on their handbrakes and crossing their arms.

To be priviledged enough to be here compiling a book commemorating 30 years of the World Rally Championship is thrilling and the perfect way to off-load a little bit of that 'sideways fever' – there never was an Escort with my name on it!

As the adage goes: those who can do, and those who can't write about it. That applies very aptly to me but not in any way to John Davenport, my learned co-writer. John has been there, sat in it, won it, organised it and written about it. It's been a very great pleasure to work with a man who won the 1000 Lakes when I was three (sorry, John!) and who knows more about this great sport than I ever will. Thanks JD, hope you enjoyed it as much as I did?

Thanks also to my 66 'heroes' and their co-drivers who have entertained, enthralled and inspired for 30 years.

Henry Hope-Frost London, February 2004

HENRY HOPE-FROST

JOHN DAVENPORT

01

THE HISTORY

World Championship rallying in the 21st century is as high-tech a global sport as anything else on the calendar. The cars bristle with cutting-edge electronics and exotic materials. The drivers and co-drivers are, in the main, finely honed athletes paid handsomely for their efforts. But it was not always like this and in its 30-year history, the World Rally Championship has undergone a wide range of evolutions, not always painless. There was a time when followers of the sport were lucky to hear the results of an event within a week of it finishing, assuming they knew it had even started, but now they can enjoy the action as it happens thanks to increasingly sophisticated technology.

This technology includes satellites that track each car and transmit times to computers to provide instant information and results. On-board cameras, as well as those in helicopters and on the ground provide thrills on TV. But rallying, in short, is not as easy to televise or to present in a coherent fashion as racing where, unless one has the complication of pit stops, almost anyone can see who is leading at any moment. Thus it is

Some things never change. Whether it was 1973 or 2003, rallying has always been about drivers making cars do impossible things in extreme conditions. Airborne in the snow - impossible. Not for a rally driver it's not...

SWEDEN
PA57006
SAAB V4
PA·57006

Throughout its 30-year history the World Rally Championship has been contested by the supercars of the day, even though some may have been considered pretty basic by modern standards. Without a doubt, however, Lancia's Stratos (below right) and Audi's fearsome Quattro (top right) qualify as supercars by any standards. And at the end of the day the thing that mattered most was who got to open the champagne (above)!

"In its 30-year history, the World Rally Championship has undergone a wide range of evolutions, not always painless"

surprising – and a measure of the strength of appeal that rallying possesses – that a World Rally Championship has existed for very much longer than world-wide television coverage of the sport.

In the beginning of the 20th century when rallying – and motor racing – were in their cradle, there was no such thing as global or even regional championships. Even in the period up to World War II, rallies stood on their individual reputation and car manufacturers would advertise their success in a Monte Carlo Rally, Liège-Rome-Liège, RAC Rally of Great Britain or an Alpine Rally on its own merits. For a time, this was also the case in the post-war era when the big rallies revived and lots of new events – Acropolis (Greece), Rally to the Midnight Sun (Sweden), 1000 Lakes (Finland), Tulip (Holland), Viking (Norway) and Sestriere (Italy) joined the established pre-war events.

From the very early days, car manufacturers had supported rallying and in some cases gone so far as to enter teams. The Rolls Royce factory sent cars to the 1914 Austrian Alpenfahrt, the forerunner of the Alpine Rally, to take on the might of Austro-Daimler, Fiat, Benz, Opel, Mercedes and Horch.

Rallying is a sport of contrasts with the stars and their cars contesting events on a variety of surfaces that are constantly changing. Mud and dust call for different tactics but the challenge remains the same

Overleaf: Some of the biggest contrasts ever seen in the sport came on the African events such as the Safari. Where else would you see 21st century technology rubbing shoulders with the most basic lifestyle, epitomised by this Subaru passing the mud huts of a Kenyan village

MICHELIN
HB Audi TEAM
Castrol

Such interest continued through the inter-war years but it was not the kind of manufacturer involvement that we now know.The cars were not highly developed versions bearing but a passing resemblance to a road car – they were relatively unmodified. Thus it was relatively cheap to lend them to private individuals and enter as a team under the factory name. If they won or did well, then the manufacturer could use the results in its advertisements. The whole thing was not much more than an extension of the press fleet.

As rallying began to take off in quite a big way at the start of the 1950s, manufacturers were involved but not committed. The important thing for the rally organisers was still the individual entry and the individual driver. When the idea of a European Championship was first mooted, the governing body, the FIA (Federation Internationale de l'Automobile) and its Sporting Committee (the CSI – Commission Sportive International) who comprised many people involved in the organisation of events, quite naturally came up with the concept of a championship for drivers. People were more important than cars.

Interestingly, its title was 'The European Touring Car Championship'. Today, we would think that this meant that it was restricted to saloon cars but in fact the adjective 'touring' meant any car in which you might go driving round the mountains. 'Grand touring cars' in the shape of sports cars of all shapes and sizes were equally acceptable. The championship comprised 10 'classic' rallies – Monte Carlo, Sestriere, RAC, Tulip, German, Swedish, Alpine, Liège, Viking and Portugal. For each driver, the best four results counted, so by winning the German and the Alpine - and finishing second on the Viking and third in Portugal - Helmut Polensky emerged as the clear victor. Interestingly he had used a Fiat 1100, a Lancia Aurelia and a Porsche 1500 Super to claim the title.

This championship went from strength to strength during the 1950s. By the time the 1960s and the first proper works teams had arrived it had done a wonderful job in strengthening the public appreciation of rallying as well as

Far left above and below: Rally cars fight for seconds through the African bush or narrow ribbons of Alpine asphalt

Left: The World Rally Championship attracts the biggest car manufacturers in the world with European car giants rubbing shoulders with their Japanese counterparts

Overleaf: Battered and bruised they rise to the challenge

Eriksson
Parmander
SUBARU
RALLIART

TOYOTA

making each event more attractive to competitors. In 1960, there were 12 rallies with names now familiar to us such as Acropolis and 1000 Lakes joining the original list.

Two other events, which would have made the total 14, were included but were not held. Walter Schock won the championship for Mercedes driving a 220SE but he was chased hard by René Trautmann in a Citröen ID19 in the latter part of the season. In fact, the championship all came down to who would do best on the final event of the season, the RAC Rally, now moved from its March date.

When Trautmann crashed on the first night, Schock did not endear himself to the rally world by packing up and going home with his title secure. This was the first sign, perhaps, that professionalism had arrived and that people were competing more for the title than for the sport.

More signs were evident the following year. On the Tulip Rally, Geoff Mabbs was able to win outright in his Triumph Herald by the sacrifice of team mate 'Tiny' Lewis since the results were based on class improvement or, in simple terms, the size of the gap between the fastest and next fastest in the class. By withdrawing, Lewis gave Mabbs the victory.

Japanese manufacturers have been winning events throughout the championship's history but as title-winners they only sprang to the fore in the late nineties. Bizarrely there was never a Japanese round of the series in the first 30 years of the championship but that has now been rectified

Opposite page: Tommi Makinen's four consecutive World Championship crowns between 1996-1998 is a record that is unlikely to be beaten for some time. Despite hitting the big time relatively late, the Mitsubishi-driving Finn was a dominant force once he arrived on the scene although, as the picture (bottom right) shows he wasn't completely infallible!

This page: The China Rally (above) made a one-off appearance in the series in 1999 but Australia (left) has establisheditself as one of the most popular events on the calendar

And on the Mille Miglia, revived after its 1955 debacle as a rally, Volvo works driver, Gunnar Andersson, bought a Ferrari and won the event. Andersson scored the points alongside those accumulated in his Volvo to lead at the halfway point and wind up second in the championship, just 11 points behind the winner, Hans-Joachim Walter, driving a Porsche.

The European Championship continued through the 1960s. It lost some of its traditional events when the Liège ceased running as a road event after 1964 and the Alpine ran into financial problems that saw it finally fail in the early 1970s. It gained some events from behind the Iron Curtain like the East German, Polish and Czechoslovakian rallies and normally counted 16 events towards its titles. Yes, that was 'titles' in the plural. When the FIA introduced their new Groups for cars in 1966, they also decided that there should be a European Rally Championship title for each of the Groups.

Gone but not forgotten. The recent trend towards compact routes taking no more than three days means that many classic images of the sport have sadly been consigned to the history books. Parc ferme in historic towns in Tuscany (right) and spectacular roads along the Corsican coastline (above) are no longer accessible to modern WRC events - more's the pity

Overleaf: Whether it is sunlit hillsides in Wales or the snow and ice of the famous Col du Turini (on the Monte Carlo Rally), spectators will trek for miles to see their heroes in action

Agip

TOYOTA
Castrol

MICHELIN
P4 MRE

This meant that the unmodified cars of Group 1 had a champion, as did the tuned saloon cars of Group 2 and the standard GT cars of Group 3.

This was not one of the great success stories of our time. It diminished the value of a single title and diversified the efforts of an increasing number of works teams. Many of them who had no budget to contest 16 rallies decided to revert to the old idea of just doing those events where a good result could be trumpeted in its own right. It took a couple of years and then the FIA acted. Half the events in 1968 would count for a European Drivers' Championship while the other half would count for a European Constructors Championship. As it turned out, 15 events ran of the 17 chosen with the split going seven to the drivers and eight to the manufacturers.

The problem was that the Drivers' events included the Monte, the Acropolis and the 1000 Lakes while the Swedish, San Remo and RAC were Constructors' events. What should a factory team do ? Miss key events and go for the manufacturers' crown ? It was not a happy solution even though it was an improvement and went a long way towards satisfying a genuine need for the car manufacturers to have something positive to say about their product. Ford of Britain won that year and could thus happily put a sticker on all Ford Escorts saying that the Escort had won the European Rally Championship.

The 1969 season was definitely non-vintage as far as the European

"Rallying went from strength to strength during the 1950s and by the 1960s the first proper works teams had arrived"

Images of a championship: Rally cars blasting through dusty bush-lined roads, on snow and ice or through muddy watersplashes are familiar scenes to those who have followed the series around the World. A door number hastily unveiled through its veil of dirt, Saabs on a transporter in the 1970s or the vast army of Toyota drivers and mechanics needed to do battle on the Safari capture the essence of this incredible global sport that combines technical wizardry with human endeavour

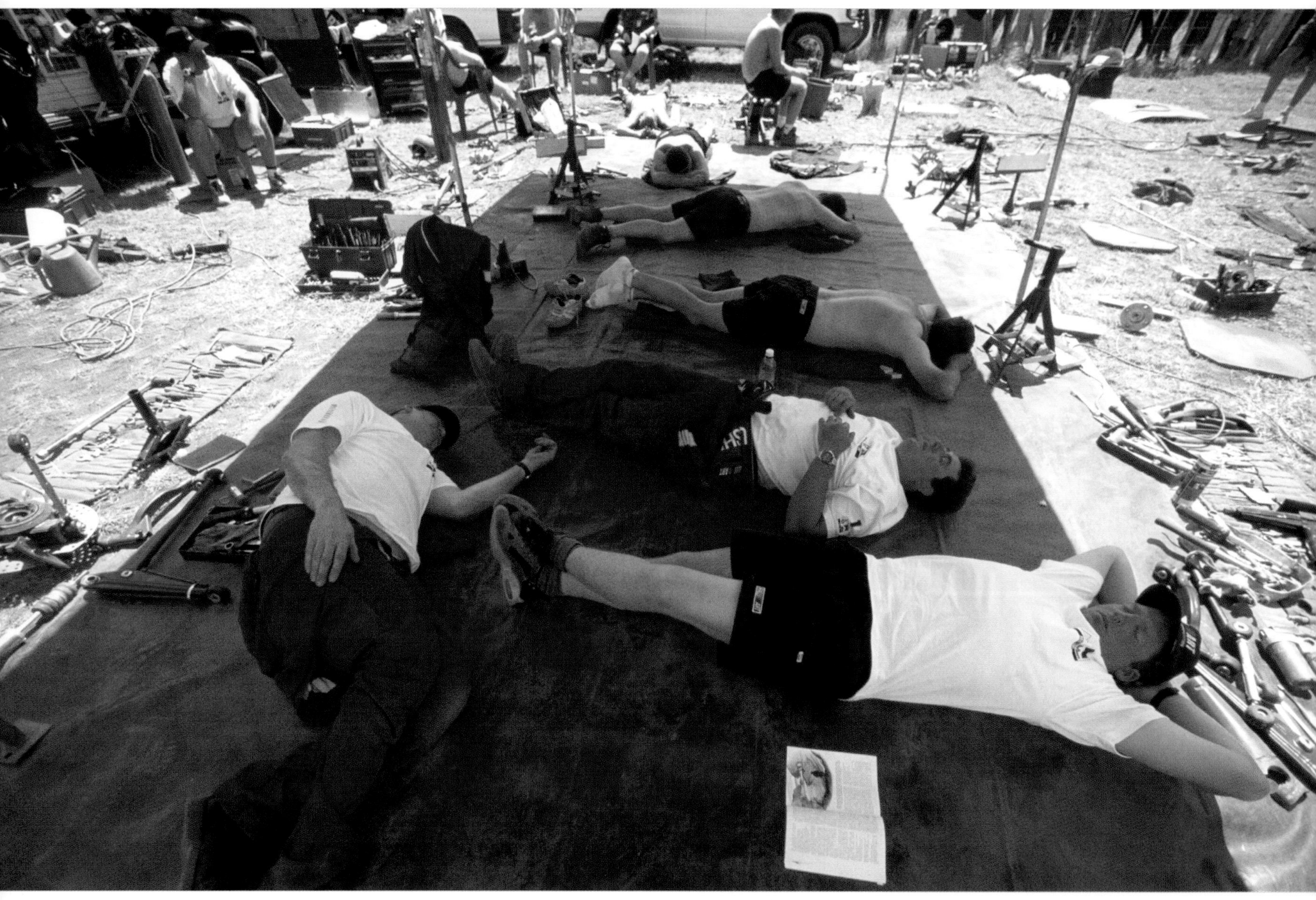

Championship was concerned. The Monte Carlo had been included in the Constructors' championship but the results of that event were retrospectively removed from the championship by the FIA because the ACM had allowed cars of Groups 5 and 6 to enter, something not allowed by championship rules. Then the Geneva and German rallies were not held and thus the title – Ford again, but this time Ford Europe – was decided on just five events. The Drivers' Championship was better but then only one manufacturer, Lancia, really put any effort into it and that resulted in their driver, Harry Källström, winning by a good margin.

New thinking was required and the FIA came up with the solution. What they did was to create a new championship called the International Rally Championship for Makes. This would comprise just eight events, the best of Europe plus the East African Safari. Hence the "International" sobriquet. As it turned out, it was only eight events in total since the Alpine Rally was cancelled at the last minute because the police would not sanction it. This was designed to be a championship in which any manufacturer with a works team should be able to send a couple of cars to all the rounds and so create something of real interest within the rally world.

Of course, it did not quite work out like that because old habits die hard and some teams were ready and able to do that while others were not. Porsche

took the championship by winning Monte and Sweden and adding Austria in the latter part of the year. Alpine-Renault finished second by winning San Remo and Acropolis while the Safari was won by Datsun which failed to score anywhere else. Statistics make it sound dreadfully dull but in fact it was a very lively season, with the title being decided on the last event. At least it was a simple championship for the media to follow with a scoring system based on Formula One.

The same could not be said for the European Drivers' Championship that also ran and now occupied a slightly inferior position to the new IRCM. During the 1960s, rallying had become immensely popular and every European country

Oposite page: Time out for the service team. Their frantic activity done they can relax while the drivers are away on the stages battling the elements before returning to have the damage fixed once again. These are rallying's unsung heroes

Above: Servicing the inner man. Carlos Sainz takes a welcome drink to replace the fluid lost from his exertions on the special stages. Modern rally drivers are finely honed athletes, a far cry from the stars of the early years who were more likely to grab a cigarette and a beer!

was licensing a score or so of international permit rallies and wanted its best rallies to be recognised on an international rather than just a national basis. So, to satisfy this demand and to mollify those traditional events that had not been chosen for the IRCM, the European championship was expanded to 22 rallies. These events varied enormously in length and severity, so a complicated method of scoring was created. It was based on the number of starters in each class and few people understood it fully. It would be fair to say that it was at this point that the European Championship passed into a dark night from which it has not, even after 33 years, fully emerged.

The IRCM, however, had a much brighter future but its growing pains were by no means over. For 1971, it grew again to eight events with Morocco coming in. The Alpine Rally was initially nominated but when it ran with insufficient starters, the points from it were not allowed. The problem was the calendar itself for six of the eight events took place in the first half of the year. This was chronological crowding of the worst type and did nothing to encourage manufacturer teams to do all the events. As it was, Alpine-Renault won four of those six events and had the title wrapped up before July. By the end of the season the team still had twice as many points as Saab in second place.

The 1972 championship was better in many respects. The points system was changed with more points available on each event so that 17 manufacturers scored rather than just 10 the year before. The American event, the Press on Regardless Rally, was added so that there were now nine events – six in Europe, two in Africa and one in the USA. Lancia finally won Monte Carlo with the Fulvia after six years of trying and went on to storm the championship despite the close attentions of Fiat.

Behind the scenes, the FIA had been consulting with representatives of the manufacturers and the organisers of the major rallies about the next step. They all wanted a World Rally Championship.

The loneliness of the long distance rally driver. No other sport in the world offers images such as this, nor does it pitch man against the elements in anything like the same way

HYUNDAI

The investments that were now being made in factory teams, with their specialised cars and the sponsorship needed to run major events with proper timing equipment and teams of marshals, meant that the championship demanded that status if it was going to progress. Famous events had sunk without trace through lack of funds and it was felt that more would go if they did not have the aura of a World title membership.

In 1973, the World Rally Championship for Manufacturers came into being although rather ominously it was for 13 events. The additions were the Polish Rally, the TAP Portuguese Rally, the 1000 Lakes and the Tour de Corse. It was a pretty good selection and it instantly brought a higher level of public attention and manufacturer participation. In the event, Renault-Alpine (the little company had now been swallowed by the big one) romped home scoring six wins from the eight events that they could count towards their total. Sadly the year saw the end of the Austrian Alpine as a major European Rally after a bitter dispute about time controls and route blocking between BMW and Renault-Alpine which was only resolved in BMW's favour months after the event.

And there was something significant missing from the format of the World Rally Championship. There was no title associated with the men and women who drove the cars. The omission of a World Drivers' title was something that

"In 1973, the World Rally Championship came into being and instantly brought a higher level of public attention and manufacturer participation"

Changes to the technical regulations for 1997 brought smaller manufacturers like Hyundai (left) in from the cold and ensured that the sport became global on several levels; events, manufacturers and drivers

took the FIA some six years to redress when it should not have taken them more than six minutes when they had the example of the Formula One championship in front of them. For prestige advertising and model endorsement, the Manufacturers' title was very important, but it is stories about people that sell newspapers and magazines. For a long period, the media had little to work with. To be fair, it was major achievement to get all the factions within the FIA to agree to the principle of a World Rally Championship, so maybe they can be forgiven one omission when they got so much else right.

The following year should have been a time of consolidation, improvement and general polishing up of the WCR act. The 1970s Middle East oil crisis that did not stop planes flying but brought cars to a standstill, and lost the championship a lot of events in the first half of the year. There were only eight events that counted and five of those took place after Lancia had homologated their new supercar, the Stratos, on October 1, 1974. Lancia won three of these second-half rallies and took the World title for the first time from Fiat with Ford in third place.

With no more artificial fuel shortages, the WRC strode out in the latter part of the 1970s with a spring in its step. Even the banning of some of the more outrageous concessions of Groups 2 and 4, such as non-production four valve cylinder heads, did not turn out to be a major brake on its expansion.

A spectacular power slide on the unique and treacherous ball-bearing gravel of Australia (above, left) and the precise threading of the needle across a bridge in Turkey (above)

Overleaf: Spectator safety has become a major issue since the dark days of the 1986 season. Crowds are much more tightly controlled but, in the right circumstances, this can contribute to the atmosphere

"Then the FIA finally got the message and for 1979 introduced the World Rally Championship for Drivers"

Lombard
lift trucks
from Eaton Yale
EATON
PIRELLI

Clockwise from bottom left: The World Rally Championship draws a crowd wherever it goes; Ford service area in the late 1970s; Finland, with its spectacular high-speed jumps, is rallying's spiritual home; sideways on the snow at close to 100mph – achieving the impossible is an everyday feat to a top-line rally driver

Manufacturers were almost queuing up to produce cars with a sporting pedigree with which to compete. Lancia, Fiat, Ford, Opel, Datsun, Chrysler (soon to be Talbot), Renault, Peugeot, Porsche, Toyota, VW and Triumph were all at the party though, of course, with varying degrees of success. The rally drivers finally got some recognition with the introduction of the FIA Cup in 1977, This was based on the WRC with some additional events like the Tour de France and Giro d'Italia added for good measure. Sandro Munari was its first recipient in 1977 and Markku Alén in 1978. Then the FIA got the message and for 1979 introduced the World Rally Championship for Drivers. To start with, it used the same 12 events as the Manufacturers' championship. Later, in order to satisfy political needs within the FIA, the two championships became overlapping with some events counting for the Manufacturers' title and some additional ones – a kind of lower rank of first-class events – counting for the Drivers' championship as well. This came in for 1980 and during this period when the replacement for the old CSI, FISA (Federation Internationale du Sport Automobile) was in power, there was endless tinkering with the events, the scoring system and even the requirement to register for the titles.

Man-made items of beauty rub shoulders with nature itself to create the unique blend of visual images that distinguishes rallying from any other form of motorsport

Overleaf: The Rally of Argentina is famous for its myriad of watersplashes, this one being the longest and most spectacular of them all and always draws a crowd

"The biggest boost– or upheaval, depending on your opinion – to the WRC came in the period between 1983 and 1986"

sparco
Marlboro
TOTAL
MICHELIN

CITROEN

The biggest boost– or upheaval, depending on your opinion – to the WRC came in the period between 1983 and 1986 when FISA introduced Group B and then dramatically banned it. The Group B era had in practice already arrived when Audi took the step of manufacturing enough turbocharged, 4WD Quattros to be able to run them in 1981 under the old Group 4 rules. As with the Lancia Stratos, the Opel Ascona and the Escort RS1800, a minimum of 400 cars had to be made in 12 months before they were accepted in WRC events. Audi had done it with a 4WD machine but few other companies were ready to produce so many cars in what was then such a radical format. Group B was ideal. It only needed 200 production cars and 20 specials evolved from that.

By 1984, Peugeot had joined Audi while by the end of 1985, Ford, Lancia, Citröen and Austin Rover all had 4WD machines ready to go rallying.

The spectacle of powerful, purpose-built, quirky cars tackling special stages

Crowds gather in the rain (below) or cling to the hillsides to see their heroes in action

Overleaf: The rolling hills of New Zealand have traditionally offered some of the most enjoyable roads for the drivers to master with their constant twists and turns. The event itself often played something of a minor role in the championship during its formative years but has now become one of its most popular rallies

was irresistible - spectator interest rocketed, and so did the standing of the WRC. Two things had been overlooked. The rally organisers were not ready to deal with hoardes of people on their stages and the cars were not subjected to a rigorous safety regime, particularly in respect of the fuels being used to produce all that horsepower. The result was fatalities to both spectators and crews. Instead of tackling the real problems, FISA decided to tackle the perceived problem and took it out on the manufacturers who were, at that time, being difficult in other areas of motor sport and needed teaching a lesson.

Losing the Group B cars was almost a fatal blow for the WRC. Fortunately, those who had suffered most, the manufacturers and the rally organisers, got the show back on the road using Group A cars. The late 1980s and early 1990s was a time of recuperation. The Japanese manufacturers – Toyota, Mazda, Nissan, Mitsubishi and Subaru – proved to be the saviour of the WRC as all of them produced winning Group A cars during that period to rival the acknowledged top dog, the Lancia Delta. The reason that the Japanese were so successful during the 1990s was that they had the resources to produce 5000 turbocharged 4WD cars – the basic requirement for Group A – and the markets in which to sell them.

The time had come for another change in the technical regulations. The

"Losing the Group B cars was almost a fatal blow for the WRC"

Threading the needle! Unlike Formula One, rally drivers don't have crash barriers to stop them when they make a mistake and those trees can be awfully close at times

European manufacturers suggested that the central idea of Group B could be adopted but with its dangerous elements eliminated, accompanied by safety regulations applied with vigour. The result was the World Rally Car, now universally used in WRC events of the 21st century. The manufacturer only needs to build a car by installing a turbocharger and 4WD in one of its normal production cars, and to have available 19 kits to accomplish the same transformation. The manufacturer cannot relocate the engine to another part of the car, keeping fuel and hot engines well separated. The result is a safe but spectacular rally car that any manufacturer may build and enter in the WRC.

At the same time, the regulations and requirements governing the events forming the championship were reformed. This was a process that had started after the accidents of 1986 when stage lengths were reduced and organisers were encouraged to make their events shorter and safer with better provision for, and control of, spectators. All this was accelerated as the importance of television coverage was recognised. The standardisation of events now went far beyond the efforts of the 1970s when events had to use the same signs at time controls and adopt certain common regulations. Now the whole format of a WRC event was to fit a fixed pattern and even the inspection of the rally route by the crews prior to the event was to be brought into that format.

As we entered a new millennium, the face the World Rally Championship presented to the world was that of a fully comprehensible championship with all events counting for both titles. It is something that is attractive for a manufacturer to enter and it is one that can be enjoyed as much by the non-expert as by the rally fanatic. There are signs that it is still evolving and there will be changes in the choice of events and the technical regulations in the years to come. But it has already come a long way over the last 30 years.

John Davenport

This page (top to bottom): Two forms of wildlife; Citroen rounded off the WRC's first 30 years as champions; sometimes a pilot's licence would seem more appropriate than a driver's licence

Far right: Cars in parc ferme during the 1970s

Overleaf: A motorway bridge in Catalunya provides arguably the most famous grandstand in modern World Championship rallying, allowing literally thousands of fans a prized vantage point from which to cheer on their heroes

It's the real thing.
PEUGEOT
O. ANDERSSON
A. HERTZ
ENTRANT MARSHALLS (E.A) LTD.
BCAL
LANCIA-ITALIA
MICHELIN
elf
Alpine Renault
2

WWW.RACING-FILES.COM

inmarsat
inmarsat
TOTAL
clarion
Marlboro
3

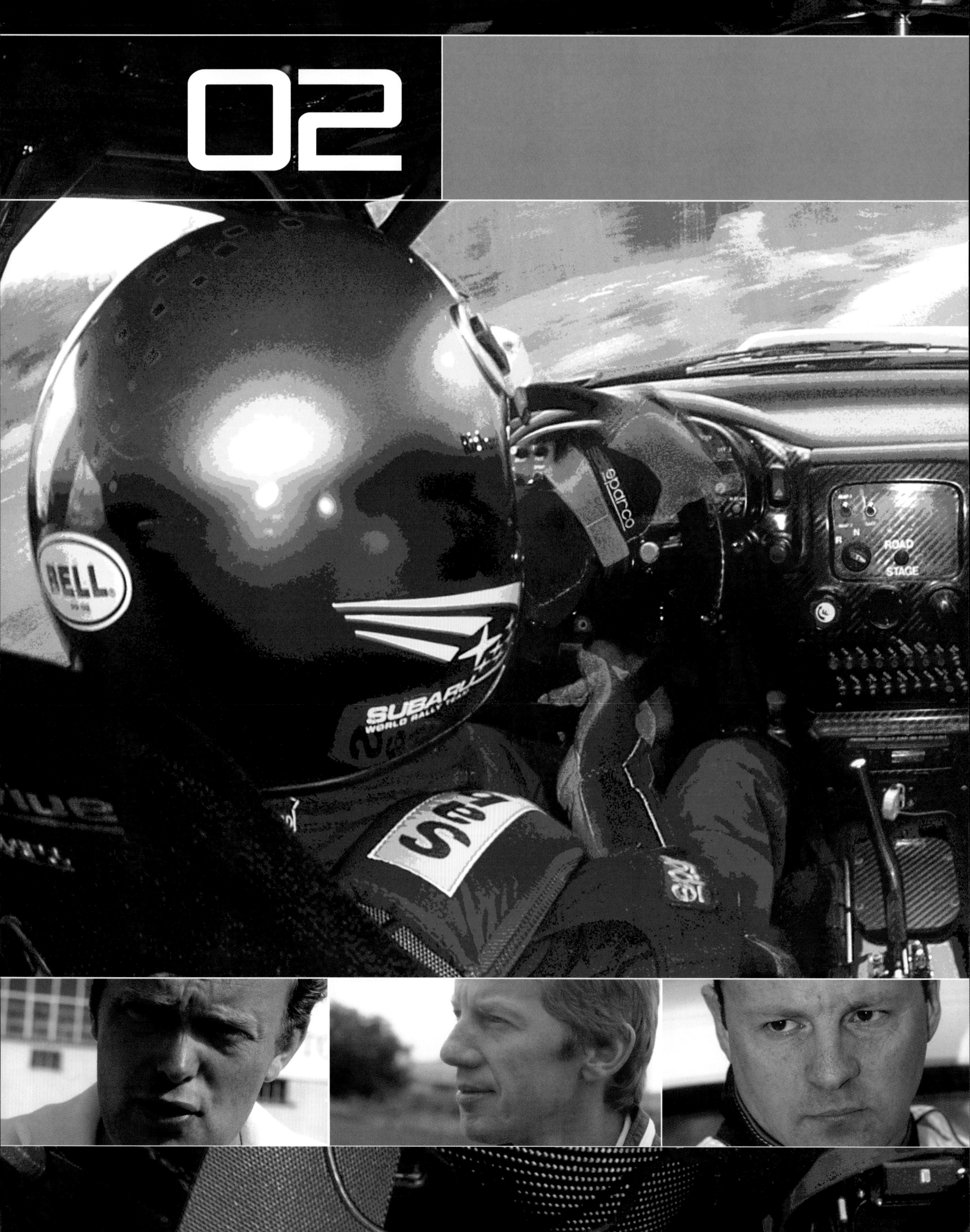
02
BELL
SUBARU
WORLD RALLY TEAM
sparco
R
N
ROAD
STAGE

THE DRIVERS

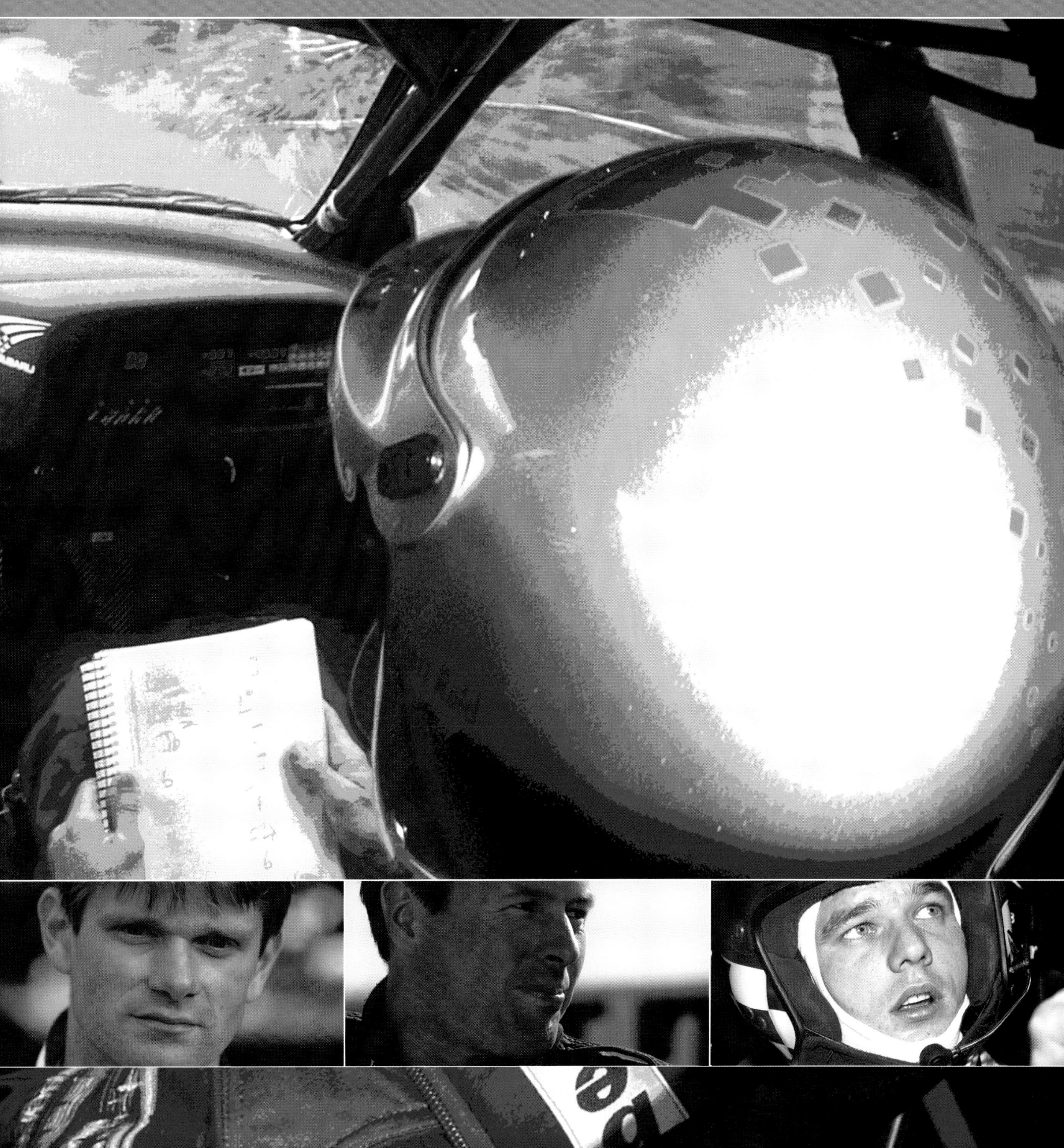

AGHINI, ANDREA

(I) BORN: 29 DECEMBER, 1963, LIVORNO, ITALY

When Lancia started its quest for rallying supremacy in the 1960s, there was a dearth of Italian drivers capable of winning internationally. By the 1980s, the upswing in the fortunes of Lancia and Fiat meant that Italian rallying was very healthy, with excellent home-grown drivers. Andrea Aghini was a perfect example.

His career started in 1984 on national events with a Peugeot 205 GTi. His WRC debut came two years later in a one-off drive in a Renault 5 GT Turbo on the 1986 San Remo Rally when the turbo failed. For the first year of the post-Group B scene, he was back in a Group N (production-based) 205 GTi before winning the class the following year in San Remo. with a 309 GTi. Two more years were spent at the wheel of a Group A 405 Mi16 in which he finished third in the 1989 Italian Championship and won two of its events outright in 1990.

His big break came in the form of a call from the Jolly Club to drive a Lancia Delta Integrale. Two WRC events, and two good performances, lead to an invitation to drive for the Lancia factory. His single WRC victory came on the San Remo after Lancia lost number one driver Didier Auriol on the very first stage. It was left to Aghini and Juha Kankkunen to uphold Lancia honour. Aghini led initially with Kankkunen realising that he was unable to catch Aghini on his home soil, the gravel roads of Tuscany.

Sadly, this was Lancia's swansong and for the ensuing season Aghini was back driving for the Jolly Club. A year later he followed Kankkunen to Toyota for a couple of events and then drove the Japanese cars for the Grifone team. He tried a year with Mitsubishi where he had a 100% finishing record but then it was back to Grifone with whom he won the Italian Championship in 1998 and 1999. His final fling in the WRC was with Mitsubishi in 2000.

AGHINI, ANDREA - CAREER RECORD

YEAR	RALLY	TEAM /ENTRANT	CAR	NO.	CO-DRIVER	RESULT
1987	**0 points**					
1	Sanremo		Peugeot 205 GTI	113	Sauro Farnocchia	Retired
1988	**13 points (6th)**					
2	Sanremo	Peugeot Talbot Sport	Peugeot 309 GTI	32	Sauro Farnocchia	12th
1989	**0 points**					
3	Sanremo	Peugeot Team Italia	Peugeot 405 Mi16	14	Sauro Farnocchia	Retired
1991	**16 points (14th)**					
4	Sanremo	Jolly Club	Lancia Delta Integrale 16V	19	Sauro Farnocchia	5th
5	Catalunya	Jolly Club	Lancia Delta Integrale 16V	3	Sauro Farnocchia	5th
1992	**39 points (7th)**					
6	Portugal	Martini Lancia	Lancia Delta HF Integrale	16	Sauro Farnocchia	Retired
7	Corsica	Martini Lancia	Lancia Delta HF Integrale	12	Sauro Farnocchia	6th
8	**Sanremo**	**Martini Lancia**	**Lancia Delta HF Integrale**	**5**	**Sauro Farnocchia**	**1st**
9	Catalunya	Martini Lancia	Lancia Delta HF Integrale	7	Sauro Farnocchia	3rd
10	Great Britain	Martini Lancia	Lancia Delta HF Integrale	15	Sauro Farnocchia	10th
1993	**22 points (14th)**					
11	Monte Carlo	Jolly Club	Lancia Delta HF Integrale	5	Sauro Farnocchia	Retired
12	Portugal	Jolly Club	Lancia Delta HF Integrale	6	Sauro Farnocchia	3rd
13	Corsica	Jolly Club	Lancia Delta HF Integrale	6	Sauro Farnocchia	Retired
14	Greece	Jolly Club	Lancia Delta HF Integrale	8	Sauro Farnocchia	4th
15	Sanremo	Jolly Club	Lancia Delta HF Integrale	1	Sauro Farnocchia	Retired
1994	**12 points (14th)**					
16	Portugal	Toyota Castrol Team	Toyota Celica Turbo 4WD	8	Sauro Farnocchia	Retired
17	Corsica	Toyota Castrol Team	Toyota Celica Turbo 4WD	8	Sauro Farnocchia	3rd
18	Sanremo	HF Grifone	Toyota Celica Turbo 4WD	10	Sauro Farnocchia	Retired
1995	**26 points (7th)**					
19	Monte Carlo	Mitsubishi Ralliart	Mitsubishi Lancer Evo 3	12	Sauro Farnocchia	6th
20	Corsica	Mitsubishi Ralliart	Mitsubishi Lancer Evo 3	12	Sauro Farnocchia	3rd
21	Catalunya	Mitsubishi Ralliart	Mitsubishi Lancer Evo 3	12	Sauro Farnocchia	5th
1997	**0 points**					
22	Sanremo	HF Grifone	Toyota Celica GT-Four	11	Loris Roggia	7th
1998	**0 points**					
23	Sanremo	HF Grifone	Toyota Corolla WRC	15	Loris Roggia	9th
1999	**2 points (18th)**					
24	Sanremo	HF Grifone	Toyota Corolla WRC	16	Loris Roggia	5th
2000	**0 points**					
25	Argentina	Ralliart Italia	Mitsubishi Carisma GT	28	Loris Roggia	Retired
26	Sanremo	Ralliart Italia	Mitsubishi Carisma GT	25	Dario D'Esposita	15th

AIRIKKALA, PENTTI (FIN) BORN: 4 SEPTEMBER 1945, HELSINKI, FINLAND

If you hailed from Finland and you lived next door to future rally legend Hannu Mikkola, you'd be expected to develop an interest in the sport. This is exactly what happened to Pentti Airikkala. His father ran a bus company and Pentti developed his techniques by driving coaches – sideways! He also got some instruction from the young Mikkola and soon purchased his first rally car, a rather old Volvo PV544. He immediately made an impression in local events before entering Finland's – and arguably rallying's – biggest event: the 1000 Lakes. He finished a respectable 20th overall and fourth in class.

"Pentti developed his technique by driving coaches – sideways!"

However, his first supported drive was actually in circuit racing, His Volvo 122S, although prepared by the importers, was unreliable and Airikkala found the business of racing too boring when compared with that of rallying. He got drives in Isuzu Bellets and Renault R8 Gordinis with which he distinguished himself in Finnish rallies.

Curiously, he was then offered the post of Opel Finland team manager, a job he did with great success, but realised that he missed driving.

He entered the 1971 RAC Rally with an Opel Kadett and discovered that he'd lost none of his flair – he ran in the top 10 but the car broke. A return to Finland meant more outings locally with Renaults and Opels and it was to signal the start of Airikkala's arrival in the big time.

The Finnish Alfa Romeo importer decided to lend him a Group 1 car for the 1974 Welsh Rally where Airikkala finished a close second to the winning Vauxhall Magnum. A talk with Vauxhall boss Bill Blydenstein led to a Vauxhall Viva for the 1000 Lakes where he won his class. Also on the Welsh, he met Ford preparation wizard David Sutton and was offered an Escort RS for the RAC Rally. He won the shakedown event but the engine failed on the event proper.

For 1975 Airikkala drove works Vauxhall Magnums in anticipation of the arrival of the all-new Chevette. The Chevette was not ready for Finland so Airikkala again drove an Escort for the Sutton team and came as close as he ever did to winning the famous Finnish event.

For the next four years, Airikkala's name became synonymous with the Chevette in both HS and HSR forms. He moved to England and won many British Championship events and the title in 1979. When Vauxhall were swamped by the Group B tide, Airikkala at first reverted to an Escort RS and then tried Mitsubishis for size – first the Lancer Turbo and then the Starion. For 1989, he got his hands on the new Galant VR-4 and won the Group N category of the British Championship. At the last minute, he stepped in to replace Mikael Eriksson on the RAC Rally and, with a Group A VR-4, had a major battle with the three works Toyotas to win outright.

This victory should have led to greater things, but Airikkala was already 46-years-old. He netted a drive with Ford in their Sierra Cosworth 4x4, but it would not prove to be a winner. For Pentti that 1989

RAC win had come too late.

Since his last forays on the world championship scene in 1990 Airikkala has spent the majority of his time teaching others the art of rally driving, although the chance to put his money where his mouth was came in the form of a one-off appearance on Rally GB at the end of 2003. A first-day retirement at the wheel of the Mitsubishi Lancer has probably persuaded Pentti that from now on it's 'do as I say, not as I do!'

Right: Pentti Airikkala took this Mitsubishi Galant VR-4 to victory on the RAC Rally in 1989. The result was against the perceived form guide and at the expense of the mighty Toyota team but it gave Pentti his one and only win at the highest level

AIRIKKALA, PENTTI – CAREER RECORD

YEAR	RALLY	TEAM/ENTRANT	CAR	NO.	CO-DRIVER	RESULT
1973						
1	Finland	Opel Finland	Opel Kadett	22	Heikki Haaksiala	Retired
1974						
2	Finland	Dealer Team Vauxhall	Vauxhall Magnum Coupe	29	Heikki Haaksiala	16th
3	Great Britain	Centre Hotels/Clarke & Simpson	Ford Escort RS1600	24	Heikki Haaksiala	Retired
1975						
4	Finland	Dealer Team Vauxhall	Vauxhall Magnum Coupe	9	Heikki Haaksiala	Retired
5	Great Britain	Dealer Team Vauxhall	Vauxhall Magnum Coupe	19	John Davenport	20th
1976						
6	Finland		Ford Escort RS1800	12	Risto Virtanen	2nd
7	Great Britain	Team Avon Tyres	Ford Escort RS1800	22	Mike Greasley	Retired
1977						
8	Sweden	Toyota Team Europe	Toyota Celica	6	Risto Virtanen	Retired
9	Finland	Dealer Team Vauxhall	Vauxhall Chevette 2300HSR	2	Risto Virtanen	Retired
10	Great Britain	Dealer Team Vauxhall	Vauxhall Chevette 2300HSR	4	Risto Virtanen	16th
1978						
11	Sweden	Dealer Team Vauxhall	Vauxhall Chevette 2300HSR	4	Risto Virtanen	Retired
12	Finland	Dealer Team Vauxhall	Vauxhall Chevette 2300HSR	5	Risto Virtanen	3rd
13	Great Britain	Dealer Team Vauxhall/Castrol	Vauxhall Chevette 2300HSR	11	Mike Nicholson	Retired
1979	16 points (15th)					
14	Sweden	Dealer Team Vauxhall	Vauxhall Chevette 2300HSR	5	Risto Virtanen	3rd
15	New Zealand	Dealer Team Vauxhall	Vauxhall Chevette 2300HSR	2	Rodger Freeth	Retired
16	Finland	Dealer Team Vauxhall	Vauxhall Chevette 2300HSR	3	Risto Virtanen	Retired
17	Great Britain	Dealer Team Vauxhall/Castrol	Vauxhall Chevette 2300HSR	7	Risto Virtanen	7th
1980	6 points (36th)					
18	Sweden	Dealer Team Vauxhall	Vauxhall Chevette 2300HSR	3	Risto Virtanen	6th
19	Finland	Dealer Team Vauxhall	Vauxhall Chevette 2300HSR	5	Risto Virtanen	Retired
20	New Zealand	Masport	Ford Escort RS2000	4	Chris Porter	Retired
21	Great Britain	Dealer Team Vauxhall/Castrol	Vauxhall Chevette 2300HSR	9	Risto Virtanen	Retired
1981	30 points (9th)					
22	Sweden	Rothmans Rally Team	Ford Escort RS1800	8	Risto Virtanen	3rd
23	Finland	Rothmans Rally Team	Ford Escort RS1800	8	Risto Virtanen	5th
24	Great Britain	Rothmans Rally Team	Ford Escort RS1800	12	Phil Short	4th
1982	12 points (15th)					
25	Finland	Team Ralliart	Mitsubishi Lancer Turbo	7	Juha Piironen	3rd
26	Great Britain	Team Ralliart	Mitsubishi Lancer Turbo	10	Juha Piironen	Retired
1983	8 points (21st)					
27	Finland	Martini Racing	Lancia Rally 037	5	Juha Piironen	5th
1984	0 points					
28	Finland	Team Nissan Europe	Nissan 240RS	8	Seppo Harjanne	Retired
1985	0 points					
29	Great Britain	British Telecom Mobile Phone	Vauxhall Astra GT/E	27	Ronan McNamee	Retired
1986	0 points					
30	Great Britain	British Telecom Mobile Phone	Vauxhall Astra GT/E	29	Ronan McNamee	16th
1987	0 points					
31	Great Britain	GM Dealersport	Opel Kadett GSi	58	Ronan McNamee	Retired
1988	10 points (30th)					
32	Great Britain	Safety Devices	Lancia Delta Integrale	20	Brian Murphy	4th
1989	20 points (14th)					
33	**Great Britain**	**Mitsubishi Ralliart Europe**	**Mitsubishi Galant VR-4**	**19**	**Ronan McNamee**	**1st**
1990	0 points					
34	Finland	Q8 Team Ford	Ford Sierra Cosworth 4x4	8	Ronan McNamee	Retired
35	Sanremo	Q8 Team Ford	Ford Sierra Cosworth 4x4	5	Ronan McNamee	11th
36	Great Britain	Q8 Team Ford	Ford Sierra Cosworth 4x4	1	Ronan McNamee	Retired
2003	0 points					
37	Great Britain	Fairfield Motorsport	Mitsubishi Lancer Evo 6	107	Nigel Gardner	Retired

ALÉN, MARKKU (FIN) BORN: 15 FEBRUARY 1951, HELSINKI, FINLAND

"His phrase of 'now maximum attack' became well known"

Tall and dark, Markku Alén is no Nordic cliché and, with a Mediterranean temperament to match, it is no surprise that he drove 16 years for the Fiat empire. In that period he won more WRC events than any of his contemporaries but was never officially crowned World Champion. Son of a Finnish ice-racing champion, Markku started rallying in 1969 with a Renault R8 Gordini and finished ninth on the 1000 Lakes at his first attempt. A short period in an Opel Kadett was followed by a contract with the Finnish Volvo importer to drive a Volvo 142. He was third twice on the 1000 Lakes, 12th on the RAC Rally in 1972 and then in 1973 was second overall on the 1000 Lakes.

These results drew the attention of both Ford and Fiat. Ford fixed him up with an Escort RS on the 1973 RAC Rally where, in a truly remarkable display of ability and determination, he recovered from a first day excursion that dropped him to 177th overall to finish third. But Fiat also had an offer of a programme in their Abarth 124 Spyder so 1974 was a year spent in both cars. He showed well in Portugal and 1000 Lakes for Fiat and won at home for Ford. But it was Fiat that came with the full programme for 1975 and that was where Alén went.

The 124 Abarth Spyder was not really a winning car though, on a rally like Portugal that Alén liked, he showed he could master the car. But when the Fiat Abarth 131 arrived, just in time for the 1000 Lakes 1976, Alén could show who was king. It was not all roses however but Alén was discovering that the elan and dedication in the Fiat team was just what he needed to perform at the highest level. His phrase of "now maximum attack" became well known.

In 1978, he won the FIA Driver's Cup, a sop to the World Drivers' Championship that was to be created the following year and had his first drives in a supercar, the Lancia Stratos, winning both San Remo and the Giro d'Italia. For the next three years he stayed at the wheel of an 131 Abarth chasing the World Championship and regularly winning Portugal and the 1000 Lakes.

Then came the supercar that he had been waiting for: the Lancia Rally 037. Working with the same engineers from the 131, this was the car that was to be Alén's favourite. He extended his range of victories winning tarmac events like Corsica and benefiting from a career-long relationship with his co-driver, Ilkka Kivimäki. But it was with the even more exotic Delta S4 that Alén came closest to winning the World Championship. In 1986, he held the title for just 11 days before the points from the San Remo Rally - that he had won - were disallowed and the crown went to Juha Kankkunen instead...

When the Group A era arrived, Alén distinguished himself with the Delta HF and Integrale and finally won an RAC Rally, though Monte Carlo continued to elude him. When Lancia reduced its programme, he signed with Subaru for two years and then did a year at Toyota finishing his WRC career with a handful of drives in 1993. A one-off outing in Finland at the wheel of a privately-entered but contemporary Ford Focus WRC netted 16th place. It was only really for fun but proved that Alén could still just about cut it in the modern-day, cut-and-thrust of the WRC.

More recently he has been employed as a TV pundit in his homeland's coverage of the Rally Finland.

Right: Markku Alén, Safari Rally 1979. The Fiat 131 Abarth helped establish Markku's name although it was its successor within the Fiat group, the Lancia Rally 037, that was arguably his favourite car

ALÉN, MARKKU - CAREER RECORD

YEAR	RALLY	TEAM/ENTRANT	CAR	NO.	CO-DRIVER	RESULT
1973						
1	Finland		Volvo 142	29	Juhani Toivonen	2nd
2	Great Britain	Motorcraft	Ford Escort RS1600	18	Ilkka Kivimaki	3rd
1974						
3	Portugal	Fiat SpA	Fiat 124 Abarth	6	Ilkka Kivimaki	3rd
4	Finland	Fiat SpA	Fiat 124 Abarth	3	Ilkka Kivimaki	3rd
5	Sanremo	Fiat SpA	Fiat 124 Abarth	3	Ilkka Kivimaki	Retired
6	Canada	Fiat SpA	Fiat 124 Abarth	102	Ilkka Kivimaki	Retired
7	United States	Fiat SpA	Fiat 124 Abarth	7	Atso Aho	2nd
8	Great Britain	Ford Motor Company	Ford Escort RS1600	15	Paul White	Retired
9	Corsica	Fiat SpA	Fiat 124 Abarth	1	Ilkka Kivimaki	Retired
1975						
10	Monte Carlo	Fiat SpA	Fiat 124 Abarth	10	Ilkka Kivimaki	3rd
11	Sweden	Fiat SpA	Fiat 124 Abarth	5	Ilkka Kivimaki	6th
12	Morocco	Fiat SpA	Fiat 124 Abarth	1	Ilkka Kivimaki	Retired
13	**Portugal**	**Fiat SpA**	**Fiat 124 Abarth**	**4**	**Ilkka Kivimaki**	**1st**
14	Finland		Datsun 160J	3	Ilkka Kivimaki	Retired
15	Sanremo	Fiat SpA	Fiat 124 Abarth	2	Ilkka Kivimaki	Retired
16	Great Britain	Fiat SpA	Fiat 124 Abarth	7	Ilkka Kivimaki	Retired
1976						
17	Monte Carlo	Fiat SpA	Fiat 124 Abarth	7	Ilkka Kivimaki	6th
18	Morocco	Fiat SpA	Fiat 131 Abarth	8	Ilkka Kivimaki	12th
19	**Finland**	**Fiat SpA**	**Fiat 131 Abarth**	**3**	**Ilkka Kivimaki**	**1st**
20	Sanremo	Fiat SpA	Fiat 131 Abarth	2	Ilkka Kivimaki	Retired
21	Great Britain	Fiat SpA	Fiat 131 Abarth	3	Ilkka Kivimaki	Retired
1977						
22	Monte Carlo	Olio Fiat	Fiat 131 Abarth	4	Ilkka Kivimaki	Retired
23	Sweden	Olio Fiat	Fiat 131 Abarth	2	Ilkka Kivimaki	Retired
24	**Portugal**	**Olio Fiat**	**Fiat 131 Abarth**	**3**	**Ilkka Kivimaki**	**1st**
25	New Zealand	Olio Fiat	Fiat 131 Abarth	3	Ilkka Kivimaki	3rd
26	Greece	Olio Fiat	Fiat 131 Abarth	9	Ilkka Kivimaki	Retired
27	Finland	Olio Fiat	Fiat 131 Abarth	1	Ilkka Kivimaki	Retired
28	Canada	Olio Fiat	Fiat 131 Abarth	5	Ilkka Kivimaki	Retired
29	Great Britain	Olio Fiat	Fiat 131 Abarth	3	Ilkka Kivimaki	Retired
1978						
30	Sweden	Fiat SpA	Fiat 131 Abarth	3	Ilkka Kivimaki	3rd
31	**Portugal**	**Fiat SpA**	**Fiat 131 Abarth**	**4**	**Ilkka Kivimaki**	**1st**
32	Greece	Fiat SpA	Fiat 131 Abarth	7	Ilkka Kivimaki	2nd
33	**Finland**	**Fiat SpA**	**Fiat 131 Abarth**	**3**	**Ilkka Kivimaki**	**1st**
34	Canada	Fiat SpA	Fiat 131 Abarth	2	Ilkka Kivimaki	2nd

ALÉN, MARKKU CAREER RECORD (CONT'D)

YEAR	RALLY	TEAM/ENTRANT	CAR	NO.	CO-DRIVER	RESULT
35	**Sanremo**	**Alitalia Lancia/Pirelli**	**Lancia Stratos**	**4**	**Ilkka Kivimaki**	**1st**
36	Great Britain	Alitalia Lancia/Pirelli	Lancia Stratos	3	Ilkka Kivimaki	Retired
1979	**68 points (3rd)**					
37	Monte Carlo	Alitalia Fiat	Fiat 131 Abarth	3	Ilkka Kivimaki	3rd
38	Sweden	Alitalia Fiat	Fiat 131 Abarth	2	Ilkka Kivimaki	4th
39	Safari	Alitalia Fiat	Fiat 131 Abarth	3	Ilkka Kivimaki	3rd
40	**Finland**	**Alitalia Fiat**	**Fiat 131 Abarth**	**1**	**Ilkka Kivimaki**	**1st**
41	Sanremo	Alitalia Fiat	Fiat 131 Abarth	1	Ilkka Kivimaki	6th
42	Great Britain	Lancia GB	Lancia Stratos	2	Ilkka Kivimaki	5th
1980	**47 points (6th)**					
43	Monte Carlo	Fiat Italia	Fiat 131 Abarth	3	Ilkka Kivimaki	Retired
44	Portugal	Fiat Italia	Fiat 131 Abarth	2	Ilkka Kivimaki	2nd
45	Greece	Fiat Italia	Fiat 131 Abarth	7	Ilkka Kivimaki	3rd
46	Argentina	Fiat Italia	Fiat 131 Abarth	4	Ilkka Kivimaki	Retired
47	**Finland**	**Fiat Rally/ASA**	**Fiat 131 Abarth**	**1**	**Ilkka Kivimaki**	**1st**
48	Sanremo	4 Rombi	Fiat 131 Abarth	7	Ilkka Kivimaki	Retired
1981	**56 points (4th)**					
49	Monte Carlo	Fiat Auto Torino	Fiat 131 Abarth	2	Ilkka Kivimaki	7th
50	**Portugal**	**Fiat Auto Torino**	**Fiat 131Abarth**	**1**	**Ilkka Kivimaki**	**1st**
51	Greece	Fiat Auto Torino	Fiat 131 Abarth	4	Ilkka Kivimaki	2nd
52	Finland	Fiat Auto Torino	Fiat 131 Abarth	1	Ilkka Kivimaki	2nd
53	Sanremo	Fiat Auto Torino	Fiat 131 Abarth	2	Ilkka Kivimaki	9th
54	Great Britain	Team Chardonnet	Lancia Stratos HF	3	Ilkka Kivimaki	Retired
1982	**12 points (21st)**					
55	Corsica	Martini Racing	Lancia Rally 037	6	Ilkka Kivimaki	9th
56	Greece	Martini Racing	Lancia Rally 037	2	Ilkka Kivimaki	Retired
57	Finland	Martini Racing	Lancia Rally 037	2	Ilkka Kivimaki	Retired
58	Sanremo	Martini Racing	Lancia Rally 037	2	Ilkka Kivimaki	Retired
59	Great Britain	Martini Racing	Lancia Rally 037	3	Ilkka Kivimaki	4th
1983	**100 points (3rd)**					
60	Monte Carlo	Martini Racing	Lancia Rally 037	4	Ilkka Kivimaki	2nd
61	Portugal	Martini Racing	Lancia Rally 037	4	Ilkka Kivimaki	4th
62	**Corsica**	**Martini Racing**	**Lancia Rally 037**	**9**	**Ilkka Kivimaki**	**1st**
63	Greece	Martini Racing	Lancia Rally 037	7	Ilkka Kivimaki	2nd
64	Argentina	Martini Racing	Lancia Rally 037	7	Ilkka Kivimaki	5th
65	Finland	Martini Racing	Lancia Rally 037	2	Ilkka Kivimaki	3rd
66	**Sanremo**	**Martini Racing**	**Lancia Rally 037**	**6**	**Ilkka Kivimaki**	**1st**
1984	**90 points (3rd)**					
67	Monte Carlo	Martini Racing	Lancia Rally 037	2	Ilkka Kivimaki	8th
68	Portugal	Martini Racing	Lancia Rally 037	2	Ilkka Kivimaki	2nd
69	Safari	Martini Racing	Lancia Rally 037	7	Ilkka Kivimaki	4th
70	**Corsica**	**Martini Racing**	**Lancia Rally 037**	**5**	**Ilkka Kivimaki**	**1st**
71	Greece	Martini Racing	Lancia Rally 037	2	Ilkka Kivimaki	3rd
72	New Zealand	Martini Racing	Lancia Rally 037	6	Ilkka Kivimaki	2nd
73	Finland	Martini Racing	Lancia Rally 037	2	Ilkka Kivimaki	2nd
74	Sanremo	Martini Racing	Lancia Rally 037	1	Ilkka Kivimaki	Retired
1985	**37 points (7th)**					
75	Safari	Lancia Martini	Lancia Rally 037	5	Ilkka Kivimaki	Retired
76	Corsica	Lancia Martini	Lancia Rally 037	1	Ilkka Kivimaki	Retired
77	Finland	Lancia Martini	Lancia Rally 037	2	Ilkka Kivimaki	3rd
78	Sanremo	Lancia Martini	Lancia Rally 037	6	Ilkka Kivimaki	4th
79	Great Britain	Lancia Martini	Lancia Rally 037	3	Ilkka Kivimaki	2nd
1986	**104 points (2nd)**					
80	Monte Carlo	Martini Lancia	Lancia Delta S4	3	Ilkka Kivimaki	Retired
81	Sweden	Martini Lancia	Lancia Delta S4	3	Ilkka Kivimaki	2nd
82	Portugal	Martini Lancia	Lancia Delta S4	2	Ilkka Kivimaki	Retired
83	Safari	Martini Lancia	Lancia Rally 037	3	Ilkka Kivimaki	3rd
84	Corsica	Martini Lancia	Lancia Delta S4	1	Ilkka Kivimaki	Retired
85	Greece	Martini Lancia	Lancia Delta S4	3	Ilkka Kivimaki	Retired
86	New Zealand	Martini Lancia	Lancia Delta S4	2	Ilkka Kivimaki	2nd
87	Argentina	Martini Lancia	Lancia Delta S4	3	Ilkka Kivimaki	2nd
88	Finland	Martini Lancia	Lancia Delta S4	2	Ilkka Kivimaki	3rd
89	Great Britain	Martini Lancia	Lancia Delta S4	3	Ilkka Kivimaki	2nd
90	**United States**	**Martini Lancia**	**Lancia Delta S4**	**2**	**Ilkka Kivimaki**	**1st**
1987	**99 points (3rd)**					
91	Sweden	Martini Lancia	Lancia Delta HF 4WD	4	Ilkka Kivimaki	5th
92	**Portugal**	**Martini Lancia**	**Lancia Delta HF 4WD**	**3**	**Ilkka Kivimaki**	**1st**
93	**Greece**	**Martini Lancia**	**Lancia Delta HF 4WD**	**3**	**Ilkka Kivimaki**	**1st**
94	United States	Martini Lancia	Lancia Delta HF 4WD	1	Ilkka Kivimaki	3rd
95	**Finland**	**Martini Lancia**	**Lancia Delta HF 4WD**	**4**	**Ilkka Kivimaki**	**1st**
96	Sanremo	Martini Lancia	Lancia Delta HF 4WD	1	Ilkka Kivimaki	Retired
97	Great Britain	Martini Lancia	Lancia Delta HF 4WD	2	Ilkka Kivimaki	5th
1988	**86 points (2nd)**					
98	Sweden	Martini Lancia	Lancia Delta HF 4WD	4	Ilkka Kivimaki	1st
99	Portugal	Martini Lancia	Lancia Delta Integrale	1	Ilkka Kivimaki	6th
100	Greece	Martini Lancia	Lancia Delta Integrale	1	Ilkka Kivimaki	4th
101	**Finland**	**Martini Lancia**	**Lancia Delta Integrale**	**1**	**Ilkka Kivimaki**	**1st**
102	Sanremo	Martini Lancia	Lancia Delta Integrale	5	Ilkka Kivimaki	4th
103	**Great Britain**	**Martini Lancia**	**Lancia Delta Integrale**	**2**	**Ilkka Kivimaki**	**1st**
1989	**27 points (9th)**					
104	Portugal	Martini Lancia	Lancia Delta Integrale	3	Ilkka Kivimaki	2nd
105	Finland	Martini Lancia	Lancia Delta Integrale	1	Ilkka Kivimaki	Retired
106	Australia	Martini Lancia	Lancia Delta Integrale	2	Ilkka Kivimaki	3rd
1990	**10 points (20th)**					
107	Safari	Subaru Technica International	Subaru Legacy RS	1	Ilkka Kivimaki	Retired
108	Greece	Subaru Technica International	Subaru Legacy RS	5	Ilkka Kivimaki	Retired
109	Finland	Subaru Technica International	Subaru Legacy RS	3	Ilkka Kivimaki	4th
110	Sanremo	Subaru Technica International	Subaru Legacy RS	3	Ilkka Kivimaki	Retired
111	Great Britain	Subaru Technica International	Subaru Legacy RS	5	Ilkka Kivimaki	Retired
1991	**40 points (8th)**					
112	Sweden	Subaru Rally Team Europe	Subaru Legacy RS	5	Ilkka Kivimaki	3rd
113	Portugal	Subaru Rally Team Europe	Subaru Legacy RS	3	Ilkka Kivimaki	5th
114	Greece	Subaru Rally Team Europe	Subaru Legacy RS	3	Ilkka Kivimaki	Retired
115	New Zealand	Subaru Rally Team Europe	Subaru Legacy RS	3	Ilkka Kivimaki	4th
116	Finland	Subaru Rally Team Europe	Subaru Legacy RS	4	Ilkka Kivimaki	Retired
117	Australia	Subaru Rally Team Europe/Markku Alén	Subaru Legacy RS	5	Ilkka Kivimaki	4th
118	Great Britain	Subaru Rally Team Europe	Subaru Legacy RS	6	Ilkka Kivimaki	Retired
1992	**50 points (5th)**					
119	Monte Carlo	Toyota Team Europe	Toyota Celica Turbo 4WD	10	Ilkka Kivimaki	Retired
120	Sweden	Toyota Team Sweden	Toyota Celica GT-Four	2	Ilkka Kivimaki	4th
121	Portugal	Toyota Team Europe	Toyota Celica Turbo 4WD	9	Ilkka Kivimaki	4th
122	Safari	Toyota Team Kenya	Toyota Celica Turbo 4WD	6	Ilkka Kivimaki	5th
123	Greece	Toyota Team Europe	Toyota Celica Turbo 4WD	7	Ilkka Kivimaki	Retired
124	Finland	Toyota Team Europe	Toyota Celica Turbo 4WD	5	Ilkka Kivimaki	3rd
125	Great Britain	Toyota Team Europe	Toyota Celica Turbo 4WD	7	Ilkka Kivimaki	4th
1993	**25 points (11th)**					
126	Portugal	555 Subaru World Rally Team	Subaru Legacy RS	8	Ilkka Kivimaki	4th
127	Safari	Toyota Castrol Team	Toyota Celica Turbo 4WD	2	Ilkka Kivimaki	2nd
128	Finland	555 Subaru World Rally Team	Subaru Impreza 555	5	Ilkka Kivimaki	Retired
2001	**0 points**					
129	Finland	Blue Rose Team	Ford Focus WRC	29	Ilkka Riipinen	16th

AMBROSINO, ALAIN (F) BORN: 15 MAY 1951, CASABLANCA, MOROCCO

For years, only local drivers won the Safari Rally, but on the other side of Africa at the Bandama Rally, later known as the Ivory Coast Rally, the habit was for European drivers to win. That stopped when Alain Ambrosino won the event in 1988.

At home in Morocco, Ambrosino started out with a Renault R8 Gordini but a move to West Africa allowed him to chose the slower, but more sturdy, Peugeot 504. With that model, he notched up the national championship – winning himself a drive with Bob Neyret's Renault Alpine team in America's round of the 1974 WRC – the Press on Regardless Rally.

Ambrosino campaigned the trusty Peugeot – with reasonable success on the Ivory Coast – until 1984, whereupon he switched to an Opel Manta 400 and got one of his best results – fourth – on the African event, as well as winning the national title again. Added to that, he secured FIA African championships in 1983, 1986 and 1987.

He switched allegiance to Nissan and drove in both East and West Africa in a Group B 240RS. However, it was in the Group A 200SX with which he finally won the Ivory Coast at his 20th attempt. When the unloved Ivory Coast Rally was eventually dropped from the World Championship, Ambrosino found a useful career in driving long distance Rally-Raids for first Peugeot and then Citroën.

AMBROSINO, ALAIN – CAREER RECORD

YEAR	RALLY	TEAM/ENTRANT	CAR	NO.	CO-DRIVER	RESULT
1974						
1	United States	Team Aseptogyl	Alpine-Renault A110	27	Jean-Jacques Regnier	Retired
1978						
2	Ivory Coast		Peugeot 104	11	Jean-Robert Bureau	Retired
1979	6 points (34th)					
3	Ivory Coast		Peugeot 504 V6 Coupe	9	Robert Schneck	6th
1980	12 points (21st)					
4	Ivory Coast	SARI	Peugeot 504 V6 Coupe	12	Jean-Robert Bureau	3rd
1981	6 points (33rd)					
5	Safari	Marshalls	Peugeot 504 V6 Coupe	3	Jean-Francois Fauchille	Retired
6	Ivory Coast	SARI Peugeot	Peugeot 504 V6 Coupe	5	Daniel le Saux	6th
1982	8 points (26th)					
7	Ivory Coast	Peugeot Nigeria	Peugeot 504 V6 Coupe	15	Jean-Francois Fauchille	5th
1983	10 points (17th)					
8	Ivory Coast	D.T.Dobie & Co. Ltd	Peugeot 504 V6 Coupe	7	Daniel Le Saux	5th
1984	10 points (19th)					
9	Ivory Coast		Opel Manta 400	4	Daniel Le Saux	4th
1985	18 points (15th)					
10	Safari		Nissan 240 RS	20	Daniel Le Saux	6th
11	Ivory Coast		Nissan 240 RS	5	Daniel Le Saux	3rd
1986	3 points (49th)					
12	Ivory Coast		Nissan 240 RS	4	Daniel Le Saux	8th
1987	0 points					
13	Ivory Coast	Nissan Motorsports International	Nissan 200SX	6	Daniel Le Saux	Retired
1988	20 points (14th)					
14	Safari	Marlboro Africa Team	Nissan 200SX	16	Daniel Le Saux	Retired
15	**Ivory Coast**		**Nissan 200SX**	**3**	**Daniel Le Saux**	**1st**
1989	0 points					
16	Ivory Coast		Nissan 200SX	1	Daniel Le Saux	Retired
1990	10 points (20th)					
17	Ivory Coast		Nissan March Super Turbo	2	Daniel Le Saux	4th

ANDERSSON, OVE

(S) BORN: 3 JANUARY 1938, UPPSALA, SWEDEN

"If the WRC had been invented in 1971, he would surely have won the drivers' title"

Perhaps better known recently for his team management of Toyota in Formula One, Ove Andersson had a long and distinguished career in rallying.

The son of a farmer in Central Sweden, Andersson's first driving skills were acquired on tractors. Motor bikes followed and were succeeded by cars when he opened his own garage. From there, it was a short step to rallying in a Saab 96 two-stroke. An introduction to BMC Sweden saw him driving a Cooper S in 1963. He nearly won the Swedish Rally, at that time a summer event, and was promptly offered a works drive with Saab. His programme was Swedish events but, when he won one of the biggest, he got a chance to drive the Acropolis Rally where he was 10th and the 1000 Lakes where he came seventh. On the Monte of 1965, he would have been third but for a broken gear lever and he finished well on the Swedish and 1000 Lakes again.

During 1965, he wrote to Lancia asking them for a drive and was astounded when, four months later, he got a positive answer. For 1966, he drove the Flavia Coupe most of the year, regularly getting on the podium and then with the new Fulvia, things improved further. He was seventh on the 1966 RAC Rally and then second, by only 13 seconds, on the Monte Carlo of 1967. He followed that up with a third at San Remo, second in Acropolis, and won the Spanish Rally. He also did some British and Scandinavian events as a freelance in a Ford Cortina, winning the Gulf London and finishing fourth on the 1000 Lakes.

Ford had their new Escort Twin Cam for 1968 and wooed Andersson away from Lancia. He was third with it on its debut international at San Remo but, after that, luck seemed to desert him. The 1970 season was even worse and Ford let him know that his contract would not be renewed. At that point, he had an approach from Alpine. They lent him an A110 for Portugal and the RAC Rally. He was not successful on either losing the clutch on the first and being hit by another car on the second, but had impressed sufficiently to be drafted into the French team for 1971.

It was a good choice all round. Andersson won four events outright: Monte Carlo, Acropolis, San Remo and Austrian Alpine. If the WRC had been invented, he would surely have won the drivers' title. In any case, Alpine won its predecessor, the International Championship for Makes and he stayed on for 1972. Sadly, the Alpine gearbox was in need of up rating when they went to the 1800cc engine and a spate of retirements filled his year. He made contact with Toyota at about the time Renault took over Alpine and decided they only wanted French drivers. He drove a Celica on the 1972 RAC Rally, won his class and beat the Datsuns. In Toyota's language, this was good news. They supported his efforts with a small European team that gradually grew into the behemoth that was Toyota Team Europe.

Andersson's driving duties gradually diminished but not before he had a freelance outing with Peugeot to win the Safari. He finally hung up his helmet at the end of 1982 after driving a chase car on the Ivory Coast Rally.

After switching to team management he was to oversee three Toyota victories on that event, eight on the Safari plus three WRC Manufacturers' and four Drivers' titles.

Ove Andersson competing on the 1976 RAC Rally. His only WRC win came with Peugeot on the 1975 Safari but the Swede will be forever associated with Toyota, both as a driver and highly successful team manager

ANDERSSON, OVE – CAREER RECORD

YEAR	RALLY	TEAM/ENTRANT	CAR	NO.	CO-DRIVER	RESULT
1973						
1	Monte Carlo	Renault-Alpine	Renault-Alpine A110	15	Jean Todt	2nd
2	Sweden		Lancia Fulvia	6	Piero Sodana	Retired
3	Portugal		Toyota Celica	9	Jean Todt	Retired
4	Safari	Marshalls (EA) Ltd	Peugeot 504	7	Jean Todt	3rd
5	Greece		Toyota Celica	4	Gunnar Haggbom	Retired
6	Austria		Toyota Celica	9	Gunnar Haggbom	8th
7	Great Britain		Toyota Celica	9	Geraint Phillips	12th
1974						
8	Portugal		Toyota Corolla	3	Arne Hertz	4th
9	Safari	Marshalls (EA) Ltd.	Peugeot 504	4	Arne Hertz	Retired
10	Great Britain	Dealer Team Toyota	Toyota Corolla	14	Arne Hertz	Retired
1975						
11	**Safari**	**Marshalls (EA) Ltd.**	**Peugeot 504**	**26**	**Arne Hertz**	**1st**
12	Greece		Toyota Corolla	6	Arne Hertz	Retired
13	Portugal		Toyota Corolla	3	Arne Hertz	3rd
14	Great Britain	Toyota (GB) Ltd	Toyota Celica	5	Arne Hertz	Retired
1976						
15	Portugal		Toyota Celica	2	Arne Hertz	2nd
16	Greece		Toyota Celica	2	Claes Billstam	Retired
17	Great Britain	Team Toyota	Toyota Corolla	8	Martin Holmes	5th
1977						
18	Portugal		Toyota Celica	4	Henry Liddon	3rd
19	Greece		Toyota Celica	4	Henry Liddon	Retired
1978						
20	Portugal	Toyota Team Europe	Toyota Celica	6	Henry Liddon	4th
21	Greece	Toyota Team Europe	Toyota Celica	2	Henry Liddon	Retired
1979	20 points (13th)					
22	Portugal	Toyota Team Europe	Toyota Celica 2000GT	4	Henry Liddon	3rd
23	Greece	Toyota Team Europe	Toyota Celica 2000GT	5	Henry Liddon	Retired
24	Ivory Coast	Toyota Team Europe	Toyota Celica 2000GT	5	Henry Liddon	5th
1980	12 points (24th)					
25	Portugal	Toyota Team Europe	Toyota Celica 2000GT	6	Henry Liddon	6th
26	Greece	Toyota Team Europe	Toyota Celica 2000GT	6	Henry Liddon	6th
27	Ivory Coast	Premoto Toyota	Toyota Celica 2000GT	1	Henry Liddon	Retired
1982	0 points					
28	Ivory Coast		Toyota Celica 2000GT	10	Robbie Grondahl	Retired

ANDRUET, JEAN-CLAUDE (F) BORN: 13 AUGUST 1942, MONTREUIL, FRANCE

Brilliant but ever so slightly eccentric, Jean-Claude Andruet was a stalwart of the Alpine Renault team in the 1960s. Nicknamed the 'Ball of Nerves' by his team mates, he was the first driver to win a WRC rally.

Andruet was a lawyer and married with a family before he was a rally driver. He was not seduced by motor sport until, aged 22, he went to a driving school with fellow pupil, Henri Pescarolo. At the end of 1964, he bought one of the new Renault R8 1100cc Gordinis and started rallying. He was pretty much an instant success winning the French novices title. In 1966 he competed in the Coupe Gordini, a mixture of races and rallies. He might have won but his car was disqualified thanks to an error of his mechanic. But he had come to the notice of Alpine – at that time still separate from Renault – and for 1967 they lent him an A110. He won his class seven times including the Coupe des Alpes and won the Challenge Shell Berre. For 1968, he moved into their factory team, winning the French championship, including the Tour de Corse.

The early 1970s were an unlucky period for Andruet although he still won a string of rallies outside France and became both French and European champion. His eccentricity was often marked by a failure to follow the instructions of his co-driver, thinking that he knew best, but he had a glorious victory on the 1973 Monte Carlo, the first time a French crew in a French car had won it since the Panhard of Martin and Bateau 12 years earlier.

Andruet later drove privately sponsored Ferraris and factory entered Fiats and Lancias. With the advent of Group B, he drove Citroën's ill-conceived BX4TC and, when the programme was mercifully terminated, so effectively were Andruet's WRC efforts.

ANDRUET, JEAN-CLAUDE - CAREER RECORD

YEAR	RALLY	TEAM/ENTRANT	CAR	NO.	CO-DRIVER	RESULT
1973						
1	**Monte Carlo**	**Renault-Alpine**	**Renault-Alpine A110**	**18**	**'Biche'**	**1st**
1974						
2	**Corsica**	**Marlboro Lancia Italia**	**Lancia Stratos**	**2**	**'Biche'**	**1st**
1975						
3	Monte Carlo		Lancia Stratos	1	Yves Jouanny	Retired
4	Corsica		Alfa Romeo Alfetta GT	3	Yves Jouanny	3rd
1976						
5	Monte Carlo		Renault-Alpine A310	1	Yves Jouanny	Retired
6	Corsica		Renault-Alpine A310	2	'Biche'	Retired
1977						
7	Monte Carlo	Fiat-Alitalia	Fiat 131 Abarth	2	'Biche'	2nd
8	Portugal		Fiat 131 Abarth	5	Christian Delferrier	4th
9	Greece		Fiat 131 Abarth	7	Christian Delferrier	Retired
10	**Sanremo**		**Fiat 131 Abarth**	**9**	**Christian Delferrier**	**1st**
11	Corsica		Fiat 131 Abarth	7	Christian Delferrier	Retired
1978						
12	Monte Carlo	Fiat-Alitalia	Fiat 131 Abarth	4	'Biche'	6th
13	Corsica		Fiat 131 Abarth	3	'Biche'	2nd
1979	10 points (22nd)					
14	Monte Carlo	Fiat France	Fiat 131 Abarth	9	Chantal Lienard	4th
15	Corsica		Fiat 131 Abarth	5	'Biche'	Retired
1980	0 points					
16	Monte Carlo	Fiat France	Fiat 131 Abarth	9	'Biche'	Retired
17	Corsica	Fiat France	Fiat 131 Abarth	6	'Biche'	Retired
1981	0 points					
18	Monte Carlo	Charles Pozzi	Ferrari 308GTB	14	'Biche'	Retired
1982	15 points (13th)					
19	Monte Carlo	Charles Pozzi	Ferrari 308GTB	3	'Biche'	Retired
20	Corsica	Charles Pozzi	Ferrari 308GTB	12	'Biche'	2nd
1983	3 points (41st)					
21	Monte Carlo	Martini Racing	Lancia Rally 037	7	'Biche'	8th
22	Corsica	Martini Racing	Lancia Rally 037	1	'Biche'	Retired
1984	6 points (30th)					
23	Monte Carlo	Martini Racing	Lancia Rally 037	5	Sergio Cresto	Retired
24	Corsica	Total Chardonnet	Lancia Rally 037	11	Martine Rick	6th
1985	3 points (51st)					
25	Monte Carlo	Citroen Competition	Citroen Visa 1000 Pistes	7	Annick Peuvergne	8th
1986	6 points (36th)					
26	Monte Carlo	Citroen Competition	Citroen BX4TC	15	Annick Peuvergne	Retired
27	Sweden	Citroen Competition	Citroen BX4TC	10	Annick Peuvergne	6th
28	Greece	Citroen Competition	Citroen BX4TC	14	Annick Peuvergne	Retired
1995	0 points					
29	Monte Carlo		Mini Cooper 1.3i	32	'Biche'	Retired

AURIOL, DIDIER

(F) BORN: 18 AUGUST 1958, MONTPELLIER, FRANCE

"He drove taxis and ambulances for four years to earn money for his first rally car"

Didier Auriol's first contact with rallying was as a spectator on his local event, the Criterium des Cevennes. It fired his imagination to the point where he drove taxis and ambulances for four years to earn money for his first rally car. That vehicle was a Simca Rallye 2 and he did his first event with it in 1979.

By 1982, he had graduated to an Escort RS 2000 and won his first national event, the Ronde du Quercy. This success led him to make contact with his long-term sponsor, the French beer, 33 Export, and it was with their backing that he drove a Renault 5 Turbo in 1984 and made his WRC debut in Corsica, retiring with a turbo fire. He moved up to a Maxi Turbo for the following year and accepted an offer from Austin Rover to drive their Metro 6R4 in the French Championship. Auriol duly won it for them and when Group B disappeared for 1987, he drove a Sierra Cosworth run by RED, the same company that had run his Metro. He got solid results on the WRC events that he tackled and twice more won the French Championship.

Ford gave him a works car for Corsica in 1988 and he won it, so he stayed with them and even managed to finish third at his first attempt at the 1000 Lakes Rally, normally an exclusively Scandinavian affair. Lancia snapped him up for 1989 and it proved to be a good choice since his results helped them to yet another WRC Manufacturers' crown. He won the three classic Mediterranean events in 1990 but could only claim a distant second place in the championship. The following year he drove a Lancia for the Jolly Club and was a consistent finisher. For 1992, he got into the works Lancia team but despite winning six events outright, including the 1000 Lakes, they were almost his only results and the WRC title eluded him.

When Martini Lancia stopped at the end of 1992, Auriol moved to Toyota and won Monte Carlo for the third time on his debut with the team. The ensuing event in Sweden was not so nice thanks to an 'illegal supply' of oil that saw the team fined $300,000 and his engine expiring for lack of the fluid. Good results but no wins brought him third place in the Championship for the third year in a row. But in 1994, it all came right despite retirement on Monte Carlo and Auriol finally claimed the Drivers' Championship.

He won Corsica for the sixth time in 1995 but this was a black year for Toyota who lost all its points and was banned for 12 months after the turbo scandal in Catalunya. There followed a two-year period of picking up drives where he could find them until, with the arrival of the Corolla WRC, he went back into the Toyota fold. The car was what Toyota should have had years earlier but now the competition had moved on. After two and half seasons (that included victory on the sport's only visit to China), so did Auriol, accepting a drive first with SEAT and then with Peugeot. For 2002, there was only a private entry on the Monte Carlo but he came back with Skoda for 2003 with the promise of a much quicker Fabia WRC by mid-season although he was discarded by the team at the end of the season. With over 150 WRC starts to his name, the young man from Millau is now a veteran.

Right: Didier Auriol, Catalunya 1992. The Frenchman won a record six events during the year but poor results on his remaining starts meant that he missed out on the title

AURIOL, DIDIER - CAREER RECORD

YEAR	RALLY	TEAM/ENTRANT	CAR	NO.	CO-DRIVER	RESULT
1984	**0 points**					
1	Corsica		Renault 5 Turbo	32	Bernard Occelli	Retired
1985	**0 points**					
2	Corsica		Renault 5 Maxi Turbo	27	Bernard Occelli	Retired
1986	**0 points**					
3	Corsica	Austin Rover Team	MG Metro 6R4	12	Bernard Occelli	Retired
1987	**13 points (22nd)**					
4	Corsica	Ford France	Ford Sierra RS Cosworth	11	Bernard Occelli	8th
5	Sanremo	Ford France	Ford Sierra RS Cosworth	8	Bernard Occelli	4th
1988	**32 points (6th)**					
6	Portugal	Ford France	Ford Sierra RS Cosworth	11	Bernard Occelli	Retired
7	**Corsica**	**Ford Motor Company**	**Ford Sierra RS Cosworth**	**8**	**Bernard Occelli**	**1st**
8	Finland	Ford Motor Company	Ford Sierra RS Cosworth	9	Bernard Occelli	3rd
9	Sanremo	Ford Motor Company	Ford Sierra RS Cosworth	4	Bernard Occelli	Retired
1989	**50 points (5th)**					
10	Monte Carlo	Martini Lancia	Lancia Delta Integrale	6	Bernard Occelli	2nd
11	Portugal	Martini Lancia	Lancia Delta Integrale	5	Bernard Occelli	Retired
12	**Corsica**	**Martini Lancia**	**Lancia Delta Integrale**	**1**	**Bernard Occelli**	**1st**
13	Greece	Martini Lancia	Lancia Delta Integrale	6	Bernard Occelli	2nd
14	Finland	Martini Lancia	Lancia Delta Integrale	5	Bernard Occelli	Retired
15	Sanremo	Martini Lancia	Lancia Delta Integrale	5	Bernard Occelli	Retired
1990	**95 points (2nd)**					
16	**Monte Carlo**	**Martini Lancia**	**Lancia Delta Integrale 16V**	**7**	**Bernard Occelli**	**1st**
17	Portugal	Martini Lancia	Lancia Delta Integrale 16V	4	Bernard Occelli	2nd
18	**Corsica**	**Martini Lancia**	**Lancia Delta Integrale 16V**	**1**	**Bernard Occelli**	**1st**
19	Greece	Martini Lancia	Lancia Delta Integrale 16V	7	Bernard Occelli	Retired
20	Argentina	Martini Lancia	Lancia Delta Integrale 16V	5	Bernard Occelli	3rd
21	Finland	Martini Lancia	Lancia Delta Integrale 16V	7	Bernard Occelli	Retired
22	Australia	Martini Lancia	Lancia Delta Integrale 16V	7	Bernard Occelli	Retired
23	**Sanremo**	**Martini Lancia**	**Lancia Delta Integrale 16V**	**11**	**Bernard Occelli**	**1st**
24	Great Britain	Martini Lancia	Lancia Delta Integrale 16V	11	Bernard Occelli	5th
1991	**101 points (3rd)**					
25	Monte Carlo	Jolly Club	Lancia Delta Integrale 16V	1	Bernard Occelli	Retired
26	Sweden	Jolly Club	Lancia Delta Integrale 16V	10	Bernard Occelli	9th
27	Portugal	Jolly Club	Lancia Delta Integrale 16V	7	Bernard Occelli	2nd
28	Corsica	Jolly Club	Lancia Delta Integrale 16V	1	Bernard Occelli	2nd
29	Greece	Jolly Club	Lancia Delta Integrale 16V	6	Bernard Occelli	4th
30	New Zealand	Jolly Club	Lancia Delta Integrale 16V	4	Bernard Occelli	3rd
31	Argentina	Jolly Club	Lancia Delta Integrale 16V	6	Bernard Occelli	3rd
32	Finland	Jolly Club	Lancia Delta Integrale 16V	6	Bernard Occelli	2nd
33	Australia	Jolly Club	Lancia Delta Integrale 16V	6	Bernard Occelli	Retired
34	**Sanremo**	**Jolly Club**	**Lancia Delta Integrale 16V**	**1**	**Bernard Occelli**	**1st**
35	Great Britain	Jolly Club	Lancia Delta Integrale 16V	4	Bernard Occelli	12th
1992	**121 points (3rd)**					
36	**Monte Carlo**	**Martini Lancia**	**Lancia Delta HF Integrale**	**4**	**Bernard Occelli**	**1st**
37	Portugal	Martini Lancia	Lancia Delta HF Integrale	2	Bernard Occelli	Retired
38	**Corsica**	**Martini Lancia**	**Lancia Delta HF Integrale**	**3**	**Bernard Occelli**	**1st**
39	**Greece**	**Martini Lancia**	**Lancia Delta HF Integrale**	**6**	**Bernard Occelli**	**1st**
40	**Argentina**	**Martini Lancia**	**Lancia Delta HF Integrale**	**3**	**Bernard Occelli**	**1st**
41	**Finland**	**Martini Lancia**	**Lancia Delta HF Integrale**	**3**	**Bernard Occelli**	**1st**
42	**Australia**	**Martini Lancia**	**Lancia Delta HF Integrale**	**3**	**Bernard Occelli**	**1st**
43	Sanremo	Martini Lancia	Lancia Delta HF Integrale	3	Bernard Occelli	Retired
44	Catalunya	Martini Lancia	Lancia Delta HF Integrale	3	Bernard Occelli	10th
45	Great Britain	Martini Lancia	Lancia Delta HF Integrale	6	Bernard Occelli	Retired
1993	**92 points (3rd)**					
46	**Monte Carlo**	**Toyota Castrol Team**	**Toyota Celica Turbo 4WD**	**3**	**Bernard Occelli**	**1st**
47	Sweden	Toyota Castrol Team	Toyota Celica Turbo 4WD	6	Bernard Occelli	Retired
48	Corsica	Toyota Castrol Team	Toyota Celica Turbo 4WD	1	Bernard Occelli	2nd
49	Greece	Toyota Castrol Team	Toyota Celica Turbo 4WD	1	Bernard Occelli	Retired
50	Argentina	Toyota Castrol Team	Toyota Celica Turbo 4WD	1	Bernard Occelli	3rd

AURIOL, DIDIER - CAREER RECORD (CONT'D)

YEAR	RALLY	TEAM/ENTRANT	CAR	NO.	CO-DRIVER	RESULT
51	New Zealand	Toyota Castrol Team	Toyota Celica Turbo 4WD	2	Bernard Occelli	3rd
52	Finland	Toyota Castrol Team	Toyota Celica Turbo 4WD	1	Bernard Occelli	3rd
53	Australia	Toyota Castrol Team	Toyota Celica Turbo 4WD	3	Bernard Occelli	Retired
54	Catalunya	Toyota Castrol Team	Toyota Celica Turbo 4WD	4	Bernard Occelli	2nd
55	Great Britain	Toyota Castrol Team	Toyota Celica Turbo 4WD	6	Bernard Occelli	6th
1994	**116 points (WORLD CHAMPION)**					
56	Monte Carlo	Toyota Castrol Team	Toyota Celica Turbo 4WD	3	Bernard Occelli	Retired
57	Portugal	Toyota Castrol Team	Toyota Celica Turbo 4WD	6	Bernard Occelli	2nd
58	Safari	Toyota Castrol Team	Toyota Celica Turbo 4WD	2	Bernard Occelli	3rd
59	**Corsica**	**Toyota Castrol Team**	**Toyota Celica Turbo 4WD**	**5**	**Bernard Occelli**	**1st**
60	Greece	Toyota Castrol Team	Toyota Celica Turbo 4WD	2	Bernard Occelli	Retired
61	**Argentina**	**Toyota Castrol Team**	**Toyota Celica Turbo 4WD**	**4**	**Bernard Occelli**	**1st**
62	New Zealand	Toyota Castrol Team	Toyota Celica Turbo 4WD	5	Bernard Occelli	5th
63	Finland	Toyota Castrol Team	Toyota Celica Turbo 4WD	4	Bernard Occelli	2nd
64	**Sanremo**	**Toyota Castrol Team**	**Toyota Celica Turbo 4WD**	**8**	**Bernard Occelli**	**1st**
65	Great Britain	Toyota Castrol Team	Toyota Celica Turbo 4WD	6	Bernard Occelli	6th
1995	**51 points (Disqualified)**					
66	Monte Carlo	Toyota Castrol Team	Toyota Celica GT-Four	1	Bernard Occelli	Retired
67	Sweden	Toyota Castrol Team	Toyota Celica GT-Four	1	Bernard Occelli	5th
68	Portugal	Toyota Castrol Team	Toyota Celica GT-Four	1	Bernard Occelli	5th
69	**Corsica**	**Toyota Castrol Team**	**Toyota Celica GT-Four**	**1**	**Denis Giraudet**	**1st**
70	New Zealand	Toyota Castrol Team	Toyota Celica GT-Four	1	Denis Giraudet	2nd
71	Australia	Toyota Castrol Team	Toyota Celica GT-Four	1	Denis Giraudet	Retired
72	Catalunya	Toyota Castrol Team	Toyota Celica GT-Four	1	Denis Giraudet	Disqualified
1996	**4 points (24th)**					
73	Sweden	555 Subaru World Rally Team	Subaru Impreza 555	3	Bernard Occelli	10th
74	Sanremo	Winfield Mitsubishi Ralliart	Mitsubishi Lancer EVO 3	8	Denis Giraudet	8th
1997	**6 points (11th)**					
75	Monte Carlo	RAS Sport	Ford Escort RS Cosworth	7	Jean-Marc Andrie	Retired
76	Argentina	HF Grifone	Toyota Celica GT-Four	7	Denis Giraudet	5th
77	Finland	Toyota Castrol Team	Toyota Corolla WRC	7	Denis Giraudet	8th
78	Indonesia	Toyota Castrol Team	Toyota Corolla WRC	7	Denis Giraudet	Retired
79	Sanremo	Toyota Castrol Team	Toyota Corolla WRC	7	Denis Giraudet	8th
80	Australia	Toyota Castrol Team	Toyota Corolla WRC	7	Denis Giraudet	3rd
81	Great Britain	Toyota Castrol Team	Toyota Corolla WRC	7	Denis Giraudet	Retired
1998	**34 points (5th)**					
82	Monte Carlo	Toyota Castrol Team	Toyota Corolla WRC	6	Denis Giraudet	14th
83	Sweden	Toyota Castrol Team	Toyota Corolla WRC	9	Denis Giraudet	6th
84	Safari	Toyota Castrol Team	Toyota Corolla WRC	6	Denis Giraudet	4th
85	Portugal	Toyota Castrol Team	Toyota Corolla WRC	6	Denis Giraudet	Retired
86	**Catalunya**	**Toyota Castrol Team**	**Toyota Corolla WRC**	**9**	**Denis Giraudet**	**1st**
87	Corsica	Toyota Castrol Team	Toyota Corolla WRC	6	Denis Giraudet	6th
88	Argentina	Toyota Castrol Team	Toyota Corolla WRC	6	Denis Giraudet	Retired
89	Greece	Toyota Castrol Team	Toyota Corolla WRC	6	Denis Giraudet	2nd
90	New Zealand	Toyota Castrol Team	Toyota Corolla WRC	6	Denis Giraudet	2nd
91	Finland	Toyota Castrol Team	Toyota Corolla WRC	6	Denis Giraudet	4th
92	Sanremo	Toyota Castrol Team	Toyota Corolla WRC	6	Denis Giraudet	Retired
93	Australia	Toyota Castrol Team	Toyota Corolla WRC	6	Denis Giraudet	3rd
94	Great Britain	Toyota Castrol Team	Toyota Corolla WRC	6	Denis Giraudet	Retired
1999	**52 points (3rd)**					
95	Monte Carlo	Toyota Castrol Team	Toyota Corolla WRC	4	Denis Giraudet	4th
96	Sweden	Toyota Castrol Team	Toyota Corolla WRC	4	Denis Giraudet	4th
97	Safari	Toyota Castrol Team	Toyota Corolla WRC	4	Denis Giraudet	2nd
98	Portugal	Toyota Castrol Team	Toyota Corolla WRC	4	Denis Giraudet	3rd
99	Catalunya	Toyota Castrol Team	Toyota Corolla WRC	4	Denis Giraudet	2nd
100	Corsica	Toyota Castrol Team	Toyota Corolla WRC	4	Denis Giraudet	5th

YEAR	RALLY	TEAM/ENTRANT	CAR	NO.	CO-DRIVER	RESULT
101	Argentina	Toyota Castrol Team	Toyota Corolla WRC	4	Denis Giraudet	3rd
102	Greece	Toyota Castrol Team	Toyota Corolla WRC	4	Denis Giraudet	Retired
103	New Zealand	Toyota Castrol Team	Toyota Corolla WRC	4	Denis Giraudet	4th
104	Finland	Toyota Castrol Team	Toyota Corolla WRC	4	Denis Giraudet	Retired
105	**China**	**Toyota Castrol Team**	**Toyota Corolla WRC**	**4**	**Denis Giraudet**	**1st**
106	Sanremo	Toyota Castrol Team	Toyota Corolla WRC	4	Denis Giraudet	3rd
107	Australia	Toyota Castrol Team	Toyota Corolla WRC	4	Denis Giraudet	Retired
108	Great Britain	Toyota Castrol Team	Toyota Corolla WRC	4	Denis Giraudet	Retired
2000	**4 points (12th)**					
109	Monte Carlo	SEAT Sport	SEAT Cordoba WRC E2	7	Denis Giraudet	Retired
110	Sweden	SEAT Sport	SEAT Cordoba WRC E2	7	Denis Giraudet	10th
111	Safari	SEAT Sport	SEAT Cordoba WRC E2	7	Denis Giraudet	3rd
112	Portugal	SEAT Sport	SEAT Cordoba WRC E2	7	Denis Giraudet	10th
113	Catalunya	SEAT Sport	SEAT Cordoba WRC E2	7	Denis Giraudet	13th
114	Argentina	SEAT Sport	SEAT Cordoba WRC E2	7	Denis Giraudet	Retired
115	Greece	SEAT Sport	SEAT Cordoba WRC E2	7	Denis Giraudet	Retired
116	New Zealand	SEAT Sport	SEAT Cordoba WRC E2	7	Denis Giraudet	Retired
117	Finland	SEAT Sport	SEAT Cordoba WRC E2	7	Denis Giraudet	11th
118	Cyprus	SEAT Sport	SEAT Cordoba WRC E2	7	Denis Giraudet	Retired
119	Corsica	SEAT Sport	SEAT Cordoba WRC E2	7	Denis Giraudet	8th
120	Sanremo	SEAT Sport	SEAT Cordoba WRC E2	7	Denis Giraudet	17th
121	Australia	SEAT Sport	SEAT Cordoba WRC E2	7	Denis Giraudet	8th
122	Great Britain	SEAT Sport	SEAT Cordoba WRC E2	7	Denis Giraudet	9th
2001	**23 points (7th)**					
123	Monte Carlo	Peugeot Total	Peugeot 206 WRC	2	Denis Giraudet	Retired
124	Sweden	Peugeot Total	Peugeot 206 WRC	2	Denis Giraudet	Retired
125	Portugal	Peugeot Total	Peugeot 206 WRC	2	Denis Giraudet	8th
126	**Catalunya**	**Peugeot Total**	**Peugeot 206 WRC**	**2**	**Denis Giraudet**	**1st**
127	Argentina	Peugeot Total	Peugeot 206 WRC	2	Denis Giraudet	Retired
128	Cyprus	Peugeot Total	Peugeot 206 WRC	2	Denis Giraudet	Retired
129	Greece	Peugeot Total	Peugeot 206 WRC	2	Denis Giraudet	Retired
130	Safari	Peugeot Total	Peugeot 206 WRC	2	Denis Giraudet	Retired
131	Finland	Peugeot Total	Peugeot 206 WRC	2	Denis Giraudet	Retired
132	New Zealand	Peugeot Total	Peugeot 206 WRC	2	Denis Giraudet	6th
133	Sanremo	Peugeot Total	Peugeot 206 WRC	2	Denis Giraudet	3rd
134	Corsica	Peugeot Total	Peugeot 206 WRC	2	Denis Giraudet	3rd
135	Australia	Peugeot Total	Peugeot 206 WRC	2	Denis Giraudet	3rd
136	Great Britain	Peugeot Total	Peugeot 206 WRC	2	Denis Giraudet	7th
2002	**0 points**					
137	Monte Carlo	Privateer	Toyota Corolla WRC	24	Jack Boyere	Retired
2003	**4 points (13th)**					
138	Monte Carlo	Skoda Motorsport	Skoda Octavia WRC	14	Denis Giraudet	9th
139	Sweden	Skoda Motorsport	Skoda Octavia WRC	14	Denis Giraudet	18th
140	Turkey	Skoda Motorsport	Skoda Octavia WRC	14	Denis Giraudet	Retired
141	New Zealand	Skoda Motorsport	Skoda Octavia WRC	14	Denis Giraudet	8th
142	Argentina	Skoda Motorsport	Skoda Octavia WRC	14	Denis Giraudet	6th
143	Greece	Skoda Motorsport	Skoda Octavia WRC	14	Denis Giraudet	9th
144	Cyprus	Skoda Motorsport	Skoda Octavia WRC	14	Denis Giraudet	Retired
145	Germany	Skoda Motorsport	Skoda Fabia WRC	14	Denis Giraudet	Retired
146	Finland	Skoda Motorsport	Skoda Fabia WRC	14	Denis Giraudet	Withdrawn
147	Australia	Skoda Motorsport	Skoda Fabia WRC	14	Denis Giraudet	12th
148	Sanremo	Skoda Motorsport	Skoda Fabia WRC	14	Denis Giraudet	12th
149	Corsica	Skoda Motorsport	Skoda Fabia WRC	14	Denis Giraudet	Retired
150	Catalunya	Skoda Motorsport	Skoda Fabia WRC	14	Denis Giraudet	Retired
151	Great Britain	Skoda Motorsport	Skoda Fabia WRC	14	Denis Giraudet	11th

BACCHELLI, FULVIO (I) BORN: 22 JANUARY 1951, TRIESTE, FRANCE

If anyone was to be nominated as the male pin-up of rally drivers, then it would probably be Fulvio Bacchelli who, with his blonde hair and Hollywood looks, was an untypical Italian. But looks are deceptive and Bacchelli's one WRC win was on one of the longest and psychologically most demanding events in the 30 years of the championship.

Bacchelli started rallying in 1971 with a Porsche and was sufficiently successful that he was recruited into the burgeoning Fiat team in 1974. Bacchelli tackled a mixture of European and World Championship events winning in San Marino and Bulgaria. He was one of the two drivers chosen to take the 131 Abarth on its Elba Rally debut where he finished second to Markku Alén's similar car. And in Morocco, the 131 Abarth's second event, Bacchelli led for most of the way, driving to what looked like his first WRC win. But on the last night, the suspension started to fall apart.

A year later, Fiat was fighting with Ford for the WRC and both decided to go to the newly elected New Zealand Rally. At seven days, five nights, 243 km of tarmac stages and 1,823 km of gravel stages it was a monster. Alén lost a water hose on the first night and Ari Vatanen put his Escort off the road. Bacchelli took the lead that he was to hold to the finish as the two Finns continued to make rods for their own backs. In the last leg of the rally, Bacchelli's engine started to give out and he had the additional worry of whether or not it would last. It did and he won by a mere minute and half from Vatanen.

At the end of the year, the Fiat and Lancia departments merged and gradually the total number of works drivers was reduced.

Bacchelli today runs a successful business for franchising electronics stores.

BACCHELLI, FULVIO – CAREER RECORD

YEAR	RALLY	TEAM /ENTRANT	CAR	NO.	CO-DRIVER	RESULT
1973						
1	Sanremo		Fiat 124 Abarth	19	Francesco Rossetti	Retired
1974						
2	Sanremo	Fiat SpA	Fiat 124 Abarth	7	Bruno Scabini	Retired
3	Corsica	Fiat SpA	Fiat 124 Abarth	5	Bruno Scabini	6th
1975						
4	Monte Carlo	Fiat SpA	Fiat 124 Abarth	12	Bruno Scabini	4th
1976						
5	Morocco	Fiat SpA	Fiat 131 Abarth	9	Francesco Rossetti	Retired
6	Sanremo	Fiat SpA	Fiat 131 Abarth	7	Francesco Rossetti	Retired
7	Great Britain	Fiat SpA	Fiat 131 Abarth	14	Francesco Rossetti	11th
1977						
8	Monte Carlo	Fiat SpA	Fiat 131 Abarth	9	Francesco Rossetti	Retired
9	Portugal	Fiat SpA	Fiat 131 Abarth	8	Francesco Rossetti	Retired
10	**New Zealand**	**Fiat SpA**	**Fiat 131 Abarth**	**1**	**Francesco Rossetti**	**1st**
11	Greece	Fiat SpA	Fiat 131 Abarth	12	Francesco Rossetti	Retired
12	Sanremo	Fiat SpA	Fiat 131 Abarth	3	Francesco Rossetti	Retired
13	Corsica	Fiat SpA	Fiat 131 Abarth	3	Bruno Scabini	3rd
14	Great Britain	Fiat SpA	Fiat 131 Abarth	17	Francesco Rossetti	17th
1978						
15	Monte Carlo	Lancia-Pirelli	Lancia Stratos	5	Arnaldo Bernacchini	10th
1979	**0 points**					
16	Monte Carlo		Lancia Stratos	6	Bruno Scabini	Retired
1982	**0 points**					
17	Sanremo	Volta	Lancia Rally 037	20	Paolo Spollon	Retired

BEGUIN, BERNARD (F) BORN: 24 SEPTEMBER 1947, GRENOBLE, FRANCE

In a rally career spanning more than 20 years, Bernard Beguin frequently showed that he was a top performer on tarmac, but, by never competing on WRC events other than Monte Carlo and Corsica, he was never able to land a full works drive.

Beguin was born in the heart of French rally territory at Grenoble and made his rally debut in 1973 with an Alfa Romeo. He continued to drive Alfas of various types for the next three years before acquiring a Porsche 911. His fortunes improved on French national events but on the Monte Carlo he retired with the car on fire in 1977 and broke the gearbox the following year. He tried a Christine Laure Alpine Renault 310 in Corsica and was up to sixth and mixing it with the Fiat Abarth 131s when the gearbox broke.

He started 1979 by driving a Ford France Escort RS2000 on the Monte Carlo but could not defeat the Opel Kadetts. He went on to win the French Championship with his Porsche, now a SC version. The next step was to try for the European Championship. The year started badly with an accident in Monte Carlo but he then won his first three EC events and eventually finished second in the championship.

Beguin tried one of the massive 430 bhp BMW M1s but project went nowhere. He had better luck with his Porsche in 1985 when he finished third. This, plus his previous BMW connection, got him into a Prodrive BMW M3 with which he won in 1987.

When the BMW programme stopped he renewed acquaintance with Ford and was French champion three times from 1991 in first a Sierra RS Cosworth and then an Escort RS Cosworth. Since then, Beguin has driven a Peugeot 306 Maxi and a Subaru Impreza 555 but his true ability clearly lay with more powerful machinery.

BEGUIN, BERNARD – CAREER RECORD

YEAR	RALLY	TEAM/ENTRANT	CAR	NO.	CO-DRIVER	RESULT
1974						
1	Corsica		Alfa Romeo Alfetta	23	Jacques Delaval	Retired
1976						
2	Monte Carlo		Alfa Romeo 2000 GTV	45	Jean-Francois Fauchille	10th
1977						
3	Monte Carlo		Porsche 911	19	Guy Gillot	Retired
4	Corsica		Renault-Alpine A310	14	Willy Huret	Retired
1978						
5	Monte Carlo	Christine Laure/BP	Porsche 911	16	Willy Huret	Retired
1979	0 points					
6	Monte Carlo	KWS	Ford Escort RS2000	30	Philippe Ozoux	16th
7	Corsica		Porsche 911SC	10	Jean-Jacques Lenne	Retired
1980	0 points					
8	Monte Carlo		Porsche 911SC	6	Jean-Jacques Lenne	Retired
1982	12 points (15th)					
9	Corsica	Sonauto Porsche	Porsche 911SC	16	Jean-Jacques Lenne	3rd
1983	0 points					
10	Corsica	BMW Motul	BMW M1	3	Jean-Jacques Lenne	Retired
1985	12 points (18th)					
11	Corsica	Rothmans Porsche Rally Team	Porsche 911SC RS	10	Jean-Jacques Lenne	3rd
1987	20 points (14th)					
12	**Corsica**	**Prodrive BMW**	**BMW M3**	**10**	**Jean-Jacques Lenne**	**1st**
1988	4 points (50th)					
13	Corsica	Bastos Motul BMW	BMW M3	1	Jean-Jacques Lenne	7th
1989	8 points (34th)					
14	Corsica	Bastos Motul BMW	BMW M3	3	Jean-Bernard Vieu	5th
1991	0 points					
15	Corsica	R.A.S Sport	Ford Sierra Cosworth 4x4	9	Jean-Marc Andrie	Retired
1993	6 points (31st)					
16	Corsica		Ford Escort RS Cosworth	15	Jean-Paul Chiaroni	6th

BIASION, MASSIMO (MIKI)

(I) BORN: 7 JANUARY 1958, BASSANO DEL GRAPPA, ITALY

A double World Rally Champion and the darling of Lancia's Group A domination in the late 1980s, Miki Biasion will be most remembered for his crucial wins on the Safari Rally which finally gave Lancia the glittering prize they had sought for over 20 years.

"Biasion's ability to consistently place himself on the podium helped Lancia to win the championship"

Biasion's first interests lay with motocross but then, in 1979, in company with his school friend and long-term co-driver-to-be, Tiziano Siviero, he tried his hand at a rally with an Opel Kadett GT/E. They were 38th overall but, not discouraged, he sought the backing of a local GM dealer, improved the car and by the end of the year had won the Group 1 section of the Italian championship. This enabled him to move up to an Opel Ascona for 1980 with which he won the Group 2 section. The next step was an Ascona 400 and though he did not win the championship with it, Biasion did make people sit up by finishing sixth in San Remo ahead of Markku Alén, Ari Vatanen and Timo Salonen.

He had one more year with Opel and was then offered a Lancia Rally 037 from the Jolly Club. He stormed the Italian championship with it, took fifth place in San Remo as well as winning the European championship. The time had now come for him to try the big events and so for two seasons, the Jolly Club took their young driver to a selection of European WRC events as a back-up to the main factory effort with the 037. He only posted one retirement out of nine events and one withdrawal following the death of Attilio Bettega in Corsica in 1985. He moved to the Lancia team at the same time that it had its first full season with the fearsome four-wheel drive Delta S4. The car took some getting used to and it did not help in a season that also saw his debut on the Safari Rally with an 037. But, in the second half of the year, Biasion got on the podium twice and then won in Argentina.

Having just got used to the raw power of a Group B car, it was down market to a Group A car for 1987 but Biasion was fortunate in that Lancia had the best Group A car around with the Delta HF. It was reliable and it was fast, and Biasion was the right man, in the right car, at the right time. He was second in the World championship to team mate Juha Kankkunen but in the following two years, there was no error and he was not only the first Italian World champion, but did it twice. The Delta was less competitive in 1990 but Biasion's ability to consistently place himself on the podium helped Lancia to win the Manufacturers' title for another two years.

Then with the Lancia programme terminating, Biasion signed with Ford to drive their uncompetitive Sierra. He racked up a good finishing record but it was not a winning car. The Escort Cosworth that replaced it could have been and Biasion gave it one of its few victories (Acropolis 1993), but the team and the car were going nowhere and after 1994, Biasion left the WRC for Rally Raids.

BIASION, MASSIMO – CAREER RECORD

YEAR	RALLY	TEAM / ENTRANT	CAR	NO.	CO-DRIVER	RESULT
1980	**0 points**					
1	Sanremo	Conrero Squadra Corse	Opel Ascona	31	Tiziano Siviero	Retired
1981	**6 points (33rd)**					
2	Sanremo	Hawk Racing Team	Opel Ascona 400	25	Tiziano Siviero	6th
1982	**3 points (49th)**					
3	Sanremo	Conrero Squadra Corse	Opel Ascona 400	18	Tiziano Siviero	8th
1983	**8 points (21st)**					
4	Sanremo	Jolly Club Totip	Lancia Rally 037	18	Tiziano Siviero	5th
1984	**43 points (6th)**					
5	Monte Carlo	Jolly Club	Lancia Rally 037	9	Tiziano Siviero	6th
6	Portugal	Jolly Club	Lancia Rally 037	8	Tiziano Siviero	4th
7	Corsica	Jolly Club	Lancia Rally 037	9	Tiziano Siviero	2nd
8	Greece	Jolly Club	Lancia Rally 037	9	Tiziano Siviero	Retired
9	Sanremo	Jolly Club	Lancia Rally 037	6	Tiziano Siviero	3rd
1985	**23 points (12th)**					
10	Monte Carlo	Jolly Club	Lancia Rally 037	5	Tiziano Siviero	9th
11	Portugal	Jolly Club	Lancia Rally 037	4	Tiziano Siviero	2nd
12	Corsica	Jolly Club	Lancia Rally 037	7	Tiziano Siviero	Withdrawn
13	Sanremo	Jolly Club	Lancia Rally 037	4	Tiziano Siviero	6th
1986	**47 points (5th)**					
14	Monte Carlo	Martini Lancia	Lancia Delta S4	9	Tiziano Siviero	Retired
15	Portugal	Martini Lancia	Lancia Delta S4	5	Tiziano Siviero	Withdrawn
16	Safari	Martini Lancia	Lancia Rally 037	4	Tiziano Siviero	Retired
17	Corsica	Martin Lancia	Lancia Delta S4	6	Tiziano Siviero	Retired
18	Greece	Martini Lancia	Lancia Delta S4	8	Tiziano Siviero	2nd
19	New Zealand	Martini Lancia	Lancia Delta S4	4	Tiziano Siviero	3rd
20	Argentina	Martini Lancia	Lancia Delta S4	5	Tiziano Siviero	1st
1987	**94 points (2nd)**					
21	Monte Carlo	Martini Lancia	Lancia Delta HF 4WD	6	Tiziano Siviero	1st
22	Portugal	Martini Lancia	Lancia Delta HF 4WD	6	Tiziano Siviero	8th
23	Corsica	Martini Lancia	Lancia Delta HF 4WD	6	Tiziano Siviero	3rd
24	Greece	Martini Lancia	Lancia Delta HF 4WD	5	Tiziano Siviero	7th
25	United States	Martini Lancia	Lancia Delta HF 4WD	6	Tiziano Siviero	2nd
26	Argentina	Martini Lancia	Lancia Delta HF 4WD	1	Tiziano Siviero	1st
27	Sanremo	Martini Lancia	Lancia Delta HF 4WD	3	Tiziano Siviero	1st
1988	**115 points (WORLD CHAMPION)**					
28	Monte Carlo	Martini Lancia	Lancia Delta HF 4WD	1	Tiziano Siviero	Retired
29	Portugal	Martini Lancia	Lancia Delta Integrale	4	Carlo Cassina	1st
30	Safari	Martini Lancia	Lancia Delta Integrale	6	Tiziano Siviero	1st
31	Greece	Martini Lancia	Lancia Delta Integrale	4	Tiziano Siviero	1st
32	United States	Martini Lancia	Lancia Delta Integrale	1	Tiziano Siviero	1st
33	Argentina	Martini Lancia	Lancia Delta Integrale	2	Tiziano Siviero	2nd
34	Sanremo	Martini Lancia	Lancia Delta Integrale	1	Tiziano Siviero	1st
1989	**106 points (WORLD CHAMPION)**					
35	Monte Carlo	Martini Lancia	Lancia Delta Integrale	4	Tiziano Siviero	1st
36	Portugal	Martini Lancia	Lancia Delta Integrale	1	Tiziano Siviero	1st
37	Safari	Martini Lancia	Lancia Delta Integrale	2	Tiziano Siviero	1st
38	Greece	Martini Lancia	Lancia Delta Integrale	1	Tiziano Siviero	1st
39	Finland	Martini Lancia	Lancia Delta Integrale	3	Tiziano Siviero	6th
40	Sanremo	Martini Lancia	Lancia Delta Integrale 16V	1	Tiziano Siviero1st	
1990	**76 points (4th)**					
41	Monte Carlo	Martini Lancia	Lancia Delta Integrale 16V	1	Tiziano Siviero	3rd
42	Portugal	Martini Lancia	Lancia Delta Integrale 16V	1	Tiziano Siviero	1st
43	Safari	Martini Lancia	Lancia Delta Integrale 16V	2	Tiziano Siviero	Retired
44	Greece	Martini Lancia	Lancia Delta Integrale 16V	1	Tiziano Siviero	3rd
45	Argentina	Martini Lancia	Lancia Delta Integrale 16V	3	Tiziano Siviero	1st
46	Sanremo	Martini Lancia	Lancia Delta Integrale 16V	1	Tiziano Siviero	Retired
47	Great Britain	Martini Lancia	Lancia Delta Integrale 16V	7	Tiziano Siviero	3rd
1991	**69 points (4th)**					
48	Monte Carlo	Martini Lancia	Lancia Delta Integrale 16V	3	Tiziano Siviero	2nd
49	Portugal	Martini Lancia	Lancia Delta Integrale 16V	1	Tiziano Siviero	3rd
50	Safari	Martini Lancia	Lancia Delta Integrale 16V	7	Tiziano Siviero	Retired
51	Greece	Martini Lancia	Lancia Delta Integrale 16V	2	Tiziano Siviero	3rd
52	Argentina	Martini Lancia	Lancia Delta Integrale 16V	1	Tiziano Siviero	2nd
53	Sanremo	Martini Lancia	Lancia Delta Integrale 16V	9	Tiziano Siviero	2nd
54	Great Britain	Martini Lancia	Lancia Delta Integrale 16V	7	Tiziano Siviero	Retired
1992	**60 points (4th)**					
55	Monte Carlo	Ford Motor Company	Ford Sierra Cosworth 4x4	3	Tiziano Siviero	8th
56	Portugal	Ford Motor Company	Ford Sierra Cosworth 4x4	7	Tiziano Siviero	2nd
57	Corsica	Ford Motor Company	Ford Sierra Cosworth 4x4	2	Tiziano Siviero	7th
58	Greece	Ford Motor Company	Ford Sierra Cosworth 4x4	8	Tiziano Siviero	3rd
59	Finland	Ford Motor Company	Ford Sierra Cosworth 4x4	4	Tiziano Siviero	5th
60	Sanremo	Ford Motor Company	Ford Sierra Cosworth 4x4	2	Tiziano Siviero	4th
61	Great Britain	Ford Motor Company	Ford Sierra Cosworth 4x4	3	Tiziano Siviero	5th
1993	**76 points (4th)**					
62	Monte Carlo	Ford Motor Company	Ford Escort RS Cosworth	2	Tiziano Siviero	3rd
63	Potugal	Ford Motor Company	Ford Escort RS Cosworth	2	Tiziano Siviero	2nd
64	Corsica	Ford Motor Company	Ford Escort RS Cosworth	7	Tiziano Siviero	7th
65	Greece	Ford Motor Company	Ford Escort RS Cosworth	7	Tiziano Siviero	1st
66	Argentina	Ford Motor Company	Ford Escort RS Cosworth	3	Tiziano Siviero	2nd
67	New Zealand	Ford Motor Company	Ford Escort RS Cosworth	6	Tiziano Siviero	Retired
68	Australia	Ford Motor Company	Ford Escort RS Cosworth	2	Tiziano Siviero	Retired
69	Sanremo	Ford Motor Company	Ford Escort RS Cosworth	5	Tiziano Siviero	Retired
70	Catalunya	Ford Motor Company	Ford Escort RS Cosworth	5	Tiziano Siviero	4th
1994	**42 points (6th)**					
71	Monte Carlo	Ford Motor Company	Ford Escort RS Cosworth	4	Tiziano Siviero	4th
72	Portugal	Ford Motor Company	Ford Escort RS Cosworth	4	Tiziano Siviero	3rd
73	Corsica	Ford Motor Company	Ford Escort RS Cosworth	2	Tiziano Siviero	5th
74	Greece	Ford Motor Company	Ford Escort RS Cosworth	1	Tiziano Siviero	Retired
75	Argentina	Ford Motor Company	Ford Escort RS Cosworth	3	Tiziano Siviero	Retired
76	New Zealand	Ford Motor Company	Ford Escort RS Cosworth	3	Tiziano Siviero	Retired
77	Sanremo	Ford Motor Company	Ford Escort RS Cosworth	5	Tiziano Siviero	3rd
78	Great Britain	Ford Motor Company	Ford Escort RS Cosworth	5	Tiziano Siviero	Retired

BLOMQVIST, STIG (S) BORN: 29 JULY 1946, OREBRO, SWEDEN

"In a career spanning almost 40 years, Stig Blomqvist has shown versatility and skill at the wheel of a wide variety of cars"

In a career spanning almost 40 years, Stig Blomqvist has shown versatility and skill at the wheel of a wide variety of cars, everything from front-wheel drive through rear-wheel drive to four-wheel drive.

He started out as a 19 year-old driving a Saab 96 in the Swedish Junior class from which he graduated in 1966. The following year he was fourth in the T-race championship, attracted some help from the Saab factory and went outside Sweden for the first time to the Austrian Alpine. For two more years, he stayed with national events in Sweden finishing fourth and then third in the national championship. He did the RAC Rally in 1969 unsuccessfully but returned in 1970 as a full works driver to lead the event until his transmission failed. His promotion had taken place at the beginning of 1970 when he had taken second place on the Swedish Rally which he was to go on to win in 1971, 72 and 73. He also added the RAC to his collection in 1971.

His career was linked to Saab right up until 1981. The 99 EMS and then the 99 Turbo replaced the 96 V4 but there proved to be a limit to the power that a front-wheel drive car could handle, and to Saab's resources. He continued to win the Swedish Rally – eventually totting up seven victories – but it would be fair to say that the cars were no longer matching his talent. When Saab closed its competition department in 1980, Blomqvist signed with the English Talbot team and drove a Sunbeam Lotus for a year. For 1982, he was offered some drives with Audi and at once he won the Swedish Rally for them. He continued to drive the Sunbeam but it was in the Audi Quattro that he really made an impression. He won the Finnish Hankirally in the winter and the South Swedish in the summer, finished second on the 1000 Lakes to team mate, Mikkola, and then, on his first ever visit to San Remo, won outright.

For 1982, he was a full factory driver for Audi but it was not until the last event of the year, that he won again. He would probably have won Sweden but part of his deal with Audi was that he would drive a non-turbocharged 80 Quattro so as not threaten Mikkola. He surprised everyone by finishing second, less than a minute behind. The following year, Audi were not quite so harsh. Mikkola had won his World crown and now Blomqvist was released to do the same. He won five events on his way to the title, even the Ivory Coast which he had never visited before.

In 1985, the Quattro – despite growing wings and losing weight – was dropping behind the new Group B cars so, after modest results in 1985, Blomqvist signed for Ford in 1986 to drive its new RS200. It was a bit of a disaster and his only result of the year was when Peugeot invited him to a one-off drive in Argentina. With the end of Group B, Blomqvist stayed with Ford, driving a succession of Sierras until a year of freelancing in 1989 when he put a VW Golf on the Safari podium. His next relationship was with the ill-fated Nissan Sunny GTI-R for two years. When that programme stopped, he went back to freelancing and, in a sensational drive for Skoda, gave them a third overall and best 2-litre car on the non-championship RAC Rally of 1996. Latterly, he has driven privately-run Mitsubishis and Subarus in the WRC Group N Championship, finishing fifth in 2001 and third in 2003.

Right: Stig Blomqvist, Sanremo 1984. He didn't manage to make the finish of this event but it mattered not in a season where the Swede lifted his one and only world championship crown with five event wins

BLOMQVIST, STIG – CAREER RECORD

YEAR	RALLY	TEAM /ENTRANT	CAR	NO.	CO-DRIVER	RESULT
1973						
1	**Sweden**	**Saab-Scania**	**Saab 96 V4**	**1**	**Arne Hertz**	**1st**
2	Finland	Saab-Scania	Saab 96 V4	2	Arne Hertz	Retired
3	Austria	Saab-Scania	Saab 96 V4	7	Arne Hertz	Retired
4	Great Britain	Saab-Scania	Saab 96 V4	2	Arne Hertz	Retired
1974						
5	Finland	Saab-Scania	Saab 96 V4	2	Hans Sylvan	4th
6	Great Britain	Saab-Scania	Saab 96 V4	2	Hans Sylvan	2nd
1975						
7	Sweden	Saab-Scania	Saab 96 V4	1	Hans Sylvan	2nd
8	Finland	Saab-Scania	Saab 96 V4	2	Hans Sylvan	Retired
9	Great Britain	Saab-Scania	Saab 96 V4	3	Hans Sylvan	Retired
1976						
10	Sweden	Saab-Scania	Saab 96 V4	2	Hans Sylvan	2nd
11	Finland	Saab-Scania	Saab 99 EMS	2	Hans Sylvan	Retired
12	Great Britain	Saab-Scania	Saab 99 EMS	4	Hans Sylvan	2nd
1977						
13	**Sweden**	**Saab-Scania**	**Saab 99 EMS**	**4**	**Hans Sylvan**	**1st**
14	Finland	Saab-Scania	Saab 99 EMS	3	Hans Sylvan	Retired
15	Great Britain	Saab-Scania	Saab 99 EMS	2	Hans Sylvan	Retired
1978						
16	Sweden	Lancia/Pirelli	Lancia Stratos	1	Hans Sylvan	4th
17	Canada	SAS	Saab 99 EMS	5	'Vicki'	Retired
18	Great Britain	Saab-Scania	Saab 99 Turbo	2	Hans Sylvan	Retired
1979	20 points (10th)					
19	**Sweden**	**Saab-Scania AB**	**Saab 99 Turbo**	**3**	**Bjorn Cederberg**	**1st**
20	Great Britain	Saab-Scania AB	Saab 99 Turbo	5	Bjorn Cederberg	Retired
1980	15 points (16th)					
21	Sweden	Saab-Scania AB	Saab 99 Turbo	1	Bjorn Cederberg	2nd
22	Great Britain	Saab Sport	Saab 99 Turbo	8	Bjorn Cederberg	Retired
1981	23 points (13th)					
23	Sweden	Publimo Racing	Saab 99 Turbo	3	Bjorn Cederberg	5th
24	Finland	Talbot Sport	Talbot Sunbeam Lotus	9	Bjorn Cederberg	8th
25	Great Britain	Talbot Sport	Talbot Sunbeam Lotus	14	Bjorn Cederberg	3rd
1982	58 points (4th)					
26	**Sweden**	**Audi Sport Sweden**	**Audi Quattro**	**4**	**Bjorn Cederberg**	**1st**
27	Finland	Audi Sport	Audi Quattro	5	Bjorn Cederberg	2nd
28	**Sanremo**	**Audi Sport**	**Audi Quattro**	**9**	**Bjorn Cederberg**	**1st**
29	Great Britain	Peugeot Talbot Sport	Talbot Sunbeam Lotus	6	Bjorn Cederberg	8th
1983	89 points (4th)					
30	Monte Carlo	Audi Sport	Audi Quattro A1	8	Bjorn Cederberg	3rd
31	Sweden	Audi Sport	Audi 80 Quattro	1	Bjorn Cederberg	2nd
32	Portugal	Audi Sport	Audi Quattro A1	6	Bjorn Cederberg	Retired
33	Greece	Audi Sport	Audi Quattro A2	8	Bjorn Cederberg	3rd
34	New Zealand	Audi Sport	Audi Quattro A2	4	Bjorn Cederberg	Retired
35	Argentina	Audi Sport	Audi Quattro A2	1	Bjorn Cederberg	2nd
36	Finland	Audi Sport	Audi Quattro A2	3	Bjorn Cederberg	2nd
37	Sanremo	Audi Sport	Audi Quattro A2	1	Bjorn Cederberg	Retired
38	**Great Britain**	**Audi Sport**	**Audi Quattro A2**	**3**	**Bjorn Cederberg**	**1st**
1984	125 points (WORLD CHAMPION)					
39	Monte Carlo	Audi Sport	Audi Quattro A2	7	Bjorn Cederberg	2nd
40	**Sweden**	**Audi Sport**	**Audi Quattro A2**	**1**	**Bjorn Cederberg**	**1st**
41	Portugal	Audi Sport	Audi Quattro A2	7	Bjorn Cederberg	Retired
42	Safari	Audi Sport	Audi Quattro A2	8	Bjorn Cederberg	Retired
43	Corsica	Audi Sport	Audi Quattro A2	6	Bjorn Cederberg	5th
44	**Greece**	**Audi Sport**	**Audi Quattro A2**	**10**	**Bjorn Cederberg**	**1st**
45	**New Zealand**	**Audi Sport**	**Audi Quattro A2**	**3**	**Bjorn Cederberg**	**1st**
46	**Argentina**	**Audi Sport**	**Audi Quattro A2**	**1**	**Bjorn Cederberg**	**1st**

STIG BLOMQVIST CAREER RECORD (CONTD)

YEAR	RALLY	TEAM/ENTRANT	CAR	NO.	CO-DRIVER	RESULT
47	Finland	Audi Sport	Audi Quattro A2	3	Bjorn Cederberg	4th
48	Sanremo	Audi Sport	Audi Sport Quattro	2	Bjorn Cederberg	Retired
49	**Ivory Coast**	**Audi Sport**	**Audi Sport Quattro**	**1**	**Bjorn Cederberg**	**1st**
1985	**75 points (2nd)**					
50	Monte Carlo	Audi Sport	Audi Sport Quattro	1	Bjorn Cederberg	4th
51	Sweden	Audi Sport	Audi Sport Quattro	1	Bjorn Cederberg	2nd
52	Portugal	Audi Sport	Audi Sport Quattro	3	Bjorn Cederberg	4th
53	Safari	Audi Sport	Audi Sport Quattro	11	Bjorn Cederberg	Retired
54	Greece	Audi Sport	Audi Sport Quattro	1	Bjorn Cederberg	2nd
55	New Zealand	Audi Sport	Audi Sport Quattro	1	Bjorn Cederberg	4th
56	Argentina	Audi Sport	Audi Sport Quattro E2	5	Bjorn Cederberg	Retired
57	Finland	Audi Sport	Audi Sport Quattro E2	4	Bjorn Cederberg	2nd
1986	**22 points (11th)**					
58	Sweden	Ford Motor Company	Ford RS200	1	Bruno Berglund	Retired
59	Portugal	Ford Motor Company	Ford RS200	4	Bruno Berglund	Withdrawn
60	Greece	Ford Motor Company	Ford RS200	2	Bruno Berglund	Retired
61	Argentina	Peugeot Talbot Sport	Peugeot 205 T16 E2	2	Bruno Berglund	3rd
62	Finland	Ford Motor Company	Peugeot 205 T16 E2	5	Bruno Berglund	4th
63	Great Britain	Ford Motor Company	Ford RS200	2	Bruno Berglund	Retired
1987	**33 points (7th)**					
64	Monte Carlo	Ford Motor Company	Ford Sierra XR 4x4	5	Bruno Berglund	Disqualified
65	Sweden	Ford Motor Company	Ford Sierra XR 4x4	2	Bruno Berglund	6th
66	Safari	Ford Motor Company	Ford Sierra RS Cosworth	6	Bruno Berglund	Retired
67	Corsica	Ford Motor Company	Ford Sierra RS Cosworth	2	Bruno Berglund	Withdrawn
68	New Zealand	Motogard Rallysport Team	Ford Sierra XR 4x4	1	Bjorn Cederberg	Retired
69	Finland	Ford Motor Company	Ford Sierra RS Cosworth	3	Bruno Berglund	3rd
70	Great Britain	Ford Motor Company	Ford Sierra RS Cosworth	3	Bruno Berglund	2nd
1988	**41 points (4th)**					
71	Sweden	Rallysport Sweden	Ford Sierra XR 4x4	3	Benny Melander	2nd
72	Portugal	Mike Little Preparations	Ford Sierra RS Cosworth	3	Benny Melander	5th
73	Corsica	Ford Motor Company	Ford Sierra RS Cosworth	4	Benny Melander	5th
74	Sanremo	Ford Motor Company	Ford Sierra RS Cosworth	6	Benny Melander	7th
75	Great Britain	Ford Motor Company	Ford Sierra RS Cosworth	3	Benny Melander	6th
1989	**20 points (15th)**					
76	Sweden	Team VAG Sweden	Audi 200 Quattro	1	Benny Melander	5th
77	Safari	Volkswagen Motorsport	Volkswagen Golf GTi 16V	6	Bjorn Cederberg	3rd
1991	**11 points (24th)**					
78	Safari	Nissan Motorsports Europe	Nissan Sunny GTI-R	5	Benny Melander	5th
79	Greece	Nissan Motorsports Europe	Nissan Sunny GTI-R	9	Benny Melander	Retired
80	Finland	Nissan Motorsports Europe	Nissan Sunny GTI-R	11	Benny Melander	8th
81	Great Britain	Nissan Motorsports Europe	Nissan Sunny GTI-R	12	Benny Melander	Retired
1992	**12 points (21st)**					
82	Sweden	Nissan Motorsports Europe	Nissan Sunny GTI-R	6	Benny Melander	3rd
83	Finland	Nissan Motorsports Europe	Nissan Sunny GTI-R	10	Benny Melander	Retired
84	Great Britain	Nissan Motorsports Europe	Nissan Sunny GTI-R	12	Benny Melander	Retired
1993	**0 points**					
85	Sweden	Opel Team Sweden	Opel Calibra Turbo 4x4	4	Benny Melander	Retired
1994	**10 points (15th)**					
86	Great Britain	Ford Motor Company	Ford Escort RS Cosworth	12	Benny Melander	4th
1995	**4 points (14th)**					
87	Sweden	RAS-Ford	Ford Escort RS Cosworth	9	Benny Melander	7th
88	Great Britain	Trigard Team Skoda	Skoda Felicia Kit Car	20	Benny Melander	21st
1996	**7 points (18th)**					
89	Sweden	Ford Motor Company	Ford Escort RS Cosworth	6	Benny Melander	8th
90	Safari	Ford Motor Company	Ford Escort RS Cosworth	5	Benny Melander	7th
91	Australia	Skoda Motorsport	Skoda Felicia Kit Car	23	Benny Melander	Retired
1997	**0 points**					
92	Sweden	Mobil Ford Motorsport	Ford Escort RS Cosworth	9	Benny Melander	10th
1999	**0 points**					
93	Sweden	Ford Motor Company	Ford Puma Kit Car	34	Benny Melander	Retired
2000	**0 points**					
94	Great Britain	David Sutton Cars Ltd.	Mitsubishi Lancer Evo 6	32	Ana Goni	Retired
2001	**0 points**					
95	Sweden	David Sutton Cars Ltd.	Mitsubishi Lancer Evo 6	40	Ana Goni	18th
96	Portugal	David Sutton Cars Ltd.	Mitsubishi Lancer Evo 6	43	Ana Goni	Retired
97	Catalunya	David Sutton Cars Ltd.	Mitsubishi Lancer Evo 6	28	Ana Goni	21st
98	Argentina	David Sutton Cars Ltd.	Mitsubishi Lancer Evo 6	23	Ana Goni	Retired
99	Cyprus	David Sutton Cars Ltd.	Mitsubishi Lancer Evo 6	31	Ana Goni	Retired
100	Greece	David Sutton Cars Ltd.	Mitsubishi Lancer Evo 6	34	Ana Goni	Retired
101	Safari	David Sutton Cars Ltd.	Mitsubishi Lancer Evo 6	23	Ana Goni	Retired
102	Finland	Skoda Motorsport	Skoda Octavia WRC E2	21	Ana Goni	22nd
103	New Zealand	David Sutton Cars Ltd.	Mitsubishi Lancer Evo 6	26	Ana Goni	21st
104	Sanremo	David Sutton Cars Ltd.	Mitsubishi Lancer Evo 6	41	Ana Goni	30th
105	Australia	David Sutton Cars Ltd.	Mitsubishi Lancer Evo 6	34	Ana Goni	23rd
106	Great Britain	David Sutton Cars Ltd.	Mitsubishi Lancer Evo 6	31	Ana Goni	16th
2002	**0 points**					
107	Sweden	Skoda Motorsport	Skoda Octavia WRC	16	Ana Goni	15th
108	Catalunya	Skoda Motorsport	Skoda Octavia WRC	16	Ana Goni	Retired
109	Greece	Skoda Motorsport	Skoda Octavia WRC	16	Ana Goni	17th
110	New Zealand	David Sutton Cars Ltd.	Mitsubishi Lancer Evo 7	110	Ana Goni	19th
111	Australia	David Sutton Cars Ltd.	Mitsubishi Lancer Evo 7	106	Ana Goni	22nd
112	Great Britian	David Sutton Cars Ltd.	Mitsubishi Lancer Evo 6	104	Ana Goni	Retired
2003						
113	Sweden	David Sutton Cars Ltd.	Subaru Impreza WRX STi	65	Ana Goni	27th
114	New Zealand	David Sutton Cars Ltd.	Subaru Impreza WRX STi	65	Ana Goni	24th
115	Cyprus	David Sutton Cars Ltd.	Subaru Impreza WRX STi	65	Ana Goni	11th
116	Germany	David Sutton Cars Ltd.	Subaru Impreza WRX STi	65	Ana Goni	29th
117	Australia	David Sutton Cars Ltd.	Subaru Impreza WRX STi	65	Rob Scott	19th
118	Corsica	David Sutton Cars Ltd.	Subaru Impreza WRX STi	65	Ana Goni	20th

BOYCE, WALTER (CDN) BORN: 29 OCTOBER 1946, OTTAWA, CANADA

Winning a World Championship Rally in a car owned by you is rare, but to win one in your own car that you have prepared and maintained yourself is truly exceptional. No surprise then that Walter Boyce claimed his lone WRC win in the very first year of the Championship.

Boyce started rallying in his native Canada when stage rallying was very much a minority sport. Most North American rallies prior to the mid-1960s were speed-time-distance events or strict regularity. Boyce was one of the new breed who wanted to drive fast and in the early 1970s, he emerged as the one to beat. He had two things going for him. The first was his co-driver, Doug Woods, whose experience in stage events was enough for him to be appointed Clerk of the Course of the first Canadian rally admitted to the WRC, the 1974 Rideau Lakes. Secondly, Boyce had a good relationship with the Toyota importer in Canada. This was before Toyota's factory involvement in rallying and there was plenty of scope for Boyce's own development skills.

His win on the Press on Regardless Rally in 1973 was against the best North American opposition as the European teams stayed away since Alpine Renault had already clinched the WRC title from Fiat, and Lancia were awaiting the Stratos. Polski Fiat sent a team of three 125Ps and both Dodge and Jeep – the winners in 1972 – entered cars. But Boyce came home a clear winner, 24 minutes ahead after 80 stages contained in 1,700 miles of rough Michigan back roads.

The following year, the Europeans came in strength. Lancia had a 1-2 in Canada with Boyce third in his Celica . The following year neither the Rideau Lakes nor the POR were in the WRC and Boyce concentrated on national rallies. Sadly his potential was never fulfilled with a truly competitive car.

BOYCE, WALTER - CAREER RECORD

YEAR	RALLY	TEAM/ENTRANT	CAR	NO.	CO-DRIVER	RESULT
1973						
1	United States		Toyota Corolla	110	Doug Woods	1st
1974						
2	Canada		Toyota Celica	101	Stuart Gray	3rd
3	United States		Toyota Celica	2	Doug Woods	Retired
1977						
4	Canada		Triumph TR7	9	Robin Edwardes	8th
1978						
5	Canada		Saab 99 EMS	12	Robin Edwardes	10th
1986	0 points					
6	United States		Volkswagen Golf GTi	20	Martin Headland	Retired

BUGALSKI, PHILIPPE (F) BORN: 12 JUNE 1963, CUSSET, FRANCE

A Frenchman's Frenchman, Philippe Bugalski has driven French manufactured cars for nearly his entire career and is best known for giving the WRC entrants a bloody nose in 1999 by winning two tarmac events with a two-litre, front-wheel drive Citroën Xsara Kit Car.

Bugalski's rally career started at the age of 19 when he rallied a VW Golf in his local region of the Auvergne. He was bold enough to enter the 1984 Monte Carlo Rally and learned how hard it is to succeed. He changed to a Renault 5 Turbo and, in 1988 struck up a deal with one of Renault's biggest dealerships to drive an R21 Turbo. He regularly won his class on French events and thus was moved into the semi-works team for 1991 with a 16-valve Clio.

For 1992, he was offered a deal to drive a Jolly Club Lancia Delta Integrale on selected WRC events. He acquitted himself extremely well but with Lancia pulling out at the end of the year and the Jolly Club going the Repsol/Sainz route for 1993, it meant a year's holiday for Bugalski. He re-established the Renault link and for 1995 was back rallying a Clio Maxi when he had a big accident on the Criterium Alpin in which his co-driver, Thierry Renaud, lost his life. It took time to recover but he came back with a Megane Maxi in which he won the F2 Corsica Rally in 1996 and finished second in the French series.

The call came from Citroën for the 1998 season. Bugalski and the Xsara Kit Car were made for one another. Citroen also did selected WRC events and it was here that Bugalski struck with his two remarkable victories over the 4WD brigade. He won a third French title in 2000 but this was with the as-yet unhomologated Xsara WRC. Bugalski joined the official Citroen team but had an unlucky time and was dropped from the main team for 2003.

BUGALSKI, PHILIPPE – CAREER RECORD

YEAR	RALLY	TEAM/ENTRANT	CAR	NO.	CO-DRIVER	RESULT
1984	**0 points**					
1	Monte Carlo		Volkswagen Golf GTi	192	Dominique Perruchon	88th
1988	**0 points**					
2	Corsica	Renault Chartres	Renault 21 Turbo	21	Jean-Marc Andrie	Retired
1989	**0 points**					
3	Monte Carlo	Renault Chartres	Renault 21 Turbo	25	Denis Giraudet	Retired
1991	**3 points (49th)**					
4	Corsica	Societe Diac	Renault Clio 16V	19	Denis Giraudet	8th
1992	**22 points (13th)**					
5	Monte Carlo	Jolly Club	Lancia Delta HF Integrale	11	Denis Giraudet	5th
6	Corsica	Martini Racing	Lancia Delta HF Integrale	7	Denis Giraudet	3rd
7	Finland	Martini Racing	Lancia Delta HF Integrale	11	Denis Giraudet	9th
1994	**0 points**					
8	Corsica	Societe Diac	Renault Clio Williams	20	Thierry Renaud	Retired
1995	**2 points (27th)**					
9	Monte Carlo	Societe Diac	Renault Clio Maxi	15	Thierry Renaud	Retired
10	Corsica	Societe Diac	Renault Clio Maxi	21	Jean-Paul Chiaroni	9th
1997	**1 point (26th)**					
11	Corsica	Societe Diac	Renault Megane Maxi	8	Jean-Paul Chiaroni	6th
1998	**2 points (16th)**					
12	Catalunya	Automobiles Citroen	Citroen Xsara Kit Car	17	Jean-Paul Chiaroni	5th
13	Corsica	Automobiles Citroen	Citroen Xsara Kit Car	9	Jean-Paul Chiaroni	Retired
14	Sanremo	Automobiles Citroen	Citroen Xsara Kit Car	12	Jean-Paul Chiaroni	Retired
1999	**20 points (7th)**					
15	Monte Carlo	Automobiles Citroen	Citroen Saxo Kit Car	23	Jean-Paul Chiaroni	Retired
16	**Catalunya**	**Automobiles Citroen**	**Citroen Xsara Kit Car**	**16**	**Jean-Paul Chiaroni**	**1st**
17	**Corsica**	**Automobiles Citroen**	**Citroen Xsara Kit Car**	**16**	**Jean-Paul Chiaroni**	**1st**
18	Sanremo	Automobiles Citroen	Citroen Xsara Kit Car	18	Jean-Paul Chiaroni	Retired
2000	**0 points**					
19	Greece	Automobiles Citroen	Citroen Saxo Kit Car	38	Jean-Paul Chiaroni	16th
20	Corsica	Automobiles Citroen	Citroen Saxo Kit Car	28	Jean-Paul Chiaroni	16th
21	Sanremo	Automobiles Citroen	Citroen Saxo Kit Car	45	Jean-Paul Chiaroni	Retired
2001	**1 point (21st)**					
22	Monte Carlo	Automobiles Citroen	Citroen Saxo Kit Car	20	Jean-Paul Chiaroni	14th
23	Portugal	Automobiles Citroen	Citroen Saxo Kit Car	54	Jean-Paul Chiaroni	Retired
24	Catalunya	Automobiles Citroen	Citroen Xsara WRC	14	Jean-Paul Chiaroni	8th
25	Greece	Automobiles Citroen	Citroen Xsara WRC	14	Jean-Paul Chiaroni	6th
26	Sanremo	Automobiles Citroen	Citroen Xsara WRC	14	Jean-Paul Chiaroni	Retired
27	Corsica	Automobiles Citroen	Citroen Xsara WRC	14	Jean-Paul Chiaroni	Retired
2002	**7 points (11th)**					
28	Monte Carlo	Automobiles Citroen	Citroen Xsara WRC	22	Jean-Paul Chiaroni	Retired
29	Corsica	Piedrafita Sport	Citroen Xsara WRC	25	Jean-Paul Chiaroni	4th
30	Catalunya	Automobiles Citroen	Citroen Xsara WRC	22	Jean-Paul Chiaroni	3rd
31	Deutschland	Automobiles Citroen	Citroen Xsara WRC	22	Jean-Paul Chiaroni	Retired
32	Sanremo	Piedrafita Sport	Citroen Xsara WRC	24	Jean-Paul Chiaroni	Retired
2003	**1 point (23rd)**					
33	Deutschland	Piedrafita Sport	Citroen Xsara WRC	20	Jean-Paul Chiaroni	Retired
34	Sanremo	Citroen Total	Citroen Xsara WRC	20	Jean-Paul Chiaroni	8th
35	Corsica	Citroen Total	Citroen Xsara WRC	20	Jean-Paul Chiaroni	9th
36	Catalunya	Citroen Total	Citroen Xsara WRC	20	Jean-Paul Chiaroni	10th

BURNS, RICHARD

(GB) BORN: 17 JANUARY 1971, READING, GREAT BRITAIN

"Richard Burns is the Thinking Man's rally driver"

In many ways, Richard Burns is the Thinking Man's rally driver. Not short of speed, but capable of a coolly analytical approach to most problems thrown up by this unpredictable sport.

Burns started his rally career when his father took him to a rally school in 1986. As soon as he was in possession of driving licence, he did local events in a Talbot Sunbeam. In 1990, with the help of David Williams of Genesis Design, he got the use of a Peugeot GTi in which he entered and won the 205 GTi Rally Cup. The following year, he won the GTi Challenge and his results in the British Championship rounds were sufficient to make him sixth overall and second in Group N. He also drove a Group N Subaru loaned by Prodrive on two national events but the highlight of the year was the RAC Rally. Here he drove a works Peugeot 309 GTi – his prize for winning the GTi Challenge – winning his class and finishing second in Group N.

The next move was into a Group N Subaru Legacy for the British National Championship. He invariably won Group N finishing ahead of cars in Groups A and B, won one event outright, and took the championship. Prodrive could not ignore this and signed him up as team mate to Alister McRae to drive a Group A Legacy for the 1993 British Championship. Burns won four of the five events and took the title with ease and even finished well on the RAC Rally. Thus for 1994, Prodrive allowed him to spread his wings to events like the Safari where he finished second in Group N and fifth overall. He did the Asia Pacific Championship in 1995 and got on the podium for the RAC Rally, but his future with Subaru looked uncertain.

The answer was Mitsubishi who gave him a modest programme for 1996, a better one in 1997 and then a full year as team mate to Tommi Mäkinen in 1998. Burns took full advantage of the opportunities this presented and won his first Safari. But being in the same team as a consistent World Champion is restrictive and when Colin McRae departed Subaru for Ford at the end of 1998, Burns had the call to return. He had an excellent season, finishing strongly with wins in Australia and Britain and only just failing to wrest the title from Mäkinen.

It was much the same story in 2000 where he won four WRC rallies, including getting his hat-trick on the RAC Rally, but it was not enough to depose the new threat from Finland, Marcus Grönholm. Burns had to be content once again with second place. As it turned out, 2001 was to be his year though it was a close call. At the RAC Rally, three drivers could have denied him but all three obligingly retired and his third place on the event was sufficient to clinch the title.

As World Champion, Burns was sought by many and accepted a drive from World Champion Manufacturers, Peugeot. But somehow he struggled to make the 206 WRC work for him. In 2003 with a new points scoring system rewarding consistency, he adopted an 'always finish' policy and led the championship until the last but one round where he crashed out. Once again the RAC Rally was to be the decider but this time serious illness intervened and Burns did not compete. With a Subaru contract for 2004, it was devastating for him to learn that his treatment for a brain tumour would preclude driving for as much as 12 months.

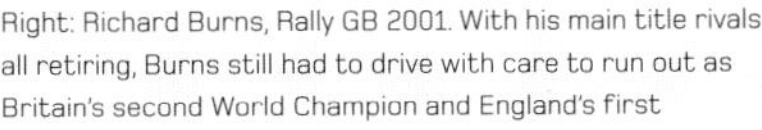

Right: Richard Burns, Rally GB 2001. With his main title rivals all retiring, Burns still had to drive with care to run out as Britain's second World Champion and England's first

BURNS, RICHARD – CAREER RECORD

YEAR	RALLY	TEAM/ENTRANT	CAR	NO.	CO-DRIVER	RESULT
1990	**0 points**					
1	Great Britain		Peugeot 309 GTI	81	Wayne Goble	28th
1991	**0 points**					
2	Great Britain		Peugeot 309 GTI	59	Robert Reid	16th
1992	**0 points**					
3	Great Britain		Peugeot 309 GTI	29	Robert Reid	Retired
1993	**4 points (38th)**					
4	Great Britain	555 Subaru World Rally Team	Subaru Legacy RS	10	Robert Reid	7th
1994	**8 points (19th)**					
5	Safari	Subaru Motor Sports Group/N.Koseki	Subaru Impreza WRX-RA	7	Robert Reid	5th
6	New Zealand	555 Subaru World Rally Team	Subaru Impreza 555	11	Robert Reid	Retired
7	Great Britain	555 Subaru World Rally Team	Subaru Impreza 555	9	Robert Reid	Retired
1995	**16 points (9th)**					
8	Portugal	555 Subaru World Rally Team	Subaru Impreza 555	6	Robert Reid	7th
9	New Zealand	555 Subaru World Rally Team	Subaru Impreza 555	14	Robert Reid	Retired
10	Great Britain	555 Subaru World Rally Team	Subaru Impreza 555	6	Robert Reid	3rd
1996	**18 points (9th)**					
11	Indonesia	Mitsubishi Ralliart	Mitsubishi Lancer Evo 3	8	Robert Reid	Retired
12	Argentina	Mitsubishi Ralliart	Mitsubishi Lancer Evo 3	8	Robert Reid	4th
13	Australia	Team Petronas Mitsubishi Ralliart	Mitsubishi Lancer Evo 3	8	Robert Reid	5th
14	Catalunya	Winfield Mitsubishi Ralliart	Mitsubishi Lancer Evo 3	8	Robert Reid	Retired
1997	**21 points (7th)**					
15	Safari	Mitsubishi Ralliart	Mitsubishi Carisma GT	2	Robert Reid	2nd
16	Portugal	Mitsubishi Ralliart	Mitsubishi Carisma GT	2	Robert Reid	Retired
17	Argentina	Mitsubishi Ralliart	Mitsubishi Carisma GT	2	Robert Reid	Retired
18	Greece	Mitsubishi Ralliart	Mitsubishi Carisma GT	2	Robert Reid	4th
19	New Zealand	Mitsubishi Ralliart	Mitsubishi Carisma GT	2	Robert Reid	4th
20	Indonesia	Mitsubishi Ralliart	Mitsubishi Carisma GT	2	Robert Reid	4th
21	Australia	Mitsubishi Ralliart	Mitsubishi Carisma GT	2	Robert Reid	4th
22	Great Britain	Mitsubishi Ralliart	Mitsubishi Carisma GT	2	Robert Reid	4th
1998	**33 points (6th)**					
23	Monte Carlo	Mitsubishi Ralliart Europe	Mitsubishi Carisma GT	2	Robert Reid	5th
24	Sweden	Mitsubishi Ralliart Europe	Mitsubishi Carisma GT	2	Robert Reid	15th
25	**Safari**	**Mitsubishi Ralliart Europe**	**Mitsubishi Carisma GT**	**2**	**Robert Reid**	**1st**
26	Portugal	Mitsubishi Ralliart Europe	Mitsubishi Carisma GT	2	Robert Reid	4th
27	Catalunya	Mitsubishi Ralliart Europe	Mitsubishi Carisma GT	2	Robert Reid	4th
28	Corsica	Mitsubishi Ralliart Europe	Mitsubishi Carisma GT	2	Robert Reid	Retired
29	Argentina	Mitsubishi Ralliart Europe	Mitsubishi Carisma GT	2	Robert Reid	4th
30	Greece	Mitsubishi Ralliart Europe	Mitsubishi Carisma GT	2	Robert Reid	Retired
31	New Zealand	Mitsubishi Ralliart Europe	Mitsubishi Carisma GT	2	Robert Reid	9th
32	Finland	Mitsubishi Ralliart Europe	Mitsubishi Carisma GT	2	Robert Reid	5th
33	Sanremo	Mitsubishi Ralliart Europe	Mitsubishi Carisma GT	2	Robert Reid	
34	Australia	Mitsubishi Ralliart Europe	Mitsubishi Carisma GT	2	Robert Reid	Retired
35	**Great Britain**	**Mitsubishi Ralliart Europe**	**Mitsubishi Carisma GT**	**2**	**Robert Reid**	**1st**
1999	**55 points (2nd)**					
36	Monte Carlo	Subaru World Rally Team	Subaru Impreza WRC	5	Robert Reid	8th
37	Sweden	Subaru World Rally Team	Subaru Impreza WRC	5	Robert Reid	5th
38	Safari	Subaru World Rally Team	Subaru Impreza WRC	5	Robert Reid	Retired
39	Portugal	Subaru World Rally Team	Subaru Impreza WRC	5	Robert Reid	4th
40	Catalunya	Subaru World Rally Team	Subaru Impreza WRC	5	Robert Reid	5th
41	Corsica	Subaru World Rally Team	Subaru Impreza WRC	5	Robert Reid	7th
42	Argentina	Subaru World Rally Team	Subaru Impreza WRC	5	Robert Reid	2nd
43	**Greece**	**Subaru World Rally Team**	**Subaru Impreza WRC**	**5**	**Robert Reid**	**1st**
44	New Zealand	Subaru World Rally Team	Subaru Impreza WRC	5	Robert Reid	Retired
45	Finland	Subaru World Rally Team	Subaru Impreza WRC	5	Robert Reid	2nd
46	China	Subaru World Rally Team	Subaru Impreza WRC	5	Robert Reid	2nd
47	Sanremo	Subaru World Rally Team	Subaru Impreza WRC	5	Robert Reid	Retired
48	**Australia**	**Subaru World Rally Team**	**Subaru Impreza WRC**	**5**	**Robert Reid**	**1st**

BURNS, RICHARD - CAREER RECORD (CONTD)

YEAR	RALLY	TEAM/ENTRANT	CAR	NO.	CO-DRIVER	RESULT
49	Great Britain	Subaru World Rally Team	Subaru Impreza WRC	5	Robert Reid	1st
2000	60 points (2nd)					
50	Monte Carlo	Subaru World Rally Team	Subaru Impreza WRC	3	Robert Reid	Retired
51	Sweden	Subaru World Rally Team	Subaru Impreza WRC	3	Robert Reid	5th
52	Safari	Subaru World Rally Team	Subaru Impreza WRC	3	Robert Reid	1st
53	Portugal	Subaru World Rally Team	Subaru Impreza WRC	3	Robert Reid	1st
54	Catalunya	Subaru World Rally Team	Subaru Impreza WRC	3	Robert Reid	2nd
55	Argentina	Subaru World Rally Team	Subaru Impreza WRC	3	Robert Reid	1st
56	Greece	Subaru World Rally Team	Subaru Impreza WRC	3	Robert Reid	Retired
57	New Zealand	Subaru World Rally Team	Subaru Impreza WRC	3	Robert Reid	Retired
58	Finland	Subaru World Rally Team	Subaru Impreza WRC	3	Robert Reid	Retired
59	Cyprus	Subaru World Rally Team	Subaru Impreza WRC	3	Robert Reid	4th
60	Corsica	Subaru World Rally Team	Subaru Impreza WRC	3	Robert Reid	4th
61	Sanremo	Subaru World Rally Team	Subaru Impreza WRC	3	Robert Reid	Retired
62	Australia	Subaru World Rally Team	Subaru Impreza WRC	3	Robert Reid	2nd
63	Great Britain	Subaru World Rally Team	Subaru Impreza WRC	3	Robert Reid	1st
2001	44 points (WORLD CHAMPION)					
64	Monte Carlo	Subaru World Rally Team	Subaru Impreza WRC	5	Robert Reid	Retired
65	Sweden	Subaru World Rally Team	Subaru Impreza WRC	5	Robert Reid	16th
66	Portugal	Subaru World Rally Team	Subaru Impreza WRC	5	Robert Reid	4th
67	Catalunya	Subaru World Rally Team	Subaru Impreza WRC	5	Robert Reid	7th
68	Argentina	Subaru World Rally Team	Subaru Impreza WRC	5	Robert Reid	2nd
69	Cyprus	Subaru World Rally Team	Subaru Impreza WRC	5	Robert Reid	2nd
70	Greece	Subaru World Rally Team	Subaru Impreza WRC	5	Robert Reid	Retired
71	Safari	Subaru World Rally Team	Subaru Impreza WRC	5	Robert Reid	Retired
72	Finland	Subaru World Rally Team	Subaru Impreza WRC	5	Robert Reid	2nd
73	New Zealand	Subaru World Rally Team	Subaru Impreza WRC	5	Robert Reid	1st
74	Sanremo	Subaru World Rally Team	Subaru Impreza WRC	5	Robert Reid	Retired
75	Corsica	Subaru World Rally Team	Subaru Impreza WRC	5	Robert Reid	4th
76	Australia	Subaru World Rally Team	Subaru Impreza WRC	5	Robert Reid	2nd
77	Great Britain	Subaru World Rally Team	Subaru Impreza WRC	5	Robert Reid	3rd
2002	34 points (5th)					
78	Monte Carlo	Peugeot Total	Peugeot 206 WRC	1	Robert Reid	8th
79	Sweden	Peugeot Total	Peugeot 206 WRC	1	Robert Reid	4th
80	Corsica	Peugeot Total	Peugeot 206 WRC	1	Robert Reid	3rd
81	Catalunya	Peugeot Total	Peugeot 206 WRC	1	Robert Reid	2nd
82	Cyprus	Peugeot Total	Peugeot 206 WRC	1	Robert Reid	2nd
83	Argentina	Peugeot Total	Peugeot 206 WRC	1	Robert Reid	Retired
84	Greece	Peugeot Total	Peugeot 206 WRC	1	Robert Reid	Retired
85	Safari	Peugeot Total	Peugeot 206 WRC	1	Robert Reid	Retired
86	Finland	Peugeot Total	Peugeot 206 WRC	1	Robert Reid	2nd
87	Germany	Peugeot Total	Peugeot 206 WRC	1	Robert Reid	2nd
88	Sanremo	Peugeot Total	Peugeot 206 WRC	1	Robert Reid	4th
89	New Zealand	Peugeot Total	Peugeot 206 WRC	1	Robert Reid	Retired
90	Australia	Peugeot Total	Peugeot 206 WRC	1	Robert Reid	Retired
91	Great Britain	Peugeot Total	Peugeot 206 WRC	1	Robert Reid	Retired
2003	58 points (4th)					
92	Monte Carlo	Marlboro Peugeot Total	Peugeot 206 WRC	2	Robert Reid	5th
93	Sweden	Marlboro Peugeot Total	Peugeot 206 WRC	2	Robert Reid	3rd
94	Turkey	Marlboro Peugeot Total	Peugeot 206 WRC	2	Robert Reid	2nd
95	New Zealand	Marlboro Peugeot Total	Peugeot 206 WRC	2	Robert Reid	2nd
96	Argentina	Marlboro Peugeot Total	Peugeot 206 WRC	2	Robert Reid	3rd
97	Greece	Marlboro Peugeot Total	Peugeot 206 WRC	2	Robert Reid	4th
98	Cyprus	Marlboro Peugeot Total	Peugeot 206 WRC	2	Robert Reid	Retired
99	Germany	Marlboro Peugeot Total	Peugeot 206 WRC	2	Robert Reid	3rd
100	Finland	Marlboro Peugeot Total	Peugeot 206 WRC	2	Robert Reid	3rd
101	Australia	Marlboro Peugeot Total	Peugeot 206 WRC	2	Robert Reid	3rd
102	Sanremo	Marlboro Peugeot Total	Peugeot 206 WRC	2	Robert Reid	7th
103	Corsica	Marlboro Peugeot Total	Peugeot 206 WRC	2	Robert Reid	8th
104	Catalunya	Marlboro Peugeot Total	Peugeot 206 WRC	2	Robert Reid	Retired

CARLSSON, INGVAR (S) BORN: 2 APRIL 1947, NYKOPING, SWEDEN

Despite his surname, it was not with a Saab that Ingvar Carlsson started his career in rallying but with an ageing Volvo PV 544.

That was in 1968 and by 1971, Carlsson had won support from the BMW importer in Sweden and had started competing regularly with a BMW 2002Ti. On the Swedish Rally of 1971, he was 10th in class and the following year had moved up to sixth overall. This was sufficient for Datsun to offer him a seat in a 240Z in Portugal 1974 and for Fiat to try him out on first the RAC Rally and then on the Swedish. On his home event, he finished a very creditable fifth ahead of team mate, Markku Alén.

He continued to drive BMW in Sweden until being invited to join a semi-works Mercedes effort for Monte Carlo in 1980. Once the connection was made, it led to other drives behind a three-pointed star. When Hannu Mikkola was not available for Portugal, Carlsson took over and brought the 450SLC home fifth just behind teammate Bjorn Waldegård. When Mercedes pulled the plug, it was back to BMWs for three seasons and the programme included his first try at the 1000 Lakes.

Then along came Mazda where Carlsson was a full works driver and tester. Early efforts were almost pointless but Mazda did homologate the 323 4WD so that when Group A ruled the roost onwards from 1987, they had – potentially – a winning car. Carlsson took to the new challenge like a duck to water but, sadly, the car was never fully developed. Carlsson was still able to extract two WRC victories from the 323 in 1989. However, it was a brief reprieve as Toyota, Ford, Subaru and Mitsubishi all came with competitive 4WD cars and when Mazda decided not to go ahead with its striking Familia Sport-4, MRTE disappeared and with it, Carlsson's WRC drive.

CARLSSON, INGVAR – CAREER RECORD

YEAR	RALLY	TEAM/ENTRANT	CAR	NO.	CO-DRIVER	RESULT
1974						
1	Portugal		Datsun 260Z	10	Solve Andreasson	Retired
2	Great Britain		Fiat 124 Abarth	47	Bo Reinicke	Retired
1975						
3	Sweden		Fiat 124 Abarth	6	Claes Billstam	5th
1976						
4	Sweden	Dealer Team BMW Sweden	BMW 2002	19	Roine Hasselstrom	Retired
1977						
5	Sweden		BMW 2002		Sven-Roine Hasselberg	Retired
1980	**9 points (31st)**					
6	Monte Carlo	Senderia Kassel	Mercedes 280CE	30	Claes Billstam	11th
7	Sweden		BMW 320	10	Sven-Roine Hasselberg	10th
8	Portugal	C.Santos Mercedes	Mercedes 450SLC	17	Claes Billstam	5th
9	Greece	Daimler-Benz	Mercedes 280CE	27	Claes Billstam	Retired
10	New Zealand	Cable-Price Corporation	Mercedes 280CE	16	Claes Billstam	Retired
1981	**0 points**					
11	Sweden	Publimo Racing	BMW 323i	10	Sven-Roine Hasselberg	Retired
1982	**0 points**					
12	Sweden	FIB Aktuellt	BMW 323i	12	Christian Boden	Retired
1983	**0 points**					
13	Sweden	Forenade Oil	BMW 323i	26	Christian Boden	11th
14	Finland	Forenade Oil	BMW 323i	96	Christian Boden	Retired
1984	**0 points**					
15	Monte Carlo	Ingvar Carlsson	Mazda 323	24	Ragnar Spjuth	Retired
16	Sweden	Ingvar Carlsson	Mazda 323	10	Ragnar Spjuth	13th
17	Greece	Mazda Rally Team Europe	Mazda RX7	20	Benny Melander	Retired
18	Great Britain	Mazda Rally Team Europe	Mazda RX7	26	Benny Melander	Retired
1985	**16 points (6th)**					
19	Sweden	Mazda Rally Team Europe	Mazda RX7	8	Benny Melander	8th
20	Greece	Mazda Rally Team Europe	Mazda RX7	9	Benny Melander	3rd
21	Great Britain	Mazda Rally Team Europe	Mazda RX7	9	Benny Melander	10th
1986	**1 point (70th)**					
22	Monte Carlo	Mazda Rally Team Europe	Mazda Familia 4WD	14	Jan-Olof Bohlin	Retired
23	Sweden	Mazda Rally Team Europe	Mazda Familia 4WD	6	Jan-Olof Bohlin	Retired
24	Finland	Mazda Rally Team Europe	Mazda 323 4WD	6	Jan-Olof Bohlin	Retired
25	Great Britain	Mazda Rally Team Europe	Mazda 323 4WD	7	Jan-Olof Bohlin	10th
1987	**20 points (17th)**					
26	Monte Carlo	Mazda Rally Team Europe	Mazda 323 4WD	14	Per Carlsson	4th
27	Sweden	Mazda Rally Team Europe	Mazda 323 4WD	9	Per Carlsson	4th
28	Portugal	Mazda Rally Team Europe	Mazda 323 4WD	10	Per Carlsson	Retired
29	Argentina	Mazda Rally Team Europe	Mazda 323 4WD	4	Per Carlsson	Retired
30	Finland	Mazda Rally Team Europe	Mazda 323 4WD	9	Per Carlsson	Retired
1988	**0 points**					
31	Monte Carlo	Mazda Rally Team Europe	Mazda 323 4WD	8	Per Carlsson	Retired
32	Portugal	Mazda Rally Team Europe	Mazda 323 4WD	12	Per Carlsson	Retired
1989	**43 points (7th)**					
33	**Sweden**	**Mazda Rally Team Europe**	**Mazda 323 4WD**	**7**	**Per Carlsson**	**1st**
34	**New Zealand**	**Mazda Rally Team Belgium**	**Mazda 323 4WD**	**1**	**Per Carlsson**	**1st**
35	Australia	Mazda Rally Team Belgium	Mazda 323 4WD	6	Per Carlsson	Retired
36	Great Britain	Mazda Rally Team Europe	Mazda 323 4WD	9	Per Carlsson	8th
1990	**23 points (10th)**					
37	New Zealand	Mazda Rally Team Europe	Mazda 323 4WD	1	Per Carlsson	2nd
38	Australia	Mazda Rally Team Europe	Mazda 323 4WD	5	Per Carlsson	5th
1991	**13 points (16th)**					
39	Sweden	Mazda Rally Team Europe	Mazda 323 GTX	1	Per Carlsson	4th
40	New Zealand	Mazda Rally Team Europe	Mazda 323 GTX	5	Per Carlsson	8th
41	Australia	Mazda Rally Team Europe	Mazda 323 GTX	4	Per Carlsson	Retired

CLARK, ROGER

(GB) BORN: 5 AUGUST 1939, NARBOROUGH, ENGLAND; DIED: 12 JANUARY 1998

"Roger Clark was the icon of British rallying"

Before the advent of Colin McRae and Richard Burns, Roger Clark was the icon of British rallying. But despite an enormous natural talent and a string of major wins, the doors never opened onto a major WRC title chase.

The son of a garage proprietor selling Renaults and then Fords, his first competition experiences were with a Ford 100E van. He tried a Renault Dauphine but the 850cc rear engined car was not competitive on British rallies. His first and last international with it was the Circuit of Ireland in 1961 where he finished 51st overall. Next was a Mini 850 for the RAC Rally and then a Cooper with which he took fourth place on the Circuit of Ireland in 1962 and a year later was second on the Scottish. It was this drive that got him noticed and he was instantly offered a works Reliant for the Alpine Rally and a Triumph TR4 for the Liège-Sofia-Liège.

In 1964 he got his first Cortina GT and promptly started winning national rallies and, more importantly, the Scottish. A series of works drives in Rovers was then offered which gave experience but did not produce much in the way of results until the 1965 Monte Carlo when Clark not only won Group 1 but finished sixth overall in a Rover 2000. This was a truly remarkable drive in awful conditions. Steady finishes in Acropolis, Alpine and RAC rallies followed. At home, he was unbeatable in the Cortina winning the Scottish, the Gulf London and the Welsh on his way to his first British title.

It came as no surprise then that he started 1966 as a full works driver for Ford in Lotus Cortinas. When the car lasted, he was on the podium though not on the 1000 Lakes where at his first attempt at that specialised event he finished 19th…

For 1967, Ford had only a small programme but Clark added the Safari to his experience and won in Canada as well as Scotland. In 1968 came the Escort Twin Cam and for Clark, it was sheer heaven. He won just about everything in Britain plus the Tulip and the Acropolis. The following year was not quite so good. There was a smaller programme from Ford and they used Clark in some strange cars like a Zodiac Mk4 and an Escort V6.

In 1970, the BDA Escort arrived and Clark gave it its first win on the Circuit of Ireland. But there were other new arrivals at Ford, the Finnish drivers Timo Mäkinen and Hannu Mikkola. Clark was given a largely British programme with an occasional foreign event thrown in. He did not disappoint at home, winning the British title in 1972, 1973 and 1975 and on top of that, he won the RAC Rally twice, in 1972 and again in 1976 when it was now a WRC qualifier.

But it was not enough to get him the role that all his fans desired: number one at Ford. Clark continued to drive for the factory on and off until the team was stood down at the end of 1979. He did a final and frustrating season with a TR7 V8 and then largely called it a day.

Right: Roger Clark's RAC Rally win in 1976 was the first WRC success for a British driver, a record that stood for 17 years until Colin McRae came along. Despite his lack of success on the World stage, Clark remained a true British rally hero

CLARK, ROGER – CAREER RECORD

YEAR	RALLY	TEAM/ENTRANT	CAR	NO.	CO-DRIVER	RESULT
1973						
1	Safari	Ford Motor Company	Ford Escort RS1600	2	Jim Porter	Retired
2	Great Britain	Ford Motor Company	Ford Escort RS1600	1	Tony Mason	2nd
1974						
3	Great Britain	Ford Motor Company	Ford Escort RS1600	5	Tony Mason	7th
1975						
4	Sanremo	Ford Motor Company	Ford Escort RS1800	9	Jim Porter	Retired
5	Great Britain	Ford Motor Company	Ford Escort RS1800	6	Tony Mason	2nd
1976						
6	Monte Carlo	Ford Motor Company	Ford Escort RS1800	11	Jim Porter	5th
7	Morocco	Ford Motor Company	Ford Escort RS1800	7	Jim Porter	Retired
8	**Great Britain**	**Ford Motor Company**	**Ford Escort RS1800**	**6**	**Stuart Pegg**	**1st**
1977						
9	Portugal	Ford Motor Company	Ford Escort RS1800	6	Jim Porter	Retired
10	Safari	Ford Motor Company	Ford Escort RS1800	2	Jim Porter	Retired
11	Greece	Ford Motor Company	Ford Escort RS1800	2	Jim Porter	2nd
12	Canada	Ford Motor Company	Ford Escort RS1800	3	Jim Porter	3rd
13	Great Britain	Ford Motor Company	Ford Escort RS1800	1	Stuart Pegg	4th
1978						
14	Great Britain	Ford Motor Company	Ford Escort RS	9	Neil Wilson	Retired
1979	0 points					
15	Monte Carlo	Ford Motor Company	Ford Fiesta	15	Jim Porter	13th
16	Greece	Rothmans	Ford Escort RS1800	7	Jim Porter	Retired
17	Great Britain	Ford Motor Company	Ford Escort RS1800	8	Neil Wilson	Retired
1980	0 points					
18	Great Britain	British Leyland Cars	Triumph TR7 V8	20	Neil Wilson	Retired
1981	1 point (63rd)					
19	Great Britain	MCD Services	Ford Escort RS1800	22	Chris Searle	10th
1984	0 points					
20	Great Britain	Rothmans Porsche Rally Team	Porsche 911SC RS	31	Ian Grindrod	12th

CUNICO, GIANFRANCO

(I) BORN: 11 OCTOBER 1957, VICENZA, ITALY

In 1993, it might have seemed that Gianfranco Cunico was the Man of the Moment for Ford having just won them the San Remo Rally after both their works cars had retired. But Ford's Boreham team was in decline and no great future beckoned for the Italian.

Cunico was one of the graduates of the Autobianchi A112 rally championship started back in the 1970s to encourage young Italian drivers. He won the A112 Trophy in 1979 and, rather quickly found himself at the wheel of a Lancia Rally 037. He was good enough to finish second in the 1983 Italian Championship with that car but then he had, like so many others, to wait for the end of the ill-starred Group B to get his next chance. He was offered a semi-works Lancia Delta HF for the 1987 Italian championship in which he won Group N and he was also best in that category on the San Remo despite a bizarre attempt by someone to sabotage his car by putting sugar in the petrol tank.

Ford Italy snapped him up for 1988 and he won the Group N title for them with a Sierra Cosworth, a feat he repeated for the next two years. He got some trial runs with the works Ford team but made no lasting impression. Moving to a Group A Sierra 4x4 in the early 1990s saw him winning national events and always being in the hunt for the Italian title. This was true even in the year he won San Remo with an Escort Cosworth. But then for three years, he was undisputed champion with an Escort Cosworth run now by the Jolly Club. Most recently he has driven a Mitsubishi Evo VII.

CUNICO, GIANFRANCO – CAREER RECORD

YEAR	RALLY	TEAM/ENTRANT	CAR	NO.	CO-DRIVER	RESULT
1981	0 points					
1	Sanremo	Gianfranco Cunico	Ford Fiesta 1600	31	Eraldo Mussa	Retired
1982	0 points					
2	Sanremo	Gianfranco Cunico	Fiat Ritmo Abarth 125 TC	15	Maurizio Perissinot	12th
1984	0 points					
3	Sanremo	Bologna Corse	Lancia Rally 037	9	Max Sghedoni	Retired
1987	0 points					
4	Sanremo	Concess. Lancia	Lancia Delta HF 4WD	29	Stefano Evangelisti	12th
1988	0 points					
5	Sanremo	Ford Italia	Ford Sierra RS Cosworth	16	Max Sghedoni	Retired
1989	4 points (52nd)					
6	Corsica	Q8 Team Ford	Ford Sierra RS Cosworth	15	Max Sghedoni	7th
7	Great Britain	Q8 Team Ford	Ford Sierra RS Cosworth	25	Terry Harryman	Retired
1990	0 points					
8	Finland	Q8 Team Ford	Ford Sierra Cosworth 4x4	20	Stefano Evangelisti	Retired
9	Sanremo	Q8 Team Ford	Ford Sierra Cosworth 4x4	20	Stefano Evangelisti	Retired
1991	12 points (19th)					
10	Corsica	Ford Italia	Ford Sierra Cosworth 4x4	16	Stefano Evangelisti	3rd
11	Sanremo	Ford Italia/Mike Little Preparations	Ford Sierra Cosworth 4x4	8	Stefano Evangelisti	Retired
1992	0 points					
12	Sanremo	Ford Italia/Mike Little Preparations	Ford Sierra Cosworth 4x4	6	Stefano Evangelisti	Retired
1993	20 points (15th)					
13	**Sanremo**	**Ford Italia**	**Ford Escort RS Cosworth**	**7**	**Stefano Evangelisti**	**1st**
1994	6 points (25th)					
14	Corsica	Ford Motor Company	Ford Escort RS Cosworth	9	Stefano Evangelisti	Retired
15	Sanremo	Jolly Club	Ford Escort RS Cosworth	6	Stefano Evangelisti	6th
1996	6 points (20th)					
16	Sanremo	Jolly Club	Ford Escort RS Cosworth	14	Stefano Evangelisti	6th
1997	0 points					
17	Sanremo	Jolly Club	Ford Escort WRC	9	Pierangelo Scalvini	Retired
1998	0 points					
18	Sanremo	Jolly Club	Ford Escort WRC	18	Luigi Pirollo	Retired
1999	0 points					
19	Sanremo	Aimont Racing	Subaru Impreza WRC	24	Luigi Pirollo	9th
2000	0 points					
20	Sanremo	Aimont Racing	Subaru Impreza WRC	23	Luigi Pirollo	Retired

Darniche, Bernard

(F) BORN: 28 MARCH 1942, CENON, FRANCE

"He never said very much but he got the job done"

Perhaps the least extrovert of the French rally drivers, Bernard Darniche was someone who had learned the skills of a racing cyclist. He never said very much but he got the job done – as his long list of victories can testify.

When he returned from service in the army, Darniche became a racing cyclist and for some years, the world of the automobile passed him by. Then in the spring of 1965, just two months after Timo Mäkinen had won the Monte Carlo in a Cooper S, Darniche was invited to co-drive in just such a car. He soon wanted to drive and he acquired an NSU 1000 in 1966. He was soon winning his class in national events and moved up to an Alpine A110 for 1967. He set a lot of fastest times but the car failed to finish on almost every occasion. For 1968, he tried the Coupe Gordini with an R8 Gordini and was third. He also won a rally with the Alpine, now works supported, and was third at the Spa 24 Hours in a Porsche 911S. At the same time, he signed two contracts : one of marriage to Françoise and one with NSU France.

For NSU he was sixth overall in Corsica and did well for them in 1969 but without repeating his Corsican success. For 1970 he went to Alpine on a three year deal and for them he delivered that elusive Corsican win but had a terrifying accident a month later on the Criterium des Cevennes when he and his co-driver, Bernard Demange were badly hurt. He came back for 1971, winning the Coupe des Alpes and then on the Monte Carlo 1972 led until the last night when he fell prey to Alpine gearbox malaise. He won the French championship in 1972 and was second in Portugal and fourth in Corsica. He played his part in Renault Alpine gaining the World Manufacturers' title in 1973 by winning in Morocco, about his only gravel rally victory, and nearly winning the Austrian Alpine.

In 1974, he did the Safari and the Press on Regardless for Renault but was already starting to look elsewhere as his three-year contract was at an end. He was second on the Tour de France with a Ligier JS2 and then tried Italian cars.

His first event was Corsica in a Fiat 124 Abarth but he and that car did not get on. It did however lead to a drive in a Stratos for the Lancia importer in France. After coming second again on the 1975 Tour de France with a Fiat X1/9 prototype, he won in Corsica with the Stratos. He was totally at home with that car on asphalt and proved it with two more wins in Corsica and one in Monte Carlo plus two French championship titles in 1976 and 1978. He also drove a Fiat France 131 Abarth and was given a works car for Corsica in 1978 where he promptly won again. His total number of wins on that event eventually came to six.

During the Group B era, he had a brief dalliance with Audi through their French importer and drove a private Peugeot 205 T16 in Corsica, but these were not machines for a man who had been brought up on a diet of powerful rear-wheel drive cars.

Right: Bernard Darniche's name will forever be associated with the awesome Lancia Stratos. Here he kicks up the dust with a spectacular powerslide on the 1979 Acropolis Rally

DARNICHE, BERNARD – CAREER RECORD

YEAR	RALLY	TEAM/ENTRANT	CAR	NO.	CO-DRIVER	RESULT
1973						
1	Monte Carlo	Renault-Alpine	Renault-Alpine A110	1	Alain Mahe	10th
2	Sweden	Renault-Alpine	Renault 12 Gordini	21	Alain Mahe	Retired
3	Portugal	Renault-Alpine	Renault-Alpine A110	3	Alain Mahe	Retired
4	**Morocco**	**Renault-Alpine**	**Renault-Alpine A110**	**1**	**Alain Mahe**	**1st**
5	Greece	Renault-Alpine	Renault-Alpine A110	10	Alain Mahe	Retired
6	Austria	Renault-Alpine	Renault-Alpine A110	2	Alain Mahe	2nd
7	Sanremo	Renault-Alpine	Renault-Alpine A110	5	Alain Mahe	Retired
8	Corsica	Renault-Alpine	Renault-Alpine A110	3	Alain Mahe	Retired
1974						
9	Safari	Renault-Alpine	Renault-Alpine A110	2	Alain Mahe	Retired
10	United States		Renault 17 Gordini	4	Alain Mahe	6th
11	Corsica		Fiat 124 Abarth	8	Alain Mahe	Retired
1975						
12	Monte Carlo		Fiat 124 Abarth	6	Alain Mahe	Retired
13	Morocco		Fiat 124 Abarth	3	Alain Mahe	Retired
14	**Corsica**	**Team Chardonnet**	**Lancia Stratos**	**6**	**Alain Mahe**	**1st**
1976						
15	Monte Carlo		Lancia Stratos	12	Alain Mahe	3rd
16	Corsica		Lancia Stratos	5	Alain Mahe	2nd
1977						
17	Monte Carlo		Lancia Stratos	8	Alain Mahe	Retired
18	**Corsica**	**Olio Fiat**	**Fiat 131 Abarth**	**5**	**Alain Mahe**	**1st**
1978						
19	Monte Carlo	Fiat-Alitalia	Fiat 131 Abarth	8	Alain Mahe	5th
20	Portugal		Lancia Stratos	3	Alain Mahe	Retired
21	**Corsica**	**Fiat Alitalia**	**Fiat 131 Abarth**	**1**	**Alain Mahe**	**1st**
1979	**40 points (6th)**					
22	**Monte Carlo**	**Team Chardonnet**	**Lancia Stratos**	**4**	**Alain Mahe**	**1st**
23	Portugal	Team Chardonnet	Lancia Stratos	2	Alain Mahe	Retired
24	Greece	Team Chardonnet	Lancia Stratos	2	Alain Mahe	Retired
25	**Corsica**	**Team Chardonnet**	**Lancia Stratos**	**1**	**Alain Mahe**	**1st**
1980	**15 points (16th)**					
26	Monte Carlo	Team Chardonnet	Lancia Stratos	1	Alain Mahe	2nd
27	Portugal	Team Chardonnet	Lancia Stratos	3	Alain Mahe	Retired
28	Greece	Team Chardonnet	Lancia Stratos	2	Alain Mahe	Retired
29	Corsica	Fiat Italia	Fiat 131 Abarth	5	Alain Mahe	Retired
1981	**26 points (12th)**					
30	Monte Carlo	Team Chardonnet	Lancia Stratos	4	Alain Mahe	6th
31	**Corsica**	**Team Chardonnet**	**Lancia Stratos**	**10**	**Alain Mahe**	**1st**
1982	0 points					
32	Corsica	BMW France	BMW M1	10	Alain Mahe	Retired
1983	**2 points (50th)**					
33	Sanremo	Audi Sport	Audi Quattro A2	11	Alain Mahe	9th
1984	**4 points (36th)**					
34	Monte Carlo	Yacco	Audi 80 Quattro	10	Alain Mahe	7th
35	Corsica	Yacco	Audi Quattro A2	8	Alain Mahe	Retired
1985	**0 points**					
36	Corsica	Team Gauloises Blondes	Peugeot 205 T16	14	Alain Mahe	Retired
1987	**0 points**					
37	Monte Carlo		Mercedes 190E 2.3 16V	20	Alain Mahe	Retired
38	Corsica		Mercedes 190E 2.3 16V	12	Alain Mahe	Retired

DELECOUR, FRANCOIS (F) BORN: 28 MARCH 1942, CENON, FRANCE

For François Delecour, many of the adjectives that one could apply to his driving also apply to the man himself : explosive, fully committed and on line.

"Delecour was explosive, fully committed and on line"

His rally career started on a French national rally in 1981 with an Autobianchi A112 and he later drove a Peugeot 104ZS and a Talbot Samba. He did his first Monte Carlo Rally in 1984, and he won Group A on two French rallies. For the next two years, he drove a Peugeot 205 GTi in the Peugeot Cup finishing third both years. He obtained support from Peugeot Concessionaires plus a new 205 GTi 1900c which he took to ninth overall in the French Championship. It was not enough to bring sponsorship for 1988 so he drove a private BMW M3.

Then for 1989, Peugeot fixed him up with a works 309 GTi in which he finished fourth in the French Championship and took three podiums on major French internationals. The following year, he made his mark by finishing ninth on the Monte as best two-wheel drive and non-turbo car. He was signed by Ford to drive their Sierra Cosworth for 1991. He so nearly won the Monte Carlo for them on his first outing. He set 11 fastest times and was pulling away from Carlos Sainz on the last night when the rear suspension broke. As the Sierra improved, so did the results but, typical of Delecour's luck was Greece where a marshal triggered the car's automatic fire extinguisher at the start of a stage, the engine stopped, and Delecour not only lost time but was docked two minutes for not starting the stage when instructed.

With the arrival of the Escort Cosworth, results got better. Delecour nearly won the 1993 Monte Carlo on the car's debut. He led most of the way and went into the last night a clear minute in the lead, but Didier Auriol overtook him and won by a mere 15 seconds. There was no such error on three other WRC rounds that year. In 1994, he finally won the Monte Carlo and put himself and Ford firmly in the record books. It was 41 years since Ford last won the event. But in April, someone crashed into a Ferrari F40 that he was driving. He broke both his ankles and nearly lost his left foot.

It was not until the end of the year that he was anything like fully fit and at that time Ford handed over their programme to the RAS Sport team. The results were there but perhaps not the development of the car or the old verve from the driver. Eventually, Delecour accepted a drive with Peugeot in their 306 Maxi Kit Car. He went well with it, finishing second overall on a wet Corsica and was given a full drive in their new 206WRC for 1999. The season only started in May and the car was initially unreliable but, in 2000, Delecour showed he could get the results. Dropped for 2001, he sought refuge at Ford as team mate to Carlos Sainz and Colin McRae. Like them he found unreliability but unlike them he just could not settle in the car and for 2002 he went to Mitsubishi. Sadly the Evo WRC was at the end of its life and there was no joy there either, or any drive for 2003.

Right: Francois Delecour in New Zealand 1993 on his way to second in the championship for Ford. Delecour's career has been synonymous with bad luck and a different turn of the cards could have seen him hit greater heights

DELECOUR, FRANCOIS – CAREER RECORD

YEAR	RALLY	TEAM/ENTRANT	CAR	NO.	CO-DRIVER	RESULT
1984	**0 points**					
1	Monte Carlo		Talbot Samba	165	Anne-Chantal Pauwels	67th
1986	**0 points**					
2	Monte Carlo		Peugeot 205 GTI	132	Anne-Chantal Pauwels	Retired
1987	**0 points**					
3	Monte Carlo	Peugeot Concessionaires	Peugeot 205 GTI	155	Anne-Chantal Pauwels	20th
1989	**0 points**					
4	Corsica		Peugeot 309 GTI	23	'Tilber'	Retired
1990	**2 points (54th)**					
5	Monte Carlo	Peugeot France	Peugeot 309 GTI	20	'Tilber'	9th
6	Corsica	Peugeot France	Peugeot 309 GTI	15	'Tilber'	Retired
1991	**40 points (7th)**					
7	Monte Carlo	Q8 Team Ford	Ford Sierra Cosworth 4x4	12	Anne-Chantal Pauwels	3rd
8	Portugal	Q8 Team Ford	Ford Sierra Cosworth 4x4	4	Anne-Chantal Pauwels	Retired
9	Corsica	Q8 Team Ford	Ford Sierra Cosworth 4x4	5	Anne-Chantal Pauwels	Retired
10	Greece	Q8 Team Ford	Ford Sierra Cosworth 4x4	5	Anne-Chantal Pauwels	Retired
11	Sanremo	Q8 Team Ford	Ford Sierra Cosworth 4x4	6	Anne-Chantal Pauwels	4th
12	Catalunya	Q8 Team Ford	Ford Sierra Cosworth 4x4	4	Daniel Grataloup	3rd
13	Great Britain	Q8 Team Ford	Ford Sierra Cosworth 4x4	8	Daniel Grataloups	6th
1992	**45 points (6th)**					
14	Monte Carlo	Ford Motor Company	Ford Sierra Cosworth 4x4	7	Daniel Grataloup	4th
15	Portugal	Ford Motor Company	Ford Sierra Cosworth 4x4	3	Daniel Grataloup	Retired
16	Corsica	Ford Motor Company	Ford Sierra Cosworth 4x4	6	Daniel Grataloup	2nd
17	Greece	Ford Motor Company	Ford Sierra Cosworth 4x4	3	Daniel Grataloup	5th
18	Finland	Ford Motor Company	Ford Sierra Cosworth 4x4	8	Daniel Grataloup	Retired
19	Sanremo	Ford Motor Company	Ford Sierra Cosworth 4x4	4	Daniel Grataloup	3rd
20	Catalunya	Ford Motor Company	Ford Sierra Cosworth 4x4	2	Daniel Grataloup	Retired
1993	**112 points (2nd)**					
21	Monte Carlo	Ford Motor Company	Ford Escort RS Cosworth	6	Daniel Grataloup	2nd
22	**Portugal**	**Ford Motor Company**	**Ford Escort RS Cosworth**	**5**	**Daniel Grataloup**	**1st**
23	Corsica	Ford Motor Company	Ford Escort RS Cosworth	3	Daniel Grataloup	1st
24	Greece	Ford Motor Company	Ford Escort RS Cosworth	2	Daniel Grataloup	Retired
25	New Zealand	Ford Motor Company	Ford Escort RS Cosworth	3	Daniel Grataloup	2nd
26	Australia	Ford Motor Company	Ford Escort RS Cosworth	5	Daniel Grataloup	3rd
27	Sanremo	Ford Motor Company	Ford Escort RS Cosworth	2	Daniel Grataloup	Retired
28	**Catalunya**	**Ford Motor Company**	**Ford Escort RS Cosworth**	**3**	**Daniel Grataloup**	**1st**
29	Great Britain	Ford Motor Company	Ford Escort RS Cosworth	3	Daniel Grataloup	4th
1994	**30 points (8th)**					
30	**Monte Carlo**	**Ford Motor Company**	**Ford Escort RS Cosworth**	**6**	**Daniel Grataloup**	**1st**
31	Portugal	Ford Motor Company	Ford Escort RS Cosworth	1	Daniel Grataloup	Retired
32	Finland	Ford Motor Company	Ford Escort RS Cosworth	5	Daniel Grataloup	4th
33	Sanremo	Ford Motor Company	Ford Escort RS Cosworth	1	Daniel Grataloup	Retired
34	Great Britain	Ford Motor Company	Ford Escort RS Cosworth	3	Daniel Grataloup	Retired
1995	**46 points (4th)**					
35	Monte Carlo	RAS-Ford	Ford Escort RS Cosworth	7	Catherine Francois	2nd
36	Sweden	RAS-Ford	Ford Escort RS Cosworth	7	Catherine Francois	Retired
37	Portugal	RAS-Ford	Ford Escort RS Cosworth	7	Catherine Francois	Retired
38	Corsica	RAS-Ford	Ford Escort RS Cosworth	7	Catherine Francois	2nd
39	New Zealand	RAS-Ford	Ford Escort RS Cosworth	7	Catherine Francois	6th
40	Australia	RAS-Ford	Ford Escort RS Cosworth	7	Catherine Francois	Retired
41	Catalunya	RAS-Ford	Ford Escort RS Cosworth	7	Catherine Francois	4th
42	Great Britain	RAS-Ford	Ford Escort RS Cosworth	7	Catherine Francois	Retired
1996	**0 points**					
43	Sweden	Ford Motor Company	Ford Escort RS Cosworth	5	Daniel Grataloup	11th
1997	**3 points (17th)**					
44	Catalunya	Peugeot Sport	Peugeot 306 Maxi	8	Daniel Grataloup	Retired
45	Corsica	Peugeot Sport	Peugeot 306 Maxi	9	Daniel Grataloup	4th
1998	**6 points (10th)**					

DELECOUR, FRANCOIS CAREER RECORD (CONTD)

YEAR	RALLY	TEAM/ENTRANT	CAR	NO.	CO-DRIVER	RESULT
46	Monte Carlo	Peugeot Sport	Peugeot 306 Maxi	14	Daniel Grataloup	10th
47	Catalunya	Peugeot Sport	Peugeot 306 Maxi	12	Daniel Grataloup	8th
48	Corsica	Peugeot Sport	Peugeot 306 Maxi	14	Daniel Grataloup	2nd
49	Sanremo	Peugeot Sport	Peugeot 306 Maxi	11	Daniel Grataloup	Retired
1999	**3 points (16th)**					
50	Monte Carlo	Privateer	Ford Escort WRC	19	Dominique Savignoni	4th
51	Corsica	Peugeot Esso	Peugeot 206 WRC	14	Daniel Grataloup	Retired
52	Greece	Peugeot Esso	Peugeot 206 WRC	14	Daniel Grataloup	Retired
53	Finland	Peugeot Esso	Peugeot 206 WRC	14	Daniel Grataloup	9th
54	Sanremo	Peugeot Esso	Peugeot 206 WRC	14	Daniel Grataloup	Retired
55	Australia	Peugeot Esso	Peugeot 206 WRC	14	Daniel Grataloup	Retired
56	Great Britain	Peugeot Esso	Peugeot 206 WRC	14	Daniel Grataloup	Retired
2000	**24 points (6th)**					
57	Monte Carlo	Peugeot Esso	Peugeot 206 WRC	9	Daniel Grataloup	Retired
58	Sweden	Peugeot Esso	Peugeot 206 WRC	9	Daniel Grataloup	7th
59	Portugal	Peugeot Esso	Peugeot 206 WRC	9	Daniel Grataloup	5th
60	Catalunya	Peugeot Esso	Peugeot 206 WRC	9	Daniel Grataloup	7th
61	Argentina	Peugeot Esso	Peugeot 206 WRC	9	Daniel Grataloup	13th
62	Greece	Peugeot Esso	Peugeot 206 WRC	9	Daniel Grataloup	9th
63	New Zealand	Peugeot Esso	Peugeot 206 WRC	9	Daniel Grataloup	Retired
64	Finland	Peugeot Esso	Peugeot 206 WRC	18	Daniel Grataloup	6th
65	Cyprus	Peugeot Esso	Peugeot 206 WRC	9	Daniel Grataloup	3rd
66	Corsica	Peugeot Esso	Peugeot 206 WRC	9	Daniel Grataloup	2nd
67	Sanremo	Peugeot Esso	Peugeot 206 WRC	9	Daniel Grataloup	2nd
68	Australia	Peugeot Esso	Peugeot 206 WRC	9	Daniel Grataloup	3rd
69	Great Britain	Peugeot Esso	Peugeot 206 WRC	9	Daniel Grataloup	6th
2001	**15 points (9th)**					
70	Monte Carlo	Ford Motor Company	Ford Focus WRC	17	Daniel Grataloup	3rd
71	Sweden	Ford Motor Company	Ford Focus WRC	17	Daniel Grataloup	5th
72	Portugal	Ford Motor Company	Ford Focus WRC	17	Daniel Grataloup	5th
73	Catalunya	Ford Motor Company	Ford Focus WRC	17	Daniel Grataloup	6th
74	Argentina	Ford Motor Company	Ford Focus WRC	17	Daniel Grataloup	7th
75	Cyprus	Ford Motor Company	Ford Focus WRC	17	Daniel Grataloup	Retired
76	Greece	Ford Motor Company	Ford Focus WRC	17	Daniel Grataloup	5th
77	Safari	Ford Motor Company	Ford Focus WRC	17	Daniel Grataloup	4th
78	Finland	Ford Motor Company	Ford Focus WRC	17	Daniel Grataloup	Retired
79	New Zealand	Ford Motor Company	Ford Focus WRC	17	Daniel Grataloup	12th
80	Sanremo	Ford Motor Company	Ford Focus WRC	17	Daniel Grataloup	6th
81	Corsica	Ford Motor Company	Ford Focus WRC	17	Daniel Grataloup	10th
82	Australia	Ford Motor Company	Ford Focus WRC	17	Daniel Grataloup	Retired
2002	**0 points**					
83	Monte Carlo	Marlboro Mitsubishi Ralliart	Mitsubishi Lancer Evo WRC	7	Daniel Grataloup	9th
84	Sweden	Marlboro Mitsubishi Ralliart	Mitsubishi Lancer Evo WRC	7	Daniel Grataloup	Retired
85	Corsica	Marlboro Mitsubishi Ralliart	Mitsubishi Lancer Evo WRC	7	Daniel Grataloup	7th
86	Catalunya	Marlboro Mitsubishi Ralliart	Mitsubishi Lancer Evo WRC	7	Daniel Grataloup	9th
87	Cyprus	Marlboro Mitsubishi Ralliart	Mitsubishi Lancer Evo WRC	7	Daniel Grataloup	13th
88	Argentina	Marlboro Mitsubishi Ralliart	Mitsubishi Lancer Evo WRC	7	Daniel Grataloup	Retired
89	Greece	Marlboro Mitsubishi Ralliart	Mitsubishi Lancer Evo WRC	7	Daniel Grataloup	11th
90	Safari	Marlboro Mitsubishi Ralliart	Mitsubishi Lancer Evo WRC	7	Daniel Grataloup	Retired
91	Finland	Marlboro Mitsubishi Ralliart	Mitsubishi Lancer Evo WRC	7	Daniel Grataloup	Retired
92	Germany	Marlboro Mitsubishi Ralliart	Mitsubishi Lancer Evo WRC	7	Daniel Grataloup	9th
93	Sanremo	Marlboro Mitsubishi Ralliart	Mitsubishi Lancer Evo WRC	7	Daniel Grataloup	10th
94	New Zealand	Marlboro Mitsubishi Ralliart	Mitsubishi Lancer Evo WRC	7	Daniel Grataloup	9th
95	Australia	Marlboro Mitsubishi Ralliart	Mitsubishi Lancer Evo WRC	7	Daniel Grataloup	Retired
96	Great Britain	Marlboro Mitsubishi Ralliart	Mitsubishi Lancer Evo WRC	7	Dominique Savignoni	Retired

DUNCAN, IAN (EAK) BORN: 22 FEBRUARY 1961, NAIROBI, KENYA

Born and bred in Nairobi, Ian Duncan's interest in the Safari Rally is understandable and he was to be the only East African driver to win it in the last 20 years of its existence.

The son of an electrical engineer who had himself done the Safari, Duncan learned to drive cars at 11 years of age at their farm in Limuru and soon after was racing bikes in motocross. When he started work with a construction firm, his company car was a Nissan 1200 Pickup that was soon being 'borrowed' at weekends to do small rallies. By 1982, he was using it to do the national rally series but when he decided to make his first entry in the Safari, a new Pickup was obtained and prepared He finished ninth and this was to be his best result on his home international for five years. These were spent learning the hard way just how unreliable rally cars could be.

For 1988, he got involved in Subaru's testing for the Safari and was given an RX Turbo for the rally and did well. But for national events, he was still using a Toyota and when TTE wanted some extended testing of their new Supra, they left him one and also provided a car for the Safari. Subaru came to him again with their new Legacy in 1990 and, like Toyota, left him one to play with. They also lent him a Group N Legacy to go to the Acropolis where he revelled in the car's speed on the rough. Finally in 1992 he made a permanent connection with TTE and drove a rebuilt recce car on the event where, after the first leg, he was lying third.

The following year he was third in a Celica Turbo and then won outright in 1994 when the official cars failed. After that, he relied on Toyota Kenya for cars and was a frequent visitor to the podium for them. recently he has contested the Kenyan championship with a turbocharged Toyota Land Cruiser VX, winning events regularly.

DUNCAN, IAN – CAREER RECORD

YEAR	RALLY	TEAM/ENTRANT	CAR	NO.	CO-DRIVER	RESULT
1983	**0 points**					
1	Safari		Nissan 1200 Pickup	29	Gavin Bennett	9th
1984	**0 points**					
2	Safari		Daihatsu Charade	31	Ian Munro	Retired
1985	**0 points**					
3	Safari		Toyota Corolla	80	Ian Munro	Retired
1986	**0 points**					
4	Safari		Toyota Corolla	23	Ian Munro	Retired
1987	**0 points**					
5	Safari		Toyota Celica TCT	70	Ian Munro	Retired
1988	**6 points (43rd)**					
6	Safari	Fuji Heavy Industries	Subaru RX Turbo	15	Ian Munro	6th
1989	**8 points (34th)**					
7	Safari	Toyota Team Kenya	Toyota Supra Turbo	10	Ian Munro	5th
1990	**3 points (47th)**					
8	Safari	Subaru Technica International	Subaru Legacy RS	10	Ian Munro	Retired
9	Greece		Subaru Legacy RS (GpN)	24	Yvonne Mehta	8th
1991	**6 points (36th)**					
10	Safari		Subaru Legacy RS	10	David Williamson	6th
1992	**6 points (34th)**					
11	Safari	Toyota Team Kenya	Toyota Celica GT-Four	9	David Williamson	6th
1993	**12 points (19th)**					
12	Safari	Toyota Castrol Team	Toyota Celica Turbo 4WD	3	Ian Munro	3rd
1994	**20 points (11th)**					
13	**Safari**	**Toyota Castrol Team**	**Toyota Celica Turbo 4WD**	**3**	**David Williamson**	**1st**
1996	**12 points (12th)**					
14	Safari	Toyota Kenya	Toyota Celica GT-Four	10	David Williamson	3rd
1997	**4 points (13th)**					
15	Safari	Toyota Kenya	Toyota Celica GT-Four	7	David Williamson	3rd
1999	**3 points (16th)**					
16	Safari	Toyota Kenya	Toyota Corolla WRC	12	David Williamson	4th

EKLUND, PER (S) BORN: 26 JUNE 1946, ARVIKA, SWEDEN

One of the sport's most versatile and likeable drivers, Per Eklund started out as a navigator for his elder brother and then, when he reached 18, borrowed his father's Volvo PV544 to branch out as a driver. His first rally car was a VW Beetle but this was changed for a two-stroke Saab 96 in 1966 and to a V4 the year after.

He distinguished himself in Swedish national rallies and, by 1970 joined the Saab works team. He and fellow Swede Stig Blomqvist formed the junior squad but their talents soon moved them up into the front line.

The Blomqvist-versus-Eklund battle not only did a lot for Saab's profile but also enlivened rallying for almost 10 years. Sadly for Eklund, it was his rival who got the upper hand and winning the Swedish Rally just once was not enough to redress the balance. Eklund would also have won in Austria in 1973 without a controversial protest by BMW .

Once his Saab contract ceased at the end of the 1970s, he drove a wide range of cars, though it was with a 750bhp Saab 9-3 Viggen that he became FIA Rallycross champion in 1999.

Since 1978 he has been seen at the wheel of cars from Porsche, Fiat, VW and a Triumph TR7 V8 before Eklund began arelationship with Toyota. He distinguished himself in the African Ivory Coast Rally, finishing on the podium three years in a row.

With the backing of long-term sponsor, Clarion, he drove Audi Quattros and MG Metro 6R4s during the early 1980s. He then chose Nissans, Lancias and Subarus after Group B was killed off at the end of 1986. Nearly all Eklund's cars were self-prepared, though it was a factory Nissan that gave him his final podium – third on the 1987 Safari.

Eklund can still be seen muscling powerful rallycross machines in the European Series. And he's still as enthusiastic as the day he started.

"The Blomqvist-versus-Eklund battle not only did a lot for Saab's profile but also enlivened rallying for almost 10 years"

Below: Per Eklund has enjoyed sponsorship from Clarion throughout his rally and rallycross career. Here the company's name is emblazoned on his Audi Quattro on the 1987 RAC Rally

EKLUND, PER – CAREER RECORD

YEAR	RALLY	TEAM/ENTRANT	CAR	NO.	CO-DRIVER	RESULT
1973						
1	Sweden	Saab-Scania	Saab 96 V4	7	Rolf Carlsson	2nd
2	Finland	Saab-Scania	Saab 96 V4	8	Bjorn Cederberg	Retired
3	Austria	Saab-Scania	Saab 96 V4	15	Bo Reinicke	3rd
4	Great Britain	Saab-Scania	Saab 96 V4	7	Bo Reinicke	Retired
1974						
5	Finland	Saab-Scania	Saab 96 V4	12	Bjorn Cederberg	Retired
6	Great Britain	Saab-Scania	Saab 96 V4	7	Bjorn Cederberg	Retired
1975						
7	Sweden	Saab-Scania	Saab 96 V4	8	Bjorn Cederberg	4th
8	Finland	Saab-Scania	Saab 96 V4	13	Bjorn Cederberg	4th
9	Great Britain	Saab-Scania	Saab 96 V4	9	Bjorn Cederberg	Retired
1976						
10	**Sweden**	**Saab-Scania**	**Saab 96 V4**	**4**	**Bjorn Cederberg**	**1st**
11	Finland	Saab-Scania	Saab 99 EMS	6	Bjorn Cederberg	Retired
12	Great Britain	Saab-Scania	Saab 99 EMS	17	Bjorn Cederberg	Retired
1977						
13	Sweden	Saab-Scania	Saab 99 EMS	1	Bjorn Cederberg	Retired
14	Finland	Saab-Scania	Saab 99 EMS	9	Bjorn Cederberg	Retired
15	Great Britain	Saab-Scania	Saab 99 EMS	11	Bjorn Cederberg	9th
1978						
16	Sweden	Saab-Scania	Saab 96 EMS	11	Bjorn Cederberg	Retired
17	Finland		Porsche 911	2	Bjorn Cederberg	4th
18	Great Britain	Saab-Scania	Saab 96 Turbo	8	Bjorn Cederberg	Retired
1979	3 points (54th)					
19	Monte Carlo	Fiat-Alitalia	Fiat Ritmo Abarth 75	7	Hans Sylvan	Retired
20	Sweden		Saab 99 Turbo	8	Hans Sylvan	Retired
21	Finland		Triumph TR7 V8	4	Hans Sylvan	8th
22	Sanremo		Triumph TR7 V8	10	Hans Sylvan	Retired
23	Great Britain	BL Cars	Triumph TR7 V8	7	Hans Sylvan	13th
1980	27 points (11th)					
24	Monte Carlo	Pierburg	VW Golf GTi	26	Hans Sylvan	5th
25	Sweden	Team Datsun Sweden	Datsun 160J	9	Hans Sylvan	8th
26	Portugal	British Leyland Cars	Triumph TR7 V8	14	Hans Sylvan	Retired
27	Finland	British Leyland Cars	Triumph TR7 V8	15	Hans Sylvan	3rd
28	Great Britain	British Leyland Cars	Triumph TR7 V8	11	Hans Sylvan	Retired
29	Ivory Coast	Premoto Toyota	Toyota Celica 2000GT	10	Hans Sylvan	7th
1981	29 points (10th)					
30	Monte Carlo	Pierburg	Volkswagen Golf GTi	12	Ragnar Spjuth	Retired
31	Sweden	Publimo Racing/Clarion	Porsche 911SC	5	Ragnar Spjuth	9th
32	Portugal	Toyota Team Europe	Toyota Celica	10	Ragnar Spjuth	Retired
33	Corsica	Toyota Team Europe	Toyota Celica	7	Jan-Olaf Bohlin	6th
34	Greece	Toyota Team Europe	Toyota Celica	9	Bjorn Cederberg	Retired
35	Finland	Rallysport News Team	Porsche 911SC	10	Ragnar Spjuth	Retired
36	Ivory Coast	Premoto Toyota	Toyota Celica	1	Ragnar Spjuth	2nd
37	Great Britain	Toyota Team GB	Toyota Celica	13	Ragnar Spjuth	6th
1982	57 points (5th)					
38	Sweden	Saab Sport	Saab 99 Turbo	6	Ragnar Spjuth	4th
39	Portugal	Toyota Team Europe	Toyota Celica	8	Ragnar Spjuth	2nd
40	New Zealand	Toyota New Zealand	Toyota Celica	7	Ragnar Spjuth	2nd
41	Finland	Rallysport News Team	Porsche 911SC	9	Ragnar Spjuth	Retired
42	Sanremo	Volkswagen Motorsport	Volkswagen Golf 16S	5	Ragnar Spjuth	Retired
43	Ivory Coast	Premoto Toyota	Toyota Celica	6	Ragnar Spjuth	2nd
44	Great Britain	Toyota Team GB	Toyota Celica	14	Dave Whittock	9th
1983	22 points (10th)					
45	Sweden	Saab Sport	Saab 99 Turbo	5	Ragnar Spjuth	Retired
46	Finland	Sesab Service	Audi Quattro ????	9	Ragnar Spjuth	4th
47	Ivory Coast	Premoto Toyota	Toyota Celica TC Turbo	4	Ragnar Spjuth	3rd
48	Great Britain	Toyota Team GB	Toyota Celica TC Turbo	4	Ragnar Spjuth	Retired
1984	30 points (7th)					
49	Sweden	Clarion	Audi Quattro	2	Dave Whittock	3rd
50	Safari	Westlands Motors	Toyota Celica TC Turbo	4	Dave Whittock	Retired
51	Finland	Clarion	Audi Quattro	6	Dave Whittock	6th
52	Great Britain	Toyota Team GB	Toyota Celica TC Turbo	8	Dave Whittock	3rd
1985	24 points (10th)					
53	Sweden		Audi Quattro	4	Dave Whittock	5th
54	Finland	Clarion Svenska	Audi Quattro	8	Bruno Berglund	6th
55	Great Britain	Clarion Svenska	Audi Quattro	8	Bjorn Cederberg	4th
1986	8 points (34th)					
56	Sweden	Austin Rover World Rally Team	MG Metro 6R4	7	Dave Whittock	Retired
57	Finland	Clarion Team Europe	MG Metro 6R4	8	Dave Whittock	7th
58	Great Britain	Austin Rover World Rally Team	MG Metro 6R4	17	Dave Whittock	7th
1987	25 points (12th)					
59	Monte Carlo	Subaru Deutschland	Subaru RX Turbo	16	Dave Whittock	12th
60	Sweden	Clarion Team Europe	Audi Coupe Quattro	10	Dave Whittock	7th
61	Safari	Fuji Heavy Industries	Subaru RX Turbo	15	Dave Whittock	5th
62	United States	Nissan Motorsports International	Nissan 200SX	11	Dave Whittock	8th
63	Finland	Clarion Team Europe	Audi Coupe Quattro	8	Dave Whittock	4th
64	Great Britain	Clarion Team Europe	Audi Coupe Quattro	17	Dave Whittock	Disqualified
1988	12 points (20th)					
65	Sweden	Clarion Team Europe	Lancia Delta HF 4WD	9	Dave Whittock	Retired
66	Safari	Nissan Motorsports International	Nissan 200SX	14	Dave Whittock	3rd
67	Great Britain	Clarion Team Europe	Nissan March	16	Dave Whittock	21st
1989	16 points (19th)					
68	Sweden	Clarion Team Europe	Lancia Delta Integrale	4	Dave Whittock	2nd
69	Monte Carlo	Clarion Team Europe	Nissan March Turbo	9	Dave Whittock	Retired
70	Safari	Nissan Motorsports International	Nissan 200SX	1	Dave Whittock	Retired
71	Greece	Clarion Team Europe	Nissan March Turbo	12	Bjorn C/Dave W?	10th
72	Finland	Clarion Team Europe	Lancia Delta Integrale	11	Dave Whittock	Retired
73	Great Britain	Clarion Team Europe	Lancia Delta Integrale ????	11	Bjorn Cederberg	Disqualified
1990	0 points					
74	Finland	Clarion Team Europe	Lancia Delta Integrale	13	Jan-Olaf Bohlin	Retired
75	Great Britain	Clarion Team Europe	Lancia Delta Integrale	14	Jan-Olaf Bohlin	12th
1991	3 points (49th)					
76	Sweden		Lancia Delta Integrale	14	Jan-Olaf Bohlin	8th
77	Great Britain		Lancia Delta Integrale	27	Jan-Olaf Bohlin	Retired
1992	8 points (32nd)					
78	Sweden	Clarion Svenska	Subaru Legacy RS	11	Johnny Johansson	6th
79	Safari	Noriyuki Koseki	Subaru Legacy RS (GpN)	11	Johnny Johansson	9th
80	Great Britain		Subaru Legacy RS	20	Johnny Johansson	12th
1993	6 points (31st)					
81	Sweden	Eklund Team Europe	Subaru Legacy RS	10	Johnny Johansson	6th
1996	0 points					
82	Sweden	Clarion Team Europe	Subaru Legacy RS	27	Anders Olsson	17th
1997	0 points					
83	Great Britain		Saab 900 Turbo	39	Johnny Johansson	Retired

ERICSSON, MIKAEL (S) BORN: 28 FEBRUARY 1960, UMEA, SWEDEN

Mikael Ericsson was the third Swede to go to Finland and win an event that the Finns considered their own personal property, but, despite 10 attempts, he never quite got his hands on the winner's laurels for his own event. A man with oodles of talent, he found it difficult to settle in a team long enough to be able to establish himself.

His first rallies were in VW Golfs in 1978 with which he contested national rallies and it was with a Golf that he made his WRC debut on the Swedish Rally of 1981. Ericsson was good enough to land a deal with the VAG importer to drive an Audi but on the 1983 Swedish Rally, it was Stig Blomqvist who got the 80 Quattro and Ericsson was left with the two-wheel drive Coupe. The following year, he got a 90 Quattro, finished fourth overall and won Group A.

It was 1986, the last year of Group B, before Ericsson got his chance in a works Lancia Delta S4. On his debut at the Acropolis, the suspension failed while in New Zealand and Finland, he finished respectfully behind his team leaders. On the RAC Rally he was leading on the third leg only to have the engine fail just two stages from the finish.

In 1989 he netted the big win in Argentina in a Lancia-dominated event giving them the WRC Manufacturers' title as early as August. But Ericsson's victory meant that he could have messed things up for Lancia's chosen hope for the Drivers' title so he did not get a car for Finland. The free agent chose Mitsubishi and took the lead after Carlos Sainz rolled and he won for the second time that year.

Superfluous to Lancia's needs for 1990, he closed a deal with Toyota and did three Safaris for them with a 100% finishing record but nothing seemed right after those two wins and his motivation dwindled.

ERICSSON, MIKAEL - CAREER RECORD

YEAR	RALLY	TEAM/ENTRANT	CAR	NO.	CO-DRIVER	RESULT
1981	0 points					
1	Sweden		Volkswagen Golf GTi	90	Hans Bonnedal	28th
1982	1 point (66th)					
2	Sweden	Audi Sport Sweden	Audi 80 Coupe	45	Jan Sandström	10th
3	Great Britain	Audi Sport Sweden	Audi Coupe Quattro	104	Jan Sandström	21st
1983	3 points (41st)					
4	Sweden	Audi Team Sweden	Audi 80 Coupe	32	Bo Thorszelius	8th
5	Finland	Audi Team Sweden	Audi 80 Quattro	44	Rolf Melleroth	Retired
1984	1 point (62nd)					
6	Sweden	Team VAG Sweden	Audi 80 Quattro	9	Rolf Melleroth	Retired
7	Finland	Team VAG Sweden	Audi 80 Quattro	19	Rolf Melleroth	Retired
8	Great Britain		Audi 80 Quattro	22	Claes Billstam	10th
1985	7 points (33rd)					
9	Sweden		Audi 80 Quattro	12	Johnny Johansson	7th
10	Finland	Blue Rose Team	Audi 80 Quattro	18	Reinhard Michel	8th
11	Great Britain		Audi 80 Quattro	20	Claes Billstam	Retired
1986	28 points (8th)					
12	Sweden	Audi Sport	Audi 90 Quattro	12	Reinhard Michel	4th
13	Greece	Martini Lancia	Lancia Delta S4	11	Claes Billstam	Retired
14	New Zealand	Martini Lancia	Lancia Delta S4	6	Claes Billstam	4th
15	Finland	Martini Lancia	Lancia Delta S4	7	Claes Billstam	5th
16	Great Britain	Martini Lancia	Lancia Delta S4	9	Claes Billstam	Retired
1987	28 points (10th)					
17	Sweden	Martini Lancia	Lancia Delta HF 4WD	8	Claes Billstam	2nd
18	Greece	Jolly Club	Lancia Delta HF 4WD	6	Claes Billstam	Retired
19	United States	Nissan Motorsports International	Nissan 200 SX	7	Claes Billstam	Retired
20	Sanremo	Jolly Club Totip	Lancia Delta HF 4WD	7	Claes Billstam	8th
21	Great Britain	Martini Lancia	Lancia Delta HF 4WD	7	Claes Billstam	4th
1988	30 points (8th)					
22	Sweden	Martini Lancia	Lancia Delta HF 4WD	2	Claes Billstam	Retired
23	Portugal	Martini Lancia	Lancia Delta Integrale	6	Claes Billstam	Retired
24	Greece	Martini Lancia	Lancia Delta Integrale	8	Claes Billstam	2nd
25	Finland	Martini Lancia	Lancia Delta Integrale	6	Claes Billstam	2nd
26	Great Britain	Martini Lancia	Lancia Delta Integrale	7	Claes Billstam	Retired
1989	50 points (4th)					
27	Sweden	Astra Team Italia	Lancia Delta Integrale	3	Claes Billstam	4th
28	**Argentina**	**Martini Lancia**	**Lancia Delta Integrale**	**3**	**Claes Billstam**	**1st**
29	**Finland**	**Mitsubishi Ralliart Europe**	**Mitsubishi Galant VR-4**	**9**	**Claes Billstam**	**1st**
1990	32 points (5th)					
30	Monte Carlo	Toyota Team Europe	Toyota Celica GT-Four	5	Claes Billstam	7th
31	Safari	Toyota Team Kenya	Toyota Celica GT-Four	6	Claes Billstam	3rd
32	Greece	Toyota Team Europe	Toyota Celica GT-Four	6	Claes Billstam	4th
33	Finland	Toyota Team Europe	Toyota Celica GT-Four	1	Claes Billstam	Retired
34	Australia	Toyota Team Europe	Toyota Celica GT-Four	6	Claes Billstam	Retired
35	Sanremo	Toyota Team Europe	Toyota Celica GT-Four	7	Claes Billstam	6th
1991	27 points (10th)					
36	Safari	Toyota Team Kenya	Toyota Celica GT-Four	4	Claes Billstam	2nd
37	Greece	Toyota Team Europe	Toyota Celica GT-Four	8	Claes Billstam	6th
38	Argentina	Toyota Team Europe	Toyota Celica GT-Four	7	Claes Billstam	6th
1992	10 points (26th)					
39	Safari	Toyota Team Kenya	Toyota Celica Turbo 4WD	2	Nicky Grist	4th
1993	0 points					
40	Sweden	Ford Motor Company	Ford Escort RS Cosworth	7	Tina Thorner	Retired

ERIKSSON, KENNETH

(S) BORN: 13 MAY 1956, APPELBO, SWEDEN

Not too many rally drivers have a personal entry in the Guinness Book of Records but, back in 1985, that is just what Kenneth Eriksson could claim. He drove an Opel Kadett round the trotting track at Karlstad – well known to Swedish Rally fans – on two wheels for a distance of 20 kilometres.

"Not too many rally drivers have a personal entry in the Guinness Book of Records"

For 20 years or more, if you were Swedish and wanted to take up rallying, a Saab was a good place to start. There were plenty of them and they were cheap. Starting in 1977, Eriksson drove a Saab 96 V4 on Swedish national rallies before changing to an Opel Ascona in 1983. He was given help with a Kadett GT/E for 1984 and came third in the Swedish Championship. As a full driver for GM Sweden, he won the championship in 1985 using a Kadett GSi and was promptly signed up by Volkswagen Motorsport to drive its new Golf GTi 16v on the 1986 WRC.

At this moment, Eriksson's only WRC experience outside Sweden was a single appearance on the RAC Rally two years earlier. So to take a two-wheel drive Group A car among all the Group B cars and rack up the result that he did on rallies as diverse as Monte Carlo, Corsica and 1000 Lakes was a truly remarkable performance. His results were good enough to clinch the World Group A title and VW were delighted to continue for 1987. The problem was that too many people now had 4WD cars in Group A, but again Eriksson's results were of a high standard considering the competition. He won the Ivory Coast Rally, again a remarkable thing to win an African rally in a front-wheel drive car, and was fourth overall in the WRC Driver standing at the end of the year.

Toyota signed him for 1988 but, as the junior in the team, he did not get a full season and the same consideration applied the following year. Thus when he got an offer to join Mitsubishi and possibly do some Rally-Raid events as well, he leapt at the chance. At first the Galant VR-4 proved unreliable but the second half of the year was better. He started 1991 by coming fourth on the Paris-Dakar and winning the Swedish Rally, and finished it by winning the Baja Aragon and taking second place on the RAC Rally.

Four more years with Mitsubishi followed but the programme never encompassed more that half a dozen WRC rallies. This was compensated by sending Eriksson to the Asia Pacific series in 1994. He won that title in 1995 and had his best ever result in the WRC Driver's Championship coming third with only three results. He moved to Subaru for 1996 when he only had one retirement from nine events – an accident with a bridge in Indonesia – but it was not enough for a title challenge. It was similar story in 1997 but he did win in Sweden and New Zealand. And Eriksson also won the Asia Pacific series for Subaru in 1996 and 1997.

Eriksson went on to drive four years for Hyundai and a further year for Skoda but neither car was a real success and for 2003 he was left on the sidelines.

Right: Victory for Kenneth Eriksson in Australia 1995 aboad the Mitusbishi led to the Swede taking third overall in that season's drivers' world championship

ERIKSSON, KENNETH – CAREER RECORD

YEAR	RALLY	TEAM/ENTRANT	CAR	NO.	CO-DRIVER	RESULT
1980	**0 points**					
1	Sweden		Saab 96 V4	150	Lennart Larsson	51st
1981	**0 points**					
2	Sweden		Saab 96 V4	122	Lennart Larsson	31st
1982	**0 points**					
3	Sweden		Saab 96 V4	52	Sven-Erik Heinstedt	15th
1983	**0 points**					
4	Sweden		Opel Ascona	38	Sven-Erik Heinstedt	16th
1984	**4 points (36th)**					
5	Sweden	Opel Team Sweden	Opel Kadett GT/E	24	Lennart Larsson	7th
6	Great Britain		Opel Kadett GSi	52	Ragnar Spjuth	Retired
1985	**1 point (68th)**					
7	Sweden	Opel Team Sweden	Opel Kadett GSi	23	Bo Thorszelius	10th
1986	**25 points (10th)**					
8	Monte Carlo	Volkswagen Motorsport	Volkswagen Golf GTi 16V	22	Peter Diekmann	9th
9	Sweden	Volkswagen Motorsport	Volkswagen Golf GTi 16V	15	Peter Diekmann	7th
10	Portugal	Volkswagen Motorsport	Volkswagen Golf GTi 16V	21	Peter Diekmann	Retired
11	Safari	Volkswagen Motorsport	Volkswagen Golf GTi 16V	17	Peter Diekmann	Retired
12	Corsica	Volkswagen Motorsport	Volkswagen Golf GTi 16V	19	Peter Diekmann	8th
13	Greece	Volkswagen Motorsport	Volkswagen Golf GTi 16V	23	Peter Diekmann	7th
14	New Zealand	Volkswagen Motorsport	Volkswagen Golf GTi 16V	11	Peter Diekmann	7th
15	Argentina	Volkswagen Motorsport	Volkswagen Golf GTi 16V	10	Peter Diekmann	5th
16	Finland	Volkswagen Motorsport	Volkswagen Golf GTi 16V	12	Peter Diekmann	12th
17	Great Britain	Volkswagen Motorsport	Volkswagen Golf GTi 16V	27	Peter Diekmann	11th
1987	**70 points (4th)**					
18	Monte Carlo	Volkswagen Motorsport	Volkswagen Golf GTi 16V	7	Peter Diekmann	5th
19	Sweden	Volkswagen Motorsport	Volkswagen Golf GTi 16V	7	Peter Diekmann	8th
20	Portugal	Volkswagen Motorsport	Volkswagen Golf GTi 16V	5	Peter Diekmann	3rd
21	Safari	Volkswagen Motorsport	Volkswagen Golf GTi 16V	8	Peter Diekmann	Retired
22	Corsica	Volkswagen Motorsport	Volkswagen Golf GTi 16V	5	Peter Diekmann	Retired
23	Greece	Volkswagen Motorsport	Volkswagen Golf GTi 16V	8	Peter Diekmann	Retired
24	New Zealand	Volkswagen Motorsport	Volkswagen Golf GTi 16V	2	Peter Diekmann	2nd
25	Argentina	Volkswagen Motorsport	Volkswagen Golf GTi 16V	3	Peter Diekmann	4th
26	**Ivory Coast**	**Volkswagen Motorsport**	**Volkswagen Golf GTi 16V**	**4**	**Peter Diekmann**	**1st**
27	Great Britain	Volkswagen Motorsport UK	Volkswagen Golf GTi 16V	5	Peter Diekmann	9th
1988	**22 points (12th)**					
28	Safari	Toyota Team Europe	Toyota Supra Turbo	7	Peter Diekmann	4th
29	Corsica	Toyota Team Europe	Toyota Celica GT-Four	5	Peter Diekmann	6th
30	Finland	Toyota Team Europe	Toyota Celica GT-Four	8	Peter Diekmann	Retired
31	Sanremo	Toyota Team Europe	Toyota Celica GT-Four	8	Peter Diekmann	6th
32	Great Britain	Toyota Team GB	Toyota Celica GT-Four	6	Peter Diekmann	Retired
1989	**47 points (6th)**					
33	Sweden	Toyota Team Sweden	Toyota Celica GT-Four	6	Staffan Parmander	3rd
34	Greece	Toyota Team Europe	Toyota Celica GT-Four	5	Staffan Parmander	Retired
35	Finland	Toyota Team Europe	Toyota Celica GT-Four	10	Staffan Parmander	4th
36	Australia	Toyota Team Europe	Toyota Celica GT-Four	3	Staffan Parmander	2nd
37	Great Britain	Toyota Team Europe	Toyota Celica GT-Four	5	Staffan Parmander	4th
1990	**27 points (8th)**					
38	Monte Carlo	Mitsubishi Ralliart Europe	Mitsubishi Galant VR-4	9	Staffan Parmander	Retired
39	Portugal	Mitsubishi Ralliart Europe	Mitsubishi Galant VR-4	7	Staffan Parmander	Retired
40	Greece	Mitsubishi Ralliart Europe	Mitsubishi Galant VR-4	8	Staffan Parmander	Retired
41	Finland	Mitsubishi Ralliart Europe	Mitsubishi Galant VR-4	9	Staffan Parmander	3rd
42	Australia	Mitsubishi Ralliart Europe	Mitsubishi Galant VR-4	3	Staffan Parmander	Retired
43	Great Britain	Mitsubishi Ralliart Europe	Mitsubishi Galant VR-4	9	Staffan Parmander	2nd
1991	**66 points (5th)**					
44	Monte Carlo	Mitsubishi Ralliart Europe	Mitsubishi Galant VR-4	8	Staffan Parmander	Retired
45	**Sweden**	**Mitsubishi Ralliart Europe**	**Mitsubishi Galant VR-4**	**4**	**Staffan Parmande**	**1st**
46	Greece	Mitsubishi Ralliart Europe	Mitsubishi Galant VR-4	4	Staffan Parmander	7th

ERIKKSON, KENNETH CAREER RECORD (CONT'D)

YEAR	RALLY	TEAM/ENTRANT	CAR	NO.	CO-DRIVER	RESULT
47	Finland	Mitsubishi Ralliart Europe	Mitsubishi Galant VR-4	3	Staffan Parmander	3rd
48	Australia	Mitsubishi Ralliart Europe	Mitsubishi Galant VR-4	3	Staffan Parmander	2nd
49	Great Britain	Mitsubishi Ralliart Europe	Mitsubishi Galant VR-4	3	Staffan Parmander	2nd
1992	**4 points (41st)**					
50	Monte Carlo	Mitsubishi Ralliart	Mitsubishi Galant VR-4	5	Staffan Parmander	Retired
51	Portugal	Mitsubishi Ralliart	Mitsubishi Galant VR-4	6	Staffan Parmander	Retired
52	Greece	Mitsubishi Ralliart	Mitsubishi Galant VR-4	4	Staffan Parmander	Retired
53	Great Britain	Mitsubishi Ralliart	Mitsubishi Galant VR-4	9	Staffan Parmander	7th
1993	**41 points (6th)**					
54	Monte Carlo	Mitsubishi Ralliart	Mitsubishi Lancer RS	8	Staffan Parmander	4th
55	Portugal	Mitsubishi Ralliart	Mitsubishi Lancer RS	3	Staffan Parmander	5th
56	Greece	Mitsubishi Ralliart	Mitsubishi Lancer RS	4	Staffan Parmander	Retired
57	Finland	Mitsubishi Ralliart	Mitsubishi Lancer RS	3	Staffan Parmander	5th
58	Great Britain	Mitsubishi Ralliart	Mitsubishi Lancer RS	4	Staffan Parmander2nd	
1994	**18 points (12th)**					
59	Monte Carlo	Team Mitsubishi Ralliart	Mitsubishi Lancer RS	9	Staffan Parmander	5th
60	Greece	Team Mitsubishi Ralliart	Mitsubishi Lancer Evo 2	4	Staffan Parmander	Retired
61	New Zealand	Team Mitsubishi Ralliart	Mitsubishi Lancer Evo 2	8	Staffan Parmander	4th
1995	**48 points (3rd)**					
62	**Sweden**	**Team Mitsubishi Ralliart**	**Mitsubishi Lancer Evo 2**	**10**	**Staffan Parmander**	**1st**
63	New Zealand	Team Mitsubishi Ralliart	Mitsubishi Lancer Evo 3	10	Staffan Parmander	5th
64	**Australia**	**Team Mitsubishi Ralliart**	**Mitsubishi Lancer Evo 3**	**10**	**Staffan Parmander**	**1st**
65	Great Britain	Team Mitsubishi Ralliart	Mitsubishi Lancer Evo 3	10	Staffan Parmander	Retired
1996	**78 points (4th)**					
66	Sweden	555 Subaru World Rally Team	Subaru Impreza 555	2	Staffan Parmander	5th
67	Safari	555 Subaru World Rally Team	Subaru Impreza 555	2	Staffan Parmander	2nd
68	Indonesia	555 Subaru World Rally Team	Subaru Impreza 555	2	Staffan Parmander	Retired
69	Greece	555 Subaru World Rally Team	Subaru Impreza 555	2	Staffan Parmander	5th
70	Argentina	555 Subaru World Rally Team	Subaru Impreza 555	2	Staffan Parmander	3rd
71	Finland	555 Subaru World Rally Team	Subaru Impreza 555	2	Staffan Parmander	5th
72	Australia	555 Subaru World Rally Team	Subaru Impreza 555	2	Staffan Parmander	2nd
73	Sanremo	555 Subaru World Rally Team	Subaru Impreza 555	2	Staffan Parmander	4th
74	Catalunya	555 Subaru World Rally Team	Subaru Impreza 555	2	Staffan Parmander	7th
1997	**28 points (5th)**					
75	**Sweden**	**555 Subaru World Rally Team**	**Subaru Impreza WRC**	**4**	**Staffan Parmander**	**1st**
76	Safari	555 Subaru World Rally Team	Subaru Impreza WRC	4	Staffan Parmander	Retired
77	Portugal	555 Subaru World Rally Team	Subaru Impreza WRC	4	Staffan Parmander	Retired
78	Argentina	555 Subaru World Rally Team	Subaru Impreza WRC	4	Staffan Parmander	3rd
79	Greece	555 Subaru World Rally Team	Subaru Impreza WRC	4	Staffan Parmander	Retired
80	**New Zealand**	**555Subaru World Rally Team**	**Subaru Impreza WRC**	**4**	**Staffan Parmander**	**1st**
81	Finland	555 Subaru World Rally Team	Subaru Impreza WRC	4	Staffan Parmander	Retired
82	Indonesia	555 Subaru World Rally Team	Subaru Impreza WRC	4	Staffan Parmander	3rd
83	Australia	555 Subaru World Rally Team	Subaru Impreza WRC	4	Staffan Parmander	Retired
84	Great Britain	555 Subaru World Rally Team	Subaru Impreza WRC	4	Staffan Parmander	Retired
1998	**3 points (13th)**					
85	Sweden	555 Subaru World Rally Team	Subaru Impreza WRC	4	Staffan Parmander	4th
86	Portugal	Hyundai Motor Sport	Hyundai Coupe Kit Car	18	Staffan Parmander	Retired
87	Catalunya	Hyundai Motor Sport	Hyundai Coupe Kit Car	27	Staffan Parmander	21st
88	Argentina	Hyundai Motor Sport	Hyundai Coupe Kit Car	12	Staffan Parmander	Retired
89	Greece	Hyundai Motor Sport	Hyundai Coupe Kit Car	26	Staffan Parmander	Retired
90	New Zealand	Hyundai Motor Sport	Hyundai Coupe Kit Car	24	Staffan Parmander	21st
91	Finland	Hyundai Motor Sport	Hyundai Coupe Kit Car	24	Staffan Parmander	Retired
92	Sanremo	Hyundai Motor Sport	Hyundai Coupe Kit Car	30	Staffan Parmander	Retired
93	Australia	Hyundai Motor Sport	Hyundai Coupe Kit Car	19	Staffan Parmander	22nd
94	Great Britain	Hyundai Motor Sport	Hyundai Coupe Kit Car	20	Staffan Parmander	Retired
1999	**0 points**					
95	Sweden	Hyundai Motor Sport	Hyundai Coupe Kit Car E2	27	Staffan Parmander	Retired
96	Portugal	Hyundai Motor Sport	Hyundai Coupe Kit Car E2	29	Staffan Parmander	14th
97	Catalunya	Hyundai Motor Sport	Hyundai Coupe Kit Car E2	21	Staffan Parmander	Retired
98	Greece	Hyundai Motor Sport	Hyundai Coupe Kit Car E2	27	Staffan Parmander	15th
99	New Zealand	Hyundai Motor Sport	Hyundai Coupe Kit Car E2	22	Staffan Parmander	17th
100	Finland	Hyundai Motor Sport	Hyundai Coupe Kit Car E2	28	Staffan Parmander	Retired
101	China	Hyundai Motor Sport	Hyundai Coupe Kit Car E2	24	Staffan Parmander	11th
102	Sanremo	Hyundai Motor Sport	Hyundai Coupe Kit Car E2	40	Staffan Parmander	Retired
103	Australia	Hyundai Motor Sport	Hyundai Coupe Kit Car E2	30	Staffan Parmander	9th
104	Great Britain	Hyundai Motor Sport	Hyundai Coupe Kit Car E2	26	Staffan Parmander	25th
2000	**5 points (11th)**					
105	Sweden	Hyundai Castrol World Rally Team	Hyundai Accent WRC	14	Staffan Parmander	13th
106	Portugal	Hyundai Castrol World Rally Team	Hyundai Accent WRC	14	Staffan Parmander	Retired
107	Catalunya	Hyundai Castrol World Rally Team	Hyundai Accent WRC	14	Staffan Parmander	23rd
108	Argentina	Hyundai Castrol World Rally Team	Hyundai Accent WRC	14	Staffan Parmander	8th
109	Greece	Hyundai Castrol World Rally Team	Hyundai Accent WRC	14	Staffan Parmander	Retired
110	New Zealand	Hyundai Castrol World Rally Team	Hyundai Accent WRC	14	Staffan Parmander	5th
111	Finland	Hyundai Castrol World Rally Team	Hyundai Accent WRC	14	Staffan Parmander	15th
112	Corsica	Hyundai Castrol World Rally Team	Hyundai Accent WRC	14	Staffan Parmander	Retired
113	Sanremo	Hyundai Castrol World Rally Team	Hyundai Accent WRC	14	Staffan Parmander	45th
114	Australia	Hyundai Castrol World Rally Team	Hyundai Accent WRC	14	Staffan Parmander	4th
115	Great Britain	Hyundai Castrol World Rally Team	Hyundai Accent WRC	14	Staffan Parmander	Retired
2001	**1 point (21st)**					
116	Sweden	Hyundai Castrol World Rally Team	Hyundai Accent WRC	9	Staffan Parmander	8th
117	Portugal	Hyundai Castrol World Rally Team	Hyundai Accent WRC	9	Staffan Parmander	7th
118	Argentina	Hyundai Castrol World Rally Team	Hyundai Accent WRC	9	Staffan Parmander	Retired
119	Cyprus	Hyundai Castrol World Rally Team	Hyundai Accent WRC	9	Staffan Parmander	Retired
120	Greece	Hyundai Castrol World Rally Team	Hyundai Accent WRC	9	Staffan Parmander	Retired
121	Finland	Hyundai Castrol World Rally Team	Hyundai Accent WRC	9	Staffan Parmander	12th
122	New Zealand	Hyundai Castrol World Rally Team	Hyundai Accent WRC	9	Staffan Parmander	10th
123	Australia	Hyundai Castrol World Rally Team	Hyundai Accent WRC	9	Staffan Parmander	12th
124	Great Britain	Hyundai Castrol World Rally Team	Hyundai Accent WRC	9	Staffan Parmander	6th
2002	**1 point (17th)**					
125	Monte Carlo	Skoda Motorsport	Skoda Octavia WRC	14	Tina Thorner	13th
126	Sweden	Skoda Motorsport	Skoda Octavia WRC	14	Tina Thorner	Retired
127	Corsica	Skoda Motorsport	Skoda Octavia WRC	14	Tina Thorner	Retired
128	Catalunya	Skoda Motorsport	Skoda Octavia WRC	14	Tina Thorner	17th
129	Cyprus	Skoda Motorsport	Skoda Octavia WRC	14	Tina Thorner	9th
130	Argentina	Skoda Motorsport	Skoda Octavia WRC	14	Tina Thorner	6th
131	Greece	Skoda Motorsport	Skoda Octavia WRC	14	Tina Thorner	14th
132	Safari	Skoda Motorsport	Skoda Octavia WRC	14	Tina Thorner	Retired
133	Finland	Skoda Motorsport	Skoda Octavia WRC	14	Tina Thorner	Retired
134	Germany	Skoda Motorsport	Skoda Octavia WRC	14	Tina Thorner	10th
135	Sanremo	Skoda Motorsport	Skoda Octavia WRC	14	Tina Thorner	11th
136	New Zealand	Skoda Motorsport	Skoda Octavia WRC	14	Tina Thorner	Retired
137	Australia	Skoda Motorsport	Skoda Octavia WRC	14	Tina Thorner	8th
138	Great Britain	Skoda Motorsport	Skoda Octavia WRC	14	Tina Thorner	13th

FASSINA, TONY

(I) BORN: 26 JULY 1945, TREVISO, ITALY

Famous for beating Walter Röhrl's Fiat 131 Abarth on the San Remo of 1979 in a Lancia Stratos, Tony Fassina had quite a small CV in the WRC but, like the iceberg, that was just the tip.

Born in the southern foothills of the Dolomites, Fassina was a car dealer before he acquired an interest in rallying. When he did, in 1969, he bought an Alfa Romeo 1750 and did the Coppa Piave. The following year, he moved to a Renault R8 Gordini and then for three years to an Alpine A110 and it was with this that he won his first national event in 1971, the Monti Savonesi. For 1975, he got a Lancia Stratos and quickly got used to the powerful car, winning the national rally trophy that year. He followed it up by winning the Italian rally championship in 1976 at which point, he was persuaded to swap to a Fiat 131 Abarth.

It was not as successful and, for 1979, he returned to a Stratos with support from the Jolly Club and won both the Italian rally championship and the San Remo. This was one of the very few victories for a privately-entered car in the WRC and was taken in the teeth of some hard pressure from three factory Fiat 131 Abarths. To add insult to injury, Fassina was driving on Michelins and not the national product, Pirelli, and it was the Fiats that were in problems with punctures.

For 1980, Fassina was offered a semi-works Opel Ascona 400 by the Italian tuner, Conrero. In 1981, Fassina was Italian champion again, while in 1982 he took the Ascona to victory in the European Championship winning the Costa Brava and CS rallies in Spain and topping the bill in Cyprus. Fassina briefly dallied with Ferrari but for the first Italian rally of 1984, Targa Florio, he drove a Lancia 037 Rallye and won outright. However, his car dealership was now growing fast and he decided to retire on a high.

FASSINA, TONY - CAREER RECORD

YEAR	RALLY	TEAM/ENTRANT	CAR	NO.	CO-DRIVER	RESULT
1976						
1	Sanremo		Lancia Stratos	11	Mauro Mannini	4th
1977						
2	Sanremo		Fiat 131 Abarth	14	Mauro Mannini	3rd
1979	**20 points (10th)**					
3	**Sanremo**	**Jolly Club**	**Lancia Stratos**	**2**	**Mauro Mannini**	**1st**
1980	**0 points**					
4	Sanremo	Conrero	Opel Ascona 400	1	'Rudy'	Retired
1981	**12 points (20th)**					
5	Sanremo	Conrero	Opel Ascona 400	6	'Rudy'	3rd
6	Great Britain	Renault Dealer Rallying	Renault Clio Maxi	19	Jack Boyere	10th

FRÉQUELIN, GUY (F) BORN: 2 APRIL 1945, LANGRES, FRANCE

Nowadays Guy Fréquelin is the director of Citroën's highly successful rally team where he has used the knowledge gained as a works driver in the 1970s and 1980s to very good advantage.

He first started rallying with a Renault R8 Gordini in 1967 when the Coupe Gordini was drawing many young Frenchmen into motor sport. But it was with an Audi 80 that he made his debut on the WRC in Corsica. Shortly after that, he started driving Alfa Romeos for the French importer and had two seasons with them chasing the French championship and winning Group 1 on Monte Carlo. In 1976, he freelanced and opened people's eyes by leading the Monte Carlo after eight stages in a Group 3 Porsche Carrera.

For 1977, Frequelin drove a works Renault Alpine 310-V6 in Calberson colours. He won his debut event with the car, the Critérium Neige et Glace, and with eight further national wins wound up as French rally champion. The following year, he was retained by Renault and drove an R5 Alpine in which he again led the Monte and had the pleasure of passing Walter Röhrl's Fiat on one stage in all the snow. Then he paired up with Jean Todt and they went to drive in the new Sunbeam Lotus. For the first time, Fréquelin spread his wings and did more events in the WRC. A bigger programme in 1980 gave him Peugeot drives in Africa and he very nearly won the World title the following season.

When Talbot effectively stopped their programme at the end of 1982, Frequelin did a couple of rallies in a Porsche for Almeras before clinching a deal to drive for GM. He twice more won the French championship but then took a sabbatical in 1986, returning briefly to drive a Kadett GSi for GM in 1987 before taking up the post he holds today at Citroën.

FRÉQUELIN, GUY – CAREER RECORD

YEAR	RALLY	TEAM/ENTRANT	CAR	NO.	CO-DRIVER	RESULT
1973						
1	Corsica		Audi 80	15	Jean Marcoup	Retired
1974						
2	Corsica		Alfa Romeo Alfetta	19	Jean Thimonier	10th
1975						
3	Monte Carlo		Alfa Romeo 2000 GTV	40	Christian Delferrier	8th
1976						
4	Monte Carlo		Porsche 911	23	Jacques Delaval	7th
5	Corsica		Opel Kadett GT/E	12	Jacques Delaval	Retired
1977						
6	Monte Carlo		Alpine-Renault A310	11	Jacques Delaval	Retired
7	Sanremo		Renault 5 Alpine	16	Jacques Delaval	Retired
1978						
8	Monte Carlo	Renault Elf Calberson	Renault 5 Alpine	12	Jacques Delaval	3rd
9	Ivory Coast		Renault 5 Alpine	5	Jacques Delaval	5th
1979	**3 points (54th)**					
10	Monte Carlo	Renault Elf Calberson	Renault 5 Alpine	16	Jacques Delaval	8th
1980	**34 points (8th)**					
11	Monte Carlo	Talbot Sport	Talbot Sunbeam Lotus	18	Jean Todt	Retired
12	Portugal	Talbot GB	Talbot Sunbeam Lotus	16	Jean Todt	3rd
13	Sanremo	Talbot GB	Talbot Sunbeam Lotus	5	Jean Todt	4th
14	Corsica	Talbot France	Talbot Sunbeam Lotus	2	Jean Todt	Retired
15	Great Britain	Talbot GB	Talbot Sunbeam Lotus	10	Jean Todt	3rd
1981	**89 points (2nd)**					
16	Monte Carlo	Talbot Sport	Talbot Sunbeam Lotus	16	Jean Todt	2nd
17	Portugal	Talbot Sport	Talbot Sunbeam Lotus	3	Jean Todt	6th
18	Safari	Marshalls	Peugeot 504 Coupe V6	6	Jean Todt	Retired
20	Corsica	Talbot Sport	Talbot Sunbeam Lotus	2	Jean Todt	2nd
21	Greece	Talbot Sport	Talbot Sunbeam Lotus	6	Jean Todt	4th
22	**Argentina**	**Talbot Sport**	**Talbot Sunbeam Lotus**	**2**	**Jean Todt**	**1st**
23	Brazil	Talbot Sport	Talbot Sunbeam Lotus	1	Jean Todt	2nd
24	Sanremo	Talbot Sport	Talbot Sunbeam Lotus	3	Jean Todt	Retired
25	Ivory Coast	SARI Peugeot	Peugeot 504 Coupe V6	2	Jean Todt	5th
26	Great Britain	Talbot Sport	Talbot Sunbeam Lotus	4	Jean Todt	Retired
1982	**16 points (12th)**					
27	Monte Carlo	Porsche Almeras	Porsche 911SC	4	Jean-Francois Fauchille	4th
28	Corsica	Porsche Almeras	Porsche 911SC	2	Jean-Francois Fauchille	6th
29	Great Britain	Peugeot Talbot Sport	Talbot Sunbeam Lotus	13	Jean-Francois Fauchille	11th
1983	**0 points**					
30	Monte Carlo	Rothmans Opel Rally Team	Opel Ascona 400	10	Jean-Francois Fauchille	Retired
31	Corsica	Rothmans Opel Rally Team	Opel Ascona 400	6	Jean-Francois Fauchille	Retired
1984	**2 points (53rd)**					
32	Safari	Opel Euro Team	Opel Manta 400	6	Bruno Berglund	Retired
33	Corsica	Opel Euro Team	Opel Manta 400	3	'Tilber'	9th
1985	**0 points**					
34	Corsica	Opel Euro Team	Opel Manta 400	8	'Tilber'	Retired
1987	**6 points (36th)**					
35	Corsica	GM Euro Sport	Opel Kadett GSi 16v	17	'Tilber'	Retired
36	Sanremo	GM Euro Sport	Opel Kadett GSi 16v	10	Didier Breton	6th

GRÖNHOLM, MARCUS

(FIN) BORN: 5 FEBRUARY 1968, ESPOO, FINLAND

"Rallying was not the young Grönholm's first choice for a career"

Marcus Grönholm was only 12 years old when his rally driver father, Ulf, was killed in a collision with a snow plough while testing a Fiat 131 Abarth. It is perhaps understandable that rallying was not the young Grönholm's first choice for a career.

He started his motorsport career on motorcycles and for almost 10 years rode motorcross. Then accumulated injuries to his knees forced him to give up. He tried rallying as an alternative and after early experiments with a Ford Escort in 1987, he got an Opel Kadett for 1988 and, with his sister, Mia, as co-driver, won the Finnish Junior Championship. The following year, with a Group N Lancia Integrale, he made his WRC debut on the 1000 Lakes in Finland. Then with help from Robbie Gröndahl at Toyota Team Europe, he acquired a Celica GT-Four for the 1990 season and the following year won the Finnish Group N Championship.

He tried a Group A Celica Turbo 4WD on the 1000 Lakes and was quick from the outset but had to withdraw after five stages. If international success eluded him for the moment, there was plenty of action in Finland – he won the Group A Championship four times (1994, 1996, 1997-1998). He had started to travel outside Finland with the Swedish Rally a regular port of call. During 1997 and 1998, he was offered several drives by Toyota with their new Corolla WRC and also drove for their Italian satellite team, Grifone. He was the first Toyota driver to gain them points with the Corolla WRC when he finished fifth on the 1997 Rally of Great Britain.

This expansion of his programme enabled Grönholm to meet other teams so, when Toyota had no offer for 1999, he picked up a drive with SEAT in Sweden. Sadly that only lasted one stage before the engine let go while in Portugal, when standing in for the injured Freddy Loix, the clutch on his Mitsubishi Carisma GT cried enough after 15 stages. Next up was a drive for Peugeot in Greece and things looked equally bad when the 206WRC's clutch broke after the first stage. But Peugeot had faith and his next three events for them all netted good results. Better was to come.

The 206WRC had only made its debut during 1999 so Grönholm was with it almost from the start. By winning the Swedish Rally, he put himself in the record books by winning his first WRC rally and Peugeot's first since 1986. He showed what the 206 – and he – could do by winning the 2000 World Championship and contributing to Peugeot's own manufacturers' title. The farmer from Finland was the apple of Peugeot's eye.

But 2001 turned out to be the year from hell. From the first eight events, he retired seven times before winning in Finland. From then on, it was situation normal for the Finn in the 206. He could not do anything about the 2001 championship, but he made no mistake about 2002. Five outright victories and a second world title. He started his 2003 season in fine style by winning three events but then a string of retirements followed. It was not to be Grönholm's or Peugeot's year. He finished it with an accident on Rally GB after which he was ignominiously prevented by the police from driving his damaged car on the public road. This was a nadir from which Grönholm will undoubtedly bounce back to add to his tally of wins and possibly titles.

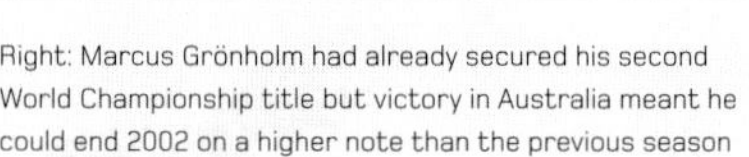

Right: Marcus Grönholm had already secured his second World Championship title but victory in Australia meant he could end 2002 on a higher note than the previous season

GRÖNHOLM, MARCUS – CAREER RECORD

YEAR	RALLY	TEAM/ENTRANT	CAR	NO.	CO-DRIVER	RESULT
1989	**0 points**					
1	Finland		Lancia Delta Integrale	45	Ilkka Riipinen	23rd
1990	**0 points**					
2	Finland		Toyota Celica GT-Four	51	Timo Rautiainen	Retired
1991	**0 points**					
3	Finland		Toyota Celica GT-Four	26	Juha Repo	13th
1992	**0 points**					
4	Sweden		Toyota Celica GT-Four	18	Ilkka Riipinen	Retired
5	Finland	Toyota Team Europe	Toyota Celica Turbo 4WD	21	Ilkka Riipinen	Retired
1993	**1 point (65th)**					
6	Finland		Toyota Celica Turbo 4WD	16	Voitto Silander	10th
1994	**8 points (19th)**					
7	Finland		Toyota Celica Turbo 4WD	12	Voitto Silander	5th
1995	**0 points**					
8	Sweden		Toyota Celica Turbo 4WD	17	Voitto Silander	Retired
9	Portugal	HF Grifone	Toyota Celica Turbo 4WD	16	Voitto Silander	Retired
10	New Zealand		Toyota Celica Turbo 4WD	16	Timo Rautiainen	Retired
1996	**14 points (10th)**					
11	Sweden		Toyota Celica Turbo 4WD	17	Timo Rautiainen	7th
12	Finland	Team Toyota Castrol Finland	Toyota Celica GT-Four	16	Timo Rautiainen	4th
1997	**5 points (12th)**					
13	Sweden	Toyota Castrol Team Sweden	Toyota Celica GT-Four	12	Timo Rautiainen	8th
14	Portugal	Team Toyota Castrol Finland	Toyota Celica GT-Four	10	Timo Rautiainen	Retired
15	Argentina	HF Grifone	Toyota Celica GT-Four	8	Timo Rautiainen	4th
16	Finland	Toyota Castrol Team	Toyota Corolla WRC	8	Timo Rautiainen	Retired
17	Great Britain	Toyota Castrol Team	Toyota Corolla WRC	9	Timo Rautiainen	5th
1998	**2 points (16th)**					
18	Sweden	H.F Grifone	Toyota Celica GT-Four	11	Timo Rautiainen	5th
19	Portugal	H.F Grifone	Toyota Corolla WRC	10	Timo Rautiainen	Retired
20	Catalunya	H.F Grifone	Toyota Corolla WRC	11	Timo Rautiainen	Retired
21	New Zealand	H.F Grifone	Toyota Corolla WRC	10	Timo Rautiainen	Retired
22	Finland	Toyota Castrol Team	Toyota Corolla WRC	12	Timo Rautiainen	7th
23	Great Britain	Toyota Castrol Team	Toyota Corolla WRC	11	Timo Rautiainen	Retired
1999	**5 points (15th)**					
24	Sweden	SEAT Sport	SEAT Cordoba WRC	10	Timo Rautiainen	Retired
25	Portugal	Marlboro Mitsubishi Ralliart	Mitsubishi Carisma GT	2	Timo Rautiainen	Retired
26	Greece	Peugeot Esso	Peugeot 206 WRC	15	Timo Rautiainen	Retired
27	Finland	Peugeot Esso	Peugeot 206 WRC	15	Timo Rautiainen	4th
28	Sanremo	Peugeot Esso	Peugeot 206 WRC	21	Timo Rautiainen	8th
29	Australia	Peugeot Esso	Peugeot 206 WRC	15	Timo Rautiainen	5th
30	Great Britain	Peugeot Esso	Peugeot 206 WRC	15	Timo Rautiainen	Retired
2000	**65 points (WORLD CHAMPION)**					
31	Monte Carlo	Peugeot Esso	Peugeot 206 WRC	17	Timo Rautiainen	Retired
32	**Sweden**	**Peugeot Esso**	**Peugeot 206 WRC**	**10**	**Timo Rautiainen**	**1st**
33	Safari	Peugeot Esso	Peugeot 206 WRC	10	Timo Rautiainen	Retired
34	Portugal	Peugeot Esso	Peugeot 206 WRC	10	Timo Rautiainen	2nd
35	Catalunya	Peugeot Esso	Peugeot 206 WRC	16	Timo Rautiainen	5th
36	Argentina	Peugeot Esso	Peugeot 206 WRC	10	Timo Rautiainen	2nd
37	Greece	Peugeot Esso	Peugeot 206 WRC	10	Timo Rautiainen	Retired
38	**New Zealand**	**Peugeot Esso**	**Peugeot 206 WRC**	**10**	**Timo Rautiainen**	**1st**
39	**Finland**	**Peugeot Esso**	**Peugeot 206 WRC**	**10**	**Timo Rautiainen**	**1st**
40	Cyprus	Peugeot Esso	Peugeot 206 WRC	10	Timo Rautiainen	Retired
41	Corsica	Peugeot Esso	Peugeot 206 WRC	16	Timo Rautiainen	5th
42	Sanremo	Peugeot Esso	Peugeot 206 WRC	16	Timo Rautiainen	4th
43	**Australia**	**Peugeot Esso**	**Peugeot 206 WRC**	**10**	**Timo Rautiainen**	**1st**
44	Great Britain	Peugeot Esso	Peugeot 206 WRC	10	Timo Rautiainen	2nd
2001	**36 points (4th)**					
45	Monte Carlo	Peugeot Total	Peugeot 206 WRC	1	Timo Rautiainen	Retired

GRÖNHOLM, MARCUS CAREER RECORD (CONT'D)

YEAR	RALLY	TEAM / ENTRANT	CAR	NO.	CO-DRIVER	RESULT
46	Sweden	Peugeot Total	Peugeot 206 WRC	1	Timo Rautiainen	Retired
47	Portugal	Peugeot Total	Peugeot 206 WRC	1	Timo Rautiainen	3rd
48	Catalunya	Peugeot Total	Peugeot 206 WRC	1	Timo Rautiainen	Retired
49	Argentina	Peugeot Total	Peugeot 206 WRC	1	Timo Rautiainen	Retired
50	Cyprus	Peugeot Total	Peugeot 206 WRC	1	Timo Rautiainen	Retired
51	Greece	Peugeot Total	Peugeot 206 WRC	1	Timo Rautiainen	Retired
52	Safari	Peugeot Total	Peugeot 206 WRC	1	Timo Rautiainen	Retired
53	Finland	Peugeot Total	Peugeot 206 WRC	1	Timo Rautiainen	1st
54	New Zealand	Peugeot Total	Peugeot 206 WRC	1	Timo Rautiainen	3rd
55	Sanremo	Peugeot Total	Peugeot 206 WRC	1	Timo Rautiainen	7th
56	Corsica	Peugeot Total	Peugeot 206 WRC	1	Timo Rautiainen	Retired
57	Australia	Peugeot Total	Peugeot 206 WRC	1	Timo Rautiainen	1st
58	Great Britain	Peugeot Total	Peugeot 206 WRC	1	Timo Rautiainen	1st
2002	77 points (WORLD CHAMPION)					
59	Monte Carlo	Peugeot Total	Peugeot 206 WRC	2	Timo Rautiainen	5th
60	Sweden	Peugeot Total	Peugeot 206 WRC	2	Timo Rautiainen	1st
61	Corsica	Peugeot Total	Peugeot 206 WRC	2	Timo Rautiainen	2nd
62	Catalunya	Peugeot Total	Peugeot 206 WRC	2	Timo Rautiainen	4th
63	Cyprus	Peugeot Total	Peugeot 206 WRC	2	Timo Rautiainen	1st
64	Argentina	Peugeot Total	Peugeot 206 WRC	2	Timo Rautiainen	Retired
65	Greece	Peugeot Total	Peugeot 206 WRC	2	Timo Rautiainen	2nd
66	Safari	Peugeot Total	Peugeot 206 WRC	2	Timo Rautiainen	Retired
67	Finland	Peugeot Total	Peugeot 206 WRC	2	Timo Rautiainen	1st
68	Germany	Peugeot Total	Peugeot 206 WRC	2	Timo Rautiainen	3rd
69	Sanremo	Peugeot Total	Peugeot 206 WRC	2	Timo Rautiainen	2nd
70	New Zealand	Peugeot Total	Peugeot 206 WRC	2	Timo Rautiainen	1st
71	Australia	Peugeot Total	Peugeot 206 WRC	2	Timo Rautiainen	1st
72	Great Britain	Peugeot Total	Peugeot 206 WRC	2	Timo Rautiainen	RtdAccdt
2003	46 points (6th)					
73	Monte Carlo	Marlboro Peugeot Total	Peugeot 206 WRC	1	Timo Rautiainen	13th
74	Sweden	Marlboro Peugeot Total	Peugeot 206 WRC	1	Timo Rautiainen	1st
75	Turkey	Marlboro Peugeot Total	Peugeot 206 WRC	1	Timo Rautiainen	9th
76	New Zealand	Marlboro Peugeot Total	Peugeot 206 WRC	1	Timo Rautiainen	1st
77	Argentina	Marlboro Peugeot Total	Peugeot 206 WRC	1	Timo Rautiainen	1st
78	Greece	Marlboro Peugeot Total	Peugeot 206 WRC	1	Timo Rautiainen	Retired
79	Cyprus	Marlboro Peugeot Total	Peugeot 206 WRC	1	Timo Rautiainen	Retired
80	Deutschland	Marlboro Peugeot Total	Peugeot 206 WRC	1	Timo Rautiainen	2nd
81	Finland	Marlboro Peugeot Total	Peugeot 206 WRC	1	Timo Rautiainen	Retired
82	Australia	Marlboro Peugeot Total	Peugeot 206 WRC	1	Timo Rautiainen	Retired
73	Sanremo	Marlboro Peugeot Total	Peugeot 206 WRC	1	Timo Rautiainen	Retired
74	Corsica	Marlboro Peugeot Total	Peugeot 206 WRC	1	Timo Rautiainen	4th
75	Catalunya	Marlboro Peugeot Total	Peugeot 206 WRC	1	Timo Rautiainen	6th
76	Great Britain	Marlboro Peugeot Total	Peugeot 206 WRC	1	Timo Rautiainen	Retired

HAIDER, JOSEF 'SEPP' (A) B: 26 AUGUST 1953, DIENTEN, AUSTRIA

Owning half a hotel is one thing, but having a brother who owns the other half – and will run it while you have a career rally driving – is quite another. Sepp Haider managed to do just that. His introduction to the sport came when Walter Röhrl went skiing close to the family hotel in Saalbach and then Jorg Pattermann took him to see a rally. Haider had tried a lot of sports, principally skiing, but this was something that really caught his imagination.

He tried a VW 1600 in local rallies and then for 1977, bought an Opel Kadett GT/E and did three World Championship rallies. There was no success at that level but his determination was now roused. He worked his way through the Kadett to an Opel Ascona 400, a Mercedes and a Citroën. The two latter choices were Group A cars and when Group B tumbled, Haider was able to take advantage of the swing to Group A.

For 1987, he was signed up by GM Euro Sport and, as well as contesting the German and Austrian Rally Championships, he drove three WRC rallies towards the end of the year. The front-wheel drive Kadett GSi was a bit fragile but in 1988, GM decided to go for the Safari where they got Hannu Mikkola as Haider's team mate. The pair both retired so it was a very pleasant surprise to go as the lone Opel driver in New Zealand and come away with a victory. In the heavy rain of the third leg, he kept his head, regained the lead and held it through to the end. The departure of Tony Fall from Opel's competition department meant that his programme stopped there. But next year, Haider won the German Championship and did three more WRC events for Opel. He then drove a semi-works Audi S2 for SMS in 1993 and did much of the testing on VW's aborted A59 Golf project. Since then, he has taken a more active interest in the hotel business.

HAIDER, JOSEF 'SEPP' – CAREER RECORD

YEAR	RALLY	TEAM/ENTRANT	CAR	NO.	CO-DRIVER	RESULT
1977						
1	Sweden		Opel Kadett GT/E		Jorg Pattermann	Retired
2	Portugal		Opel Kadett GT/E		Jorg Pattermann	Retired
3	Greece		Opel Kadett GT/E		Jorg Pattermann	Retired
1987	1 points (66th)					
4	Finland	GM Euro Sport	Opel Kadett GSi	16	Ferdi Hinterlaitner	Retired
5	Sanremo	GM Euro Sport	Opel Kadett GSi	15	Jorg Pattermann	10th
6	Great Britain	GM Euro Sport	Opel Kadett GSi	25	Rob Arthur	Retired
1988	20 points (14th)					
7	Safari	GM Euro Sport	Opel Kadett GSi 16V	10	Lofty Drews	Retired
8	**New Zealand**	**GM Euro Sport**	**Opel Kadett GSi 16V**	**3**	**Ferdi Hinterlaitner**	**1st**
1989	0 points					
9	Finland	GM Euro Sport	Opel Kadett GSi 16V	13	Ferdi Hinterlaitner	Retired
10	Australia	GM Euro Sport	Opel Kadett GSi 16V	8	Ferdi Hinterlaitner	Retired
11	Great Britain	GM Euro Sport	Opel Kadett GSi 16V	10	Mike Nicholson	Retired
1993	12 points (23rd)					
12	Sweden	SMS Revo Ingenieure	Audi Coupe S2	12	Klaus Wendel	7th
13	New Zealand	SMS Revo Ingenieure	Audi Coupe S2	15	Klaus Wendel	Retired
14	Australia	SMS Revo Ingenieure	Audi Coupe S2	12	Klaus Wendel	5th

HÄMÄLÄINEN, KYÖSTI (FIN) B: 16 SEPTEMBER 1945, HELSINKI, FINLAND

It would be easy to dismiss Kyösti Hämäläinen as a one-off victor of the 1000 Lakes Rally but it has to be taken into account that he was also 13 times Finnish Rally Champion.

Hämäläinen's career was forged by hard work and persuading other people to provide him with a car. His first outings were in a VW in 1969 and the same year, he did his first 1000 Lakes in a BMW 2002 but did not finish. The next year he drove a Mercedes 200 diesel and finished 41st. After more outings in a BMW 2002 Ti with which he won Group 1 on the 1972 1000 Lakes, he got a 2000 GTV from the Alfa Romeo importer for 1973. He won the Group 1 Finnish Championship but retired on the 1000 Lakes.

In 1975, he drove a Group 1 Sunbeam Avenger, won his home series and led Group 1 on the RAC Rally until a roll made him more cautious. During 1976, when Avenger drives dried up, he got a deal to complete the season with Ford Finland, and for the 1977 season. He was offered a works RS1800 for the 1000 Lakes but first he did a Finnish national rally, confusingly called the Swiss Rally, and won it outright. With Ari Vatanen retiring early on the 1000 Lakes, Ford's hopes rested on Hämäläinen to fight the Fiats, which he did to such good effect that he won the rally.

For the RAC Rally of 1977, Hämäläinen got a RS1800 sponsored by Total and had a clean run to finish sixth. He was now 32 but three things counted against him: he did not speak English, he did not use pace notes and Ford had a full complement of experienced Scandinavians. For the 1978 1000 Lakes, he got a works RS1800 as a 'thank you', but by the following year, he was driving a Mercedes diesel. He took eight more titles for Ford Finland, but never made it into the international scene.

HÄMÄLÄINEN, KYÖSTI – CAREER RECORD

YEAR	RALLY	TEAM/ENTRANT	CAR	NO.	CO-DRIVER	RESULT
1973						
1	Finland		Alfa Romeo 2000 GTV	47	Veijo Aho	Retired
1974						
2	Finland		Alfa Romeo 2000 GTV	31	Veijo Aho	17th
1975						
3	Finland		Chrysler Avenger	16	Urpo Vihervaara	9th
4	Great Britain		Sunbeam Avenger	30	Urpo Vihervaara	36th
1976						
5	Finland	Ford Finland	Ford Escort RS2000	17	Urpo Vihervaara	Retired
6	Great Britain	Peter Clarke Autos/Ford Sure Service	Ford Escort RS2000	39	Urpo Vihervaara	Retired
1977						
7	Sweden	Ford Finland	Ford Escort RS2000	10	Juhani Korhonen	5th
8	**Finland**	**Ford Motor Companny**	**Ford Escort RS1800**	**14**	**Martti Tiukkanen**	**1st**
9	Great Britain	Peter Clarke/Total Oil GB	Ford Escort RS1800	20	Howard Scott	6th
1978						
10	Finland	Ford Motor Company	Ford Escort RS	1	Juhani Korhonen	8th
1979	0 points					
11	Finland		Mercedes-Benz 300D	12	Matti Lammi	31st
1980	0 points					
12	Finland		Lada 130 Rallye	7	Lionel Hennebel	18th
1981	0 points					
13	Sweden	VMJ Racing	Ford Escort RS	11	Juhani Korhonen	
14	Finland	Team Ralliart	Mitsubishi Lancer 2000	13	Tapio Vanhala	11th
1982	0 points					
15	Finland	Autoracing Oy	Ford Escort RS1800	21	Tapio Vanhala	Retired
1985	0 points					
16	Finland	Ford Finland	Ford Escort RS Turbo	56	Esa Virrankalpi	28th
1986	0 points					
17	Finland		Ford Sierra XR4x4	44	Martti Putkonen	Retired
1987	0 points					
18	Finland		Ford Sierra RS Cosworth	104	Ossi Nurminen	Retired
1988	0 points					
19	Finland		Ford Sierra RS Cosworth	51	Martti Putkonen	15th

JONSSON, MATS

(S) B: 28 NOVEMBER 1957, KARLSTAD, SWEDEN

Mats Jonsson is living proof that, no matter how good you are, you need two things for major success. One is to have the luck to pick the team that is going places and the other is determination to compete worldwide.

Like so many successful Swedes, Jonsson was born in Karlstad, home to the Swedish Rally, and started his rally career in a Volvo PV544. Three years later in 1979, he was still in a Volvo but now a 142S, the weapon of choice for drivers like Hannu Mikkola and Markku Alén. He finished seventh in class and with the same car was fourth in class in 1981. A contract with GM Sweden saw him next in a Group 2 Opel Ascona with which he was third in class in 1982 and won the class in 1983 on his way to his first Swedish championship. When GM Sweden got their hands on a Group B Ascona 400, it was Jonsson who got to drive it and he took fourth overall behind three Quattros on the 1984 Swedish.

By 1985, the four-wheel drive revolution was in full flood and the the policy of GM Sweden was to revert to Group A. In Sweden, he drove the new Kadett GSi and was Swedish champion in 1986 and 1987. GM Euro Sport took Jonsson into their plans for a bigger WRC effort and he started to travel more widely, taking a commendable fourth place in the 1989 New Zealand Rally. But then GM stopped.

In Sweden, Jonsson moved to Toyota for whom he won four consecutive Swedish titles. During that period, he also won the Swedish Rally twice and, when Toyota Sweden stopped their support at the end of 1993, he found no difficulty in getting drives for his home international or for campaigns for the Swedish title which he has won twice since in Ford Escorts. He is still rallying and his current mount is a Group N Mitsubishi Lancer Evo 6.

JONSSON, MATS – CAREER RECORD

YEAR	RALLY	TEAM/ENTRANT	CAR	NO.	CO-DRIVER	RESULT
1979	0 points					
1	Sweden		Volvo 142		Per Hansson	16th
2	Finland		Volvo 142	44	Magnus Olsson	25th
1980	**0 points**					
3	Sweden		Volvo 142	22	Sven-Olov Kvamlov	22nd
1981	**0 points**					
4	Sweden		Volvo 142	32	Sven-Olov Kvamlov	22nd
5	Great Britain		Volvo 142	56	Johnny Johansson	16th
1982	**0 points**					
6	Sweden		Opel Ascona	27	Sven-Olov Kvamlov	12th
7	Great Britain		Opel Ascona	60	Johnny Johansson	16th
1983	**0 points**					
8	Sweden		Opel Ascona	27	Ake Gustavsson	13th
9	Finland		Opel Ascona	91	Ake Gustavsson	Retired
10	Great Britain		Opel Ascona	31	Johnny Johansson	10th
1984	**10 points (19th)**					
11	Sweden	Opel Team Sweden	Opel Ascona 400	6	Ake Gustavsson	4th
12	Great Britain	Opel Team Sweden/Autoservice	Opel Ascona 400	24	Johnny Johansson	Retired
1985	**2 points (60th)**					
13	Sweden		Opel Ascona 400	9	Ake Gustavsson	9th
14	Great Britain	Opel Team Sweden/Autoservice	Opel Ascona	24	Johnny Johansson	13th
1986	**0 points**					
15	Sweden		Opel Kadett GSi	29	Johnny Johansson	12th
16	Great Britain	Team Autoservice/Colway Tyres	Opel Ascona	67	Johnny Johansson	13th
1987	**4 points (46th)**					
17	Sweden	GM Euro Sport	Opel Kadett GSi	16	Lars Backman	13th
18	Finland	GM Euro Sport	Opel Kadett GSi	14	Lars Backman	Retired
19	Great Britain	GM Euro Sport	Opel Kadett GSi	21	Johnny Johansson	7th
1988	**3 points (70th)**					
20	Sweden	GM Euro Sport	Opel Kadett GSi	13	Lars Backman	Retired
21	Finland	GM Euro Sport	Opel Kadett GSi	18	Lars Backman	10th
22	Great Britain	GM Euro Sport	Opel Kadett GSi	23	Lars Backman	9th
1989	**10 points (29th)**					
23	Sweden	GM Euro Sport	Opel Kadett GSi	21	Lars Backman	12th
24	New Zealand	GM Euro Sport	Opel Kadett GSi	18	Lars Backman	4th
25	Finland	GM Euro Sport	Opel Kadett GSi	17	Lars Backman	Retired
26	Great Britain	GM Euro Sport	Opel Kadett GSi 16V	26	Lars Backman	13th
1990	**10 points (20th)**					
27	Great Britain	Toyota Team Sweden	Toyota Celica GT-Four	26	Lars BackmanCHECK!	4th
1991	**21 points (12th)**					
28	Sweden	Toyota Team Europe	Toyota Celica GT-Four	15	Lars Backman	2nd
29	Finland		Toyota Celica GT-Four	12	Lars Backman	6th
1992	**20 points (15th)**					
30	**Sweden**		**Toyota Celica GT-Four**	**4**	**Lars Backman**	**1st**
1993	**22 points (13th)**					
31	**Sweden**	**Toyota Castrol Team**	**Toyota Celica Turbo 4WD**	**1**	**Lars Backman**	**1st**
32	Great Britain	Toyota Team Sweden	Toyota Celica Turbo 4WD	9	Lars Backman	9th
1995	**0 points**					
33	Sweden	555 Subaru World Rally Team	Subaru Impreza 555	6	Johnny Johansson	Retired
1996	**0 points**					
34	Sweden	Opel Team Sweden	Opel Astra GSi 16V	32	Johnny Johanssonn	Retired
1997	**0 points**					
35	Sweden		Ford Escort RS Cosworth	14	Johnny Johanssonn	9th
1998	**0 points**					
36	Sweden	Bo-Be Plastindustri	Ford Escort RS Cosworth	15	Johnny Johanssonn	10th
1999	**0 points**					
37	Sweden	Bo-Be Plastindustri	Ford Escort WRC	16	Johnny Johanssonn	Retired
2000	**0 points**					
38	Sweden		Ford Escort WRC	20	Johnny Johanssonn	Retired
2001	**0 points**					
39	Sweden		Mitsubishi Lancer Evo 6	29	Johnny Johanssonn	20th

KÄLLSTRÖM, HARRY (S) B: 30 JUNE 1939, SODERTELJE, SWEDEN

The most gentle and enigmatic of men, Harry Källström was also one of the most highly regarded rally drivers at the end of the 1960s. Never fluent in much else than his native Swedish and some expressive hand gestures, he let his driving do the talking.

Källström's father was a well-known rally driver and was the first winner of the Swedish T-race championship in 1952, driving a VW Beetle. Six years later, his son entered his first rally in the old car and came home ahead of his father in a newer one. On his second event, he won the Junior class and was third overall. In 1959 he won the T-race championship and was promptly nicknamed 'Sputnik' for his swift rise to fame. In 1963, his first acquaintance with the RAC Rally resulted in a second place with a VW after which he swapped to BMC Sweden and drove Mini Coopers for two years.

For 1967, he was signed up by Renault Sweden and drove R8 Gordinis with one of which he won a Coupe des Alpes. The following year, he joined Lancia and nearly won on his debut at the Sestriere Rally. He won the European Championship in 1969 which included winning the San Remo, Spanish and RAC Rallies. He won the RAC again the following year, a truly impressive performance against much more powerful opposition.

Källström continued to drive Lancia Fulvias but left when it was clear they had no place for him in the Stratos line-up and took up an offer to drive a Datsun on Safari. He did well enough to tie for first place with Shekhar Mehta and only lose the win on a tiebreak. Källström loved the rear swing axle layout of the Violet 160J and, once the car was sorted out was successful with it. He never liked the solid axle version that followed and shortly after the Acropolis Rally in 1978, he retired.

KÄLLSTRÖM, HARRY – CAREER RECORD

YEAR	RALLY	TEAM /ENTRANT	CAR	NO.	CO-DRIVER	RESULT
1973						
1	Monte Carlo	Lancia-Marlboro	Lancia Fulvia	16	Claes Billstam	8th
2	Sweden		Lancia Fulvia	3	Claes Billstam	4th
3	Portugal	Porsche Salzburg	Volkswagen Beetle 1303S	10	Claes Billstam	Retired
4	Safari	Nissan Motor Company	Datsun 1800SSS	9	Claes Billstam	2nd
5	Greece	Porsche Salzburg	Volkswagen Beetle 1303S	7	Claes Billstam	Retired
6	Austria	Porsche Salzburg	Volkswagen Beetle 1303S	6	Claes Billstam	11th
7	Great Britain		Datsun 240Z	5	Claes Billstam	14th
1974						
8	Portugal		Datsun 260Z	4	Claes Billstam	5th
9	Safari		Datsun 260Z	14	Claes Billstam	4th
10	Finland		Datsun 160J	10	Claes Billstam	21st
11	Great Britain	Datsun Dealers	Datsun 160J	13	Claes Billstam	15th
1975						
12	Sweden		Datsun 160J	9	Sture Bostrom	Retired
13	Safari	D.T Dobie & Co. Ltd	Datsun 160J	11	Sture Bostrom	Retired
14	Great Britain	Old Woking Service Station	Datsun 160J	15	Stedt	11th
1976						
15	Safari	D.T Dobie & Co. Ltd	Datsun 160J	10	Leif Lindqvist	7th
16	**Greece**		**Datsun 160J**	**14**	**Claes-Goran Andersson**	**1st**
17	Great Britain	Team Sanyo	Datsun 160J	13	Gerry Phillips	Retired
1977						
18	Safari	D.T Dobie & Co. Ltd	Datsun 160J	8	Claes Billstam	Retired
19	Greece		Datsun 160J	1	Claes Billstam	3rd
1978						
20	Safari	D.T Dobie & Co. Ltd	Datsun 160J	7	Claes Billstam	Retired
21	Greece		Datsun 160J	4	Claes Billstam	4th

KANKKUNEN, JUHA (FIN) B: 2 APRIL 1959, LAUKAA, FINLAND

"Kankkunen's first claim to fame was winning the Safari Rally at his very first attempt"

Four World Championships with three different teams is a pretty strong record. But Juha Kankkunen's first claim to fame was winning the gruelling Safari Rally at his very first attempt.

Born near Jyväskylä, home of the 1000 Lakes Rally, it was hardly surprising that Kankkunen developed an interest in rallying. When he was 19 years old, he made his debut in a Ford Escort RS2000 and a year later did his first 1000 Lakes. It was not until he got an Opel Kadett GT/E in 1982 that he came to the notice of Toyota Team Europe. His first drive for them was in Finland in 1983 where he wrestled the unwieldy Celica Turbo to sixth place overall. He had his first experience of Africa in the Ivory Coast and did the RAC Rally before getting a more formal role with TTE in 1984. It was not a good year but Kankkunen got the experience he needed.

It paid off as Kankkunen showed that the Celica was supreme in Africa, winning both Safari and Ivory Coast and taking a very commendable fifth place on the RAC Rally amidst the 4WD cars. For 1986, Kankkunen was recruited to Peugeot and teamed up with Juha Piironen. They started carefully on Monte Carlo, won Sweden and at the end of the year were declared champions 11 days after the last round when the San Remo results were annulled. With the ending of Group B, the only team with a fully competitive car out of the box was Lancia and that was where Kankkunen found himself for 1987 and his second World title.

Then it was back to TTE for two seasons driving their new Celica GT-4 but though it promised much it did not deliver as quickly. A better offer from Lancia for the 1990 season in their well-developed Integrale 16v saw Kankkunen back with the Italians and in 1991 clinching his third World Championship. Never the fastest on tarmac, Kankkunen largely avoided events like Corsica and San Remo and blitzed his way to success on the classic gravel rallies. At the end of 1992, he and Carlos Sainz swapped teams with Kankkunen returning to Toyota. It was a sad year because his friend and co-driver, Juha Piironen, fell ill in Argentina and could not continue his career. When Kankkunen became champion for the fourth time, he had won events that year with three different co-drivers.

In 1994, it was team mate Didier Auriol who made the running but the following year it looked like Kankkunen might just make it a fifth title. He came away from Australia with a seven-point lead, but in Spain he crashed after leading and then the FIA decided to eject Toyota from the whole championship for using illegal turbochargers. Bang went his chance and the following year, he did events in a Toyota when they could be entered by someone other than the works team. He tried two years with Ford and, though frequently on the podium, wins eluded him. For 1999 he moved to Subaru, his seventh team change. Things went better and he won in Argentina and at home but still not enough to give him that elusive fifth title. For 2001 he effectively retired but found indolence not to his liking and made a brief comeback with Hyundai in 2002.

KANKKUNEN, JUHA - CAREER RECORD

YEAR	RALLY	TEAM/ENTRANT	CAR	NO.	CO-DRIVER	RESULT
1979	0 points					
1	Finland		Ford Escort RS2000	43	Timo Hantunen	14th
1982	0 points					
2	Finland	Intereconomics	Opel Manta GT/E	38	Timo Hantunen	Retired
3	Great Britain	Intereconomics	Opel Manta GT/E	103	Rolf Mesteron	Retired
1983	10 points (19th)					
4	Finland	Toyota Team Europe	Toyota Celica TCT	12	Staffan Pettersson	6th
5	Ivory Coast	Premoto Toyota	Toyota Celica TCT	6	Dave Whittock	Retired
6	Great Britain	Toyota Team Great Britain	Toyota Celica TCT	16	Juha Piironen	7th
1984	80 points (24th)					
7	Portugal	Toyota Team Europe	Toyota Celica TCT	11	Fred Gallagher	Retired
8	New Zealand	Toyota New Zealand	Toyota Celica TCT	8	Fred Gallagher	Retired
9	Finland	Toyota Team Europe	Toyota Celica TCT	11	Fred Gallagher	5th
10	Great Britain	Toyota Team GB	Toyota Celica TCT	15	Fred Gallagher	Retired
1985	48 points (5th)					
11	**Safari**	**Westland Motors**	**Toyota Celica TCT**	**21**	**Fred Gallagher**	**1st**
12	New Zealand	Toyota New Zealand	Toyota Celica TCT	7	Fred Gallagher	Retired
13	Finland	Toyota Team Europe	Toyota Celica TCT	7	Fred Gallagher	Retired
14	**Ivory Coast**	**Premoto Toyota**	**Toyota Celica TCT**	**3**	**Fred Gallagher**	**1st**
15	Great Britain	Toyota Team Europe	Toyota Celica TCT	5	Fred Gallagher	5th
1986	118 points (WORLD CHAMPION)					
16	Monte Carlo	Peugeot Talbot Sport	Peugeot 205 T16 E2	4	Juha Piironen	5th
17	**Sweden**	**Peugeot Talbot Sport**	**Peugeot 205 T16 E2**	**4**	**Juha Piironen**	**1st**
18	Portugal	Peugeot Talbot Sport	Peugeot 205 T16 E2	7	Juha Piironen	Retired
19	Safari	Peugeot Talbot Sport	Peugeot 205 T16 E2	1	Juha Piironen	5th
20	**Greece**	**Peugeot Talbot Sport**	**Peugeot 205 T16 E2**	**5**	**Juha Piironen**	**1st**
21	**New Zealand**	**Peugeot Talbot Sport**	**Peugeot 205 T16 E2**	**3**	**Juha Piironen**	**1st**
22	Argentina	Peugeot Talbot Sport	Peugeot 205 T16 E2	1	Juha Piironen	Retired
23	Finland	Peugeot Talbot Sport	Peugeot 205 T16 E2	3	Juha Piironen	2nd
24	Great Britain	Peugeot Talbot Sport	Peugeot 205 T16 E2	5	Juha Piironen	3rd
25	United States	Peugeot Talbot Sport	Peugeot 205 T16 E2	1	Juha Piironen	2nd
1987	100 points (WORLD CHAMPION)					
26	Monte Carlo	Martini Lancia	Lancia Delta HF 4WD	1	Juha Piironen	2nd
27	Sweden	Martini Lancia	Lancia Delta HF 4WD	1	Juha Piironen	3rd
28	Portugal	Martini Lancia	Lancia Delta HF 4WD	1	Juha Piironen	4th
29	Greece	Martini Lancia	Lancia Delta HF 4WD	1	Juha Piironen	2nd
30	**United States**	**Martini Lancia**	**Lancia Delta HF 4WD**	**3**	**Juha Piironen**	**1st**
31	Finland	Martini Lancia	Lancia Delta HF 4WD	2	Juha Piironen	5th
32	**Great Britain**	**Martini Lancia**	**Lancia Delta HF 4WD**	**4**	**Juha Piironen**	**1st**
1988	8 points (37th)					
33	Safari	Toyota Team Europe	Toyota Supra Turbo	2	Juha Piironen	5th
34	Corsica	Toyota Team Europe	Toyota Celica GT-Four	2	Juha Piironen	Retired
35	Greece	Toyota Team Europe	Toyota Celica GT-Four	2	Juha Piironen	Retired
36	Finland	Toyota Team Europe	Toyota Celica GT-Four	3	Juha Piironen	Retired
37	Sanremo	Toyota Team Europe	Toyota Celica GT-Four	2	Juha Piironen	Retired
38	Great Britain	Toyota Team GB	Toyota Celica GT-Four	1	Juha Piironen	Retired
1989	60 points (3rd)					
39	Monte Carlo	Toyota Team Europe	Toyota Celica GT-Four	2	Juha Piironen	5th
40	Portugal	Toyota Team Europe	Toyota Celica GT-Four	2	Juha Piironen	Retired
41	Corsica	Toyota Team Europe	Toyota Celica GT-Four	2	Juha Piironen	3rd
42	Greece	Toyota Team Europe	Toyota Celica GT-Four	2	Juha Piironen	Retired
43	Finland	Toyota Team Europe	Toyota Celica GT-Four	2	Juha Piironen	Retired
44	**Australia**	**Toyota Team Europe**	**Toyota Celica GT-Four**	**1**	**Juha Piironen**	**1st**
45	Sanremo	Toyota Team Europe	Toyota Celica GT-Four	4	Juha Piironen	5th
46	Great Britain	Toyota Team Europe	Toyota Celica GT-Four	1	Juha Piironen	3rd
1990	85 points (3rd)					
47	Monte Carlo	Martini Lancia	Lancia Delta Integrale 16V	4	Juha Piironen	Retired
48	Portugal	Martini Lancia	Lancia Delta Integrale 16V	5	Juha Piironen	3rd
49	Safari	Martini Lancia	Lancia Delta Integrale 16V	5	Juha Piironen	2nd
50	Greece	Martini Lancia	Lancia Delta Integrale 16V	4	Juha Piironen	2nd
51	Argentina	Martini Lancia	Lancia Delta Integrale 16V	2	Juha Piironen	Retired
52	Finland	Martini Lancia	Lancia Delta Integrale 16V	2	Juha Piironen	5th
53	**Australia**	**Martini Lancia**	**Lancia Delta Integrale 16V**	**1**	**Juha Piironen**	**1st**
54	Sanremo	Martini Lancia	Lancia Delta Integrale 16V	6	Juha Piironen	2nd
55	Great Britain	Martini Lancia	Lancia Delta Integrale 16V	3	Juha Piironen	Retired
1991	150 points (WORLD CHAMPION)					
56	Monte Carlo	Martini Lancia	Lancia Delta Integrale 16V	9	Juha Piironen	5th
57	Portugal	Martini Lancia	Lancia Delta Integrale 16V	5	Juha Piironen	4th
58	**Safari**	**Martini Lancia**	**Lancia Delta Integrale 16V**	**6**	**Juha Piironen**	**1st**
59	**Greece**	**Martini Lancia**	**Lancia Delta Integrale 16V**	**7**	**Juha Piironen**	**1st**
60	New Zealand	Martini Lancia	Lancia Delta Integrale 16V	2	Juha Piironen	2nd
61	Argentina	Martini Lancia	Lancia Delta Integrale 16V	8	Juha Piironen	4th

KANKKUNEN, JUHA CAREER RECORD (CONT'D)

YEAR	RALLY	TEAM/ENTRANT	CAR	NO.	CO-DRIVER	RESULT
62	Finland	Martini Lancia	Lancia Delta Integrale 16V	2	Juha Piironen	1st
63	Australia	Martini Lancia	Lancia Delta Integrale 16V	1	Juha Piironen	1st
64	Sanremo	Martini Lancia	Lancia Delta Integrale 16V	4	Juha Piironen	Retired
65	Catalunya	Martini Lancia	Lancia Delta Integrale 16V	2	Juha Piironen	2nd
66	Great Britain	Martini Lancia	Lancia Delta Integrale 16V	2	Juha Piironen	1st
1992	134 points (2nd)					
67	Monte Carlo	Martini Lancia	Lancia Delta HF Integrale	1	Juha Piironen	3rd
68	Portugal	Martini Lancia	Lancia Delta HF Integrale	4	Juha Piironen	1st
69	Safari	Martini Lancia	Lancia Delta HF Integrale	1	Juha Piironen	2nd
70	Greece	Martini Lancia	Lancia Delta HF Integrale	1	Juha Piironen	2nd
71	Finland	Martini Lancia	Lancia Delta HF Integrale	1	Juha Piironen	2nd
72	Australia	Martini Lancia	Lancia Delta HF Integrale	1	Juha Piironen	2nd
73	Sanremo	Martini Lancia	Lancia Delta HF Integrale	1	Juha Piironen	2nd
74	Catalunya	Martini Lancia	Lancia Delta HF Integrale	5	Juha Piironen	2nd
75	Great Britain	Martini Lancia	Lancia Delta HF Integrale	1	Juha Piironen	3rd
1993	135 points (WORLD CHAMPION)					
76	Monte Carlo	Toyota Castrol Team	Toyota Celica Turbo 4WD	7	Juha Piironen	5th
77	Sweden	Toyota Castrol Team	Toyota Celica Turbo 4WD	3	Juha Piironen	2nd
78	Safari	Toyota Castrol Team	Toyota Celica Turbo 4WD	1	Juha Piironen	1st
79	Greece	Toyota Castrol Team	Toyota Celica Turbo 4WD	6	Juha Piironen	Retired
80	Argentina	Toyota Castrol Team	Toyota Celica Turbo 4WD	4	Nicky Grist	1st
81	New Zealand	Toyota Castrol Team	Toyota Celica Turbo 4WD	5	Nicky Grist	5th
82	Finland	Toyota Castrol Team	Toyota Celica Turbo 4WD	4	Denis Giraudet	1st
83	Australia	Toyota Castrol Team	Toyota Celica Turbo 4WD	6	Nicky Grist	1st
84	Catalunya	Toyota Castrol Team	Toyota Celica Turbo 4WD	2	Nicky Grist	3rd
85	Great Britain	Toyota Castrol Team	Toyota Celica Turbo 4WD	1	Nicky Grist	1st
1994	93 points (3rd)					
86	Monte Carlo	Toyota Castrol Team	Toyota Celica Turbo 4WD	1	Nicky Grist	2nd
87	Portugal	Toyota Castrol Team	Toyota Celica Turbo 4WD	2	Nicky Grist	1st
88	Safari	Toyota Castrol Team	Toyota Celica Turbo 4WD	1	Nicky Grist	Retired
89	Corsica	Toyota Castrol Team	Toyota Celica Turbo 4WD	1	Nicky Grist	4th
90	Greece	Toyota Castrol Team	Toyota Celica Turbo 4WD	6	Nicky Grist	3rd
91	Argentina	Toyota Castrol Team	Toyota Celica Turbo 4WD	1	Nicky Grist	Retired
92	New Zealand	Toyota Castrol Team	Toyota Celica Turbo 4WD	1	Nicky Grist	2nd
93	Finland	Toyota Castrol Team	Toyota Celica Turbo 4WD	1	Nicky Grist	9th
94	Sanremo	Toyota Castrol Team	Toyota Celica GT-Four	3	Nicky Grist	7th
95	Great Britain	Toyota Castrol Team	Toyota Celica GT-Four	1	Nicky Grist	2nd
1995	62 points (Disqualified)					
96	Monte Carlo	Toyota Castrol Team	Toyota Celica GT-Four	2	Nicky Grist	3rd
97	Sweden	Toyota Castrol Team	Toyota Celica GT-Four	2	Nicky Grist	4th
98	Portugal	Toyota Castrol Team	Toyota Celica GT-Four	2	Nicky Grist	2nd
99	Corsica	Toyota Castrol Team	Toyota Celica GT-Four	2	Nicky Grist	10th
100	New Zealand	Toyota Castrol Team	Toyota Celica GT-Four	2	Nicky Grist	3rd
101	Australia	Toyota Castrol Team	Toyota Celica GT-Four	2	Nicky Grist	3rd
102	Catalunya	Toyota Castrol Team	Toyota Celica GT-Four	2	Nicky Grist	Retired
1996	37 points (7th)					
103	Sweden	Toyota Castrol Team Sweden	Toyota Celica GT-Four	12	Nicky Grist	4th
104	Indonesia	Toyota Australia	Toyota Celica GT-Four	10	Nicky Grist	3rd
105	Finland	Team Toyota Castrol Finland	Toyota Celica GT-Four	11	Nicky Grist	2nd
1997	29 points (4th)					
106	Argentina	Ford Motor Company	Ford Escort WRC	6	Juha Repo	Retired
107	Greece	Ford Motor Company	Ford Escort WRC	6	Juha Repo	2nd
108	New Zealand	Ford Motor Company	Ford Escort WRC	6	Juha Repo	3rd
109	Finland	Ford Motor Company	Ford Escort WRC	6	Juha Repo	2nd
110	Indonesia	Ford Motor Company	Ford Escort WRC	6	Juha Repo	2nd
111	Sanremo	Ford Motor Company	Ford Escort WRC	6	Juha Repo	6th
112	Australia	Ford Motor Company	Ford Escort WRC	6	Juha Repo	Retired
113	Great Britain	Ford Motor Company	Ford Escort WRC	6	Juha Repo	2nd
1998	39 points (4th)					
114	Monte Carlo	Ford Motor Company	Ford Escort WRC	7	Juha Repo	2nd
115	Sweden	Ford Motor Company	Ford Escort WRC	7	Juha Repo	3rd
116	Safari	Ford Motor Company	Ford Escort WRC	7	Juha Repo	2nd
117	Portugal	Ford Motor Company	Ford Escort WRC	7	Juha Repo	7th
118	Catalunya	Ford Motor Company	Ford Escort WRC	7	Juha Repo	Retired
119	Corsica	Ford Motor Company	Ford Escort WRC	7	Juha Repo	9th
120	Argentina	Ford Motor Company	Ford Escort WRC	7	Juha Repo	3rd
121	Greece	Ford Motor Company	Ford Escort WRC	7	Juha Repo	3rd
122	New Zealand	Ford Motor Company	Ford Escort WRC	7	Juha Repo	4th
123	Finland	Ford Motor Company	Ford Escort WRC	7	Juha Repo	3rd
124	Sanremo	Ford Motor Company	Ford Escort WRC	7	Juha Repo	Retired
125	Australia	Ford Motor Company	Ford Escort WRC	7	Juha Repo	5th
126	Great Britain	Ford Motor Company	Ford Escort WRC	7	Juha Repo	2nd
1999	44 points (4th)					
127	Monte Carlo	Subaru World Rally Team	Subaru Impreza WRC	6	Juha Repo	2nd
128	Sweden	Subaru World Rally Team	Subaru Impreza WRC	6	Juha Repo	6th
129	Safari	Subaru World Rally Team	Subaru Impreza WRC	6	Juha Repo	Retired
130	Portugal	Subaru World Rally Team	Subaru Impreza WRC	6	Juha Repo	Retired
131	Catalunya	Subaru World Rally Team	Subaru Impreza WRC	14	Juha Repo	6th
132	Argentina	Subaru World Rally Team	Subaru Impreza WRC	6	Juha Repo	1st
133	Greece	Subaru World Rally Team	Subaru Impreza WRC	6	Juha Repo	Retired
134	New Zealand	Subaru World Rally Team	Subaru Impreza WRC	6	Juha Repo	2nd
135	Finland	Subaru World Rally Team	Subaru Impreza WRC	6	Juha Repo	1st
136	China	Subaru World Rally Team	Subaru Impreza WRC	6	Juha Repo	4th
137	Sanremo	Subaru World Rally Team	Subaru Impreza WRC	6	Juha Repo	6th
138	Australia	Subaru World Rally Team	Subaru Impreza WRC	6	Juha Repo	Retired
139	Great Britain	Subaru World Rally Team	Subaru Impreza WRC	6	Juha Repo	2nd
2000	20 points (8th)					
140	Monte Carlo	Subaru World Rally Team	Subaru Impreza WRC	4	Juha Repo	3rd
141	Sweden	Subaru World Rally Team	Subaru Impreza WRC	4	Juha Repo	6th
142	Safari	Subaru World Rally Team	Subaru Impreza WRC	4	Juha Repo	2nd
143	Portugal	Subaru World Rally Team	Subaru Impreza WRC	4	Juha Repo	Retired
144	Catalunya	Subaru World Rally Team	Subaru Impreza WRC	4	Juha Repo	Retired
145	Argentina	Subaru World Rally Team	Subaru Impreza WRC	4	Juha Repo	4th
146	Greece	Subaru World Rally Team	Subaru Impreza WRC	4	Juha Repo	3rd
147	New Zealand	Subaru World Rally Team	Subaru Impreza WRC	4	Juha Repo	Retired
148	Finland	Subaru World Rally Team	Subaru Impreza WRC	4	Juha Repo	8th
149	Cyprus	Subaru World Rally Team	Subaru Impreza WRC	4	Juha Repo	7th
150	Australia	Subaru World Rally Team	Subaru Impreza WRC	4	Juha Repo	Retired
151	Great Britain	Subaru World Rally Team	Subaru Impreza WRC	4	Juha Repo	5th
2001	0 points					
152	Finland	Hyundai Castrol World Rally Team	Hyundai Accent WRC2	20	Juha Repo	Retired
2002	2 points (14th)					
153	Sweden	Hyundai Castrol World Rally Team	Hyundai Accent WRC2	19	Juha Repo	8th
154	Cyprus	Hyundai Castrol World Rally Team	Hyundai Accent WRC3	19	Juha Repo	Retired
155	Argentina	Hyundai Castrol World Rally Team	Hyundai Accent WRC3	19	Juha Repo	7th
156	Greece	Hyundai Castrol World Rally Team	Hyundai Accent WRC3	19	Juha Repo	Retired
157	Safari	Hyundai Castrol World Rally Team	Hyundai Accent WRC3	19	Juha Repo	8th
158	Finland	Hyundai Castrol World Rally Team	Hyundai Accent WRC3	19	Juha Repo	Retired
159	New Zealand	Hyundai Castrol World Rally Team	Hyundai Accent WRC3	19	Juha Repo	5th
160	Australia	Hyundai Castrol World Rally Team	Hyundai Accent WRC3	19	Juha Repo	Retired
161	Great Britain	Hyundai Castrol World Rally Team	Hyundai Accent WRC3	19	Juha Repo	9th

KULLÄNG, ANDERS

(S) B: 28 SEPTEMBER 1943, KARLSTAD, SWEDEN

Anders Kulläng is one of those drivers of whom one thinks that it would have been nice to have seen him drive a fully competitive car at the peak of his career.

Born the son of a parish priest in the heart of Swedish Rally territory at Karlstad, Kulläng started rallying in 1962 with a Volvo PV544. His first break came when GM Sweden gave him some help to run a Kadett and in 1969 he posted his first major result with a fourth place on the Swedish Rally. He was seventh on the Swedish Rally in both 1970 and 1971 and in that second year also won the Swedish championship. In 1972, he drove an Ascona for Opel on the Olympia Rally and finished second overall while he was fourth on the Swedish and third at the RAC Rally.

He was now inducted into the Opel Europe team with whom he posted good results in Sweden and Finland and seemed to be the only man who could get a Group 2 Kadett GT/E to the finish of the RAC Rally. Had he not been put off the road by a lack of brakes on the 1976 event, he could have been third among the Escorts and Stratoses.

He stayed with Opel knowing that they were brewing up the Ascona 400 which was launched at the Monte Carlo 1980 where he promptly finished fourth overall. In Sweden it was even better and he won outright, justly rewarding all those years of trial and aspiration. The following year started well in Monte Carlo and Sweden. Then came a wonderful Safari where Kulläng led for almost two-thirds of the event before hitting a herd of cows and retiring. When his sponsor, Publimmo, withdrew he was left without a drive. He took up with the new Mitsubishi team and drove their largely uncompetitive Lancer Turbo for two seasons. After that, his WRC career was at an end at the age of 40.

KULLÄNG, ANDERS - CAREER RECORD

YEAR	RALLY	TEAM/ENTRANT	CAR	NO.	CO-DRIVER	RESULT
1973						
1	Monte Carlo	General Motors	Opel Ascona	44	Claes-Goran Andersson	13th
2	Great Britain		Opel Ascona	15	Donald Karlsson	Retired
1974						
3	Finland		Opel Ascona	13	Claes-Goran Andersson	8th
1975						
4	Monte Carlo		Opel Ascona	24	Claes-Goran Andersson	Retired
5	Sweden		Opel Ascona	11	Claes-Goran Andersson	Retired
6	Finland		Opel Ascona	8	Claes-Goran Andersson	5th
7	Great Britain	Opel Euro Händler Team	Opel Kadett GT/E	17	Claes-Goran Andersson	Retired
1976						
8	Monte Carlo		Opel Kadett GT/E	28	Claes-Goran Andersson	Retired
9	Sweden		Opel Ascona	7	Claes-Goran Andersson	3rd
10	Portugal		Opel Kadett GT/E	7	Claes-Goran Andersson	7th
11	Finland		Opel Kadett GT/E	11	Claes-Goran Andersson	Retired
12	Great Britain	Opel Euro Händler Team	Opel Kadett GT/E	19	Claes-Goran Andersson	7th
1977						
13	Sweden		Opel Kadett GT/E	8	Bruno Berglund	3rd
14	Great Britain		Opel Kadett GT/E	19	Bruno Berglund	15th
1978						
15	Monte Carlo	Opel Euro Händler	Opel Kadett GT/E	7	Bruno Berglund	9th
16	Sweden		Opel Kadett GT/E	7	Bruno Berglund	Retired
17	Portugal		Opel Kadett GT/E	10	Bruno Berglund	6th
18	Greece		Opel Kadett GT/E	2	Bruno Berglund	Retired
19	Finland		Opel Kadett GT/E	9	Bruno Berglund	7th
20	Canada		Opel Kadett GT/E	6	Bruno Berglund	3rd
21	Great Britain		Opel Kadett GT/E	17	Bruno Berglund	5th
1979	**0 points**					
22	Monte Carlo	Opel Dealer Team Holland	Opel Kadett GT/E	10	Bob de Jong	Retired
22	Sweden	Opel Team Sweden	Opel Kadett GT/E	7	Bruno Berglund	Retired
24	Portugal	Opel Dealer Team Holland	Opel Kadett GT/E	6	Bob de Jong	Retired
25	Greece	Opel Dealer Team Holland	Opel Kadett GT/E	6	Bob de Jong	Retired
26	Finland	Opel Dealer Team Holland	Opel Kadett GT/E	10	Bruno Berglund	Retired
1980	**48 points (5th)**					
27	Monte Carlo	Opel Euro Händler	Opel Ascona 400	4	Bruno Berglund	4th
28	**Sweden**	**Opel Euro Händler**	**Opel Ascona 400**	**7**	**Bruno Berglund**	**1st**
29	Portugal	Opel Euro Händler	Opel Ascona 400	12	Bruno Berglund	Retired
30	Greece	Opel Euro Händler	Opel Ascona 400	4	Bruno Berglund	4th
31	Finland	Opel Euro Händler	Opel Ascona 400	4	Bruno Berglund	Retired
32	Sanremo	Opel Euro Händler	Opel Ascona 400	6	Bruno Berglund	Retired
33	Great Britain	Opel Euro Händler	Opel Ascona 400	7	Bruno Berglund	5th
1981	**22 points (15th)**					
34	Monte Carlo	Publimmo Racing	Opel Ascona 400	11	Bruno Berglund	4th
35	Sweden	Publimmo Racing	Opel Ascona 400	1	Bruno Berglund	4th
36	Portugal	Publimmo Racing	Opel Ascona 400	7	Bruno Berglund	Retired
37	Safari	Publimmo Racing	Opel Ascona 400	4	Bruno Berglund	Retired
38	Greece	Team Ralliart	Mitsubishi Lancer Turbo	7	Bruno Berglund	Retired
39	Finland	Team Ralliart	Mitsubishi Lancer Turbo	7	Bruno Berglund	12th
40	Great Britain	Team Ralliart	Mitsubishi Lancer Turbo	11	Bruno Berglund	9th
1982	**4 points (41st)**					
41	Finland	Team Ralliart	Mitsubishi Lancer Turbo	10	Bruno Berglund	Retired
42	Sanremo	Team Ralliart	Mitsubishi Lancer Turbo	8	Bruno Berglund	7th
43	Great Britain	Team Ralliart	Mitsubishi Lancer Turbo	15	Bruno Berglund	Retired
1984	**0 points**					
44	Sweden	Team Volvo	Volvo 240 Turbo	7	Lars-Ove Larsson	Retired
1988	**0 points**					
45	Sweden		BMW 325iX	46	Jorgen Skallman	28th

LIATTI, PIERO

(I) B: 7 MARCH 1962, BIELLA, ITALY

"Liatti's excellent tarmac results helped Subaru to the 1997 Manufacturers' title"

Most rally drivers dream of winning the Monte Carlo Rally and, even for some of the most eminent, a dream is all it remains. Piero Liatti has only won one WRC event and that was the Monte Carlo Rally.

Born in Northern Italy, Liatti did his first rally during 1982 in a Renault 5 but later changed to a Fiat Uno. He was studying mathematics but never finished his degree and joined his father's garage as a salesman. He won the Fiat Uno Trophy in 1986 and graduated to a Lancia Rally 037 in which he finished second in the Italian Championship of 1987. The following year he drove a Lancia Delta and won the Group N category.

He moved up to a Group A Delta for 1989 and finished fifth in the European Championship. The following year he finished second in the Italian Championship. In 1991, with a fully supported Delta Integrale, he won the European Championship.

This victory enabled him to spread his wings a little and, in 1992, he competed in Corsica and New Zealand. His ability to drive fast on tarmac was recognised and for two years he was given a Subaru, first a Legacy and then an Impreza, to go after the Italian title where, in 1993, he was fifth. He impressed sufficiently that when Prodrive were looking for a 'back-up' driver in 1995, Liatti got the seat.

He had three solid results from three WRC starts with the team and was also second in the Italian Championship and won the F2-only San Remo.

He got a bigger programme for 1996 when Fabrizia Pons joined him in the Impreza. A year with but a single retirement was followed by his win in Monte Carlo on the debut of the Impreza WRC97, the first rally for the new WRC car era.

Liatti's excellent tarmac results helped Subaru to the 1997 WRC Manufacturer's title. However 1998 was not quite as good and he was released at the end of the year. Liatti then spent unconvincing year's each with SEAT, Ford and Hyundai.

He continued rallying, finishing seventh in the European Championship of 2000 and making an appearance in Super 1600 on the 2003 San Remo. His role these days is as an instructor at the National School of Driving run by the CSAI.

Right: Piero Liatti was a vital part of Subaru's successful 1997 campaign although team orders forced him to sacrifice a likely second career victory at the final control of the San Remo Rally to help Colin McRae's title aspirations

LIATTI, PIERO - CAREER RECORD

YEAR	RALLY	TEAM/ENTRANT	CAR	NO.	CO-DRIVER	RESULT
1990	**8 points (27th)**					
1	Sanremo		Lancia Delta Integrale	21	Luciano Tedeschini	5th
1991	**4 points (40th)**					
2	Sanremo	A.R.T Engineering	Lancia Delta Integrale 16V	12	Luciano Tedeschini	7th
1992	**22 points (12th)**					
3	Corscia	A.R.T Engineering	Lancia Delta HF Integrale	8	Luciano Tedeschini	8th
4	New Zealand		Lancia Delta HF Integrale	3	Luciano Tedeschini	2nd
5	Sanremo		Lancia Delta HF Integrale	7	Luciano Tedeschini	7th
1993	**10 points (24th)**					
6	Sanremo	A.R.T Engineering	Subaru Legacy RS	3	Alex Alessandrini	4th
1994	**0 points**					
7	Sanremo		Subaru Impreza 555	18	Luigi Pirollo	Retired
1995	**21 points (8th)**					
8	Monte Carlo	555 Subaru World Rally Team	Subaru Impreza 555	6	Alex Alessandrini	8th
9	Corsica	555 Subaru World Rally Team	Subaru Impreza 555	6	Alex Alessandrini	6th
10	Catalunya	555 Subaru World Rally Team	Subaru Impreza 555	6	Alex Alessandrini	3rd
1996	**56 points (5th)**					
11	Sweden	555 Subaru World Rally Team	Subaru Impreza 555	10	Mario Fertoglia	12th
12	Safari	555 Subaru World Rally Team	Subaru Impreza 555	3	Mario Fertoglia	5th
13	Indonesia	555 Subaru World Rally Team	Subaru Impreza 555	3	Fabrizia Pons	2nd
14	Greece	555 Subaru World Rally Team	Subaru Impreza 555	3	Fabrizia Pons	4th
15	Argentina	555 Subaru World Rally Team	Subaru Impreza 555	3	Fabrizia Pons	7th
16	Australia	555 Subaru World Rally Team	Subaru Impreza 555	3	Fabrizia Pons	7th
17	Sanremo	555 Subaru World Rally Team	Subaru Impreza 555	3	Fabrizia Pons	Retired
18	Catalunya	555 Subaru World Rally Team	Subaru Impreza 555	3	Fabrizia Pons	2nd
1997	**24 points (6th)**					
19	**Monte Carlo**	**555 Subaru World Rally Team**	**Subaru Impreza WRC**	**4**	**Fabrizia Pons**	**1st**
20	Catalunya	555 Subaru World Rally Team	Subaru Impreza WRC	4	Fabrizia Pons	2nd
21	Corsica	555 Subaru World Rally Team	Subaru Impreza WRC	4	Fabrizia Pons	5th
22	Sanremo	555 Subaru World Rally Team	Subaru Impreza WRC	4	Fabrizia Pons	2nd
23	Great Britain	555 Subaru World Rally Team	Subaru Impreza WRC	8	Fabrizia Pons	7th
1998	**17 points (7th)**					
24	Monte Carlo	555 Subaru World Rally Team	Subaru Impreza WRC	4	Fabrizia Pons	4th
25	Sweden	555 Subaru World Rally Team	Subaru Impreza WRC	10	Fabrizia Pons	9th
26	Safari	555 Subaru World Rally Team	Subaru Impreza WRC	4	Fabrizia Pons	Retired
27	Portugal	555 Subaru World Rally Team	Subaru Impreza WRC	4	Fabrizia Pons	6th
28	Catalunya	555 Subaru World Rally Team	Subaru Impreza WRC	4	Fabrizia Pons	Retired
29	Corsica	555 Subaru World Rally Team	Subaru Impreza WRC	4	Fabrizia Pons	3rd
30	Argentina	555 Subaru World Rally Team	Subaru Impreza WRC	4	Fabrizia Pons	6th
31	Greece	555 Subaru World Rally Team	Subaru Impreza WRC	4	Fabrizia Pons	6th
32	New Zealand	555 Subaru World Rally Team	Subaru Impreza WRC	4	Fabrizia Pons	6th
33	Sanremo	555 Subaru World Rally Team	Subaru Impreza WRC	4	Fabrizia Pons	2nd
34	Australia	555 Subaru World Rally Team	Subaru Impreza WRC	4	Fabrizia Pons	Retired
1999	**1 point (22nd)**					
35	Monte Carlo	SEAT Sport	SEAT Cordoba WRC	10	Carlo Cassina	6th
36	Safari	SEAT Sport	SEAT Cordoba WRC	10	Carlo Cassina	Retired
37	Portugal	SEAT Sport	SEAT Cordoba WRC	10	Carlo Cassina	Retired
38	Catalunya	SEAT Sport	SEAT Cordoba WRC	10	Carlo Cassina	10th
39	Corsica	SEAT Sport	SEAT Cordoba WRC	10	Carlo Cassina	9th
40	Argentina	SEAT Sport	SEAT Cordoba WRC	10	Carlo Cassina	Retired
41	Greece	SEAT Sport	SEAT Cordoba WRC	10	Carlo Cassina	Retired
42	China	SEAT Sport	SEAT Cordoba WRC E2	10	Carlo Cassina	Retired
43	Sanremo	SEAT Sport	SEAT Cordoba WRC E2	10	Carlo Cassina	Retired
2000	**1 point (21st)**					
44	Corsica	Ford Motor Company	Ford Focus WRC	17	Carlo Cassina	6th
45	Sanremo	Ford Motor Company	Ford Focus WRC	18	Carlo Cassina	Retired
2001						
46	Monte Carlo	Hyundai Castrol World Rally Team	Hyundai Accent WRC	9	Carlo Cassina	Retired
47	Catalunya	Hyundai Castrol World Rally Team	Hyundai Accent WRC2	9	Carlo Cassina	Retired
48	Cyprus	Hyundai Castrol World Rally Team	Hyundai Accent WRC2	20	Carlo Cassina	Retired
49	Sanremo	Hyundai Castrol World Rally Team	Hyundai Accent WRC2	9	Carlo Cassina	Retired
50	Corsica	Hyundai Castrol World Rally Team	Hyundai Accent WRC2	9	Carlo Cassina	8th
51	Great Britain	Hyundai Castrol World Rally Team	Hyundai Accent WRC2	19	Carlo Cassina	Retired
2003						
52	Sanremo	Privateer	Peugeot 206 S1600	101	Vanda Geninatti	15th

LOEB, SÉBASTIEN

(F) B: 26 FEBRUARY 1974, OBERHOFFEN-LES-WISSEMBOURG, FRANCE

The progress of Sébastien Loeb up the ladder of success has been like that of a precision rocket and the cool young man from Alsace now stands at the very pinnacle of his sport though, as yet, he is an uncrowned prince.

"The cool young man from Alsace now stands at the very pinnacle of his sport"

His first taste of motor sport came when he entered a regional competition called the Volant Rally Jeunes in 1995. He reached the final which encouraged him go back for more when he was again a finalist, this time in the national section. He also acquired a Peugeot 106 and did his first proper rally, the Rallye de Florival. With the Peugeot, he entered the 1997 Volant Peugeot 106 and finished eighth, winning his class three times. The next move was to Citroën and a Saxo Kit Car with which he won two small rallies outright and finished sixth in the Citroën Saxo Cup. At this point, he was 'adopted' by the FFSA, the French national motorsport body and was supported by them in three WRC rounds. In France, he won the Saxo Cup and was an amazing third overall with the Saxo on the Rallye Alsace-Vosges.

Now came a key decision for Loeb. He decided to persevere with the Saxo but to migrate with it to the French gravel championship. He rapidly learnt how to cope with the new surfaces and won his class seven times and took the F2 gravel title. He was also busy on tarmac competing in the main French championship with his Saxo and a Renault Maxi Megane while for the last round, the Rally du Var, Citroën lent him a Xsara Kit car with which he won outright. He had also benefited from his FFSA association by driving a rented Toyota Corolla on two tarmac WRC rounds.

For 2001, Citroën put him in a Xsara Kit car for the French tarmac championship, which he won and supported his efforts with a new Saxo Kit car in the Junior WRC where again he proved invincible. He won the WRC Super 1600 class five times out of six and the only rally on which he failed to score in that category was San Remo where Citroën had been given permission by the FIA to enter him in a Xsara WRC instead. He came second overall, just 11 seconds behind the winner. After that, there could be no doubt that Loeb was destined for a place in the full works team for 2002.

He won his first WRC rally on the new Rallye Deutschland but the whole season was a matter of gaining experience on rallies like the Safari and Australia that he had never seen before. His ability to learn and to handle himself under pressure was never more evident than on the first event of 2003, the Monte Carlo Rally. He had been denied victory the previous year thanks to an unauthorised tyre change by the team that had not given him any advantage so the expectation was high and Loeb fulfilled it. He retired in Turkey thanks to a lack of fuel but won again in Deutschland and then added San Remo to his total. He came to the Rally GB equal on points with teammate, Carlos Sainz, and one ahead of Petter Solberg. By mid-way, it was down to Loeb and Solberg with the Norwegian leading by just 40 seconds. However, for Citroën, the Manufacturers' title was more important and Loeb had to sacrifice his Drivers' title bid to make sure of finishing second which he did. One suspects that in future there will be no reining him in.

Right: Sebastien Loeb's win on Sanremo in 2003 was his third win in a season that came very close to seeing the Frenchman claim his first worldchampionship crown. No one doubts that the sport's ultimate prize isn't far away

LOEB, SEBASTIEN - CAREER RECORD

YEAR	RALLY	TEAM /ENTRANT	CAR	NO.	CO-DRIVER	RESULT
1999	**0 points**					
1	Catalunya	Equipe de France FFSA	Citroen Saxo Kit Car	44	Daniel Elena	Retired
2	Corsica	Equipe de France FFSA	Citroen Saxo Kit Car	49	Daniel Elena	19th
3	Sanremo	Equipe de France FFSA	Citroen Saxo Kit Car	107	Daniel Elena	21st
2000	**0 points**					
4	Finland		Citroen Saxo Kit Car	84	Daniel Elena	Retired
5	Corsica	Equipe de France FFSA	Toyota Corolla WRC	33	Daniel Elena	9th
6	Sanremo	Equipe de France FFSA	Toyota Corolla WRC	43	Daniel Elena	10th
7	Great Britain		Citroen Saxo Kit Car	62	Daniel Elena	38th
2001	**6 points (14th)**					
8	Monte Carlo		Citroen Saxo Kit Car	37	Daniel Elena	15th
9	Sweden		Citroen Saxo Kit Car	64	Daniel Elena	Retired
10	Catalunya		Citroen Saxo Kit Car	53	Daniel Elena	15th
11	Greece		Citroen Saxo Kit Car	53	Daniel Elena	19th
12	Finland		Citroen Saxo Kit Car	53	Daniel Elena	28th
13	Sanremo	Automobiles Citroen	Citroen Xsara WRC	20	Daniel Elena	2nd
14	Corsica		Citroen Saxo Kit Car	53	Daniel Elena	13th
15	Great Britain		Citroen Saxo Kit Car	53	Daniel Elena	15th
2002	**18 points (10th)**					
16	Monte Carlo	Automobiles Citroen	Citroen Xsara WRC	21	Daniel Elena	2nd
17	Sweden	Automobiles Citroen	Citroen Xsara WRC	21	Daniel Elena	17th
18	Catalunya	Automobiles Citroen	Citroen Xsara WRC	21	Daniel Elena	Retired
19	Greece	Automobiles Citroen	Citroen Xsara WRC	21	Daniel Elena	7th
20	Safari	Automobiles Citroen	Citroen Xsara WRC	21	Daniel Elena	5th
21	Finland	Automobiles Citroen	Citroen Xsara WRC	21	Daniel Elena	10th
22	**Germany**	**Automobiles Citroen**	**Citroen Xsara WRC**	**21**	**Daniel Elena**	**1st**
23	Australia	Piedrafita Sport	Citroen Xsara WRC	21	Daniel Elena	7th
24	Great Britain	Automobiles Citroen	Citroen Xsara WRC	21	Daniel Elena	Retired
2003	**71 points (2nd)**					
25	**Monte Carlo**	**Citroen Total**	**Citroen Xsara WRC**	**18**	**Daniel Elena**	**1st**
26	Sweden	Citroen Total	Citroen Xsara WRC	18	Daniel Elena	7th
27	Turkey	Citroen Total	Citroen Xsara WRC	18	Daniel Elena	Retired
28	New Zealand	Citroen Total	Citroen Xsara WRC	18	Daniel Elena	4th
29	Argentina	Citroen Total	Citroen Xsara WRC	18	Daniel Elena	Retired
30	Greece	Citroen Total	Citroen Xsara WRC	18	Daniel Elena	Retired
31	Cyprus	Citroen Total	Citroen Xsara WRC	18	Daniel Elena	3rd
32	**Germany**	**Citroen Total**	**Citroen Xsara WRC**	**18**	**Daniel Elena**	**1st**
33	Finland	Citroen Total	Citroen Xsara WRC	18	Daniel Elena	5th
34	Australia	Citroen Total	Citroen Xsara WRC	18	Daniel Elena	2nd
35	**Sanremo**	**Citroen Total**	**Citroen Xsara WRC**	**18**	**Daniel Elena**	**1st**
36	Corsica	Citroen Total	Citroen Xsara WRC	18	Daniel Elena	13th
37	Catalunya	Citroen Total	Citroen Xsara WRC	18	Daniel Elena	2nd
38	Great Britain	Citroen Total	Citroen Xsara WRC	18	Daniel Elena	2nd

MÄKINEN, TIMO

(FIN) B: 18 MARCH 1939, HELSINKI, FINLAND

"One of very few rally drivers to achieve legendary status"

One of very few rally drivers to achieve legendary status, Timo Mäkinen was an idol to both rally men and spectators during the 1960s and '70s. The stories that surrounded him – both behind the wheel and away from it – were numerous.

His first driving experiences were taking newspaper delivery vans for his father's company from one end of Finland to the other in all weathers. Mäkinen started driving in competition in 1960 using such diverse cars as a Triumph TR3, a Volvo PV444, a Saab 96 850 and, for one ice race, a D-type Jaguar. His car control and versatility got him a regular drive in a Mini Cooper – and a sales job – with the BMC agent in Helsinki. His first proper works drive was when he was invited to drive a Mini Cooper on the 1962 RAC Rally. The idea was to spike Erik Carlsson's guns, in which he failed, but he did set some very fast times, finished and won his class. Thus began a working relationship with the then BMC competition manager, Stuart Turner, that was to last almost 15 years.

Now part of the BMC line-up, his first job was to take an Austin Healey 3000 on the Monte Carlo with Mini racer, Christabel Carlisle. They won their class and Mäkinen spent most the rest of the year driving the big Healey. The following year he was 'promoted' to the Cooper S and promptly won the Tulip Rally. He sensationally won the Monte Carlo of 1965, the little Cooper S punching its way through the blizzards to victory. The French were surprised by this and when he won again the following year, they were sure that there was something more than just Mäkinen Magic at work. The cars were stripped naked and eventually all the British works cars were excluded for an alleged lighting infringement.

Undaunted, Mäkinen went on to take a hat-trick of wins on the 1000 Lakes with the Cooper S but now BMC were to close their competition department and Mäkinen was destined to become a nomad for a few years. He drove Lancias, Peugeots, BMWs and, most notably, a private Ford Escort TC on the 1968 RAC Rally. He loved the car and was leading until it broke down. This was what he wanted to drive and, by good fortune, Stuart Turner was now in a position at Ford to renew their relationship.

There followed six years of highly productive rallying. Mäkinen added another 1000 Lakes win to his previous three and also collected a hat-trick of RAC Rally wins. A repeat victory at Monte Carlo always eluded him but the Escort RS was being eclipsed on tarmac rallies by cars like the Alpine Renault and the Lancia Stratos.

In his latter years at Ford, Mäkinen also did some African rallies with Peugeot and Mercedes with whom he also drove in South American events.

Always the extrovert, Mäkinen was hugely popular everywhere and was always the one to be photographed wearing the oxygen equipment, the wetsuit or whatever the latest gimmick happened to be.

Right: Timo Makinen rattled off a hat-trick of RAC Rally wins from 1973-1975. Here he is taking the second of the trio that came amid Ford's eight-year domination of the event from 1972-1979

MÄKINEN, TIMO – CAREER RECORD

YEAR	RALLY	TEAM/ENTRANT	CAR	NO.	CO-DRIVER	RESULT
1973						
1	Monte Carlo	Ford Motor Company	Ford Escort RS1600	3	Henry Liddon	11th
2	Safari	Ford Motor Company	Ford Escort RS1600	16	Henry Liddon	Retired
3	Morocco	Peugeot	Peugeot 504	13	Henry Liddon	Retired
4	**Finland**	**Ford Motor Company**	**Ford Escort RS1600**	**4**	**Henry Liddon**	**1st**
5	**Great Britain**	**Ford/Milk Marketing Board**	**Ford Escort RS1600**	**13**	**Henry Liddon**	**1st**
1974						
6	Safari	Marshalls (EA) Ltd.	Peugeot 504	5	John Davenport	Retired
7	Finland	Ford Motor Company	Ford Escort RS1600	1	Henry Liddon	2nd
8	**Great Britain**	**Ford Motor Company/Colibri Lighters**	**Ford Escort RS1600**	**1**	**Henry Liddon**	**1st**
1975						
9	Safari	Marshalls (EA) Ltd.	Peugeot 504	1	Henry Liddon	Retired
10	Morocco	Ford Motor Company	Ford Escort RS1800	4	Henry Liddon	5th
11	Finland	Ford Motor Company	Ford Escort RS1800	4	Henry Liddon	3rd
12	Sanremo	Ford Motor Company	Ford Escort RS1800	3	Henry Liddon	Retired
13	**Great Britain**	**Ford/Allied Polymer Group**	**Ford Escort RS1800**	**1**	**Henry Liddon**	**1st**
1976						
14	Monte Carlo	Ford Motor Company	Ford Escort RS1800	14	Henry Liddon	Retired
15	Safari	Marshalls (EA) Ltd.	Peugeot 504 V6 Coupe	3	Henry Liddon	Retired
16	Morocco	Ford Motor Company	Ford Escort RS1800	4	Henry Liddon	Retired
17	Finland	Ford Motor Company	Ford Escort RS1800	4	Henry Liddon	4th
18	Corsica		Peugeot 104 ZS	4	Henry Liddon	Retired
19	Great Britain	Ford Motor Company	Ford Escort RS1800	1	Henry Liddon	Retired
1977						
20	Sweden		Fiat 131 Abarth	5	Henry Liddon	Retired
21	Safari	Marshalls (EA) Ltd.	Peugeot 504 V6 Coupe	9	Henry Liddon	Retired
22	Finland	Olio Fiat	Fiat 131 Abarth	6	Henry Liddon	Retired
23	Canada		Fiat 131 Abarth	7	Henry Liddon	Retired
24	Corsica		Peugeot 104 ZS	8	Henry Liddon	Retired
25	Great Britain	Chequered Flag	Fiat 131 Abarth	6	Henry Liddon	11th
1978						
26	Safari	Marshalls (EA) Ltd.	Peugeot 504 V6 Coupe	11	Jean Todt	Retired
27	Portugal		Peugeot 104ZS	12	Jean Todt	7th
28	Ivory Coast		Peugeot 504 V6 Coupe	1	Jean Todt	2nd
1979	0 points					
29	Safari	Marshalls (EA) Ltd.	Peugeot 504 V6 Coupe	8	Jean Todt	Retired
30	Finland	Toyota Team Europe	Toyota Celica 2000GT	7	Henry Liddon	Retired
31	Ivory Coast		Peugeot 504 V6 Coupe	2	Jean Todt	Retired
1980	7 points (35th)					
32	Monte Carlo	BMW France	BMW 320i	17	Henry Liddon	14th
33	Greece	Automobiles Peugeot	Peugeot 504 V6 Coupe	17	Jean Todt	10th
34	Argentina	Automobiles Peugeot	Peugeot 504 V6 Coupe	16	Jean Todt	Retired
35	Finland	Timo Makinen Racing	Triumph TR7 V8	11	Erkki Salonen	22nd
36	Great Britain	Rothmans Rally Team	Ford Escort RS1800	19	Martin Holmes	6th
37	Ivory Coast	Automobiles Peugeot	Peugeot 504 V6 Coupe	14	Jean Todt	Retired
1981	0 points					
38	Safari	Marshalls (EA) Ltd.	Peugeot 504 V6 Coupe	10	Atso Aho	Retired
39	Finland		Talbot Sunbeam Lotus	22	Juhani Korhonen	Retired

MÄKINEN, TOMMI

(FIN) B: 26 JUNE 1964, PUUPPOLA, FINLAND

"The only major rallies he failed to conquer were Acropolis and Corsica"

It is all too easy to look at Tommi Mäkinen's four world championship titles and remember him only for that. He also won Monte Carlo four times in a row, three of those coming outside his championship years. He has won rallies as diverse as Sweden and the Safari, Portugal and San Remo, Catalunya and Australia. In fact, the only major rallies he failed to conquer were Acropolis and Corsica. So not only brilliant but an all-rounder as well.

Mäkinen's driving career started on tractors and he won the Finnish national ploughing championship in 1982 and again in 1985, the same year that he started rallying. The chosen car was a Ford Escort 2000 and within a year, he was Finnish Junior Champion. The next move was to acquire a Group N Lancia Delta HF. He was unsuccessful in the big rallies but in 1988, he won the Finnish Group N title. The following year, still in Group N he won the Arctic Rally outright and, with the help of his Italian suppliers, won an Italian Championship event.

Then came his meeting with Seppo Harjanne, previously co-driver to Timo Salonen and immensely experienced. Harjanne persuaded Mäkinen to spread his wings and chase the FIA Group N title. The car they chose was a Mitsubishi Galant VR-4 and, at once Mäkinen made his mark finishing in the top 10 in both Australia and New Zealand. Despite starting his campaign mid-season, Mäkinen was third in the championship and ready for more. He did three rallies at the start of 1991 in rented Group N cars before being offered a Group A Mazda for the 1000 Lakes. He drove well in a less-than-competitive car and finished fifth but in a second outing with Mazda slid off in Kielder Forest on the RAC Rally.

Promotion to full works driver in the Nissan team for 1992 was not all it sounded. The Sunny GTI-R was not competitive but somehow Mäkinen got top 10 placings on Monte Carlo and RAC Rallies. With Nissan 'resting' the GTI-R, his next season was in a Lancia Delta run by an Italian team with good results from too few rallies. Nissan offered him an F2 Sunny for Portugal in 1994 where he led F2 until the engine failed and he drove for them in the British Championship finishing eighth overall. But for the 1000 Lakes, Ford asked him to become their eighth works driver in one year in their Escort Cosworth. He returned the favour by winning the rally outright. From then on, his career never looked back.

Ford was not in a position to sign him so he tried a Mitsubishi – unsuccessfully – in San Remo and then signed a contract that was to keep him with the Japanese company for seven years. During that time, he carried out a personal blitz on the World Championship and on the third occasion, his five wins were enough to give Mitsubishi the Manufacturer's title as well. At the end of 1997, Harjanne retired and Risto Mannisenmaki stepped in. The winning continued until Mäkinen had a bad accident in Corsica 2001 where

Mannisenmaki was injured. Just prior to that, he had decided to change teams for next year to improve his motivation. Mitsubishi had hit a bit of a wall with its first World Rally Car and it was retirement or Subaru for Mäkinen. On his debut event in the Impreza WRC he won the Monte Carlo but after that retirements outweighed successes and at the Rally GB of 2003, he confirmed his own retirement.

Right: Tommi Makinen won't look back on Australia 2000 with much joy as his car was disqualified for a technical infringement. By then, however, he had already racked up four world titles and had little to prove to the world, himself or his peers

MÄKINEN, TOMMI – CAREER RECORD

YEAR	RALLY	TEAM /ENTRANT	CAR	NO.	CO-DRIVER	RESULT
1987	**0 points**					
1	Finland		Lancia Delta HF 4WD	120	Jari Nieminen	Retired
1988	**0 points**					
2	Finland		Lancia Delta HF 4WD	36	Risto Mannisenmaki	Retired
3	Great Britain	Mu-Uutiset 4 Rombi Corse	Lancia Delta Integrale	85	Rodney Spokes	Retired
1989	**0 points**					
4	Sweden		Lancia Delta Integrale	28	Timo Hantunen	Retired
5	Finland		Lancia Delta Integrale	26	Timo Hantunen	Retired
1990	**10 points (24th)**					
6	New Zealand	Pro Sport Rally Team	Mitsubishi Galant VR-4	21	Seppo Harjanne	6th
7	Finland	Pro Sport Rally Team	Mitsubishi Galant VR-4	18	Seppo Harjanne	11th
8	Australia	Pro Sport Rally Team	Mitsubishi Galant VR-4	22	Seppo Harjanne	7th
9	Sanremo	Pro Sport Rally Team	Mitsubishi Galant VR-4	25	Seppo Harjanne	13th
10	Great Britain	Pro Sport Rally Team	Mitsubishi Galant VR-4	29	Seppo Harjanne	Retired
1991	**80 points (30th)**					
11	Sweden	Promo Racing S.A	Ford Sierra RS Cosworth 4x4	12	Seppo Harjanne	13th
12	Portugal	Mike Little Preparations	Ford Sierra RS Cosworth 4x4	11	Seppo Harjanne	Retired
13	New Zealand	Promo Racing S.A	Mitusbishi Galant VR-4	6	Seppo Harjanne	Retired
? 14	Finland	Mazda Rally Team Europe	Mazda 323 GTX	10	Seppo Harjanne	5th
15	Great Britain	Mazda Rally Team Europe	Mazda 323 GTX	9	Seppo Harjanne	Retired
1992	**5 points (40th)**					
16	Monte Carlo	Nissan Motorsports Europe	Nissan Sunny GTI-R	12	Seppo Harjanne	9th

YEAR	RALLY	TEAM /ENTRANT	CAR	NO.	CO-DRIVER	RESULT
17	Portugal	Nissan Motorsports Europe	Nissan Sunny GTI-R	8	Seppo Harjanne	Retired
18	Finland	Nissan Motorsports Europe	Nissan Sunny GTI-R	7	Seppo Harjanne	Retired
19	Great Britain	Nissan Motorsports Europe	Nissan Sunny GTI-R	5	Seppo Harjanne	8th
1993	**26 points (10th)**					
20	Sweden	Astra	Lancia Delta HF Integrale	9	Seppo Harjanne	4th
21	Greece	Astra	Lancia Delta HF Integrale	18	Seppo Harjanne	6th
22	Finland	Astra	Lancia Delta HF Integrale	13	Seppo Harjanne	4th
1994	**22 points (10th)**					
23	Portugal	Nissan F2	Nissan Sunny GTI	12	Seppo Harjanne	Retired
24	**Finland**	**Ford Motor Company**	**Ford Escort RS Cosworth**	**7**	**Seppo Harjanne**	**1st**
25	Sanremo	Mitsubishi Ralliart	Mitsubishi Lancer Evo 2	2	Seppo Harjanne	Retired
26	Great Britain	Nissan F2	Nissan Sunny GTI	18	Seppo Harjanne	9th
1995	**38 points (5th)**					
27	Monte Carlo	Mitsubishi Ralliart	Mitsubishi Lancer Evo 2	11	Seppo Harjanne	4th
28	Sweden	Mitsubishi Ralliart	Mitsubishi Lancer Evo 2	11	Seppo Harjanne	2nd
29	Corsica	Mitsubishi Ralliart	Mitsubishi Lancer Evo 3	11	Seppo Harjanne	8th
30	New Zealand	Mitsubishi Ralliart	Mitsubishi Lancer Evo 3	11	Seppo Harjanne	Retired
31	Australia	Mitsubishi Ralliart	Mitsubishi Lancer Evo 3	11	Seppo Harjanne	4th
32	Catalunya	Mitsubishi Ralliart	Mitsubishi Lancer Evo 3	11	Seppo Harjanne	Retired
33	Great Britain	Mitsubishi Ralliart	Mitsubishi Lancer Evo 3	11	Seppo Harjanne	Retired
1996	**123 points (WORLD CHAMPION)**					
34	**Sweden**	**Mitsubishi Ralliart**	**Mitsubishi Lancer Evo 3**	**7**	**Seppo Harjanne**	**1st**

MÄKINEN, TOMMI CAREER RECORD (CONT'D)

YEAR	RALLY	TEAM/ENTRANT	CAR	NO.	CO-DRIVER	RESULT
35	Safari	Mitsubishi Ralliart	Mitsubishi Lancer Evo 3	7	Seppo Harjanne	1st
36	Indonesia	Mitsubishi Ralliart	Mitsubishi Lancer Evo 3	7	Seppo Harjanne	Retired
37	Greece	Mitsubishi Ralliart	Mitsubishi Lancer Evo 3	7	Seppo Harjanne	2nd
38	Argentina	Mitsubishi Ralliart	Mitsubishi Lancer Evo 3	7	Seppo Harjanne	1st
39	Finland	Mitsubishi Ralliart	Mitsubishi Lancer Evo 3	7	Seppo Harjanne	1st
40	Australia	Petronas Mitsubishi Ralliart	Mitsubishi Lancer Evo 3	7	Seppo Harjanne	1st
41	Sanremo	Mitsubishi Ralliart	Mitsubishi Lancer Evo 3	7	Seppo Harjanne	Retired
42	Catalunya	Winfield Mitsubishi Ralliart	Mitsubishi Lancer Evo 3	7	Juha Repo	5th
1997	63 points (WORLD CHAMPION)					
43	Monte Carlo	Mitsubishi Ralliart	Mitsubishi Lancer Evo 4	1	Seppo Harjanne	3rd
44	Sweden	Mitsubishi Ralliart	Mitsubishi Lancer Evo 4	1	Seppo Harjanne	3rd
45	Safari	Mitsubishi Ralliart	Mitsubishi Lancer Evo 4	1	Seppo Harjanne	Retired
46	Portugal	Mitsubishi Ralliart	Mitsubishi Lancer Evo 4	1	Seppo Harjanne	1st
47	Catalunya	Mitsubishi Ralliart	Mitsubishi Lancer Evo 4	1	Seppo Harjanne	1st
48	Corsica	Mitsubishi Ralliart	Mitsubishi Lancer Evo 4	1	Seppo Harjanne	Retired
49	Argentina	Mitsubishi Ralliart	Mitsubishi Lancer Evol 4	1	Seppo Harjanne	1st
50	Greece	Mitsubishi Ralliart	Mitsubishi Lancer Evo 4	1	Seppo Harjanne	3rd
51	New Zealand	Mitsubishi Ralliart	Mitsubishi Lancer Evo 4	1	Seppo Harjanne	Retired
52	Finland	Mitsubishi Ralliart	Mitsubishi Lancer Evo 4	1	Seppo Harjanne	1st
53	Indonesia	Mitsubishi Ralliart	Mitsubishi Lancer Evo 4	1	Seppo Harjanne	Retired
54	Sanremo	Mitsubishi Ralliart	Mitsubishi Lancer Evo 4	1	Seppo Harjanne	3rd
55	Australia	Mitsubishi Ralliart	Mitsubishi Lancer Evo 4	1	Seppo Harjanne	2nd
56	Great Britain	Mitsubishi Ralliart	Mitsubishi Lancer Evo 4	1	Seppo Harjanne	6th
1998	58 points (WORLD CHAMPION)					
57	Monte Carlo	Mitsubishi Ralliart Europe	Mitsubishi Lancer Evo 4	1	Risto Mannisenmaki	Retired
58	Sweden	Mitsubishi Ralliart Europe	Mitsubishi Lancer Evo 4	1	Risto Mannisenmaki	1st
59	Safari	Mitsubishi Ralliart Europe	Mitsubishi Lancer Evo 4	1	Risto Mannisenmaki	Retired
60	Portugal	Mitsubishi Ralliart Europe	Mitsubishi Lancer Evo 4	1	Risto Mannisenmaki	Retired
61	Catalunya	Mitsubishi Ralliart Europe	Mitsubishi Lancer Evo 4	1	Risto Mannisenmaki	3rd
62	Corsica	Mitsubishi Ralliart Europe	Mitsubishi Lancer Evo 5	1	Risto Mannisenmaki	Retired
63	Argentina	Mitsubishi Ralliart Europe	Mitsubishi Lancer Evo 5	1	Risto Mannisenmaki	1st
64	Greece	Mitsubishi Ralliart Europe	Mitsubishi Lancer Evo 5	1	Risto Mannisenmaki	Retired
65	New Zealand	Mitsubishi Ralliart Europe	Mitsubishi Lancer Evo 5	1	Risto Mannisenmaki	3rd
66	Finland	Mitsubishi Ralliart Europe	Mitsubishi Lancer Evo 5	1	Risto Mannisenmaki	1st
67	Sanremo	Mitsubishi Ralliart Europe	Mitsubishi Lancer Evo 5	1	Risto Mannisenmaki	1st
68	Australia	Mitsubishi Ralliart Europe	Mitsubishi Lancer Evo 5	1	Risto Mannisenmaki	1st
69	Great Britain	Mitsubishi Ralliart Europe	Mitsubishi Lancer Evo 5	1	Risto Mannisenmaki	Retired
1999	62 points (WORLD CHAMPION)					
70	Monte Carlo	Marlboro Mitsubishi Ralliart	Mitsubishi Lancer Evo 5	1	Risto Mannisenmaki	1st
71	Sweden	Marlboro Mitsubishi Ralliart	Mitsubishi Lancer Evo 5	1	Risto Mannisenmaki	1st
72	Safari	Marlboro Mitsubishi Ralliart	Mitsubishi Lancer Evo 5	1	Risto Mannisenmaki	Retired
73	Portugal	Marlboro Mitsubishi Ralliart	Mitsubishi Lancer Evo 5	1	Risto Mannisenmaki	5th
74	Catalunya	Marlboro Mitsubishi Ralliart	Mitsubishi Lancer Evo 5	1	Risto Mannisenmaki	3rd
75	Corsica	Marlboro Mitsubishi Ralliart	Mitsubishi Lancer Evo 5	1	Risto Mannisenmaki	6th
76	Argentina	Marlboro Mitsubishi Ralliart	Mitsubishi Lancer Evo 5	1	Risto Mannisenmaki	4th
77	Greece	Marlboro Mitsubishi Ralliart	Mitsubishi Lancer Evo 5	1	Risto Mannisenmaki	3rd
78	New Zealand	Marlboro Mitsubishi Ralliart	Mitsubishi Lancer Evo 5	1	Risto Mannisenmaki	1st
79	Finland	Marlboro Mitsubishi Ralliart	Mitsubishi Lancer Evo 5	1	Risto Mannisenmaki	Retired
80	China	Marlboro Mitsubishi Ralliart	Mitsubishi Lancer Evo 5	1	Risto Mannisenmaki	Retired
81	Sanremo	Marlboro Mitsubishi Ralliart	Mitsubishi Lancer Evo 5	1	Risto Mannisenmaki	1st
82	Australia	Marlboro Mitsubishi Ralliart	Mitsubishi Lancer Evo 5	1	Risto Mannisenmaki	3rd
83	Great Britain	Marlboro Mitsubishi Ralliart	Mitsubishi Lancer Evo 5	1	Risto Mannisenmaki	Retired
2000	36 points (5th)					
84	Monte Carlo	Marlboro Mitsubishi Ralliart	Mitsubishi Lancer Evo 6	1	Risto Mannisenmaki	1st
85	Sweden	Marlboro Mitsubishi Ralliart	Mitsubishi Lancer Evo 6	1	Risto Mannisenmaki	2nd
86	Safari	Marlboro Mitsubishi Ralliart	Mitsubishi Lancer Evo 6	1	Risto Mannisenmaki	Retired
87	Portugal	Marlboro Mitsubishi Ralliart	Mitsubishi Lancer Evo 6	1	Risto Mannisenmaki	Retired
88	Catalunya	Marlboro Mitsubishi Ralliart	Mitsubishi Lancer Evo 6	1	Risto Mannisenmaki	4th
89	Argentina	Marlboro Mitsubishi Ralliart	Mitsubishi Lancer Evo 6	1	Risto Mannisenmaki	3rd
90	Greece	Marlboro Mitsubishi Ralliart	Mitsubishi Lancer Evo 6	1	Risto Mannisenmaki	Retired
91	New Zealand	Marlboro Mitsubishi Ralliart	Mitsubishi Lancer Evo 6	1	Risto Mannisenmaki	Retired
92	Finland	Marlboro Mitsubishi Ralliart	Mitsubishi Lancer Evo 6	1	Risto Mannisenmaki	4th
93	Cyprus	Marlboro Mitsubishi Ralliart	Mitsubishi Lancer Evo 6	1	Risto Mannisenmaki	5th
94	Corsica	Marlboro Mitsubishi Ralliart	Mitsubishi Lancer Evo 6	1	Risto Mannisenmaki	Retired
95	Sanremo	Marlboro Mitsubishi Ralliart	Mitsubishi Lancer Evo 6	1	Risto Mannisenmaki	3rd
96	Australia	Marlboro Mitsubishi Ralliart	Mitsubishi Lancer Evo 6	1	Risto Mannisenmaki	Disqualified
97	Great Britain	Marlboro Mitsubishi Ralliart	Mitsubishi Lancer Evo 6	1	Risto Mannisenmaki	3rd
2001	41 points (3rd)					
98	Monte Carlo	Marlboro Mitsubishi Ralliart	Mitsubishi Lancer Evo 6	7	Risto Mannisenmaki	1st
99	Sweden	Marlboro Mitsubishi Ralliart	Mitsubishi Lancer Evo 6	7	Risto Mannisenmaki	Retired
100	Portugal	Marlboro Mitsubishi Ralliart	Mitsubishi Lancer Evo 6	7	Risto Mannisenmaki	1st
101	Catalunya	Marlboro Mitsubishi Ralliart	Mitsubishi Lancer Evo 6	7	Risto Mannisenmaki	3rd
102	Argentina	Marlboro Mitsubishi Ralliart	Mitsubishi Lancer Evo 6	7	Risto Mannisenmaki	4th
103	Cyprus	Marlboro Mitsubishi Ralliart	Mitsubishi Lancer Evo 6	7	Risto Mannisenmaki	Retired
104	Greece	Marlboro Mitsubishi Ralliart	Mitsubishi Lancer Evo 6	7	Risto Mannisenmaki	4th
105	Safari	Marlboro Mitsubishi Ralliart	Mitsubishi Lancer Evo 6	7	Risto Mannisenmaki	1st
106	Finland	Marlboro Mitsubishi Ralliart	Mitsubishi Lancer Evo 6	7	Risto Mannisenmaki	Retired
107	New Zealand	Marlboro Mitsubishi Ralliart	Mitsubishi Lancer Evo 6	7	Risto Mannisenmaki	8th
108	Sanremo	Marlboro Mitsubishi Ralliart	Mitsubishi Lancer Evo WRC	7	Risto Mannisenmaki	Retired
109	Corsica	Marlboro Mitsubishi Ralliart	Mitsubishi Lancer Evo WRC	7	Risto Mannisenmaki	Retired
110	Australia	Marlboro Mitsubishi Ralliart	Mitsubishi Lancer Evo WRC	7	Timo Hantunen	6th
111	Great Britain	Marlboro Mitsubishi Ralliart	Mitsubishi Lancer Evo WRC	7	Kaj Lindstrom	Retired
2002	22 points (8th)					
112	Monte Carlo	Subaru World Rally Team	Subaru Impreza WRC	10	Kaj Lindstrom	1st
113	Sweden	555 Subaru World Rally Team	Subaru Impreza WRC	10	Kaj Lindstrom	Retired
114	Corsica	555 Subaru World Rally Team	Subaru Impreza WRC	10	Kaj Lindstrom	Retired
115	Catalunya	555 Subaru World Rally Team	Subaru Impreza WRC	10	Kaj Lindstrom	Retired
116	Cyprus	555 Subaru World Rally Team	Subaru Impreza WRC	10	Kaj Lindstrom	3rd
117	Argentina	555 Subaru World Rally Team	Subaru Impreza WRC	10	Kaj Lindstrom	Retired
118	Greece	555 Subaru World Rally Team	Subaru Impreza WRC	10	Kaj Lindstrom	Retired
119	Safari	555 Subaru World Rally Team	Subaru Impreza WRC	10	Kaj Lindstrom	Retired
120	Finland	555 Subaru World Rally Team	Subaru Impreza WRC	10	Kaj Lindstrom	6th
121	Germany	555 Subaru World Rally Team	Subaru Impreza WRC	10	Kaj Lindstrom	7th
122	Sanremo	555 Subaru World Rally Team	Subaru Impreza WRC	10	Kaj Lindstrom	Retired
123	New Zealand	555 Subaru World Rally Team	Subaru Impreza WRC	10	Kaj Lindstrom	3rd
124	Australia	555 Subaru World Rally Team	Subaru Impreza WRC	10	Kaj Lindstrom	Excluded
125	Great Britian	555 Subaru World Rally Team	Subaru Impreza WRC	10	Kaj Lindstrom	4th
2003	30 points (8th)					
126	Monte Carlo	555 Subaru World Rally Team	Subaru Impreza WRC	8	Kaj Lindstrom	Retired
127	Sweden	555 Subaru World Rally Team	Subaru Impreza WRC	8	Kaj Lindstrom	2nd
128	Turkey	555 Subaru World Rally Team	Subaru Impreza WRC	8	Kaj Lindstrom	8th
129	New Zealand	555 Subaru World Rally Team	Subaru Impreza WRC	8	Kaj Lindstrom	7th
130	Argentina	555 Subaru World Rally Team	Subaru Impreza WRC	8	Kaj Lindstrom	Retired
131	Greece	555 Subaru World Rally Team	Subaru Impreza WRC	8	Kaj Lindstrom	5th
132	Cyprus	555 Subaru World Rally Team	Subaru Impreza WRC	8	Kaj Lindstrom	Retired
133	Deutschland	555 Subaru World Rally Team	Subaru Impreza WRC	8	Kaj Lindstrom	Retired
134	Finland	555 Subaru World Rally Team	Subaru Impreza WRC	8	Kaj Lindstrom	6th
135	Australia	555 Subaru World Rally Team	Subaru Impreza WRC	8	Kaj Lindstrom	6th
136	Sanremo	555 Subaru World Rally Team	Subaru Impreza WRC	8	Kaj Lindstrom	10th
137	Corsica	555 Subaru World Rally Team	Subaru Impreza WRC	8	Kaj Lindstrom	7th
138	Catalunya	555 Subaru World Rally Team	Subaru Impreza WRC	8	Kaj Lindstrom	8th
139	Great Britain	555 Subaru World Rally Team	Subaru Impreza WRC	8	Kaj Lindstrom	3rd

MÄRTIN, MARKKO

(EE) B: 11 NOVEMBER 1975, TARTU, ESTONIA

"Nowadays the young Estonian does not find many people joking about the cars he drives or the way he drives them"

In Western Europe, a Lada is often the butt of jokes about slow, unreliable cars. However, for Markko Märtin it was his first rally car and nowadays the young Estonian does not find many people joking about the cars he drives or the way he drives them.

His career started in 1993 when he acquired a Lada Samara from his uncle, prepared it himself and competed in the Estonian national championship. In only his second year, he was good enough to win his class and in 1995 ventured over to Finland to drive in the Mantta Rally, a national rally used by the works teams to try out their cars for the 1000 Lakes Rally. To everyone's surprise, the young Estonian finished 12th overall.

A better car was needed and with help from his ex-rally driving father, he bought a Group N Ford Escort Cosworth with which he finished second in his national championship in 1996. He also won his first outright victory when he borrowed an ex-factory Toyota Celica and won a rally in Latvia. He bought his own Celica for 1997 and won the Estonian championship. He also got some backing from the Estonian Oil Service and with the additional funds took the Celica to Finland as well as to rallies in Lithuania and Holland. A Celica GT-4 obtained for the 1998 season burnt out in Portugal but, with support from TTE, he was able to hire a GT-4 from Grifone for Finland where he finished just outside the top 10. He was back in his own car for the RAC Rally and did even better by finishing ninth.

It was now a case of what next ? He hired an Escort WRC for two rallies and shone with it in Sweden before getting back into the Toyota fold with a Corolla WRC prepared by Toyota Team Sweden. He made steady progress with excellent results in Acropolis and Cyprus. He won his first major international rally driving a Subaru on the Azores Rally in 2000 and it was Subaru that gave him his first works drive when they signed him for 2001. For results, it was not the best of years but he gained experience of many of the rallies, like Monte Carlo, that he had not tackled before.

For 2002, Ford took a gamble on this young man and it paid off. He had only one retirement in 12 rallies and by the end of the year had got to grips with the Focus WRC to the point where he could finish a close second on the Rally GB, a result decided only on the final stage.

With Colin McRae and Carlos Sainz leaving Ford, Märtin found himself promoted to team leader and, with the new Focus WRC 03, he proved that he was worthy of the elevation. He looked like a winner in both New Zealand and Argentina but it all finally came good on the Acropolis where he led nearly all the way. His most effective demonstration of his abilities, however, was in Finland where he drove superbly in a long battle with Marcus Grönholm, winning a third of the stages to become only the third non-Scandinavian to win this event.

The World title now looked a possibility but a bizarre exclusion in Australia for allegedly carrying a rock as ballast was a setback. Indifferent luck in San Remo was followed by an accident in Corsica that left Märtin with an injured neck. Despite the pain, he still took third place. Engine failure before the fourth stage of Rally GB ended his season on a low note but there are no doubt better things to come.

Right: Markko Märtin flying high in Australia 2003. It all came to nought with a bizarre exclusion but by now the Estonian was being tipped as a future world champion

MÄRTIN, MARKKO – CAREER RECORD

YEAR	RALLY	TEAM/ENTRANT	CAR	NO.	CO-DRIVER	RESULT
1997	0 points					
1	Finland		Toyota Celica Turbo 4WD	53	Toomas Kitsing	Retired
1998	0 points					
2	Portugal		Toyota Celica GT-4	41	Toomas Kitsing	Retired
3	Finland	H.F Grifone	Toyota Celica GT-4	19	Toomas Kitsing	12th
4	Sanremo	E.O.S Team Toyota	Toyota Celica GT-4	46	Toomas Kitsing	Retired
5	Great Britain		Toyota Celica GT-4	33	Toomas Kitsing	9th
1999	2 points (18th)					
6	Sweden		Ford Escort WRC	36	Toomas Kitsing	8th
7	Portugal		Ford Escort WRC	17	Toomas Kitsing	Retired
8	Greece		Toyota Corolla WRC	23	Toomas Kitsing	5th
9	Finland		Toyota Corolla WRC	18	Toomas Kitsing	Retired
10	Sanremo		Toyota Corolla WRC	22	Toomas Kitsing	Retired
11	Great Britain		Toyota Corolla WRC	17	Toomas Kitsing	8th
2000	1 point (21st)					
12	Sweden	Lukoil-E.O.S Rally	Toyota Corolla WRC	18	Michael Park	9th
13	Portugal	Lukoil-E.O.S Rally	Toyota Corolla WRC	25	Michael Park	7th
14	Catalunya	Lukoil-E.O.S Rally	Toyota Corolla WRC	23	Michael Park	10th
15	Greece	Lukoil-E.O.S Rally	Toyota Corolla WRC	17	Michael Park	Retired
16	Finland	Lukoil-E.O.S Rally	Toyota Corolla WRC	20	Michael Park	10th
17	Cyprus	Lukoil-E.O.S Rally	Toyota Corolla WRC	17	Michael Park	6th
18	Sanremo	Lukoil-E.O.S Rally	Toyota Corolla WRC	30	Michael Park	Retired
19	Australia	Lukoil-E.O.S Rally	Toyota Corolla WRC	18	Michael Park	Retired
20	Great Britain	Lukoil-E.O.S Rally	Toyota Corolla WRC	21	Michael Park	7th
2001	3 points (19th)					
21	Monte Carlo	Subaru World Rally Team	Subaru Impreza WRC	6	Michael Park	Retired
22	Sweden	Subaru World Rally Team	Subaru Impreza WRC	18	Michael Park	12th
23	Portugal	Subaru World Rally Team	Subaru Impreza WRC	18	Michael Park	Retired
24	Catalunya	Subaru World Rally Team	Subaru Impreza WRC	18	Michael Park	Retired
25	Greece	Subaru World Rally Team	Subaru Impreza WRC	18	Michael Park	Retired
26	Finland	Subaru World Rally Team	Subaru Impreza WRC	18	Michael Park	5th
27	Sanremo	Subaru World Rally Team	Subaru Impreza WRC	18	Michael Park	Retired
28	Corsica	Subaru World Rally Team	Subaru Impreza WRC	18	Michael Park	6th
29	Great Britain	Subaru World Rally Team	Subaru Impreza WRC	18	Michael Park	Retired
2002	20 points (9th)					
30	Monte Carlo	Ford Motor Company	Ford Focus WRC	6	Michael Park	12th
31	Corsica	Ford Motor Company	Ford Focus WRC	6	Michael Park	8th
32	Catalunya	Ford Motor Company	Ford Focus WRC	6	Michael Park	8th
33	Cyprus	Ford Motor Company	Ford Focus WRC	6	Michael Park	8th
34	Argentina	Ford Motor Company	Ford Focus WRC	6	Michael Park	4th
35	Greece	Ford Motor Company	Ford Focus WRC	6	Michael Park	6th
36	Safari	Ford Motor Company	Ford Focus WRC	6	Michael Park	4th
37	Finland	Ford Motor Company	Ford Focus WRC	6	Michael Park	5th
38	Germany	Ford Motor Company	Ford Focus WRC	6	Michael Park	6th
39	Sanremo	Ford Motor Company	Ford Focus WRC	6	Michael Park	5th
40	New Zealand	Ford Motor Company	Ford Focus WRC	6	Michael Park	Retired
41	Australia	Ford Motor Company	Ford Focus WRC	6	Michael Park	5th
42	Great Britain	Ford Motor Company	Ford Focus WRC	6	Michael Park	2nd
2003	49 points (5th)					
43	Monte Carlo	Ford Motor Company	Ford Focus WRC	4	Michael Park	4th
44	Sweden	Ford Motor Company	Ford Focus WRC	4	Michael Park	4th
45	Turkey	Ford Motor Company	Ford Focus WRC	4	Michael Park	6th
46	New Zealand	Ford Motor Company	Ford Focus WRC	4	Michael Park	Retired
47	Argentina	Ford Motor Company	Ford Focus WRC	4	Michael Park	Retired
48	**Greece**	**Ford Motor Company**	**Ford Focus WRC**	**4**	**Michael Park**	**1st**
49	Cyprus	Ford Motor Company	Ford Focus WRC	4	Michael Park	Retired
50	Germany	Ford Motor Company	Ford Focus WRC	4	Michael Park	5th
51	**Finland**	**Ford Motor Company**	**Ford Focus WRC**	**4**	**Michael Park**	**1st**
52	Australia	Ford Motor Company	Ford Focus WRC	4	Michael Park	Disqualified
53	Sanremo	Ford Motor Company	Ford Focus WRC	4	Michael Park	3rd
54	Corsica	Ford Motor Company	Ford Focus WRC	4	Michael Park	Retired
55	Catalunya	Ford Motor Company	Ford Focus WRC	4	Michael Park	3rd
56	Great Britain	Ford Motor Company	Ford Focus WRC	4	Michael Park	Retired

McRae, Colin (GB) b: 5 August 1968, Lanark, Scotland

In his early days, it seemed as if Colin McRae believed that finishing rallies with cars that looked decidedly second-hand was the recipe for success. It is to his credit that in 1995 he overcame this reputation to become Britain's first World Rally Champion.

"McRae became Britain's first World Rally Champion"

Long before his father Jimmy took up rallying, Colin McRae was into all things mechanical. At 10, he got his first motor bike and was soon collecting national championships in trials and scrambling. His first car was a Mini in which he won the 1985 West Scotland Autotest Championship. He was still 16 but the instant his driving licence was available, he did his first rallies in a borrowed Talbot Avenger.

For 1986, he bought a Talbot Sunbeam Ti and went after the Scottish Championship. On the Scottish Rally itself, he was fast enough to lead Group A before retiring with broken suspension. He drove a Vauxhall Nova for two seasons, twice won his class on the British Championship, and got the backing of the British Junior Team for two WRC events. Towards the end of 1988, he drove a Group N Sierra Cosworth RS and finished the year runner up to Pentti Airikkala for the Group N title.

The following year, he drove a two-wheel drive Group A Sierra Cosworth and was second in the British Championship. On the RAC Rally, where he drove a new Sierra Cosworth 4x4, McRae was a sensation. He finished sixth among the Lancia and Toyotas and well clear of the Ford works cars but with the Sierra looking like a stylist's nightmare, one rear door held on by tape and another closed only with a bolt from a garden shed. For 1991, he signed a deal with Prodrive that was to last eight years. McRae ran in the British Championship with a Subaru Legacy and won in both 1991 and 1992. In that second year, the team took him abroad on some WRC outings, the most memorable of which was his Finnish debut. He had three major accidents, any one of which should have caused retirement, but McRae was determined to finish. The car was so badly knocked about that the organisers had to be persuaded to let it continue, but they did and he was eighth.

Now in the full Subaru WRC team, McRae finally netted his first win in New Zealand and won there again before finally adding the RAC Rally to his CV. The 1995 season started badly with retirements in Monte Carlo and Sweden but he clinched the title with a second RAC win after reluctantly yielding to Carlos Sainz in Catalunya. In 1997, McRae fought back to win the RAC Rally after dropping to eighth with a loose wheel and only lost the championship by a single point.

He left Subaru to Ford – and a very much enhanced salary – at the end of 1998. He won Safari and Portugal but the Focus WRC was a bit too new to grab a title. In 2001, he had his best year with it winning three rallies mid-season and finishing second in the title race. Unsure whether he had a place with Ford for 2003 because of financial cutbacks, he moved to Citroën to drive the Xsara WRC. His debut event, Monte Carlo was the best result. At the end of 2003, the FIA announced that only two drivers would need to be registered by each team and McRae found himself without a works drive for the first time in 14 years. He promptly signed to do the 2004 Paris-Dakar with Nissan.

Right: Victory on the 1996 Acropolis made up for the frustration of being excluded on his previous visit (in 1994) after event officials failed to secure the car's bonnet and then refused to let him have extra time allowance to rectify the damage caused

McRAE, COLIN – CAREER RECORD

YEAR	RALLY	TEAM /ENTRANT	CAR	NO.	CO-DRIVER	RESULT
1987	**0 points**					
1	Sweden	British Junior Rally Team	Vauxhall Nova	107	Mike Broad	36th
2	Great Britain	British Junior Rally Team	Vauxhall Nova	85	Derek Ringer	Retired
1988	**0 points**					
3	Great Britain	Peugeot Talbot Sport	Peugeot 205 GTI	111	Derek Ringer	Retired
1989	**8 points (34th)**					
4	Sweden	Mike Little Preparations	Ford Sierra XR 4x4	55	Derek Ringer	15th
5	New Zealand	Gary Smith Motorsport	Ford Sierra RS Cosworth	19	Derek Ringer	5th
6	Great Britain	R.E.D	Ford Sierra RS Cosworth	27	Derek Ringer	Retired
1990	**6 points (34th)**					
7	Great Britain	Shell UK Oil	Ford Sierra Cosworth 4x4	27	Derek Ringer	6th
1991	**0 points**					
8	Great Britain	Subaru Rally Team Europe	Subaru Legacy RS	21	Derek Ringer	Retired
1992	**34 points (8th)**					
9	Sweden	Subaru Rally Team Europe	Subaru Legacy RS	7	Derek Ringer	2nd
10	Greece	Subaru Rally Team Europe	Subaru Legacy RS	9	Derek Ringer	4th
11	New Zealand	Subaru Rally Team Europe	Subaru Legacy RS	4	Derek Ringer	Retired
12	Finland	Subaru Rally Team Europe	Subaru Legacy RS	9	Derek Ringer	8th
13	Great Britain	Subaru Rally Team Europe	Subaru Legacy RS	4	Derek Ringer	6th
1993	**50 points (5th)**					
14	Sweden	555 Subaru World Rally Team	Subaru Legacy RS	2	Derek Ringer	3rd
15	Portugal	555 Subaru World Rally Team	Subaru Legacy RS	4	Derek Ringer	7th
16	Safari	Subaru Motor Sports Group/N.Koseki	Subaru Vivio Sedan	6	Derek Ringer	Retired
17	Corsica	555 Subaru World Rally Team	Subaru Legacy RS	8	Derek Ringer	5th
18	Greece	555 Subaru World Rally Team	Subaru Legacy RS	5	Derek Ringer	Retired
19	**New Zealand**	**555 Subaru World Rally Team**	**Subaru Legacy RS**	**7**	**Derek Ringer**	**1st**
20	Australia	555 Subaru World Rally Team	Subaru Legacy RS	7	Derek Ringer	6th
21	Great Britain	555 Subaru World Rally Team	Subaru Legacy RS	2	Derek Ringer	Retired
1994	**49 points (4th)**					
22	Monte Carlo	555 Subaru World Rally Team	Subaru Impreza 555	7	Derek Ringer	10th
23	Portugal	555 Subaru World Rally Team	Subaru Impreza 555	5	Derek Ringer	Retired
24	Corsica	555 Subaru World Rally Team	Subaru Impreza 555	7	Derek Ringer	Retired
25	Greece	555 Subaru World Rally Team	Subaru Impreza 555	7	Derek Ringer	Excluded
26	Argentina	555 Subaru World Rally Team	Subaru Impreza 555	6	Derek Ringer	Retired
27	**New Zealand**	**555 Subaru World Rally Team**	**Subaru Impreza 555**	**2**	**Derek Ringer**	**1st**
28	Sanremo	555 Subaru World Rally Team	Subaru Impreza 555	4	Derek Ringer	5th
29	**Great Britain**	**555 Subaru World Rally Team**	**Subaru Impreza 555**	**4**	**Derek Ringer**	**1st**
1995	**90 points (WORLD CHAMPION)**					
30	Monte Carlo	555 Subaru World Rally Team	Subaru Impreza 555	4	Derek Ringer	Retired
31	Sweden	555 Subaru World Rally Team	Subaru Impreza 555	4	Derek Ringer	Retired
32	Portugal	555 Subaru World Rally Team	Subaru Impreza 555	4	Derek Ringer	3rd
33	Corsica	555 Subaru World Rally Team	Subaru Impreza 555	4	Derek Ringer	5th
34	**New Zealand**	**555 Subaru World Rally Team**	**Subaru Impreza 555**	**4**	**Derek Ringer**	**1st**
35	Australia	555 Subaru World Rally Team	Subaru Impreza 555	4	Derek Ringer	2nd
36	Catalunya	555 Subaru World Rally Team	Subaru Impreza 555	4	Derek Ringer	2nd
37	**Great Britain**	**555 Subaru World Rally Team**	**Subaru Impreza 555**	**4**	**Derek Ringer**	**1st**
1996	**92 points (2nd)**					
38	Sweden	555 Subaru World Rally Team	Subaru Impreza 555	1	Derek Ringer	3rd
39	Safari	555 Subaru World Rally Team	Subaru Impreza 555	1	Derek Ringer	4th
40	Indonesia	555 Subaru World Rally Team	Subaru Impreza 555	1	Derek Ringer	Retired
41	**Greece**	**555 Subaru World Rally Team**	**Subaru Impreza 555**	**1**	**Derek Ringer**	**1st**
42	Argentina	555 Subaru World Rally Team	Subaru Impreza 555	1	Derek Ringer	Retired
43	Finland	555 Subaru World Rally Team	Subaru Impreza 555	1	Derek Ringer	Retired
44	Australia	555 Subaru World Rally Team	Subaru Impreza 555	1	Derek Ringer	4th
45	**Sanremo**	**555 Subaru World Rally Team**	**Subaru Impreza 555**	**1**	**Derek Ringer**	**1st**
46	**Catalunya**	**555 Subaru World Rally Team**	**Subaru Impreza 555**	**1**	**Derek Ringer**	**1st**

MCRAE, COLIN CAREER RECORD

YEAR	RALLY	TEAM / ENTRANT	CAR	NO.	CO-DRIVER	RESULT
1997	**62 points (2nd)**					
47	Monte Carlo	555 Subaru World Rally Team	Subaru Impreza WRC	3	Nicky Grist	Retired
48	Sweden	555 Subaru World Rally Team	Subaru Impreza WRC	3	Nicky Grist	4th
49	**Safari**	**555 Subaru World Rally Team**	**Subaru Impreza WRC**	**3**	**Nicky Grist**	**1st**
50	Portugal	555 Subaru World Rally Team	Subaru Impreza WRC	3	Nicky Grist	Retired
51	Catalunya	555 Subaru World Rally Team	Subaru Impreza WRC	3	Nicky Grist	4th
52	**Corsica**	**555 Subaru World Rally Team**	**Subaru Impreza WRC**	**3**	**Nicky Grist**	**1st**
53	Argentina	555 Subaru World Rally Team	Subaru Impreza WRC	3	Nicky Grist	2nd
54	Greece	555 Subaru World Rally Team	Subaru Impreza WRC	3	Nicky Grist	Retired
55	New Zealand	555 Subaru World Rally Team	Subaru Impreza WRC	3	Nicky Grist	Retired
56	Finland	555 Subaru World Rally Team	Subaru Impreza WRC	3	Nicky Grist	Retired
57	Indonesia	555 Subaru World Rally Team	Subaru Impreza WRC	3	Nicky Grist	Retired
58	**Sanremo**	**555 Subaru World Rally Team**	**Subaru Impreza WRC**	**3**	**Nicky Grist**	**1st**
59	**Australia**	**555 Subaru World Rally Team**	**Subaru Impreza WRC**	**3**	**Nicky Grist**	**1st**
60	**Great Britain**	**555 Subaru World Rally Team**	**Subaru Impreza WRC**	**3**	**Nicky Grist**	**1st**
1998	**45 points (3rd)**					
61	Monte Carlo	555 Subaru World Rally Team	Subaru Impreza WRC	3	Nicky Grist	3rd
62	Sweden	555 Subaru World Rally Team	Subaru Impreza WRC	3	Nicky Grist	Retired
63	Safari	555 Subaru World Rally Team	Subaru Impreza WRC	3	Nicky Grist	Retired
64	**Portugal**	**555 Subaru World Rally Team**	**Subaru Impreza WRC**	**3**	**Nicky Grist**	**1st**
65	Catalunya	555 Subaru World Rally Team	Subaru Impreza WRC	3	Nicky Grist	Retired
66	**Corsica**	**555 Subaru World Rally Team**	**Subaru Impreza WRC**	**3**	**Nicky Grist**	**1st**
67	Argentina	555 Subaru World Rally Team	Subaru Impreza WRC	3	Nicky Grist	5th
68	**Greece**	**555 Subaru World Rally Team**	**Subaru Impreza WRC**	**3**	**Nicky Grist**	**1st**
69	New Zealand	555 Subaru World Rally Team	Subaru Impreza WRC	3	Nicky Grist	5th
70	Finland	555 Subaru World Rally Team	Subaru Impreza WRC	3	Nicky Grist	Retired
71	Sanremo	555 Subaru World Rally Team	Subaru Impreza WRC	3	Nicky Grist	3rd
72	Australia	555 Subaru World Rally Team	Subaru Impreza WRC	3	Nicky Grist	4th
73	Great Britain	555 Subaru World Rally Team	Subaru Impreza WRC	3	Nicky Grist	Retired
1999	**23 points (6th)**					
74	Monte Carlo	Ford Motor Company	Ford Focus WRC	7	Nicky Grist	Excluded
75	Sweden	Ford Motor Company	Ford Focus WRC	7	Nicky Grist	Retired
76	**Safari**	**Ford Motor Company**	**Ford Focus WRC**	**7**	**Nicky Grist**	**1st**
77	**Portugal**	**Ford Motor Company**	**Ford Focus WRC**	**7**	**Nicky Grist**	**1st**
78	Catalunya	Ford Motor Company	Ford Focus WRC	7	Nicky Grist	Retired
79	Corsica	Ford Motor Company	Ford Focus WRC	7	Nicky Grist	4th
80	Argentina	Ford Motor Company	Ford Focus WRC	7	Nicky Grist	Retired
81	Greece	Ford Motor Company	Ford Focus WRC	7	Nicky Grist	Retired
82	New Zealand	Ford Motor Company	Ford Focus WRC	7	Nicky Grist	Retired
83	Finland	Ford Motor Company	Ford Focus WRC	7	Nicky Grist	Retired
84	China	Ford Motor Company	Ford Focus WRC	7	Nicky Grist	Retired
85	Sanremo	Ford Motor Company	Ford Focus WRC	7	Nicky Grist	Retired
86	Australia	Ford Motor Company	Ford Focus WRC	7	Nicky Grist	Retired
87	Great Britain	Ford Motor Company	Ford Focus WRC	7	Nicky Grist	Retired
2000	**43 points (4th)**					
88	Monte Carlo	Ford Motor Company	Ford Focus WRC	5	Nicky Grist	Retired
89	Sweden	Ford Motor Company	Ford Focus WRC	5	Nicky Grist	3rd
90	Safari	Ford Motor Company	Ford Focus WRC	5	Nicky Grist	Retired
91	Portugal	Ford Motor Company	Ford Focus WRC	5	Nicky Grist	Retired
92	**Catalunya**	**Ford Motor Company**	**Ford Focus WRC**	**5**	**Nicky Grist**	**1st**
93	Argentina	Ford Motor Company	Ford Focus WRC	5	Nicky Grist	Retired
94	**Greece**	**Ford Motor Company**	**Ford Focus WRC**	**5**	**Nicky Grist**	**1st**
95	New Zealand	Ford Motor Company	Ford Focus WRC	5	Nicky Grist	2nd
96	Finland	Ford Motor Company	Ford Focus WRC	5	Nicky Grist	2nd
97	Cyprus	Ford Motor Company	Ford Focus WRC	5	Nicky Grist	2nd

MEHTA, SHEKHAR (EAK) B: 20 JUNE 1945, KAMPALA, EAST AFRICA

For most drivers, winning the Safari Rally once is a lifetime achievement. Shekhar Mehta won it five times and did enough on other events around the world to demonstrate that it was no narrow speciality.

The Mehta family imported BMWs into Uganda and it was in a BMW 1800 that he launched his motor sport career in 1966. He followed it with a year driving a Renault 16 and then chose a Peugeot 204. His Safari debut was on the 1968 event when only seven cars finished and the Peugeot was not one of them. He bought a second-hand Datsun 1600 SSS for 1970 that broke down but not before Mehta had driven well enough to come to the attention of Datsun. When their first choice, Joginder Singh, decided to drive Ford in 1971, Mehta got the offer of a works 240Z and he finished second.

In 1973, it all came good when he finished dead level on points with Harry Källström. The decision went to Mehta on a tiebreak and suddenly he was a wanted man. Datsun ran him in three WRC events but the 240Z was ageing so when Lancia offered him a deal for 1974, he jumped at the chance. He got a Fulvia home on Safari just outside the top 10 and notched up an excellent result on his first attempt at the San Remo. He drifted back to Datsun and their new 160J that was a turning point for both Mehta and Datsun. The five Safari wins followed as did excellent results on gravel rallies in Greece, Argentina and other parts of Africa.

A deal to drive the Peugeot 205 T16 was done for the 1986 Safari and his was one of the two Peugeots to finish. When Group B was stopped at the end of the year, Peugeot and Mehta went off to do Rally Raids, a move that ended in hospital after an accident in Egypt that ended his career. He is now President of the FIA Rallies Commission.

MEHTA, SHEKHAR – CAREER RECORD

YEAR	RALLY	TEAM/ENTRANT	CAR	NO.	CO-DRIVER	RESULT
1973						
1	**Safari**	**Nissan Motor Company**	**Datsun 240Z**	**1**	**Lofty Drews**	**1st**
2	Morocco		Datsun 240Z	5	Geraint Phillips	Retired
3	Finland		Datsun 240Z	6	Ensio Mikander	Retired
4	Great Britain		Datsun Sunny	27	Keith Wood	37th
1974						
5	Safari	Lancia Marlboro	Lancia Fulvia	7	Mike Doughty	11th
6	Sanremo		Lancia Beta Coupe	14	Martin Holmes	4th
1975						
7	Safari	Lancia Alitalia	Lancia Beta Coupe	2	Mike Doughty	Retired
8	Morocco		Datsun Violet	5	Bob Bean	6th
9	Portugal		Datsun Violet	7	Yvonne Pratt	7th
1976						
10	Safari	D.T. Dobie & Co. Ltd.	Datsun Violet	5	Mike Doughty	Retired
11	Greece		Datsun Violet	5	Henry Liddon	3rd
1977						
12	Safari	D.T. Dobie & Co. Ltd.	Datsun Violet	5	Mike Doughty	Retired
1978						
13	Safari	D.T. Dobie & Co. Ltd.	Datsun 160J	11	Mike Doughty	Retired
14	Greece		Datsun 160J	12	Yvonne Mehta	3rd
15	Ivory Coast		Opel Ascona	6	Mike Doughty	Retired
1979	20 points (10th)					
16	**Safari**	**D.T. Dobie & Co. Ltd.**	**Datsun 160J**	**9**	**Mike Doughty**	**1st**
1980	30 points (9th)					
17	**Safari**	**D.T. Dobie & Co. Ltd.**	**Datsun 160J**	**1**	**Mike Doughty**	**1st**
18	Greece	Opel Euro Händler	Opel Ascona	9	Yvonne Mehta	Retired
19	Ivory Coast	Comafrique	Datsun 160J	3	Mike Doughty	Retired
1981	55 points (5th)					
20	**Safari**	**D.T. Dobie & Co. Ltd.**	**Datsun Violet GT**	**7**	**Mike Doughty**	**1st**
21	Greece	Team Datsun Europe	Datsun 160J	10	Yvonne Mehta	5th
22	Argentina	Team Datsun Europe	Datsun Violet GT	1	Yvonne Mehta	2nd
23	Brazil	Team Datsun Europe	Datsun Violet GT	3	Yvonne Mehta	Retired
24	Ivory Coast	Comafrique	Datsun Violet GT	6	Mike Doughty	3rd
1982	30 points (8th)					
25	**Safari**	**D.T. Dobie & Co. Ltd.**	**Nissan Violet GT**	**1**	**Mike Doughty**	**1st**
26	Greece	Nissan Motorsports Europe	Nissan Violet GT	12	Yvonne Mehta	4th
27	New Zealand	Dealer Team Nissan	Nissan Violet GT	6	Yvonne Mehta	Retired
28	Brazil	Nissan Motorsports Europe	Nissan Violet GTS	4	Yvonne Mehta	Retired
1983	26 points (9th)					
29	Safari	D.T. Dobie & Co. Ltd.	Nissan 240RS	4	Rob Combes	Retired
30	Greece	N.I Theocharakis	Nissan 240RS	10	Yvonne Mehta	6th
31	New Zealand	Dealer Team Nissan	Nissan 240RS	6	Yvonne Mehta	4th
32	Argentina	Audi Sport	Audi Quattro A2	3	Yvonne Mehta	4th
1984	27 points (9th)					
33	Monte Carlo		Subaru Leone 1800	11	Yvonne Mehta	14th
34	Safari	D.T. Dobie & Co. Ltd.	Nissan 240RS	2	Rob Combes	5th
35	Greece	N.I Theocharakis	Nissan 240RS	8	Yvonne Mehta	7th
36	Ivory Coast		Nissan 240RS	2	Rob Combes	3rd
37	Great Britain	Team Nissan Europe	Nissan 240RS	10	Yvonne Mehta	8th
1985	20 points (14th)					
38	Safari	D.T. Dobie & Co. Ltd.	Nissan 240RS	4	Rob Combes	Retired
39	Greece	N.I Theocharakis	Nissan 240RS	4	Yvonne Mehta	4th
40	New Zealand	Nissan New Zealand	Nissan 240RS	6	Yvonne Mehta	Retired
41	Argentina		Nissan 240RS	2	Yvonne Mehta	4th
1986	3 points (49th)					
42	Safari	Peugeot Talbot Sport	Peugeot 205 T16	6	Rob Combes	8th
1987	18 points (18th)					
43	Safari	Nissan Motorsports International	Nissan 200SX	12	Rob Combes	Retired
44	Greece	Nissan Motorsports International	Nissan 200SX	11	Yvonne Mehta	Retired
45	United States	Nissan Motorsports International	Nissan 200SX	9	Yvonne Mehta	8th
46	Ivory Coast	Nissan Motorsports International	Nissan 200SX	10	Rob Combes	2nd

MIKKOLA, HANNU (FIN) B: 24 MAY 1942, JOENSUU, FINLAND

"Mikkola bought himself a Volvo PV444 and went rallying"

In 1963, Hannu Mikkola bought himself a Volvo PV444 and went rallying. In the best tradition, he did not tell his father until he had something to show him, which was after the first event in which he finished fourth overall. By 1966, he and the old Volvo were second in the Finnish Rally Championship. The Volvo importer gave him a works 122S for Finland and Lancia invited him to Monte Carlo in 1967 to drive a Fulvia Coupe where Mikkola was lying sixth before a spectator stole his time card on the last night.

Datsun signed him to drive their Fairlady sports car on the 1968 Monte Carlo where he was ninth overall and he drove for them again on the Tulip and Acropolis rallies. Just before the latter, he drove a Lancia in Austria and nearly beat the factory Ford Escort TC. So impressed were Ford that they gave him an Escort for the 1000 Lakes, which he promptly won. He also netted the Finnish championship that year.

Such a hot property could not be allowed to freelance and Ford signed him for 1969. It was not one of Ford's best years, nor his, despite winning 1000 Lakes again. It was 1970 when he leapt to fame by winning the London-Mexico for Ford and nailing his hat-trick on the 1000 Lakes. The following year, he led the East African Safari in a Escort TC but it was his return and victory on that event the following year - the first for a European driver - that set him on course for stardom.

But Ford still did not offer him a full programme so Mikkola started to add drives elsewhere. He developed a nice sideline in driving Peugeot 504s on African rallies. He won the 1000 Lakes for a fourth time for Ford in 1974 but had no contract for 1975. He promptly joined Fiat and had his best result on Monte Carlo. Winning the 1000 Lakes for the fifth time, in a 1600cc Toyota Corolla, was an outstanding result and thus, in 1976, drives in Celicas were added to his Peugeot obligations.

A change of management at Ford for 1978 saw Mikkola returning. The Ford programme did not cover all events and again, Mikkola found a second employer. This time it was the emergent Mercedes team. As the new decade started, things looked good since both Ford and Mercedes offered him ongoing contracts and both had projects for new rally cars to suit Group B regulations.

Out of the blue came a phone call asking him to try a new 4WD car from Audi. A drive in the prototype Quattro convinced him and the rest is history. He was a sensation on the 1981 Monte Carlo until gremlins intervened but he was soon winning. However, the points never seemed to add up and, though Audi won the manufacturer's title in 1982, it was not until 1983 that Mikkola finally managed to collect the drivers' title.

From being the leader, Audi was overtaken by Peugeot and Lancia. Mikkola won one more WRC event and then the Group B cars disappeared at the end of 1986. Mikkola stayed with Audi for the first Group A year but then went racing. For four years,

Mikkola drove for Mazda but the car was never a match for his talents His final serious appearances were one-offs for Subaru and Toyota in 1993.

Right: By 1981 the four-wheel drive revolution in rallying was a year old and Mikkola rounded off the season with victory on the RAC Rally

MIKKOLA, HANNU – CAREER RECORD

YEAR	RALLY	TEAM/ENTRANT	CAR	NO.	CO-DRIVER	RESULT
1973						
1	Monte Carlo	Ford Motor Company	Ford Escort RS1600	20	Jim Porter	4th
2	Safari	Ford Motor Company	Ford Escort RS1600	4	John Davenport	Retired
3	Morocco		Peugeot 504	10	Atso Aho	Retired
4	Finland		Volvo 142	5	Erkki Rautanen	Retired
5	Great Britain	Ford Motor Company	Ford Escort RS1600	6	John Davenport	Retired
1974						
6	Safari	Marshalls (EA) Ltd.	Peugeot 504	1	Jean Todt	Retired
7	**Finland**		**Ford Escort RS1600**	**6**	**John Davenport**	**1st**
8	Great Britain	Ford Motor Company	Ford Escort RS1600	10	John Davenport	Retired
1975						
9	Monte Carlo		Fiat 131 Abarth	2	Jean Todt	2nd
10	Sweden		Fiat 131 Abarth	3	Jean Todt	Retired
11	Safari	Marshalls (EA) Ltd.	Peugeot 504	12	Jean Todt	Retired
12	**Morocco**		**Peugeot 504**	**6**	**Jean Todt**	**1st**
13	Portugal		Fiat 124 Abarth	1	Jean Todt	2nd
14	**Finland**	**Toyota Team Europe**	**Toyota Corolla**	**1**	**Atso Aho**	**1st**
15	Great Britain	Toyota GB Ltd	Toyota Celica	10	Jean Todt	Retired
1976						
16	Monte Carlo		Opel Kadett GT/E	3	Claes Billstam	Retired
17	Portugal		Toyota Corolla	5	Jean Todt	Retired
18	Safari	Marshalls (EA) Ltd.	Peugeot 504 Coupe	4	Jean Todt	Retired
19	Greece		Toyota Corolla	6	Jean Todt	Retired
20	Morocco		Peugeot 504 Coupe	2	Jean Todt	Retired
21	Finland		Toyota Celica	1	Atso Aho	3rd
22	Corsica		Peugeot 104 ZS	7	Jean Todt	10th
23	Great Britain	Team Toyota	Toyota Celica	5	Jean Todt	Retired
1977						
24	Sweden		Toyota Corolla	3	Arne Hertz	Retired
25	Portugal		Toyota Celica	7	Arne Hertz	Retired
26	Safari	Marshalls (EA) Ltd.	Peugeot 504	12	Arne Hertz	Retired
27	Greece		Toyota Celica	8	Arne Hertz	Retired
28	Finland		Toyota Celica	7	Arne Hertz	Retired
29	Great Britain		Toyota Celica	8	Arne Hertz	2nd
1978						
30	Sweden		Ford Escort RS	5	Arne Hertz	2nd
31	Portugal		Ford Escort RS	8	Arne Hertz	2nd
32	Finland		Ford Escort RS	4	Arne Hertz	Retired
33	**Great Britain**	**Eaton Yale**	**Ford Escort RS**	**4**	**Arne Hertz**	**1st**
1979	111 points (2nd)					
34	Monte Carlo	Ford Motor Company	Ford Escort RS1800	5	Arne Hertz	5th
35	Sweden	Ford Motor Company	Ford Escort RS1800	5	Arne Hertz	5th
36	**Portugal**	**Ford Motor Company**	**Ford Escort RS1800**	**1**	**Arne Hertz**	**1st**
37	Safari	D.T. Dobie & Co. Ltd./Daimler-Benz	Mercedes-Benz 450SLC	14	Arne Hertz	2nd
38	Greece	Ford Motor Company	Ford Escort RS1800	4	Arne Hertz	Retired
39	**New Zealand**	**Ford Motor Company**	**Ford Escort RS1800**	**1**	**Arne Hertz**	**1st**
40	Finland	Ford Motor Company	Ford Escort RS1800	2	Arne Hertz	Retired
41	**Great Britain**	**Ford Motor Company**	**Ford Escort RS1800**	**1**	**Arne Hertz**	**1st**
42	**Ivory Coast**	**SEACI**	**Mercedes-Benz 450SLC**	**6**	**Arne Hertz**	**1st**
1980	64 points (2nd)					
43	Monte Carlo	Esso	Porsche 911SC	2	Arne Hertz	Retired
44	Sweden	Privateer	Ford Escort RS	2	Arne Hertz	4th
45	Portugal	Rothmans Rally Team	Ford Escort RS	1	Arne Hertz	Retired
46	Safari	D.T. Dobie & Co. Ltd./Daimler-Benz	Mercedes-Benz 450SLC	7	Arne Hertz	Retired
47	Greece	Rothmans Rally Team	Ford Escort RS	5	Arne Hertz	Retired
48	Argentina	Daimler-Benz	Mercedes-Benz 500SLC	3	Arne Hertz	2nd
49	Finland	Toyota Team Europe	Toyota Celica 2000GT	2	Arne Hertz	Retired
50	New Zealand	Cable-Price Corporation	Mercedes-Benz 500SLC	3	Arne Hertz	3rd

MIKKOLA, HANNU CAREER RECORD (CONT'D)

YEAR	RALLY	TEAM/ENTRANT	CAR	NO.	CO-DRIVER	RESULT
51	Sanremo	Rothmans Rally Team	Ford Escort RS	8	Arne Hertz	3rd
52	Great Britain	Eaton Yale	Ford Escort RS	1	Arne Hertz	2nd
53	Ivory Coast	SEACI	Mercedes-Benz 500SLC	4	Arne Hertz	Retired
1981	62 points (3rd)					
54	Monte Carlo	Audi Sport	Audi Quattro	5	Arne Hertz	Retired
55	**Sweden**	**Audi Sport**	**Audi Quattro**	**2**	**Arne Hertz**	**1st**
56	Portugal	Audi Sport	Audi Quattro	2	Arne Hertz	Retired
57	Corsica	Audi Sport	Audi Quattro	3	Arne Hertz	Retired
58	Greece	Audi Sport	Audi Quattro	8	Arne Hertz	Retired
59	Finland	Audi Sport	Audi Quattro	3	Arne Hertz	3rd
60	Sanremo	Audi Sport	Audi Quattro	5	Arne Hertz	4th
61	**Great Britain**	**Audi Sport**	**Audi Quattro**	**5**	**Arne Hertz**	**1st**
1982	70 points (3rd)					
62	Monte Carlo	Audi Sport	Audi Quattro	1	Arne Hertz	2nd
63	Sweden	Audi Sport	Audi Quattro	1	Arne Hertz	16th
64	Portugal	Audi Sport	Audi Quattro	2	Arne Hertz	Retired
65	Corsica	Audi Sport	Audi Quattro	8	Arne Hertz	Retired
66	Greece	Audi Sport	Audi Quattro	3	Arne Hertz	Retired
67	New Zealand	Audi Sport	Audi Quattro	3	Arne Hertz	Retired
68	Brazil	Audi Sport	Audi Quattro	1	Arne Hertz	Retired
69	**Finland**	**Audi Sport**	**Audi Quattro**	**3**	**Arne Hertz**	**1st**
70	Sanremo	Audi Sport	Audi Quattro	4	Arne Hertz	2nd
71	Ivory Coast	Audi Sport	Audi Quattro	5	Roland Gumpert	Retired
72	**Great Britain**	**Audi Sport**	**Audi Quattro**	**1**	**Arne Hertz**	**1st**
1983	125 points (WORLD CHAMPION)					
73	Monte Carlo	Audi Sport	Audi Quattro A1	2	Arne Hertz	4th
74	**Sweden**	**Audi Sport**	**Audi Quattro A1**	**3**	**Arne Hertz**	**1st**
75	**Portugal**	**Audi Sport**	**Audi Quattro A1**	**3**	**Arne Hertz**	**1st**
76	Safari	Audi Sport	Audi Quattro A1	6	Arne Hertz	2nd
77	Corsica	Audi Sport	Audi Quattro A2	4	Arne Hertz	Retired
78	Greece	Audi Sport	Audi Quattro A2	4	Arne Hertz	Retired
79	New Zealand	Audi Sport	Audi Quattro A2	2	Arne Hertz	Retired
80	**Argentina**	**Audi Sport**	**Audi Quattro A2**	**2**	**Arne Hertz**	**1st**
81	**Finland**	**Audi Sport**	**Audi Quattro A2**	**1**	**Arne Hertz**	**1st**
82	Sanremo	Audi Sport	Audi Quattro A2	5	Arne Hertz	Retired
83	Ivory Coast	Audi Sport	Audi Quattro A2	1	Arne Hertz	2nd
84	Great Britain	Audi Sport	Audi Quattro A2	1	Arne Hertz	2nd
1984	104 points (2nd)					
85	Monte Carlo	Audi Sport	Audi Quattro A2	4	Arne Hertz	3rd
86	**Portugal**	**Audi Sport**	**Audi Quattro A2**	**1**	**Arne Hertz**	**1st**
87	Safari	Audi Sport	Audi Quattro A2	1	Arne Hertz	3rd
88	Greece	Audi Sport	Audi Quattro A2	7	Arne Hertz	2nd
89	New Zealand	Audi Sport	Audi Quattro A2	4	Arne Hertz	3rd
90	Argentina	Audi Sport	Audi Quattro A2	2	Arne Hertz	2nd
91	Finland	Audi Sport	Audi Sport Quattro	1	Arne Hertz	Retired
92	Ivory Coast	Audi Sport	Audi Quattro A2	3	Arne Hertz	2nd
93	Great Britain	Audi Sport	Audi Quattro A2	3	Arne Hertz	2nd
1985	10 points (22nd)					
94	Sweden	Audi Sport	Audi Sport Quattro	3	Arne Hertz	4th
95	Safari	Audi Sport	Audi Sport Quattro	1	Arne Hertz	Retired
96	Finland	Audi Sport	Audi Sport Quattro E2	6	Arne Hertz	Retired
97	Great Britain	Audi Sport	Audi Sport Quattro E2	2	Arne Hertz	Retired
1986	12 points (18th)					
98	Monte Carlo	Audi Sport	Audi Sport Quattro E2	6	Arne Hertz	3rd
1987	32 points (8th)					
99	**Safari**	**Audi Sport**	**Audi 200 Quattro**	**7**	**Arne Hertz**	**1st**
100	Greece	Audi Sport	Audi 200 Quattro	4	Arne Hertz	3rd
101	Finland	Audi Sport	Audi 200 Quattro	5	Arne Hertz	Retired
1988	10 points (30th)					
102	Monte Carlo	Mazda Team Europe	Mazda 323 HB 4WD	4	Christian Geistdorfer	Retired
103	Sweden	Mazda Team Europe	Mazda 323 HB 4WD	5	Christian Geistdorfer	Retired
104	Portugal	Mazda Team Europe	Mazda 323 HB 4WD	2	Christian Geistdorfer	4th
105	Safari	GM Euro Sport	Opel Kadett GSi 16V	3	Seppo Harjanne	Retired
106	Greece	Mazda Team Europe	Mazda 323 HB 4WD	6	Christian Geistdorfer	Retired
107	Finland	Mazda Team Europe	Mazda 323 HB 4WD	7	Christian Geistdorfer	Retired
108	Great Britain	Mazda Team Europe	Mazda 323 HB 4WD	10	Christian Geistdorfer	Retired
1989	12 points (27th)					
109	Monte Carlo	Mazda Rally Team Europe	Mazda 323 HB 4WD	7	Christian Geistdorfer	4th
110	Finland	Mazda Rally Team Europe	Mazda 323 HB 4WD	8	Christian Geistdorfer	Retired
111	Great Britain	Mazda Rally Team Europe	Mazda 323 HB 4WD	6	Arne Hertz	9th
1990	6 points (34th)					
112	Monte Carlo	Mazda Rally Team Europe	Mazda 323 HB 4WD	6	Arne Hertz	Retired
113	Portugal	Mazda Rally Team Europe	Mazda 323 HB 4WD	8	Arne Hertz	6th
114	Finland	Mazda Rally Team Europe	Mazda 323 1.8 GTX	11	Arne Hertz	Retired
115	Great Britain	Mazda Rally Team Europe	Mazda 323 1.8 GTX	10	Arne Hertz	Retired
1991	11 points (25th)					
116	Monte Carlo	Mazda Rally Team Europe	Mazda 323 1.8 GTX	10	Johnny Johansson	Retired
117	Sweden	Mazda Rally Team Europe	Mazda 323 1.8 GTX	7	Johnny Johansson	7th
118	Portugal	Mazda Rally Team Europe	Mazda 323 1.8 GTX	9	Johnny Johansson	Retired
119	Greece	Mazda Rally Team Europe	Mazda 323 1.8 GTX	11	Johnny Johansson	8th
120	Finland	Mazda Rally Team Europe	Mazda 323 1.8 GTX	7	Johnny Johansson	Retired
121	Great Britain	Mazda Rally Team Europe	Mazda 323 1.8 GTX	15	Johnny Johansson	7th
1993	4 points (38th)					
122	Sweden	555 Subaru World Rally Team	Subaru Legacy RS	5	Bruno Berglund	Retired
123	Finland	Toyota Castrol Team	Toyota Celica Turbo 4WD	8	Arne Hertz	7th

MOUTINHO, JOACHIM (P) B: 14 DECEMBER 1951, PORTO, PORTUGAL

Not many top class rally drivers can say that their WRC debut was made at the wheel of an Austin Maxi but that is one claim to fame for Joachim Moutinho. He had started rallying a year before that, in 1972, driving a Datsun 1200 on a local rally in the north west of Portugal. Over the next few years, he tried various rally cars, finishing up with an Opel Kadett.

He next appeared in a Group 1 Ford Escort run by a private team before reverting to a Group 2 Kadett for a season. He then got a factory specification R5 Turbo from the Portuguese Renault importers and rewarded them with two national championship titles in 1985 and 1986.

It was also 1986 when Moutinho won the Portuguese Rally. It was a sad affair.

Serious accidents on the first day, one of which had resulted in the deaths of several spectators, had caused all the factory drivers to withdraw their services when the organisers refused to give any assurances about spectator control for the rest of the event.

With only a handful of Group B cars left running, Moutinho came home an easy winner some 15 minutes ahead of a Lancia Rally 037 driven by another local driver, Carlos Bica.

MOUTINHO, JOACHIM - CAREER RECORD

YEAR	RALLY	TEAM/ENTRANT	CAR	NO.	CO-DRIVER	RESULT
1973						
1	Portugal		Austin Maxi	65	Edgar Fortes	Retired
1978						
2	Portugal		Opel Kadett GT/E	27	Edgar Fortes	Retired
1979	0 points					
3	Portugal	Team Lopes Correia	Ford Escort RS2000	20	Miguel Sottomayor	Retired
1980	0 points					
4	Portugal	Team Lopes Correia	Ford Escort RS2000	34	Miguel Sottomayor	Retired
1981	2 points (56th)					
5	Portugal		Opel Kadett GT/E	28	Antonio Morais	9th
1984	0 points					
6	Portugal	Renault Galp	Renault 5 Turbo	18	Edgar Fortes	Retired
1985	0 points					
7	Portugal	Renault Galp	Renault 5 Turbo	8	Edgar Fortes	Retired
1986	20 points (13th)					
8	**Portugal**	**Renault Galp**	**Renault 5 Turbo**	**14**	**Edgar Fortes**	**1st**

Mouton, Michèle (F) B: 23 June 1951, Grasse, France

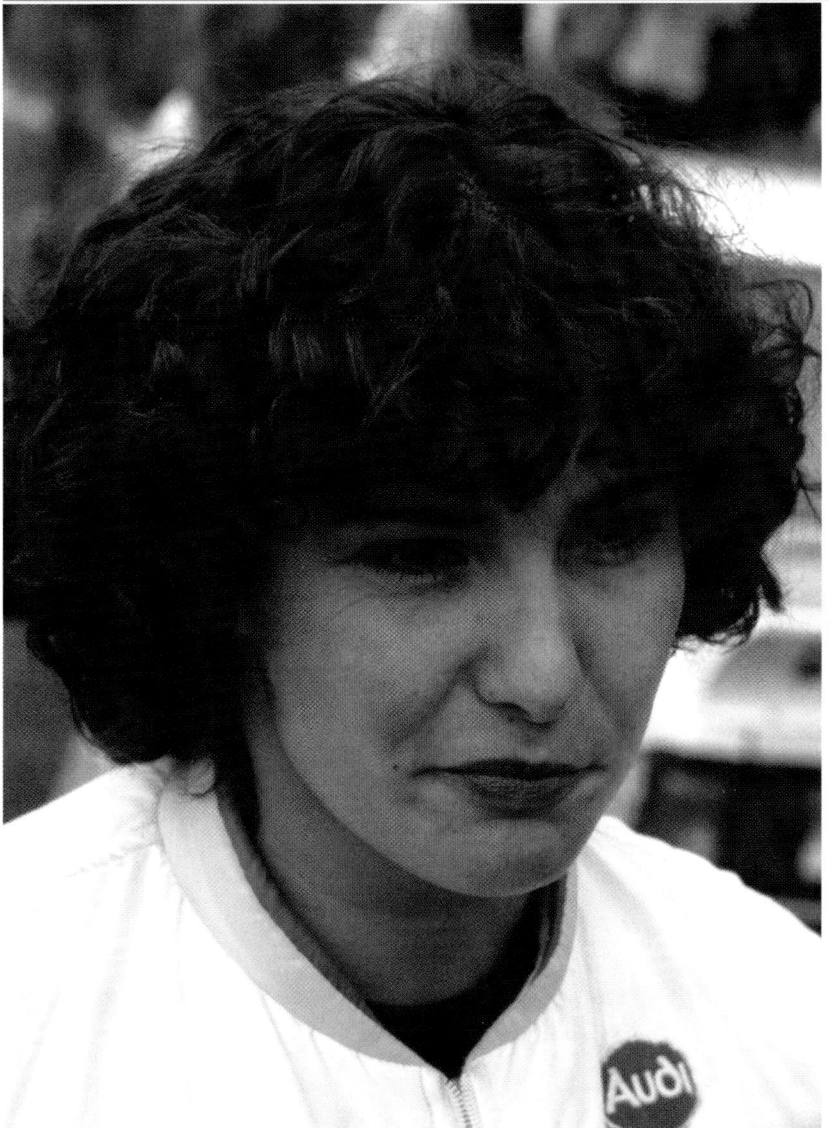

Right from the start of Michèle Mouton's career, she considered herself as first among equals and, at the height of her career, she showed that she was quite capable of winning WRC events and nearly grabbed the world title.

"At the height of her career, she showed that she was quite capable of winning WRC events"

This dynamic young lady started driving at the age of 14 in her father's Citroen 2CV. An interest in motorsport was generated when, seven years later, a friend suggested she might like to come and practice the Tour de Corse. He later invited Mouton to co-drive on the Monte Carlo Rally of 1973. She did that and three more rallies before her father intervened. He had been a prisoner of war during WWII and the opportunity to indulge his love of driving was denied him. But now he suggested that his daughter might like to take the wheel. He bought her an Alpine Renault A110 and she entered first the Criterium Feminin Paris-St Raphael and then the Tour de France.

All went well and at the end of the year she finished eighth overall on the Ilê de Beauté, the national rally run alongside the Tour de Corse. After successful seasons in 1974 and 1975 where she became French Ladies Champion, she was offered financial help from Elf and thus became semi-professional. She continued with the Alpine A110 for the 1976 season, widening her WRC experience with outings on the Monte Carlo and San Remo rallies, but the Alpine was getting a bit passé.

For 1977, she had the opportunity to work with Fiat France who initially put her in a Group 1 Autobianchi A112 for the Monte Carlo where she finished 22 places behind Jean-Claude Andruet in his Fiat France Abarth 131. For the rest of the season, she was to have a similar mount and proved her worth by winning the Tour de France. The following year, it was in a Lancia Stratos that she took seventh place on Monte Carlo but she used an Abarth 131 for the rest of that year and the two following seasons.

Then came the life-changing offer to join Hannu Mikkola in the new Audi team with their turbocharged, 4WD Quattro. It is to Mouton's eternal credit that, like Mikkola, she could see the future of such a car. Sadly she seemed accident-prone on the Monte Carlo Rally, but elsewhere – even on the 1000 Lakes and in Sweden – she showed her ability with a car that, in 1981, was still undeveloped. It was no great surprise, except to some of the other drivers, when she won Sanremo. The following year, she notched up three outright WRC wins plus a second place on the RAC Rally and, had it not been for failing to score in the Ivory Coast, she would have been World Champion. The title lay between her and Walter Röhrl, a man who disliked African rallies. However, he won the Ivory Coast when Mouton went off the road in fog on the last night. It was a doubly sad rally for her as she had learned just before the start that her father had died. For her, losing her father and mentor was far worse than losing the World title.

She continued to drive Audi for three more years, including setting a new record at Pike's Peak, before moving to Peugeot for a year in which she won the German Rally Championship. Her retirement at the end of the Group B era was purely voluntary. Since then she has created the Race of Champions, an annual TV spectacular featuring the world's top rally drivers.

Right: Michèle Mouton was more than just a makeweight female driver. She proved repeatedly that she could win rallies and came within a whisker of winning the 1982 World Championship. She is pictured here on the following season's Safari Rally

MOUTON, MICHÈLE – CAREER RECORD

YEAR	RALLY	TEAM/ENTRANT	CAR	NO.	CO-DRIVER	RESULT
1974						
1	Corsica		Alpine-Renault A110	65	Annie Arrii	12th
1975						
2	Corsica		Alpine-Renault A110	20	Francoise Conconi	7th
1976						
3	Monte Carlo		Alpine-Renault A110	19	Francoise Conconi	11th
4	Sanremo		Alpine-Renault A110	31	'Biche'	Retired
5	Corsica		Alpine-Renault A310	20	Francoise Conconi	Retired
1977						
6	Monte Carlo		Autobianchi A112	37	Francoise Conconi	24th
7	Corsica		Fiat 131 Abarth	20	Francoise Conconi	8th
1978						
8	Monte Carlo	Team Chardonnet	Lancia Stratos	10	Francoise Conconi	7th
9	Corsica	Fiat France	Fiat 131 Abarth	10	Francoise Conconi	5th
1979	12 points (21st)					
10	Monte Carlo	Fiat France	Fiat 131 Abarth	12	Francoise Conconi	7th
11	Corsica	Fiat France	Fiat 131 Abarth	3	Francoise Conconi	5th
1980	12 points (23rd)					
12	Monte Carlo	Fiat France	Fiat 131 Abarth	12	Annie Arrii	7th
13	Corsica	Fiat France	Fiat 131 Abarth	15	Annie Arrii	5th
1981	30 points (8th)					
14	Monte Carlo	Audi Sport	Audi Quattro	15	Fabrizia Pons	Retired
15	Portugal	Audi Sport	Audi Quattro	12	Fabrizia Pons	4th
16	Corsica	Audi Sport	Audi Quattro	15	Fabrizia Pons	Retired
17	Greece	Audi Sport	Audi Quattro	20	Fabrizia Pons	Retired
18	Finland	Audi Sport	Audi Quattro	14	Fabrizia Pons	13th
19	**Sanremo**	**Audi Sport**	**Audi Quattro**	**14**	**Fabrizia Pons**	**1st**
20	Great Britain	Audi Sport	Audi Quattro	10	Fabrizia Pons	Retired
1982	97 points (2nd)					
21	Monte Carlo	Audi Sport	Audi Quattro	5	Fabrizia Pons	Retired
22	Sweden	Audi Sport	Audi Quattro	5	Fabrizia Pons	5th
23	**Portugal**	**Audi Sport**	**Audi Quattro**	**7**	**Fabrizia Pons**	**1st**
24	Corsica	Audi Sport	Audi Quattro	9	Fabrizia Pons	7th
25	**Greece**	**Audi Sport**	**Audi Quattro**	**9**	**Fabrizia Pons**	**1st**
26	New Zealand	Audi Sport	Audi Quattro	9	Fabrizia Pons	Retired
27	**Brazil**	**Audi Sport**	**Audi Quattro**	**3**	**Fabrizia Pons**	**1st**
28	Finland	Audi Sport	Audi Quattro	8	Fabrizia Pons	Retired
29	Sanremo	Audi Sport	Audi Quattro	1	Fabrizia Pons	4th
30	Ivory Coast	Audi Sport	Audi Quattro	2	Fabrizia Pons	Retired
31	Great Britain	Audi Sport	Audi Quattro	5	Fabrizia Pons	2nd
1983	53 points (5th)					
32	Monte Carlo	Audi Sport	Audi Quattro A1	5	Fabrizia Pons	Retired
33	Sweden	Audi Sport	Audi Quattro A1	4	Fabrizia Pons	4th
34	Portugal	Audi Sport	Audi Quattro A1	1	Fabrizia Pons	2nd
35	Safari	Audi Sport	Audi Quattro A1	1	Fabrizia Pons	3rd
36	Corsica	Audi Sport	Audi Quattro A2	10	Fabrizia Pons	Retired
38	Greece	Audi Sport	Audi Quattro A2	1	Fabrizia Pons	Retired
29	New Zealand	Audi Sport	Audi Quattro A2	5	Fabrizia Pons	Retired
39	Argentina	Audi Sport	Audi Quattro A2	5	Fabrizia Pons	3rd
40	Finland	Audi Sport	Audi Quattro A2	6	Fabrizia Pons	16th
41	Sanremo	Audi Sport	Audi Quattro A2	8	Fabrizia Pons	7th
42	Great Britain	Audi Sport	Audi Quattro A2	5	Fabrizia Pons	Retired
1984	25 points (12th)					
43	Sweden	Audi Sport	Audi Quattro A2	3	Fabrizia Pons	2nd
44	Safari	Audi Sport	Audi Quattro A2	3	Fabrizia Pons	Retired
45	Greece	Audi Sport	Audi Sport Quattro	4	Fabrizia Pons	Retired
46	Finland	Audi Sport	Audi Sport Quattro	7	Fabrizia Pons	Retired
47	Great Britain	Audi Sport	Audi Sport Quattro	6	Fabrizia Pons	4th
1985	0 points					
48	Ivory Coast	Audi Sport	Audi Sport Quattro E2	2	Arne Hertz	Retired
1986	0 points					
49	Monte Carlo	Peugeot Talbot Deutschland	Peugeot 205 Turbo 16	10	Terry Harryman	Retired
50	Corsica	Peugeot Talbot Sport	Peugeot 205 Turbo 16	10	Fabrizia Pons	Retired

MUNARI, SANDRO (I) B: 27 MARCH 1940, CAVARZERE, ITALY

The first and greatest Italian superstar of rallying is Sandro Munari. He rose to stand alongside the Scandinavians and showed his mastery of the Monte Carlo, the hardest rally to win in the WRC calendar, by winning it four times in six years.

"The first and greatest Italian superstar of rallying"

In the 1960s, the Po delta was the cradle of Italian rallying and Munari was born in the heart of that region. His first driving skills were acquired with lorries and tractors on his father's farm and then in 1964, he built and raced a go-kart with Arnaldo Cavallari, triple Italian rally champion. About the same time, he dabbled with hill-climbing in a Fiat 850 but then started co-driving for Cavallari in an Alfa GTA. This was 1965 and they won several Italian international rallies.

At this point, the nascent Lancia team invited him to become one of its drivers and threw him in at the deep end by sending him to rallies like the 1000 Lakes. He impressed sufficiently to have a full contract for 1966 and started by holding down second place on the Monte Carlo before having an accident on the last night. The rest of the year was full of retirements, largely mechanical, as Lancia struggled with thc unwieldy Flavia. For 1967, Munari had a Fulvia Coupé and took fifth place on the Monte and won the Italian Championship. But his most sensational result was to win the Tour de Corse and miss being unpenalised on the road sections by a few seconds.

That win launched Lancia, the Fulvia and Munari into serious rallying. But before he could take advantage of his new reputation, his car was involved in a road accident in Yugoslavia on the 1968 Monte Carlo concentration that killed his co-driver, Luciano Lombardini, and put Munari out of action for fully six months. When he came back in 1969, he teamed up with John Davenport and they won the rejuvenated Sestriere Rally and the Italian Championship. By now, the Fulvia was getting eclipsed and 1970 and 1971 were not easy years for a driver who wanted to win. However, Munari could pull some amazing performances out of the hat as on the Safari of 1970 where he led the event right up until the last night when he slid off in fog.

Like Corsica in 1967, the 1972 season was to lift Munari clear off the ground. Against all odds, he won the Monte Carlo in a Fulvia. That win boosted his career and gave Lancia the spur to create the Stratos. He drove a Ferrari 512S and won the Targa Florio but for rallying, it was still a Fulvia for Munari. He won the European Championship in 1973 and put one on the Safari podium in 1974. Once the Stratos was homologated, there was no stopping him. He won with it on its debut in San Remo 1974 and followed up with a hat trick of Monte Carlo victories. He even took a third place on the Safari.

But when Lancia and its new owner Fiat consolidated their competition departments for 1978, the Stratos took a back seat and Munari found he was not the flavour of the month. For one reason or another, he could not wrest the same performances from the 131 Abarth and he gradually slipped out of the mainstream. For some years he continued to find entries on the Safari which he was determined to win, but that goal eluded him.

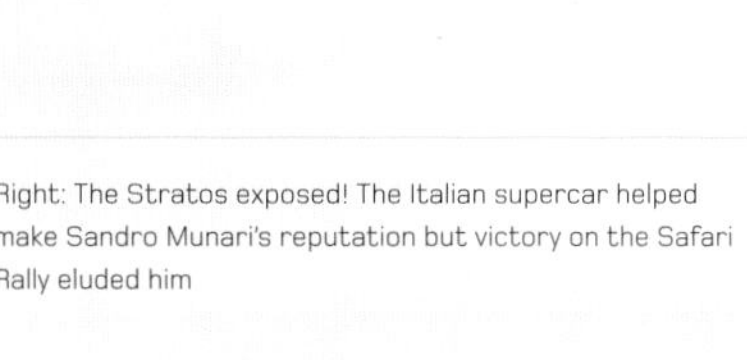

Right: The Stratos exposed! The Italian supercar helped make Sandro Munari's reputation but victory on the Safari Rally eluded him

MUNARI, SANDRO – CAREER RECORD

YEAR	RALLY	TEAM/ENTRANT	CAR	NO.	CO-DRIVER	RESULT
1973						
1	Monte Carlo	Lancia Marlboro	Lancia Fulvia	11	Mario Mannucci	Retired
1974						
2	Safari	Lancia Marlboro	Lancia Fulvia	10	Lofty Drews	3rd
3	**Sanremo**	**Lancia Alitalia**	**Lancia Stratos**	**2**	**Mario Munnucci**	**1st**
4	**Canada**	**Lancia Alitalia**	**Lancia Stratos**	**103**	**Mario Mannucci**	**1st**
5	United States	Lancia Alitalia	Lancia Stratos	64	Mario Mannucci	Retired
6	Great Britain	Lancia Alitalia	Lancia Stratos	3	Piero Sodano	3rd
7	Corsica	Lancia Alitalia	Lancia Stratos	6	Mario Mannucci	Retired
1975						
8	**Monte Carlo**	**Lancia Alitalia**	**Lancia Stratos**	**14**	**Mario Mannucci**	**1st**
9	Safari	Lancia Alitalia	Lancia Stratos	3	Lofty Drews	2nd
10	Sanremo	Lancia Alitalia	Lancia Stratos	1	Mario Mannucci	Retired
11	Corsica	Lancia Alitalia	Lancia Stratos	1	Mario Mannucci	Retired
12	Great Britain	Lancia Alitalia	Lancia Stratos	8	Mario Mannucci	Retired
1976						
13	**Monte Carlo**	**Lancia Alitalia**	**Lancia Stratos**	**10**	**Silvio Maiga**	**1st**
14	**Portugal**	**Lancia Alitalia**	**Lancia Stratos**	**1**	**Silvio Maiga**	**1st**
15	Safari	Lancia Alitalia	Lancia Stratos	6	Silvio Maiga	Retired
16	Morocco	Lancia Alitalia	Lancia Stratos	3	Silvio Maiga	3rd
17	Sanremo	Lancia Alitalia	Lancia Stratos	1	Silvio Maiga	2nd
18	**Corsica**	**Lancia Alitalia**	**Lancia Stratos**	**1**	**Silvio Maiga**	**1st**
19	Great Britain	Lancia Alitalia	Lancia Stratos	7	Silvio Maiga	4th
1977						
20	**Monte Carlo**	**Lancia Alitalia**	**Lancia Stratos**	**1**	**Silvio Maiga**	**1st**
21	Safari	Lancia Alitalia	Lancia Stratos	7	Piero Sodano	3rd
22	Sanremo	Lancia Alitalia	Lancia Stratos	2	Piero Sodano	Retired
23	Corsica	Lancia Alitalia	Lancia Stratos	1	Piero Sodano	Retired
24	Great Britain	Lancia Alitalia	Lancia Stratos	7	Piero Sodano	25th
1978						
25	Monte Carlo	Lancia Alitalia	Lancia Stratos	1	Piero Sodano	Retired
26	Portugal	Fiat Alitalia	Fiat 131 Abarth	1	Piero Sodano	Retired
27	Greece	Fiat Alitalia	Fiat 131 Abarth	1	Mario Mannucci	Retired
28	Sanremo	Fiat Alitalia	Fiat 131 Abarth	5	Mario Mannucci	Retired
29	Corsica	Fiat Alitalia	Fiat 131 Abarth	5	Mario Mannucci	3rd
30	Great Britain	Lancia Alitalia	Lancia Stratos	10	Piero Sodano	Retired
1979	1 point (73rd)					
31	Safari	Fiat Alitalia	Fiat 131 Abarth	7	Silvio Maiga	10th
1980	6 points (36th)					
32	Ivory Coast		Fiat 131 Abarth	2	Jacques Jaubert	6th
1981	0 points					
33	Safari		Dodge Ramcharger	16	Piero Sodano	Retired
1982	0 points					
34	Safari		Porsche 911SC	11	Ian Street	Retired
1983	0 points					
35	Safari	Autodelta	Alfa Romeo GTV6	15	Ian Street	Retired
1984	0 points					
36	Safari	International Casino	Toyota Celica TCT	18	Ian Street	Retired

NICOLAS, JEAN-PIERRE (F) B: 22 JANUARY 1945, MARSEILLE, FRANCE

Jean-Pierre Nicolas may not have been the most svelte member of the Alpine Renault "Musketeers" but he was nonetheless a keen player.

The son of Georges Nicolas, former member of the Renault works team, Nicolas was born in Aix-en-Provence where the family ran a Renault dealership. Nicolas's first rallies were attempted in 1963 at the wheel of a Dauphine 1093 with his father co-driving and even in that first year, he won the Rallye Mistral. He moved to an R8 Gordini before military service interrupted and on his return in 1966 used to win the Tour de Madeira and a Coupe des Alpes.

Nicolas was inducted into the Alpine team for 1968 but it was not until 1970 that the pairing got into their stride. In 1972, he gained international fame by winning the Olympia Rally in Germany while in 1973, he proved a solid performer on all surfaces to take four WRC podiums plus a win in Corsica to gain the makes' title for Alpine-Renault.

He used the A110 to win Morocco again in 1974 and shared a Ligier JS2 with Gerard Larrousse to win the Tour de France. He now started to diversify and drove for Peugeot in African rallies, finishing the Safari for the first time and winning in Morocco. With only days to go to the start of the 1978 Monte Carlo, money from Gitanes enabled him to drive the Almeras Porsche and, with no time to recce, he won against an armada of Fiats and Renaults. He then won both African WRC events with Peugeot, which so nearly enabled him to win the FIA Cup for Drivers, the forerunner of the WRC title.

As Group B loomed, Nicolas rejoined his old co-driver, Jean Todt and went to Peugeot to test and compete with the new 205 T16. He did two WRC rallies in 1984 but then hung up his helmet to become Sporting Director for Peugeot.

NICOLAS, JEAN-PIERRE - CAREER RECORD

YEAR	RALLY	TEAM /ENTRANT	CAR	NO.	CO-DRIVER	RESULT
1973						
1	Monte Carlo	Renault-Alpine	Renault-Alpine A110	21	Michel Vial	3rd
2	Sweden	Renault-Alpine	Renault 12 Gordini	8	Michel Vial	14th
3	Portugal	Renault-Alpine	Renault-Alpine A110	1	Michel Vial	2nd
4	Morocco	Renault-Alpine	Renault-Alpine A110	4	Michel Vial	5th
5	Greece	Renault-Alpine	Renault-Alpine A110	5	Michel Vial	3rd
6	Austria	Renault-Alpine	Renault-Alpine A110	11	Michel Vial	5th
7	Sanremo	Renault-Alpine	Renault-Alpine A110	8	Michel Vial	3rd
8	Great Britain	Renault-Alpine	Renault-Alpine A110	8	Claude Roure	5th
9	**Corsica**	**Renault-Alpine**	**Renault-Alpine A110**	**1**	**Michel Vial**	**1st**
1974						
10	Safari	Renault-Alpine	Renault 17 Gordini	17	Christian Delferrier	Retired
11	United States	Renault-Alpine	Renault 17 Gordini	9	Geraint Phillips	3rd
12	Corsica	Renault-Alpine	Renault-Alpine A110	10	Vincent Laverne	2nd
1975						
13	Monte Carlo	Renault-Alpine	Renault-Alpine A110	8	Vincent Laverne	Retired
14	Sanremo	Renault-Alpine	Renault-Alpine A110	12	Vincent Laverne	Retired
15	Corsica	Renault-Alpine	Renault-Alpine A110	7	Vincent Laverne	2nd
1976						
16	Monte Carlo	Renault-Alpine	Alpine-Renault A310	4	Vincent Laverne	Retired
17	Safari	Marshalls (EA) Ltd.	Peugeot 504	2	Jean-Claude Lefebvre	9th
18	**Morocco**		**Peugeot 504**	**6**	**Michel Gamet**	**1st**
19	Sanremo		Opel Kadett GT/E	5	Vincent Laverne	Retired
20	Corsica		Opel Kadett GT/E	6	Vincent Laverne	Retired

YEAR	RALLY	TEAM /ENTRANT	CAR	NO.	CO-DRIVER	RESULT
1977						
21	Monte Carlo		Opel Kadett GT/E	7	Jean Todt	Retired
22	Safari	Marshalls (EA) Ltd.	Peugeot 504 V6 Coupe	11	Jean Todt	Retired
23	Corsica		Ford Escort RS1800	2	Vincent Laverne	Retired
24	Great Britain		Renault 5 Alpine	59	Michel Vial	Retired
1978						
25	**Monte Carlo**	**Porsche Almeras**	**Porsche 911**	**3**	**Vincent Laverne**	**1st**
26	**Safari**	**Marshalls (EA) Ltd.**	**Peugeot 504 V6 Coupe**	**4**	**Jean-Claude Lefebvre**	**1st**
27	Portugal	Ford Motor Company	Ford Escort RS	5	Vincent Laverne	3rd
28	Greece	Automobiles Citroen	Citroen CX2400 GTi	6	Vincent Laverne	Retired
29	**Ivory Coast**		**Peugeot 504 V6 Coupe**	**2**	**Michel Gamet**	**1st**
30	Corsica		Opel Kadett GT/E	7th	Vincent Laverne	7th
1979	**6 points (34th)**					
31	Monte Carlo	Porsche Almeras	Porsche Carrera RS	1	Jean Todt	6th
32	Safari	Marshalls (EA) Ltd.	Peugeot 504 V6 Coupe	12	Henry Liddon	Retired
33	Sanremo	Talbot France	Talbot Sunbeam Lotus	4	Jean Todt	Retired
34	Corsica	Talbot France	Talbot Sunbeam Lotus	4	Jean Todt	Retired
35	Ivory Coast		Peugeot 504 V6 Coupe	1	Jean de Alexandris	Retired
1980	**8 points (33rd)**					
36	Safari	Opel Euro Händler	Opel Ascona 400	2	Henry Liddon	5th
1984	**18 points (14th)**					
37	Corsica	Peugeot Talbot Sport	Peugeot 205 T16	12	Charley Pasquier	4th
38	Greece	Peugeot Talbot Sport	Peugeot 205 T16	12	Charley Pasquier	Retired
39	Sanremo	Peugeot Talbot Sport	Peugeot 205 T16	8	Charley Pasquier	5th
40	Safari	International Casino	Toyota Celica TCT	18	Ian Street	Retired

Oreille, Alain (F) b: 22 April 1953, Sarre-Union, France

No one was more surprised than Alan Oreille when he won the 1989 Ivory Coast Rally. He had gone to that African event with no greater intention than getting to the finish and so winning the FIA Group N Cup.

Oreille's rally career started in 1972 with a BMW 1600 but when he started competing seriously, co-driven by his wife, Sylvie, it was in a Group 2 Simca Rallye. He regularly won his category in French national rallies between 1978 and 1980 before changing to a French dealer supported Opel Kadett GT/E in 1981. He regularly won the Group 1 category in French international rallies before moving up to a Group 2 Kadett in 1982. By 1983, he was winning national rallies outright and, at the end of the season, Greder Racing let him loose in an Opel Ascona with which he was third overall on the Cevennes.

A lasting connection with Renault was forged in 1984 when he drove a Group N R5 Alpine Turbo with which he finished fifth overall in the French championship. Renault also gave him the chance to make international appearances with a R11 Turbo and the following year he moved to a Group A version in France. He finished second twice in the championship before reverting to Group N with a R5 GT Turbo in 1988.

For 1989, the Renault France Network backed an attempt at the FIA Group N Cup, created at the same time as the WRC Driver's championship. Oreille only did five of the events but won the FIA Cup helped in no small measure by his Ivory Coast win. He repeated the FIA Cup win the following year.

He carried on doing French championship events with a Diac backed Clio and in 1995 did a British Championship season with a Clio Maxi where he finished fourth in the championship.

Oreille, Alain – Career Record

YEAR	RALLY	TEAM/ENTRANT	CAR	NO.	CO-DRIVER	RESULT
1984	0 points					
1	Corsica		Renault 11 Turbo	119	Sylvie Oreille	21st
1985	0 points					
2	Monte Carlo		Renault 11 Turbo	31	Sylvie Oreille	16th
3	Corsica		Renault 11 Turbo	24	Sylvie Oreille	Retired
1986	3 points (49th)					
4	Monte Carlo	Renault France	Renault 11 Turbo	25	Sylvie Oreille	8th
5	Corsica	Renault France	Renault 11 Turbo	16	Sylvie Oreille	Retired
1987	2 points (58th)					
6	Monte Carlo		Renault 11 Turbo	15	Sylvie Oreille	Retired
7	Corsica	Phillips Renault Elf	Renault 11 Turbo	16	Sylvie Oreille	9th
1988	11 points (28th)					
8	Monte Carlo	Renault France	Renault 11 Turbo	10	Jean-Marc Andrie	4th
9	Corsica	Simon Racing	Renault 5 GT Turbo	10	Sylvie Oreille	10th
1989	26 points (10th)					
10	Monte Carlo	Renault France	Renault 5 GT Turbo (GpN)	19	Gilles Thimonier	10th
11	Corsica	Simon Racing	Renault 5 GT Turbo (GpN)	17	Gilles Thimonier	8th
12	Australia	Simon Racing	Renault 5 GT Turbo (GpN)	17	Gilles Thimonier	12th
13	Sanremo	Simon Racing	Renault 5 GT Turbo (GpN)	21	Gilles Thimonier	9th
14	**Ivory Coast**	**Simon Racing**	**Renault 5 GT Turbo (GpN)**	**9**	**Gilles Thimonier**	**1st**
1990	22 points (11th)					
15	Monte Carlo	Simon Racing	Renault 5 GT Turbo (GpN)	11	Michel Roissard	13th
16	Portugal	Simon Racing	Renault 5 GT Turbo (GpN)	11	Michel Roissard	14th
17	Corsica	Simon Racing	Renault 5 GT Turbo (GpN)	7	Michel Roissard	8th
18	Greece	Simon Racing	Renault 5 GT Turbo (GpN)	10	Michel Roissard	13th
19	New Zealand	Simon Racing	Renault 5 GT Turbo (GpN)	7	Michel Roissard	10th
20	Argentina	Simon Racing	Renault 5 GT Turbo (GpN)	6	Michel Roissard	6th
21	Australia	Simon Racing	Renault 5 GT Turbo (GpN)	14	Michel Roissard	Retired
22	Sanremo	Simon Racing	Renault 5 GT Turbo (GpN)	16	Michel Roissard	17th
23	Ivory Coast	Simon Racing	Renault 5 GT Turbo (GpN)	4	Michel Roissard	3rd
1992	1 point (68th)					
24	Corsica	Societe Diac	Renault Clio 16V	9	Jean-Marc Andrie	10th
1993	2 points (55th)					
25	Corsica	Societe Diac	Renault Clio 16V	16	Jean-Marc Andrie	10th
1994	0 points					
26	Monte Carlo	Societe Diac	Renault Clio Williams	11	Jean-Marc Andrie	Retired
27	Corsica	Societe Diac	Renault Clio Williams	10	Jean-Marc Andrie	Retired
1995	1 point (32nd)					
28	Great Britain	Renault Dealer Rallying	Renault Clio Maxi	19	Jack Boyere	10th

PANIZZI, GILLES

(F) B: 19 SEPTEMBER 1965, MENTON, FRANCE

"It was prehaps inevitable that Gilles Panizzi would at some point drive a rally car"

Born in Menton, halfway between Monte Carlo and San Remo, and into a family already passionate about rallying, it was perhaps inevitable that Gilles Panizzi would at some point drive a rally car.

When he started out in an Opel Manta GT/E bought with his own savings in 1987, there was no immediate sign that he was going to be acknowledged as one of the top drivers on asphalt. He finished 23rd on the Rally de Nice. The following year, still in the Manta, he took his brother, Herve, with him and this was the beginning of a very effective partnership that has lasted ever since. For 1989, Panizzi hired a Renault 5GT Turbo from Automeca and made an impression on French national rallies, winning the Aspirant title from Echappement magazine. The following year, he made his WRC debut on the Monte Carlo with a rented Lancia Integrale and finished 16th. Then in 1992, the brothers decided to do the Peugeot Shell Cup and went sufficiently well to get some additional help from Peugeot towards the end of the season. They soon began to win their class regularly and this continued throughout 1993. They also hired a Lancia again for three rallies to widen their experience.

In 1994, they became part of the official Peugeot line-up and were given the task of developing the Group A 306 S16. By 1995, this was a very competitive car and Panizzi finished third in the F2 category in Corsica with one. The following year, he drove the 306 Maxi to outright victory in the French Championship winning six of the 11 rallies. He repeated his championship win in 1997 and was leading Catalunya before a puncture dropped him to third.

Now came another learning process as Peugeot built up to their WRC programme. Panizzi did four conventional European rallies in the 306 Maxi and was then sent to do his first gravel event in Finland with a Group N 106. To widen his knowledge even further, he hired a Group N Subaru for the RAC Rally and then an Impreza WRC for Monte Carlo in 1999. The Peugeot 206 WRC was ready to roll in Corsica but Panizzi discovered that it was not going to be a winner straight out of the box.

The year 2000 started with a brace of retirements. None of the Peugeots would restart from an icy overnight halt on the Monte while on the Safari the suspension broke. To add to his woes, Panizzi was fined $50,000 for remonstrating with a slower driver who would not pull over. The 206WRC was becoming competitive and he soon proved it by winning, in rapid succession, two tarmac rallies – Corsica and San Remo. Over the next two years, these were to become a Panizzi speciality and Peugeot came to count on them.

Panizzi, however, was keen to break out of the asphalt-only mould and drove as many gravel events as he could. In 2003, he was not on the pace in San Remo but a late charge in the rain saw him rise to second in the last two stages. Then a below par showing in Corsica was followed by another astounding drive in the rain of Spain, but his non-finish on the Rally GB left Peugeot with no title for the year.

Right: San Remo is as much Gilles Panizzi's home event as Monte Carlo. Here, in 2002, the acknowledged asphalt expert took his third sealed surface win of the season

PANIZZI, GILLES – CAREER RECORD

YEAR	RALLY	TEAM/ENTRANT	CAR	NO.	CO-DRIVER	RESULT
1990	**0 points**					
1	Monte Carlo		Lancia Delta HF Integrale	40	Herve Panizzi	16th
1993	**0 points**					
2	Corsica		Peugeot 106 XSi	22	Herve Panizzi	Retired
1995	**0 points**					
3	Corsica	Peugeot Sport	Peugeot 306 S16	27	Herve Panizzi	12th
1997	**8 points (10th)**					
4	Catalunya	Peugeot Sport	Peugeot 306 Maxi	11	Herve Panizzi	3rd
5	Corsica	Peugeot Sport	Peugeot 306 Maxi	7	Herve Panizzi	3rd
1998	**6 points (12th)**					
6	Monte Carlo	Peugeot Sport	Peugeot 306 Maxi	16	Herve Panizzi	9th
7	Catalunya	Peugeot Sport	Peugeot 306 Maxi	15	Herve Panizzi	9th
8	Corsica	Peugeot Sport	Peugeot 306 Maxi	10	Herve Panizzi	9th
9	Finland	Peugeot Sport	Peugeot 106 Rallye S20	71	Herve Panizzi	35th
10	Sanremo	Peugeot Sport	Peugeot 306 Maxi	14	Herve Panizzi	5th
11	Great Britain		Subaru Impreza WRX	21	Herve Panizzi	Retired
1999	**6 points (10th)**					
12	Monte Carlo		Subaru Impreza WRC	17	Herve Panizzi	Retired
13	Corsica	Peugeot Esso	Peugeot 206 WRC	15	Herve Panizzi	Retired
14	Finland	Peugeot Esso	Peugeot 206 WRC	16	Herve Panizzi	33rd
15	Sanremo	Peugeot Esso	Peugeot 206 WRC	15	Herve Panizzi	2nd
16	Great Britain	Peugeot Esso	Peugeot 206 WRC	22	Herve Panizzi	7th
2000	**21 points (7th)**					
17	Monte Carlo	Peugeot Esso	Peugeot 206 WRC	10	Herve Panizzi	Retired
18	Safari	Peugeot Esso	Peugeot 206 WRC	9	Herve Panizzi	Retired
19	Catalunya	Peugeot Esso	Peugeot 206 WRC	10	Herve Panizzi	6th
20	**Corsica**	**Peugeot Esso**	**Peugeot 206 WRC**	**10**	**Herve Panizzi**	**1st**
21	**Sanremo**	**Peugeot Esso**	**Peugeot 206 WRC**	**10**	**Herve Panizzi**	**1st**
22	Australia	Peugeot Esso	Peugeot 206 WRC	16	Herve Panizzi	Retired
23	Great Britain	Peugeot Esso	Peugeot 206 WRC	19	Herve Panizzi	8th
2001	**22 points (8th)**					
24	Monte Carlo	Peugeot Total	Peugeot 206 WRC	16	Herve Panizzi	Retired
25	Portugal	HF Grifone srl	Peugeot 206 WRC	20	Herve Panizzi	12th
26	Catalunya	Peugeot Total	Peugeot 206 WRC	16	Herve Panizzi	2nd
27	Cyprus	HF Grifone srl	Peugeot 206 WRC	21	Herve Panizzi	Retired
28	Greece	HF Grifone srl	Peugeot 206 WRC	28	Herve Panizzi	Retired
29	Finland	HF Grifone srl	Peugeot 206 WRC	25	Herve Panizzi	14th
30	**Sanremo**	**Peugeot Total**	**Peugeot 206 WRC**	**16**	**Herve Panizzi**	**1st**
31	Corsica	Peugeot Total	Peugeot 206 WRC	16	Herve Panizzi	2nd
32	Australia	Peugeot Total	Peugeot 206 WRC	19	Herve Panizzi	9th
33	Great Britain	HF Grifone srl	Peugeot 206 WRC	22	Herve Panizzi	Retired
2002	**31 points (6th)**					
34	Monte Carlo	Peugeot Total	Peugeot 206 WRC	3	Herve Panizzi	7th
35	Sweden	Bozian Racing	Peugeot 206 WRC	24	Herve Panizzi	16th
36	**Corsica**	**Peugeot Total**	**Peugeot 206 WRC**	**3**	**Herve Panizzi**	**1st**
37	**Catalunya**	**Peugeot Total**	**Peugeot 206 WRC**	**3**	**Herve Panizzi**	**1st**
38	Cyprus	Peugeot Total	Peugeot 206 WRC	23	Herve Panizzi	10th
39	Argentina	Peugeot Total	Peugeot 206 WRC	23	Herve Panizzi	Retired
40	Greece	Bozian Racing	Peugeot 206 WRC	23	Herve Panizzi	Retired
41	Safari	Peugeot Total	Peugeot 206 WRC	23	Herve Panizzi	6th
42	Sanremo	Peugeot Total	Peugeot 206 WRC	3	Herve Panizzi	1st
43	New Zealand	Peugeot Total	Peugeot 206 WRC	23	Herve Panizzi	7th
44	Great Britain	Bozian Racing	Peugeot 206 WRC	23	Herve Panizzi	11th
2003	**27 points (10th)**					
45	Monte Carlo	Marlboro Peugeot Total	Peugeot 206 WRC	3	Herve Panizzi	Withdrawn
46	Turkey	Bozian Racing	Peugeot 206 WRC	21	Herve Panizzi	5th
47	Greece	Bozian Racing	Peugeot 206 WRC	21	Herve Panizzi	7th
48	Cyprus	Bozian Racing	Peugeot 206 WRC	20	Herve Panizzi	Retired
49	Germany	Marlboro Peugeot Total	Peugeot 206 WRC	3	Herve Panizzi	10th
50	Sanremo	Marlboro Peugeot Total	Peugeot 206 WRC	3	Herve Panizzi	2nd
51	Corsica	Marlboro Peugeot Total	Peugeot 206 WRC	3	Herve Panizzi	6th
52	**Catalunya**	**Marlboro Peugeot Total**	**Peugeot 206 WRC**	**3**	**Herve Panizzi**	**1st**
53	Great Britain	Bozian Racing	Peugeot 206 WRC	21	Herve Panizzi	Retired

PINTO, RAFFAELE (I) B: 23 APRIL 1945, COMO, ITALY

One of the Old Boys of Italian rallying, Raffaele Pinto proved that he could hold his own with front or rear wheel drive and was often the backroom boy behind someone else's victory.

Pinto made his first appearances in the emerging Lancia team of the late 1960s. One of his roles was to help with test-driving and sorting out the rally cars in the days before specialist engineers and electronics. He got his own chance to drive a Fulvia and had an excellent record in Spain finishing fourth and then third in 1968 and 1969. However, when Lancia got Sandro Munari back and added a couple of Finns to its team, the new Fiat team snapped up Pinto to help with their new 124 Spyder.

By 1971, he was winning events in Italy and Austria for Fiat. For 1972, he was put at the head of Fiat's charge for the European Championship and duly won it, taking outright victories in six rallies.

One of those wins was particularly difficult as, on the Yugoslav Rally, Pinto collided with a cow on the very first special stage and the Fiat mechanics had to almost completely rebuild his car.

His win in Poland was particularly good as he had a hard fight with Walter Röhrl in a Cologne Capri all the way to the finish.

The first year of the WRC saw him score points for Fiat in Monte Carlo but it was not until Portugal, the first WRC rally to be run in 1974 after the fuel crisis, that he finally got the win his hard work deserved.

In 1975, he went back to Lancia and drove a Stratos without success in the WRC but he did win San Marino and a couple of other Italian rallies. He took a Stratos to third on San Remo 1976 behind the similar cars of Bjorn Waldegård and Sandro Munari and upheld Lancia honour in Corsica 1977 where he was second to Bernard Darniche's Fiat.

PINTO, RAFFAELE - CAREER RECORD

YEAR	RALLY	TEAM/ENTRANT	CAR	NO.	CO-DRIVER	RESULT
1973						
1	Monte Carlo		Fiat 124 Abarth	5	Arnaldo Bernacchini	7th
2	Portugal		Fiat 124 Abarth	6	Arnaldo Bernacchini	Retired
3	Austria		Fiat 124 Abarth	10	Arnaldo Bernacchini	Retired
4	Sanremo		Fiat 124 Abarth	4	Arnaldo Bernacchini	Retired
1974						
5	**Portugal**		**Fiat 124 Abarth**	**2**	**Arnaldo Bernacchini**	**1st**
6	Sanremo		Fiat 124 Abarth	3	Arnaldo Bernacchini	Retired
7	Corsica		Fiat 124 Abarth	11	Arnaldo Bernacchini	Retired
1975						
8	Monte Carlo		Lancia Stratos	17	Arnaldo Bernacchini	Retired
9	Greece		Lancia Stratos	4	Arnaldo Bernacchini	Retired
10	Sanremo		Lancia Stratos	7	Arnaldo Bernacchini	Retired
11	Corsica		Lancia Stratos	4	Arnaldo Bernacchini	Retired
1976						
12	Monte Carlo		Lancia Stratos	3	Arnaldo Bernacchini	Retired
13	Portugal		Lancia Stratos	4	Arnaldo Bernacchini	4th
14	Greece		Lancia Stratos	7	Arnaldo Bernacchini	Retired
15	Sanremo		Lancia Stratos	6	Arnaldo Bernacchini	3rd
1977						
16	Monte Carlo		Lancia Stratos	5	Arnaldo Bernacchini	Retired
17	Sanremo		Lancia Stratos	4	Arnaldo Bernacchini	Retired
18	Corsica		Lancia Stratos	4	Arnaldo Bernacchini	2nd
1978						
19	Sanremo		Ferrari 308GTB	23	Fabio Penariol	Retired

PURAS, JESÚS (E) B: 16 MARCH 1963, SANTANDER, SPAIN

Sometimes no matter how hard you try, you just can't break through the glass ceiling. Jesús Puras has been Spanish Rally Champion eight times, twice in Lancias and six times in Citroens but he has not been permanently signed up at WRC level.

His first taste of rallying came in 1982 with a Renault 5TS and he stayed faithful to the marque until 1988 when he swapped to a Ford Sierra in the year that Carlos Sainz drove one to his second Spanish title. The following year, Puras drove a Lancia Delta Integrale and became Spanish Champion for the first time. He promptly signed for Mazda until MRTE folded and he returned to the. Lancia and a second Spanish title.

The next move was to try his fortunes in the WRC with a Group N Ford Escort RS Cosworth, winning the FIA Group N title despite not even starting the Safari, Acropolis and 1000 Lakes.

Then came the call to join the SEAT WRC team in 1996. He did eight of the WRC 2-litre rounds with his best result coming in Portugal where he won the 2-litre category. SEAT won the F2 Manufacturers title but Puras got little credit after five mechanical retirements.

Reunited with Citroën, he won repeatedly in Spain but retirements plagued his WRC record with the shining exception of Corsica in 1999 where he was second overall. For 2001, Citroën gave him the chance to show what he could do on tarmac by giving him a Xsara WRC car for three events. He led in Catalunya but retired with a fuel problem while in San Remo, under some pressure to perform, he went off the road. However, it finally came good in Corsica where he won easily.

However, this win was too little too late and Citroën saw him as being a tarmac-only driver. When he failed to win again in 2002, he was dropped.

PURAS, JESUS - CAREER RECORD

YEAR	RALLY	TEAM/ENTRANT	CAR	NO.	CO-DRIVER	RESULT
1991	**4 points (40th)**					
1	Monte Carlo	Mazda Rally Team Europe	Mazda 323 GTX	16	Jose Arrarte	Retired
2	Portugal	Mazda Rally Team Europe	Mazda 323 GTX	16	Jose Arrarte	7th
3	Catalunya		Lancia Delta Integrale	8	Jose Arrarte	Retired
1992	**6 points (34th)**					
4	Catalunya	Mauro Rallye Team	Lancia Delta HF Integrale	18	Alex Romani	6th
1994	**5 points (30th)**					
5	Monte Carlo		Ford Escort RS Cosworth (GpN)	23	Alex Romani	9th
6	Portugal		Ford Escort RS Cosworth (GpN)	26	Carlos del Barrio	8th
7	Corsica		Ford Escort RS Cosworth (GpN)	15	Carlos del Barrio	12th
8	Argentina		Ford Escort RS Cosworth (GpN)	9	Carlos del Barrio	Retired
9	New Zealand		Ford Escort RS Cosworth (GpN)	19	Carlos del Barrio	Retired
10	Sanremo		Ford Escort RS Cosworth (GpN)	26	Carlos del Barrio	27th
11	Great Britain		Ford Escort RS Cosworth (GpN)	26	Alex Romani	15th
1995	**0 points**					
12	Catalunya	Citroen Hispania	Citroen ZX 16V	18	Carlos del Barrio	Retired
1996	**0 points**					
13	Argentina	SEAT Sport	SEAT Ibiza Kit Car	15	Carlos del Barrio	Retired
14	Australia	SEAT Sport	SEAT Ibiza Kit Car	20	Carlos del Barrio	Reired
15	Catalunya	SEAT Sport	SEAT Ibiza Kit Car	19	Carlos del Barrio	15th
1997	**0 points**					
16	Catalunya	Citroen Hispania	Citroen ZX 16V	15	Carlos del Barrio	Retired
1998	**0 points**					
17	Cataluya	Automobiles Citroen	Citroen Xsara Kit Car	19	Carlos del Barrio	Retired
18	Sanremo	Automobiles Citroen	Citroen Xsara Kit Car	16	Carlos del Barrio	Retired
1999	**6 points (10th)**					
19	Monte Carlo	Automobiles Citroen	Citroen Saxo Kit Car	25	Marc Marti	Retired
20	Catalunya	Citroen Hispania	Citroen Xsara Kit Car	17	Marc Marti	Retired
21	Corsica	Automobiles Citroen	Citroen Xsara Kit Car	17	Marc Marti	2nd
22	Finland		Subaru Impreza WRX	40	Marc Marti	Retired
23	China	Privateer	Toyota Corolla WRC	13	Marc Marti	Retired
24	Sanremo	Automobiles Citroen	Citroen Xsara Kit Car	19	Marc Marti	Retired
25	Great Britain	Privateer	Toyota Corolla WRC	21	Marc Marti	16th
2000	**0 points**					
26	Portugal		Mitsubishi Carisma GT Evo 6	18	Marc Marti	Retired
27	Catalunya	Automobiles Citroen	Citroen Xsara Kit Car	17	Marc Marti	Retired
28	Finland		Mitsubishi Lancer Evo 6	41	Marc Marti	Retired
29	Corsica		Citroen Saxo Kit Car	30	Marc Marti	28th
30	Sanremo		Citroen Saxo Kit Car	48	Marc Marti	35th
2001	**10 points (11th)**					
31	Monte Carlo	Privateer	Citroen Saxo Kit Car	21	Marc Marti	Retired
32	Catalunya	Automobiles Citroen	Citroen Xsara WRC	15	Marc Marti	Retired
33	Sanremo	Automobiles Citroen	Citroen Xsara WRC	15	Marc Marti	Retired
34	**Corsica**	**Automobiles Citroen**	**Citroen Xsara WRC**	**15**	**Marc Marti**	**1st**
2002	**1 point (17th)**					
35	Catalunya	Duriforte Gigante	Citroen Xsara WRC	25	Carlos del Barrio	12th
36	Deutschland	Automobiles Citroen	Citroen Xsara WRC	20	Marc Marti	Retired
37	Sanremo	Piedrafita Sport	Citroen Xsara WRC	27	Carlos del Barrio	6th

Ragnotti, Jean

(F) B: 29 August 1945, Carpentras, France

It is almost true to say that Jean Ragnotti spells his surname R-e-n-a-u-l-t as he has been driving and working with its products since the beginning of his career.

His first rally car in 1967 was his own Fiat 850 but he quickly progressed to an R8 Gordini while also driving Lancias and NSUs in hill climbs. His brother-in-law's transport business ran Bedford trucks and the GM dealer was interested enough to support Ragnotti in 1969 with an Opel Kadett GT/E. He won Group 1 on the Coupe des Alpes and in Corsica, following that up with a similar result on the Monte Carlo of 1970. He finished the year second in the French series. GM France offered him a drive in a Group 2 Kadett for 1970 but it proved unreliable and Ragnotti had more than his fair share of retirements.

He launched his racing career by driving a huge Opel Commodore at a German GP support race and drove a Lancia Fulvia at the Targa Florio. When an Ascona replaced the Kadett for 1972, he won Group 1 on the Monte and was ninth overall. But the GM cars were rapidly being outclassed. He drove a Fulvia in San Remo and was lying second until retirement.

Ragnotti briefly turned to racing but started rallying again in 1976.

When Renault homologated the R5 Alpine Ragnotti's rally career lifted off. Then the R5 got muscle with a Turbo and the engine migrated to the back. Ragnotti sensationally won Monte Carlo in 1981 and Corsica in 1982, repeating the latter result with the R5 Maxi Turbo in 1985. He was French champion in 1980 and again in 1984. After Group B died, Ragnotti became the star of Renault rally programmes with a succession of front wheel drive cars and today helps their Clio Super 1600 JWRC efforts from the sidelines.

Ragnotti, Jean – Career Record

YEAR	RALLY	TEAM/ENTRANT	CAR	NO.	CO-DRIVER	RESULT
1973						
1	Monte Carlo		Renault 12 Gordini	7	Jacques Jaubert	15th
1975						
2	Monte Carlo	Renault-Alpine	Renault-Alpine A110	23	Pierre Thimonier	Retired
1976						
3	Monte Carlo		Renault-Alpine A310	31	Jean-Marc Andrie	50th
4	Portugal		Renault-Alpine A310	6	Jacques Jaubert	Retired
5	Greece		Renault-Alpine A310	16	Jacques Jaubert	Retired
6	Corsica		Renault-Alpine A310	8	Jacques Jaubert	4th
7	Great Britain	Equipe Gitanes	Renault-Alpine A310	30	Jacques Jaubert	Retired
1977						
8	Sanremo		Renault 5 Alpine	23	Jean-Marc Andrie	7th
9	Great Britain		Renault 5 Alpine	38	Jean-Marc Andrie	Retired
1978						
10	Monte Carlo	Renault Elf Calberson	Renault 5 Alpine	19	Jean-Marc Andrie	2nd
11	Ivory Coast		Renault 5 Alpine	4	Jean-Marc Andrie	3rd
1979	**25 points (7th)**					
12	Monte Carlo	Renault Elf Calberson	Renault 5 Alpine	11	Jean-Marc Andrie	11th
13	Greece	Renault Elf Calberson	Renault 5 Alpine	9	Jean-Marc Andrie	4th
14	Corsica		Renault 5 Alpine	6	Jean-Marc Andrie	2nd
1980	**0 points**					
15	Corsica	Renault Elf Calberson	Renault 5 Turbo	4	Jean-Marc Andrie	Retired
1981	**28 points (11th)**					
16	**Monte Carlo**	**Renault Sport**	**Renault 5 Turbo**	**9**	**Jean-Marc Andrie**	**1st**
17	Corsica	Renault Sport	Renault 5 Turbo	11	Jean-Marc Andrie	Retired
18	Great Britain	Renault Sport	Renault 5 Turbo	9	Martin Holmes	5th
1982	**20 points (10th)**					
19	**Corsica**	**Renault Elf**	**Renault 5 Turbo**	**7**	**Jean-Marc Andrie**	**1st**
20	Ivory Coast	Renault Elf	Renault 5 Turbo	1	Jean-Marc Andrie	Retired
1983	**4 points (35th)**					
21	Monte Carlo	Renault Elf	Renault 5 Turbo	9	Jean-Marc Andrie	7th
22	Corsica	Renault Elf	Renault 5 Turbo	2	Jean-Marc Andrie	Retired
23	Greece	Renault Elf	Renault 5 Turbo	14	Jean-Marc Andrie	Retired
1984	**20 points (13th)**					
24	Portugal	Renault Portuguese	Renault 5 Turbo	9	Pierre Thimonier	5th
25	Corsica	Equipe Renault Elf	Renault 5 Turbo	10	Pierre Thimonier	3rd
1985	**20 points (13th)**					
26	**Corsica**	**Renault Elf Philips**	**Renault 5 Maxi Turbo**	**3**	**Pierre Thimonier**	**1st**
1986	**10 points (22nd)**					
27	Corsica	Renault Elf Philips	Renault 11 Turbo	7	Pierre Thimonier	4th
1987	**51 points (5th)**					
28	Monte Carlo	Philips Renault Elf	Renault 11 Turbo	3	Pierre Thimonier	8th
29	Portugal	Renault Sport Elf	Renault 11 Turbo	4	Pierre Thimonier	2nd
30	Corsica	Philips Renault Elf	Renault 11 Turbo	3	Pierre Thimonier	4th
31	Greece	Renault Sport Elf	Renault 11 Turbo	7	Pierre Thimonier	5th
32	Sanremo	Renault Sport Elf	Renault 11 Turbo	2	Pierre Thimonier	3rd
1990	**0 points**					
33	Corsica	Societe Diac	Renault 5 GT Turbo	14	Gilles Thimonier	Retired
1991	**0 points**					
34	Corsica	Societe Diac	Renault Clio 16V	10	Gilles Thimonier	Retired
1992	**2 points (58th)**					
35	Corsica	Societe Diac	Renault Clio 16V	15	Gilles Thimonier	9th
1993	**3 points (45th)**					
36	Corsica	Societe Diac	Renault Clio Williams	17	Gilles Thimonier	8th
1994	**3 points (36th**					
37	Monte Carlo	Societe Diac	Renault Clio Williams	10	Gilles Thimonier	13th
38	Corsica	Societe Diac	Renault Clio Williams	11	Gilles Thimonier	8th
1995	**4 points (14th)**					
39	Monte Carlo	Societe Diac	Renault Clio Maxi	14	Gilles Thimonier	7th
40	Corsica	Societe Diac	Renault Clio Maxi	17	Gilles Thimonier	11th

RECALDE, JORGE

(RA) B: 9 AUGUST 1951, MINA CLAVERO, ARGENTINA; D: 10 MARCH 2001

How better to get started in rallying than to beat four top European drivers in a staged event over 120kms of road near your home. That is what Jorge Recalde did in 1972 – and was given the Fiat 125 he drove as a prize.

Recalde's motor sport career had started two years earlier when he borrowed a Renault Gordini 1093 to enter an event. It continued in borrowed cars with hill-climbs, rallies and races, even driving the Argentine equivalent of an F1 car, a single-seater with a four-litre engine. On the Tour of South America in 1978, Recalde was sixth in a 1400cc Renault 12 behind five works Mercedes. Through local contacts in Ford, he crossed to Europe and drove private Escorts in Portugal and Acropolis and was invited, at the instigation of Juan-Manuel Fangio, to join the Mercedes effort for his home event where a driveshaft broke. But he was given a second chance and drove brilliantly to second on the Ivory Coast, his first African rally.

In 1983 he was Argentine champion in a Renault 18GTX and the following year got a one-off drive for Audi where he finished third, less than two minutes behind the other works Audis and having set fastest time on a quarter of the stages. In 1986, he guested with Lancia and brought his S4 home in fourth place after suffering a puncture and then setting a string of fastest times. The quiet Argentinean struck up a good relationship with the Lancia team and continued to work for them right up until they retired at the end of 1993. During 1988, he did almost a full season with them and won the Argentina Rally.

He did an enormous amount of testing for the 1989 Safari and was tipped as a likely winner. Indeed he led most of the way when right at the end of the second leg the 'spotter'

RECALDE, JORGE – CAREER RECORD

YEAR	RALLY	TEAM/ENTRANT	CAR	NO.	CO-DRIVER	RESULT
1980	18 points (14th)					
1	Portugal		Ford Escort RS	25	Hector Moyana	8th
2	Greece		Ford Escort RS	25	Eduardo Tettamanti	12th
3	Argentina	Daimler-Benz	Mercedes-Benz 500 SLC	14	Nestor Straimel	Retired
4	Ivory Coast		Mercedes-Benz 500 SLC	15	Nestor Straimel	2nd
1981	22 points (14th)					
5	Argentina	Ma.Ma.Sa	Datsun 160J	5	Jorge del Buono	3rd
6	Brazil		Datsun 160J	4	Jorge del Buono	4th
1983	3 points (41st)					
7	Argentina		Renault 18 GTX	10	Jorge del Buono	Retired
1984	12 points (16th)					
8	Argentina	Audi Sport	Audi Quattro A2	3	Jorge del Buono	3rd
1985	0 points					
9	Argentina	Renault Argentina	Renault 18 GTX	6	Jorge del Buono	Retired
1986	10 points (22nd)					
10	Argentina	Martini Lancia	Lancia Delta S4	6	Jorge del Buono	4th
1987	30 points (9th)					
11	Portugal	Jolly Club	Fiat Uno Turbo	12	Jorge del Buono	10th
12	Greece		Audi Coupe Quattro	12	Jorge del Buono	4th
13	United States	Jolly Club	Lancia Delta HF 4WD	16	Jorge del Buono	7th
14	Argentina	Martini Lancia	Lancia Delta HF 4WD	5	Jorge del Buono	2nd
1988	27 points (9th)					
15	Portugal		Lancia Delta Integrale	10	Jorge del Buono	10th
16	Corsica		Lancia Delta Integrale	7	Jorge del Buono	Retired
17	Greece		Lancia Delta Integrale	10	Jorge del Buono	Retired
18	United States		Lancia Delta Integrale	3	Jorge del Buono	6th
19	**Argentina**	**Martini Lancia**	**Lancia Delta Integrale**	**2**	**Jorge del Buono**	**1st**
20	Finland		Lancia Delta Integrale	11	Jorge del Buono	13th
21	Sanremo		Lancia Delta Integrale	10	Jorge del Buono	Retired
22	Great Britain	Top Run	Lancia Delta Integrale	14	Jorge del Buono	18th
1989	20 points (15th)					
23	Safari	Martini Lancia	Lancia Delta Integrale	3	Jorge del Buono	Retired
24	Greece		Lancia Delta Integrale	10	Jorge del Buono	5th
25	Argentina	Martini Lancia	Lancia Delta Integrale	1	Jorge del Buono	3rd
26	Australia	Top Run	Lancia Delta Integrale	7	Jorge del Buono	Retired
27	Great Britain	Top Run	Lancia Delta Integrale	12	Pierangelo Scalvini	15th
1990	7 points (33rd)					
28	Portugal	Top Run	Lancia Delta Integrale 16V	12	Martin Christie	7th
29	Greece	Top Run	Lancia Delta Integrale 16V	11	Martin Christie	Retired
30	New Zealand	Top Run	Lancia Delta Integrale 16V	5	Martin Christie	8th
31	Argentina	Recalde Alpitour	Toyota Celica GT-Four	4	Martin Christie	Retired
32	Finland	Top Run	Lancia Delta Integrale 16V	15	Martin Christie	22nd
33	Australia	Top Run	Lancia Delta Integrale 16V	12	Martin Christie	11th
1991	29 points (9th)					
34	Safari	Martini Lancia	Lancia Delta Integrale 16V	1	Martin Christie	3rd
35	Greece	Martini Lancia/Cyclon Rally Team	Lancia Delta Integrale 16V	12	Martin Christie	Retired
36	Argentina	Martini Lancia	Lancia Delta Integrale 16V	3	Martin Christie	5th
37	Australia	Martini Lancia	Lancia Delta Integrale 16V	9	Martin Christie	8th
38	Catalunya		Lancia Delta Integrale 16V	6	Martin Christie	6th
1992	28 points (10th)					
39	Safari	Martini Lancia	Lancia Delta HF Integrale	5	Martin Christie	3rd
40	Greece	Martini Lancia	Lancia Delta HF Integrale	11	Martin Christie	6th
41	Argentina	Martini Lancia	Lancia Delta HF Integrale	2	Martin Christie	Retired
42	Australia	Martini Lancia	Lancia Delta HF Integrale	7	Martin Christie	4th
1993	0 points					
43	Portugal	Astra	Lancia Delta HF Integrale	15	Martin Christie	Retired
44	Greece	Top Run	Lancia Delta HF Integrale	14	Martin Christie	Retired
45	Argentina	Top Run	Lancia Delta HF Integrale	7	Martin Christie	Retired

helicopter frightened some sheep into his path, the radiator was broken and the engine expired. Between 1994 and 1999, Recalde drove Mitsubishis in Group N but then in 2000 he started in Argentina with Ford and won the national championship. For the first round in 2001, he had taken charge of an Escort WRC but on a very hot day in which he had had many troubles with the car, he collapsed and died from a heart attack in his motorhome.

Right: Jorge Recalde was loyal to Lancia and was rewarded with an emotional victory on his home event in 1988. When the Italian team withdrew he turned his attention to the Group N Championship with Mitsubishi

RECALDE, JORGE – CAREER RECORD (CONT'D)

YEAR	RALLY	TEAM/ENTRANT	CAR	NO.	CO-DRIVER	RESULT
46	New Zealand	Top Run	Lancia Delta HF Integrale	11	Martin Christie	Retired
47	Australia	Top Run	Lancia Delta HF Integrale	11	Martin Christie	Retired
1994	**8 points (19th)**					
48	Portugal	Team Mitsubishi Ralliart Germany	Mitsubishi Lancer RS	19	Martin Christie	Retired
49	Corsica	Team Mitsubishi Ralliart Germany	Mitsubishi Lancer RS	18	Martin Christie	17th
50	Argentina	Team Mitsubishi Ralliart Germany	Mitsubishi Lancer Evo 2	11	Martin Christie	5th
51	New Zealand	Team Mitsubishi Ralliart Germany	Mitsubishi Lancer Evo 2	17	Martin Christie	Retired
52	Finland	Team Mitsubishi Ralliart Germany	Mitsubishi Lancer Evo 2	16	Martin Christie	Retired
1995	**4 points (20th)**					
53	Portugal	Team Mitsubishi Ralliart Germany	Mitsubishi Lancer Evo 2	11	Martin Christie	10th
54	Corsica	Team Mitsubishi Ralliart Germany	Mitsubishi Lancer Evo 2	15	Martin Christie	20th
55	New Zealand	Team Mitsubishi Ralliart Germany	Mitsubishi Lancer Evo 2	18	Martin Christie	9th
56	Australia	Team Mitsubishi Ralliart Germany	Mitsubishi Lancer Evo 2	15	Martin Christie	10th
57	Catalunya	Team Mitsubishi Ralliart Germany	Mitsubishi Lancer Evo 2	17	Martin Christie	Retired
1996	**0 points**					
58	Greece		Mitsubishi Lancer Evo 3	14	Martin Christie	Retired
59	Argentina		Mitsubishi Lancer Evo 3	12	Martin Christie	Retired
60	Finland		Mitsubishi Lancer Evo 3	11	Martin Christie	Retired
61	Sanremo		Mitsubishi Lancer Evo 3	19	Martin Christie	Retired
62	Catalunya		Mitsubishi Lancer Evo 3	15	Martin Christie	26th
1997	**0 points**					
63	Argentina		Mitsubishi Lancer Evo 4	18	Jose Garcia	14th
1998	**0 points**					
64	Argentina		Mitsubishi Lancer Evo 4	20	Jose Garcia	Retired
65	Australia		Mitsubishi Lancer Evo 5	35	Jorge del Buono	18th
1999	**0 points**					
66	Argentina	Ralliart America	Mitsubishi Lancer Evo 5	19	Jose Garcia	8th
2000	**0 points**					
67	Argentina		Ford Escort RS Cosworth	21	Diego Curletto	Retired

RÖHRL, WALTER

(D) B: 7 MARCH 1947, REGENSBURG, GERMANY

It is said that "genius does what it must, and talent does what it can". Walter Röhrl was a genius among rally drivers.

"Walter Röhrl was a genius among rally drivers"

Röhrl's rally career started in 1968 when he entered the Bavarian Rally in a borrowed Fiat 850 Coupé. He did not win but he set some impressive times downhill. He returned with a BMW 2002ti in 1969 but was disqualified for missing a passage control. Röhrl used an Alfa and Porsche during 1970 and came to the notice of Ford Cologne who gave him a Group 1 Capri for the German Championship. After three rallies, this became a Group 2 Capri and he went on to finish third in the German Championship. There were fewer rallies in 1972 but more important ones. Röhrl was second in Poland, led the Olympia Rally and won the Baltic.

For 1973, he got an Opel contract, drove a Commodore on his Monte Carlo and then chased both German and European titles in an Ascona. The following year he won a string of rallies to take the European title and came fifth on his first shot at the RAC Rally. For 1975, his outstanding result was to win the Acropolis in the ageing Ascona. Sadly, the keyword for the new Kadett GT/E was unreliability and a fourth place in Monte Carlo plus a win in Yprès were highlights of 1976. Towards the end of 1977, he drove a couple of rallies for Fiat and went into their team for 1978. For the WRC he drove the Fiat 131 Abarth and won twice, while on German events he drove a Stratos and won five times.

In 1979, he raced in the World Championship for Makes with the Beta Montecarlo as well as driving rallies with the 131 Abarth. He won four rallies in Germany and was second in San Remo but it was hardly a real push for the title. Despite doing five WCM races in 1980, he got the rally programme that he wanted and, in just seven events, he took four outright wins, two second places and a fifth to become World Champion. He signed a contract to go with Mercedes in 1981, but, before the season could start, Mercedes had withdrawn. Röhrl cut a deal with Porsche for a limited number of events with a 911SC and rallied a 924 Carrera GTS in Germany. He also raced a 935 for the factory .

For 1982, Röhrl was back with Opel now in the Ascona 400. He started by winning the Monte Carlo and finished by, very reluctantly, winning the Ivory Coast Rally and clinching the World title for the second time. A dispute with Opel management over his refusal to attend a sponsor function at the RAC Rally saw the new World Champion go home without competing – and without a contract. He was instantly snapped up by Lancia to drive their new Rally 037, won three times with it, never failed to finish and nearly took a third championship title.

He moved to Audi who were desperate to win the WRC. He triumphed in Monte Carlo but it was Stig Blomqvist's year and four retirements consigned Röhrl to a lowly place. He bounced back in 1985, giving the Quattro Sport E2 its only WRC victory at San Remo. Audi pulled out of rallying after the accidents in Portugal 1986 but returned briefly with the Group A 200 Quattro. Röhrl went extremely well in Monte Carlo and finished second to his team mate on the Safari. Audi took the Group B car to Pikes Peak for Röhrl where he beat Ari Vatanen by just seven seconds.

When Audi retired definitively from rallying Röhrl raced for them in IMSA and the DTM. He left at the end of 1991 and since then has been a test driver and guru at Porsche.

Right: Walter Röhrl won with several different makes in many disciplines but he is most closely associated with Audi. He is seen here on his way to winning the 1985 San Remo rally with the Sport Quattro

RÖHRL, WALTER - CAREER RECORD

YEAR	RALLY	TEAM/ENTRANT	CAR	NO.	CO-DRIVER	RESULT
1973						
1	Monte Carlo	Opel Euro Händler Team	Opel Commodore	22	Jochen Berger	45th
2	Austria	Opel Euro Händler Team	Opel Ascona	4	Jochen Berger	Retired
3	Great Britain	Opel Euro Händler Team	Opel Ascona	26	Jochen Berger	Retired
1974						
4	Portugal	Opel Euro Händler Team	Opel Ascona	5	Jochen Berger	Retired
5	Great Britain	Opel Euro Händler Team	Opel Ascona	4	Jochen Berger	5th
1975						
6	Monte Carlo	Opel Euro Händler Team	Opel Ascona	5	Jochen Berger	Retired
7	**Greece**	**Opel Euro Händler Team**	**Opel Ascona**	**2**	**Jochen Berger**	**1st**
8	Morocco	Opel Euro Händler Team	Opel Ascona	7	Jochen Berger	Retired
9	Portugal	Opel Euro Händler Team	Opel Ascona	3	Jochen Berger	Retired
10	Sanremo	Opel Euro Händler Team	Opel Kadett GT/E	4	Jochen Berger	Retired
11	Great Britain	Opel Euro Händler Team	Opel Kadett GT/E	4	Jochen Berger	Retired
1976						
12	Monte Carlo	Opel Euro Händler Team	Opel Kadett GT/E	16	Jochen Berger	4th
13	Portugal	Opel Euro Händler Team	Opel Kadett GT/E	3	Claes Billstam	Retired
14	Safari	Opel Euro Händler Team	Opel Kadett GT/E	9	Claes Billstam	Retired
15	Sanremo	Opel Euro Händler Team	Opel Kadett GT/E	8	Willi-Peter Pitz	Retired
16	Corsica	Opel Euro Händler Team	Opel Kadett GT/E	3	Jochen Berger	Retired
17	Great Britain	Opel Euro Händler Team	Opel Kadett GT/E	11	Jochen Berger	Retired
1977						
18	Monte Carlo	Opel Euro Händler Team	Opel Kadett GT/E	3	Willi-Peter Pitz	Retired
19	Greece	Opel Euro Händler Team	Opel Kadett GT/E	3	Willi-Peter Pitz	Retired
20	Canada	Olio Fiat	Fiat 131 Abarth	4	Christian Geistdorfer	Retired
21	Sanremo	Olio Fiat	Fiat 131 Abarth	5	Willi-Peter Pitz	Retired
22	Great Britain	Opel Euro Händler Team	Opel Kadett GT/E	12	Willi-Peter Pitz	Retired
1978						
23	Monte Carlo	Fiat Alitalia	Fiat 131 Abarth	2	Christian Geistdorfer	4th
24	Portugal	Fiat Alitalia	Fiat 131 Abarth	9	Christian Geistdorfer	Retired
25	**Greece**	**Fiat Alitalia**	**Fiat 131 Abarth**	**5**	**Christian Geistdorfer**	**1st**
26	**Canada**	**Fiat Alitalia**	**Fiat 131 Abarth**	**3**	**Christian Geistdorfer**	**1st**
27	Sanremo	Fiat Alitalia	Fiat 131 Abarth	2	Christian Geistdorfer	Retired
28	Great Britain	Fiat Alitalia	Fiat 131 Abarth	5	Christian Geistdorfer	6th
1979	**21 points (9th)**					
29	Monte Carlo	Alitalia Fiat	Fiat 131 Abarth	14	Christian Geistdorfer	Retired
30	Safari	Alitalia Fiat	Fiat 131 Abarth	11	Christian Geistdorfer	8th
31	Sanremo	Alitalia Fiat	Fiat 131 Abarth	6	Christian Geistdorfer	2nd
32	Great Britain	Alitalia Fiat	Fiat 131 Abarth	3	Christian Geistdorfer	8th
1980	**118 points (WORLD CHAMPION)**					
33	**Monte Carlo**	**Fiat Italia**	**Fiat 131 Abarth**	**10**	**Christian Geistdorfer**	**1st**
34	**Portugal**	**Fiat Italia**	**Fiat 131 Abarth**	**5**	**Christian Geistdorfer**	**1st**
35	Greece	Fiat Italia	Fiat 131 Abarth	3	Christian Geistdorfer	5th
36	**Argentina**	**Fiat Italia**	**Fiat 131 Abarth**	**2**	**Christian Geistdorfer**	**1st**
37	New Zealand	Fiat Italia	Fiat 131 Abarth	2	Christian Geistdorfer	2nd
38	**Sanremo**	**Jolly Club**	**Fiat 131 Abarth**	**2**	**Christian Geistdorfer**	**1st**
39	Corsica	Fiat Italia	Fiat 131 Abarth	3	Christian Geistdorfer	2nd
1981	**0 points**					
40	Sanremo	Eminance	Porsche 911SC	1	Christian Geistdorfer	Retired
1982	**109 points (WORLD CHAMPION)**					
41	**Monte Carlo**	**Rothmans Opel Rally Team**	**Opel Ascona 400**	**2**	**Christian Geistdorfer**	**1st**
42	Sweden	Rothmans Opel Rally Team	Opel Ascona 400	3	Christian Geistdorfer	3rd
43	Portugal	Rothmans Opel Rally Team	Opel Ascona 400	1	Christian Geistdorfer	Retired
44	Safari	Rothmans Opel Rally Team	Opel Ascona 400	5	Christian Geistdorfer	2nd
45	Corsica	Rothmans Opel Rally Team	Opel Ascona 400	5	Christian Geistdorfer	4th
46	Greece	Rothmans Opel Rally Team	Opel Ascona 400	1	Christian Geistdorfer	2nd
47	New Zealand	Rothmans Opel Rally Team	Opel Ascona 400	2	Christian Geistdorfer	3rd
48	Brazil	Rothmans Opel Rally Team	Opel Ascona 400	2	Christian Geistdorfer	2nd

RÖHRL, WALTER CAREER RECORD (CONT'D)

YEAR	RALLY	TEAM/ENTRANT	CAR	NO.	CO-DRIVER	RESULT
49	Sanremo	Rothmans Opel Rally Team	Opel Ascona 400	3	Christian Geistdorfer	3rd
50	**Ivory Coast**	**Rothmans Opel Rally Team**	**Opel Ascona 400**	**4**	**Christian Geistdorfer**	**1st**
1983	**102 points (2nd)**					
51	**Monte Carlo**	**Martini Racing**	**Lancia Rally 037**	**1**	**Christian Geistdorfer**	**1st**
52	Portugal	Martini Racing	Lancia Rally 037	2	Christian Geistdorfer	3rd
53	Corsica	Martini Racing	Lancia Rally 037	5	Christian Geistdorfer	2nd
54	**Greece**	**Martini Racing**	**Lancia Rally 037**	**3**	**Christian Geistdorfer**	**1st**
55	**New Zealand**	**Martini Racing**	**Lancia Rally 037**	**1**	**Christian Geistdorfer**	**1st**
56	Sanremo	Martini Racing	Lancia Rally 037	2	Christian Geistdorfer	2nd
1984	**26 points (11th)**					
57	**Monte Carlo**	**Audi Sport**	**Audi Quattro A2**	**1**	**Christian Geistdorfer**	**1st**
58	Portugal	Audi Sport	Audi Quattro A2	4	Christian Geistdorfer	6th
59	Corsica	Audi Sport	Audi Sport Quattro	2	Christian Geistdorfer	Retired
60	Greece	Audi Sport	Audi Sport Quattro	1	Christian Geistdorfer	Retired
61	New Zealand	Audi Sport	Audi Quattro A2	1	Christian Geistdorfer	Retired
62	Sanremo	Audi Sport	Audi Sport Quattro	5	Christian Geistdorfer	Retired
1985	**59 points (3rd)**					
63	Monte Carlo	Audi Sport	Audi Sport Quattro	3	Christian Geistdorfer	2nd
64	Sweden	Audi Sport	Audi Sport Quattro	5	Christian Geistdorfer	Retired
65	Portugal	Audi Sport	Audi Sport Quattro	5	Christian Geistdorfer	3rd
66	Corsica	Audi Sport	Audi Sport Quattro	5	Christian Geistdorfer	Retired
67	Greece	Audi Sport	Audi Sport Quattro	3	Christian Geistdorfer	Retired
68	New Zealand	Audi Sport	Audi Sport Quattro	3	Christian Geistdorfer	3rd
69	**Sanremo**	**Audi Sport**	**Audi Sport Quattro E2**	**5**	**Christian Geistdorfer**	**1st**
70	Great Britain	Audi Sport	Audi Sport Quattro E2	4	Phil Short	Retired
1986	**10 points (22nd)**					
71	Monte Carlo	Audi Sport	Audi Sport Quattro E2	2	Christian Geistdorfer	4th
72	Portugal	Audi Sport	Audi Sport Quattro E2	3	Christian Geistdorfer	Retired
1987	**27 points (11th)**					
73	Monte Carlo	Audi Sport	Audi 200 Quattro	4	Christian Geistdorfer	3rd
74	Safari	Audi Sport	Audi 200 Quattro	2	Christian Geistdorfer	2nd
75	Greece	Audi Sport	Audi 200 Quattro	2	Christian Geistdorfer	Retired

Rovanperä, Harri

(FIN) B: 8 APRIL 1966, JYVASKALA, FINLAND

"He stood out for his very extrovert driving technique"

It is easier for a camel to pass through the eye of a needle ... than it is for a young man to get his hands on a rally car. But for Harri Rovanpera, living in Jyväskylä meant that he just had to have one, so he spent every available moment driving delivery vans and working to that end.

He started in a small way doing local events with a Sunbeam Avenger in 1989. He stood out for his very extrovert driving technique. Two years later, he got hold of an Escort RS2000 and drove in Group F on Finnish Championship events. He was consistently in the top 10 and in 1993, when he made his WRC debut on the 1000 Lakes with an Opel Manta, it was with the help of a Rally Finland award generated by his championship results.

During 1994, Rovanpera drove a Group N Mitsubishi Galant VR-4 and got his first WRC finish. The following year he was contracted to drive a Group A Opel Kadett GSi 16v and clinched the Finnish 2-litre Championship but went back to a Mitsubishi for the start of the next season. He drove a Group A Escort Cosworth on the 1000 Lakes and then came the call from SEAT. They had been doing WRC events with Spanish drivers but, for the RAC Rally, they invited Rovanpera to join their team. Only an F2 event, the RAC was not so well attended as normal, but his eighth place overall and best SEAT driver confirmed him as a team member for 1997.

Catapulted into a full WRC season, Rovanpera acquitted himself well with only three retirements and, most of the time, results in the top 10. This was not bad for a 2-litre kit car and when they got its major evolution through in 1998, he took it to fifth place overall on his first ever Safari. Later that same year, SEAT introduced the 4WD Cordoba WRC and Rovanpera drove it on its debut in Jyväskylä. Sadly, the Cordoba WRC was not a complete success. His best result with the car was on the last rally of 1999 when he was third on the RAC Rally. He drove a couple of rallies with SEAT in 2000 but had to go looking for other cars. He drove for Grifone in Finland and would have been second had he not checked in early at a time control.

But his speed was evident and Peugeot signed him for 2001. Like a fairytale, he won the very first WRC rally he did for them but he was not one of their nominated drivers to score manufacturer points. However, Rovanpera's programme was rapidly expanded, he was nominated as one of their scoring drivers and the result was a Manufacturer's championship for Peugeot. Rovanpera has been one of Peugeot's main assets with consistent results, though a win on his home event eludes him for the present. He started 2004 without a commitment but was recalled to drive Peugeot's new 307WRC after the first two events.

ROVANPERÄ, HARRI - CAREER RECORD

YEAR	RALLY	TEAM/ENTRANT	CAR	NO.	CO-DRIVER	RESULT
1993	0 points					
1	Finland		Opel Manta	39	Risto Pietilainen	Retired
1994	0 points					
2	Finland		Mitsubishi Galant VR-4	30	Risto Pietilainen	12th
1996	0 points					
3	Finland	Promoracing ESTB	Ford Escort RS Cosworth	18	Juha Repo	Retired
1997	0 points					
4	Monte Carlo	SEAT Sport	SEAT Ibiza Kit Car	18	Voitto Silander	14th
5	Portugal	SEAT Sport	SEAT Ibiza Kit Car	22	Voitto Silander	Retired
6	Catalunya	SEAT Sport	SEAT Ibiza Kit Car	17	Voitto Silander	Retired
7	Argentina	SEAT Sport	SEAT Ibiza Kit Car	11	Voitto Silander	8th
8	New Zealand	SEAT Sport	SEAT Ibiza Kit Car	9	Voitto Silander	Retired
9	Finland	SEAT Sport	SEAT Ibiza Kit Car	21	Voitto Silander	10th
10	Indonesia	SEAT Sport	SEAT Ibiza Kit Car	11	Voitto Silander	7th
11	Sanremo	SEAT Sport	SEAT Ibiza Kit Car	25	Voitto Silander	10th
12	Australia	SEAT Sport	SEAT Ibiza Kit Car	16	Voitto Silander	10th
13	Great Britain	SEAT Sport	SEAT Ibiza Kit Car	27	Voitto Silander	9th
1998	3 points (15th)					
14	Monte Carlo	SEAT Sport	SEAT Ibiza Kit Car	15	Voitto Silander	11th
15	Sweden	SEAT Sport	SEAT Ibiza Kit Car	17	Voitto Silander	Retired
16	Safari	SEAT Sport	SEAT Ibiza Kit Car E2	11	Voitto Silander	5th
17	Portugal	SEAT Sport	SEAT Ibiza Kit Car E2	16	Risto Pietilainen	Retired
18	Catalunya	SEAT Sport	SEAT Ibiza Kit Car E2	18	Risto Pietilainen	Retired
19	Argentina	SEAT Sport	SEAT Ibiza Kit Car E2	14	Risto Pietilainen	Retired
20	Greece	SEAT Sport	SEAT Ibiza Kit Car E2	25	Risto Pietilainen	15th
21	New Zealand	SEAT Sport	SEAT Ibiza Kit Car E2	19	Risto Pietilainen	13th
22	Finland	SEAT Sport	SEAT Cordoba WRC	9	Risto Pietilainen	11th
23	Sanremo	SEAT Sport	SEAT Cordoba WRC	9	Risto Pietilainen	Retired
24	Australia	SEAT Sport	SEAT Cordoba WRC	9	Risto Pietilainen	11th
25	Great Britain	SEAT Sport	SEAT Cordoba WRC	9	Risto Pietilainen	6th
1999	10 points (9th)					
26	Monte Carlo	SEAT Sport	SEAT Cordoba WRC	9	Risto Pietilainen	7th
27	Sweden	SEAT Sport	SEAT Cordoba WRC	9	Risto Pietilainen	16th
28	Safari	SEAT Sport	SEAT Cordoba WRC	9	Risto Pietilainen	6th
29	Portugal	SEAT Sport	SEAT Cordoba WRC	9	Risto Pietilainen	Retired
30	Catalunya	SEAT Sport	SEAT Cordoba WRC	9	Risto Pietilainen	14th
31	Corsica	SEAT Sport	SEAT Cordoba WRC	9	Risto Pietilainen	13th
32	Argentina	SEAT Sport	SEAT Cordoba WRC	9	Risto Pietilainen	Retired
33	Greece	SEAT Sport	SEAT Cordoba WRC	9	Risto Pietilainen	Retired
34	New Zealand	SEAT Sport	SEAT Cordoba WRC	9	Risto Pietilainen	Retired
35	Finland	SEAT Sport	SEAT Cordoba WRC E2	9	Risto Pietilainen	5th
36	China	SEAT Sport	SEAT Cordoba WRC E2	9	Risto Pietilainen	5th
37	Sanremo	SEAT Sport	SEAT Cordoba WRC E2	9	Risto Pietilainen	16th
38	Australia	SEAT Sport	SEAT Cordoba WRC E2	9	Risto Pietilainen	6th
39	Great Britain	SEAT Sport	SEAT Cordoba WRC E2	9	Risto Pietilainen	3rd
2000	7 points (9th)					
40	Sweden	SEAT Sport	SEAT Cordoba WRC E2	16	Risto Pietilainen	12th
41	Portugal	HF Grifone	Toyota Corolla WRC	16	Risto Pietilainen	4th
42	Finland	HF Grifone	Toyota Corolla WRC	17	Risto Pietilainen	3rd
43	Great Britain	SEAT Sport	SEAT Cordoba WRC E3	17	Risto Pietilainen	10th
2001	36 points (5th)					
44	**Sweden**	**Peugeot Total**	**Peugeot 206 WRC**	**16**	**Risto Pietilainen**	**1st**
45	Portugal	Peugeot Total	Peugeot 206 WRC	16	Risto Pietilainen	Retired
46	Argentina	Peugeot Total	Peugeot 206 WRC	16	Risto Pietilainen	Retired
47	Cyprus	Peugeot Total	Peugeot 206 WRC	16	Risto Pietilainen	Retired
48	Greece	Peugeot Total	Peugeot 206 WRC	16	Risto Pietilainen	3rd
49	Safari	Peugeot Total	Peugeot 206 WRC	16	Risto Pietilainen	2nd
50	Finland	Peugeot Total	Peugeot 206 WRC	16	Risto Pietilainen	4th
51	New Zealand	Peugeot Total	Peugeot 206 WRC	16	Risto Pietilainen	3rd
52	Sanremo	HF Grifone	Peugeot 206 WRC	25	Risto Pietilainen	11th
53	Corsica	HF Grifone	Peugeot 206 WRC	29	Risto Pietilainen	7th
54	Australia	Peugeot Total	Peugeot 206 WRC	16	Risto Pietilainen	4th
55	Great Britain	Peugeot Total	Peugeot 206 WRC	16	Risto Pietilainen	2nd
2002	30 points (7th)					
56	Monte Carlo	Bozian Racing	Peugeot 206 WRC	25	Risto Pietilainen	Retired
57	Sweden	Peugeot Total	Peugeot 206 WRC	3	Risto Pietilainen	2nd
58	Corsica	Bozian Racing	Peugeot 206 WRC	24	Risto Pietilainen	11th
59	Catalunya	Bozian Racing	Peugeot 206 WRC	23	Risto Pietilainen	7th
60	Cyprus	Peugeot Total	Peugeot 206 WRC	3	Risto Pietilainen	4th
61	Argentina	Peugeot Total	Peugeot 206 WRC	3	Risto Pietilainen	Retired
62	Greece	Peugeot Total	Peugeot 206 WRC	3	Risto Pietilainen	4th
63	Safari	Peugeot Total	Peugeot 206 WRC	3	Risto Pietilainen	2nd
64	Finland	Peugeot Total	Peugeot 206 WRC	3	Voitto Silander	Retired
65	Germany	Peugeot Total	Peugeot 206 WRC	3	Voitto Silander	Retired
66	Sanremo	Bozian Racing	Peugeot 206 WRC	25	Voitto Silander	9th
67	New Zealand	Peugeot Total	Peugeot 206 WRC	3	Voitto Silander	2nd
68	Australia	Peugeot Total	Peugeot 206 WRC	3	Voitto Silander	2nd
69	Great Britain	Peugeot Total	Peugeot 206 WRC	3	Risto Pietilainen	7th
2003	18 points (11th)					
70	Sweden	Marlboro Peugeot Total	Peugeot 206 WRC	3	Risto Pietilainen	Retired
71	Turkey	Marlboro Peugeot Total	Peugeot 206 WRC	3	Risto Pietilainen	Retired
72	New Zealand	Marlboro Peugeot Total	Peugeot 206 WRC	3	Risto Pietilainen	Retired
73	Argentina	Marlboro Peugeot Total	Peugeot 206 WRC	3	Risto Pietilainen	4th
74	Greece	Marlboro Peugeot Total	Peugeot 206 WRC	3	Risto Pietilainen	6th
75	Cyprus	Marlboro Peugeot Total	Peugeot 206 WRC	3	Risto Pietilainen	2nd
76	Finland	Marlboro Peugeot Total	Peugeot 206 WRC	3	Risto Pietilainen	Retired
77	Australia	Marlboro Peugeot Total	Peugeot 206 WRC	3	Risto Pietilainen	7th
78	Great Britain	Marlboro Peugeot Total	Peugeot 206 WRC	3	Risto Pietilainen	Retired

SABY, BRUNO (F) B: 23 FEBRUARY 1949, GRENOBLE, FRANCE

With a driving career spanning 35 years, Bruno Saby is one of the most experienced and versatile of the second generation of French drivers in the WRC. His career started with local rallies round Grenoble in a Citroën Ami 6 in 1967. By 1973, he had acquired a Renault R12 Gordini in which he entered the Monte Carlo but had to retire through illness. He did the 1000 Lakes the following year with an Opel Ascona and was excluded for speeding. Fortunately, at this time, rallying was very much a hobby and it was not until 1978 when he won the French rallycross championship that he thought of turning professional.

He got support to drive a Renault R5 Alpine and visited Africa for the Ivory Coast Rally, getting halfway before the suspension collapsed. In 1980, he moved up to an R5 Turbo and was promptly fourth in Corsica with what was effectively a Group 3 car with 100 bhp less that the works cars. The next year, he was French Champion and by 1983 he was driving for the Renault factory team. For 1985, which was its first full season in the WRC, Peugeot wanted a French driver in their team alongside Ari Vatanen and Timo Salonen. When Vatanen was hurt in Argentina, more of the responsibility fell on Saby and he delivered with a second place in Corsica to help lift Peugeot to its Manufacturer's title.

In 1986, he was again the Third Man when Juha Kankkunen joined Peugeot. After losing a wheel on Monte Carlo and recovering to finish sixth, it was Saby's sad task to win in Corsica after Henri Toivonen's fatal accident. When Group B finished, so did Peugeot's WRC programme. Saby was joined Lancia and won Monte Carlo for them in 1988. Saby drove Lancias in rallying for another three years before discovering a new challenge in Rally Raids.

SABY, BRUNO - CAREER RECORD

YEAR	RALLY	TEAM/ENTRANT	CAR	NO.	CO-DRIVER	RESULT
1973						
1	Monte Carlo		Renault 12 Gordini	149	Jacques Penon	Retired
1974						
2	Finland		Opel Ascona	49	Jean-Christian Court-Payen	Excluded
1978						
3	Monte Carlo	Team Chardonnet	Autobianchi A112	23	Michel Guegan	Retired
4	Great Britain		Renault Alpine 1600	48	Michel Guegan	Retired
1979	**0 points**					
5	Monte Carlo	Renault Elf Calberson	Renault 5 Alpine	28	Michel Guegan	Retired
6	Ivory Coast		Renault 5 Alpine	21	Daniel le Saux	Retired
1980	**10 points (25th)**					
7	Monte Carlo		Renault 5 Alpine	35	Jean-Marc Andrie	15th
8	Corsica	Garage Galtier	Renault 5 Turbo	18	'Tilber'	4th
1981	**0 points**					
9	Monte Carlo	Renault Elf	Renault 5 Turbo	20	Daniel le Saux	Retired
10	Corsica		Renault 5 Turbo	16	Daniel le Saux	Retired
11	Great Britain		Renault 5 Turbo	23	Jean-Marc Andrie	Retired
1982	**26 points (9th)**					
12	Monte Carlo	Garage Galtier	Renault 5 Turbo	9	Francoise Sappey	5th
13	Corsica	Garage Galtier	Renault 5 Turbo	14	Francoise Sappey	5th
14	Ivory Coast	Garage Galtier	Renault 5 Turbo	8	Daniel le Saux	4th
1983	**9 points (20th)**					
15	Monte Carlo		Renault 5 Turbo	14	Francoise Sappey	13th
16	Corsica	Philips Auto Radio	Renault 5 Turbo	15	Chris Williams	5th
1984	**3 points (43rd)**					
17	Monte Carlo	Philips Auto Radio	Renault 5 Turbo	12	Jean-Marc Andrie	Retired
18	Corsica	Philips Auto Radio	Renault 5 Turbo	16	Jean-Francois Fauchille	Retired
19	Finland	Philips Auto Radio	Renault 5 Turbo	15	Jean-Francois Fauchille	8th
1985	**23 points (11th)**					
20	Monte Carlo	Peugeot Talbot Sport	Peugeot 205 T16	8	Jean-Francois Fauchille	5th
21	Safari	Peugeot Talbot Sport	Peugeot 205 T16	12	Jean-Francois Fauchille	Retired
22	Corsica	Peugeot Talbot Sport	Peugeot 205 T16 E2	11	Jean-Francois Fauchille	2nd
23	Sanremo	Peugeot Talbot Sport	Peugeot 205 T16 E2	7	Jean-Francois Fauchille	Retired
1986	**38 points (7th)**					
24	Monte Carlo	Peugeot Talbot Sport	Peugeot 205 T16 E2	8	Jean-Francois Fauchille	6th
25	**Corsica**	**Peugeot Talbot Sport**	**Peugeot 205 T16 E2**	**5**	**Jean-Francois Fauchille**	**1st**
26	Greece	Peugeot Talbot Sport	Peugeot 205 T16 E2	9	Jean-Francois Fauchille	3rd
27	Argentina	Peugeot Talbot Sport	Peugeot 205 T16 E2	4	Jean-Francois Fauchille	Retired
1987	**15 points (20th)**					
28	Monte Carlo	Martini Lancia	Lancia Delta HF 4WD	8	Jean-Francois Fauchille	Retired
29	Corsica	Martini Lancia	Lancia Delta HF 4WD	1	Jean-Francois Fauchille	Retired
30	Sanremo	Team Chardonnet	Lancia Delta HF 4WD	6	Jean-Francois Fauchille	2nd
1988	**32 points (6th)**					
31	**Monte Carlo**	**Martini Lancia**	**Lancia Delta HF 4WD**	**3**	**Jean-Francois Fauchille**	**1st**
32	Corsica	Martini Lancia	Lancia Delta Integrale	6	Jean-Francois Fauchille	3rd
1989	**12 points (25th)**					
33	Monte Carlo	Martini Lancia	Lancia Delta Integrale	1	Jean-Francois Fauchille	3rd
34	Corsica	Lancia France	Lancia Delta Integrale	5	Daniel Grataloup	Retired
1990	**16 points (15th)**					
35	Monte Carlo	Lancia Fina	Lancia Delta Integrale 16V	8	Daniel Grataloup	6th
36	Corsica	Lancia Fina	Lancia Delta Integrale 16V	6	Daniel Grataloup	4th
1991	**8 points (34th)**					
37	Monte Carlo	Lancia Fina	Lancia Delta Integrale 16V	6	Daniel Grataloup	6th
38	Corsica	Martini Lancia	Lancia Delta Integrale 16V	8	Daniel Grataloup	Retired
39	Great Britain	Privateer	Lancia Delta Integrale 16V	16	Jean-Francois Fauchille	9th

SAINZ, CARLOS

(E) B: 12 APRIL 1962, MADRID, SPAIN

To be World Rally Champion twice is an outstanding achievement, but when that could have been three – or even four – then you know this is an exceptional man. Additionally, Carlos Sainz has won on all kinds of surfaces, all kinds of rallies : three wins on Monte and Acropolis, four in New Zealand, plus Safari, 1000 Lakes, RAC, Portugal, Corsica, Turkey and Cyprus – the only ones missing are Sweden (second four times) and San Remo (second twice).

Sainz could have been a champion in several disciplines. As a young man he was a national level squash player and also distinguished himself at fencing, football and skiing. His first steps in rallying were in 1980 with a Renault R5 TS. Next he tried racing, drove in the SEAT Panda championship and won it, as well as racing in the Renault 5 Cup. He won the Marlboro Challenge and got a drive in a Formula Ford at the Brands Festival in 1983. He finished fourth in his heat but cracked the radiator in the quarter-final. Towards the end of 1984, he got a drive in the second Opel Manta 400 run by GM Spain and was second to their number one driver (and Spanish Champion that year) Salvador Servia. He was promptly offered a R5 Turbo and was runner up to Servia in 1985 and 1986.

For 1987, Ford Spain stepped in and offered Sainz a full contract. He won the Spanish Championship and made his WRC debut on the Portuguese Rally. He was Spanish Champion again in 1988 and did four WRC events with Ford in which he showed remarkable consistency. Toyota spotted his talent and he joined them for the 1989 season. The new Celica GT-4 was not fully sorted and the year started with four retirements but then changed dramatically to see Sainz on the podium three times. It thus came as no great surprise when the young Spaniard won four WRC events and the championship in 1990.

The following year was almost as good. Sainz won five events and could have claimed the title with a win on the RAC Rally but a head gasket problem delayed him. With the Celica Turbo 4WD in 1992 there was no such problem. He won Catalunya and RAC rallies to clinch the title. Out of loyalty to his long-time sponsor, Repsol, Sainz left Toyota at the end of 1992 as they had signed with Castrol and went to Lancia. The problem was that the Lancia works team had handed over to the Jolly Club. It was a dismal year for Sainz and saw him leave for Subaru for 1994. Again, he was second in the World Championship and hoped for better in 1995. His team mate was Colin McRae and they were the two men in line for the title. In an effort to keep Sainz with Subaru, team orders were applied to let Sainz win from McRae in Catalunya but then he needed to win the RAC to take the title. McRae led that one too and there was no way he could be asked to step aside in Britain. In any case, by then Sainz had decided to go to Ford.

After two years with the Escort, Sainz returned to the Toyota fold and nearly won his third World title. He

"To be World Rally Champion twice is an outstanding achievement, but when that could have been three – or even four – then you know this is an exceptional man."

only needed to finish fourth on the RAC Rally but the engine expired with 500 yards to go. The year 2000 saw him back with Ford in the Focus WRC but the wins were few and when Ford decided to go with less expensive young talent for 2003, Sainz signed with Citroën. Coming into the Rally GB, he was lying equal first in the Championship but a wiring fire on the in-car camera and a subsequent accident put him out of the rally. Retirement has been mentioned but Sainz's hunger for driving seems undiminished.

Right: Rally GB hasn't always been kind to 'El Matador' but here in 1992 he is seen heading for the victory that rounded off his second title-winning season. The 2003 event marked his 180th appearance in the WRC, making him the most experienced driver still competing

SAINZ, CARLOS - CAREER RECORD

YEAR	RALLY	TEAM/ENTRANT	CAR	NO.	CO-DRIVER	RESULT
1987	7 points (35th)					
1	Portugal	Marlboro Rally Team	Ford Sierra RS Cosworth	11	Antonio Boto	Retired
2	Corsica	Marlboro Rally Team	Ford Sierra RS Cosworth	15	Antonio Boto	7th
3	Great Britain	RACC Espana	Ford Sierra RS Cosworth	26	Antonio Boto	8th
1988	26 points (11th)					
4	Portugal	Privateer	Ford Sierra RS Cosworth	15	Luis Moya	Retired
5	Corsica	Ford Motor Company	Ford Sierra RS Cosworth	12	Luis Moya	5th
6	Finland	Ford Motor Company	Ford Sierra RS Cosworth	14	Luis Moya	6th
7	Sanremo	Ford Motor Company	Ford Sierra RS Cosworth	11	Luis Moya	5th
8	Great Britain	Ford Motor Company	Ford Sierra RS Cosworth	21	Luis Moya	7th
1989	39 points (8th)					
9	Monte Carlo	Toyota Team Europe	Toyota Celica GT-Four	15	Luis Moya	Retired
10	Portugal	Toyota Team Europe	Toyota Celica GT-Four	9	Luis Moya	Retired
11	Corsica	Toyota Team Europe	Toyota Celica GT-Four	12	Luis Moya	Retired
12	Greece	Toyota Team Europe	Toyota Celica GT-Four	8	Luis Moya	Retired
13	Finland	Toyota Team Europe	Toyota Celica GT-Four	7	Luis Moya	3rd
14	Sanremo	Toyota Team Europe	Toyota Celica GT-Four	2	Luis Moya	3rd
15	Great Britain	Toyota Team Europe	Toyota Celica GT-Four	3	Luis Moya	2nd
1990	140 points (WORLD CHAMPION)					
16	Monte Carlo	Toyota Team Europe	Toyota Celica GT-Four	2	Luis Moya	2nd
17	Portugal	Toyota Team Europe	Toyota Celica GT-Four	2	Luis Moya	Retired
18	Safari	Toyota Team Kenya	Toyota Celica GT-Four	67	Luis Moya	4th
19	Corsica	Toyota Team Europe	Toyota Celica GT-Four	2	Luis Moya	2nd
20	**Greece**	**Toyota Team Europe**	**Toyota Celica GT-Four**	**2**	**Luis Moya**	**1st**
21	**New Zealand**	**Toyota Team Europe**	**Toyota Celica GT-Four**	**2**	**Luis Moya**	**1st**
22	Argentina	Toyota Team Europe	Toyota Celica GT-Four	1	Luis Moya	2nd
23	**Finland**	**Toyota Team Europe**	**Toyota Celica GT-Four**	**4**	**Luis Moya**	**1st**
24	Australia	Toyota Team Europe	Toyota Celica GT-Four	2	Luis Moya	2nd
25	Sanremo	Toyota Team Europe	Toyota Celica GT-Four	2	Luis Moya	3rd
26	**Great Britain**	**Toyota Team Europe**	**Toyota Celica GT-Four**	**2**	**Luis Moya**	**1st**
1991	143 points (2nd)					
27	**Monte Carlo**	**Toyota Team Europe**	**Toyota Celica GT-Four**	**2**	**Luis Moya**	**1st**
28	**Portugal**	**Toyota Team Europe**	**Toyota Celica GT-Four**	**2**	**Luis Moya**	**1st**
29	Safari	Toyota Team Kenya	Toyota Celica GT-Four	2	Luis Moya	Retired
30	**Corsica**	**Toyota Team Europe**	**Toyota Celica GT-Four**	**2**	**Luis Moya**	**1st**
31	Greece	Toyota Team Europe	Toyota Celica GT-Four	1	Luis Moya	2nd
32	**New Zealand**	**Toyota Team Europe**	**Toyota Celica GT-Four**	**1**	**Luis Moya**	**1st**
33	**Argentina**	**Toyota Team Europe**	**Toyota Celica GT-Four**	**5**	**Luis Moya**	**1st**
34	Finland	Toyota Team Europe	Toyota Celica GT-Four	1	Luis Moya	4th
35	Australia	Toyota Team Europe	Toyota Celica GT-Four	2	Luis Moya	Retired
36	Sanremo	Toyota Team Europe	Toyota Celica GT-Four	2	Luis Moya	6th
37	Catalunya	Toyota Team Europe	Toyota Celica GT-Four	1	Luis Moya	Retired
38	Great Britain	Toyota Team Europe	Toyota Celica GT-Four	1	Luis Moya	3rd
1992	144 points (WORLD CHAMPION)					
39	Monte Carlo	Toyota Team Europe	Toyota Celica Turbo 4WD	2	Luis Moya	2nd
40	Portugal	Toyota Team Europe	Toyota Celica Turbo 4WD	1	Luis Moya	3rd
41	**Safari**	**Toyota Team Kenya**	**Toyota Celica Turbo 4WD**	**8**	**Luis Moya**	**1st**
42	Corsica	Toyota Team Europe	Toyota Celica Turbo 4WD	1	Luis Moya	4th
43	Greece	Toyota Team Europe	Toyota Celica Turbo 4WD	2	Luis Moya	Retired
44	**New Zealand**	**Toyota Team Europe**	**Toyota Celica Turbo 4WD**	**1**	**Luis Moya**	**1st**
45	Argentina	Toyota Team Europe	Toyota Celica Turbo 4WD	1	Luis Moya	2nd
46	Australia	Toyota Team Europe	Toyota Celica Turbo 4WD	2	Luis Moya	3rd
47	**Catlaunya**	**Toyota Team Europe**	**Toyota Celica Turbo 4WD**	**4**	**Luis Moya**	**1st**
48	**Great Britain**	**Toyota Team Europe**	**Toyota Celica Turbo 4WD**	**2**	**Luis Moya**	**1st**
1993	35 points (8th)					
49	Monte Carlo	Jolly Club	Lancia Delta HF Integrale	1	Luis Moya	14th
50	Portugal	Jolly Club	Lancia Delta HF Integrale	1	Luis Moya	Retired
51	Corsica	Jolly Club	Lancia Delta HF Integrale	2	Luis Moya	4th

SAINZ, CARLOS CAREER RECORD (CONT'D)

YEAR	RALLY	TEAM/ENTRANT	CAR	NO.	CO-DRIVER	RESULT
52	Greece	Jolly Club	Lancia Delta HF Integrale	3	Luis Moya	2nd
53	Argentina	Jolly Club	Lancia Delta HF Integrale	2	Luis Moya	Retired
54	New Zealand	Jolly Club	Lancia Delta HF Integrale	1	Luis Moya	4th
55	Australia	Jolly Club	Lancia Delta HF Integrale	1	Luis Moya	Retired
56	Sanremo	Jolly Club	Lancia Delta HF Integrale	4	Luis Moya	Retired
57	Catalunya	Jolly Club	Lancia Delta HF Integrale	1	Luis Moya	Retired
1994	**99 points (2nd)**					
58	Monte Carlo	555 Subaru World Rally Team	Subaru Impreza 555	2	Luis Moya	3rd
59	Portugal	555 Subaru World Rally Team	Subaru Impreza 555	3	Luis Moya	4th
60	Corsica	555 Subaru World Rally Team	Subaru Impreza 555	3	Luis Moya	2nd
61	**Greece**	**555 Subaru World Rally Team**	**Subaru Impreza 555**	**3**	**Luis Moya**	**1st**
62	Argentina	555 Subaru World Rally Team	Subaru Impreza 555	2	Luis Moya	2nd
63	New Zealand	555 Subaru World Rally Team	Subaru Impreza 555	6	Luis Moya	Retired
64	Finland	555 Subaru World Rally Team	Subaru Impreza 555	2	Luis Moya	3rd
65	Sanremo	555 Subaru World Rally Team	Subaru Impreza 555	10	Luis Moya	2nd
66	Great Britain	555 Subaru World Rally Team	Subaru Impreza 555	2	Luis Moya	Retired
1995	**85 points (2nd)**					
67	**Monte Carlo**	**555 Subaru World Rally Team**	**Subaru Impreza 555**	**5**	**Luis Moya**	**1st**
68	Sweden	555 Subaru World Rally Team	Subaru Impreza 555	5	Luis Moya	Retired
69	**Portugal**	**555 Subaru World Rally Team**	**Subaru Impreza 555**	**5**	**Luis Moya**	**1st**
70	Corsica	555 Subaru World Rally Team	Subaru Impreza 555	5	Luis Moya	4th
71	Australia	555 Subaru World Rally Team	Subaru Impreza 555	5	Luis Moya	Retired
72	**Catalunya**	**555 Subaru World Rally Team**	**Subaru Impreza 555**	**5**	**Luis Moya**	**1st**
73	Great Britain	555 Subaru World Rally Team	Subaru Impreza 555	5	Luis Moya	2nd
1996	**89 points (3rd)**					
74	Sweden	Ford Motor Company	Ford Escort RS Cosworth	4	Luis Moya	2nd
75	Safari	Ford Motor Company	Ford Escort RS Cosworth	4	Luis Moya	Retired
76	**Indonesia**	**Ford Motor Company**	**Ford Escort RS Cosworth**	**4**	**Luis Moya**	**1st**
77	Greece	Ford Motor Company	Ford Escort RS Cosworth	4	Luis Moya	3rd
78	Argentina	Ford Motor Company	Ford Escort RS Cosworth	4	Luis Moya	2nd
79	Finland	Ford Motor Company	Ford Escort RS Cosworth	4	Luis Moya	Retired
80	Australia	Ford Motor Company	Ford Escort RS Cosworth	4	Luis Moya	3rd
81	Sanremo	Ford Motor Company	Ford Escort RS Cosworth	4	Luis Moya	2nd
82	Catalunya	Ford Motor Company	Ford Escort RS Cosworth	4	Luis Moya	Retired
1997	**51 points (3rd)**					
83	Monte Carlo	Ford Motor Company	Ford Escort WRC	5	Luis Moya	2nd
84	Sweden	Ford Motor Company	Ford Escort WRC	5	Luis Moya	2nd
85	Safari	Ford Motor Company	Ford Escort WRC	5	Luis Moya	Retired
86	Portugal	Ford Motor Company	Ford Escort WRC	5	Luis Moya	Retired
87	Catalunya	Ford Motor Company	Ford Escort WRC	5	Luis Moya	10th
88	Corsica	Ford Motor Company	Ford Escort WRC	5	Luis Moya	2nd
89	Argentina	Ford Motor Company	Ford Escort WRC	5	Luis Moya	Retired
90	**Greece**	**Ford Motor Company**	**Ford Escort WRC**	**5**	**Luis Moya**	**1st**
91	New Zealand	Ford Motor Company	Ford Escort WRC	5	Luis Moya	2nd
92	Finland	Ford Motor Company	Ford Escort WRC	5	Luis Moya	Retired
93	**Indonesia**	**Ford Motor Company**	**Ford Escort WRC**	**5**	**Luis Moya**	**1st**
94	Sanremo	Ford Motor Company	Ford Escort WRC	5	Luis Moya	4th
95	Australia	Ford Motor Company	Ford Escort WRC	5	Luis Moya	Retired
96	Great Britain	Ford Motor Company	Ford Escort WRC	5	Luis Moya	3rd
1998	**56 points (2nd)**					
97	**Monte Carlo**	**Toyota Castrol Team**	**Toyota Corolla WRC**	**5**	**Luis Moya**	**1st**
98	Sweden	Toyota Castrol Team	Toyota Corolla WRC	5	Luis Moya	2nd
99	Safari	Toyota Castrol Team	Toyota Corolla WRC	5	Luis Moya	Retired
100	Portugal	Toyota Castrol Team	Toyota Corolla WRC	5	Luis Moya	2nd
101	Catalunya	Toyota Castrol Team	Toyota Corolla WRC	5	Luis Moya	7th
102	Corsica	Toyota Castrol Team	Toyota Corolla WRC	5	Luis Moya	8th
103	Argentina	Toyota Castrol Team	Toyota Corolla WRC	5	Luis Moya	2nd
104	Greece	Toyota Castrol Team	Toyota Corolla WRC	5	Luis Moya	4th
105	**New Zealand**	**Toyota Castrol Team**	**Toyota Corolla WRC**	**5**	**Luis Moya**	**1st**
106	Finland	Toyota Castrol Team	Toyota Corolla WRC	5	Luis Moya	2nd
107	Sanremo	Toyota Castrol Team	Toyota Corolla WRC	5	Luis Moya	4th
108	Australia	Toyota Castrol Team	Toyota Corolla WRC	5	Luis Moya	2nd
109	Great Britain	Toyota Castrol Team	Toyota Corolla WRC	5	Luis Moya	Retired
1999	**44 points (5th)**					
110	Monte Carlo	Toyota Castrol Team	Toyota Corolla WRC	3	Luis Moya	Retired
111	Sweden	Toyota Castrol Team	Toyota Corolla WRC	3	Luis Moya	2nd
112	Safari	Toyota Castrol Team	Toyota Corolla WRC	3	Luis Moya	3rd
113	Portugal	Toyota Castrol Team	Toyota Corolla WRC	3	Luis Moya	2nd
114	Catalunya	Toyota Castrol Team	Toyota Corolla WRC	3	Luis Moya	Retired
115	Corsica	Toyota Castrol Team	Toyota Corolla WRC	3	Luis Moya	3rd
116	Argentina	Toyota Castrol Team	Toyota Corolla WRC	3	Luis Moya	5th
117	Greece	Toyota Castrol Team	Toyota Corolla WRC	3	Luis Moya	2nd
118	New Zealand	Toyota Castrol Team	Toyota Corolla WRC	3	Luis Moya	6th
119	Finland	Toyota Castrol Team	Toyota Corolla WRC	3	Luis Moya	3rd
120	China	Toyota Castrol Team	Toyota Corolla WRC	3	Luis Moya	3rd
121	Sanremo	Toyota Castrol Team	Toyota Corolla WRC	3	Luis Moya	Retired
122	Australia	Toyota Castrol Team	Toyota Corolla WRC	3	Luis Moya	2nd
123	Great Britain	Toyota Castrol Team	Toyota Corolla WRC	3	Luis Moya	Retired
2000	**46 points (3rd)**					
124	Monte Carlo	Ford Motor Company	Ford Focus WRC	6	Luis Moya	2nd
125	Sweden	Ford Motor Company	Ford Focus WRC	6	Luis Moya	Retired
126	Safari	Ford Motor Company	Ford Focus WRC	6	Luis Moya	4th
127	Portugal	Ford Motor Company	Ford Focus WRC	6	Luis Moya	3rd
128	Catalunya	Ford Motor Company	Ford Focus WRC	6	Luis Moya	3rd
129	Argentina	Ford Motor Company	Ford Focus WRC	6	Luis Moya	Retired
130	Greece	Ford Motor Company	Ford Focus WRC	6	Luis Moya	2nd
131	New Zealand	Ford Motor Company	Ford Focus WRC	6	Luis Moya	3rd
132	Finland	Ford Motor Company	Ford Focus WRC	6	Luis Moya	14th
133	**Cyprus**	**Ford Motor Company**	**Ford Focus WRC**	**6**	**Luis Moya**	**1st**
134	Corsica	Ford Motor Company	Ford Focus WRC	6	Luis Moya	3rd
135	Sanremo	Ford Motor Company	Ford Focus WRC	6	Luis Moya	5th
136	Australia	Ford Motor Company	Ford Focus WRC	6	Luis Moya	Retired
137	Great Britain	Ford Motor Company	Ford Focus WRC	6	Luis Moya	4th
2001	**33 points (6th)**					
138	Monte Carlo	Ford Motor Company	Ford Focus WRC	3	Luis Moya	2nd
139	Sweden	Ford Motor Company	Ford Focus WRC	3	Luis Moya	3rd
140	Portugal	Ford Motor Company	Ford Focus WRC	3	Luis Moya	2nd
141	Catalunya	Ford Motor Company	Ford Focus WRC	3	Luis Moya	5th
142	Argentina	Ford Motor Company	Ford Focus WRC	3	Luis Moya	3rd
143	Cyprus	Ford Motor Company	Ford Focus WRC	3	Luis Moya	3rd
144	Greece	Ford Motor Company	Ford Focus WRC	3	Luis Moya	Retired
145	Safari	Ford Motor Company	Ford Focus WRC	3	Luis Moya	Retired
146	Finland	Ford Motor Company	Ford Focus WRC	3	Luis Moya	6th
147	New Zealand	Ford Motor Company	Ford Focus WRC	3	Luis Moya	4th
148	Sanremo	Ford Motor Company	Ford Focus WRC	3	Luis Moya	4th
149	Corsica	Ford Motor Company	Ford Focus WRC	3	Luis Moya	Retired
150	Australia	Ford Motor Company	Ford Focus WRC	3	Luis Moya	8th
151	Great Britain	Ford Motor Company	Ford Focus WRC	3	Luis Moya	Retired
2002	**36 points (3rd)**					
152	Monte Carlo	Ford Motor Company	Ford Focus WRC	4	Luis Moya	3rd
153	Sweden	Ford Motor Company	Ford Focus WRC	4	Luis Moya	3rd
154	Corsica	Ford Motor Company	Ford Focus WRC	4	Luis Moya	6th

SAINZ, CARLOS CAREER RECORD (CONT'D)

YEAR	RALLY	TEAM/ENTRANT	CAR	NO.	CO-DRIVER	RESULT
155	Catalunya	Ford Motor Company	Ford Focus WRC	4	Marc Marti	Retired
156	Cyprus	Ford Motor Company	Ford Focus WRC	4	Luis Moya	11th
157	**Argentina**	**Ford Motor Company**	**Ford Focus WRC**	**4**	**Luis Moya**	**1st**
158	Greece	Ford Motor Company	Ford Focus WRC	4	Luis Moya	3rd
159	Safari	Ford Motor Company	Ford Focus WRC	4	Luis Moya	Retired
160	Finland	Ford Motor Company	Ford Focus WRC	4	Luis Moya	4th
161	Germany	Ford Motor Company	Ford Focus WRC	4	Luis Moya	8th
162	Sanremo	Ford Motor Company	Ford Focus WRC	4	Luis Moya	Retired
163	New Zealand	Ford Motor Company	Ford Focus WRC	4	Luis Moya	4th
164	Australia	Ford Motor Company	Ford Focus WRC	4	Luis Moya	4th
165	Great Britain	Ford Motor Company	Ford Focus WRC	4	Luis Moya	3rd
2003	**63 points (3rd)**					
166	Monte Carlo	Citroen Total	Citroen Xsara WRC	19	Marc Marti	3rd
167	Sweden	Citroen Total	Citroen Xsara WRC	19	Marc Marti	9th
168	**Turkey**	**Citroen Total**	**Citroen Xsara WRC**	**19**	**Marc Marti**	**1st**
169	New Zealand	Citroen Total	Citroen Xsara WRC	19	Marc Marti	12th
170	Argentina	Citroen Total	Citroen Xsara WRC	19	Marc Marti	2nd
171	Greece	Citroen Total	Citroen Xsara WRC	19	Marc Marti	2nd
172	Cyprus	Citroen Total	Citroen Xsara WRC	19	Marc Marti	5th
173	Germany	Citroen Total	Citroen Xsara WRC	19	Marc Marti	6th
174	Finland	Citroen Total	Citroen Xsara WRC	19	Marc Marti	4th
175	Australia	Citroen Total	Citroen Xsara WRC	19	Marc Marti	5th
176	Sanremo	Citroen Total	Citroen Xsara WRC	19	Marc Marti	4th
177	Sanremo	Citroen Total	Citroen Xsara WRC	19	Marc Marti	4th
178	Corsica	Citroen Total	Citroen Xsara WRC	19	Marc Marti	2nd
179	Catalunya	Citroen Total	Citroen Xsara WRC	19	Marc Marti	7th
180	Great Britain	Citroen Total	Citroen Xsara WRC	19	Marc Marti	Retired

SALONEN, TIMO

(FIN) B: 8 OCTOBER 1951, HELSINKI, FINLAND

"Salonen started driving on ice-covered lakes long before he was allowed out on the road"

It is hard to know for what Timo Salonen is most famous. It could be his amazing drives on European rallies with Datsun, or his blitz on the World championship in a Peugeot...or it could be his famous devotion to the product of his long-time sponsor, Marlboro.

Like most of Finnish contemporaries, Salonen started driving on ice-covered lakes long before he was allowed out on the road. When he did so, it was at the wheel of a Datsun 1600SSS that was also used as his first rally car.

He later started working for a Mazda dealer and chose a Mazda 1300 to make his WRC debut on the 1000 Lakes in 1974 where he won his class. He then made contact with Datsun and drove for them netting a brace of top 10 finishes on the 1000 Lakes.

In 1977, he caught the eye of Danielle Audetto at Fiat and took a 131 Abarth to second place on the 1000 Lakes before winning the Quebec Rally for them.

By 1979, he was back with Datsun but this time in a full works car. He opened his account by taking second place on the tough Acropolis Rally and getting on the podium in both Canada and Britain. The following year, Datsun did more WRC events with their reliable if less-than powerful cars. In New Zealand, Salonen was at his very best on this secret rally, leading nearly all the way and taking one of his best wins. The opposition was not standing still and in 1981, it was the African rallies where Datsun strength and reliability came into play and where Salonen scored. He stayed with Nissan – as the company now was – right through to the end of 1984 when he was recruited to Peugeot for their new 205 T16.

Salonen took to the car and the team instantly and, after two snow rallies to run himself in, won decisively in Portugal after a steady drive. He finished the Safari, retired in Corsica with electrical failure and then won four WRC rallies on the trot.

Ari Vatanen's accident in Argentina shifted a lot of responsibility onto Salonen's shoulders but, after winning Finland's 1000 Lakes Rally, he was in the lead of the championship and second place in San Remo was enough to confirm the title.

The following year started well in Monte Carlo but retirements and withdrawal in Portugal did nothing to help his efforts towards a second title. He won in Finland and Great Britain – the last rally of the Group B era – but an unwarranted exclusion in San Remo soured the end of the year.

For 1987, in the aftermath of the cancellation of Group B and the proposed Group S, Peugeot went to play in the desert with their cars while Salonen found a new home with the company with which he had started his WRC career, Mazda. At first it all looked good as he won in Sweden and the Mazda 323 4WD seemed to be competitive. However, transmission problems dogged the team. It was hard to get finishes let alone results. When MRTE folded,

Salonen found a drive with Mitsubishi but the new breed of 4WD Group A cars was not to his liking and he retired during 1992 to concentrate on his car business in Finland. In 2002, he made a one-off comeback in a Peugeot 206WRC to celebrate his 50th birthday.

Right: Finland 1986 and Timo Salonen is on his way to yet another victory for the Peugeot 205T16. It was the final year of Group B and when Salonen won the RAC Rally later that same season he became the final winner of this flawed, but awesome, category

SALONEN, TIMO – CAREER RECORD

YEAR	RALLY	TEAM/ENTRANT	CAR	NO.	CO-DRIVER	RESULT
1974						
1	Finland		Mazda 1300	43	Seppo Harjanne	22nd
1975						
2	Finland		Datsun 160J	15	Jaakko Markkula	6th
1976						
3	Finland		Datsun Violet	13	Jaakko Markkula	6th
1977						
4	Finland	Olio Fiat	Fiat 131 Abarth	13	Jaakko Markkula	2nd
5	**Canada**	**Olio Fiat**	**Fiat 131 Abarth**	**8**	**Jaakko Markkula**	**1st**
6	Great Britain	Olio Fiat	Fiat 131 Abarth	10	Jaakko Markkula	Retired
1978						
7	Sweden	Fiat SpA	Fiat 131 Abarth	9	Jaakko Markkula	Retired
8	Finland	Fiat SpA	Fiat 131 Abarth	6	Erkki Nyman	2nd
9	Canada	Fiat SpA	Fiat 131 Abarth	1	Erkki Nyman	Retired
1979	**50 points (4th)**					
10	Greece	Team Datsun Europe	Datsun 160J	8	Seppo Harjanne	2nd
11	New Zealand	Team Datsun Europe	Datsun 160J	4	Seppo Harjanne	Disqualified
12	Finland	Team Datsun Europe	Datsun 160J	6	Seppo Harjanne	5th
13	Canada	Team Datsun Europe	Datsun 160J	3	Seppo Harjanne	2nd
14	Sanremo	Team Datsun Europe	Datsun 160J	9	Seppo Harjanne	Retired
15	Great Britain	Team Datsun Europe	Datsun 160J	12	Stuart Pegg	3rd
1980	**45 points (7th)**					
16	Sweden	Team Datsun Sweden	Datsun 160J	5	Seppo Harjanne	7th
17	Portugal	Team Datsun Europe	Datsun 160J	11	Seppo Harjanne	Retired
18	Greece	N.I Theocharakis	Datsun 160J	14	Seppo Harjanne	2nd
19	Finland	Aroyhtyma	Datsun 160J	6	Seppo Harjanne	6th
20	**New Zealand**	**Team Datsun**	**Datsun 160J**	**5**	**Seppo Harjanne**	**1st**
21	Sanremo	Team Datsun Europe	Datsun 160J	3	Seppo Harjanne	Retired
22	Corsica	Team Datsun Europe	Datsun 160J	1	Seppo Harjanne	Retired
23	Great Britain	Team Datsun Europe	Datsun 160J	4	Seppo Harjanne	Retired
1981	**40 points (6th)**					
24	Portugal	Team Datsun Europe	Datsun Violet GT	8	Seppo Harjanne	Retired
25	Safari	D.T Dobie & Co. Ltd/Datsun	Datsun Silvia 200SX	2	Seppo Harjanne	4th
26	Corsica	Team Datsun Europe	Datsun Violet GT	1	Seppo Harjanne	Retired
27	Greece	Team Datsun Europe	Datsun Violet GT	3	Seppo Harjanne	Retired
28	Argentina	Team Datsun Europe	Datsun Violet GT	6	Seppo Harjanne	Retired
29	Finland	Team Datsun Europe	Datsun Violet GT	5	Seppo Harjanne	4th
30	Sanremo	Team Datsun Europe	Datsun Violet GT	7	Seppo Harjanne	12th
31	**Ivory Coast**	**Comafrique**	**Datsun Violet GT**	**4**	**Seppo Harjanne**	**1st**
32	Great Britain	Team Datsun Europe	Datsun Violet GT	7	Seppo Harjanne	Retired
1982	**20 points (11th)**					
33	Portugal	Team Nissan Europe	Nissan Violet GTS	3	Seppo Harjanne	Retired
34	Safari	Nissan Motorsports Europe	Nissan Violet GTS	3	Seppo Harjanne	Retired
35	Greece	Team Nissan Europe	Nissan Violet GTS	4	Seppo Harjanne	Retired
36	New Zealand	Team Nissan Europe	Nissan Violet GTS	1	Seppo Harjanne	4th
37	Finland	Team Nissan Europe	Nissan Silvia Turbo	6	Seppo Harjanne	4th
38	Great Britain	Team Nissan Europe	Nissan Violet GT	12	Seppo Harjanne	Retired
1983	**18 points (13th)**					
39	Monte Carlo	Team Nissan Europe	Nissan 240 RS	12	Seppo Harjanne	14th
40	Portugal	Team Nissan Europe	Nissan 240 RS	8	Seppo Harjanne	Retired
41	Safari	D.T Dobie & Co. Ltd	Nissan 240 RS	3	Seppo Harjanne	Retired
42	Greece	N.I Theocharakis	Nissan 240 RS	5	Seppo Harjanne	Retired
43	New Zealand	Dealer Team Nissan	Nissan 240 RS	3	Seppo Harjanne	2nd
44	Finland	Auto Keskus	Nissan 240 RS	8	Seppo Harjanne	8th
45	Great Britain	Team Nissan Europe	Nissan 240 RS	9	Seppo Harjanne	Retired
1984	**27 points (10th)**					
46	Monte Carlo	Nissan Motor Company	Nissan 240 RS	3	Seppo Harjanne	10th
47	Safari	D.T Dobie	Nissan 240 RS	9	Seppo Harjanne	7th

CAREER RECORD

YEAR	RALLY	TEAM/ENTRANT	CAR	NO.	CO-DRIVER	RESULT
48	Greece	N.I Theocharakis	Nissan 240 RS	5	Seppo Harjanne	6th
49	New Zealand	Dealer Team Nissan	Nissan 240 RS	5	Seppo Harjanne	4th
50	Great Britain	Team Nissan Europe	Nissan 240 RS	7	Seppo Harjanne	6th
1985	127 points (WORLD CHAMPION)					
51	Monte Carlo	Peugeot Talbot Sport	Peugeot 205 T16	6	Seppo Harjanne	3rd
52	Sweden	Peugeot Talbot Sport	Peugeot 205 T16	6	Seppo Harjanne	3rd
53	**Portugal**	**Peugeot Talbot Sport**	**Peugeot 205 T16**	**6**	**Seppo Harjanne**	**1st**
54	Safari	Peugeot Talbot Sport	Peugeot 205 T16	6	Seppo Harjanne	7th
55	Corsica	Peugeot Talbot Sport	Peugeot 205 T16	6	Seppo Harjanne	Retired
56	**Greece**	**Peugeot Talbot Sport**	**Peugeot 205 T16 E2**	**5**	**Seppo Harjanne**	**1st**
57	**New Zealand**	**Peugeot Talbot Sport**	**Peugeot 205 T16 E2**	**5**	**Seppo Harjanne**	**1st**
58	**Argentina**	**Peugeot Talbot Sport**	**Peugeot 205 T16 E2**	**3**	**Seppo Harjanne**	**1st**
59	**Finland**	**Peugeot Talbot Sport**	**Peugeot 205 T16 E2**	**3**	**Seppo Harjanne**	**1st**
60	Sanremo	Peugeot Talbot Sport	Peugeot 205 T16 E2	3	Seppo Harjanne	2nd
61	Great Britain	Peugeot Talbot Sport	Peugeot 205 T16 E2	1	Seppo Harjanne	Retired
1986	63 points (3rd)					
62	Monte Carlo	Peugeot Talbot Sport	Peugeot 205 T16 E2	1	Seppo Harjanne	2nd
63	Sweden	Peugeot Talbot Sport	Peugeot 205 T16 E2	2	Seppo Harjanne	Retired
64	Portugal	Peugeot Talbot Sport	Peugeot 205 T16 E2	1	Seppo Harjanne	Withdrawn
65	Corsica	Peugeot Talbot Sport	Peugeot 205 T16 E2	2	Seppo Harjanne	Retired
66	Greece	Peugeot Talbot Sport	Peugeot 205 T16 E2	1	Seppo Harjanne	Retired
67	New Zealand	Peugeot Talbot Sport	Peugeot 205 T16 E2	1	Seppo Harjanne	5th
68	**Finland**	**Peugeot Talbot Sport**	**Peugeot 205 T16 E2**	**1**	**Seppo Harjanne**	**1st**
69	**Great Britain**	**Peugeot Talbot Sport**	**Peugeot 205 T16 E2**	**1**	**Seppo Harjanne**	**1st**
1987	20 points (14th)					
70	Monte Carlo	Mazda Rally Team Europe	Mazda 323 HB 4WD	2	Seppo Harjanne	Retired
71	**Sweden**	**Mazda Rally Team Europe**	**Mazda 323 HB 4WD**	**3**	**Seppo Harjanne**	**1st**
72	Portugal	Mazda Rally Team Europe	Mazda 323 HB 4WD	2	Seppo Harjanne	Retired
73	Finland	Mazda Rally Team Europe	Mazda 323 HB 4WD	1	Seppo Harjanne	Retired
1988	33 points (5th)					
74	Monte Carlo	Mazda Rally Team Europe	Mazda 323 HB 4WD	2	Seppo Harjanne	5th
75	Sweden	Mazda Rally Team Europe	Mazda 323 HB 4WD	1	Seppo Harjanne	Retired
76	Greece	Mazda Rally Team Europe	Mazda 323 HB 4WD	3	Seppo Harjanne	Retired
77	Finland	Mazda Rally Team Europe	Mazda 323 HB 4WD	2	Seppo Harjanne	4th
78	Great Britain	Mazda Rally Team Europe	Mazda 323 HB 4WD	4	Voitto Silander	2nd
1989	21 points (12th)					
79	Sweden	Mazda Rally Team Europe	Mazda 323 HB 4WD	2	Voitto Silander	22nd
80	Monte Carlo	Mazda Rally Team Europe	Mazda 323 HB 4WD	3	Voitto Silander	Retired
81	Finland	Mazda Rally Team Europe	Mazda 323 HB 4WD	4	Voitto Silander	2nd
82	Great Britain	Mazda Rally Team Europe	Mazda 323 HB 4WD	4	Voitto Silander	6th
1990	9 points (25th)					
83	Monte Carlo	Mazda Rally Team Europe	Mazda 323 HB 4WD	3	Voitto Silander	8th
84	Portugal	Mazda Rally Team Europe	Mazda 323 HB 4WD	5	Voitto Silander	Retired
85	Finland	Mazda Rally Team Europe	Mazda 323 1.8 GTX	5	Voitto Silander	6th
86	Great Britain	Mazda Rally Team Europe	Mazda 323 1.8 GTX	6	Voitto Silander	Retired
1991	21 points (13th)					
87	Monte Carlo	Mitsubishi Ralliart Europe	Mitsubishi Galant VR-4	4	Voitto Silander	8th
88	Sweden	Mitsubishi Ralliart Europe	Mitsubishi Galant VR-4	6	Voitto Silander	Retired
89	Greece	Mitsubishi Ralliart Europe	Mitsubishi Galant VR-4	15	Voitto Silander	Retired
90	Finland	Mitsubishi Ralliart Europe	Mitsubishi Galant VR-4	5	Voitto Silander	Retired
91	Australia	Mitsubishi Ralliart Europe	Mitsubishi Galant VR-4	7	Voitto Silander	5th
92	Great Britain	Mitsubishi Ralliart Europe	Mitsubishi Galant VR-4	10	Voitto Silander	4th
1992	14 points (20th)					
93	Monte Carlo	Mitsubishi Ralliart	Mitsubishi Galant VR-4	9	Voitto Silander	6th
94	Portugal	Mitsubishi Ralliart	Mitsubishi Galant VR-4	10	Voitto Silander	5th
2002	0 points					
95	Finland	Bozian Racing	Peugeot 206WRC	33	Launo Heinonen	14th

SCHWARZ, ARMIN

(D) B: 16 JULY 1963, OBERREICHHENBACH, GERMANY

"Armin Schwarz has earned his place in the top echelon of rally drivers"

A Bavarian rally driver? One instinctively thinks of Walter Röhrl, but Armin Schwarz has also earned his place in the top echelon of rally drivers. Born just 20 kilometres west of Nürnberg, he started out as an apprentice mechanic and worked on his own rally cars. His first car was a Fiat 131, which he made as much like an Abarth as he could.

By 1986, he was rallying an Audi 80 Quattro, prepared with some help from Schmidt Motorsport. He entered the Mitropa Cup, a series involving rallies in Italy, Austria and Germany but needed to swap cars for the last round. This was the Three Cities Rally that was also a round of the German Championship. Prime contender for that title was Michele Mouton in a Peugeot 205 T16 E2. Young Schwarz hired a MG Metro 6R4 and very nearly beat the lady. But finishing second, however, was enough to win him the Mitropa title and win him a seat in what was effectively a works Audi 200 Quattro for the ensuing seasons.

Entered and run by Schmidt, he won the German Rally Championship in 1987 and 1988 and took the unwieldy 200 to fifth place overall on the 1988 RAC Rally with Arne Hertz. For 1989, the team spread their wings and travelled to a selection of WRC events that started well but finished with elimination on the RAC Rally thanks to a no-blame road accident.

At this point, Schmidt Motorsport went into racing but Schwarz's talent had been sufficiently widely noticed for him to be offered a drive with Toyota Team Europe. Though Schwarz drove well, two accidents suggested that he was trying too hard. The following year he was paired once again with Arne Hertz and they were immediately successful on the Monte Carlo. His programme was much bigger but the Celica GT-4 was now getting a bit long in the tooth. Schwarz won the Catalunya Rally by leading from start to finish in this mixed gravel and tarmac event.

For 1992, TTE were equipped with the Celica Turbo 4WD but Lancia had their fifth evolution of the Integrale. Results were hard to come by and Schwarz took a two-year contract with Mitsubishi. On the 1994 Monte, he set more fastest times than anyone else but went off the road thanks to spectators throwing snow on the road. He was back with Toyota for 1995 but it was bad timing. TTE was thrown out of the series and banned for a year after the discovery of illegal turbochargers in Catalunya. Schwarz entered and won the 1996 European Championship. He also won a very snowy RAC Rally, an event only counting for the F2 Championship.

A year with Ford was short-lived when Schwarz was summarily dropped mid-season and he signed for Skoda for 1999. Three years with the Octavia WRC saw promise but no big results and for 2002, Schwarz moved again to Hyundai. Even that story did not have a happy ending as towards the end of 2003, the team imploded and he returned to Skoda for 2004.

SCHWARZ, ARMIN – CAREER RECORD

YEAR	RALLY	TEAM / ENTRANT	CAR	NO.	CO-DRIVER	RESULT
1988	**8 points (37th)**					
1	Great Britain	Schmidt Motorsport	Audi 200 Quattro	36	Arne Hertz	5th
1989	**7 points (41st)**					
2	Greece	Schmidt Motorsport	Audi 200 Quattro	18	Klaus Wicha	8th
3	Finland	Schmidt Motorsport	Audi 200 Quattro	16	Klaus Wicha	7th
4	Sanremo	Schmidt Motorsport	Audi 200 Quattro	11	Klaus Wicha	Retired
5	Great Britain	Schmidt Motorsport	Audi 200 Quattro	22	Klaus Wicha	Retired
1990	**12 points (19th)**					
6	Monte Carlo	Toyota Team Europe	Toyota Celica GT-Four	12	Klaus Wicha	5th
7	Portugal	Toyota Team Europe	Toyota Celica GT-Four	15	Klaus Wicha	Retired
8	Corsica	Toyota Team Europe	Toyota Celica GT-Four	9	Klaus Wicha	Retired
9	Sanremo	Toyota Team Europe	Toyota Celica GT-Four	19	Klaus Wicha	Retired
10	GB	Toyota Team Europe	Toyota Celica GT-Four	21	Klaus Wicha	7th
1991	**55 points (6th)**					
11	Monte Carlo	Toyota Team Europe	Toyota Celica GT-Four	7	Arne Hertz	4th
12	Portugal	Toyota Team Europe	Toyota Celica GT-Four	6	Arne Hertz	Retired
13	Corsica	Toyota Team Europe	Toyota Celica GT-Four	7	Arne Hertz	Retired
14	Greece	Toyota Team Europe	Toyota Celica GT-Four	14	Arne Hertz	5th
15	Finland	Toyota Team Europe	Toyota Celica GT-Four	9	Arne Hertz	9th
16	Australia	Toyota Team Europe	Toyota Celica GT-Four	8	Arne Hertz	3rd
17	Sanremo	Toyota Team Europe	Toyota Celica GT-Four	5	Arne Hertz	8th
18	**Catalunya**	**Toyota Team Europe**	**Toyota Celica GT-Four**	**5**	**Arne Hertz**	**1st**
1992	**16 points (9th)**					
19	Monte Carlo	Toyota Team Europe	Toyota Celica Turbo 4WD	6	Arne Hertz	Retired
20	Portugal	Toyota Team Europe	Toyota Celica Turbo 4WD	5	Arne Hertz	Retired
21	Corsica	Toyota Team Europe	Toyota Celica Turbo 4WD	5	Arne Hertz	5th
22	Greece	Toyota Team Europe	Toyota Celica Turbo 4WD	10	Arne Hertz	Retired
23	Catalunya	Toyota Team Europe	Toyota Celica Turbo 4WD	1	Arne Hertz	5th
1993	**23 points (12th)**					
24	Monte Carlo	Mitsubishi Ralliart	Mitsubishi Lancer RS	4	Nicky Grist	6th
25	Portugal	Mitsubishi Ralliart	Mitsubishi Lancer RS	7	Nicky Grist	Retired
26	Greece	Mitsubishi Ralliart	Mitsubishi Lancer RS	9	Nicky Grist	3rd
27	Finland	Mitsubishi Ralliart	Mitsubishi Lancer RS	6	Nicky Grist	9th
28	Great Britain	Mitsubishi Ralliart	Mitsubishi Lancer RS	7	Peter Thul	8th
1994	**31 points (7th)**					
29	Monte Carlo	Mitsubishi Ralliart Europe	Mitsubishi Lancer Evo 2	5	Klaus Wicha	7th
30	Greece	Mitsubishi Ralliart	Mitsubishi Lancer Evo 2	8	Klaus Wicha	2nd
31	New Zealand	Mitsubishi Ralliart	Mitsubishi Lancer Evo 2	4	Klaus Wicha	3rd
32	Sanremo	Mitsubishi Ralliart	Mitsubishi Lancer Evo 2	7	Klaus Wicha	Retired
1995	**8 points (Disqualified)**					
33	Monte Carlo	Toyota Castrol Team	Toyota Celica GT-Four	3	Klaus Wicha	Retired
34	Sweden	Toyota Castrol Team	Toyota Celica GT-Four	3	Klaus Wicha	9th
35	Portugal	Toyota Castrol Team	Toyota Celica GT-Four	3	Klaus Wicha	4th
36	Corsica	Toyota Castrol Team	Toyota Celica GT-Four	3	Klaus Wicha	Retired
37	New Zealand	Toyota Castrol Team	Toyota Celica GT-Four	3	Klaus Wicha	4th
38	Australia	Toyota Castrol Team	Toyota Celica GT-Four	3	Klaus Wicha	5th
39	Catalunya	Toyota Castrol Team	Toyota Celica GT-Four	3	Klaus Wicha	Retired
1997	**11 points (8th)**					
40	Monte Carlo	Ford Motor Company	Ford Escort WRC	6	Denis Giraudet	4th
41	Sweden	Ford Motor Company	Ford Escort WRC	6	Denis Giraudet	6th
42	Safari	Ford Motor Company	Ford Escort WRC	6	Denis Giraudet	4th
43	Portugal	Ford Motor Company	Ford Escort WRC	6	Denis Giraudet	3rd
44	Catalunya	Ford Motor Company	Ford Escort WRC	6	Denis Giraudet	Retired
45	Corsica	Ford Motor Company	Ford Escort WRC	6	Philip Mills	9th
1998	**0 points**					
46	Great Britain	R.E.D	Ford Escort WRC	14	Manfred Hiemer	7th
1999	**0 points**					
47	Monte Carlo	Skoda Motorsport	Skoda Octavia WRC	11	Manfred Hiemer	Retired
48	Portugal	Skoda Motorsport	Skoda Octavia WRC	11	Manfred Hiemer	Retired
49	Catalunya	Skoda Motorsport	Skoda Octavia WRC	11	Manfred Hiemer	Retired
50	Greece	Skoda Motorsport	Skoda Octavia WRC	11	Manfred Hiemer	12th
51	Finland	Skoda Motorsport	Skoda Octavia WRC	11	Manfred Hiemer	Retired
52	Sanremo	Skoda Motorsport	Skoda Octavia WRC	11	Manfred Hiemer	Retired
53	Great Britain	Skoda Motorsport	Skoda Octavia WRC	11	Manfred Hiemer	Retired
2000	**2 points (17th)**					
54	Monte Carlo	Skoda Motorsport	Skoda Octavia WRC	11	Manfred Hiemer	7th
55	Safari	Skoda Motorsport	Skoda Octavia WRC	11	Manfred Hiemer	7th
56	Portugal	Skoda Motorsport	Skoda Octavia WRC	11	Manfred Hiemer	8th
57	Catalunya	Skoda Motorsport	Skoda Octavia WRC	11	Manfred Hiemer	11th
58	Greece	Skoda Motorsport	Skoda Octavia WRC	11	Manfred Hiemer	5th
59	Cyprus	Skoda Motorsport	Skoda Octavia WRC	11	Manfred Hiemer	Retired
60	Sanremo	Skoda Motorsport	Skoda Octavia WRC	11	Manfred Hiemer	12th
61	Great Britain	Skoda Motorsport	Skoda Octavia WRC	11	Manfred Hiemer	13th
2001	**9 points (12th)**					
62	Monte Carlo	Skoda Motorsport	Skoda Octavia WRC	11	Manfred Hiemer	4th
63	Sweden	Skoda Motorsport	Skoda Octavia WRC	11	Manfred Hiemer	Retired
64	Portugal	Skoda Motorsport	Skoda Octavia WRC	11	Manfred Hiemer	Retired
65	Catalunya	Skoda Motorsport	Skoda Octavia WRC	11	Manfred Hiemer	Retired
66	Argentina	Skoda Motorsport	Skoda Octavia WRC	11	Manfred Hiemer	Retired
67	Cyprus	Skoda Motorsport	Skoda Octavia WRC	11	Manfred Hiemer	9th
68	Greece	Skoda Motorsport	Skoda Octavia WRC	11	Manfred Hiemer	7th
69	Safari	Skoda Motorsport	Skoda Octavia WRC	11	Manfred Hiemer	3rd
70	Finland	Skoda Motorsport	Skoda Octavia WRC	11	Manfred Hiemer	15th
71	Sanremo	Skoda Motorsport	Skoda Octavia WRC	11	Manfred Hiemer	Retired
72	Corsica	Skoda Motorsport	Skoda Octavia WRC	11	Manfred Hiemer	Retired
73	Great Britain	Skoda Motorsport	Skoda Octavia WRC	11	Manfred Hiemer	5th
2002	**0 points**					
74	Monte Carlo	Hyundai Castrol World Rally Team	Hyundai Accent WRC	17	Manfred Hiemer	Retired
75	Sweden	Hyundai Castrol World Rally Team	Hyundai Accent WRC	17	Manfred Hiemer	Retired
76	Corsica	Hyundai Castrol World Rally Team	Hyundai Accent WRC	17	Manfred Hiemer	13th
77	Catalunya	Hyundai Castrol World Rally Team	Hyundai Accent WRC	17	Manfred Hiemer	16th
78	Cyprus	Hyundai Castrol World Rally Team	Hyundai Accent WRC	17	Manfred Hiemer	7th
79	Argentina	Hyundai Castrol World Rally Team	Hyundai Accent WRC	17	Manfred Hiemer	Retired
80	Greece	Hyundai Castrol World Rally Team	Hyundai Accent WRC	17	Manfred Hiemer	9th
81	Safari	Hyundai Castrol World Rally Team	Hyundai Accent WRC	17	Manfred Hiemer	Retired
82	Finland	Hyundai Castrol World Rally Team	Hyundai Accent WRC	17	Manfred Hiemer	13th
83	Germany	Hyundai Castrol World Rally Team	Hyundai Accent WRC	17	Manfred Hiemer	Retired
84	Sanremo	Hyundai Castrol World Rally Team	Hyundai Accent WRC	17	Manfred Hiemer	Retired
85	New Zealand	Hyundai Castrol World Rally Team	Hyundai Accent WRC	17	Manfred Hiemer	10th
86	Australia	Hyundai Castrol World Rally Team	Hyundai Accent WRC	17	Manfred Hiemer	Retired
87	Great Britain	Hyundai Castrol World Rally Team	Hyundai Accent WRC	17	Manfred Hiemer	Retired
2003	**3 points (18th)**					
88	Monte Carlo	Hyundai World Rally Team	Hyundai Accent WRC	10	Manfred Hiemer	8th
89	Sweden	Hyundai World Rally Team	Hyundai Accent WRC	10	Manfred Hiemer	13th
90	Turkey	Hyundai World Rally Team	Hyundai Accent WRC	10	Manfred Hiemer	Retired
91	New Zealand	Hyundai World Rally Team	Hyundai Accent WRC	10	Manfred Hiemer	Retired
92	Argentina	Hyundai World Rally Team	Hyundai Accent WRC	10	Manfred Hiemer	Retired
93	Greece	Hyundai World Rally Team	Hyundai Accent WRC	10	Manfred Hiemer	Retired
94	Cyprus	Hyundai World Rally Team	Hyundai Accent WRC	10	Manfred Hiemer	7th
95	Deutschland	Hyundai World Rally Team	Hyundai Accent WRC	10	Manfred Hiemer	12th
96	Finland	Hyundai World Rally Team	Hyundai Accent WRC	10	Manfred Hiemer	12th
97	Australia	Hyundai World Rally Team	Hyundai Accent WRC	10	Manfred Hiemer	13th

SHINOZUKA, KENJIRO (J) B: 20 NOVEMBER 1948, TOKYO, JAPAN

Not everyone finds it easy to convert between the demands of Rally-Raids and conventional rallying but Kenjiro Shinozuka is certainly one driver who has the secret.

He started rallying in Japan with an Isuzu Bellet in 1968 and by 1976 had shone sufficiently to get funding to take part in the Safari with a Mitsubishi Lancer. He finished a creditable sixth overall behind works Mitsubishis and Peugeots. He was then considered part of the Mitsubishi set-up though, until 1988, his only European entry was in a hired Ford Escort. The same year he won the Asia Pacific Championship with a Galant VR-4. After that, Mitsubishi started to support him in various WRC events round the world where his best result was a fifth place on the 1990 Safari. All this was a prelude to Mitsubishi Ralliart's major participation in the WRC that would finally, in 1996, lead to their first WRC title.

But Shinozuka was about to make his own contribution to the firm's WRC statistics. He narrowly missed winning the 1990 Ivory Coast Rally when, after leading for most of the event, he hit an unmarked hole and broke the car. He made no such mistake for the following two years gaining back-to-back victories in what was now the toughest rally on the WRC calendar and becoming the first Japanese driver to win a WRC event. It was the year of his second WRC victory, 1992, that Shinozuka started being successful in Rally-Raids with a third place on the Paris-Cape Town. He won Paris-Dakar in 1997 and the same year, drove his last WRC rally in Australia but continued for some years with his Rally-Raid programme.

SHINOZUKA, KENJIRO - CAREER RECORD

YEAR	RALLY	TEAM/ENTRANT	CAR	NO.	CO-DRIVER	RESULT
1976						
1	Safari	Colt Motorsports Club	Mitsubishi Lancer	33	Bob Graham	6th
1977						
2	Safari	Colt Motorsports Club	Mitsubishi Colt Lancer	27	Quentin Thompson	10th
3	Canada		Mitsubishi Colt Lancer	38	Ron Richardson	6th
1981	**1 point (63rd)**					
4	Portugal		Ford Escort RS1800	31	Bryan Harris	10th
1988	**0 points**					
5	New Zealand	Team Mitsubishi Oil Ralliart	Mitsubishi Galant VR-4	7	Fred Gocentas	Retired
6	Great Britain	Mitsubishi Ralliart	Mitsubishi Galant VR-4	45	John Meadows	26th
1989	**14 points (24th)**					
7	Portugal		Mitsubishi Galant VR-4	12	John Meadows	18th
8	Greece	Mitsubishi Ralliart Europe	Mitsubishi Galant VR-4	19	John Meadows	7th
9	New Zealand	Team Miitsubishi Oil Citizen	Mitsubishi Galant VR-4	8	Fred Gocentas	6th
10	Australia	Team Miitsubishi Oil Citizen	Mitsubishi Galant VR-4	14	Fred Gocentas	7th
1990	**8 points (27th)**					
11	Safari	Team Miitsubishi Oil Citizen	Mitsubishi Galant VR-4	12	John Meadows	5th
12	Ivory Coast	Team Miitsubishi Oil Citizen	Mitsubishi Galant VR-4	9	John Meadows	Retired
1991	**23 points (11th)**					
13	Safari	Team Mitsubishi Oil Ralliart	Mitsubishi Galant VR-4	12	John Meadows	8th
14	**Ivory Coast**	**Team Mitsubishi Oil Ralliart**	**Mitsubishi Galant VR-4**	**7**	**John Meadows**	**1st**
1992	**21 points (14th)**					
15	Safari	Mitsubishi Ralliart	Mitsubishi Galant VR-4	7	John Meadows	10th
16	**Ivory Coast**		**Mitsubishi Galant VR-4**	**1**	**John Meadows**	**1st**
1993	**0 points**					
17	Safari	Team Mitsubishi Oil Ralliart	Mitsubishi Lancer RS	4	Pentti Kuukkala	Retired
1994	**15 points (13th)**					
18	Safari	Team Mitsubishi Ralliart	Mitsubishi Lancer Evo 2	4	Pentti Kuukkala	2nd
1996	**6 points (20th)**					
19	Safari	Mitsubishi Lancer Dealer Team	Mitsubishi Lancer Evo 3	8	Pentti Kuukkala	6th
1997						
20	Australia	Team Mitsubishi Ralliart	Mitsubishi Lancer Evo 3	13	Fred Gocentas	Retired

SINGH, JOGINDER

(EAK) B: 9 FEBRUARY 1932, KERICHO, KENYA

If you were searching for an example of determination and perseverance, you could pick no better man than Joginder Singh. In his 22 consecutive attempts at the Safari Rally he posted three wins, only three retirements and 11 times he finished inside the top five.

Born in Kericho, high up among the tea plantations of western Kenya, Joginder learnt his automobile engineering in his father's workshop before moving to Nairobi where he landed a job as Kenya's first mobile EAA patrolman. He started rallying in 1958 with a friend in a Morris Minor. He took a private VW to ninth place on the 1959 Safari and got support from Cooper Motors for whom he drove for the next three years, finishing every time and fifth in 1962.

For 1964, Joginder was signed to drive one of the Lincoln Mercury Comets brought from Detroit with much razzmatazz but which went home rather subdued. The Comet gave Joginder his worst Safari result but he was able to buy two of the works Volvos PV544s that were deemed not worth shipping back to Sweden. In 1965 he pulled start number one out of the hat and drove brilliantly to win by a country mile.

He drove Volvos for the next two years and always finished well. He was second for Datsun in 1969 and a contract loomed but he chose Ford instead and posted his first retirement ever in 1972. Short of a drive for 1973 he looked around and chose the 1600cc Mitsubishi Galant, preparing it himself. He became Mitsubishi's advance guard on the WRC scene winning the Safari twice. His rally career finished in works Mercedes, on the last occasion being partnered by an American TV star from Baywatch to whom he gave a lesson in stoicism by contriving to remove the passenger window and most of the door in an early accident.

SINGH, JOGINDER - CAREER RECORD

YEAR	RALLY	TEAM/ENTRANT	CAR	NO.	CO-DRIVER	RESULT
1973						
1	Safari	Simba Motors Ltd	Mitsubishi Colt Galant	18	Tim Samuels	7th
1974						
2	**Safari**		**Mitsubishi Colt Lancer**	**46**	**David Doig**	**1st**
1975						
3	Safari	Joginder's Rally Team	Mitsubishi Colt Lancer	4	David Doig	Retired
1976						
4	**Safari**	**Simba Motors Ltd**	**Mitsubishi Lancer**	**8**	**David Doig**	**1st**
1977						
5	Safari	Dia Star International Corporation	Mitsubishi Colt Lancer	10	David Doig	5th
1978						
6	Safari	D.T Dobie & Co. Ltd	Mercedes-Benz 280E	2	David Doig	Retired
1979	0 points					
7	Safari	D.T Dobie & Co. Ltd	Mercedes 280E	2	David Doig	11th
1980	0 points					
8	Safari	American Sports Sales Inc.	Mercedes 450SLC	8	Parker Stevenson	14th

Solberg, Petter (N) B: 18 November 1974, Spydeberg, Norway

One is always amazed by Olympic high jumpers, the lazy way they run up and then soar over the pole. Watching Petter Solberg take the WRC Drivers' Championship in 2003 was a bit like that, a slow run up and then soaring to a title for which he had been considered an outsider.

"Solberg soared to a title for which he was considered an outsider"

Solberg comes from a motor sporting family but it was not rallies right from the start. His earliest experiences were with Ford Escorts and then a Volvo 240 Turbo in hill-climbing and rallycross. He was twice Norwegian double champion in those disciplines in 1995 and 1996. He did his first rally in 1996 with his brother's Toyota Celica, crashed and wrote it off. Nothing daunted, he tried more rallying with a Celica in 1997 while still hill-climbing with the same car. In 1998, young Solberg made his WRC debut on the Swedish Rally and clinched his national championship with four wins from six rallies. With the help of Norwegian veteran, John Haugland, he persuaded Ford to give him a test drive in England and they were sufficiently impressed to offer him a limited contract for 1999.

To everyone's surprise, the effervescent young Norwegian finished every WRC event he drove for Ford. That included a fifth place on the Safari where he stood in at the last moment for Thomas Rådström. Part of the reason for his consistency then and now was his acquisition from M-Sport's staff of Philip Mills as co-driver. The year 2000 looked as if it was going to be even better for Solberg and the Focus WRC. He finished Safari again in fifth but retirements were as frequent as finishes and, after the Rally Finland, he split with Ford and went to Subaru taking Mills with him.

To start with, the change of team did not look to have benefited his results but at least he was speeding up, reaching the podium in Greece and setting good times on other events. Indeed, he often led an event before having some confrontation with the scenery. His first full season with Subaru was his first full year of WRC. Subaru was not at the top of its form and had not won a World Championship since 1997. When Richard Burns left them to go to Peugeot for 2002, Solberg did not automatically rise to be Number One in the team, as Burns' replacement was four times World Champion, Tommi Mäkinen. What Solberg did do was move into that position by his results. During the year, he was on the podium four times before finishing the year with his first WRC win on the Rally GB.

2003 started badly with a crash on the Monte Carlo and a bad tyre experience in Sweden. It was not until New Zealand that he started to acquire points at a reasonable rate. A trip on the roof in Argentina did not stop him adding to his score. A broken driveshaft in Greece cost him a win but he won in Cyprus. A brilliant drive in Finland to displace Burns from second place was followed by a win in Australia. Most satisfying of all was Corsica where this Scandinavian won by faultless driving in the rain after nearly writing the car off in a pre-event test.

He came to the last round one point behind the two leaders, Sebastian Loeb and Carlos Sainz. Could he win the Rally GB for the second time running and clinch the title just 12 months after winning his first WRC event ? He did and he has.

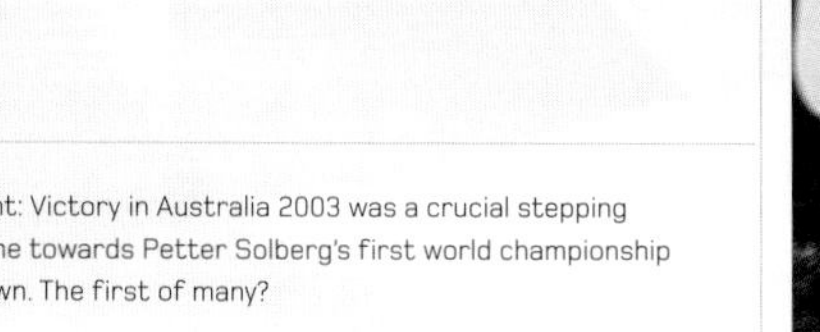

Right: Victory in Australia 2003 was a crucial stepping stone towards Petter Solberg's first world championship crown. The first of many?

SOLBERG, PETTER – CAREER RECORD

YEAR	RALLY	TEAM/ENTRANT	CAR	NO.	CO-DRIVER	RESULT
1998	**0 points**					
1	Sweden	Shell Norge	Toyota Celica GT-Four	34	Egil Soltat	16th
2	Great Britain		Toyota Celica GT-Four	45	Cato Menkerud	Retired
1999	**2 points (18th)**					
3	Sweden	Ford Motor Company	Ford Escort WRC	14	Philip Mills	11th
4	Safari	Ford Motor Company	Ford Escort WRC	8	Fred Gallagher	5th
5	Portugal	Ford Motor Company	Ford Escort WRC	8	Philip Mills	11th
6	Finland		Ford Escort WRC	17	Philip Mills	12th
7	Sanremo	Ford Motor Company	Ford Escort WRC	25	Philip Mills	27th
8	Great Britain	Ford Motor Company	Ford Escort WRC	20	Philip Mills	9th
2000	**6 points (10th)**					
9	Safari	Ford Motor Company	Ford Focus WRC	16	Philip Mills	5th
10	Portugal	Ford Motor Company	Ford Focus WRC	19	Philip Mills	Retired
11	Argentina	Ford Motor Company	Ford Focus WRC	16	Philip Mills	6th
12	Greece	Ford Motor Company	Ford Focus WRC	16	Philip Mills	Retired
13	New Zealand	Ford Motor Company	Ford Focus WRC	16	Philip Mills	4th
14	Finland	Ford Motor Company	Ford Focus WRC	16	Philip Mills	Retired
15	Corsica	Subaru World Rally Team	Subaru Impreza WRC	18	Philip Mills	Retired
16	Sanremo	Subaru World Rally Team	Subaru Impreza WRC	19	Philip Mills	9th
17	Australia	Subaru World Rally Team	Subaru Impreza WRC	17	Philip Mills	Retired
18	Great Britain	Subaru World Rally Team	Subaru Impreza WRC	16	Philip Mills	Retired
2001	**11 points (10th)**					
19	Monte Carlo	Subaru World Rally Team	Subaru Impreza WRC	18	Philip Mills	Retired
20	Sweden	Subaru World Rally Team	Subaru Impreza WRC	6	Philip Mills	6th
21	Portugal	Subaru World Rally Team	Subaru Impreza WRC	6	Philip Mills	Retired
22	Catalunya	Subaru World Rally Team	Subaru Impreza WRC	6	Philip Mills	Retired
23	Argentina	Subaru World Rally Team	Subaru Impreza WRC	6	Philip Mills	5th
24	Cyprus	Subaru World Rally Team	Subaru Impreza WRC	6	Philip Mills	Retired
25	Greece	Subaru World Rally Team	Subaru Impreza WRC	6	Philip Mills	2nd
26	Safari	Subaru World Rally Team	Subaru Impreza WRC	6	Philip Mills	Retired
27	Finland	Subaru World Rally Team	Subaru Impreza WRC	6	Philip Mills	7th
28	New Zealand	Subaru World Rally Team	Subaru Impreza WRC	6	Philip Mills	7th
29	Sanremo	Subaru World Rally Team	Subaru Impreza WRC	6	Philip Mills	9th
30	Corsica	Subaru World Rally Team	Subaru Impreza WRC	6	Philip Mills	5th
31	Australia	Subaru World Rally Team	Subaru Impreza WRC	6	Philip Mills	7th
32	Great Britain	Subaru World Rally Team	Subaru Impreza WRC	6	Philip Mills	Retired
2002	**37 points (2nd)**					
33	Monte Carlo	555 Subaru World Rally Team	Subaru Impreza WRC	11	Philip Mills	6th
34	Sweden	555 Subaru World Rally Team	Subaru Impreza WRC	11	Philip Mills	Retired
35	Corsica	555 Subaru World Rally Team	Subaru Impreza WRC	11	Philip Mills	5th
36	Catalunya	555 Subaru World Rally Team	Subaru Impreza WRC	11	Philip Mills	5th
37	Cyprus	555 Subaru World Rally Team	Subaru Impreza WRC	11	Philip Mills	5th
38	Argentina	555 Subaru World Rally Team	Subaru Impreza WRC	11	Philip Mills	2nd
39	Greece	555 Subaru World Rally Team	Subaru Impreza WRC	11	Philip Mills	5th
40	Safari	555 Subaru World Rally Team	Subaru Impreza WRC	11	Philip Mills	Retired
41	Finland	555 Subaru World Rally Team	Subaru Impreza WRC	11	Philip Mills	3rd
42	Germany	555 Subaru World Rally Team	Subaru Impreza WRC	11	Philip Mills	Retired
43	Sanremo	555 Subaru World Rally Team	Subaru Impreza WRC	11	Philip Mills	3rd
44	New Zealand	555 Subaru World Rally Team	Subaru Impreza WRC	11	Philip Mills	Retired
45	Australia	555 Subaru World Rally Team	Subaru Impreza WRC	11	Philip Mills	3rd
46	**Great Britain**	**555 Subaru World Rally Team**	**Subaru Impreza WRC**	**11**	**Philip Mills**	**1st**
2003	**72 points (WORLD CHAMPION)**					
47	Monte Carlo	555 Subaru World Rally Team	Subaru Impreza WRC	7	Philip Mills	Retired
48	Sweden	555 Subaru World Rally Team	Subaru Impreza WRC	7	Philip Mills	6th
49	Turkey	555 Subaru World Rally Team	Subaru Impreza WRC	7	Philip Mills	Retired
50	New Zealand	555 Subaru World Rally Team	Subaru Impreza WRC	7	Philip Mills	3rd
51	Argentina	555 Subaru World Rally Team	Subaru Impreza WRC	7	Philip Mills	5th
52	Greece	555 Subaru World Rally Team	Subaru Impreza WRC	7	Philip Mills	3rd
53	**Cyprus**	**555 Subaru World Rally Team**	**Subaru Impreza WRC**	**7**	**Philip Mills**	**1st**
54	Germany	555 Subaru World Rally Team	Subaru Impreza WRC	7	Philip Mills	8th
55	Finland	555 Subaru World Rally Team	Subaru Impreza WRC	7	Philip Mills	2nd
56	**Australia**	**555 Subaru World Rally Team**	**Subaru Impreza WRC**	**7**	**Philip Mills**	**1st**
57	Sanremo	555 Subaru World Rally Team	Subaru Impreza WRC	7	Philip Mills	Retired
58	**Corsica**	**555 Subaru World Rally Team**	**Subaru Impreza WRC**	**7**	**Philip Mills**	**1st**
59	Catalunya	555 Subaru World Rally Team	Subaru Impreza WRC	7	Philip Mills	5th
60	**Great Britain**	**555 Subaru World Rally Team**	**Subaru Impreza WRC**	**7**	**Philip Mills**	**1st**

Tauziac, Patrick (F) B: 18 January 1955, Saigon, Vietnam

Patrick Tauziac did his first major rally, the 1983 Ivory Coast, in a Mitsubishi Colt and, throughout his rally career, which never ventured outside his adopted country, he remained faithful to the Japanese marque.

Born in Saigon of mixed parentage the year after the fall of Dien Bien Phu, Tauziac came to the Ivory Coast when he was still a child. In his teens, he developed an interest in cars and tried his hand at rallycross using a rather gaudily painted Renault 4L.

His rally debut came on a local event in 1983 where he drove a front wheel drive Colt. In 1984 he won Group A, the last of six finishers, 19 hours behind the winning Quattro.

With the Mitsubishi Starion Turbo he gradually improved his results, finishing fourth in 1987 and then third and then second.

When he got a Mitsubishi Galant VR-4 for the 1990 event, the outcome might have seemed a foregone conclusion in the absence of both Lancia and Toyota. However, team mate Kenjiro Shinozuka gave him a hard fight until he buried his VR-4 in an enormous hole and lost the chance of being the first Japanese driver to win a World Championship event.

Tauziac came through to become the first Asian-born driver to do just that. Two years later, the Ivory Coast Rally was no longer in the WRC, proving that, for Tauziac at least, timing is everything.

Tauziac, Patrick Career Record

YEAR	RALLY	TEAM/ENTRANT	CAR	NO.	CO-DRIVER	RESULT
1983						
1	Ivory Coast		Mitsubishi Colt	47	Louis Cournil	Retired
1984	6 points (30th)					
2	Ivory Coast		Mitsubishi Colt	18	Louis Cournil	6th
1985	0 points					
3	Ivory Coast		Mitsubishi Lancer Turbo	6	Alain Olinger	Retired
1986	0 points					
4	Ivory Coast		Mitsubishi Starion Turbo	11	Claude Papin	Retired
1987	10 points (26th)					
5	Ivory Coast	Ralliart/CFAO	Mitsubishi Starion Turbo	17	Claude Papin	4th
1988	12 points (20th)					
6	Ivory Coast		Mitsubishi Starion Turbo	5	Claude Papin	3rd
1989	15 points (20th)					
7	Ivory Coast		Mitsubishi Starion Turbo	9	Claude Papin	2nd
1990	20 points (12th)					
8	**Ivory Coast**		**Mitsubishi Galant VR-4**	**1**	**Claude Papin**	**1st**
1991	15 points (15th)					
9	Ivory Coast		Mitsubishi Galant VR-4	1	Claude Papin	2nd
1992	0 points					
10	Ivory Coast		Mitsubishi Galant VR-4	2	Christian Boy	Retired

THÉRIER, JEAN-LUC (F) B: 7 OCTOBER 1945, HODENG-AU-BOSC, FRANCE

If rallying is fun, then that spirit is encapsulated in one man: Jean-Luc Thérier. A comedian out of the car, he was a formidable opponent in it, as natural a driver as he was a joker.

His career started in karts in 1960 and in 1966 he tried his hand at the Coupe Gordini, a mixture of rallies and races with Renault R8s, and won it. He won a seat in a works Alpine A210 for the 1968 Le Mans where he finished 10th and won the Index of Performance. He finished an amazing fifth overall on the Monte Carlo of 1969 with a Group 1 R8 and promptly signed to drive rallies for Alpine Renault. In 1970, he won the San Remo and the Acropolis rallies and would have been third overall on the RAC Rally but got stuck on the very last stage.

He started 1971 by finishing second in Monte Carlo but, for the next two years, had a mixed programme of rallies and hillclimbs. It was good preparation for the first year of the WRC when Renault Alpine won. And it was Thérier who did much of the work. After that triumph, Renault reduced their involvement but he stayed with them for a further two years.

At a loose end in 1976, Thérier was signed up by the nascent Toyota team and, in France at least, he was invincible, twice winning the gravel championship. At the end of 1980, he won Corsica with a Porsche 911SC but failed to repeat that success on the other WRC events he drove in the car. For 1982, he signed to drive a Renault R5 Turbo for Lamirault in Chartres and won his second French tarmac title. He looked set for a major comeback with Renault but during the 1985 Paris-Dakar in which he was making a one-off appearance in a Citroën Visa 4x4, he had a big accident, the effects of which have prevented any possibility of his driving again.

THÉRIER, JEAN-LUC – CAREER RECORD

YEAR	RALLY	TEAM/ENTRANT	CAR	NO.	CO-DRIVER	RESULT
1973						
1	Monte Carlo	Renault Alpine	Renault-Alpine A110	4	Marcel Callewaert	5th
2	Sweden	Renault Alpine	Renault-Alpine A110	11	Marcel Callewaert	3rd
3	**Portugal**	**Renault Alpine**	**Renault-Alpine A110**	**5**	**Jacques Jaubert**	**1st**
4	Morocco	Renault Alpine	Renault-Alpine A110	3	Christian Delferrier	7th
5	**Greece**	**Renault Alpine**	**Renault-Alpine A110**	**1**	**Christian Delferrier**	**1st**
6	Poland	Renault Alpine	Renault-Alpine A110	2	Alain Mahe	Retired
7	**Sanremo**	**Renault Alpine**	**Renault-Alpine A110**	**1**	**Jacques Jaubert**	**1st**
8	Great Britain	Renault Alpine	Renault-Alpine A110	3	Michel Vial	Retired
9	Corsica	Renault Alpine	Renault-Alpine A110	7	Marcel Callewaert	3rd
1974						
10	Safari	Renault Alpine	Renault-Alpine A110	15	Vincent Laverne	Retired
11	**United States**	**Renault**	**Renault 17 Gordini**	**12**	**Christian Delferrier**	**1st**
12	Corsica	Renault Alpine	Renault-Alpine A310	7	Michel Vial	3rd
1975						
13	Monte Carlo	Renault Alpine	Renault-Alpine A110	5	Michel Vial	Retired
14	Safari	Renault Alpine	Renault-Alpine A110	5	Michel Vial	Retired
15	Sanremo	Renault Alpine	Renault-Alpine A110	5	Michel Vial	3rd
16	Corsica	Renault Alpine	Renault-Alpine A110	2	Michel Vial	Retired
1976						
17	Monte Carlo	Renault Alpine	Renault-Alpine A310	9	Michel Vial	Retired
18	Great Britain	Team Toyota	Toyota Celica 2000GT	12	Michel Vial	Retired
1977						
19	Great Britain	Toyota Team Europe	Toyota Celica GT	18	Michel Vial	Retired
1978						
20	Sweden	Toyota Team Europe	Toyota Celica	10	Michel Vial	Retired
21	Portugal	Toyota Team Europe	Toyota Celica	15	Michel Vial	Retired
22	Greece	Toyota Team Europe	Toyota Celica	9	Michel Vial	Retired
23	Corsica		Triumph TR7 V8	7	Michel Vial	Retired
24	Great Britain	Toyota Team Europe	Toyota Celica	22	Michel Vial	Retired
1979	**0 points**					
25	Monte Carlo	Cresson/Zenith	Volkswagen Golf GTi	19	Michel Vial	Retired
26	Sweden	Toyota Team Europe	Toyota Celica 2000GT	13	Michel Vial	Retired
27	Portugal	Toyota Team Europe	Toyota Celica 2000GT	7	Michel Vial	Retired
28	Greece	Toyota Team Europe	Toyota Celica 2000GT	11	Michel Vial	Retired
29	Great Britain	Toyota Team Europe	Toyota Celica 2000GT	21	Michel Vial	Retired
30	Ivory Coast	Toyota Team Europe	Toyota Celica 2000GT	8	Michel Vial	Retired
1980	**20 points (12th)**					
31	Monte Carlo	BP Racing Volkswagen Sport	Volkswagen Golf GTi	14	Michel Vial	Retired
32	Portugal	Toyota Team Europe	Toyota Celica 2000GT	15	Michel Vial	Retired
33	Greece	Toyota Team Europe	Toyota Celica 2000GT	16	Michel Vial	Retired
34	**Corsica**	**Porsche Almeras**	**Porsche 911SC**	**9**	**Michel Vial**	**1st**
1981	**0 points**					
35	Monte Carlo	Esso	Porsche 911SC	10	Michel Vial	Retired
36	Portugal	Porsche Almeras	Porsche 911SC	5	Michel Vial	Retired
37	Corsica	Esso	Porsche 911SC	6	Michel Vial	Retired
38	Sanremo	Eminence	Porsche 911SC	10	Michel Vial	Retired
1982	**12 points (15th)**					
39	Monte Carlo	Porsche Almeras	Porsche 911SC	8	Michel Vial	3rd
40	Portugal	Porsche Almeras	Porsche 911SC	4	Michel Vial	Retired
41	Corsica	Garage Lamirault	Renault 5 Turbo	3	Michel Vial	Retired
1983	**0 points**					
42	Monte Carlo	Lamirault	Renault 5 Turbo	11	Michel Vial	Retired
43	Portugal	Lamirault	Renault 5 Turbo	5	Michel Vial	Retired
44	Corsica	Lamirault	Renault 5 Turbo	7	Michel Vial	Retired
1984	**10 points (19th)**					
45	Monte Carlo	Societe Diac	Renault 5 Turbo	6	Michel Vial	4th

TOIVONEN, HENRI

(FIN) B: 28 AUGUST 1956, JYVASKALA, FINLAND; D: 2 MAY 1986, AJACCIO, CORSICA

"His death robbed us of the chance to see how great he really could have been"

When your father is a famous rally driver who has won the 1000 Lakes, Monte Carlo and been European Rally Champion for Porsche, your aspirations may be high but the chances are that you may not make it. Henri Toivonen was the exception that proves the rule. The sadness is the use of the past tense since his death robbed us of the chance to see how great he really could have been.

His father, Pauli Toivonen, worked for the Finnish importer of Citroën, VW, Porsche and Chrysler and thus his son's debut car happened to be a Simca Rallye 2. One of his very first events was the 1975 1000 Lakes where he failed to finish. A Chrysler Avenger was his next car and, with a fifth place on the 1977 1000 Lakes plus local success, he was offered drives the following year with a works Group 1 Citroën 2400 CX in Portugal and Greece. He tried a Porsche 911 on the 1000 Lakes until the engine blew and with his own Avenger finished in the top 10 on the RAC Rally.

There was not much happening in his career in 1979 but he did get a works Fiat 131 for the 1000 Lakes where, despite lack of match experience, he was right up with the leaders until he left the road. He did some British events in a rented Escort RS and though he took home no prizes from the RAC Rally, he did take home a contract to drive Talbot's new Sunbeam Lotus in 1980. Toivonen won the Arctic Rally in January but abroad, he and the car took time to settle. It was not until the San Remo that he got a result and then a superb win on the RAC Rally at the tender age of 24 years and three months - at the time making him the youngest WRC event winner of all time.

In 1981 he did a full season as team mate to Guy Frequelin to take the Manufacturer's WRC title for Talbot. On that high note, their Sunbeam Lotus programme stopped as the company swung into developing the Peugeot 205 T16 so Toivonen sought refuge with Opel for whom he did a mixture of WRC and British events. His only win was on the Manx in 1983, but his speed was never in doubt and he seemed to have discovered the happy habit of finishing on the podium. In 1984, he was signed up by Lancia to drive their Rally 037 and he filled out an already busy year by driving a Rothmans Porsche 911 SC in the European Championship. As before, he was either winning or in the first three, though early season form showed that he could still have the occasional accident.

The 1985 season proved his new found maturity with steadily improving results in the 037 and then a win in the Delta S4 on its debut at the RAC Rally. The S4 seemed to be his ideal companion. He started the next year by winning Monte Carlo and won again in Costa Smeralda after the Portuguese debacle only to crash in Corsica and lose his life along with co-driver Sergio Cresto. This accident, coupled with the spectator fatalities in Portugal, spelled the end for Group B and its proposed evolution, Group S.

Right: With victory on Monte Carlo already behind him, Henri Toivonen went to Corsica expecting to turn the screw on his 1986 title rivals. Instead he was killed when his car plunged off the road, a fatality that sent as much of a shock wave through rallying as did the death of Ayrton Senna in the Formula 1 world

TOIVONEN, HENRI - CAREER RECORD

YEAR	RALLY	TEAM/ENTRANT	CAR	NO.	CO-DRIVER	RESULT
1975						
1	Finland		Simca Rallye	36	Antero Lindqvist	Retired
1977						
2	Finland		Chrysler Avenger	25	Antero Lindqvist	5th
1978						
3	Portugal	Citroen	Citroen CX2400 GTi	24	Juha Paajanen	Retired
4	Greece	Citroen	Citroen CX2400 GTi	22	Juha Paajanen	Retired
5	Finland		Porsche 911	21	Juha Paajanen	Retired
6	Great Britain	Racing Team Toivonen	Chrysler Sunbeam	44	Juhani Korhonen	9th
1979	0 points					
7	Finland		Fiat 131 Abarth	14	Juha Paajanen	Retired
8	Great Britain	Toyota Oil	Ford Escort RS1800	20	Phil Boland	Retired
1980	28 points (10th)					
9	Portugal	Talbot GB	Talbot Sunbeam Lotus	20	Antero Lindqvist	Retired
10	Finland	Talbot Motor Company	Talbot Sunbeam Lotus	12	Antero Lindqvist	Retired
11	Sanremo	Talbot GB	Talbot Sunbeam Lotus	16	Antero Lindqvist	5th
12	**Great Britain**	**Talbot GB**	**Talbot Sunbeam Lotus**	**16**	**Paul White**	**1st**
1981	38 points (7th)					
13	Monte Carlo	Talbot Sport	Talbot Sunbeam Lotus	8	Fred Gallagher	5th
14	Portugal	Talbot Sport	Talbot Sunbeam Lotus	9	Fred Gallagher	2nd
15	Corsica	Talbot Sport	Talbot Sunbeam Lotus	9	Fred Gallagher	Retired
16	Greece	Talbot Sport	Talbot Sunbeam Lotus	11	Fred Gallagher	Retired
17	Finland	Talbot Sport	Talbot Sunbeam Lotus	6	Fred Gallagher	Retired
18	Sanremo	Talbot Sport	Talbot Sunbeam Lotus	11	Fred Gallagher	2nd
19	Great Britain	Talbot Sport	Talbot Sunbeam Lotus	1	Fred Gallagher	Retired
1982	32 points (7th)					
20	Portugal	Rothmans Opel Rally Team	Opel Ascona 400	6	Fred Gallagher	Retired
21	Greece	Rothmans Opel Rally Team	Opel Ascona 400	6	Fred Gallagher	3rd
22	Finland	Rothmans Opel Rally Team	Opel Ascona 400	4	Fred Gallagher	Retired
23	Sanremo	Rothmans Opel Rally Team	Opel Ascona 400	6	Fred Gallagher	5th
24	Great Britain	Rothmans Opel Rally Team	Opel Ascona 400	7	Fred Gallagher	3rd
1983	16 points (14th)					
25	Monte Carlo	Rothmans Opel Rally Team	Opel Ascona 400	6	Fred Gallagher	6th
26	Greece	Rothmans Opel Rally Team	Opel Manta 400	6	Fred Gallagher	Retired
27	Finland	Rothmans Opel Rally Team	Opel Manta 400	7	Fred Gallagher	Retired
28	Sanremo	Rothmans Opel Rally Team	Opel Manta 400	7	Fred Gallagher	4th
29	Great Britain	Rothmans Opel Rally Team	Opel Manta 400	2	Fred Gallagher	Retired
1984	12 points (16th)					
30	Portugal	Martini Racing	Lancia Rally 037	10	Juha Piironen	Retired
31	Greece	Martini Racing	Lancia Rally 037	11	Juha Piironen	Reired
32	Finland	Martini Racing	Lancia Rally 037	10	Juha Piironen	3rd
1985	48 points (6th)					
33	Monte Carlo	Lancia Martini	Lancia Rally 037	4	Juha Piironen	6th
34	Finland	Lancia Martini	Lancia Rally 037	5	Juha Piironen	4th
35	Sanremo	Lancia Martini	Lancia Rally 037	1	Juha Piironen	3rd
36	**Great Britain**	**Lancia Martini**	**Lancia Delta S4**	**6**	**Neil Wilson**	**1st**
1986	20 points (13th)					
37	**Monte Carlo**	**Martini Lancia**	**Lancia Delta S4**	**7**	**Sergio Cresto**	**1st**
38	Sweden	Martini Lancia	Lancia Delta S4	5	Sergio Cresto	Retired
39	Portugal	Martini Lancia	Lancia Delta S4	8	Sergio Cresto	Retired
40	Corsica	Martini Lancia	Lancia Delta S4	4	Sergio Cresto	Fatal accident

VATANEN, ARI (FIN) B: 27 APRIL 1952, JOENSUU, FINLAND

"He thrived on adversity, fighting back on numerous occasions to snatch victory from the jaws of defeat"

For sheer brilliance and charisma, it would be hard to surpass Ari Vatanen. With an attacking driving style that made him the darling of rally fans in the 1970s and 1980s, he always seemed to bring a sense of adventure to the sport. And he thrived on adversity, fighting back on numerous occasions to snatch victory from the jaws of defeat.

Vatanen's rally career started when he was just 18. He acquired an Opel Ascona and by 1974 was optimistic enough to enter it on the 1000 Lakes where it promptly lost a wheel. He brought it to Britain and astounded people with his speed. An offer to drive a Ford Escort soon followed but, in two years, there were no results to show. Even a full season in 1977 only netted him a second place in New Zealand and third in the European Championship. And most of the retirements were self-inflicted.

But while he was going, Vatanen was a joy to behold. In 1979, David Richards joined him as co-driver and in 1980 he won the Acropolis Rally at only his second attempt. But then Ford pulled out of rallying and Vatanen was left to run for the WRC with David Sutton's private team. After a year of considerable drama and success, Vatanen won the World Drivers' title - the only time a 'privateer' has ever achieved the feat. It had been touch and go and even the points from the Ivory Coast where he finished ninth and dead last, 22 hours behind the winner, were useful - indeed vital - to the cause.

In 1982, he did two WRC events with Ford but then signed for the Rothmans Opel Team in time for the RAC Rally and drove for Opel throughout the next season.

At only his second appearance on the Safari, he won, driving an Ascona 400. The new Manta 400 was not so kind to him and at the end of the year he was approached by Peugeot to driveits new Group B rally car. He had to wait until Corsica to take the 205 T16 on its first WRC outing where both he and the car impressed, leading before retirement.

The same happened in Greece until the engine failed. But then Vatanen embarked on a run of success that eclipsed even his World Championship year. He won five WRC events in a row despite rolling on the RAC Rally and being checked in four minutes early on the Monte Carlo. Both times he fought through to win.

After suffering a bout of mechanical failures, he went to Argentina and had a horrific high speed accident. For weeks it was thought that he might not live; for months that he might not recover. But a year and a bit later, Vatanen was back behind the wheel of a Peugeot and winning. The only difference was that Peugeot had pulled out of the WRC and this was the Paris-Dakar of 1987. Vatanen went on to win this desert event three more times, along with the Pikes Peak hill climb.

As the 1990s kicked in, he drove for Mitsubishi, Subaru and finally back at Ford. He stood in at short notice for an injured Bruno Thiry on the 1998

Safari and would have been second had he not yielded the place to team mate, Juha Kankkunen.

His last factory drive was with Subaru in 1998, his 100th WRC start, but he entered Rally Finland 2003 for fun and finished a spectacular 11th, waving to the fans as he went.

Always the gentleman, Vatanen now has a new career in politics as a Member of the European Parliament.

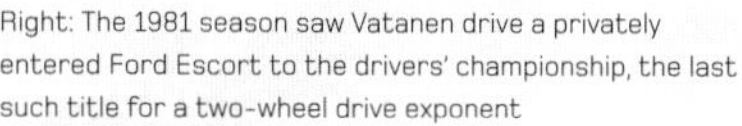

Right: The 1981 season saw Vatanen drive a privately entered Ford Escort to the drivers' championship, the last such title for a two-wheel drive exponent

VATANEN, ARI – CAREER RECORD

YEAR	RALLY	TEAM/ENTRANT	CAR	NO.	CO-DRIVER	RESULT
1974						
1	Finland		Opel Ascona	28	Alf Krogell	Retired
1975						
2	Finland	Ford Motor Company	Ford Escort RS1600	11	Geraint Phillips	Retired
3	Great Britain	Independent Radio News/Motorcraft	Ford Escort RS1600	14	Peter Bryant	Retired
1976						
4	Finland	Ford Motor Company	Ford Escort RS1800	9	Atso Aho	Retired
5	Great Britain	Allied Polymer Group	Ford Escort RS1800	15	Peter Bryant	Retired
1977						
6	Portugal	Ford Motor Company	Ford Escort RS1800	9	Peter Bryant	Retired
7	Safari	Ford Motor Company	Ford Escort RS1800	14	Atso Aho	Retired
8	New Zealand	Masport	Ford Escort RS1800	2	Jim Scott	2nd
9	Greece	Ford Motor Company	Ford Escort RS1800	16	Atso Aho	Retired
10	Finland	Ford Motor Company	Ford Escort RS1800	4	Atso Aho	Retired
11	Canada	Ford Motor Company	Ford Escort RS1800	6	Atso Aho	Retired
12	Sanremo	Ford Motor Company	Ford Escort RS1800	6	Peter Bryant	Retired
13	Great Britain	Ford Motor Company	Ford Escort RS1800	9	Peter Bryant	Retired
1978						
14	Sweden	Ford Motor Company	Ford Escort RS	8	Atso Aho	5th
15	Portugal	Ford Motor Company	Ford Escort RS	11	Peter Bryant	Retired
16	Finland	Ford Motor Company	Ford Escort RS	7	Atso Aho	Retired
17	Great Britain	Marlboro	Ford Escort RS	6	Peter Bryant	Retired
1979	50 points (5th)					
18	Monte Carlo	Rothmans Rally Team	Ford Fiesta 1600	17	David Richards	10th
19	Sweden	Rothmans Rally Team	Ford Escort RS1800	6	David Richards	Retired
20	Portugal	Rothmans Rally Team	Ford Escort RS1800	5	Peter Bryant	Retired
21	New Zealand	Rothmans Rally Team	Ford Escort RS1800	3	David Richards	3rd
22	Finland	Rothmans Rally Team	Ford Escort RS1800	8	David Richards	2nd
23	Canada	Rothmans Rally Team	Ford Escort RS1800	1	David Richards	3rd
24	Great Britain	Rothmans Rally Team	Ford Escort RS1800	6	David Richards	4th
1980	50 points (4th)					
25	Monte Carlo	Publimo Racing	Ford Escort RS1800	5	David Richards	Retired
26	Portugal	Rothmans Rally Team	Ford Escort RS1800	7	David Richards	Retired
27	**Greece**	**Rothmans Rally Team**	**Ford Escort RS1800**	**10**	**David Richards**	**1st**
28	Finland	Rothmans Rally Team	Ford Escort RS1800	3	David Richards	2nd
29	Sanremo	Rothmans Rally Team	Ford Escort RS1800	4	David Richards	2nd
30	Great Britain	Rothmans Rally Team	Ford Escort RS1800	5	David Richards	Retired
1981	96 points (WORLD CHAMPION)					
31	Monte Carlo	Rothmans Rally Team	Ford Escort RS1800	3	David Richards	Retired
32	Sweden	Rothmans Rally Team	Ford Escort RS1800	4	David Richards	2nd
33	Portugal	Rothmans Rally Team	Ford Escort RS1800	6	David Richards	Retired
34	**Greece**	**Rothmans Rally Team**	**Ford Escort RS1800**	**1**	**David Richards**	**1st**
35	Argentina	Rothmans Rally Team	Ford Escort RS1800	3	David Richards	Retired
36	**Brazil**	**Rothmans Rally Team**	**Ford Escort RS1800**	**2**	**David Richards**	**1st**
37	**Finland**	**Rothmans Rally Team**	**Ford Escort RS1800**	**2**	**David Richards**	**1st**
38	Sanremo	Rothmans Rally Team	Ford Escort RS1800	4	David Richards	7th
39	Ivory Coast	Rothmans Rally Team	Ford Escort RS1800	7	David Richards	9th
40	Great Britain	Rothmans Rally Team	Ford Escort RS1800	2	David Richards	2nd
1982	15 points (13th)					
41	Sweden	David Sutton Cars	Ford Escort RS1800	2	Terry Harryman	2nd
42	Finland	David Sutton Cars	Ford Escort RS1800	1	Terry Harryman	Retired
43	Great Britain	Rothmans Opel Rally Team	Opel Ascona 400	2	Terry Harryman	Retired
1983	44 points (6th)					
44	Monte Carlo	Rothmans Opel Rally Team	Opel Ascona 400	3	Terry Harryman	5th
45	Sweden	Rothmans Opel Rally Team	Opel Ascona 400	2	Terry Harryman	6th
46	**Safari**	**Rothmans Opel Rally Team**	**Opel Ascona 400**	**2**	**Terry Harryman**	**1st**
47	Greece	Rothmans Opel Rally Team	Opel Manta 400	2	Terry Harryman	4th
48	Finland	Rothmans Opel Rally Team	Opel Manta 400	4	Terry Harryman	Retired

VATANEN, ARI - CAREER RECORD (CONT'D)

YEAR	RALLY	TEAM/ENTRANT	CAR	NO.	CO-DRIVER	RESULT
49	Sanremo	Rothmans Opel Rally Team	Opel Manta 400	4	Terry Harryman	Retired
50	Great Britain	Rothmans Opel Rally Team	Opel Manta 400	6	Terry Harryman	Retired
1984	**60 points (4th)**					
51	Corsica	Peugeot Talbot Sport	Peugeot 205 T16	4	Terry Harryman	Retired
52	Greece	Peugeot Talbot Sport	Peugeot 205 T16	3	Terry Harryman	Retired
53	**Finland**	**Peugeot Talbot Sport**	**Peugeot 205 T16**	**4**	**Terry Harryman**	**1st**
54	**Sanremo**	**Peugeot Talbot Sport**	**Peugeot 205 T16**	**3**	**Terry Harryman**	**1st**
55	**Great Britain**	**Peugeot Talbot Sport**	**Peugeot 205 T16**	**2**	**Terry Harryman**	**1st**
1985	**55 points (4th)**					
56	**Monte Carlo**	**Peugeot Talbot Sport**	**Peugeot 205 T16**	**2**	**Terry Harryman**	**1st**
57	**Sweden**	**Peugeot Talbot Sport**	**Peugeot 205 T16**	**2**	**Terry Harryman**	**1st**
58	Portugal	Peugeot Talbot Sport	Peugeot 205 T16	2	Terry Harryman	Retired
59	Safari	Peugeot Talbot Sport	Peugeot 205 T16	7	Terry Harryman	Retired
60	Corsica	Peugeot Talbot Sport	Peugeot 205 T16	2	Terry Harryman	Retired
61	Greece	Peugeot Talbot Sport	Peugeot 205 T16 E2	2	Terry Harryman	Retired
62	New Zealand	Peugeot Talbot Sport	Peugeot 205 T16 E2	2	Terry Harryman	2nd
63	Argentina	Peugeot Talbot Sport	Peugeot 205 T16 E2	4	Terry Harryman	Retired
1987	**16 points (19th)**					
64	Safari	Fuji Heavy Industries	Subaru Leone RX	1	'Tilber'	10th
65	Finland	Ford Motor Company	Ford Sierra RS Cosworth	6	Terry Harryman	2nd
1988	**0 points**					
66	Finland	Prodrive BMW	BMW M3	5	Bruno Berglund	Retired
67	Great Britain	Ralliart Europe	Mitsubishi Galant VR-4	5	Bruno Berglund	Retired
1989	**8 points (34th)**					
68	Monte Carlo	Mitsubishi Ralliart Europe	Mitsubishi Galant VR-4	16	Bruno Berglund	Retired
69	Greece	Mitsubishi Ralliart Europe	Mitsubishi Galant VR-4	7	Bruno Berglund	Retired
70	Finland	Mitsubishi Ralliart Europe	Mitsubishi Galant VR-4	6	Bruno Berglund	Retired
71	Great Britain	Mitsubishi Ralliart Europe	Mitsubishi Galant VR-4	2	Bruno Berglund	5th
1990	**15 points (16th)**					
72	Monte Carlo	Mitsubishi Ralliart Europe	Mitsubishi Galant VR-4	14	Bruno Berglund	Retired
73	Portugal	Mitsubishi Ralliart Europe	Mitsubishi Galant VR-4	3	Bruno Berglund	Retired
74	Greece	Mitsubishi Ralliart Europe	Mitsubishi Galant VR-4	3	Bruno Berglund	Retired
75	Finland	Mitsubishi Ralliart Europe	Mitsubishi Galant VR-4	6	Bruno Berglund	2nd
76	Great Britain	Mitsubishi Ralliart Europe	Mitsubishi Galant VR-4	4	Bruno Berglund	Retired
1991	**12 points (22nd)**					
77	Finland	Milk Team	Ford Sierra Cosworth 4x4	8	Bruno Berglund	7th
78	Great Britain	Subaru Rally Team Europe	Subaru Legacy RS	11	Bruno Berglund	5th
1992	**25 points (11th)**					
79	Sweden	Subaru Rally Team Europe	Subaru Legacy RS	3	Bruno Berglund	Retired
80	Greece	Subaru Rally Team Europe	Subaru Legacy RS	5	Bruno Berglund	Retired
81	New Zealand	Subaru Rally Team Europe	Subaru Legacy RS	2	Bruno Berglund	Retired
82	Finland	Subaru Rally Team Europe	Subaru Legacy RS	6	Bruno Berglund	4th
83	Australia	Subaru Rally Team Europe	Subaru Legacy RS	4	Bruno Berglund	Retired
84	Great Britain	Subaru Rally Team Europe	Subaru Legacy RS	10	Bruno Berglund	2nd
1993	**38 points (7th)**					
85	Greece	555 Subaru World Rally Team	Subaru Legacy RS	10	Bruno Berglund	Retired
86	New Zealand	555 Subaru World Rally Team	Subaru Legacy RS	4	Bruno Berglund	Retired
87	Finland	555 Subaru World Rally Team	Subaru Impreza 555	2	Bruno Berglund	2nd
88	Australia	555 Subaru World Rally Team	Subaru Legacy RS	4	Bruno Berglund	2nd
89	Great Britain	555 Subaru World Rally Team	Subaru Impreza 555	5	Bruno Berglund	5th
1994	**28 points (9th)**					
90	Greece	Ford Motor Company	Ford Escort RS Cosworth	9	Fabrizia Pons	5th
91	Aergentina	Ford Motor Company	Ford Escort RS Cosworth	5	Fabrizia Pons	3rd
92	New Zealand	Ford Motor Company	Ford Escort RS Cosworth	7	Fabrizia Pons	Retired
93	Finland	Ford Motor Company	Ford Escort RS Cosworth	3	Fabrizia Pons	Retired
94	Great Britain	Ford Motor Comapny	Ford Escort RS Cosworth	7	Fabrizia Pons	5th
1996	**0 points**					
95	Sweden	Ford Motor Company	Ford Escort RS Cosworth	14	Fabrizia Pons	Retired
1997	**0 points**					
96	Great Britain	Motorsport Consultancy	Ford Escort WRC	11	Roger Freeman	8th
1998	**6 points (11th)**					
97	Safari	Team Valvoline Ford	Ford Escort WRC	8	Fred Gallagher	3rd
98	Portugal	Team Valvoline Ford	Ford Escort WRC	8	Fred Gallagher	5th
99	Finland	Ford Motor Company	Ford Escort WRC	11	Fred Gallagher	Retired
100	Great Britain	555 Subaru World Rally Team	Subaru Impreza WRC	12	Fabrizia Pons	Retired
2003	**0 points**					
101	Finland	Bozian Racing	Peugeot 206WRC	26	Fabrizia Pons	11th

WALDEGÅRD, BJORN

(S) B: 12 NOVEMBER 1943, RO, SWEDEN

"He was promised a car if he kept away from motor bikes"

To have an international rally career spanning 27 years is not unique, but when that career includes victories in a multiplicity of cars on four Safaris, five Swedish, two Monte Carlos, two San Remos and an RAC Rally, you know you have the very best. Bjorn Waldegård, the son of a farmer from eastern Sweden, was promised a car when he was 18 if he kept away from motor bikes. That car was a VW Beetle and he started rallying it in 1962. With help from the Swedish importer, he contested national events and made his first international foray on the 1965 Acropolis Rally. The same year, he entered the RAC Rally in a VW 1600 Fastback. He hit the headlines in the Swedish press thanks mainly to the length of rope that was required to retrieve the car, but before the accident he had been setting some fast times...

He did one more year in VWs and then, in his first fully paid drive, was given a Porsche 911 and was Swedish Champion in T-race, a shorter form of rally. In 1968, he won the Swedish Rally and led the RAC until transmission failure. By now, the Porsche factory was interested and in their car he won the Monte Carlo. The rest of 1969 was an action replay with victory in Sweden and leading the RAC, this time almost to the finish. He won Monte again in a 911S in 1970 and would probably have made his hat-trick in 1971 had he not been persuaded to drive a 914/6 in which he finished equal third.

Porsche now stopped and he had a contract with BMW for whom he nearly won the RAC in 1973 but then they too stopped rallying. He picked up a couple of drives with Toyota and Opel in this contractual interregnum and, at the end of the year, after a good placing on the RAC, Lancia offered him a drive in their Stratos. First time out, he won in Sweden but the year ended with exclusion on the RAC when the supercar's bodywork could not keep up with the rest of the car. The 1976 San Remo saw him in a titanic struggle with team mate, Sandro Munari. Lancia tried to fix Munari's win by holding back Waldegård at a stage start but he was just too quick, won the rally and promptly lost his drive.

Ford immediately signed him for the 1976 RAC Rally and the relationship carried on for another three years and saw both the company and its driver winning World Rally titles.

Part of Waldegård's title chase in 1979 (to become the first ever Drivers' World Champion) was at the wheel of a Mercedes and he subsequently drove for them, and Fiat, in 1980.

When the Mercedes programme collapsed at the end of 1980, Waldegård signed with Toyota, a contract which lasted 11 years. Although he never won the World Championship again, this was his most successful period in Africa with both Safari and Ivory Coast podiums appearing regularly in his CV.

He won with the new Celica GT-Four but within a year chose retirement though he still actively competes on classic events.

WALDEGÅRD, BJORN – CAREER RECORD

YEAR	RALLY	TEAM/ENTRANT	CAR	NO.	CO-DRIVER	RESULT
1973						
1	Monte Carlo	Fiat SpA	Fiat 124 Abarth	2	Hans Thorszelius	Retired
2	Sweden	Scania Vabis or Yabis?	Volkswagen Beetle 1303S	4	Hans Thorszelius	6th
3	Portugal	Fiat SpA	Fiat 124 Abarth	4	Hans Thorszelius	Retired
4	Safari	Porsche System Engineering	Porsche 911	10	Hans Thorszelius	Retired
5	Morocco	Fiat SpA	Fiat 124 Abarth	6	Fergus Sager	6th
6	Greece	BMW Motorsport	BMW 2002	6	Hans Thorszelius	Retired
7	Austria	BMW Motorsport	BMW 2002 Tii	16	Hans Thorszelius	4th
8	Sanremo	BMW Motorsport	BMW 2002	10	Fergus Sager? Hans Thorszelius?	51st
9	Great Britain	BMW Motorsport	BMW 2002	4	Hans Thorszelius	7th
1974						
10	Portugal	Toyota Team Europe	Toyota Celica	7	Hans Thorszelius	Retired
11	Safari	Chipstead of Kensington	Porsche 911	19	Hans Thorszelius	2nd
12	Finland	???????????????	Opel Ascona	9	Arne Hertz	10th
13	Great Britain	Toyota Team Europe	Toyota Corolla	9	Hans Thorszelius	4th
1975						
14	**Sweden**	**Lancia Alitalia**	**Lancia Stratos**	**4**	**Hans Thorszelius**	**1st**
15	Safari	Lancia Alitalia	Lancia Stratos	8	Hans Thorszelius	3rd
16	Greece	Lancia Alitalia	Lancia Stratos	1	Hans Thorszelius	Retired
17	Morocco	Fiat SpA	Fiat 124 Abarth	2	Claes-Goran Andersson	Retired
18	Portugal	Toyota Team Europe	Toyota Corolla	5	Hans Thorszelius	Retired
19	**Sanremo**	**Lancia Alitalia**	**Lancia Stratos**	**11**	**Hans Thorszelius**	**1st**
20	Great Britain	Lancia Alitalia	Lancia Stratos	2	Hans Thorszelius	Retired
1976						
21	Monte Carlo	Lancia Alitalia	Lancia Stratos	6	Hans Thorszelius	2nd
22	Sweden	Lancia Alitalia	Lancia Stratos	1	Hans Thorszelius	Retired
23	Safari	Lancia Alitalia	Lancia Stratos	1	Hans Thorszelius	Retired
24	Greece	Lancia Alitalia	Lancia Stratos	3	Hans Thorszelius	Retired
25	**Sanremo**	**Lancia Alitalia**	**Lancia Stratos**	**4**	**Hans Thorszelius**	**1st**
26	Great Britain	Nigel Rockey	Ford Escort RS1800	32	Hans Thorszelius	3rd
1977						
27	Portugal	Ford Motor Company	Ford Escort RS1800	2	Hans Thorszelius	2nd
28	**Safari**	**Ford Motor Company**	**Ford Escort RS1800**	**1**	**Hans Thorszelius**	**1st**
29	**Greece**	**Ford Motor Company**	**Ford Escort RS1800**	**6**	**Hans Thorszelius**	**1st**
30	Finland	Ford Motor Company	Ford Escort RS1800	8	Hans Thorszelius	3rd
31	Sanremo	Ford Motor Company	Ford Escort RS1800	1	Hans Thorszelius	5th
32	**Great Britain**	**Ford Motor Company**	**Ford Escort RS1800**	**5**	**Hans Thorszelius**	**1st**
1978						
33	**Sweden**	**Ford Motor Company**	**Ford Escort RS1800**	**2**	**Hans Thorszelius**	**1st**
34	Safari	Martini Racing/Porsche System Engineering	Porsche 911	5	Hans Thorszelius	4th
35	Portugal	Ford Motor Company	Ford Escort RS1800	2	Hans Thorszelius	Retired
36	Great Britain	Eaton Yale	Ford Escort RS1800	1	Hans Thorszelius	2nd
1979	**112 points (WORLD CHAMPION)**					
37	Monte Carlo	Ford Motor Company	Ford Escort RS1800	2	Hans Thorszelius	2nd
38	Sweden	Ford Motor Company	Ford Escort RS1800	1	Hans Thorszelius	2nd
39	Portugal	Ford Motor Company	Ford Escort RS1800	3	Hans Thorszelius	2nd
40	Safari	D.T Dobie/Daimler-Benz	Mercedes-Benz 450SLC	10	Hans Thorszelius	6th
41	**Greece**	**Ford Motor Company**	**Ford Escort RS1800**	**1**	**Hans Thorszelius**	**1st**
42	Finland	Ford Motor Company	Ford Escort RS1800	5	Claes Billstam	3rd
43	**Canada**	**Ford Motor Company**	**Ford Escort RS1800**	**2**	**Hans Thorszelius**	**1st**
44	Great Britain	Ford Motor Company	Ford Escort RS1800	4	Hans Thorszelius	9th
45	Ivory coast	SEACI	Mercedes-Benz 450SLC	4	Hans Thorszelius	2nd
1980	**63 points (3rd)**					
46	Monte Carlo	Fiat Italia	Fiat 131 Abarth	7	Hans Thorszelius	3rd
47	Sweden	Fiat Sweden	Fiat 131 Abarth	4	Hans Thorszelius	3rd
48	Portugal	C.Santos Mercedes	Mercedes-Benz 450SLC	4	Hans Thorszelius	4th
49	Safari	D.T. Dobie/Daimler-Benz	Mercedes-Benz 450SLC	3	Hans Thorszelius	10th
50	Greece	Daimler-Benz	Mercedes-Benz 450SLC	1	Hans Thorszelius	Retired
51	Argentina	Daimler-Benz	Mercedes-Benz 500SLC	8	Hans Thorszelius	Retired
52	New Zealand	Cable-Price Corporation	Mercedes-Benz 500SLC	1	Hans Thorszelius	5th
53	Great Britain	Toyota Team Europe	Toyota Celica 2000GT	3	Hans Thorszelius	Retired
54	**Ivory Coast**	**SEACI**	**Mercedes-Benz 500SLC**	**8**	**Hans Thorszelius**	**1st**
1981	**17 points (18th)**					
55	Monte Carlo	Toyota Team Europe	Ford Escort RS1800	1	Hans Thorszelius	8th
56	Portugal	Toyota Team Europe	Toyota Celica 2000GT	4	Hans Thorszelius	3rd
57	Corsica	Toyota Team Europe	Toyota Celica 2000GT	8	Hans Thorszelius	Retired
58	Greece	Toyota Team Europe	Toyota Celica 2000GT	2	Hans Thorszelius	Retired
59	Finland	Toyota Team Europe	Toyota Celica 2000GT	4	Hans Thorszelius	9th
60	Ivory Coast	Toyota Team Europe	Toyota Celica 2000GT	3	Hans Thorszelius	Retired
61	Great Britain	Toyota Team GB	Toyota Celica 2000GT	8	Hans Thorszelius	Retired
1982	**36 points (6th)**					
62	Monte Carlo	Porsche Almeras	Porsche 911SC	6	Hans Thorszelius	Retired
63	Portugal	Toyota Team Europe	Toyota Celica 2000GT	5	Hans Thorszelius	Retired
64	**New Zealand**	**Toyota Team Europe**	**Toyota Celica 2000GT**	**4**	**Hans Thorszelius**	**1st**
65	Ivory Coast	Toyota Team Europe	Toyota Celica 2000GT	3	Hans Thorszelius	3rd
66	Great Britain	Toyota Team GB	Toyota Celica 2000GT	8	Ragnar Spjuth	7th
1983	**20points (11th)**					
67	Finland	Toyota Team Europe	Toyota Celica TCT	10	Hans Thorszelius	12th
68	Sanremo	ProMotor Sport	Ferrari 308 GTB	3	Claes Billstam	Retired
69	**Ivory Coast**	**Premoto Toyota**	**Toyota Celica TCT**	**3**	**Hans Thorszelius**	**1st**
70	Great Britain	Toyota Team GB	Toyota Celica TCT	7	Hans Thorszelius	Retired
1984	**28 points (8th)**					
71	Portugal	Toyota Team Europe	Toyota Celica TCT	3	Hans Thorszelius	Retired
72	**Safari**	**Westlands Motors**	**Toyota Celica TCT**	**5**	**Hans Thorszelius**	**1st**
73	New Zealand	Toyota New Zealand	Toyota Celica TCT	2	Hans Thorszelius	5th
74	Finland	Toyota Team Europe	Toyota Celica TCT	5	Claes Billstam	Retired
75	Great Britain	Toyota Team GB	Toyota Celica TCT	5	Hans Thorszelius	Retired
1985	**34 points (8th)**					
76	Safari	Westlands Motors	Toyota Celica TCT	3	Hans Thorszelius	2nd
77	New Zealand	Toyota New Zealand	Toyota Celica TCT	4	Michel Lizin	Retired
78	Finland	Toyota Team Europe	Toyota Celica TCT	9	Hans Thorszelius	7th
79	Ivory Coast	Premoto Toyota	Toyota Celica TCT	1	Hans Thorszelius	2nd
80	Great Britain	Toyota Team Europe	Toyota Celica TCT	7	Hans Thorszelius	Retired
1986	**48 points (4th)**					
81	**Safari**	**Toyota Team Europe**	**Toyota Celica TCT**	**2**	**Fred Gallagher**	**1st**
82	**Ivory Coast**	**Toyota Team Europe**	**Toyota Celica TCT**	**3**	**Fred Gallagher**	**1st**
83	United States	Toyota Team Europe	Toyota Celica TCT	3	Fred Gallagher	5th
1987	**6 points (36th)**					
84	Safari	Toyota Team Europe	Toyota Supra 3.0i	3	Fred Gallagher	Retired
85	United States	Toyota Team Europe	Toyota Supra 3.0i	4	Fred Gallagher	6th
86	Ivory Coast	Toyota Team Europe	Toyota Supra 3.0i	3	Fred Gallagher	5th
1988	**16 points (17th)**					
87	Safari	Toyota Team Europe	Toyota Supra Turbo	8	Fred Gallagher	7th
88	Greece	Toyota Team Europe	Toyota Celica GT-Four	5	Fred Gallagher	Retired
89	Great Britain	Toyota Team GB	Toyota Celica GT-Four	11	Fred Gallagher	3rd
1989	**10 points (29th)**					
90	Monte Carlo	Toyota Team Europe	Toyota Celica GT-Four	5	Fred Gallagher	Retired
91	Portugal	Toyota Team Europe	Toyota Celica GT-Four	4	Fred Gallagher	Retired
92	Safari	Toyota Team Kenya	Toyota Supra Turbo	5	Fred Gallagher	4th
1990	**20 points (12th)**					
93	**Safari**	**Toyota Team Kenya**	**Toyota Celica GT-Four**	**3**	**Fred Gallagher**	**1st**
1991	**10 points (26th)**					
94	Safari	Toyota Team Kenya	Toyota Celica GT-Four	3	Fred Gallagher	4th
1992	**0 points**					

WARMBOLD, ACHIM (D) B: 17 JULY 1941, DUISBURG, GERMANY

Nominated by Jean-Luc Thérier as the quickest rally driver, Achim Warmbold was never quite able to fulfil his initial promise. The son of a Duisborg novelist, an interest in cars only developed late.

He was 28 when he made the jump from navigating to driving and in 1969 drove a Steinmetz Opel to second place in the German Championship. He moved to BMW and won the German Championship twice before tackling major internationals in 1972, leading many and winning the TAP Rally of Portugal.

He stayed with BMW for 1973 and did four rallies, filling in time with a couple of successful drives with Fiat. He was offered a Fiat contract for 1974 but, with the promise of a better BMW on the way, he stayed in Munich. Sadly, the new car only did one rally before BMW stopped. Warmbold became a peripatetic mercenary, picking up drives where he could. The talent was still there but not the cars.

In 1981, he created Mazda Rally Team Europe (MRTE) and started preparing and driving for the Japanese manufacturer. His best results were with the rotary engined RX7 but in Group B this was no match for the supercars.

The advent of Group A promised better things for Mazda but the 323 4WD never quite made it and the team withdrew after five years.

Nowadays Warmbold overseas the WRC programme of his son, Anthony, who is campaigning privateer Fords and showing some promise.

WARMBOLD, ACHIM - CAREER RECORD

YEAR	RALLY	TEAM/ENTRANT	CAR	NO.	CO-DRIVER	RESULT
1973						
1	Portugal	KWS	BMW 2002	8	John Davenport	Retired
2	Greece	BMW Motorsport	BMW 2002	2	Jean Todt	Retired
3	**Poland**	**Fiat SpA**	**Fiat 124 Abarth**	**4**	**Jean Todt**	**1st**
4	Finland	Fiat SpA	Fiat 124 Abarth	122	Jean Todt	8th
5	**Austria**	**BMW Motorsport**	**BMW 2002Tii**	**8**	**Jean Todt**	**1st**
6	Sanremo	BMW Motorsport	BMW 2002	3	Jean Todt	Retired
7	Great Britain	BMW Motorsport	BMW 2002	11	Jean Todt	15th
1974						
8	Portugal		Opel Ascona	1	Jean Todt	Retired
9	Finland	BMW Motorsport	BMW 2002	4	Jean Todt	13th
1975						
10	Monte Carlo	Renault Alpine	Alpine-Renault A110	11	John Davenport	Retired
11	Greece	Toyota Team Europe	Toyota Corolla	3	John Davenport	Retired
12	Portugal	KWS	BMW 2002	2	John Davenport	Retired
1978						
13	Monte Carlo	Opel Euro Handler Team	Opel Kadett GT/E	14	Hanno Menne	Retired
14	Portugal	Opel Euro Handler Team	Opel Kadett GT/E	14	Claes Billstam	5th
15	Greece	Opel Euro Handler Team	Opel Kadett GT/E	10	Hans Sylvan	5th
1979	0 points					
16	Monte Carlo	Automobiles Citroën	Citroen 2500CX Diesel	21	Philippe Alessandrini	Disqualified
17	Greece		Porsche Carrera RS	10	Horst Rausch	Retired
1980	0 points					
18	Monte Carlo	Team Fischer HiFi	Toyota Celica 2000GT	11	Piero Sodano	Retired
1981	0 points					
19	Portugal	Toyota Germany	Toyota Celica 2000GT	16	Pierre Alessandri	Retired
1982	0 points					
20	Monte Carlo	Mazda Rally Team Europe	Mazda 323	15	Claes Billstam	54th
1983	0 points					
21	Monte Carlo	Mazda Rally Team Europe	Mazda 323	15	B.Schmidt	20th
22	Greece	Mazda Rally Team Europe	Mazda RX7	17	Gunter Kischkel	15th
1984	2 points (53rd)					
23	Monte Carlo	Mazda Rally Team Europe	Mazda 323 Turbo	18	Matthias Feltz	11th
24	Greece	Mazda Rally Team Europe	Mazda RX7	17	'Biche'	9th
1985	6 points (34th)					
25	Greece	Mazda Rally Team Europe	Mazda RX7	14	'Biche'	6th
1986	0 points					
26	Monte Carlo	Mazda Rally Team Europe	Mazda Familia 4WD	16	'Biche'	Retired
2000	0 points					
27	Great Britain		Toyota Corolla WRC	43	Antony Warmbold	Retired

WITTMANN, FRANZ (A) B: 7 APRIL 1950, RAMSAU, AUSTRIA

It is always nice to be first but Franz Wittmann seems to have made quite a habit of it. He was the first man to win an international rally driving an Audi Quattro. The date was January 11th, 1981, the event was the Janner Rally in Austria and the Quattro had only been homologated for 10 days. In his later career, he was also the first Austrian to win a WRC event and simultaneously the first driver to win a WRC event at the wheel of his own car since Walter Boyce won the POR Rally in 1973.

The son of wealthy timber merchants, he started out in Volkswagens and made his first appearance in the WRC on the last-ever Austrian Alpine in 1973 with a 1300S prepared by Porsche Salzburg. Two years later and he had struck up a relationship with the big GM dealer in Vienna and was driving a Kadett GT/E. He was several times Austrian Champion, won the Mitropa Cup in 1976 and 1977, and in 1978 was second in the European Championship.

In the late 1970s, he was part of the Audi 80 programme and, behind the scenes, the testing for the Quattro. Hence his appearance in the car on the Janner Rally in January 1981 and his subsequent events in similar cars. For 1985, he was drafted into the VW Motorsport team who was building up their team for an assault on the Group A World Championship in 1986. He proved to be a good team mate for Kenneth Eriksson and they took third and first places respectively in the 1986 results.

For 1987, the first full year of the new Group A regime, you had to have a Lancia Delta and through the support of an Austrian radio company, that is exactly what Wittmann was able to get. In New Zealand, he got ahead of his ex-team mate's VW and stayed there to the finish.

WITTMANN, FRANZ - CAREER RECORD

YEAR	RALLY	TEAM/ENTRANT	CAR	NO.	CO-DRIVER	RESULT
1973						
1	Austria		Volkswagen 1303S	25	Hans Siebert	12th
1975						
2	Finland	Bosch Racing Team Vienna	BMW 2002	19	Helmut Deimel	Retired
1976						
3	Portugal		BMW 2002		Traude Schatzl	Retired
4	Great Britain	Bosch Racing Team Vienna	Opel Kadett GT/E	54	John Morgan	Retired
1977						
5	Portugal		Opel Kadett GT/E	12	Kurt Nestinger	7th
6	Greece		Opel Kadett GT/E		Kurt Nestinger	Retired
7	Finland		Opel Kadett GT/E	20	Helmut Deimel	7th
1979	0 points					
8	Finland	Audi Motorsport	Audi 80 GLE	11	Helmut Deimel	26th
1980	0 points					
9	Greece		Porsche 911SC	26	Kurt Nestinger	Retired
1981	0 points					
10	Greece	Audi Sport	Audi Quattro	17	Kurt Nestinger	Retired
11	Finland	Audi Sport	Audi Quattro	18	Kurt Nestinger	Retired
1982	12 points (15th)					
12	Portugal	Audi Sport	Audi Quattro	18	Peter Diekmann	3rd
13	Corsica	Audi Sport	Audi Quattro	11	Peter Diekmann	Retired
14	Greece	Porsche Austria	Audi Quattro	11	Peter Diekmann	Retired
15	Sanremo	Porsche Austria	Audi Quattro	7	Peter Diekmann	Retired
1983	8 points (27th)					
16	Portugal	Funkberaterring Rally Team	Audi Quattro A1	9	Peter Diekmann	7th
17	Greece	Funkberaterring Rally Team	Audi Quattro A1	11	Kurt Nestinger	7th
1984	3 points (43rd)					
18	Safari	Funkberaterring Rally Team?	Audi Quattro A2	12	Peter Diekmann	8th
19	New Zealand	Funkberaterring Rally Team?	Audi Quattro A2	9	Peter Diekmann	Retired
1985	4 points (50th)					
20	Portugal	Volkswagen Motorsport	Volkswagen Golf GTi	11	Ferdi Hinterleitner	Retired
21	Corsica	Volkswagen Motorsport	Volkswagen Golf GTi	18	Ferdi Hinterleitner	Retired
22	Greece	Volkswagen Motorsport	Volkswagen Golf GTi	17	Max Ogrisek	9th
23	Finland	Volkswagen Motorsport	Volkswagen Golf GTi	20	Ferdi Hinterleitner	12th
24	Sanremo	Volkswagen Motorsport	Volkswagen Golf GTi	14	Matthias Feltz	9th
1986	7 points (35th)					
25	Monte Carlo	Volkswagen Motorsport	Volkswagen Golf GTi 16V	20	Matthias Feltz	10th
26	Portugal	Volkswagen Motorsport	Volkswagen Golf GTi 16V	23	Matthias Feltz	Retired
27	Safari	Volkswagen Motorsport	Volkswagen Golf GTi 16V	18	Matthias Feltz	12th
28	Corsica	Volkswagen Motorsport	Volkswagen Golf GTi 16V	17	Matthias Feltz	Retired
29	Greece	Volkswagen Motorsport	Volkswagen Golf GTi 16V	25	Matthias Feltz	9th
30	Argentina	Volkswagen Motorsport	Volkswagen Golf GTi 16V	9	Matthias Feltz	7th
1987	20 points (14th)					
31	**New Zealand**	**Funkberaterring Rally Team**	**Lancia Delta HF 4WD**	**4**	**Jorg Pattermann**	**1st**
1988	12 points (20th)					
32	Argentina	Lancia Rally Team Austria	Lancia Delta Integrale	1	Jorg Pattermann	3rd
1989	0 points					
33	Australia	Lancia Rally Team Austria	Lancia Delta Integrale	9	Jorg Pattermann	Retired

03

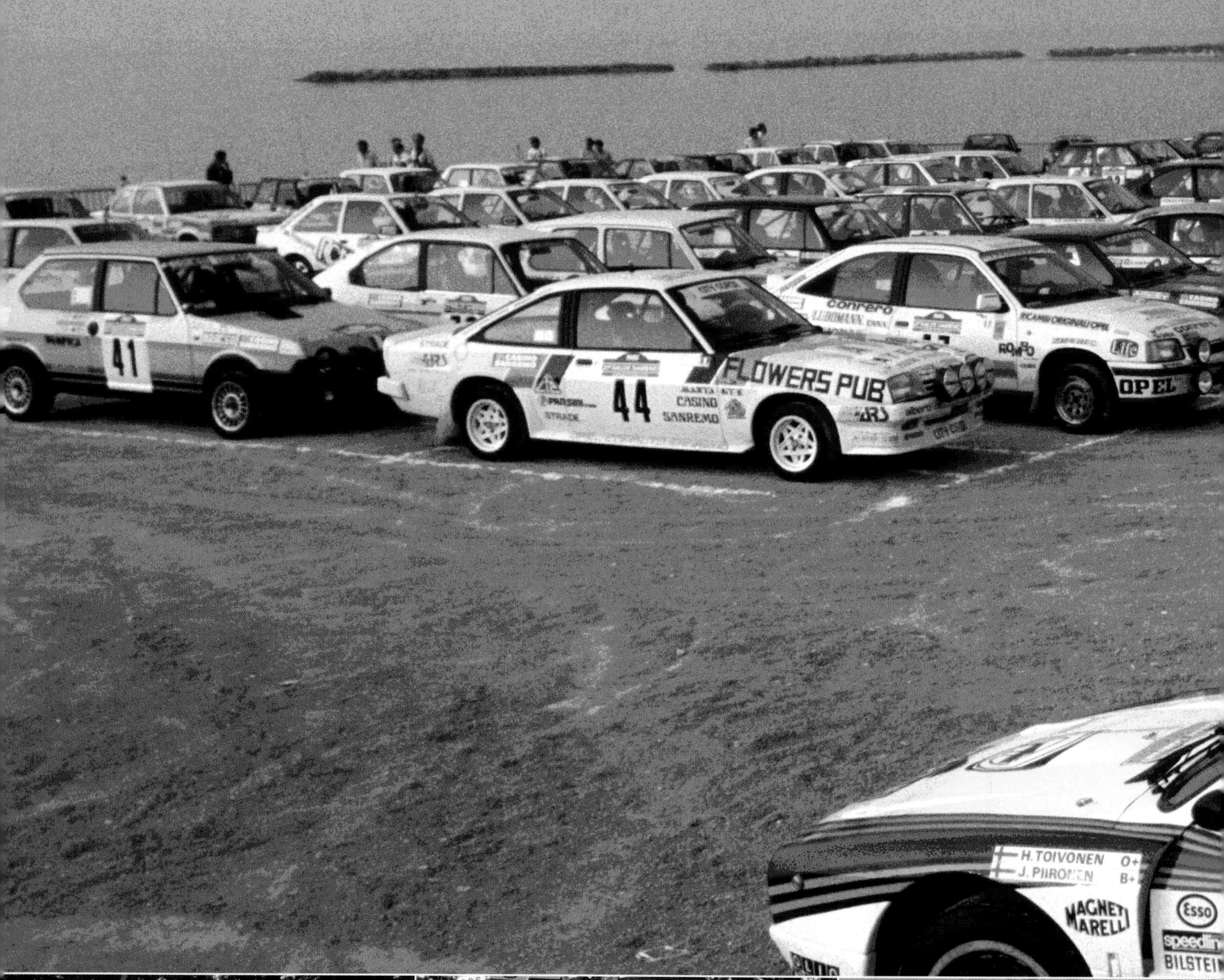
41
FLOWERS PUB
44
CASINO
SANREMO
OPEL
H.TOIVONEN O+
J. PIIRONEN B+
MAGNETI MARELLI
Esso

GITANES
8

S.O.S
MOTUL
Rothmans
BMW
10
MICHELIN

10
MICHELIN

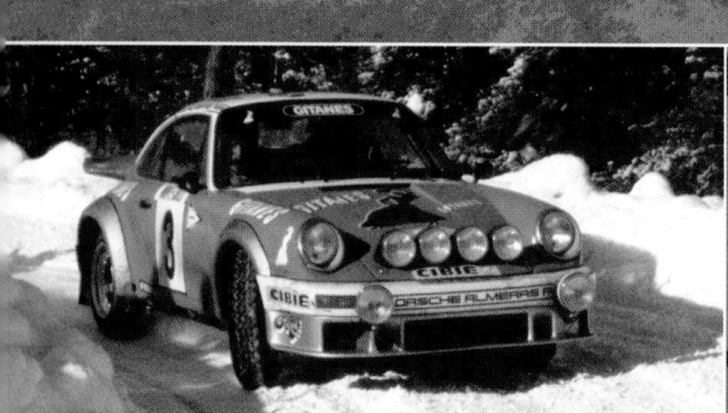

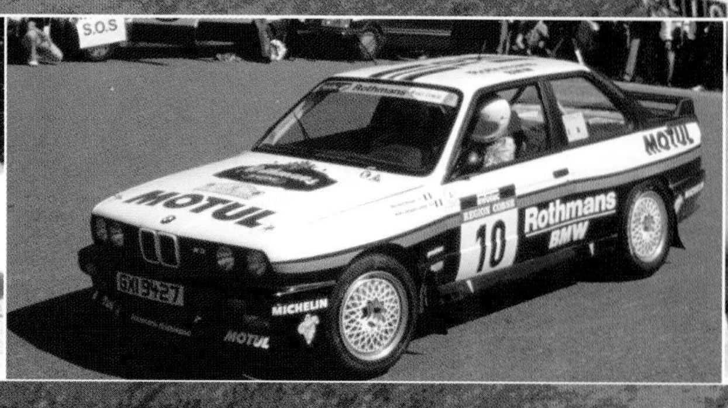

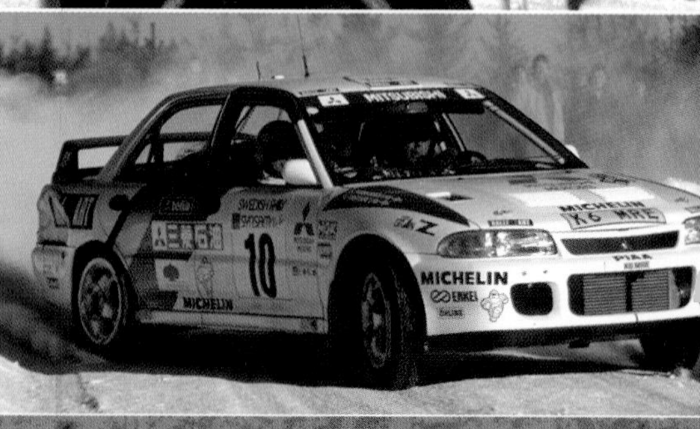

THE CARS

MAXIVIDEO
MICHELIN
aerospatiale
1985
CASINO SANREMO
SPORTLINE
MARTINI
PIRELLI
LANCIA
27°RALLYE SANREMO
CAMPIONATO DEL MONDO RALLYS
MARTINI
TOYOTA
Castrol

AUDI

Audi came into rallying with a bang in 1981 when it introduced the Quattro. The new car was fitted with technology that would become *de rigueur* throughout the sport: four-wheel drive and a turbocharged engine.

The company, in its previous incarnation as Auto Union, had been involved in rallying during the 1950s and 1960s with the 1000, an example of which actually won the Safari Rally in 1956, while DKW F11s were frighteningly quick in rallies like the Tulip. Both these cars were powered by three-cylinder, two-stroke engines. The Audi name came back in 1965 with the introduction of a front-wheel drive, four-cylinder, four-stroke model.

Audi tried out the WRC with its 80 model in the late 1970s, but its performance did not prepare anyone for the quantum leap represented by the Quattro. The German giant withdrew from rallying in 1987 and has since concentrated on touring car and sportscar racing – disciplines in which it has been equally successful. It would certainly be true to say that the high-performance image Audi enjoys today was very much created by the success of its rally programme.

QUATTRO

Rally introduced	1981 Monte Carlo
Rally wins	10
	Hannu Mikkola: 4 (1981 Sweden, GB; 1982 Finland, GB)
	Michèle Mouton: 4 (1981 Sanremo; 1982 Portugal, Greece, Brazil)
	Stig Blomqvist: 2 (1982 Sweden, Sanremo)
Engine size	5-cylinder, 2144cc, turbocharged, fuel injection
Engine position	Front, longitudinal
Transmission	5-speed, four-wheel drive
BHP/revs	360 @ 6500rpm
Length	4404mm
Width	1733mm
Height	1344mm
Wheelbase	2524mm
Weight	1150kg

QUATTRO A1

Rally introduced	1983 Monte Carlo
Rally wins	2
	Hannu Mikkola: 2 (1983 Sweden, Portugal)
Engine size	5-cylinder, 2144cc, turbocharged, fuel injection
Engine position	Front, longitudinal
Transmission	5-speed, four-wheel drive
BHP/revs	370 @ 6500rpm
Length	4404mm
Width	1733mm
Height	1344mm
Wheelbase	2524mm
Weight	1100kg

QUATTRO A2

Rally introduced	1983 Corsica
Rally wins	9
	Hannu Mikkola: 3 (1983 Argentina, Finland; 1984 Portugal)
	Stig Blomqvist: 5 (1983 GB; 1984 Sweden, Greece, New Zealand, Argentina)
	Walter Rohrl: 1 (1984 Monte Carlo)
Engine size	5-cylinder, 2109cc, turbocharged, fuel injection
Engine position	Front, longitudinal
Transmission	5-speed, four-wheel drive
BHP/revs	370 @ 6500rpm
Length	4404mm
Width	1733mm
Height	1344mm
Wheelbase	2524mm
Weight	1000kg

QUATTRO SPORT S1

Rally introduced:	1984 Corsica
Rally wins:	1
	Stig Blomqvist: 1 (1984 Ivory Coast)
Engine size	5-cylinder, 2121cc, turbocharged, fuel injection
Engine position	Front, longitudinal
Transmission	6-speed, four-wheel drive
BHP/revs	510 @ 7500rpm
Length	4160mm
Width	1790mm
Height	1344mm
Wheelbase	2204mm
Weight	1200kg

QUATTRO SPORT E2

Rally introduced:	1985 Argentina
Rally wins:	1
	Walter Rohrl: 1 (1985 Sanremo)
Engine size	5-cylinder, 2110cc, turbocharged, fuel injection
Engine position	Front, longitudinal
Transmission	6-speed, four-wheel drive
BHP/revs	550 @ 7500rpm
Length	4240mm
Width	1860mm
Height	1344mm
Wheelbase	2224mm
Weight	1090kg

200 QUATTRO

Rally introduced	1987 Monte Carlo
Rally wins	1
	Hannu Mikkola: 1 (1987 Safari)
Engine size	5-cylinder, 2144cc, turbocharged, fuel injection
Engine position	Front, longitudinal
Transmission	6-speed, four-wheel drive
BHP	240 @ 6000rpm
Length	4807mm
Width	1814mm
Height	1422mm
Wheelbase	2687mm
Weight	1250kg

BMW

As one of the great motorsporting marques, it would have been strange not to have found BMW in a list of WRC-winning manufacturers. BMWs indeed had a significant presence on many of the entry lists of major rallies during the 1960s and 1970s when they were the vehicles of choice for the privateer owner/driver.

The factory itself only had a works rally team for a relatively short time. In the late 1960s, after the introduction of the 1602 and then the 2002 models, BMW won the German championship several times and were thus inspired to set up its own rally team in 1971 using the 2002 Tii.

By 1974, it had all the requirements needed to storm the WRC – top drivers and engineers and a superb 16-valve engine – but lacked the money to do both racing and rallying.

Later attempts to rally the beautiful but ungainly M1 sportscar were unsuccessful but for a brief time during the late 80s, the 2.3-litre, four-cylinder M3 was competitive, particularly on tarmac, until it was overwhelmed by the armada of new four-wheel drive, turbocharged machinery emerging from Japan.

2002 Tii

Rally introduced	1973 Greece
Rally wins	1
	Achim Warmbold: 1 (1973 Austria)
Engine size	4-cylinder, 1998cc, carburettor
Engine position	Front, longitudinal
Transmission	4/5-speed, rear-wheel drive
BHP/revs	230 @ 7800rpm
Length	4250mm
Width	1590mm
Height	1390mm
Wheelbase	2500mm
Weight	1050kg

M3

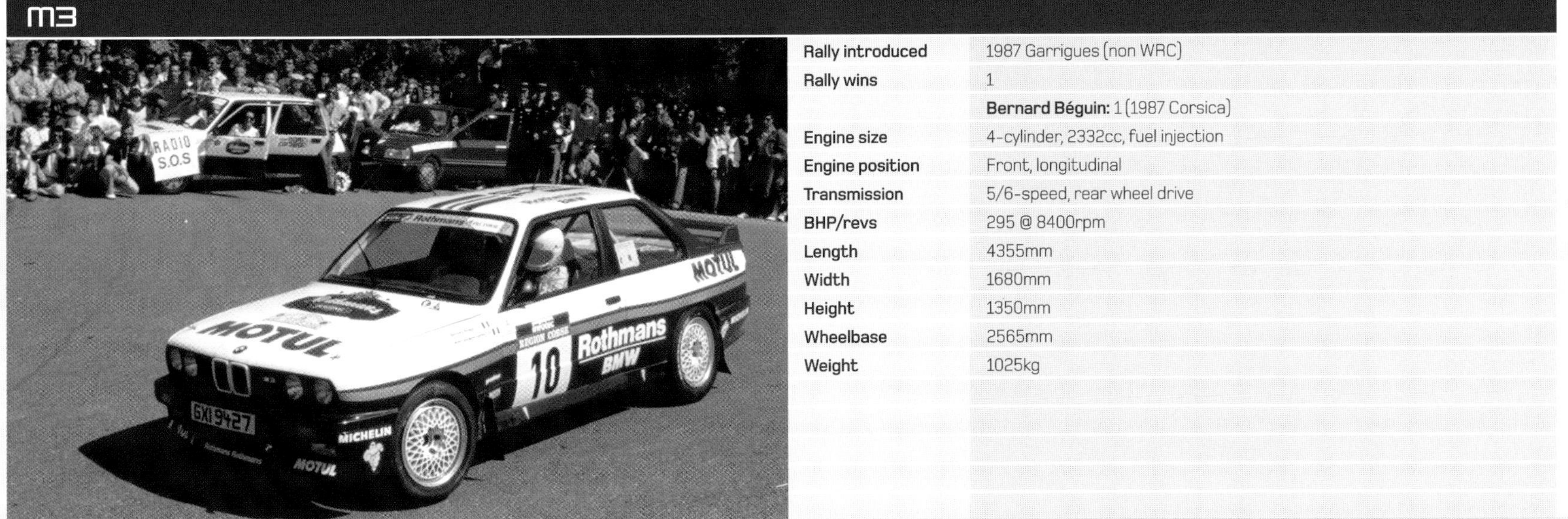

Rally introduced	1987 Garrigues (non WRC)
Rally wins	1
	Bernard Béguin: 1 (1987 Corsica)
Engine size	4-cylinder, 2332cc, fuel injection
Engine position	Front, longitudinal
Transmission	5/6-speed, rear wheel drive
BHP/revs	295 @ 8400rpm
Length	4355mm
Width	1680mm
Height	1350mm
Wheelbase	2565mm
Weight	1025kg

CITROËN

Citroën's first major involvement in rallying came about after a PR man took a gamble and lent out one of the firm's revolutionary ID19s to Paul Coltelloni for the 1959 Monte Carlo Rally. He won the event and Citroën's competition department, under the legendary René Cotton, was born. The big Citroëns were good at long distance rallies such as the Liège-Sofia-Liège and Moroccan Rally but they also won in Corsica, regularly won Coupes des Alpes and, controversially, won the Monte Carlo again in 1966 when BMC was excluded.

By the time the WRC was created in 1973, it was a bit outclassed. The factory tried first the V6 SM and then the 2400CX but they made little impression on the supercar era. Citroën did try a Group B car, the BX 4TC, in 1986 but it was a disaster and the programme only lasted a few rallies. The mini-Group B programme with the Visa Mille Pistes 4x4 did rather better.

When Citroën inherited the Rallye-Raid programme from its sister firm Peugeot in 1991, it was the start of something big. Using two-litre, Group A kit cars, Citroën developed the Xsara WRC which has since become the WRC benchmark.

XSARA KIT-CAR

Rally introduced	1998 Lyon-Charbonnieres (non WRC)
Rally wins	2
	Philippe Bugalski: 2 (1999 Catalunya, Corsica)
Engine size	4-cylinder, 1988cc, fuel injection
Engine position	Front, transverse
Transmission	6-speed, front-wheel drive
BHP/revs	290 @ 8750rpm
Length	4167mm
Width	1840mm
Height	1391mm
Wheelbase	2555mm
Weight	960kg

XSARA WRC

Rally introduced	2000 Lyon-Charbonnieres (non WRC)
Rally wins	6
	Jesus Puras: 1 (2001 Corsica)
	Sebastien Loeb: 4 (2002 Germany; 2003 Monte Carlo, Germany, Sanremo)
	Carlos Sainz: 1 (2003 Turkey)
Engine size	4-cylinder, 1988cc, turbocharged, fuel injection
Engine position	Front, longitudinal
Transmission	6-speed, four-wheel drive
BHP/revs	300 @ 5500rpm
Length	4167mm
Width	1770mm
Height	1390mm
Wheelbase	2555mm
Weight	1230kg

DATSUN

Datsun rally cars first appeared in mainstream rallying in Africa when, in 1963, the factory arrived with a brace of Bluebirds driven by Japanese crews. It could not have picked a worse year – there were only seven finishers and the Bluebird was not among them.

It would be seven years before Datsun got it right and were able to celebrate its first Safari victory with the 1600SSS. Twelve months later they won again, this time with the 240Z.

Datsun then brought the big 240Z to Europe for the Monte Carlo Rally and surprised many people by getting it home in the top three. For Africa, they developed the 1800SSS but it was with various versions of the Violet model that it dominated the Safari event in the late 1970s. It had some success with the Violet in Europe which encouraged it to build a two-wheel drive Group B car, the Nissan 240RS. This was too little too late.

A final attempt at a four-wheel drive, Group A car spawned the Sunny GTi-R in the early 1990s but it was unsuccessful. The front-wheel drive Sunny did rather better in F2 – the WRC's feeder formula of the mid 1990s.

240Z

Rally introduced	1971 Monte Carlo
Rally wins	1
	Shekhar Mehta: 1 (1973 Safari)
Engine size	6-cylinder, 2397cc, carburettor
Engine position	Front, longitudinal
Transmission	5-speed, rear-wheel drive
BHP/revs	220 @ 6500rpm
Length	4114mm
Width	1630mm
Height	1285mm
Wheelbase	2305mm
Weight	1160kg

VIOLET 160J (KP 710)

Rally introduced	1975 Great Britain
Rally wins	1
	Harry Källstrom: 1 (1976 Greece)
Engine size	4-cylinder, 1952cc, carburettor
Engine position	Front, longitudinal
Transmission	5-speed, rear-wheel drive
BHP/revs	260 @ 5000rpm
Length	3810mm
Width	1582mm
Height	1400mm
Wheelbase	2451mm
Weight	980kg

VIOLET 160J (PA 10)

Rally introduced	1978 Safari
Rally wins	3
	Shekhar Mehta: 2 (1979 Safari; 1980 Safari)
	Timo Salonen: 1 (1980 New Zealand)
Engine size	4-cylinder, 1952cc, carburettor
Engine position	Front, longitudinal
Transmission	5-speed, rear-wheel drive
BHP/revs	190 @ 7200rpm
Length	4080mm
Width	1600mm
Height	1389mm
Wheelbase	2400mm
Weight	980kg

VIOLET GT

Rally introduced	1981 Monte Carlo
Rally wins	3
	Shekhar Mehta: 2 (1981 Safari; 1982 Safari)
	Timo Salonen: 1 (1981 Ivory Coast)
Engine size	4-cylinder, 1952cc, carburettor
Engine position	Front, longitudinal
Transmission	5-speed, rear-wheel drive
BHP/revs	230 @ 7500rpm
Length	4080mm
Width	1600mm
Height	1389mm
Wheelbase	2400mm
Weight	1040kg

FIAT

Back in the early 1960s Fiat's rally cars tended to be a bit of a joke. The 125S and the 124 Sport Coupe had neither the power nor the handling to worry Lancias, Porsches and Alpines, although the Polski Fiat 125 did well in Iron Curtain rallies.

Fiat was determined to create a rally car to beat Lancia, especially after it bought its rival in 1969. The car it came up with was the 124 Sport Spyder. And it won its class on its first Monte Carlo! This was quickly followed by the Abarth 124 Rallye that, with a bigger engine, proved itself capable of winning outright, though it soon had to take a back seat to the legendary Stratos.

Fiat's next car was the 131 Abarth and company politics declared that it was the Stratos that then had to take the back seat. The 131 was a regular winner but it too suffered at the hands of the politicians with a return to the limelight for Lancia.

The Fiat name quickly disappeared from the rallying scene, until the advent of the Junior World Rally Championship in recent years. Fiat entered a Super 1600 Punto for the WRC feeder formula and enjoys reasonable success with it. A return to the WRC proper might happen but not just yet.

124 ABARTH

Rally introduced	1973 Monte Carlo
Rally wins	1
	Achim Warmbold: 1 (1973 Poland)
Engine size	4-cylinder, 1756cc, carburettor
Engine position	Front, longitudinal
Transmission	5-speed, rear-wheel drive
BHP/revs	165 @ 7200rpm
Length	3910mm
Width	1630mm
Height	1240mm
Wheelbase	2280mm
Weight	980kg

124 ABARTH 16V

Rally introduced	1974 Portugal
Rally wins	2
	Raffaele Pinto: 1 (1974 Portugal)
	Markku Alén: 1 (1975 Portugal)
Engine size	4-cylinder, 1832cc, carburettor/fuel injection
Engine position	Front, longitudinal
Transmission	5-speed, rear-wheel drive
BHP/revs	210 @ 8000rpm
Length	3910mm
Width	1730mm
Height	1240mm
Wheelbase	2280mm
Weight	980kg

131 ABARTH

Rally introduced	1976 Elba (non WRC)
Rally wins	18
	Markku Alén: 7 (1976 Finland; 1977 Portugal; 1978 Portugal, Finland; 1979 Finland; 1980 Finland; 1981 Portugal) **Fulvio Bacchelli:** 1 (1977 New Zealand) **Jean-Claude Andruet:** 1 (1977 San Remo) **Bernard Darniche:** 2 (1977 Corsica; 1978 Corsica) **Timo Salonen:** 1 (1977 Canada) **Walter Röhrl:** 6 (1978 Greece, Canada; 1980 Monte Carlo, Portugal, Argentina, San Remo)
Engine size	4-cylinder, 1995cc, fuel injection
Engine position	Front, longitudinal
Transmission	5-speed, rear-wheel drive
BHP/revs	230 @ 7500rpm
Length	4158mm
Width	1720mm
Height	1385mm
Wheelbase	2490mm
Weight	1000kg

FORD

In the 1960s the Ford name could have meant Ford America with its Falcons, Ford Germany with its Taunus 17M and 20MRS, or Ford of Britain with its Zephyrs, Cortinas and finally Escorts.

It was the twin cam Escort, first introduced in 1968, that laid the foundation for Ford's formidable reputation in rallying and the lifting of its rather mundane model image to that of sporting icon. The Escort in its various forms dominated British rallying, won the RAC Rally eight times and carried off both WRC titles in 1979.

For the turbulent Group B era of the 1980s, Ford initially came up with the never-rallied RS1700T, a front-engined, rear-gearboxed, two-wheel drive car but then scrapped it and built the 4WD RS200. Its debut came only a few months before Group B was scrapped. In Group A, Ford rallied several versions of its Sierra model before creating the Escort RS Cosworth in 1993. Its success lead to the birth of the Escort WRC, which in turn spawned the successful Focus WRC. Under the guidance of former Ford driver Malcolm Wilson's M-Sport outift, who took over the factory team responsibilities in 1997, the Focus still reigns.

ESCORT RS1600 MK I

Rally introduced	1972 Finland (non WRC)
Rally wins	4
	Timo Mäkinen: 3 (1973 Finland, GB; 1975 GB)
	Hannu Mikkola: 1 (1974 Finland)
Engine size	4-cylinder, 1993cc, carburettor
Engine position	Front, longitudinal
Transmission	5-speed, rear-wheel drive
BHP	230 @ 8000rpm
Length	3978mm
Width	1740mm
Height	1384mm
Wheelbase	2400mm
Weight	1027kg

ESCORT RS1800 MK2

Rally introduced	1975 Circuit of Ireland (non WRC)
Rally wins	17
	Timo Makinen: 1 (1975 GB) **Roger Clark:** 1 (1976 GB) **Bjorn Waldegård:** 6 (1977 Safari, Greece, GB; 1978 Sweden; 1979 Greece, Canada) **Kyösti Hämäläinen:** 1 (1977 Finland) **Hannu Mikkola:** 4 (1978 GB; 1979 Portugal, New Zealand, GB) **Ari Vatanen:** 4 (1980 Greece; 1981 Greece, Brazil, Finland)
Engine size	4-cylinder, 1993cc, carburettor
Engine position	Front, longitudinal
Transmission	5-speed, rear-wheel drive
BHP	250 @ 8000rpm
Length	3978mm
Width	1740mm
Height	1300mm
Wheelbase	2400mm
Weight	1040kg

SIERRA RS COSWORTH

Rally introduced	1987 Monte Carlo
Rally wins	1
	Didier Auriol: 1 (1988 Corsica)
Engine size	4-cylinder, 1993cc, turbocharged, fuel injection
Engine position	Front, longitudinal
Transmission	5-speed, rear-wheel drive
BHP/revs	300 @ 6500rpm
Length	4460mm
Width	1920mm
Height	1359mm
Wheelbase	2609mm
Weight	1175k

ESCORT RS COSWORTH

Rally introduced	1993 Monte Carlo
Rally wins	8
	Francois Delecour: 4 (1993 Portugal, Corsica, Catalunya; 1994 Monte Carlo) **Miki Biasion:** 1 (1993 Greece) **Gianfranco Cunico:** 1 (1993 Sanremo) **Tommi Makinen:** 1 (1994 Finland) **Carlos Sainz:** 1 (1996 Indonesia)
Engine size	4-cylinder, 1998cc, turbocharged, fuel injection
Engine position	Front, longitudinal
Transmission	7-speed, four-wheel drive
BHP/revs	300 @ 6500rpm
Length	4211mm
Width	1734mm
Height	1425mm
Wheelbase	2551mm
Weight	1220kg

ESCORT WRC

Rally introduced	1997 Monte Carlo
Rally wins	2
	Carlos Sainz: 2 (1997 Greece, Indonesia)
Engine size	4-cylinder, 1998cc, turbocharged, fuel injection
Engine position	Front, longitudinal
Transmission	6-speed sequential, four-wheel drive
BHP/revs	300 @ 5500rpm
Length	4211mm
Width	1770mm
Height	1425mm
Wheelbase	2550mm
Weight	1230kg

FOCUS WRC

Rally introduced	1999 Monte Carlo
Rally wins	11
	Colin McRae: 9 (1999 Safari, Portugal; 2000 Catalunya, Greece; 2001 Argentina, Cyprus, Greece; 2002 Greece, Safari)
	Carlos Sainz: 2 (2000 Cyprus; 2002 Argentina)
Engine size	4-cylinder, 1991cc, turbocharged, fuel injection
Engine position	Front, transverse
Transmission	6-speed sequential, four-wheel drive
BHP	300 @ 6500rpm
Length	4152mm
Width	1770mm
Height	1420mm
Wheelbase	2635mm
Weight	1260kg

FOCUS RS WRC03

Rally introduced	2003 New Zealand
Rally wins	2
	Markko Märtin: 2 (2003 Greece, Finland)
Engine size	4-cylinder, 1988cc, turbocharged, fuel injection
Engine position	Front, transverse
Transmission	6-speed sequential, four-wheel drive
BHP	300 @ 6500rpm
Length	4442mm
Width	1770mm
Height	1420mm
Wheelbase	2615mm
Weight	1230kg

LANCIA

The success of Lancia in rallying – nine manufacturers' and four drivers' titles – is centred on one man, Cesare Fiorio. He started the HF Squadra Corse in 1964 as a method of helping private owners using factory resources. This ultimately led to the creation of the factory team which ran Flavias and then Fulvias during the late 1960s.

Despite Lancia's financial difficulties, Fiorio somehow kept the flag flying, hired the top Scandinavians, encouraged a new generation of Italians and, in the early 1970s – after the company had been bought by Fiat – got the green light to build the Stratos. WRC success was instant.

Lancia had to take a back seat to Fiat for a while but Fiorio won the game of internal politics and came back with first the 037 Rally and then the S4. When Group B was banned, Lancia was the first to react and, using its knowledge of the S4, created arguably the most successful rally car of all time, the Group A Delta which, in various guises, won just about everything between 1987 and 1992.

When Fiorio left for Ferrari in 1989 things began to dwindle and, by the end of 1993, had fizzled out.

STRATOS

Rally introduced	1972 Corsica (non WRC)
Rally wins	17
	Sandro Munari: 7 (1974 Sanremo, Canada; 1975 Monte Carlo; 1976 Monte Carlo, Portugal, Corsica; 1977 Monte Carlo **Bjorn Waldegård:** 3 (1975 Sweden, Sanremo; 1976 Sanremo) **Bernard Darniche:** 4 (1975 Corsica; 1979 Monte Carlo, Corsica; 1981 Corsica) **Markku Alén:** 1 (1978 Sanremo) **Jean-Claude Andruet:** 1 (1974 Corsica) **Tony Fassina:** 1 (1979 Sanremo)
Engine size	V6, 2418cc, carburettor/fuel injection
Engine position	Mid, longitudinal
Transmission	5-speed, rear-wheel drive
BHP/revs	240 @ 7800rpm
Length	3710mm
Width	1750mm
Height	1110mm
Wheelbase	2180mm
Weight	960kg

RALLY 037

Rally introduced	1982 Corsica
Rally wins	5
	Walter Röhrl: 3 (1983 Monte Carlo, Greece, New Zealand)
	Markku Alén: 2 (1983 Corsica, Sanremo)
Engine size	4-cylinder, 1995cc, compressed, fuel injection
Engine position	Mid, longitudinal
Transmission	5-speed, rear-wheel drive
BHP/revs	305 @ 8000rpm
Length	3890mm
Width	1800mm
Height	1245mm
Wheelbase	2445mm
Weight	960kg

RALLY 037 EVO

Rally introduced	1984 Monte Carlo
Rally wins:	1
	Markku Alén: 1 (1984 Corsica)
Engine size	4-cylinder, 2111cc, compressed, fuel injection
Engine position	Mid, longitudinal
Transmission	5-speed, rear-wheel drive
BHP	325 @ 8000rpm
Length	3890mm
Width	1800mm
Height	1245mm
Wheelbase	2445mm
Weight	963kg

DELTA S4

Rally introduced	1985 Great Britain
Rally wins	4
	Henri Toivonen: 2 (1985 GB; 1986 Monte Carlo)
	Miki Biaision: 1 (1986 Argentina)
	Markku Alén: 1 (1986 USA)
Engine size	4-cylinder, 1759cc, turbocharged and compressed, fuel injection
Engine position	Mid, longitudinal
Transmission	5-speed, four-wheel drive
BHP/revs	450 @ 8000rpm
Length	3990mm
Width	1880mm
Height	1400mm
Wheelbase	2440mm
Weight	890kg

DELTA HF 4WD

Rally introduced	1987 Monte Carlo
Rally wins	11
	Miki Biasion: 3 (1987 Monte Carlo, Argentina, Sanremo) **Markku Alén:** 4 (1987 Portugal, Greece, Finland; 1988 Sweden) **Juha Kankkunen:** 2 (1987 USA, GB) **Franz Wittmann:** 1 (1987 New Zealand)
	Bruno Saby: 1 (1988 Monte Carlo)
Engine size	4-cylinder, 1995cc, turbocharged, fuel injection
Engine position	Front, transverse
Transmission	5-speed, four-wheel drive
BHP/revs	250 @ 6250rpm
Length	3895mm
Width	1620mm
Height	1360mm
Wheelbase	2475mm
Weight	1200kg

DELTA HF INTEGRALE

Rally introduced	1988 Portugal
Rally wins	14
	Miki Biasion: 9 (1988 Portugal, Safari, Greece, USA, Sanremo; 1989 Monte Carlo, Portugal, Safari, Greece) **Markku Alén:** 2 (1988 Finland, RAC) **Didier Auriol:** 1 (1989 Corsica) **Mikael Ericsson:** 1 (1989 Argentina) **Jorge Recalde:** 1 (1988 Argentina)
Engine size	4-cylinder, 1995cc, turbocharged, fuel injection
Engine position	Front, transverse
Transmission	6-speed, four-wheel drive
BHP/revs	295 @ 7000rpm
Length	3900mm
Width	1700mm
Height	1360mm
Wheelbase	2480mm
Weight	1100kg

DELTA HF INTEGRALE 16V

Rally introduced	1989 Sanremo
Rally wins	13
	Miki Biaision: 3 (1989 Sanremo; 1990 Portugal, Argentina) **Didier Auriol:** 4 (1990 Monte Carlo, Corsica, Sanremo; 1991 Sanremo) **Juha Kankkunen:** 6 (1990 Australia; 1991 Safari, Acropolis, Finland, Australia, GB)
Engine size	4-cylinder, 1995cc, turbocharged, fuel injection
Engine position	Front, transverse
Transmission	6-speed, four-wheel drive
BHP/revs	295 @ 7000rpm
Length	3900mm
Width	1700mm
Height	1360mm
Wheelbase	2480mm
Weight	1115kg

SUPER DELTA HF INTEGRALE

Rally introduced	1992 Monte Carlo
Rally wins	8
	Didier Auriol: 6 (1992 Monte Carlo, Corsica, Greece, Argentina, Finland, Australia) **Juha Kankkunen:** 1 (1992 Portugal) **Andrea Aghini:** 1 (1992 Sanremo)
Engine size	4-cylinder, 1995cc, turbocharged, fuel injection
Engine position	Front, transverse
Transmission	6-speed, four-wheel drive
BHP/revs	295 @ 7000rpm
Length	3900mm
Width	1770mm
Height	1360mm
Wheelbase	2480mm
Weight	1132kg

MAZDA

Mazda's interest in rallying was first generated in two quite different geograhical locations: the West Coast of America and in the Asia Pacific region.

The first cars to be rallied were the rotary-engined RX2 and RX3 and there was a natural progression from these 4-door saloons to the RX7 rotary-engined sports car. The RX7 emerged as a Group B car in 1984 with full factory backing. Its 300bhp, twin-rotor engine made it the most powerful normally aspirated, two-wheel drive car in rallying but the results did not match the expectation created by the car's potential.

The RX7 was soon replaced by the more marketable four-wheel drive 323. This car really should have been a great success for Mazda. In Group A specification, it had a sixteen-valve 1600cc engine at a time when even Lancia – the manufacturer that did all the winning at that time – only had an eight-valve engine. The 323 was no match for the Italian machines, despite two wins in Sweden and one in New Zealand.

A lack of support from the factory, added to homologation problems for the 323's transmission system, led to its downfall and disappearance.

323 4WD

Rally introduced	1986 Great Britain
Rally wins	3
	Ingvar Carlsson: 2 (1989 Sweden, New Zealand)
	Timo Salonen: 1 (1987 Sweden)
Engine size	4-cylinder, 1623cc, turbocharged, fuel injection
Engine position	Front, transverse
Transmission	6-speed, four-wheel drive
BHP/revs	250 @ 6000rpm
Length	3990mm
Width	1645mm
Height	1385mm
Wheelbase	2400mm
Weight	1120kg

MERCEDES-BENZ

Can Mercedes-Benz lay claim to being the first post-war factory rally team? Very possibly, and the German giant certainly had a big presence during the growth of rallying. Its 300SL of the 1950s, followed by the 220SE, the 230SL and the 300SE made sure of that.

An abortive attempt on the African Safari Rally in 1964 saw Mercedes retreat from the scene but just a decade later it was back, this time with a programme featuring the 280E and the 450SLC.

Neither model was quite the right car, especially for the European rallies but they did show some competitiveness on African events.

Undaunted, Mercedes came up with ambitious plans to build a revolutionary four-wheel drive car and went as far as signing drivers such as Ari Vatanen and Walter Röhrl – two of the sport's biggest names – but the plans were shelved at the end of 1980, leaving Vatanen to carry on winning at Ford and Rohrl to take two drivers' titles with Fiat and Opel.

Mercedes disappeared altogether from the WRC leaving a feeling of 'what might have been', although it did do rather well in touring cars and Formula 1.

450SLC 5.0

Rally introduced	1978 South America (non WRC)
Rally wins	1
	Hannu Mikkola: 1 (1979 Ivory Coast)
Engine size	V8, 5025cc, fuel injection
Engine position	Front, longitudinal
Transmission	3-speed automatic, rear-wheel drive
BHP/revs	310 @ 5400rpm
Length	4750mm
Width	1750mm
Height	1331mm
Wheelbase	2815mm
Weight	1430kg

500SLC

Rally introduced	1980 Argentina
Rally wins	1
	Bjorn Waldegård: 1 (1980 Ivory Coast)
Engine size	V8, 5025cc, fuel injection
Engine position	Front, longitudinal
Transmission	3-speed automatic, rear-wheel drive
BHP/revs	340 @ 6500rpm
Length	4750mm
Width	1750mm
Height	1331mm
Wheelbase	2815mm
Weight	1350kg

MITSUBISHI

The first steps in rallying for Mitsubishi were modest indeed. Joginder and Satwant Singh prepared a pair of second-hand Colt Lancers and finished eleventh and seventh respectively on the 1973 Safari.

The following year, Joginder won and slowly but surely, the Japanese involvement became bigger. Soon, Colts were being rallied in many parts of the world other than Japan and Kenya.

In 1981, Mitsubishi came to Europe as a fully-fledged works team with the Lancer Turbo but did not hit the headlines. It decided to retreat and compete instead in Rallye-Raids where it very rapidly learned a lot about turbocharging and four-wheel drive. It was able to come back into the WRC in 1988 with the Galant VR-4 which enjoyed modest success. Its successor, the Lancer, built upon this initial grounding and did an enormous amount of winning in the late 1990s, taking one manufacturers' title and four drivers' titles.

Mitsubishi's battles with its big Japanese rival Subaru gave the WRC much of the credibility it enjoys today, as well as creating a cult following within road car markets, too.

COLT LANCER GSR 1600

Rally introduced	1974 Safari
Rally wins	2
	Joginder Singh: 2 (1974 Safari; 1976 Safari)
Engine size	4-cylinder, 1596cc, carburettor
Transmission	5-speed, rear-wheel drive
Engine position	Front, longitudinal
BHP/revs	165 @ 7800rpm
Length	3965mm
Width	1525mm
Height	1400mm
Wheelbase	2340mm
Weight	1100kg

GALANT VR-4

Rally introduced	1989 Portugal
Rally wins	4
	Mikael Ericsson: 1 (1989 Finland) **Pentti Airikkala:** 1 (1989 GB)
	Patrick Tauziac: 1 (1990 Ivory Coast) **Kenneth Eriksson:** 1 (1991 Sweden)
Engine size	4-cylinder, 1997cc, turbocharged, fuel injection
Engine position	Front, transverse
Transmission	6-speed, four-wheel drive
BHP/revs	295 @ 7000rpm
Length	4560mm
Width	1695mm
Height	1440mm
Wheelbase	2600mm
Weight	1330kg

GALANT VR-4 EVO

Rally introduced	1991 Greece
Rally wins	2
	Kenjiro Shinozuka: 2 (1991 Ivory Coast; 1992 Ivory Coast)
Engine size	4-cylinder, 1997cc, turbocharged, fuel injection
Engine position	Front, transverse
Transmission	6-speed, four-wheel drive
BHP/revs	300 @ 7000rpm
Length	4560mm
Width	1695mm
Height	1440mm
Wheelbase	2600mm
Weight	1174kg

LANCER EVOLUTION II

Rally introduced	1994 Greece
Rally wins	1
	Kenneth Eriksson: 1 (1995 Sweden)
Engine size	4-cylinder, 1997cc, turbocharged, fuel injection
Engine position	Front, transverse
Transmission	6-speed, four-wheel drive
BHP/revs	298 @ 6000rpm
Length	4310mm
Width	1695mm
Height	1440mm
Wheelbase	2500mm
Weight	1200kg

LANCER EVOLUTION III

Rally introduced	1995 Safari
Rally wins	6
	Kenneth Eriksson: 1 (1995 Australia)
	Tommi Mäkinen: 5 (1996 Sweden, Safari, Argentina, Finland, Australia)
Engine size	4-cylinder, 1997cc, turbocharged, fuel injection
Engine position	Front, transverse
Transmission	6-speed, four-wheel drive
BHP/revs	300 @ 6000rpm
Length	4310mm
Width	1695mm
Height	1440mm
Wheelbase	2500mm
Weight	1200kg

LANCER EVOLUTION IV (AND CARISMA GT EVO IV)

Rally introduced	1997 Monte Carlo
Rally wins	6
	Tommi Mäkinen: 5 (1997 Portugal, Catalunya, Argentina, Finland; 1998 Sweden) **Richard Burns:** 1 (1998 Safari)
Engine size	4-cylinder, 1997cc, turbocharged, fuel injection
Engine position	Front, transverse
Transmission	6-speed sequential, four-wheel drive
BHP/revs	300 @ 6000rpm
Length	4310mm
Width	1695mm
Height	1395mm
Wheelbase	2500mm
Weight	1230kg

LANCER EVOLUTION V

Rally introduced	1998 Spain
Rally wins	5
	Tommi Mäkinen: 4 (1998 Argentina, Finland, Sanremo, Australia) **Richard Burns:** 1 (1998 GB)
Engine size	4-cylinder, 1997cc, turbocharged, fuel injection
Engine position	Front, transverse
Transmission	6-speed sequential, four-wheel drive
BHP/revs	300 @ 6000rpm
Length	4350mm
Width	1770mm
Height	1395mm
Wheelbase	2510mm
Weight	1230kg

LANCER EVOLUTION VI

Rally introduced	1999 Monte Carlo
Rally wins:	8
	Tommi Mäkinen: 8 (1999 Monte Carlo, Sweden, New Zealand, Sanremo; 2000 Monte Carlo; 2001 Monte Carlo, Portugal, Safari)
Engine size	4-cylinder, 1997cc, turbocharged, fuel injection
Engine position	Front, transverse
Transmission	6-speed sequential, four-wheel drive
BHP/revs	300 @ 6000rpm
Length	4350mm
Width	1770mm
Height	1395mm
Wheelbase	2510mm
Weight	1230kg

NISSAN (see Datsun)

200 SX

Rally introduced	1987 Safari	**BHP/revs**	260 @ 7000rpm
Rally wins:	1	**Length**	4460mm
	Alain Ambrosino: 1 (1988 Ivory Coast)	**Width**	1670mm
Engine size	V6, 2995cc, fuel injection	**Height**	1320mm
Engine position	Front, longitudinal	**Wheelbase**	2425mm
Transmission	5-speed, rear-wheel drive	**Weight**	1250kg

OPEL

It was initially through its Swedish arm that the German branch of General Motors known as Opel made its name in rallying. Using the Rekord and Kadett, drivers like Bosse Ericsson and Lillbror Nasenius shone in local events in Scandinavia.

It was not until the mid-1970s when it appeared with first the Ascona and then the Kadett GT/E that Opel made its presence felt more widely. The Kadett GT/E was a great car in the Group 1 class and a particluar favourite among numerous private owners, but it never enjoyed the success of the more modified Group 2 factory car.

Opel then took the big step of creating the Group 4 Ascona 400. It was a gamble that paid off and gave it a drivers' title in 1982, thanks to the talents of German ace Walter Röhrl.

The lighter Manta 400 that superceded the Ascona was no match for its Group B oppostion, though. The company was working hard on getting a four-wheel drive Astra homologated, but it came to nothing when the controversial – and dangerous – Group B formula was banned at the end of 1986.

Opel then concentrated on the two-wheel drive Kadett GSi instead which ultimately didn't set the world on fire. Most recently, Opel has developed a Corsa for use in the Junior WRC, the series to help many of tomorrow's WRC stars emerge.

OPEL ASCONA

Rally introduced	1972 (non WRC)
Rally wins	1
	Walter Röhrl: 1 (1975 Greece)
Engine size	4-cylinder, 1960cc, carburettor
Engine position	Front, longitudinal
Transmission	4-speed, rear-wheel drive
BHP/revs	206 @ 7000rpm
Length	4120mm
Width	1730mm
Height	1300mm
Wheelbase	2430mm
Weight	950kg

OPEL ASCONA 400

Rally introduced	1980 Monte Carlo
Rally wins	4
	Anders Kulläng: 1 (1980 Sweden) **Walter Röhrl:** 2 (1982 Monte Carlo, Ivory Coast) **Ari Vatanen:** 1 (1983 Safari)
Engine size	4-cylinder, 2420cc, carburettor
Engine position	Front, longitudinal
Transmission	5-speed, rear-wheel drive
BHP	270 @ 7000rpm
Length	4320mm
Width	1664mm
Height	1360mm
Wheelbase	2518mm
Weight	1050kg

KADETT GSI

Rally introduced	1987 Safari
Rally wins	1
	Sepp Haider: 1 (1988 New Zealand)
Engine size	4-cylinder, 1998cc, fuel injection
Engine position	Front, transverse
Transmission	6-speed, front-wheel drive
BHP/revs	180 @ 7200rpm
Length	3998mm
Width	1663mm
Height	1395mm
Wheelbase	2520mm
Weight	945kg

PEUGEOT

Peugeot's post-war rally reputation was first gained in Europe with the 203 in which a generation of French rally drivers learned their trade. It was in Africa that they rose to the top, though, with Bert Shankland's and Nick Nowicki's double Safari victories with the 404 and, later, Ove Andersson and Jean-Pierre Nicolas in 504s.

Morocco and Ivory Coast were also happy hunting grounds for the long-legged Peugeots. When its sister company, Talbot, took the WRC manufacturers' title in 1981, Peugeot decided that it would join the Group B race. It built one of the most successful, elegant and innovative four-wheel drive machines, the 205 T16, and deservedly took back-to-back manufacturers' and drivers' titles in 1985 and 1986. The demise of Group B saw the company in dispute with the sport's governing body, the result of which led it to leave the WRC behind and concentrate instead on Rally-Raids, something it did rather well.

Peugeot returned to rallying with the 306 kit-car in 1995. This effort expanded into a full-blown WRC programme with the 206, which enjoyed phenomenal success right up to the end of 2003.

504

Rally introduced	1972 Morocco (non WRC)
Rally wins	2
	Ove Andersson: 1 (1975 Safari) **Hannu Mikkola:** 1 (1975 Morocco)
Engine size	4-cylinder, 1995cc, fuel injection
Engine position	Front, longitudinal
Transmission	4-speed, rear-wheel drive
BHP/revs	170 @ 6500rpm
Length	4490mm
Width	1690mm
Height	1410mm
Wheelbase	2740mm
Weight	1350kg

504 V6 COUPE

Rally introduced	1976 Safari
Rally wins	3
	Jean-Pierre Nicolas: 3 (1976 Morocco; 1978 Safari, Ivory Coast)
Engine size	V6, 2664cc, carburettor
Engine position	Front, longitudinal
Transmission	4/5-speed, rear-wheel drive
BHP/revs	250 @ 7400rpm
Length	4360mm
Width	1700mm
Height	1350mm
Wheelbase	2550mm
Weight	1350kg

205 TURBO 16

Rally introduced	1984 Corsica
Rally wins	6
	Ari Vatanen: 5 (1984 Finland, Sanremo, GB; 1985 Monte Carlo, Sweden)
	Timo Salonen: 1 (1985 Portugal)
Engine size	4-cylinder, 1775cc, turbocharged, fuel injection
Engine position	Mid, transverse
Transmission	5-speed, four-wheel drive
BHP/revs	350 @ 8000rpm
Length	3825mm
Width	1674mm
Height	1410mm
Wheelbase	2540mm
Weight	940kg

205 TURBO 16 E2

Rally introduced	1985 Corsica
Rally wins	10
	Timo Salonen: 6 (1985 Greece, New Zealand, Argentina, Finland; 1986 Finland, GB) **Juha Kankkunen:** 3 (1986 Sweden, Greece, New Zealand)
	Bruno Saby: 1 (1986 Corsica)
Engine size	4-cylinder, 1775cc, turbocharged, fuel injection
Engine position	Mid, transverse
Transmission	5/6-speed, four-wheel drive
BHP/revs	500 @ 7500rpm
Length	3825mm
Width	1674mm
Height	1420mm
Wheelbase	2540mm
Weight	910kg

206 WRC

Rally introduced	1999 Corsica
Rally wins	24
	Marcus Grönholm: 15 (2000 Sweden, New Zealand, Finland, Australia; 2001 Finland, Australia, GB; 2002 Sweden, Cyprus, Finland, New Zealand, Australia; 2003 Sweden, New Zealand, Argentina)
	Gilles Panizzi: 7 (2000 Corsica, Sanremo; 2001 Sanremo; 2002 Corsica, Catalunya, Sanremo; 2003 Catalunya) **Harri Rovanpera:** 1 (2001 Sweden)
	Didier Auriol: 1 (2001 Catalunya)
Engine size	4-cylinder, 1997cc, turbocharged, fuel injection
Engine position	Front, transverse
Transmission	6-speed, four-wheel drive
BHP/revs	300 @ 5250rpm
Length	4005mm
Width	1770mm
Height	1300mm
Wheelbase	2468mm
Weight	1230kg

PORSCHE

From the 1950s right through to the middle of the 1980s, Porsche designed, built and campaigned successful rally cars.

Initially it was the 356, in all its various guises, that gave the German sportscar maker its rallying success, but from the mid 1960s, it was the legendary 911 and its numerous variants that won many of the major events. A clever piece of homologation in 1966 had enabled Porsche to put its 912 into Group 1, the 911T into Group 2 and the 911S into Group 3 so that it could dominate almost entirely. The authorities cottoned on to this cunning interpretation of the rules and put a stop to it by introducing minimum internal dimensions for Groups 1 and 2 in 1968. The 911 remained successful anyhow and, in its most powerful two-wheel drive version, the 911SC RS, won European championship tarmac rallies throughout the 1980s. The four-wheel drive 959 was principally developed for the Paris-Dakar Rally Raid but, to many people's disappointment, did not spur Porsche into committing to the WRC.

With oustanding success in circuit racing, the Porsche brand retained its sporting pedigree.

911 CARRERA RS 3.0

Rally introduced	1974 Safari
Rally wins	1
	Jean-Pierre Nicolas: 1 (1978 Monte Carlo)
Engine size	Flat 6-cylinder, 2994cc, fuel injection
Engine position	Rear, longitudinal
Transmission	5-speed, rear-wheel drive
BHP/revs	300 @ 8200rpm
Length	4291mm
Width	1652mm
Height	1320mm
Wheelbase	2271mm
Weight	1000kg

911 SC 3.0

Rally introduced	1978 Safari
Rally wins	1
	Jean-Luc Thérier: 1 (1980 Corsica)
Engine size	Flat 6-cylinder, 2994cc, fuel injection
Engine position	Rear, longitudinal
Transmission	5-speed, rear-wheel drive
BHP/revs	300 @ 8200rpm
Length	4230mm
Width	1800mm
Height	1300mm
Wheelbase	2271mm
Weight	1000kg

RENAULT-ALPINE

The Alpine company, under its founder Jean Redele, had been making fibreglass sports car bodies on Renault chassis since 1955.

During the 1960s, the A106 evolved into the A108 and finally the A110. At the same time, the engines moved up from 850cc through 1100cc, 1300cc to 1600cc and it was with this last engine configuration with which Alpine won the International Rally Championship of Makes in 1971.

A move up to an 1800cc engine for 1972 was not matched by an uprated gearbox and retirements were commonplace. At the end of 1972, Renault bought the company outright, after which the cars were then referred to and entered as Renault-Alpines. With the backing of the Regie, the 1973 season – the first in the newly-created WRC – was an enormous success, with the A110 winning the inaugural manufacturers' title with wins in Monte Carlo, Portugal, Morocco, Greece, Sanremo and Corsica.

The works team then tried both four- and six-cylinder versions of its successor, the A310, but soon turned to more production-based cars for its rally success.

A110

Rally introduced	1972 Monte Carlo (non WRC)
Rally wins	6
	Jean-Claude Andruet: 1 (1973 Monte Carlo)
	Jean-Luc Thérier: 3 (1973 Portugal, Greece, Sanremo)
	Bernard Darniche: 1 (1973 Morocco)
	Jean-Pierre Nicolas: 1 (1973 Corsica)
Engine size	4-cylinder, 1800cc, carburettor
Engine position	Rear, longitudinal
Transmission	5-speed, rear-wheel drive
BHP/revs	175 @ 7200rpm
Length	3845mm
Width	1650mm
Height	1130mm
Wheelbase	2100mm
Weight	730kg

RENAULT

Renault's roots in rallying can be traced back to the 1950s, thanks to its Dauphine 1093. With a 850cc engine, the Dauphine was a formidable rally car in its own right.

Renault campaigned a number of machines in those early forays but for the most part was happy to let Alpine carry its name in rallying. Then, in the 1970s it had some good results with the 12 and 17 Gordini models which encouraged the French firm to do more rallying, this time with versions of the 5 model. The 5 started as a simple front-wheel drive car, but then metamorphasised into a mid-engined, rear-wheel drive, turbocharged monster. The R5 Turbo and R5 Maxi Turbo had arrived. These cars were much more successful than their front-wheel drive parent car but, like many rally cars of that period, they soon became obsolete after the demise of Group B.

After that, Renault persevered with the front-wheel drive R11 Turbo in Group A until Formula 2 (a WRC junior formula) was invented.

It developed Clio Maxi and Megane Maxi kit cars which proved successful in F2. Renault currently supports the JWRC with its Clio Super 1600.

17 GORDINI

Rally introduced	1974 Safari
Rally wins	1
	Jean-Luc Thérier: 1 (1974 USA)
Engine size	4-cylinder, 1605cc, carburettor
Engine position	Front, longitudinal
Transmission	5-speed, front-wheel drive
BHP/revs	160 @ 7000rpm
Length	4260mm
Width	1630mm
Height	1310mm
Wheelbase	2440mm
Weight	980kg

5 TURBO

Rally introduced	1980 Corsica
Rally wins	2
	Jean Ragnotti: 2 (1981 Monte Carlo; 1982 Corsica)
Engine size	4-cylinder, 1397cc, turbocharged, fuel injection
Engine position	Mid, longitudinal
Transmission	5-speed, rear-wheel drive
BHP/revs	265 @ 7000rpm
Length	3664mm
Width	1752mm
Height	1323mm
Wheelbase	2430mm
Weight	900kg

5 MAXI TURBO

Rally introduced	1985 Corsica
Rally wins	2
	Jean Ragnotti: 1 (1985 Corsica) **Joachim Moutinho:** 1 (1986 Portugal)
Engine size	4-cylinder, 1527cc, turbocharged, fuel injection
Engine position	Mid, longitudinal
Transmission	5-speed, rear-wheel drive
BHP/revs	350 @ 6500rpm
Length	3664mm
Width	1752mm
Height	1323mm
Wheelbase	2430mm
Weight	905kg

5 GT TURBO

Rally introduced	1987 Corsica
Rally wins:	1
	Alain Oreille: 1 (1989 Ivory Coast)
Engine size	4-cylinder, 1397cc, turbocharged, carburettor
Engine position	Front, transverse
Transmission	5-speed, front-wheel drive
BHP/revs	100 @ 6000rpm
Length	3590mm
Width	1770mm
Height	1390mm
Wheelbase	2460mm
Weight	775kg

SAAB

It is hard to think of Saab without thinking of Erik Carlsson, that legendary figure who put the little Swedish car at the top of the rallying tree in the early 1960s.

But Saab was in fact rallying BC – before Carlsson! The two-cylinder Saab 92 carved out a competition career for itself in Sweden right from its launch in 1950 with drivers like Rolf Mellde and Greta Molander.

With the advent of the three-cylinder 93 and the aforementioned Mr Carlsson, the reputation of Saab started to spread much wider. With the 841cc 96 and then the 96 Monte Carlo, it was a force to be reckoned with. The change to a V4 engine for the 96 in 1967 gave it more power but the competition had got stiffer. That did not stop Saab constantly winning in Sweden and occasionally elsewhere.

When Saab introduced the bigger and heavier 99, things became more difficult and attempts to rally the 99 Turbo in the early 1980s showed how hard it was at the time to transmit so much power (270bhp) through the front wheels. Saab's works involvement went no further than the 99 Turbo.

96

Rally introduced	1973 Sweden
Rally wins	2
	Stig Blomqvist: 1 (1973 Sweden) **Per Eklund:** 1 (1976 Sweden)
Engine size	V4, 1815cc, carburettor
Engine position	Front, longitudinal
Transmission	4-speed, front-wheel drive
BHP/revs	170 @ 7000rpm
Length	4170mm
Width	1570mm
Height	1470mm
Wheelbase	2490mm
Weight	875kg

99 EMS

Rally introduced	1976 Boucles de Spa (non WRC)
Rally wins	1
	Stig Blomqvist: 1 (1977 Sweden)
Engine size	4-cylinder, 1999cc, carburettor
Engine position	Front, longitudinal
Transmission	4-speed, front-wheel drive
BHP/revs	225 @ 7800rpm
Length	4385mm
Width	1690mm
Height	1440mm
Wheelbase	2473mm
Weight	1080kg

99 TURBO

Rally introduced	1978 Great Britain
Rally wins	1
	Stig Blomqvist: 1 (1979 Sweden)
Engine size	4-cylinder, 1999cc, turbocharged, fuel injection
Engine position	Front, longitudinal
Transmission	4-speed, front-wheel drive
BHP/revs	270 @ 6000rpm
Length	4385mm
Width	1690mm
Height	1435mm
Wheelbase	2475mm
Weight	1080kg

SUBARU

The 'win on Sunday, sell on Monday' tag became highly apt for this former farmer's pick-up manufacturer, whose rallying exploits of the last 15 years have put the Japanese firm well and truly on the automotive map.

It all started back in 1980 when, almost unnoticed by the majority, Subaru won its class on the Safari Rally with a normally aspirated 4x4 Hatchback. Five years later, it had the RX Turbo at its disposal and got Asia-Pacific wins and top six placings on the Safari under its belt.

With the introduction of the Legacy in 1990, Subaru had a car in another league and the British-based Prodrive team soon proved it with WRC victories. Just three years later it was followed by the new Impreza. The Impreza was better still than the Legacy, with its all-alloy engine and more compact body. It won – in four- then 2-door WRC guise – three manufacturers' titles for Subaru, as well as winning all the big events on the calendar. Thanks also to Subaru, the names Colin McRae, Richard Burns and Petter Solberg have become permanently etched on the drivers' world title trophy, too.

LEGACY RS

Rally introduced	1990 Safari
Rally wins	1
	Colin McRae: 1 (1993 New Zealand)
Engine size	Flat 4-cylinder, 1994cc, turbocharged, fuel injection
Engine position	Front, longitudinal
Transmission	6-speed, four-wheel drive
BHP/revs	300 @ 6400rpm
Length	4150mm
Width	1705mm
Height	1325mm
Wheelbase	2580mm
Weight	1200kg

IMPREZA 555

Rally introduced	1993 Finland
Rally wins	11
	Colin McRae: 7 (1994 New Zealand, GB; 1995 New Zealand, GB; 1996 Greece, Sanremo, Catalunya) **Carlos Sainz:** 4 (1994 Greece; 1995 Monte Carlo, Portugal, Catalunya)
Engine size	Flat 4-cylinder, 1994cc, turbocharged, fuel injection
Engine position	Front, longitudinal
Transmission	6-speed, four-wheel drive
BHP/revs	295 @ 6500rpm
Length	4340mm
Width	1690mm
Height	1390mm
Wheelbase	2520mm
Weight	1200kg

IMPREZA WRC97

Rally introduced	1997 Monte Carlo
Rally wins	8
	Colin McRae: 5 (1997 Safari, Corsica, Sanremo, Australia, GB
	Kenneth Eriksson: 2 (1997 Sweden, New Zealand)
	Piero Liatti: 1 (1997 Monte Carlo)
Engine size	Flat 4-cylinder, 1994cc, turbocharged, fuel injection
Engine position	Front, longitudinal
Transmission	6-speed, four-wheel drive
BHP/revs	300 @ 5500rpm
Length	4340mm
Width	1770mm
Height	1390mm
Wheelbase	2520mm
Weight	1230kg

IMPREZA WRC98

Rally introduced	1998 Monte Carlo
Rally wins	3
	Colin McRae: 3 (1998 Portugal, Corsica, Greece)
Engine size	Flat 4-cylinder, 1994cc, turbocharged, fuel injection
Engine position	Front, longitudinal
Transmission	6-speed, four-wheel drive
BHP/revs	300 @ 5500rpm
Length	4340mm
Width	1770mm
Height	1390mm
Wheelbase	2520mm
Weight	1230kg

IMPREZA WRC99

Rally introduced	1999 Monte Carlo
Rally wins	6
	Richard Burns: 4 (1999 Greece, Australia, GB; 2000 Safari)
	Juha Kankkunen: 2 (1999 Argentina, Finland)
Engine size	Flat 4-cylinder, 1994cc, turbocharged, fuel injection
Engine position	Front, longitudinal
Transmission	6-speed, four-wheel drive
BHP/revs	300 @ 5500rpm
Length	4340mm
Width	1770mm
Height	1390mm
Wheelbase	2520mm
Weight	1230kg

IMPREZA WRC2000

Rally introduced	2000 Portugal
Rally wins	3
	Richard Burns: 3 (2000 Portugal, Argentina, GB)
Engine size	Flat 4-cylinder, 1994c, turbocharged, fuel injection
Engine position	Front, longitudinal
Transmission	6-speed, four-wheel drive
BHP/revs	300 @ 5500rpm
Length	4340mm
Width	1770mm
Height	1390mm
Wheelbase	2520mm
Weight	1230kg

IMPREZA WRC2001

Rally introduced	2001 Monte Carlo
Rally wins	2
	Richard Burns: 1 (2001 New Zealand)
	Tommi Mäkinen: 1 (2002 Monte Carlo)
Engine size	Flat 4-cylinder, 1994cc, turbocharged, fuel injection
Engine position	Front, longitudinal
Transmission	6-speed, four-wheel drive
BHP/revs	300 @ 5500rpm
Length	4340mm
Width	1770mm
Height	1390mm
Wheelbase	2520mm
Weight	1230kg

IMPREZA WRC2002

Rally introduced	2002 Corsica
Rally wins	1
	Petter Solberg: 1 (2002 GB)
Engine size	Flat 4-cylinder, 1994cc, turbocharged, fuel injection
Engine position	Front, longitudinal
Transmission	6-speed, four-wheel drive
BHP/revs	300 @ 5500rpm
Length	4340mm
Width	1770mm
Height	1390mm
Wheelbase	2520mm
Weight	1230kg

IMPREZA WRC2003

Rally introduced	2003 Monte Carlo
Rally wins	4
	Petter Solberg: 4 (2003 Cyprus, Australia, Corsica, GB)
Engine size	Flat 4-cylinder, 1994cc, turbocharged, fuel injection
Engine position	Front, longitudinal
Transmission	6-speed, four-wheel drive
BHP/revs	300 @ 5500rpm
Length	4340mm
Width	1770mm
Height	1390mm
Wheelbase	2520mm
Weight	1230kg

TALBOT

With cars like the Sunbeam-Talbot 90, the Sunbeam Rapier, the Hillman Imp, the Sunbeam Tiger and the Hillman Avenger, the company once known as the Rootes Group had been remarkably successful in rallying. In 1975, it became known as Chrysler UK Ltd. and its new three-door hatchback was just about to be released.

The competition department of Chrysler UK then persuaded the company bosses to produce a version of this new hatchback with a Lotus engine so that it could take on, and hopefully beat, the might of Ford's ultra-successful Escorts.

First rallied seriously in 1979, the Sunbeam-Lotus turned out to be very competitive and in 1981, with the help of Henri Toivonen and Guy Fréquelin, went on to win the WRC manufacturers' title.

However, company politics during the previous year had resulted in the company changing hands. The car was now known as the Talbot Sunbeam Lotus and once the dust had settled the new bosses were not particularly enthusiastic about rallying. After the 1982 season, the programme was canned and Peugeot was given the go-ahead to create the legendary 205 T16...

SUNBEAM LOTUS

Rally introduced	1979 West Cork (non WRC)
Rally wins	2
	Henri Toivonen: 1 (1980 GB) **Guy Fréquelin:** 1 (1981 Argentina)
Engine size	4-cylinder, 2174cc, carburettor
Engine position	Front, longitudinal
Transmission	4-speed, rear-wheel drive
BHP/revs	240 @ 7000rpm
Length	3829mm
Width	1628mm
Height	1395mm
Wheelbase	2415mm
Weight	1015kg

TOYOTA

Short of a drive for the 1972 RAC Rally, Ove Andersson accepted an offer to visit Toyota in Japan with a view to driving its Celica model on the event. He agreed to the deal, won his class and beat the highly-acclaimed Datsun opposition.

Within a short time Andersson found himself with a contract to run cars for Toyota. It was so succesful that Toyota Team Europe was formed and quickly grew into one of the biggest factory teams of the 1980s. Its Group B car was a turbocharged, rear-wheel drive Celica which proved to be good at winning in Africa but not elsewhere. A proper four-wheel drive Group B car was planned but was aborted in mid-1986 just as Group B got the chop.

The design work that had been done was put to good use in designing the Celica Turbo GT4 and its derivatives that put Toyota on the WRC map with manufacturers' titles in 1993 and 1994. The Corolla WRC gave Toyota a third title in 1999 but the Japanese giant had already decided to forsake rallying for the race track. With a big-budget, high-tech move into Formula 1 just around the corner, not even Toyota could afford to do both.

COROLLA

Rally introduced	1973
Rally wins	2
	Walter Boyce: 1 (1973 USA) **Hannu Mikkola:** 1 (1975 Finland)
Engine size	4-cylinder, 1588cc, carburettor
Engine position	Front, longitudinal
Transmission	5-speed, rear-wheel drive
BHP/revs	150 @ 6800rpm
Length	3945mm
Width	1590mm
Height	1335mm
Wheelbase	2335mm
Weight	850kg

CELICA 2000 GT

Rally introduced	1982 New Zealand
Rally wins	1
	Bjorn Waldegård: 1 (1982 New Zealand)
Engine size	4-cylinder, 1998cc, fuel injection
Engine position	Front, longitudinal
Transmission	5-speed, rear-wheel drive
BHP/revs	245 @ 9000rpm
Length	4435mm
Width	1665mm
Height	1310mm
Wheelbase	2500mm
Weight	1000kg

CELICA TWIN CAM TURBO

Rally introduced	1983 Finland
Rally wins	6
	Bjorn Waldegård: 4 (1983 Ivory Coast; 1984 Safari; 1986 Safari, Ivory Coast) **Juha Kankkunen:** 2 (1985 Safari, Ivory Coast)
Engine size	4-cylinder, 2090cc, turbocharged, fuel injection
Engine position	Front, longitudinal
Transmission	5-speed, rear-wheel drive
BHP	370 @ 8500rpm
Length	4284mm
Width	1785mm
Height	1310mm
Wheelbase	2500mm
Weight	1040kg

CELICA GT-FOUR ST165

Rally introduced	1988 Corsica
Rally wins	13
	Juha Kankkunen: 1 (1989 Australia) **Bjorn Waldegård:** 1 (1990 Safari) **Carlos Sainz:** 9 (1990 Greece, New Zealand, Finland, GB; 1991 Monte Carlo, Portugal, Corsica, New Zealand, Argentina) **Armin Schwarz:** 1 (1991 Catalunya) **Mats Jonsson:** 1 (1992 Sweden)
Engine size	4-cylinder, 1988cc, turbocharged, fuel injection
Engine position	Front, longitudinal
Transmission	6-speed, four-wheel drive
BHP	300 @ 6800rpm
Length	4365mm
Width	1710mm
Height	1300mm
Wheelbase	2525mm
Weight	1100kg

CELICA TURBO 4WD

Rally introduced	1992 Monte Carlo
Rally wins	16
	Carlos Sainz: 4 (1992 Safari, New Zealand, Catalunya, RAC) **Didier Auriol:** 4 (1993 Monte Carlo; 1994 Corsica, Argentina, Sanremo) **Mats Jonsson:** 1 (1993 Sweden) **Juha Kankkunen:** 6 (1993 Safari, Argentina, Finland, Australia, GB; 1994 Portugal) **Ian Duncan:** 1 (1994 Safari)
Engine size	4-cylinder, 1988cc, turbocharged, fuel injection
Engine position	Front, longitudinal
Transmission	6-speed, four-wheel drive
BHP/revs	300 @ 5600rpm
Length	4410mm
Width	1745mm
Height	1300mm
Wheelbase	2545mm
Weight	1120kg

CELICA GT-FOUR ST205

Rally introduced	1994 Sanremo
Rally wins	1
	Didier Auriol: 1 (1995 Corsica)
Engine size	4-cylinder, 1988cc, turbocharged, fuel injection
Engine position	Front, longitudinal
Transmission	6-speed, four-wheel drive
BHP/revs	300 @ 5600rpm
Length	4424mm
Width	1770mm
Height	1300mm
Wheelbase	2545mm
Weight	1200kg

COROLLA WRC

Rally introduced	1997 Finland
Rally wins	4
	Carlos Sainz: 2 (1998 Monte Carlo, New Zealand)
	Didier Auriol: 2 (1998 Catalunya; 1999 China)
Engine size	4-cylinder, 1998cc, turbocharged, fuel injection
Engine position	Front, longitudinal
Transmission	6-speed sequential, four-wheel drive
BHP/revs	300 @ 5700rpm
Length	4100mm
Width	1710mm
Height	1385mm
Wheelbase	2465mm
Weight	1230kg

VOLKSWAGEN

The Volkswagen Beetle enjoyed great success on rallies like the Safari during the 1950s but the early models never had enough power to be a threat anywhere else.

In the early 1970s, Porsche Salzburg persuaded the factory to homologate a 'proper' version of the 1302S and drivers such as Tony Fall and Achim Warmbold drove them successfully in European rallies. The first proper involvement by the factory was in Germany with the Golf GTi starting in 1977.

The Golf was without doubt the most successful, two-litre, front-wheel drive rally car of the era. When it got a 16-valve cylinder head for 1986, it didn't worry the Group B machinery, but it was successful in Group A, even winning the Ivory Coast Rally outright at the end of 1987 in the hands of Kenneth Eriksson. Eriksson himself was 'World Champion' in the Group A class the previous season, the only time such a title was awarded.

The supercharged Golf G60 was an aberration and VW's involvement in rallying ceased temporarily. It returned with the Golf kit car in the mid-1990s and latterly has developed a Super 1600 Polo for the Junior class of the WRC.

GOLF GTI 16V

Rally introduced	1986 Monte Carlo
Rally wins	1
	Kenneth Eriksson: 1 (1987 Ivory Coast)
Engine size	4-cylinder, 1800cc, fuel injection
Engine position	Front, transverse
Transmission	5-speed, front wheel drive
BHP/revs	200 @ 7000rpm
Length	3987mm
Width	1680mm
Height	1405mm
Wheelbase	2475mm
Weight	880kg

04
幸福
一生

THE RALLIES

ARGENTINA

1980 Rally Codasur
Walter Röhrl (D)/Christian Geistdörfer (D)
Fiat 131 Abarth

1981 Rally Codasur
Guy Fréquelin (F)/Jean Todt (F)
Talbot Sunbeam Lotus

1982
NO WRC EVENT

1983 Marlboro Rally Argentina
Hannu Mikkola (FIN)/Arne Hertz (S) Audi Quattro A2

1984 Marlboro Rally Argentina
Stig Blomqvist (S)/Björn Cederberg (S)
Audi Quattro A2

1985 Marlboro Rally Argentina
Timo Salonen (FIN)/Seppo Harjanne (FIN)
Peugeot 205 Turbo 16 E2

1986 Marlboro Rally Argentina
Miki Biasion (ITA)/Tiziano Siviero (ITA)
Lancia Delta S4

1987 Marlboro Rally Argentina
Miki Biasion (ITA)/Tiziano Siviero (ITA)
Lancia Delta HF 4WD

1988 Marlboro Rally Argentina
Jorge Recalde (RA)/Jorge del Buono (RA)
Lancia Delta Integrale

1989 Rally Argentina
Mikael Ericsson (S)/Claes Billstam (S)
Lancia Delta Integrale

1990 Rally Argentina
Miki Biasion (ITA)/Tiziano Siviero (ITA)
Lancia Delta Integrale 16V

1991 Rally Argentina
Carlos Sainz (E)/Luís Moya (E)
Toyota Celica GT-Four

1992 Rally Argentina
Didier Auriol (F)/Bernard Occelli (F)
Lancia Delta HF Integrale

1993 Rally Argentina
Juha Kankkunen (FIN)/Nicky Grist (GB)
Toyota Celica Turbo 4WD

1994 Rally Argentina
Didier Auriol (F)/Bernard Occelli (F)
Toyota Celica Turbo 4WD

1995
NO WRC EVENT

1996 Rally Argentina
Tommi Mäkinen (FIN)/Seppo Harjanne (FIN)
Mitsubishi Lancer Evo 3

1997 Rally Argentina
Tommi Mäkinen (FIN)/Seppo Harjanne (FIN)
Mitsubishi Lancer Evo 4

1998 Rally Argentina
Tommi Mäkinen (FIN)/Risto Mannisenmäki (FIN)
Mitsubishi Lancer Evo 5

1999 Rally Argentina
Juha Kankkunen (FIN)/Juha Repo (FIN)
Subaru Impreza WRC

2000 Rally Argentina
Richard Burns (GB)/Robert Reid (GB)
Subaru Impreza WRC

2001 Rally Argentina
Colin McRae (GB)/Nicky Grist (GB)
Ford Focus WRC

2002 Rally Argentina
Carlos Sainz (E)/Luís Moya (E)
Ford Focus WRC

2003 Rally Argentina
Marcus Grönholm (FIN)/Timo Rautiainen (FIN)
Peugeot 206 WRC

AUSTRALIA

1989 Commonwealth Bank Rally Australia
Juha Kankkunen (FIN)/Juha Piironen (FIN)
Toyota Celica GT-Four

1990 Commonwealth Bank Rally Australia
Juha Kankkunen (FIN)/Juha Piironen (FIN)
Lancia Delta Integrale 16V

1991 Commonwealth Bank Rally Australia
Juha Kankkunen (FIN)/Juha Piironen (FIN)
Lancia Delta Integrale 16V

1992 Telecom Rally Australia
Didier Auriol (F)/Bernard Occelli (F)
Lancia Delta HF Integrale

1993 Telecom Rally Australia
Juha Kankkunen (FIN)/Nicky Grist (GB)
Toyota Celica Turbo 4WD

1994
NO WRC EVENT

1995 Telstra Rally Australia
Kenneth Eriksson (S)/Staffan Parmander (S)
Mitsubishi Lancer Evo 3

1996 API Rally Australia
Tommi Mäkinen (FIN)/Seppo Harjanne (FIN)
Mitsubishi Lancer Evo 3

1997 API Rally Australia
Colin McRae (GB)/Nicky Grist (GB)
Subaru Impreza WRC

1998 API Rally Australia
Tommi Mäkinen (FIN)/Risto Mannisenmäki
(FIN)Mitsubishi Lancer Evo 5

1999 Telstra Rally Australia
Richard Burns (GB)/Robert Reid (GB)
Subaru Impreza WRC

2000 Telstra Rally Australia
Marcus Grönholm (FIN)/Timo Rautiainen (FIN)
Peugeot 206 WRC

2001 Telstra Rally Australia
Marcus Grönholm (FIN)/Timo Rautiainen (FIN)
Peugeot 206 WRC

2002 Telstra Rally Australia
Marcus Grönholm (FIN)/Timo Rautiainen (FIN)
Peugeot 206 WRC

2003 Telstra Rally Australia
Petter Solberg (N)/Phil Mills (GB)
Subaru Impreza WRC

AUSTRIA

1973 Osterreichische Alpenfährt
Achim Warmbold (D)/Jean Todt (F)
BMW 2002Tii

BRAZIL

1981 Marlboro Rallye do Brasil
Ari Vatanen (FIN)/David Richards (GB)
Ford Escort RS1800

1982 Marlboro Rallye do Brasil
Michèle Mouton (F)/Fabrizia Pons (ITA)
Audi Quattro

CANADA

1974 Rally Rideau Lakes
Sandro Munari (ITA)/Mauro Mannucci (ITA)
Lancia Stratos

1977 Critérium Molson du Quebec
Timo Salonen (FIN)/Jaakko Markkula (FIN)
Fiat 131 Abarth

1978 Critérium Molson du Quebec
Walter Röhrl (D)/Christian Geistdörfer (D)
Fiat 131 Abarth

1979 Critérium Molson du Quebec
Bjorn Waldegård (S)/Hans Thorszelius (S)
Ford Escort RS

CHINA

1999 China Rally
Didier Auriol (F)/Denis Giraudet (F)
Toyota Corolla WRC

CORSICA

1973 Tour de Corse
Jean-Pierre Nicolas (F)/Michel Vial (F)
Alpine-Renault A110

1974 Tour de Corse
Jean-Claude Andruet (F)/'Biche' (F)
Lancia Stratos

1975 Tour de Corse
Bernard Darniche (F)/Alain Mahé (F)
Lancia Stratos

1976 Tour de Corse
Sandro Munari (ITA)/Silvio Maiga (ITA)
Lancia Stratos

1977 Tour de Corse
Bernard Darniche (F)/Alain Mahé (F)
Fiat 131 Abarth

1978 Tour de Corse
Bernard Darniche (F)/Alain Mahé (F)
Fiat 131 Abarth

1979 Tour de Corse – Rallye de France
Bernard Darniche (F)/Alain Mahé (F)
Lancia Stratos

1980 Tour de Corse – Rallye de France
Jean-Luc Thérier (F)/Michel Vial (F)
Porsche 911 SC

1981 Tour de Corse – Rallye de France
Bernard Darniche (F)/Alain Mahé (F)
Lancia Stratos

1982 Tour de Corse – Rallye de France
Jean Ragnotti (F)/Jean-Marc Andrié (F)
Renault 5 Turbo

1983 Tour de Corse – Rallye de France
Markku Alén (FIN)/Ilkka Kivimäkl (FIN)
Lancia Rally 037

1984 Tour de Corse – Rallye de France
Markku Alén (FIN)/Ilkka Kivimäki (FIN)
Lancia Rally 037

1985 Tour de Corse – Rallye de France
Jean Ragnotti (F)/Pierre Thimonier (F)
Renault 5 Maxi Turbo

1986 Tour de Corse – Rallye de France
Bruno Saby (F)/Jean-François Fauchille (F)
Peugeot 205 Turbo 16 E2

1987 Tour de Corse – Rallye de France
Bernard Béguin (F)/Jean-Jacques Lenne (F)
BMW M3

1988 Tour de Corse – Rallye de France
Didier Auriol (F)/Bernard Occelli (F)
Ford Sierra RS Cosworth

1989 Tour de Corse – Rallye de France
Didier Auriol (F)/Bernard Occelli (F)
Lancia Delta Integrale

1990 Tour de Corse – Rallye de France
Didier Auriol (F)/Bernard Occelli (F)
Lancia Delta Integrale 16V

1991 Tour de Corse – Rallye de France
Carlos Sainz (E)/Luís Moya (E)
Toyota Celica GT-Four

1992 Tour de Corse – Rallye de France
Didier Auriol (F)/Bernard Occelli (F)
Lancia Delta HF Integrale

1993 Tour de Corse – Rallye de France
François Delecour (F)/Daniel Grataloup (F)
Ford Escort RS Cosworth

1994 Tour de Corse – Rallye de France
Didier Auriol (F)/Bernard Occelli (F)
Toyota Celica Turbo 4WD

1995 Tour de Corse – Rallye de France
Didier Auriol (F)/Denis Giraudet (F)
Toyota Celica GT-Four

1996 Tour de Corse – Rallye de France
NO WRC EVENT

1997 Tour de Corse – Rallye de France
Colin McRae GB)/Nicky Grist (GB)
Subaru Impreza WRC

1998 Tour de Corse – Rallye de France
Colin McRae (GB)/Nicky Grist (GB)
Subaru Impreza WRC

1999 Tour de Corse – Rallye de France
Philippe Bugalski (F)/Jean-Paul Chiaroni (F)
Citroën Xsara Kit Car

2000 Tour de Corse – Rallye de France
Gilles Panizzi (F)/Hervé Panizzi (F)
Peugeot 206 WRC

2001 Tour de Corse – Rallye de France
Jesús Puras (E)/Marc Martí (E)
Citroën Xsara WRC

2002 Rallye de France Tour de Corse
Gilles Panizzi (F)/Hervé Panizzi (F)
Peugeot 206 WRC

2003 Tour de Corse – Rallye de France
Petter Solberg (N)/Phil Mills (GB)
Subaru Impreza WRC

CYPRUS

www.fordracing.net
MARTINI
Valvoline
Telefonica MoviStar

2000 Cyprus Rally
Carlos Sainz (E)/Luís Moya (E)
Ford Focus WRC

2001 Cyprus Rally
Colin McRae (GB)/Nicky Grist (GB)
Ford Focus WRC

2002 Cyprus Rally
Marcus Grönholm (FIN)/Timo Rautiainen (FIN)
Peugeot 206 WRC

2003 Cyprus Rally
Petter Solberg (N)/Phil Mills (GB)
Subaru Impreza WRC

FINLAND

1973 1000 Lakes Rally
Timo Mäkinen (FIN)/Henry Liddon (GB)
Ford Escort RS1600

1974 1000 Lakes Rally
Hannu Mikkola (FIN)/John Davenport (GB)
Ford Escort RS1600

1975 1000 Lakes Rally
Hannu Mikkola (FIN)/Atso Aho (FIN)
Toyota Corolla

1976 1000 Lakes Rally
Markku Alén (FIN)/Ilkka Kivimäki (FIN)
Fiat 131 Abarth

1977 1000 Lakes Rally
Kyosti Hämäläinen (FIN)/Martti Tiukkanen (FIN)
Ford Escort RS1800

1978 1000 Lakes Rally
Markku Alén (FIN)/Ilkka Kivimäki (FIN)
Fiat 131 Abarth

1979 1000 Lakes Rally
Markku Alén (FIN)/Ilkka Kivimäki (FIN)
Fiat 131 Abarth

1980 1000 Lakes Rally
Markku Alén (FIN)/Ilkka Kivimäki (FIN)
Fiat 131 Abarth

1981 1000 Lakes Rally
Ari Vatanen (FIN)/David Richards (GB)
Ford Escort RS1800

1982 1000 Lakes Rally
Hannu Mikkola (FIN)/Arne Hertz (S)
Audi Quattro

1983 1000 Lakes Rally
Hannu Mikkola (FIN)/Arne Hertz (S)
Audi Quattro A2

1984 1000 Lakes Rally
Ari Vatanen (FIN)/Terry Harryman (GB)
Peugeot 205 Turbo 16

1985 1000 Lakes Rally
Timo Salonen (FIN)/Seppo Harjanne (FIN)
Peugeot 205 Turbo 16 E2

1986 1000 Lakes Rally
Timo Salonen (FIN)/Seppo Harjanne (FIN)
Peugeot 205 Turbo 16 E2

1987 1000 Lakes Rally
Markku Alén (FIN)/Ilkka Kivimäki (FIN)
Lancia Delta HF 4WD

1988 1000 Lakes Rally
Markku Alén (FIN)/Ilkka Kivimäki (FIN)
Lancia Delta Integrale

1989 1000 Lakes Rally
Mikael Ericsson (S)/Claes Billstam (S)
Mitsubishi Galant VR-4

1990 1000 Lakes Rally
Carlos Sainz (E)/Luis Moya (E)
Toyota Celica GT-Four

1991 1000 Lakes Rally
Juha Kankkunen (FIN)/Juha Piironen (FIN)
Lancia Delta Integrale 16V

1992 1000 Lakes Rally
Didier Auriol (F)/Bernard Occelli (F)
Lancia Delta HF Integrale

1993 1000 Lakes Rally
Juha Kankkunen (FIN)/Denis Giraudet (F)
Toyota Celica Turbo 4WD

1994 1000 Lakes Rally
Tommi Mäkinen (FIN)/Seppo Harjanne (FIN)
Ford Escort RS Cosworth

1995
NO WRC EVENT

1996 Neste 1000 Lakes Rally
Tommi Mäkinen (FIN)/Seppo Harjanne (FIN)
Mitsubishi Lancer Evo 3

1997 Neste Rally Finland
Tommi Mäkinen (FIN)/Seppo Harjanne (FIN)
Mitsubishi Lancer Evo 4

1998 Neste Rally Finland
Tommi Mäkinen (FIN)/Risto Mannisenmäki (FIN)
Mitsubishi Lancer Evo 5

1999 Neste Rally Finland
Juha Kankkunen (FIN)/Juha Repo (FIN)
Subaru Impreza WRC

2000 Neste Rally Finland
Marcus Grönholm (FIN)/Timo Rautiainen (FIN)
Peugeot 206 WRC

2001 Neste Rally Finland
Marcus Grönholm (FIN)/Timo Rautiainen (FIN)
Peugeot 206 WRC

2002 Neste Rally Finland
Marcus Grönholm (FIN)/Timo Rautiainen (FIN)
Peugeot 206 WRC

2003 Neste Rally Finland
Markko Märtin (EE)/Michael Park (GB)
Ford Focus WRC

GERMANY

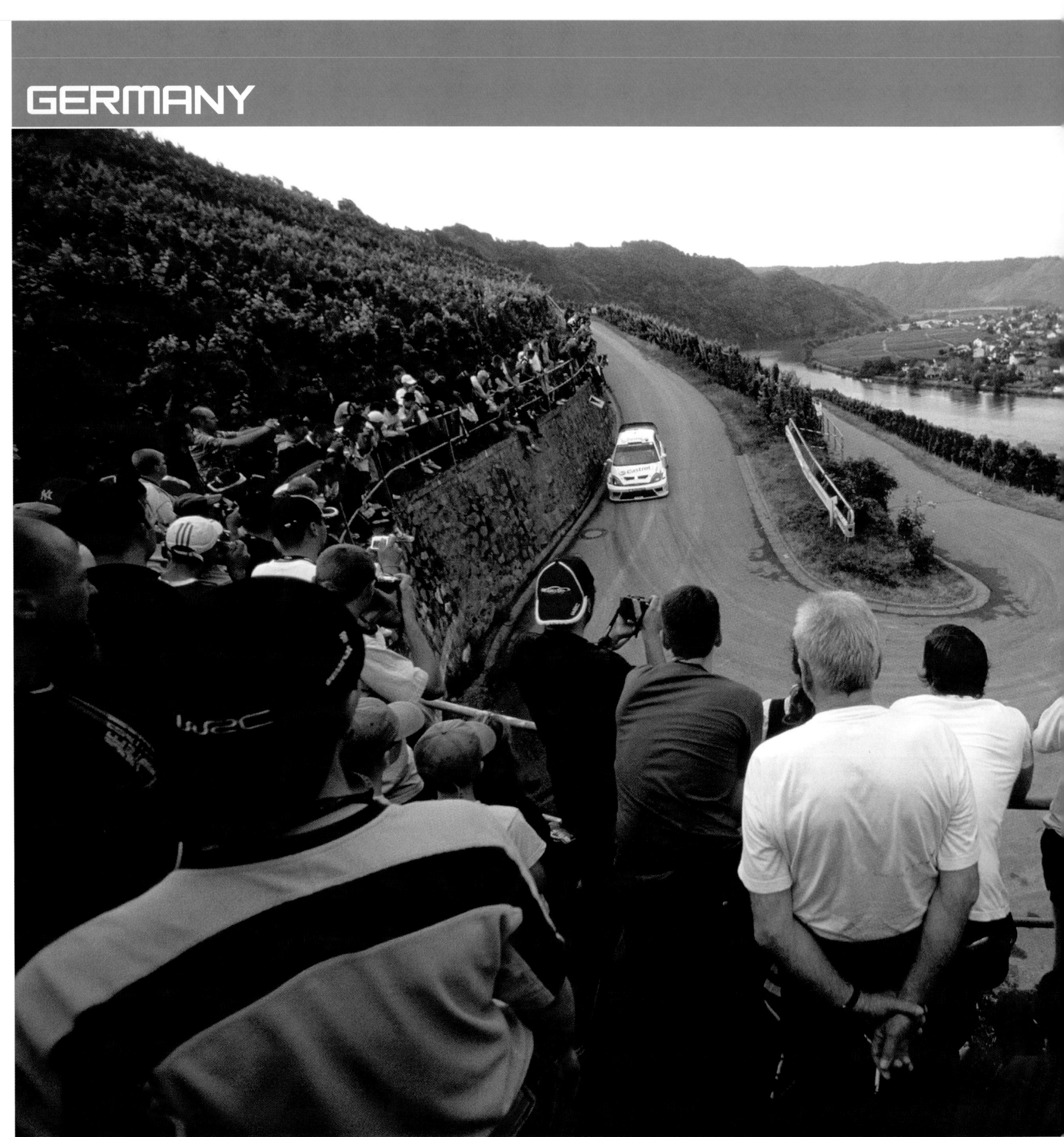

2002 ADAC Rallye Deutschland
Sébastien Loeb (F)/Daniel Elena (F)
Citroën Xsara WRC

2003 ADAC Rallye Deutschland
Sébastien Loeb (F)/Daniel Elena (F)
Citroën Xsara WRC

GREAT BRITAIN

1973 RAC Rally
Timo Mäkinen (FIN)/Henry Liddon (GB)
Ford Escort RS1600

1974 Lombard RAC Rally
Timo Mäkinen (FIN)/Henry Liddon (GB)
Ford Escort RS1600

1975 Lombard RAC Rally
Timo Mäkinen (FIN)/Henry Liddon (GB)
Ford Escort RS1800

1976 Lombard RAC Rally
Roger Clark (GB)/Stuart Pegg (RSA)
Ford Escort RS1800

1977 Lombard RAC Rally
Bjorn Waldegård (S)/Hans Thorszelius (S)
Ford Escort RS1800

1978 Lombard RAC Rally
Hannu Mikkola (FIN)/Arne Hertz (S)
Ford Escort RS

1979 Lombard RAC Rally
Hannu Mikkola (FIN)/Arne Hertz (S)
Ford Escort RS

1980 Lombard RAC Rally
Henri Toivonen (FIN)/Paul White (GB)
Talbot Sunbeam Lotus

1981 Lombard RAC Rally
Hannu Mikkola (FIN)/Arne Hertz (S)
Audi Quattro

1982 Lombard RAC Rally
Hannu Mikkola (FIN)/Arne Hertz (FIN)
Audi Quattro

1983 Lombard RAC Rally
Stig Blomqvist (S)/Björn Cederberg (S)
Audi Quattro A2

1984 Lombard RAC Rally
Ari Vatanen (FIN)/Terry Harryman (GB)
Peugeot 205 Turbo 16

1985 Lombard RAC Rally
Henri Toivonen (FIN)/Neil Wilson (GB)
Lancia Delta S4

1986 Lombard RAC Rally
Timo Salonen (FIN)/Seppo Harjanne (FIN)
Peugeot 205 Turbo 16 E2

1987 Lombard RAC Rally
Juha Kankkunen (FIN)/Juha Piironen (FIN)
Lancia Delta HF 4WD

1988 Lombard RAC Rally
Markku Alén (FIN)/Ilkka Kivimäki (FIN)
Lancia Delta Integrale

1989 Lombard RAC Rally
Pentti Airikkala (FIN)/Ronan McNamee (GB)
Mitsubishi Galant VR-4

1990 Lombard RAC Rally
Carlos Sainz (E)/Luís Moya (E)
Toyota Celica GT-Four

1991 Lombard RAC Rally
Juha Kankkunen (FIN)/Juha Piironen (FIN)
Lancia Delta Integrale 16V

1992 Lombard RAC Rally
Carlos Sainz (E)/Luís Moya (E)
Toyota Celica Turbo 4WD

1993 Network Q RAC Rally
Juha Kankkunen (FIN)/Nicky Grist (GB)
Toyota Celica Turbo 4WD

1994 Network Q RAC Rally
Colin McRae (GB)/Derek Ringer (GB)
Subaru Impreza 555

1995 Network Q RAC Rally
Colin McRae (GB)/Derek Ringer (GB)
Subaru Impreza 555

1996 Network Q RAC Rally
NO WRC EVENT

1997 Network Q RAC Rally
Colin McRae (GB)/Nicky Grist (GB)
Subaru Impreza WRC

1998 Network Q Rally of Great Britain
Richard Burns (GB)/Robert Reid (GB)
Mitsubishi Carisma GT Evo 5

1999 Network Q Rally of Great Britain
Richard Burns (GB)/Robert Reid (GB)
Subaru Impreza WRC

2000 Network Q Rally of Great Britain
Richard Burns (GB)/Robert Reid (GB)
Subaru Impreza WRC

2001 Network Q Rally of Great Britain
Marcus Grönholm (FIN)/Timo Rautiainen (FIN)
Peugeot 206 WRC

2002 Network Q Rally of Great Britain
Petter Solberg (GB)/Phil Mills (GB)
Subaru Impreza WRC

2003 Wales Rally of Great Britain
Petter Solberg (GB)/Phil Mills (GB)
Subaru Impreza WRC

GREECE

1973 Acropolis Rally
Jean-Luc Thérier (F)/Christian Delferrier (B)
Alpine-Renault A110

1974
NO WRC EVENT

1975 Acropolis Rally
Walter Röhrl (D)/Jochen Berger (D)
Opel Ascona

1976 Acropolis Rally
Harry Källström (S)/Claes-Goran Andersson (S)
Datsun 160J

1977 Acropolis Rally
Bjorn Waldegård (S)/Hans Thorszelius (S)
Ford Escort RS1800

1978 Acropolis Rally
Walter Röhrl (D)/Christian Geistdörfer (D)
Fiat 131 Abarth

1979 Acropolis Rally
Bjorn Waldegård (S)/Hans Thorszelius (S)
Ford Escort RS

1980 Acropolis Rally
Ari Vatanen (FIN)/David Richards (GB)
Ford Escort RS1800

1981 Acropolis Rally
Ari Vatanen (FIN)/David Richards (GB)
Ford Escort RS1800

1982 Acropolis Rally
Michèle Mouton (F)/Fabrizia Pons (ITA)
Audi Quattro

1983 Acropolis Rally
Walter Röhrl (D)/Christian Geistdörfer (D)
Lancia Rally 037

1984 Acropolis Rally
Stig Blomqvist (S)/Björn Cederberg (S)
Audi Quattro A2

1985 Acropolis Rally
Timo Salonen (FIN)/Seppo Harjanne (FIN)
Peugeot 205 Turbo 16

1986 Acropolis Rally
Juha Kankkunen (FIN)/Juha Piironen (FIN)
Peugeot 205 Turbo 16 E2

1987 Acropolis Rally
Markku Alén (FIN)/Ilkka Kivimäki (FIN)
Lancia Delta HF 4WD

1988 Acropolis Rally
Miki Biasion (ITA)/Tiziano Siviero (ITA)
Lancia Delta Integrale

1989 Acropolis Rally
Miki Biasion (ITA)/Tiziano Siviero (ITA)
Lancia Delta Integrale

1990 Acropolis Rally
Carlos Sainz (E)/Luís Moya (E)
Toyota Celica GT-Four

1991 Acropolis Rally
Juha Kankkunen (FIN)/Juha Piironen (FIN)
Lancia Delta Integrale 16V

1992 Acropolis Rally
Didier Auriol (F)/Bernard Occelli (F)
Lancia Delta HF Integrale

1993 Acropolis Rally
Miki Biasion (ITA)/Tiziano Siviero (ITA)
Ford Escort RS Cosworth

1994 Acropolis Rally of Greece
Carlos Sainz (E)/Luís Moya (E)
Subaru Impreza 555

1995
NO WRC EVENT

1996 Acropolis Rally of Greece
Colin McRae (GB)/Derek Ringer (GB)
Subaru Impreza 555

1997 Acropolis Rally of Greece
Carlos Sainz (E)/Luís Moya (E)
Ford Escort WRC

1998 Acropolis Rally of Greece
Colin McRae (GB)/Nicky Grist (GB)
Subaru Impreza WRC

1999 Acropolis Rally of Greece
Richard Burns (GB)/Robert Reid (GB)
Subaru Impreza WRC

2000 Acropolis Rally
Colin McRae (GB)/Nicky Grist (GB)
Ford Focus WRC

2001 Acropolis Rally
Colin McRae (GB)/Nicky Grist (GB)
Ford Focus WRC

2002 Acropolis Rally
Colin McRae (GB)/Nicky Grist (GB)
Ford Focus WRC

2003 Acropolis Rally
Markko Märtin (EE)/Michael Park (GB)
Ford Focus WRC

INDONESIA

1996 Bank Utama Rally of Indonesia
Carlos Sainz (E)/Luís Moya (E)
Ford Escort RS Cosworth

1997 Rally Indonesia
Carlos Sainz (E)/Luís Moya (E)
Ford Escort WRC

MONTE CARLO

1973 Rallye Automobile de Monte Carlo
Jean-Claude Andruet (F)/'Biche' (F)
Alpine-Renault A110

1974
NO WRC EVENT

1975 Rallye Automobile de Monte Carlo
Sandro Munari (ITA)/Mauro Mannucci (ITA)
Lancia Stratos

1976 Rallye Automobile de Monte Carlo
Sandro Munari (ITA)/Silvio Maiga (ITA)
Lancia Stratos

1977 Rallye Automobile de Monte Carlo
Sandro Munari (ITA)/Silvio Maiga (ITA)
Lancia Stratos

1978 Rallye Automobile de Monte Carlo
Jean-Pierre Nicolas (F)/Vincent Laverne (F)
Porsche 911

1979 Rallye Automobile de Monte Carlo
Bernard Darniche (F)/Alain Mahé (F)
Lancia Stratos

1980 Rallye Automobile de Monte Carlo
Walter Röhrl (D)/Christian Geistdörfer (D)
Fiat 131 Abarth

1981 Rallye Automobile de Monte Carlo
Jean Ragnotti (F)/Jean-Marc Andrié (F)
Renault 5 Turbo

1982 Rallye Automobile de Monte Carlo
Walter Röhrl (D)/Christian Geistdörfer (D)
Opel Ascona 400

1983 Rallye Automobile de Monte Carlo
Walter Röhrl (D)/Christian Geistdörfer (D)
Lancia Rally 037

1984 Rallye Automobile de Monte Carlo
Walter Röhrl (D)/Christian Geistdörfer (D)
Audi Quattro A2

1985 Rallye Automobile de Monte Carlo
Ari Vatanen (FIN)/Terry Harryman (GB)
Peugeot 205 Turbo 16

1986 Rallye Automobile de Monte Carlo
Henri Toivonen (FIN)/Sergio Cresto (USA)
Lancia Delta S4

1987 Rallye Automobile de Monte Carlo
Miki Biasion (ITA)/Tiziano Siviero (ITA)
Lancia Delta HF 4WD

1988 Rallye Automobile de Monte Carlo
Bruno Saby (F)/Jean-François Fauchille (F)
Lancia Delta HF 4WD

1989 Rallye Automobile de Monte Carlo
Miki Biasion (ITA)/Tiziano Siviero (ITA)
Lancia Delta Integrale

1990 Rallye Automobile de Monte Carlo
Didier Auriol (F)/Bernard Occelli (F)
Lancia Delta Integrale 16V

1991 Rallye Automobile de Monte Carlo
Carlos Sainz (E)/Luís Moya (E)
Toyota Celica GT-Four

1992 Rallye Automobile de Monte Carlo
Didier Auriol (F)/Bernard Occelli (F)
Lancia Delta HF Integrale

1993 Rallye Automobile de Monte Carlo
Didier Auriol (F)/Bernard Occelli (F)
Toyota Celica Turbo 4WD

1994 Rallye Automobile de Monte Carlo
François Delecour (F)/Daniel Grataloup (F)
Ford Escort RS Cosworth

1995 Rallye Automobile de Monte Carlo
Carlos Sainz (E)/Luís Moya (E)
Subaru Impreza 555

1996
NO WRC EVENT

1997 Rallye Automobile de Monte Carlo
Piero Liatti (ITA)/Fabrizia Pons (ITA)
Subaru Impreza WRC

1998 Rallye Automobile de Monte Carlo
Carlos Sainz (E)/Luís Moya (E)
Toyota Corolla WRC

1999 Rallye Automobile de Monte Carlo
Tommi Mäkinen (FIN)/Risto Mannisenmäki
(FIN)Mitsubishi Lancer Evo 6

2000 Rallye Automobile de Monte Carlo
Tommi Mäkinen (FIN)/Risto Mannisenmäki
(FIN)Mitsubishi Lancer Evo 6

2001 Rallye Automobile de Monte Carlo
Tommi Mäkinen (FIN)/Risto Mannisenmäki
(FIN)Mitsubishi Lancer Evo 6

2002 Rallye Automobile de Monte Carlo
Tommi Mäkinen (FIN)/Kaj Lindström (FIN)
Subaru Impreza WRC

2003 Rallye Automobile de Monte Carlo
Sébastien Loeb (F)/Daniel Elena (F)
Citroën Xsara WRC

MOROCCO

1973 Rallye du Maroc
Bernard Darniche (F)/Alain Mahé (F)
Alpine-Renault A110

1975 Rallye du Maroc
Hannu Mikkola (FIN)/Jean Todt (F)
Peugeot 504

1976 Rallye du Maroc
Jean-Pierre Nicolas (F)/Michel Gamet (F)
Peugeot 504

NEW ZEALAND

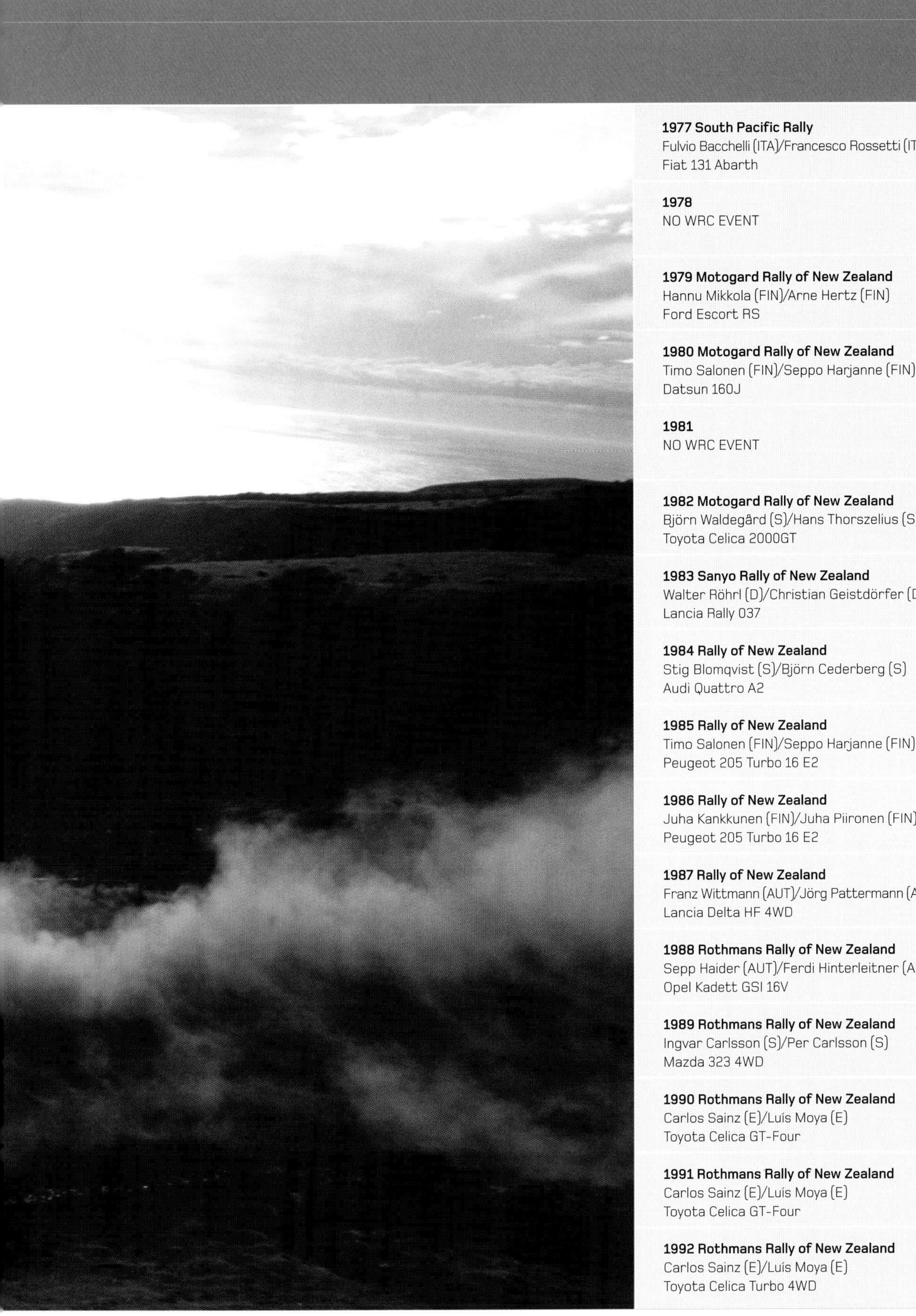

1977 South Pacific Rally
Fulvio Bacchelli (ITA)/Francesco Rossetti (ITA)
Fiat 131 Abarth

1978
NO WRC EVENT

1979 Motogard Rally of New Zealand
Hannu Mikkola (FIN)/Arne Hertz (FIN)
Ford Escort RS

1980 Motogard Rally of New Zealand
Timo Salonen (FIN)/Seppo Harjanne (FIN)
Datsun 160J

1981
NO WRC EVENT

1982 Motogard Rally of New Zealand
Björn Waldegård (S)/Hans Thorszelius (S)
Toyota Celica 2000GT

1983 Sanyo Rally of New Zealand
Walter Röhrl (D)/Christian Geistdörfer (D)
Lancia Rally 037

1984 Rally of New Zealand
Stig Blomqvist (S)/Björn Cederberg (S)
Audi Quattro A2

1985 Rally of New Zealand
Timo Salonen (FIN)/Seppo Harjanne (FIN)
Peugeot 205 Turbo 16 E2

1986 Rally of New Zealand
Juha Kankkunen (FIN)/Juha Piironen (FIN)
Peugeot 205 Turbo 16 E2

1987 Rally of New Zealand
Franz Wittmann (AUT)/Jörg Pattermann (AUT)
Lancia Delta HF 4WD

1988 Rothmans Rally of New Zealand
Sepp Haider (AUT)/Ferdi Hinterleitner (AUT)
Opel Kadett GSI 16V

1989 Rothmans Rally of New Zealand
Ingvar Carlsson (S)/Per Carlsson (S)
Mazda 323 4WD

1990 Rothmans Rally of New Zealand
Carlos Sainz (E)/Luís Moya (E)
Toyota Celica GT-Four

1991 Rothmans Rally of New Zealand
Carlos Sainz (E)/Luís Moya (E)
Toyota Celica GT-Four

1992 Rothmans Rally of New Zealand
Carlos Sainz (E)/Luís Moya (E)
Toyota Celica Turbo 4WD

1993 Rothmans Rally of New Zealand
Colin McRae (GB)/Derek Ringer (GB)
Subaru Legacy RS

1994 Rothmans Rally of New Zealand
Colin McRae (GB)/Derek Ringer (GB)
Subaru Impreza 555

1995 Smokefree Rally of New Zealand
Colin McRae (GB)/Derek Ringer (GB)
Subaru Impreza 555

1996
NO WRC EVENT

1997 Smokefree Rally of New Zealand
Kenneth Eriksson (S)/Staffan Parmander (S)
Subaru Impreza WRC

1998 Rally of New Zealand
Carlos Sainz (E)/Luís Moya (E)
Toyota Corolla WRC

1999 Rally of New Zealand
Tommi Mäkinen (FIN)/Risto Mannisenmäki (FIN)
Mitsubishi Lancer Evo 6

2000 Rally of New Zealand
Marcus Grönholm (FIN)/Timo Rautiainen (FIN)
Peugeot 206 WRC

2001 Propecia Rally of New Zealand
Richard Burns (GB)/Robert Reid (GB)
Subaru Impreza WRC

2002 Propecia Rally of New Zealand
Marcus Grönholm (FIN)/Timo Rautiainen (FIN)
Peugeot 206 WRC

2003 Propecia Rally of New Zealand
Marcus Grönholm (FIN)/Timo Rautiainen (FIN)
Peugeot 206 WRC

POLAND

1973 Rajd Polski
Achim Warmbold (D)/Jean Todt (F)
Fiat 124 Abarth

PORTUGAL

1973 TAP Rallye de Portugal
Jean-Luc Thérier (F)/Jacques Jaubert (F)
Alpine-Renault A110

1974 TAP Rallye de Portugal
Raffaele Pinto (ITA)/Arnaldo Bernacchini (ITA)
Fiat 124 Abarth

1975 Rallye de Portugal Vinho do Porto
Markku Alén (FIN)/Ilkka Kivimäki (FIN)
Fiat 124 Abarth

1976 Rallye de Portugal Vinho do Porto
Sandro Munari (ITA)/Silvio Maiga (ITA)
Lancia Stratos

1977 Rallye de Portugal Vinho do Porto
Markku Alén (FIN)/Ilkka Kivimäki (FIN)
Fiat 131 Abarth

1978 Rallye de Portugal Vinho do Porto
Markku Alén (FIN)/Ilkka Kivimaki (FIN)
Fiat 131 Abarth

1979 Rallye de Portugal Vinho do Porto
Hannu Mikkola (FIN)/Arne Hertz (S)
Ford Escort RS

1980 Rallye de Portugal Vinho do Porto
Walter Röhrl (D)/Christian Geistdörfer (D)
Fiat 131 Abarth

1981 Rallye de Portugal Vinho do Porto
Markku Alén (FIN)/Ilkka Kivimäki (FIN)
Fiat 131 Abarth

1982 Rallye de Portugal Vinho do Porto
Michèle Mouton (F)/Fabrizia Pons (ITA)
Audi Quattro

1983 Rallye de Portugal Vinho do Porto
Hannu Mikkola (FIN)/Arne Hertz (S)
Audi Quattro A1

1984 Rallye de Portugal Vinho do Porto
Hannu Mikkola (FIN)/Arne Hertz (S)
Audi Quattro A2

1985 Rallye de Portugal Vinho do Porto
Timo Salonen (FIN)/Seppo Harjanne (FIN)
Peugeot 205 Turbo 16

1986 Rallye de Portugal Vinho do Porto
Joaquim Moutinho (P)/Edgar Fortes (P)
Renault 5 Turbo

1987 Rallye de Portugal Vinho do Porto
Markku Alén (FIN)/Ilkka Kivimäki (FIN)
Lancia Delta HF 4WD

1988 Rallye de Portugal Vinho do Porto
Miki Biasion (ITA)/Carlo Cassina (ITA)
Lancia Delta Integrale

1989 Rallye de Portugal Vinho do Porto
Miki Biasion (ITA)/Tiziano Siviero (ITA)
Lancia Delta Integrale

1990 Rallye de Portugal Vinho do Porto
Miki Biasion (ITA)/Tiziano Siviero (ITA)
Lancia Delta Integrale 16V

1991 Rallye de Portugal
Carlos Sainz (E)/Luís Moya (E)
Toyota Celica GT-Four

1992 Rallye de Portugal
Juha Kankkunen (FIN)/Juha Piironen (FIN)
Lancia Delta HF Integrale

1993 Rallye de Portugal
François Delecour (F)/Daniel Grataloup (F)
Ford Escort RS Cosworth

1994 TAP Rallye de Portugal
Juha Kankkunen (FIN)/Nicky Grist (GB)
Toyota Celica Turbo 4WD

1995 TAP Rallye de Portugal
Carlos Sainz (E)/Luís Moya (E)
Subaru Impreza 555

1996
NO WRC EVENT

1997 TAP Rallye de Portugal
Tommi Mäkinen (FIN)/Seppo Harjanne (FIN)
Mitsubishi Lancer Evo 4

1998 TAP Rallye de Portugal
Colin McRae (GB)/Nicky Grist (GB)
Subaru Impreza WRC

1999 TAP Rallye de Portugal
Colin McRae (GB)/Nicky Grist (GB)
Ford Focus WRC

2000 TAP Rallye de Portugal
Richard Burns (GB)/Robert Reid (GB)
Subaru Impreza WRC

2001 TAP Rallye de Portugal
Tommi Mäkinen (FIN)/Risto Mannisenmäki (FIN)Mitsubishi Lancer Evo 6

SANREMO

1973 Rallye Sanremo
Jean-Luc Thérier (F)/Jacques Jaubert (F)
Alpine-Renault A110

1974 Rallye Sanremo
Sandro Munari (ITA)/Mauro Mannucci (ITA)
Lancia Stratos

1975 Rallye Sanremo
Bjorn Waldegård (S)/Hans Thorszelius (S)
Lancia Stratos

1976 Rallye Sanremo
Bjorn Waldegård (S)/Hans Thorszelius (S)
Lancia Stratos

1977 Rallye Sanremo
Jean-Claude Andruet (F)/Christian Delferrier (B)
Fiat 131 Abarth

1978 Rallye Sanremo
Markku Alén (FIN)/Ilkka Kivimäki (FIN)
Lancia Stratos

1979 Rallye Sanremo
'Tony' Fassina (ITA)/Mauro Mannini (ITA)
Lancia Stratos

1980 Rallye Sanremo
Walter Röhrl (D)/Christian Geistdörfer (D)
Fiat 131 Abarth

1981 Rallye Sanremo
Michèle Mouton (F)/Fabrizia Pons (ITA)
Audi Quattro

1982 Rallye Sanremo
Stig Blomqvist (S)/Björn Cederberg (S)
Audi Quattro

1983 Rallye Sanremo
Markku Alén (FIN)/Ilkka Kivimäki (FIN)
Lancia Rally 037

1984 Rallye Sanremo
Ari Vatanen (FIN)/Terry Harryman (GB)
Peugeot 205 Turbo 16

1985 Rallye Sanremo
Walter Röhrl (D)/Christian Geistdörfer (D)
Audi Sport Quattro E2

1986
EVENT ANNULLED

1987 Rallye Sanremo
Miki Biasion (ITA)/Tiziano Siviero (ITA)
Lancia Delta HF 4WD

1988 Rallye Sanremo – Rallye d'Italia
Miki Biasion (ITA)/Tiziano Siviero (ITA)
Lancia Delta Integrale

1989 Rallye Sanremo – Rallye d'Italia
Miki Biasion (ITA)/Tiziano Siviero (ITA)
Lancia Delta Integrale 16V

1990 Rallye Sanremo – Rallye d'Italia
Didier Auriol (F)/Bernard Occelli (F)
Lancia Delta Integrale 16V

1991 Rallye Sanremo – Rallye d'Italia
Didier Auriol (F)/Bernard Occelli (F)
Lancia Delta Integrale 16V

1992 Rallye Sanremo – Rallye d'Italia
Andrea Aghini (ITA)/Sauro Farnocchia (ITA)
Lancia Delta HF Integrale

1993 Rallye Sanremo – Rallye d'Italia
Gianfranco Cunico (ITA)/Stefano Evangelisti (ITA)
Ford Escort RS Cosworth

1994 Rallye Sanremo – Rallye d'Italia
Didier Auriol (F)/Bernard Occelli (F)
Toyota Celica Turbo 4WD

1995
NO WRC EVENT

1996 Rallye Sanremo – Rallye d'Italia
Colin McRae (GB)/Derek Ringer (GB)
Subaru Impreza 555

1997 Rallye Sanremo – Rallye d'Italia
Colin McRae (GB)/Nicky Grist (GB)
Subaru Impreza WRC

1998 Rallye Sanremo – Rallye d'Italia
Tommi Mäkinen (FIN)/Risto Mannisenmäki (FIN)
Mitsubishi Lancer Evo 5

1999 Rallye Sanremo – Rallye d'Italia
Tommi Mäkinen (FIN)/Risto Mannisenmäki (FIN)
Mitsubishi Lancer Evo 6

2000 Rallye Sanremo – Rallye d'Italia
Gilles Panizzi (F)/Hervé Panizzi (F)
Peugeot 206 WRC

2001 Rallye Sanremo – Rallye d'Italia
Gilles Panizzi (F)/Hervé Panizzi (F)
Peugeot 206 WRC

2002 Rallye Sanremo – Rallye d'Italia
Gilles Panizzi (F)/Hervé Panizzi (F)
Peugeot 206 WRC

2003 Rallye Sanremo – Rallye d'Italia
Sébastien Loeb (F)/Daniel Elena (F)
Citroën Xsara WRC

SPAIN

1991 Rallye Catalunya-Costa Brava (Rallye de Espana)
Armin Schwarz (D)/Arne Hertz (S)
Toyota Celica GT-Four

1992 Rallye Catalunya-Costa Brava (Rallye de Espana)
Carlos Sainz (E)/Luís Moya (E)
Toyota Celica Turbo 4WD

1993 Rallye Catalunya-Costa Brava (Rallye de Espana)
François Delecour (F)/Daniel Grataloup (F)
Ford Escort RS Cosworth

1994 Rallye Catalunya-Costa Brava (Rallye de Espana)
NO WRC EVENT

1995 Rallye Catalunya-Costa Brava (Rallye de Espana)
Carlos Sainz (E)/Luís Moya (E)
Subaru Impreza 555

1996 Rallye Catalunya-Costa Brava (Rallye de Espana)
Colin McRae (GB)/Derek Ringer (GB)
Subaru Impreza 555

1997 Rallye Catalunya-Costa Brava (Rallye de Espana)
Tommi Mäkinen (FIN)/Seppo Harjanne (FIN)
Mitsubishi Lancer Evo 4

1998 Rallye Catalunya-Costa Brava (Rallye de Espana)
Didier Auriol (F)/Denis Giraudet (F)
Toyota Corolla WRC

1999 Rallye Catalunya-Costa Brava
Philippe Bugalski (F)/Jean-Paul Chiaroni (F)
Citroën Xsara Kit Car

2000 Rallye Catalunya-Costa Brava (Rallye de Espana)
Colin McRae (GB)/Nicky Grist (GB)
Ford Focus WRC

2001 Rallye Catalunya-Costa Brava (Rallye de Espana)
Didier Auriol (F)/Denis Giraudet (F)
Peugeot 206 WRC

2002 Rallye Catalunya-Costa Brava (Rallye de Espana)
Gilles Panizzi (F)/Hervé Panizzi (F)
Peugeot 206 WRC

2003 Rallye Catalunya-Costa Brava (Rallye de Espana)
Gilles Panizzi (F)/Hervé Panizzi (F)
Peugeot 206 WRC

SWEDEN

1973 International Swedish Rally
Stig Blomqvist (S)/Arne Hertz (S)
Saab 96 V4

1974
NO WRC EVENT

1975 International Swedish Rally
Bjorn Waldegård (S)/Hans Thorszelius (S)
Lancia Stratos

1976 International Swedish Rally
Per Eklund (S)/Bjorn Cederberg (S)
Saab 96 V4

1977 International Swedish Rally
Stig Blomqvist (S)/Hans Sylvan (S)
Saab 99EMS

1978 International Swedish Rally
Bjorn Waldegård (S)/Hans Thorszelius (S)
Ford Escort RS

1979 International Swedish Rally
Stig Blomqvist (S)/Bjorn Cederberg (S)
Saab 99 Turbo

1980 International Swedish Rally
Anders Kulläng (S)/Bruno Berglund (S)
Opel Ascona 400

1981 International Swedish Rally
Hannu Mikkola (FIN)/Arne Hertz (S)
Audi Quattro

1982 International Swedish Rally
Stig Blomqvist (S)/Björn Cederberg (S)
Audi Quattro

1983 International Swedish Rally
Hannu Mikkola (FIN)/Arne Hertz (S)
Audi Quattro A1

1984 International Swedish Rally
Stig Blomqvist (S)/Björn Cederberg (S)
Audi Quattro A2

1985 International Swedish Rally
Ari Vatanen (FIN)/Terry Harryman (GB)
Peugeot 205 Turbo 16

1986 International Swedish Rally
Juha Kankkunen (FIN)/Juha Piironen (FIN)
Peugeot 205 Turbo 16 E2

1987 International Swedish Rally
Timo Salonen (FIN)/Seppo Harjanne (Fin)
Mazda 323 4WD

1988 International Swedish Rally
Markku Alén (FIN)/Ilkka Kivimäki (FIN)
Lancia Delta HF 4WD

1989 International Swedish Rally
Ingvar Carlsson (S)/Per Carlsson (S)
Mazda 323 4WD

1990
NO WRC EVENT

1991 International Swedish Rally
Kenneth Eriksson (S)/Staffan Parmander (S)
Mitsubishi Galant VR-4

1992 International Swedish Rally
Mats Jonsson (S)/Lars Bäckman (S)
Toyota Celica GT-Four

1993 International Swedish Rally
Mats Jonsson (S)/Lars Bäckman (S)
Toyota Celica Turbo 4WD

1994
NO WRC EVENT

1995 International Swedish Rally
Kenneth Eriksson (S)/Staffan Parmander (S)
Mitsubishi Lancer Evo 2

1996 International Swedish Rally
Tommi Mäkinen (FIN)/Seppo Harjanne (FIN)
Mitsubishi Lancer Evo 3

1997 International Swedish Rally
Kenneth Eriksson (S)/Staffan Parmander (S)
Subaru Impreza WRC

1998 International Swedish Rally
Tommi Mäkinen (FIN)/Risto Mannisenmäki
(FIN)Mitsubishi Lancer Evo 4

1999 International Swedish Rally
Tommi Mäkinen (FIN)/Risto Mannisenmäki (FIN)
Mitsubishi Lancer Evo 5

2000 International Swedish Rally
Marcus Grönholm (FIN)/Timo Rautiainen (FIN)
Peugeot 206 WRC

2001 International Swedish Rally
Harri Rovanperä (FIN)/Risto Pietiläinen (FIN)
Peugeot 206 WRC

2002 Uddeholm Swedish Rally
Marcus Grönholm (FIN)/Timo Rautiainen (FIN)
Peugeot 206 WRC

2003 Uddeholm Swedish Rally
Marcus Grönholm (FIN)/Timo Rautiainen (FIN)
Peugeot 206 WRC

TURKEY

2003 Rally of Turkey
Carlos Sainz (E)/Marc Martí (E)
Citroën Xsara WRC

UNITED STATES

1973 Press-on-Regardless Rally
Walter Boyce (CDN)/Doug Woods (CDN)
Toyota Corolla

1974 Press-on-Regardless Rally
Jean-Luc Thérier (F)/Christian Delferrier (B)
Renault 17 Gordini

1986 Olympus Rally
Markku Alén (FIN)/Ilkka Kivimäki (FIN)
Lancia Delta S4

1987 Olympus Rally
Juha Kankkunen (FIN)/Juha Piironen (FIN)
Lancia Delta HF 4WD

1988 Olympus Rally
Miki Biasion (ITA)/Tiziano Siviero (ITA)
Lancia Delta Integrale

05

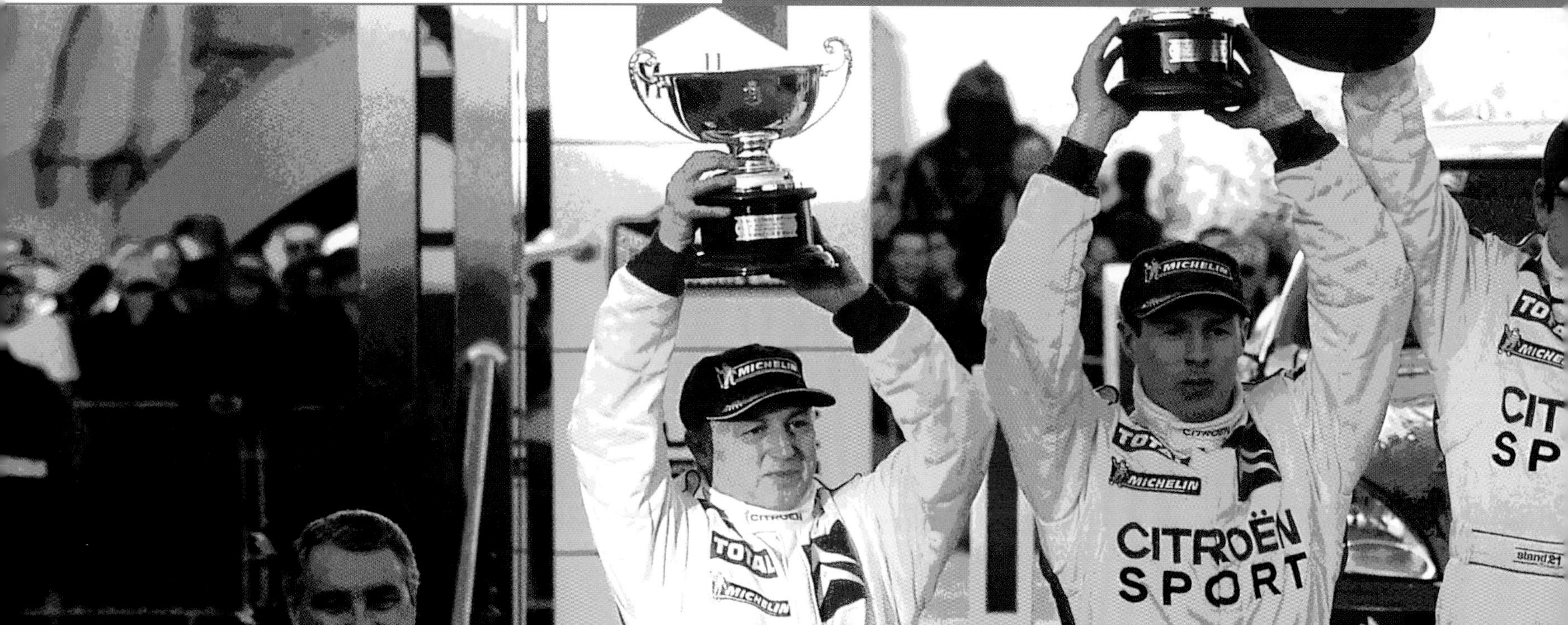
CITROËN
SPORT
MICHELIN
TOTAL
stand21
CITROËN

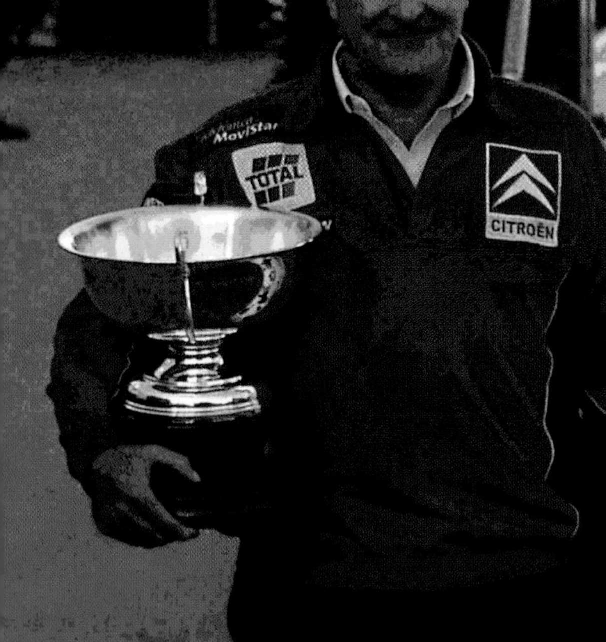
SPOLA
KROKEN
Snowgrip
Castrol
BOSCH
1

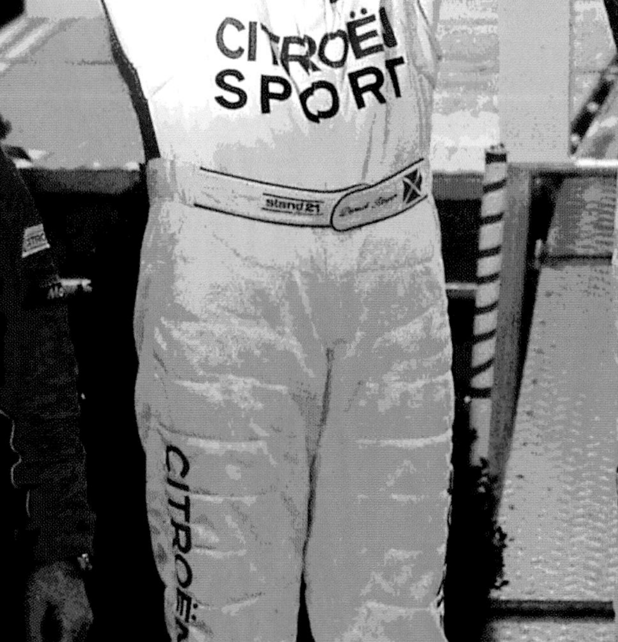
FORD ESCORT

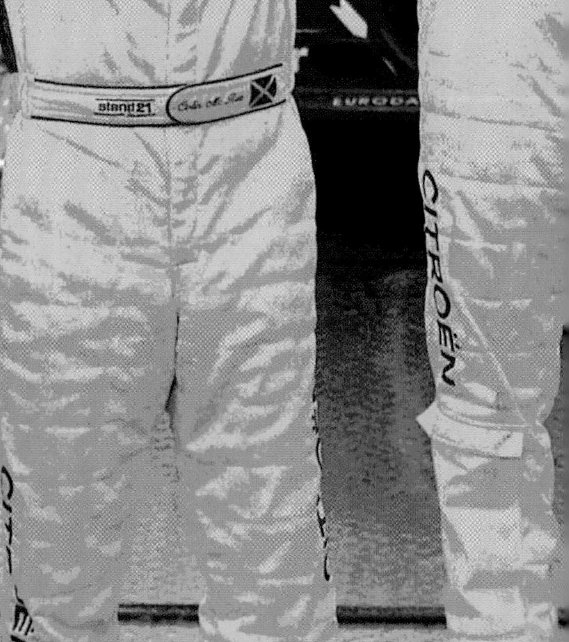

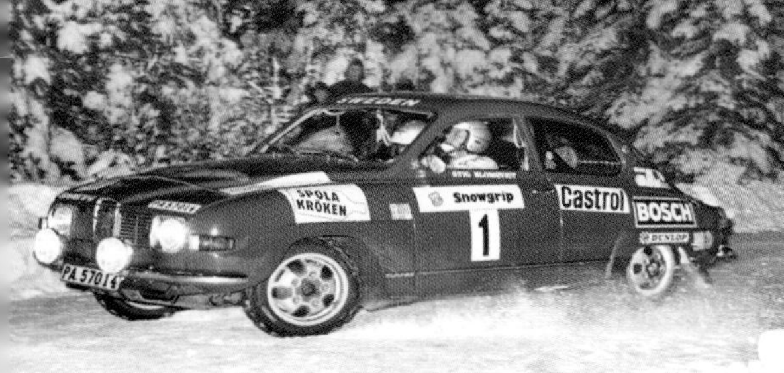

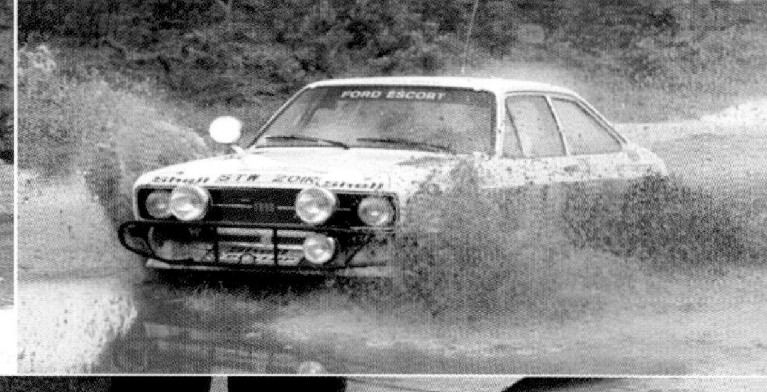

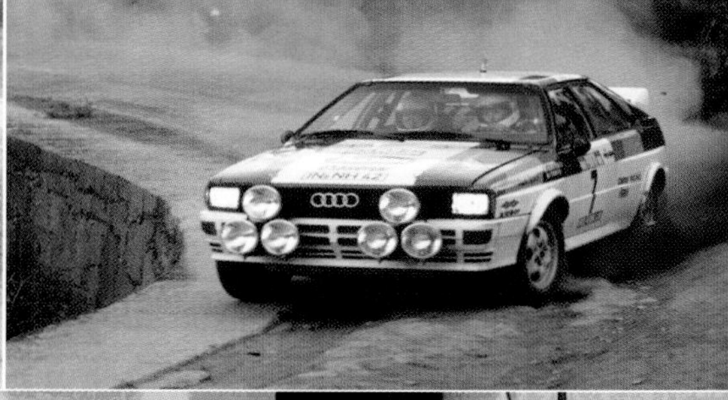

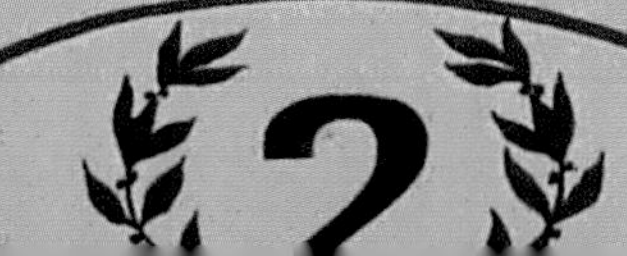

THE RESULTS

Marlboro
MICHELIN
CITROËN
TOTAL
CITROËN SPORT
stand21
CITROËN SPORT
Marlboro
CITROËN
inmarsat
555 SUBARU
REPSOL
TOTAL
3

1973

ROUND 01 – MONTE CARLO (19th-26th January)

01	Jean-Claude Andruet (F)/'Biche' (F)	Alpine-Renault A110	5h 42m 04s
02	Ove Andersson (S)/Jean Todt (F)	Alpine-Renault A110	5h 42m 30s
03	Jean-Pierre Nicolas (F)/Michel Vial (F)	Alpine-Renault A110	5h 43m 39s
04	Hannu Mikkola (FIN)/Jim Porter (NZ)	Ford Escort RS1600	5h 44m 29s
05	Jean-Luc Thérier (F)/Marcel Callewaert (F)	Alpine-Renault A110	5h 46m 01s
06	Jean-Francois Piot (F)/Jean-Louis Marnat (F)	Alpine-Renault A110	5h 46m 02s
07	Raffaele Pinto (I)/Arnaldo Bernacchini (I)	Fiat 124 Abarth	5h 52m 14s
08	Harry Källström (S)/Claes Billstam (S)	Lancia Fulvia 1.6 HF	5h 52m 15s
09	Tony Fall (GB)/Mike Wood (GB)	Datsun 240Z	5h 55m 47s
10	Bernard Darniche (F)/Alain Mahé (F)	Alpine-Renault A110	5h 57m 08s

Jean-Claude Andruet/'Biche'

ROUND 02 – SWEDEN (15th-18th February)

01	Stig Blomqvist (S)/Arne Hertz (S)	Saab 96 V4	9h 18m 31s
02	Per Eklund (S)/Rolf Carlsson (S)	Saab 96 V4	9h 20m 53s
03	Jean-Luc Thérier (F)/Marcel Callewaert	Alpine-Renault A110	9h 34m 12s
04	Harry Källström (S)/Claes Billstam (S)	Lancia Fulvia HF	9h 37m 14s
05	Hakan Lindberg (S)/Solve Andreasson (S)	Fiat 124 Abarth	9h 40m 41s
06	Bjorn Waldegård (S)/Hans Thorszelius (S)	VW Beetle 1303S	9h 57m 28s
07	Bror Danielsson (S)/Ulf Sundberg (S)	BMW 2002	10h 00m 58s
08	John Haugland (N)/Arild Antonsen (N)	Skoda 110	10h 35m 41s
09	Per-Inge Walfridsson (S)/Kjell Nilsson (S)	Volvo 142S	10h 36m 42s
10	Fredrik Donner (FIN)/Aarno Hurttia (FIN)	Opel Ascona	10h 37m 22s

Stig Blomqvist/Arne Hertz

ROUND 03 – PORTUGAL (13th-18th March)

01	Jean-Luc Thérier (F)/Jacques Jaubert (F)	Alpine-Renault A110	5h 42m 16s
02	Jean-Pierre Nicolas (F)/Michel Vial (F)	Alpine-Renault A110	5h 48m 57s
03	Francisco Romaozinho (P)/José Bernardo (P)	Citroën DS21	6h 07m 48s
04	Luis Netto (P)/Manuel Coenttro (P)	Fiat 124 Abarth	6h 10m 40s
05	Amèrico Nunes (P)/Antonio Morais (P)	Porsche 911	6h 17m 00s
06	António Borges (P)/António Lemos (P)	Alpine-Renault A110	6h 41m 00s
07	'Mêqêpê' (P)/Jorge Amaral (P)	Opel Ascona	6h 51m 40s
08	António Martorell (P)/Augusto Roxo (P)	Opel Ascona	6h 56m 09s
09	Giovanni Salvi (P)/Barbosa Gama (P)	Porsche 911	7h 05m 24s
	Only 9 finishers		

Jean-Luc Therier/Jacques Jaubert

ROUND 04 – SAFARI, AFRICA (19th-23rd April)

01	Shekhar Mehta (EAK)/Lofty Drews (EAK)	Datsun 240Z	6h 46m
02	Harry Källström (S)/Claes Billstam (S)	Datsun 1800 SSS	6h 46m
03	Ove Andersson (S)/Jean Todt (F)	Peugeot 504	8h 47m
04	Tony Fall (GB)/Mike Wood (GB)	Datsun 1800 SSS	9h 14m
05	Peter Huth (EAK)/John McConnell (EAK)	Peugeot 504	12h 07m
06	Hugh Lionnet (EAK)/Phillip Hechle (EAK)	Peugeot 504	13h 10m
07	Satwant Singh (ZAM)/John Mitchell (ZIM)	Mitsubishi Colt Galant	14h 03m
08	Robin Ulyate (EAK)/Ivan Smith (EAK)	Fiat 125S	14h 34m
09	Mike Kirkland (EAK)/Bruce Field (EAK)	Datsun 1600 SSS	14h 37m
10	Jim Noon (EAK)/Roger Barnard (GB)	Datsun 1600 SSS	15h 05m

Shekhar Mehta/Lofty Drews

ROUND 05 – MOROCCO (8th-13th May)

01	Bernard Darniche (F)/Alain Mahé (F)	Alpine-Renault A110	15h 01m 22s
02	Robert Neyret (F)/Jacques Terramorsi (F)	Citroën DS23	15h 20m 04s
03	Richard Bochnicek (A)/Sepp-Dieter Kemmayer (A)	Citroën DS23	15h 34m 37s
04	Raymond Ponnelle (MAR) /Pierre de Serpos (F)	Citroën DS23	15h 39m 56s
05	Jean-Pierre Nicolas (F)/Michel Vial (F)	Alpine-Renault A110	15h 52m 00s
06	Bjorn Waldegård (S)/Fergus Sager (S)	Fiat 124 Abarth	15h 59m 43s
07	Jean-Luc Thérier (F)/Christian Delferrier (B)	Alpine-Renault A110	16h 18m 16s
08	Jean Deschazeaux (MAR)/Jean Plassard (MAR)	Citroën DS23	16h 48m 26s
09	Lorenzo Merlone (I)/Riccardo Mortara (I)	Volvo 142S	17h 53m 47s
10	Claudine Trautmann (F)/Marie-Pierre Palayer (F)	Peugeot 504	18h 03m 33s

Bernard Darniche/Alain Mahé

ROUND 06 – ACROPOLIS, GREECE (23rd-28th May)

01	Jean-Luc Thérier (F)/Christian Delferrier (B)	Alpine-Renault A110	7h 37m 58s
02	Rauno Aaltonen (FIN)/Robin Turvey (GB)	Fiat 124 Abarth	7h 44m 59s
03	Jean-Pierre Nicolas (F)/Michel Vial (F)	Alpine-Renault A110	7h 45m 56s
04	Hakan Lindberg (S)/Arne Hertz (S)	Fiat 124 Abarth	7h 57m 21s
05	Georg Fischer (A)/Hans Siebert (A)	VW 1303S	8h 34m 57s
06	Richard Bochnicek (A)/Sepp-Dieter Kemmayer (A)	Citroën DS23	8h 40m 14s
07	Chris Sclater (GB)/Bob de Jong (NL)	Ford Escort RS1600	8h 43m 36s
08	Helmut Doppelreiter (A)/Schurek (A)	VW 1303S	9h 40m 01s
09	Ioánnis Phas (GR)/Andreas Papatriantafillou (GR)	Toyota Corolla	9h 43m 47s
10	Ioánnis Bardopoulos (GR)/Theodoros Karelas (GR)	Audi 80 GL	10h 16m 59s

Jean-Luc Thérier/Christian Delferrier

ROUND 07 – POLAND (12th-15th July)

01	Achim Warmbold (D)/Jean Todt (F)	Fiat 124 Abarth	8h 28m 14s
02	Egon Culmbacher (D)/Werner Ernst (D)	Wartburg 353	11h 15m 16s
03	Maciej Stawowiak (PL)/Jan Czyzyk yk (PL)	Fiat 125 Polski	12h 08m 31s
	Only 3 finishers		

Achim Warmbold/Jean Todt

ROUND 08 – 1000 LAKES, FINLAND (3rd-5th August)

01	Timo Mäkinen (FIN)/Henry Liddon (GB)	Ford Escort RS1600	4h 53m 50s
02	Markku Alén (FIN)/Juhani Toivonen (FIN)	Volvo 142	4h 55m 59s
03	Leo Kinnunen (FIN)/Atso Aho (FIN)	Porsche 911	4h 57m 12s
04	Simo Lampinen (FIN)/John Davenport (GB)	Saab 96 V4	4h 59m 28s
05	Antti Ojanen (FIN)/Heikki Miikki (FIN)	Opel Ascona	5h 03m 30s
06	Ulf Grönholm (FIN)/Henry Lnholm/Laine (FIN)	Opel Ascona	5h 04m 03s
07	Tapio Rainio (FIN)/Erkki Nyman (FIN)	Saab 96 V4	5h 05m 43s
08	Achim Warmbold (D)/Jean Todt (F)	Fiat Abarth 124	5h 09m 43s
09	Pertti Lehtonen (FIN)/Ilkka Kivimäki (FIN)	Saab 96 V4	5h 11m 36s
10	Hannu Pallalm (FIN)/Jyrki Ahava (FIN)	Opel Ascona	5h 18m 02s

Timo Mäkinen/Henry Liddon

ROUND 09 – AUSTRIA (12th-14th September)

01	Achim Warmbold (D)/Jean Todt (F)	BMW 2002Tii	3h 58m 55s
02	Bernard Darniche (F)/Alain Mahé (F)	Alpine-Renault A110	4h 00m 10s
03	Per Eklund (S)/Bo Reinicke (S)	Saab 96 V4	4h 00m 11s
04	Bjorn Waldegård (S)/Hans Thorszelius (S)	BMW 2002Tii	4h 01m 10s
05	Jean-Pierre Nicolas (F)/Michel Vial (F)	Alpine-Renault A110	4h 01m 25s
06	Häkan Lindberg (S)/Helmut Eisendle (I)	Fiat 124 Abarth	4h 06m 15s
07	Klaus Russling (A)/Wolfgang Weiss (A)	Porse 911	4h 06m 38s
08	Ove Andersson (S)/Gunnar Haggbom (S)	Toyota Celica	4h 09m 05s
09	Herbert Grunsteidl (A)/Georg Hopf (A)	BMW 2002	4h 10m 02s
10	Tony Fall (GB)/Mike Wood (GB)	VW Beetle 1303S	4h 11m 16s

Achim Warmbold/Jean Todt

ROUND 10 – SANREMO, ITALY (10th-13th October)

01	Jean-Luc Thérier (F)/Jacques Jaubert (F)	Alpine-Renault A110	8h 01m 32s
02	Maurizio Verini (I)/Angelo Torriani (I)	Fiat 124 Abarth	8h 07m 34s
03	Jean-Pierre Nicolas (F)/Michel Vial (F)	Alpine-Renault A110	8h 11m 37s
04	Giulio Bisulli (I)/Arturo Zanuccoli (I)	Fiat 124 Abarth	8h 13m 05s
05	Sergio Barbasio (I)/Bruno Scabini (I)	Fiat 124 Abarth	8h 13m 38s
06	Alcide Paganelli (I)/Ninni Russo (I)	Fiat 124 Abarth	8h 14m 31s
07	Mauro Pregliasco (I)/Angelo Garzoglio (I)	Lancia Fulvia HF	8h 15m 00s
08	Simo Lampinen (FIN)/Piero Sodano (I)	Lancia Fulvia HF	8h 15m 33s
09	Roberto Bauce (I)/Andrea Visconti (I)	Opel Ascona	9h 18m 17s
10	Bruno Ferraris (I)/Giorgio Vigo (I)	Lancia Fulvia HF	9h 21m 01s

Jean-Luc Thérier/Jacques Jaubert

ROUND 11 – PRESS ON REGARDLESS, UNITED STATES (31st October-4th November)			
01	Walter Boyce (CDN)/Doug Woods (CDN)	Toyota Corolla	418 pts
02	Jim Walker (USA)/Terry Palmer (USA)	Volvo 142S	439 pts
03	Jim Smiskol (USA)/Carol Smiskol (USA)	Datsun 240Z	453 pts
04	John Buffum (USA)/Wayne Zitkus (USA)	Ford Escort RS1600	459 pts
05	John Rodgers (USA)/Erik Brooks (USA)	Datsun 1600 SSS	465 pts
06	Robert Mucha (PL)/ (PL)/Ryszard Zyszkowski (PL)	Fiat 125 Polski	477 pts
07	Bill Dodd (USA)/Rudy Kren (USA)	Ford Capri 2600	484 pts
08	Jim Callon (USA)/Gary Hays (USA)	Datsun 510	488 pts
09	Steve Dorr (USA)/Rick Andersson (USA)	Datsun 510	489 pts
10	Chuck McLaren (CDN)/Doug Leverton (CDN)	Datsun 510	496 pts

Walter Boyce/Doug Woods

ROUND 12 – RAC, GREAT BRITAIN (17th-21st November)			
01	Timo Mäkinen (FIN)/Henry Liddon (GB)	Ford Escort RS1600	6h 47m 08s
02	Roger Clark (GB)/Tony Mason (GB)	Ford Escort RS1600	6h 52m 23s
03	Markku Alén (FIN)/Ilkka Kivimäki (FIN)	Ford Escort RS1600	6h 55m 26s
04	Per-Inge Walfridsson (FIN)/John Jensen (GB)	Volvo 142	7h 01m 13s
05	Jean-Pierre Nicolas (F)/Claude Roure (F)	Alpine-Renault A110	7h 03m 08s
06	Gunnar Blomqvist (S)/Ingelov Blomqvist (S)	Opel Ascona	7h 05m 44s
07	Bjorn Waldegård (S)/Hans Thorszelius (S)	BMW 2002	7h 06m 14s
08	Lars Carlsson (S)/Peter Peterson (D)	Opel Ascona	7h 09m 19s
09	Tony Fowkes (GB)/Bryan Harris (GB)	Ford Escort RS1600	7h 09m 46s
10	Sergio Barbasio (I)/Gino Macaluso (I)	BMW 2002	7h 19m 30s

Timo Mäkinen/Henry Liddon

ROUND 13 – CORSICA, FRANCE (1st-2nd December)			
01	Jean-Pierre Nicolas (F)/Michel Vial (F)	Alpine-Renault A110	5h 06m 31s
02	Jean-Francois Piot (F)/Jean de Alexandris (F)	Alpine-Renault A110	5h 14m 37s
03	Jean-Luc Thérier (F)/Mercel Callewaert (F)	Alpine-Renault A110	5h 18m 46s
04	Guy Chausseuil (F)/Christian Baron (F)	Ford Escort RS1600	5h 21m 33s
05	Francis Serpaggi (F)/Félix Mariani (F)	Alpine-Renault A110	5h 24m 37s
06	Jean-Pierre Manzagol (F)/Pierre Alessandri (F)	Alpine-Renault A110	5h 27m 31s
07	Henri Gréder (F)/'Christine' (B)	Opel Commodore	5h 52m 11s
08	'Gedehem' (F)/Vincent Laverne (F)	Porsche 911	5h 54m 13s
09	Jean-Claude Lagniez (F)/Michel Terry (F)	Alfa Romeo 2000GTV	6h 00m 06s
10	Yves Evard (F)/Gilbert Carraz (F)	Audi 80	6h 17m 47s

Jean-Pierre Nicolas/Michel Vial

FINAL MANUFACTURERS' CHAMPIONSHIP POSITIONS		
01	Alpine-Renault	147
02	Fiat	84
03	Ford	76
04	Volvo	44
05	Saab	42
06	Datsun	34
07	Citroën	33
08	BMW	28
09	Porsche	27
10	Toyota	25

1974

ROUND 01 – PORTUGAL (20th-23rd March)			
01	Raffaele Pinto (I)/Arnaldo Bernacchini (I)	Fiat 124 Abarth	6h 26m 15s
02	Acide Paganelli (I)/Ninni Russo (I)	Fiat 124 Abarth	6h 30m 12s
03	Markku Alén (FIN)/Ilkka Kivimäki (FIN)	Fiat 124 Abarth	6h 37m 17s
04	Ove Andersson (S)/Arne Hertz (S)	Toyota Corolla	6h 40m 54s
05	Harry Källström (S)/Claes Billstam (S)	Datsun 260Z	6h 54m 27s
06	Bob Neyret (F)/Yveline Vanoni (F)	Alpine Renault A110	7h 04m 18s
07	Georg Fischer (A)/Harald Gottlieb (A)	BMW 2002	7h 05m 02s
08	Francisco Romaozinho (P)/José Bernardo (P)	Citroën GS	7h 17m 04s
09	Chris Sclater (GB)/Neil Wilson (GB)	Ford Escort RS1600	7h 26m 59s
10	António Borges (P)/Miguel Sottomayor (P)	Fiat 124 Abarth	7h 27m 55s

Raffaele Pinto/Arnaldo Bernacchini

ROUND 02 – SAFARI, AFRICA (11th-15th April)			
01	Joginder Singh (EAK)/David Doig (EAK)	Mitsubishi Colt Lancer	11h 18m
02	Bjorn Waldegård (S)/Hans Thorszelius (S)	Porsche 911	11h 46m
03	Sandro Munari (I)/Lofty Drews (EAK)	Lancia Fulvia HF	12h 22m
04	Harry Källström (S)/Claes Billstam (S)	Datsun 260Z	13h 01m
05	Zully Remtulla (TAN)/Niar Jivani (TAN)	Datsun 260Z	13h 29m
06	Rauno Aaltonen (FIN)/Wolfgang Stiller (D)	Datsun 1800 SSS	13h 46m
07	Bert Shankland (TAN)/Chris Bates (EAK)	Peugeot 504	14h
08	Peter Huth (EAK)/Phillip Hechle (EAK)	Peugeot 504	14h 41m
09	Vic Preston Jr (EAK)/Roger Barnard (GB)	Ford Escort RS1600	14h 56m
10	Robin Ulyate (EAK)/Ivan Smith (EAK)	Fiat 124 Abarth	15h 13m

Joginder Singh/David Doig

ROUND 03 – 1000 LAKES, FINLAND (2nd-4th August)			
01	Hannu Mikkola (FIN)/John Davenport (GB)	Ford Escort RS1600	3h 11m 42s
02	Timo Mäkinen (FIN)/Henry Liddon (GB)	Ford Escort RS1600	3h 12m 13s
03	Markku Alén (FIN)/Ilkka Kivimäki (FIN)	Fiat Abarth 124	3h 13m 52s
04	Stig Blomqvist (S)/Hans Sylvan (S)	Saab 96 V4	3h 14m 02s
05	Simo Lampinen (FIN)/Juhani Markkanen (FIN)	Saab 96 V4	3h 17m 33s
06	Leo Kinnunen (FIN)/Atso Aho (FIN)	Fiat 124 Abarth	3h 17m 54s
07	Tapio Rainio (FIN)/Erkki Nyman (FIN)	Saab 96 V4	3h 19m 16s
08	Anders Kulläng (S)/Claes-Göran Andersson (S)	Opel Ascona	3h 21m 26s
09	Antti Ojanen (FIN)/Timo Mäkelä (FIN)	Fiat 124 Abarth	3h 21m 35s
10	Bjorn Waldegård (S)/Arnie Hertz (S)	Opel Ascona	3h 23m 05s

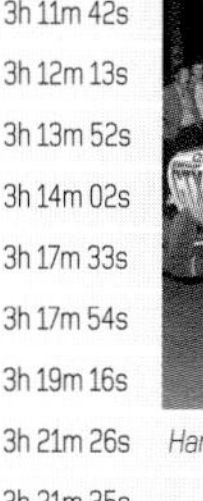

Hannu Mikkola/John Davenport

ROUND 04 – SANREMO, ITALY (2nd-5th October)			
01	Sandro Munari (I)/Mauro Mannucci (I)	Lancia Stratos	9h 12m 43s
02	Giulio Bisulli (I)/Francesco Rossetti (I)	Fiat Abarth 124	9h 20m 30s
03	Alfredo Fagnola (I)/Elvio Novarese (I)	Opel Ascona	9h 56m 09s
04	Shekhar Mehta (EAK)/Martin Holmes (GB)	Lancia Beta Coupé	9h 58m 38s
05	'Iccudrac' (I)/Dino Defendenti (I)	Porsche 911	10h 05m 59s
06	Mido Morielli (I)/Carlo Zamunaro (I)	Lancia Fulvia HF	10h 13m 12s
07	Renzo Magnani (I)/'Valentino' (I)	Lancia Fulvia HF	10h 15m 10s
08	Alain Errani (F)/Vincent Laverne (F)	Opel Ascona	10h 17m 14s
09	Paolo Isnardi (I)/Simone Scimone (I)	Opel Ascona	10h 24m 24s
10	Giorgio Bramino (I)/Giorgio d'Angelo (I)	Opel Ascona	10h 27m 15s

Sandro Munari/Mauro Mannucci

ROUND 05 – CANADA (16th-20th October)			
01	Sandro Munari (I)/Mauro Mannucci (I)	Lancia Stratos	294.53m
02	Simo Lampinen (FIN)/John Davenport (GB)	Lancia Beta Coupé	296.84m
03	Walter Boyce (CDN)/Stuart Gray (GB)	Toyota Celica	307.77m
04	Keith Billows (GB)/John Campbell (USA)	Ford Escort RS1600	316.84m
05	Eric Jones (USA)/Mark Hathaway (USA)	Datsun 510 SSS	321.17m
06	Bo Skowronnek (CDN)/Tony Woodlands (CDN)	Datsun 240Z	323.39m
07	Jacques Racine (CDN)/Michel Poirier-Defoy (CDN)	Datsun 510 SSSS10 SSS	328.03m
08	John Smiskol (USA)/Carol Smiskol (USA)	Datsun 260Z	332.52m
09	Glen Thomas (CDN)/Ron Arthur (CDN)	Datsun 510	339.74m
10	Howard Whan (CDN)/Jim Pue-Christie (CDN)	Datsun 510	353.22m

Sandro Munari/Mauro Mannucci

ROUND 06 – PRESS ON REGARDLESS, UNITED STATES (30th October-3rd November)			
01	Jean-Luc Thérier (F)/Christian Delferrier (B)	Renault 17 Gordini	5h 29m 47s
02	Markku Alén (FIN)/Atso Aho (FIN)	Fiat 124 Abarth	5h 35m 10s
03	Jean-Pierre Nicolas (F)/Geraint Phillips (GB)	Renault 17 Gordini	5h 35m 49s
04	Simo Lampinen (FIN)/John Davenport (GB)	Lancia Beta Coupé	5h 49m 48s
05	Guy Chasseuil (F)/Jean-Pierre Rouget (F)	Alpine Renault A110	5h 56m 45s
06	Bernard Darniche (F)/Alain Mahé (F)	Renault 17 Gordini	6h 05m 26s
07	Sobieslaw Zasada (PL)/Jerzy Dobrzanski (PL)	Porsche 911	6h 21m 58s
08	Bob Neyret (F)/Claudine Trautmann (F)	Alpine Renault A110	6h 22m 42s
09	Marianne Hoepfner (F)/Yveline Vanoni (F)	Alpine Renault A110	6h 35m 29s
10	Bob Hourihan (USA)/Doug Shepherd (USA)	Volvo 142	6h 40m 40s

Jean-Luc Thérier/Christian Delferrier

ROUND 07 – RAC, GREAT BRITAIN (16th - 20th November)			
01	Timo Mäkinen (FIN)/Henry Liddon (GB)	Ford Escort RS1600	8h 02m 39s
02	Stig Blomqvist (S)/Hans Sylvan (S)	Saab 96 V4	8h 04m 19s
03	Sandro Munari (I)/Piero Sodano (I)	Lancia Stratos	8h 11m 55s
04	Bjorn Waldegård (S)/Hans Thorszelius (S)	Toyota Corolla	8h 13m 54s
05	Walter Röhrl (D)/Jochen Berger (D)	Opel Ascona	8h 15m 52s
06	Per-Inge Walfridsson (FIN)/John Jensen (GB)	Volvo 142	8h 16m 09s
07	Roger Clark (GB)/Tony Mason (GB)	Ford Escort RS1600	8h 19m 06s
08	Billy Coleman (GB)/Dan O'Sullivan (GB)	Ford Escort RS1600	8h 20m 29s
09	Chris Sclater (GB)/Martin Holmes (GB)	Datsun Violet TC	8h 21m 56s
10	Simo Lampinen (FIN)/Solve Andreasson (S)	Lancia Beta Coupé	8h 21m 57s

Timo Mäkinen/Henry Liddon

ROUND 08 – CORSICA, FRANCE (30th November-1st December)			
01	Jean-Claude Andruet (F)/'Biche' (F)	Lancia Stratos	4h 49m 10s
02	Jean-Pierre Nicolas (F)/Vincent Laverne (F)	Alpine Renault A110	4h 52m 38s
03	Jean-Luc Thérier (F)/Michel Vial (F)	Alpine Renault A310	5h 12m 09s
04	Jean-Pierre Manzagol (F)/Jean-Francois Filippi (F)	Alpine Renault A110	5h 14m 43
05	Gerard Larrousse (F)/Christian Delferrier (B)	Alpine Renault A110	5h 16m 47s
06	Fulvio Bacchelli (I)/Bruno Scabini (I)	Fiat 124 Abarth	5h 26m 27s
07	Jean-Louis Clarr (F)/Jean-Francois Fauchille (F)	Opel Ascona	5h 33m 57s
08	Jean-Francois Piot (F)/Jacques Jaubert (F)	Renault 17 Gordini	5h 37m 45s
09	Jean-Marie Soriano (F)/Robert Simonetti (F)	Alpine Renault A110	6h 08m 38s
10	Guy Fréquelin/Jean Thimonier	Alfa Romeo Alfetta	6h 09m 57s

Jean-Claude Andruet/'Biche'

FINAL MANUFACTURERS' CHAMPIONSHIP POSITIONS		
01	Lancia	94
02	Fiat	69
03	Ford	54
04	Toyota	32
05	Alpine-Renault	29
06	Datsun	28
07	Porsche	27
08	Opel	27
09	Saab	25
10	Renault	23

1975

ROUND 01 – MONTE CARLO (15th-23rd January)			
01	Sandro Munari (I)/Mauro Mannucci (I)	Lancia Stratos HF	6h 25m 59s
02	Hannu Mikkola (FIN)/Jean Todt (F)	Fiat 124 Abarth	6h 29m 05s
03	Markku Alén (FIN)/Ilkka Kivimäki (FIN)	Fiat 124 Abarth	6h 29m 46s
04	Fulvio Bacchelli (I)/Bruno Scabini (I)	Fiat 124 Abarth	6h 47m 02s
05	Jean-Francois Piot (F)/Jean de Alexandris (F)	Renault 17 Gordini	6h 51m 15s
06	Jacques Henry (F)/Maurice Gélin (F)	Alpine Renault A110	6h 52m 12s
07	Jean-Pierre Rouget (F)/Patrice Chonez (F)	Porsche 911	7h 25m 00s
08	Guy Frequelin (F)/Christian Delferrier (B)	Alfa Romeo 2000GTV	7h 33m 30s
09	Noël Labaune (F)/Jean Maurin (F)	Porsche 911	7h 46m 25s
10	Christian Dorche (F)/Pierre Gertosio (F)	BMW 2002Tii	7h 49m 25s

Sandro Munari/Mauro Mannucci

ROUND 02 – SWEDEN (13th-15th February)			
01	Bjorn Waldegård (S)/Hans Thorszelius (S)	Lancia Stratos	7h 19m 46s
02	Stig Blomqvist (S)/Hans Sylvan (S)	Saab 96 V4	7h 21m 33s
03	Simo Lampinen (FIN)/Solve Andreasson	Lancia Beta Coupé	7h 31m 22s
04	Per Eklund (S)/Bjorn Cederberg (S)	Saab 96 V4	7h 33m 13s
05	Ingvar Carlsson (S)/Claes Billstam (S)	Fiat 124 Abarth	7h 39m 30s
06	Markku Alén (FIN)/Ilkka Kivimäki (FIN)	Fiat 124 Abarth	7h 49m 25s
07	John Haugland (N)/Arild Antonsen (N)	Skoda 120S	8h 14m 03s
08	Häkän Svensson (S)/Jan-Erik Andersson (S)	Opel Ascona	8h 27m 20s
09	Rune Ahlin (S)/Äke Gustavsson (S)	Volvo 142	8h 35m 34s
10	Leif Andersson (S)/Lars Nyberg (S)	Ford Escort RS2000	8h 41m 02s

Bjorn Waldegård/Hans Thorszelius

ROUND 03 – SAFARI, AFRICA (27th-31st March)			
01	Ove Andersson (S)/Arne Hertz (S)	Peugeot 504	11h 58m
02	Sandro Munari (I)/Lofty Drews (EAK)	Lancia Stratos	12h 36m
03	Bjorn Waldegård (S)/Hans Thorszelius (S)	Lancia Stratos	13h 57m
04	Andrew Cowan (GB)/John Mitchell (ZIM)	Mitsubishi Colt Lancer	14h 31m
05	Bert Shankland (TAN)/Chris Bates (EAK)	Peugeot 504	15h 01m
06	Zully Remtulla (TAN)/Nizar Jivani (TAN)	Datsun 710	16h 34m
07	John Hellier (EAK)/Kanti Shah (EAK)	Datsun 160B	18h 12m
08	Davinder Singh (EAK)/Roger Barnard (GB)	Mitsubishi Colt Lancer	19h 05m
09	Frank Tundo (EAK)/Anton Levitan (EAK)	Datsun 710	19h 15m
10	Prem Choda (EAK)/Pauru Choda (EAK)	Mitsubishi Colt Lancer	23h 01m

Ove Andersson/Arne Hertz

ROUND 04 – ACROPOLIS, GREECE (24th-31st May)			
01	Walter Röhrl (D)/Jochen Berger (D)	Opel Ascona	9h 20m 36s
02	'Siroco' (GR)/Miltos Andriopoulos (GR)	Alpine Renault A110	9h 56m 18s
03	Mihális Koumas (GR)/Pétros Dimitriadis (GR)	Mitsubishi Gallant	11h 35m 53s
04	Johnny Pesmazoglou (GR)/Dimitris Iorgitsis (GR)	Opel Ascona	11h 45m 01s
05	'Leonidas' (GR)/Ioánnis Lekkas (GR)	Audi 80GT	11h 53m 51s
06	Bernt-Inge Steffansson (S)/Ola Tholen (S)	Volvo 142GT	11h 54m 22s
07	Iórgis Moschous (GR)/Aris Stathakis (GR)	Alfa Romeo Alfetta GT	12h 03m 50s
08	Mihális Moschous (GR)/'Nikias' (GR)	Alfa Romeo Alfetta	12h 33m 12s
09	Hans-Michael Jelsdorf (DEN)/'Gliese' (DEN)	Opel Ascona	12h 42m 01s
10	'Pavlos' (GR)/Pavlos Valendis (GR)	Lada 2103	12h 53m 02s

Walter Röhrl/Jochen Berger

ROUND 05 – MOROCCO (24th-28th June)			
01	Hannu Mikkola (FIN)/Jean Todt (F)	Peugeot 504	23h 30m 48s
02	Bernard Consten (F)/Gerard Flocon (F)	Peugeot 504	25h 12m 03s
03	Robert Neyret (F)/Jacques Terramorsi (F)	Alpine Renault A110	25h 48m 19s
04	Jean Deschaseaux (MAR)/JeanPlassard (MAR)	Citroën DS23	27h 32m 52s
05	Timo Mäkinen (FIN)/Henry Liddon (GB)	Peugeot 504	28h 01m 03s
06	Shekhar Mehta (EAK)/Bob Bean (GB)	Datsun Violet	28h 09m 23s
07	Marianne Hoepfner (F)/Christine Fourton (F)	Peugeot 504	30h 51m 03s
08	Claudine Trautmann (F)/Marie-Odile Desvignes (F)	Peugeot 504	30h 5Todt6s
09	Karl Noujaim (F)/Jean-Claude Maget (F)	Peugeot 504	30h 57m 49s
10	Jacques Osstyn (MAR)/J-H Weilmann (MAR)	Volvo 142	31h 42m 53s

Hannu Mikkola/Jean Todt

ROUND 06 – PORTUGAL (18th-21st July)			
01	Markku Alén (FIN)/Ilkka Kivimäki (FIN)	Fiat 124 Abarth	6h 24m 15s
02	Hannu Mikkola (FIN)/Jean Todt (F)	Fiat 124 Abarth	6h 26m 58s
03	Ove Andersson (S)/Arne Hertz (S)	Toyota Corolla	6h 29m 29s
04	Rauno Aaltonen (FIN)/Claes Billstam (S)	Opel Ascona	6h 35m 31s
05	Pedro Cortes (P)/Teixeira Gomes (P)	Datsun 260Z	6h 45m 07s
06	Mário Figueiredo (P)/Carlos Barata (P)	Datsun 240Z	6h 53m 47s
07	Shekhar Mehta (EAK)/Yvonne Pratt (EAK)	Datsun Violet	7h 10m 30s
08	Francisco Romaozinho (P)/José Bernardo (P)	Citroën GS	7h 10m 51s
09	Fernando Lezama (E)/Javier Arnaix (E)	Ford Escort RS1600	7h 24m 53s
10	José Megre (P)/Rapso de Magalhaes (P)	Datsun 240Z	7h 38m 49s

Markku Alén/Ilkka Kivimäki

ROUND 07 – 1000 LAKES, FINLAND (29th-31st August)

Pos	Driver/Co-driver	Car	Time
01	Hannu Mikkola (FIN)/Atso Aho (FIN)	Toyota Corolla	2h 52m 33s
02	Simo Lampinen (FIN)/Juhani Markkanen (FIN)	Saab 96 V4	2h 53m 47s
03	Timo Mäkinen (FIN)/Henry Liddon (GB)	Ford Escort RS1.8	2h 54m 35s
04	Per Eklund (S)/Bjorn Cederberg (S)	Saab 96 V4	2h 54m 40s
05	Anders Kulläng (S)/Claes-Goran Andersson (S)	Opel Ascona	2h 57m 27s
06	Timo Salonen (FIN)/Jaakko Markkula (FIN)	Datsun Violet	2h 58m 11s
07	Jari Vilkas (FIN)/Juhani Soini (FIN)	Saab 96 V4	3h 00m 29s
08	Erik Aaby (N)/Monty Karlan (N)	Ford Escort RS1.6	3h 02m 26s
09	Kyösti Hamalainen (FIN)/Urpo Vihervaara (FIN)	Chrysler Avenger	3h 02m 51s
10	Antero Laine (FIN)/Raimo Alm (FIN)	Saab 96 V4	3h 04m 28s

Hannu Mikkola/Atso Aho

ROUND 08 – SANREMO, ITALY (4th-10th October)

Pos	Driver/Co-driver	Car	Time
01	Bjorn Waldegård (S)/Hans Thorszelius (S)	Lancia Stratos	10h 22m 52s
02	Maurizio Verini (I)/Francesco Rossetti (I)	Fiat 124 Abarth	10h 25m 40s
03	Jean-Luc Thérier (F)/Michel Vial (F)	Alpine Renault A110	10h 59m 04s
04	Mauro Pregliasco (I)/Piero Sodano (I)	Lancia Beta Coupé	11h 20m 11s
05	Carlo Bianchi (I)/Mauro Mannini (I)	Porsche 911 Carrera	11h 33m 29s
06	Salvatore Bray (I)/'Rudy' (I)	Opel Ascona	11h 47m 42s
07	Alberto Brambilla (I)/Giorgio Bottini (I)	Alfa Romeo Alfetta GT	12h 01m 28s
08	Georg Fischer (AUT)/Harald Gottlieb (AUT)	Opel Ascona	12h 16m 26s
09	Federico Ormezzano (I)/Enrico Cartotto (I)	Alfa Romeo 2000GTV	12h 18m 30s
10	Paolo Isnardi/Simone Scimone (I)	Opel Ascona	12h 27m 45s

Bjorn Waldegård/Hans Thorszelius

ROUND 09 – CORSICA, FRANCE (8th-9th November)

Pos	Driver/Co-driver	Car	Time
01	Bernard Darniche (F)/Alain Mahé (F)	Lancia Stratos	4h 58m 26s
02	Jean-Pierre Nicolas (F)/Vincent Laverne (F)	Alpine Renault A110	4h 58m 58s
03	Jean-Claude Andruet (F)/Yves Jouanny (F)	Alfa Romeo Alfetta GT	5h 09m 51s
04	Jean-Pierre Manzagol (F)/Jean-Francois Filippi (F)	Alpine Renault A110	5h 15m 42s
05	Jacques Henry (F)/Maurice Gelin (F)	Alpine Renault A110	5h 19m 41s
06	Francis Vincent F)/Jacques Jaubert (F)	Alpine Renault A110	5h 22m 26s
07	Michèle Mouton (F)/Francoise Conconi (F)	Alpine Renault A110	5h 33m 49s
08	Jean-Marie Soriano (F)/Robert Simonetti (F)	Alpine Renault A110	5h 52m 45s
09	Bernard Picone (F)/Robert Cianelli (F)	Alpine Renault A110	5h 52m 46s
10	Henri Gréder (F)/'Celigny' (F)	Opel Kadett GT/E	5h 58m 21s

Bernard Darniche/Alain Mahé

ROUND 10 – RAC, GREAT BRITAIN (22nd-26th November)

Pos	Driver/Co-driver	Car	Time
01	Timo Mäkinen (FIN)/Henry Liddon (GB)	Ford Escort RS1800	6h 00m 44s
02	Roger Clark (GB)/Tony Mason (GB)	Ford Escort RS1800	6h 01m 57s
03	Tony Fowkes (GB)/Bryan Harris (GB)	Ford Escort RS1600	6h 06m 11s
04	Tony Pond (GB)/David Richards (GB)	Opel Kadett GT/E	6h 12m 26s
05	Erik Aaby (N)/Per-Odnar Nyborg (N)	Ford Escort RS1600	6h 14m 14s
06	Billy Coleman (GB)/Dan O'Sullivan (GB)	Ford Escort RS1800	6h 16m 38s
07	Bengt Nilsson (S)/Lars-Erik Carlström (S)	Opel Ascona	6h 17m 53s
08	Maurizio Verini (I)/Nini Russo (I)	Fiat 124 Abarth	6h 17m 59s
09	Will Sparrow (GB)/Ron Crellin (GB)	Vauxhall Magnum	6h 18m 04s
10	Simo Lampinen (FIN)/Piero Sodano (I)	Triumph Dolomite Sprint	6h 18m 59s

Timo Mäkinen/Henry Liddon

FINAL MANUFACTURERS' CHAMPIONSHIP POSITIONS

Pos	Manufacturer	Points
01	Lancia	96
02.	Fiat	61
03.	Alpine-Renault	60
04.	Opel	58
05.	Peugeot	40
06.	Ford	35
07.	Toyota	32
08.	Saab	30
09.	Datsun	26
10.	Alfa Romeo	23

1976

ROUND 01 – MONTE CARLO (17th-24th January)

Pos	Driver/Co-driver	Car	Time
01	Sandro Munari (I)/Silvio Maiga (I)	Lancia Stratos	6h 25m 10s
02	Bjorn Waldegård (S)/Hans Thorszelius (S)	Lancia Stratos	6h 26m 37s
03	Bernard Darniche (F)/Alain Mahé (F)	Lancia Stratos	6h 31m 23s
04	Walter Röhrl (D)/Jochen Berger (D)	Opel Kadett GT/E	6h 34m 32s
05	Roger Clark (GB)/Jim Porter (GB)	Ford Escort RS1800	6h 37m 07s
06	Markku Alén (FIN)/Ilkka Kivimäki (FIN)	Fiat 124 Abarth	6h 42m 31s
07	Guy Frequelin (F)/Jacques Delaval (F)	Porsche 911	6h 44m 19s
08	Roberto Cambiaghi (I)/Bruno Scabini (I)	Fiat 124 Abarth	7h 05m 27s
09	Nicolas Koob (LUX)/Nico Demuth (LUX)	Porsche 911	7h 07m 19s
10	Bernard Beguin (F)/Jean-Francois Fauchille (F)	Alfa Romeo 2000GTV	7h 13m 47s

Sandro Munari/Silvio Maiga

ROUND 02 – SWEDEN (20th-22nd February)

Pos	Driver/Co-driver	Car	Points
01	Per Eklund (S)/Bjorn Cederberg (S)	Saab 96 V4	29,306 pts
02	Stig Blomqvist (S)/Hans Sylvan (S)	Saab 96 V4	29,402 pts
03	Anders Kulläng (S)/Claes-Goran Andersson (S)	Opel Ascona	30,670 pts
04	Simo Lampinen (FIN)/Arne Hertz (S)	Lancia Stratos	31,552 pts
05	Ulf Sundberg (S)/Mats Nordström (S)	Saab 99EMS	32,315 pts
06	Lars Carlsson (S)/Bob de Jong (NL)	Opel Kadett GT/E	32,466 pts
07	Sören Skanse (S)/Anders Johansson (S)	Volvo 142	32,727 pts
08	Sven-Inge Neby (S)/Gunnar Hendriksson (S)	Volvo 142	32,827 pts
09	Äke Gustavsson (S)/Göran Gustavsson (S)	Saab 99EMS	32,850 pts
10	Kaj Fyhrqvist (S)/Leif Malmström (FIN)	Opel Ascona	33,371 pts

Per Eklund/Bjorn Cederberg

ROUND 03 – PORTUGAL (10th-14th March)

Pos	Driver/Co-driver	Car	Time
01	Sandro Munari (I)/Silvio Maiga (I)	Lancia Stratos	5h 41m 26s
02	Ove Andersson (S)/Arne Hertz (S)	Toyota Celica	5h 44m 24s
03	'Mêqêpê' (P)/Joao Baptista (P)	Opel Kadett GT/E	6h 26m 37s
04	Raffaele Pinto (I)/Arnaldo Bernacchini (I)	Lancia Stratos	6h 33m 54s
05	Santinho Mendes (P)/Lemos Nobre (P)	Opel Kadett GT/E	6h 39m 29s
06	Georg Fischer (AUT)/Harald Gottlieb (AUT)	Datsun Violet	6h 40m 20s
07	Giovanni Salvi (P)/Pedro de Almeida (P)	Ford Escort RS2000	6h 46m 44s
08	Jorge Ortigao (P)/Pedro Abreu (P)	Mazda RX3	6h 47m 05s
09	Manuel Inácio (P)/Pina de Morais (P)	Opel Ascona	6h 52m 34s
10	Carlos Torres (P)/Augusto Roxo (P)	Mazda RX3	7h 01m 39s

Sandro Munari/Silvio Maiga

ROUND 04 – SAFARI, AFRICA (15th-19th April)

Pos	Driver/Co-driver	Car	Time
01	Joginder Singh (KEN)/David Doig (KEN)	Mitsubishi Colt Lancer	1h 57m
02	Robin Ulyate (KEN)/Chris Bates (KEN)	Mitsubishi Colt Lancer	2h 21m
03	Andrew Cowan (GB)/Johnstone Syer (KEN)	Mitsubishi Colt Lancer	2h 42m
04	Bert Shankland (TAN)/Brian Barton (KEN)	Peugeot 504	2h 52m
05	Simo Lampinen (FIN)/Arne Hertz (S)	Peugeot 504	3h 23m
06	Kenjiro Shinozuka (J)/Bob Graham (GB)	Mitsubishi Colt Lancer	4h 18m
07	Harry Källström (S)/Leif Lindqvist (S)	Datsun Violet	4h 49m
08	Zully Remtulla (TAN)/Nizar Jivani (TAN)	Datsun Violet	5h 09m
09	Jean-Pierre Nicolas (F)/Jean-Claude Lefebvre (F)	Peugeot 504	5h 11m
10	John Hellier (KEN)/Kanti Shah (KEN)	Alfa Romeo 1750	7h 14m

Joginder Singh/David Doig

ROUND 05 – ACROPOLIS, GREECE (22nd-28th May)

01	Harry Källström (S)/Claes-Goran Andersson (S)	Datsun 160J	8h 43m 14s
02	'Siroco' (GR)/Miltos Andriopoulos (GR)	Alpine Renault A110	8h 48m 38s
03	Shekhar Mehta (KEN)/Henry Liddon (GB)	Datsun 160J	9h 09m 53s
04	Iórgis Moschous (GR)/Dimitri Arvanitakis (GR)	Alfa Romeo Alfetta GT	9h 32m 23s
05	Klaus Russling (AUT)/Manfred Essig (AUT)	Opel Ascona	9h 52m 18s
06	Stasys Brundza (URS)/Arvydas Girdauskas (URS)	Lada 1500	9h 54m 16s
07	Ioánnis Papadamandiou (GR)/Kóstas Tsavos (GR)	BMW 2002Ti	10h 41m 57s
08	Leo Schirnhofer (AUT)/Harald Gottlieb (AUT)	VW Beetle 1303S	10h 42m 50s
09	Horst Rausch (D)/Jutta Fellbaum (D)	BMW 2002tii	10h 46m 19s
10	Horst Niebergall (D)/Bernd Fromann (D)	Wartburgs	

Harry Källström/Claes-Goran Andersson

ROUND 06 – MOROCCO (22nd-27th June)

01	Jean-Pierre Nicolas (F)/Michel Gamet (F)	Peugeot 504	20h 20m 15s
02	Simo Lampinen (FIN)/Atso Aho (FIN)	Peugeot 504	20h 42m 52s
03	Sandro Munari (ITA)/Silvio Maiga (ITA)	Lancia Stratos	21h 38m 38s
04	Jean Deschazeaux (MAR)/Jean Plassard (MAR)	Citroën CX2200	21h 44m 45s
05	Jean-Claude Lefebvre (F)/Gerard Flocon (F)	Peugeot 504	22h 06m 54s
06	Jacky Privé (F)/'Tilber' (MON)	Renault 17 Gordini	22h 34m 17s
07	Marianne Hoepfner (F)/'Biche'' (F)	Peugeot 504	22h 40m 51s
08	Christine Dacremont (F)/Yveline Vanoni (F)	Peugeot 504	22h 52m 07s
09	Jean Guichet (F)/Jacques Jaubert (F)	Peugeot 504	22h 59m 05s
10	Jean-Claude Briavoine (F)/Robert Schneck (F)	Renault 12 Gordini	22h 59m 08s

Jean-Pierre Nicolas/Michel Gamet

ROUND 07 – 1000 LAKES, FINLAND (27th-29th August)

01	Markku Alén (FIN)/Ilkka Kivimäki (FIN)	Fiat 131 Abarth	4h 10m 18s
02	Pentti Airikkala (FIN)/Risto Virtanen (FIN)	Ford Escort RS1800	4h 11m 03s
03	Hannu Mikkola (FIN)/Arne Hertz (S)	Toyota Celica	4h 13m 32s
04	Timo Mäkinen (FIN)/Henry Liddon (GB)	Ford Escort RS1800	4h 17m 12s
05	Simo Lampinen (FIN)/Juhani Markkanen (FIN)	Saab 96 V4	4h 20m 00s
06	Timo Salonen (FIN)/Jaakko Markkula (FIN)	Datsun Violet	4h 20m 06s
07	Tapio Rainio (FINN)/Erkki Nyman (FIN)	Saab 96 V4	4h 21m 39s
08	Jari Vilkas (FIN)/Juhani Siono (FIN)	Saab 96 V4	4h 25m 12s
09	Markku Saaristo (FIN)/Timo Alanen (FIN)	Ford Escort RS2000	4h 25m 44s
10	Leif Asterhag (S)/Claes Billstam (S)	Toyota Corolla	4h 29m 16s

Markku Alén/Ilkka Kivimaki

ROUND 08 – SANREMO, ITALY (6th-9th October)

01	Bjorn Waldegård (S)/Hans Thorszelius (S)	Lancia Stratos	10h 27m 40s
02	Sandro Munari (ITA)/Silvio Maiga (ITA)	Lancia Stratos	10h 27m 44s
03	Rafaelle Pinto (ITA)/Arnaldo Bernacchini (ITA)	Lancia Stratos	10h 37m 13s
04	'Tony' Fassina (ITA)/Mauro Mannini	Lancia Stratos	10h 59m 22s
05	Amilcare Ballestrieri (ITA)/Sergio Maiga (ITA)	Opel Kadett GT/E	11h 13m 46s
06	Livio Lorenzelli (ITA)/Mario Necco (ITA)	Fiat 124 Abarth	11h 20m 29s
07	Federico Ormezzano (ITA)/'Rudy' (ITA)	Opel Kadett GT/E	11h 35m 51s
08	'Lucky' (ITA)/Giovanni Braito (ITA)	Opel Kadett GT/E	11h 48m 42s
09	Chritian Gardavot (F)/Daniele Roux (F)	Porsche 911	11h 55m 32s
10	Angelo Presotto (ITA)/Maurizio Perissinot (ITA)	Opel Kadett GT/E	11h 58m 03s

Bjorn Waldegård/Hans Thorszelius

ROUND 09 – CORSICA, FRANCE (6th-7th November)

01	Sandro Munari (ITA)/Silvio Maiga (ITA)	Lancia Stratos	8h 23m 55s
02	Bernard Darniche (F)/Alain Mahé (F)	Lancia Strato (F)	8h 24m 12s
03	Jean-Pierre Manzagol (F)/Jean-Francois Filippi (F)	Alpine Renault A310	8h 49m 14s
04	Jean Ragnotti (F)/Jacques Jaubert (F)	Alpine Renault A310	8h 59m 28s
05	Jacques Alméras (F)/Christian Delferrier (B)	Porsche 911	9h 19m 10s
06	Pierre-Louis Moreau (F)/Patrice Baron (F)	Alpine Renault A110	9h 41m 33s
07	Daniel Rognoni (F)/Gilbert Dini (F)	Porsche 911	9h 48m 48s
08	Jean-Claude Sevelinge (ITA)/Joseph Sevelinge (F)	Opel Kadett GT/E	9h 56m 28s
09	Henri Gréder (F)/'Celigny' (ITA)	Opel Kadett GT/E	10h 06m 28s
10	Hannu Mikkola (FIN)/Jean Todt (F)	Peugeot 104ZS	10h 13m 51s

Sandro Munari/Silvio Maiga

ROUND 10 – RAC, GREAT BRITAIN (27th-30th November)

01	Roger Clark (GB)/Stuart Pegg (RSA)	Ford Escort RS1800	6h 02m 26s
02	Stig Blomqvist (S)/Hans Sylvan (S)	Saab 99EMS	6h 07m 03s
03	Bjorn Waldegård (S)/Hans Thorszelius (S)	Ford Escort RS1800	6h 07m 55s
04	Sandro Munari (ITA)/Silvio Maiga (ITA)	Lancia Stratos	6h 08m 49s
05	Ove Andersson (S)/Martin Holmes (GB)	Toyota Corolla	6h 11m 43s
06	Billy Coleman (GB)/Dan O'Sullivan (GB)	Ford Escort RS1800	6h 11m 48s
07	Anders Kulläng (S)/Claes-Göran Andersson (S)	Opel Kadett GT/E	6h 15m 13s
08	Andy Dawson (GB)/Andrew Marriott (GB)	Datsun Violet	6h 22m 07s
09	Brian Culchetlcheth (GB)/Johnstone Syer (KEN)	Triumph TR7	6h 22m 54s
10	Bror Danielsson (S)/Ulf Sundberg (S)	Opel Kadett GT/E	6h 24m 28s

Roger Clark/Stuart Pegg

FINAL MANUFACTURERS' CHAMPIONSHIP POSITIONS

01	Lancia	112
02	Opel	57
03	Ford	47
04	Saab	43
05	Datsun	39
06	Toyota	35
07	Fiat	32
08	Peugeot	31
09	Alpine-Renault	27
10	Mitsubishi	20

1977

ROUND 01 – MONTE CARLO (22nd-28th January)

01	Sandro Munari (I)/Silvio Maiga (I)	Lancia Stratos	6h 36m 13s
02	Jean-Claude Andruet (F)/'Biche' (F)	Fiat 131 Abarth	6h 38m 29s
03	Antonio Zanini (E)/Juan Petisco (E)	SEAT 124 Especial	6h 47m 07s
04	Salvador Canellas (E)/Daniel Ferrater (E)	SEAT 124 Especial	6h 55m 03s
05	Gérard Swaton (F)/Colette Galli (F)	Lancia Stratos	6h 59m 17s
06	Christine Dacremont (F)/Colette Galli (F)	Lancia Stratos	7h 01m 10s
07	Salvador Servia (E)/Jorge Sabater (E)	SEAT 1430/1800	7h 02m 08s
08	Daniel de Meyer (F)/Omer Veran (F)	Alpine Renault A110	7h 05m 15s
09	Nicolas Koob (LUX)/Nico Demuth (LUX)	Porsche 911	7h 07m 20s
10	Ingvar Carlsson (S)/Bob de Jong (NL)	Opel Kadett GT/E	7h 08m 56s

Sandro Munari/Silvio Maiga

ROUND 02 – SWEDEN (11th-13th February)

01	Stig Blomqvist (S)/Hans Sylvan (S)	Saab 99EMS	8h 02m 17s
02	Bror Danielsson (S)/Ulf Sundberg (S)	Opel Kadett GT/E	8h 08m 19s
03	Anders Kulläng (S)/Bruno Berglund (S)	Opel Kadett GT/E	8h 08m 32s
04	Simo Lampinen (FIN)/Solve Andreasson (S)	Fiat Abarth 131	8h 13m 15s
05	Kyösti Hämäläinen (FIN)/Juhani Korhonen (FIN)	Ford Escort RS2000	8h 21m 43s
06	Hans Avelin (S)/Ragnar Spjuth (S)	Opel Ascona	8h 30m 26s
07	Leif Asterhag (S)/Claes Billstam (S)	Toyota Celica	8h 34m 49s
08	Sven-Inge Neby (S)/Gunnar Hendriksson (S)	Volvo 142	8h 36m 14s
09	Ola Stromberg (S)/Per Carlsson (S)	Saab 96 V4	8h 40m 00s
10	Per Engseth (N)/Asbjorn Floene (N)	Lada 1500	8h 40m 13s

Stig Blomqvist/Hans Sylvan

ROUND 03 – PORTUGAL (1st-6th March)			
01	Markku Alén (FIN)/Ilkka Kivimäki (FIN)	Fiat 131 Abarth	6h 51m 47s
02	Bjorn Waldegård (S)/Hans Thorszelius (S)	Ford Escort RS	6h 55m 43s
03	Ove Andersson (S)/Henry Liddon (GB)	Toyota Celica	6h 56m 08s
04	Jean-Claude Andruet (F)/Christian Delferrier (B)	Fiat 131 Abarth	7h 06m 34s
05	Maurizio Verini (I)/Ninni Russo (I)	Fiat 131 Abarth	7h 07m 00s
06	'Mêqêpê' (P)/Miguel Vilar (P)	Opel Kadett GT/E	7h 28m 55s
07	Franz Wittmann (AUT)/Kurt Nestinger (AUT)	Opel Kadett GT/E	7h 38m 27s
08	Giovanni Zerla Salvi (P)/Pedro de Almeida (P)	Ford Escort RS2000	7h 44m 32s
09	Américo Nunes (P)/Mira Amaral (P)	Porsche 911	7h 46m 36s
10	Klaus Russling (AUT)/Klaus Krammer (AUT)	Opel Kadett GT/E	7h 46m 43s

Markku Alén/Ilkka Kivimäki

ROUND 04 – SAFARI, AFRICA (7th-11th April)			
01	Bjorn Waldegård (S)/Hans Thorszelius (S)	Ford Escort RS1800	11h 05m
02	Rauno Aaltonen (FIN)/Lofty Drews (EAK)	Datsun Violet	11h 40m
03	Sandro Munari (I)/Piero Sodano (I)	Lancia Stratos	13h 14m
04	Andrew Cowan (GB)/Paul White (GB)	Mitsubishi Colt Lancer	13h 16m
05	Joginder Singh (EAK)/David Doig (EAK)	Mitsubishi Colt Lancer	14h 12m
06	Davinder Singh (EAK)/Chris Bates (EAK)	Mitsubishi Colt Lancer	14h 34m
07	Bert Shankland (TAN)/Brian Barton (EAK)	Peugeot 504	17h 30m
08	Zully Remtulla (TAN)/Nizar Jivani (TAN)	Datsun Violet	18h 16m
09	Rob Collinge (EAK)/Anton Levitan (EAK)	Datsun 160J	20h 32m
10	Kenjiro Shinozuka (J)/Quentin Thompson (EAK)	Mitsubishi Colt Lancer	27h 40m

Bjorn Waldegård/Hans Thorszelius

ROUND 05 – NEW ZEALAND (1st-7th May)			
01	Fulvio Bacchelli (I)/Francesco Rossetti (I)	Fiat 131 Abarth	24h 29m 55s
02	Ari Vatanen (FIN)/Jim Scott (NZ)	Ford Escort RS1800	24h 31m 29s
03	Markku Alén (FIN)/Ilkka Kivimäki (FIN)	Fiat 131 Abarth	24h 51m 54s
04	Simo Lampinen (FIN)/Solve Andreasson (S)	Fiat 131 Abarth	24h 55m 47s
05	Rod Millen (NZ)/Mike Franchi (NZ)	Mazda RX3	25h 47m 59s
06	John Woolf (NZ)/Grant Whittaker (NZ)	Mazda RX3	26h 09m 39s
07	John Sergel (NZ)/Mike Fletcher (NZ)	Ford Escort RS1800	28h 12m 48s
08	Richard Tippett (NZ)/Adrian Hercock (NZ)	Ford Escort RS2000	28h 21m 45s
09	Morrie Chandler (NZ)/Don Campbell (NZ)	Mitsubishi Colt Lancer	28h 26m 41s
10	Alan Brough (NZ)/Mike Galvin (NZ)	Toyota Trueno	28h 45m 13s

Fulvio Bacchelli/Francesco Rossetti

ROUND 06 – ACROPOLIS, GREECE (28th May-3rd June)			
01	Bjorn Waldegård (S)/Hans Thorszelius (S)	Ford Escort RS1800	9h 31m 57s
02	Roger Clark (GB)/Jim Porter (GB)	Ford Escort RS1800	9h 37m 44s
03	Harry Källström (S)/Claes Billstam (S)	Datsun Violet	9h 47m 19s
04	Simo Lampinen (FIN)/Solve Andreasson (S)	Fiat 131 Abarth	9h 54m 42s
05	'Siroco' (GR)/Manólis Makrinos (GR)	Datsun 160J	10h 10m 27s
06	Jean-Paul Luc (F)/Michel Prud'homme (F)	Citroën CX2400	11h 27m 41s
07	Alain Oger (F)/Jean-Pierre Dupuis (F)	Renault 12 Gordini	11h 28m 32s
08	Kypros Kyprianou (CYP)/Alkis Loginos (CYP)	Chrysler Avenger	11h 48m 57s
09	Johnny Pesmazoglou (GR)/Haris Kaltsounis (GR)	Opel Ascona	11h 49m 11s
10	Roland de Libran (F)/Jean-Louis Vial (F)	Renault 17	12h 06m 11s

Bjorn Waldegård/Hans Thorszelius

ROUND 07 – 1000 LAKES, FINLAND (26th-28th August)			
01	Kyösti Hämäläinen (FIN)/Martti Tiukkanen (FIN)	Ford Escort RS1800	4h 26m 06s
02	Timo Salonen (FIN)/Jaakko Markkula (FIN)	Fiat 131 Abarth	4h 30m 31s
03	Bjorn Waldegaard (S)/Claes Billstam (S)	Ford Escort RS1800	4h 36m 22s
04	Markku Saaristo (FIN)/Timo Alanen (FIN)	Toyota Corolla	4h 45m 41s
05	Henri Toivonen (FIN)/Antero Lindqvist (FIN)	Chrysler Avenger	4h 52m 25s
06	Erkki Pitkänen (FIN)/Juhani Paalama (FIN)	Chrysler Avenger	4h 58m 29s
07	Franz Wittmann (A)/Helmut Deimel (D)	Opel Kadett GT/E	5h 01m 08s
08	Kyösti Saari (FIN)/Jorma Hakanen (FIN)	Opel Kadett GT/E	5h 05m 47s
09	Timo Jouhki (FIN)/Juha Piironen (FIN)	Opel Kadett GT/E	5h 08m 03s
10	John Haugland (N)/Bruno Berglund (S)	Skoda 130RS	5h 09m 45s

Kyösti Hämäläinen/Martti Tiukkanen

ROUND 08 – CANADA (14th-18th September)			
01	Timo Salonen (FIN)/Jaakko Markkula (FIN)	Fiat 131 Abarth	5h 13m 54s
02	Simo Lampinen (FIN)/Solve Andreasson (S)	Fiat 131 Abarth	5h 18m 31s
03	Roger Clark (GB)/Jim Porter (GB)	Ford Escort RS	5h 20m 56s
04	John Buffum (USA)/'Vicki' (USA)	Triumph TR7	5h 55m 54s
05	Jean-Paul Pérusse (CDN)/John Bellefleur (CDN)	Saab 96EMS	6h 10m 59s
06	Kenjiro Shinozuka (J)/Ron Richardson (USA)	Mitsubishi Colt Lancer	6h 12m 27s
07	Hendrik Blok (USA)/Rich Crandall (USA)	Mitsubishi Colt Lancer	6h 16m 54s
08	Walter Boyce (CDN)/Robin Edwardes (CDN)	Triumph TR7	6h 49m 46s
09	Paul Bourgeois (CDN)/Paul Normand (CDN)	Datsun 510	6h 58m 02s
10	Bob Garside (CDN)/Gary Murakami (CDN)	Toyota Corolla	7h 10m 28s

Timo Salonen/Jaakko Markkula

ROUND 09 – SANREMO, ITALY (4th-8th October)			
01	Jean-Claude Andruet (F)/Christian Delferrier (B)	Fiat 131 Abarth	10h 27m 43s
02	Maurizio Verini (I)/Bruno Scabini (I)	Fiat 131 Abarth	10h 29m 40s
03	'Tony' Fassina (I)/Mauro Mannini (I)	Fiat 131 Abarth	10h 36m 30s
04	Mauro Pregliasco (I)/Vittorio Reisoli (I)	Lancia Stratos	10h 38m 30s
05	Bjorn Waldegaard (S)/Hans Thorszelius (S)	Ford Escort RS1800	10h 41m 19s
06	Federico Ormezzano (I)/Renato Meiohas (I)	Opel Kadett GT/E	10h 57m 01s
07	Jean Ragnotti (F)/Jean-Marc Andrie (F)	Renault 5 Alpine	11h 08m 48s
08	Angelo Presotto (I)/Mirko Perissutti (I)	Opel Kadett GT/E	11h 21m 22s
09	Orlando Dall'Ava (I)/Alberto Russo (I)	Alfa Romeo Alfetta GT	11h 29m 50s
10	Christian Gardavot (F)/Gérard Otto (F)	Porsche 911	11h 32m 43s

Jean-Claude Andruet/Christian Delferrier

ROUND 10 – CORSICA, FRANCE (5th-6th November)			
01	Bernard Darniche (F)/Alain Mahé (F)	Fiat 131 Abarth	8h 13m 40s
02	Raffaele Pinto (I)/Arnaldo Bernacchini (I)	Lancia Stratos	8h 17m 07s
03	Fulvio Bacchelli (I)/Bruno Scabini (I)	Fiat 131 Abarth	8h 24m 07s
04	Tony Carello (I)/Maurizio Perissinot (I)	Lancia Stratos	8h 25m 02s
05	Francis Vincent (F) /Francis Calvier (F)	Fiat 131 Abarth	8h 30m 01s
06	Jacques Alméras (F)/'Tilber' (MON)	Porsche 911	8h 34m 24s
07	Maurizio Verini (I)/Ninni Russo (I)	Fiat 131 Abarth	8h 49m 58s
08	Michèle Mouton (F)/Francoise Conconi (F)	Fiat 131 Abarth	8h 50m 48s
09	Gérard Swaton (F)/Bernard Cordesse (F)	Porsche 911	8h 58m 39s
10	Jean-Claude Lefebvre (F)/Jean Todt (F)	Peugeot 104ZS	8h 59m 01s

Bernard Darniche/Alain Mahé

ROUND 11 – RAC, GREAT BRITAIN (20th-24th November)			
01	Bjorn Waldegård (S)/Hans Thorszelius (S)	Ford Escort RS1800	8h 21m 26s
02	Hannu Mikkola (FIN)/Arne Hertz (S)	Toyota Celica	8h 23m 49s
03	Russell Brookes (GB)/John Brown (GB)	Ford Escort RS1800	8h 31m 55s
04	Roger Clark (GB)/Stuart Pegg (RSA)	Ford Escort RS1800	8h 36m 21s
05	Andy Dawson (GB)/Andrew Marriott (GB)	Ford Escort RS1800	8h 39m 46s
06	Kyösti Hämäläinen (FIN)/Howard Scott (GB)	Ford Escort RS1800	8h 42m 17s
07	Simo Lampinen (FIN)/Solve Andreasson (S)	Fiat 131 Abarth	8h 44m 24s
08	Tony Pond (GB)/Fred Gallagher (GB)	Triumph TR7	8h 45m 04s
09	Per Eklund (S)/Bjorn Cederberg (S)	Saab 99EMS	8h 46m 02s
10	Bror Danielsson (S)/Mike Broad (GB)	Opel Kadett GT/E	8h 46m 22s

Bjorn Waldegård/Hans Thorszelius

FINAL MANUFACTURERS' CHAMPIONSHIP POSITIONS		
01	Fiat	136
02	Ford	132
03	Toyota	68
04	Opel	65
05	Lancia	60
06	Datsun	40
07	Porsche	35
08	Saab	30
09	Mitsubishi	28
10	Chrysler	24

1978

ROUND 01 – MONTE CARLO (21st-28th January)

01	Jean-Pierre Nicolas (F)/Vincent Laverne (F)	Porsche 911	6h 57m 03s
02	Jean Ragnotti (F)/Jean-Marc Andrié (F)	Renault 5 Alpine	6h 58m 55s
03	Guy Fréquelin (F)/Jacques Delaval (F)	Renault 5 Alpine	6h 59m 55s
04	Walter Röhrl (D)/Christian Geistdörfer (D)	Fiat 131 Abarth	7h 00m 22s
05	Bernard Darniche (F)/Alain Mahé (F)	Fiat 131 Abarth	7h 02m 44s
06	Jean-Claude Andruet (F)/'Biche' (F)	Fiat 131 Abarth	7h 03m 23s
07	Michèle Mouton (F)/Francoise Conconi (F)	Lancia Stratos	7h 05m 50s
08	Mauirizio Verini (I)/Francesco Rossetti (I)	Fiat 131 Abarth	7h 09m 01s
09	Anders Kulläng (S)/Bruno Berglund (S)	Opel Kadett GT/E	7h 11m 41s
10	Fulvio Bacchelli (I)/Arnaldo Bernacchini (I)	Lancia Stratos	7h 11m 58s

Jean-Pierre Nicolas/Vincent Laverne

ROUND 02 – SWEDEN (10th-12th February)

01	Bjorn Waldegård (S)/Hans Thorszelius (S)	Ford Escort RS	6h 42m 40s
02	Hannu Mikkola (FIN)/Arne Hertz (S)	Ford Escort RS	6h 44m 08s
03	Markku Alén (FIN)/Ilkka Kivimäki (FIN)	Fiat 131 Abarth	6h 45m 26s
04	Stig Blomqvist (S)/Hans Sylvan (S)	Lancia Stratos	6h 48m 11s0
05	Ari Vatanen (FIN)/Atso Aho (FIN)	Ford Escort RS	6h 50m 01s
06	Simo Lampinen (FIN)/Solve Andreasson (S)	Fiat 131 Abarth	6h 56m 15s
07.	Bror Danielsson (S)/Klas Edqvist (S)	Opel Kadett GT/E	6h 59m 45s
08	Lars-Erik Walfridsson (S)/Per-Arne Persson (S)	Volvo 142	7h 17m 11s
09	Ola Strömberg (S)/Hans-Jöran Ericson (S)	Saab 96 V4	7h 18m 02s
10	Kjell Melin (S)/Ola Hellgren (S)	VW Golf GTi	7h 19m 39s

Bjorn Waldegård/Hans Thorszelius

ROUND 03 – SAFARI, AFRICA (23rd-27th March)

01	Jean-Pierre Nicolas (F)/Jean-Claude Lefèbvre (F)	Peugeot 504 V6 Coupé	8h 18m
02	Vic Preston (EAK)/John Lyall (EAK)	Porsche 911SC	8h 55m
03	Rauno Aaltonen (FIN)/Lofty Drews (EAK)	Datsun 160J	9h 10m
04	Bjorn Waldegård (S)/Hans Thorszelius (S)	Porsche 911SC	9h 49m
05	Simo Lampinen (FIN)/Henry Liddon (GB)	Peugeot 504 V6 Coupé	13h 37m
06	Sobieslaw Zasada (PL)/Blazej Krupa (PL)	Mercedes-Benz 280	15h 30m
07	John Hellier (EAK)/Kanti Shah (EAK)	Datsun 160J	18h 26m
08	Frank Tundo (EAK)/David Haworth (EAK)	Ford Escort RS	18h 54m
09	Jayant Shah (EAK)/Najeet Eisa (EAK)	Datsun 160J	20h 44m
10	Hans-Peter Ruedin (EAK)/Ekhardt Ender (EAK)	Mitsubishi Lancer	20h 50m

Jean-Pierre Nicolas/Jean-Claude Lefèbvre

ROUND 04 – PORTUGAL (19th-23rd April)

01	Markku Alén (FIN)/Ilkka Kivimaki (FIN)	Fiat 131 Abarth	7h 45m 33s
02	Hannu Mikkola (FIN)/Arne Hertz (S)	Ford Escort RS	7h 50m 01s
03	Jean-Pierre Nicolas (F)/Vincent Laverne (F)	Ford Escort RS	8h 01m 01s
04	Ove Andersson (S)/Henry Liddon (GB)	Toyota Celica	8h 13m 27s
05	Achim Warmbold (D)/Claes Billstam (S)	Opel Kadett GT/E	8h 28m 42s
06	Anders Kulläng (S)/Bruno Berglund (S)	Opel Kadett GT/E	8h 36m 42s
07	Timo Mäkinen (FIN)/Jean Todt (F)	Peugeot 104 ZS	8h 50m 36s
08	Carlos Torres (P)/Pedro de Almeida (P)	Ford Escort RS	9h 11m 35s
09	Andre Martinho (P)/António Morais (P)	Porsche Carrera	9h 31m 24s
10	Carlos Fontainhas (P)/Rogério Seromenho (P)	Ford Escort RS	9h 46m 36s

Markku Alén/Ilkka Kivimaki

ROUND 05 – ACROPOLIS, GREECE (29th May-2nd June)

01	Walter Röhrl (D)/Christian Geistdörfer (D)	Fiat 131 Abarth	10h 00m 50s
02	Markku Alén (FIN)/Ilkka Kivimäki (FIN)	Fiat 131 Abarth	10h 10m 54s
03	Shekhar Mehta (EAK)/Yvonne Mehta (EAK)	Datsun 160J	10h 23m 36s
04	Harry Källström (S)/Claes Billstam (S)	Datsun 160J	10h 24m 01s
05	Achim Warmbold (D)/Hans Sylvan (S)	Opel Kadett GT/E	10h 54m 19s
06	'Siroco' (GR)/Manólis Makrinos (GR)	Lancia Stratos	11h 04m 17s
07	Billy Coleman (GB)/Jim Porter (GB)	Ford Escort RS	11h 13m 49s
08	Evangelos Gallo (GR)/Andreas Arkentis (GR)	Toyota Celica	11h 36m 32s
09	Miloslav Zapadlo (CZ)/Jirí Motal (CZ)	Skoda 130RS	11h 41m 23s
10	Stasys Brundza (URS)/Arvydas Girdaudskas (URS)	Lada 1600	11h 44m 49s

Walter Röhrl/Christian Geistdörfer

ROUND 06 – 1000 LAKES, FINLAND (25th-27th August)

01	Markku Alén (FIN)/Ilkka Kivimäki (FIN)	Fiat 131 Abarth	3h 30m 10s
02	Timo Salonen (FIN)/Erkki Nyman (FIN)	Fiat 131 Abarth	3h 32m 14s
03	Pentti Airikkala (FIN)/Risto Virtanen (FIN)	Vauxhall Chevette 2300HS	3h 32m 50s
04	Per Eklund (S)/Bjorn Cederberg (S)	Porsche 911	3h 38m 25s
05	Simo Lampinen (FIN)/Juhani Markkanen (FIN)	Fiat 131 Abarth	3h 40m 54s
06	Tapio Rainio (FIN)/Jaakko Markkula (FIN)	Toyota Celica	3h 42m 25s
07	Anders Kulläng (S)/Bruno Berglund (S)	Opel Kadett GT/E	3h 43m 08s
08	Kyösti Hämäläinen (FIN)/Juhani Korhonen (FIN)	Ford Escort RS	3h 46m 34s
09	Leif Asterhag (S)/Anders Gullberg (S)	Toyota Celica	3h 46m 50s
10	Markku Saaristo (FIN)/Timo Alanen (FIN)	Toyota Celica	3h 48m 47s

Markku Alén/Ilkka Kivimäki

ROUND 07 – CANADA (13th-17th September)

01	Walter Röhrl (D)/Christian Geistdörfer (D)	Fiat 131 Abarth	4h 54m 23s
02	Markku Alén (FIN)/Ilkka Kivimäki (FIN)	Fiat 131 Abarth	5h 02m 56s
03	Anders Kulläng (S)/Bruno Berglund (S)	Opel Kadett GT/E	5h 12m 46s
04	Taisto Heinonen (CDN)/John Bellefleur (CDN)	Toyota Celica	5h 34m 07s
05	Jean-Paul Pérusse (CDN)/Louis Belanger (CDN)	Triumph TR7	5h 36m 56s
06	Carlos Torres (P)/Pedro de Almeida (P)	Ford Escort RS2000	5h 58m 20s
07	Man Bergsteijn (NL)/Dirk Buwalda (NL)	Opel Kadett GT/E	6h 16m 37s
08	Hendrik Blok (USA)/Gene Hammond (USA)	Saab 99 EMS	6h 24m 26s
09	Gordon McCallum (CDN)/Linda McCallum (CDN)	VW Golf	6h 25m 24s
10	Walter Boyce (CDN)/Robin Edwardes (CDN)	Saab 99EMS	6h 29m 15s

Walter Röhrl/Christian Geistdörfer

ROUND 08 – SANREMO, ITALY (3rd-7th October)

01	Markku Alén (FIN)/Ilkka Kivimäki (FIN)	Lancia Stratos	10h 53m 28s
02	Maurizio Verini (I)/Arnaldo Bernacchini (I)	Fiat 131 Abarth	11h 04m 00s
03	Francis Vincent (F)/Willy Lux (B)	Porsche 911	11h 10m 31s
04	'Bip-Bip' (I)/Mirko Perissutti (I)	Porsche 911	11h 27m 52s
05	Mauro Pregliasco (I)/Vittorio Reisoli (I)	Alfa Romeo Alfetta GT	11h 30m 48s
06	Angelo Presotto (I)/Max Sghedoni (I)	Ford Escort RS2000	11h 46m 17s
07	Christian Gardavot (F)/Gérard Otto (F)	Porsche 911	11h 47m 26s
08	Christina Lunel (F)/Denise Emmanuelli (F)	Opel Kadett GT/E	12h 08m 16s
09	Fabrizia Pons (I)/Gabriella Zappia (I)	Opel Kadett GT/E	12h 10m 12s
10	Charles Alberti (F)/'Tout a Fond' (F)	Opel Kadett GT/E	13h 30m 56s

Markku Alén/Ilkka Kivimäki

ROUND 09 – IVORY COAST, AFRICA (21st-24th October)

01	Jean-Pierre Nicolas (F)/Michel Gamet (F)	Peugeot 504 V6 Coupé	2h 28m
02	Timo Mäkinen (FIN)/Jean Todt (F)	Peugeot 504 V6 Coupé	2h 43m
03	Jean Ragnotti (F)/Jean-Marc Andrié (F)	Renault 5 Alpine	3h 50m
04	Simo Lampinen (FIN)/Atso Aho (FIN)	Peugeot 504 V6 Coupé	5h 07m
05	Guy Fréquelin (F)/Jacques Delaval (F)	Renault 5 Alpine	5h 34m
06	Jean-Francois Vincens (F)/Felix Giallolacci (F)	Mitsubishi Colt Lancer	10h 17m
07	Kal Noujaim (F)/Jean-Claude Mages (F)	Mitsubishi Colt Lancer	11h 20m
08	Samir Assef (LEB)/Jean-Yves Burelle (CI)	Peugeot 504 V6 Coupe	12h 04m
09	Hervé Page (CI)/Philippe Saget (CI)	Datsun Violet	16h 20m
	Only 9 finishers		

Jean-Pierre Nicolas/Michel Gamet

ROUND 10 – CORSICA FRANCE (4th-5th November)

01	Bernard Darniche (F)/Alain Mahé (F)	Fiat 131 Abarth	6h 47m 34s
02	Jean-Claude Andruet (F)/'Biche' (F)	Fiat 131 Abarth	6h 51m 59s
03	Sandro Munari (I)/Mauro Mannucci (I)	Fiat 131 Abarth	6h 52m 59s
04	Jacques Alméras (F)/Jean-Claude Perramond (F)	Porsche 911	6h 57m 44s
05	Michèle Mouton (F)/Francoise Conconi (F)	Fiat 131 Abarth	6h 58m 12s
06	Pierre-Louis Moreau (F)/Patrice Baron (F)	Porsche 911	7h 05m 11s
07	Jean-Pierre Nicolas (F)/Vincent Laverne (F)	Opel Kadett GT/E	7h 06m 09s
08	Daniel Rognoni (F)/Gilbert Dini (F)	Porsche 911	7h 17m 55s
09	Claude Balesi (F)/Jean-Paul Cirindini (F)	Alpine-Renault A110	7h 19m 19s
10	Christian Dorche (F)/Jean-Francois Fauchille (F)	Opel Kadett GT/E	7h 31m 03s

Bernard Darniche/Alain Mahé

ROUND 11 – RAC, GREAT BRITAIN (19th-23rd November)

01	Hannu Mikkola (FIN)/Arne Hertz (S)	Ford Escort RS	8h 47m 23s
02	Bjorn Waldegård (S)/Hans Thorszelius (S)	Ford Escort RS	8h 52m 41s
03	Russell Brookes (GB)/Derek Tucker (GB)	Ford Escort RS	8h 58m 55s
04	Tony Pond (GB)/Fred Gallagher (GB)	Triumph TR7 V8	9h 03m 09s
05	Anders Kulläng (S)/Bruno Berglund (S)	Opel Kadett GT/E	9h 13m 48s
06	Walter Röhrl (D)/Christian Geistdorfer (D)	Fiat 131 Abarth	9h 17m 47s
07	John Taylor (GB)/Phil Short (GB)	Ford Escort RS1800	9h 19m 20s
08	Andy Dawson (GB)/Terry Harryman (GB)	Datsun 160J	9h 20m 51s
09	Henri Toivonen (FIN)/Juhani Korhonen (FIN)	Chrysler Sunbeam	9h 27m 23s
10	Bror Danielsson (S)/Bob de Jong (NL)	Opel Kadett GT/E	9h 31m 52s

Hannu Mikkola/Arne Hertz

FINAL MANUFACTURERS' CHAMPIONSHIP POSITIONS

01	Fiat	134
02.	Ford	100
03.	Opel	100
04.	Porsche	79
05.	Datsun	52
06.	Toyota	50
07.	Lancia	49
08.	Peugeot	45
09.	Renault	33
10.	British Leyland	24

1979

ROUND 01 – MONTE CARLO (20th-26th January)

01	Bernard Darniche (F)/Alain Mahé (F)	Lancia Stratos	8h 13m 38s
02	Bjorn Waldegård (S)/Hans Thorszelius (S)	Ford Escort RS	8h 13m 44s
03	Markku Alén (FIN)/Ilkka Kivimäki (FIN)	Fiat 131 Abarth	8h 17m 47s
04	Jean-Claude Andruet (F)/Chantal Lienard (F)	Fiat 131 Abarth	8h 19m 20s
05	Hannu Mikkola (FIN) Hertz (FIN)	Ford Escort RS	8h 23m 07s
06	Jean-Pierre Nicolas (F)/Jean Todt (F)	Porsche Carrera RS	8h 26m 37s
07	Michèle Mouton (F)/Francoise Conconi (F)	Fiat 131 Abarth	8h 34m 44s
08	Guy Frequelin (F)/Jacques Delaval (F)	Renault 5 Alpine	8h 44m 27s
09	Jacques Almeras (F)/Maurice Gelin (F)	Porsche Carrera RS	8h 49m 52s
10	Ari Vatanen (FIN)/David Richards (GB)	Ford Fiesta	8h 50m 11s

Bernard Darniche/Alain Mahé

ROUND 02 – SWEDEN (16th-18th February)

01	Stig Blomqvist (S)/Bjorn Cederberg (S)	Saab 99 Turbo	6h 34m 49s
02	Bjorn Waldegård (S)/Hans Thorszelius (S)	Ford Escort RS	6h 36m 09s
03	Pentti Airikkala (FIN)/Risto Virtanen (FIN)	Vauxhall Chevette 2300HS	6h 39m 31s
04	Markku Alén (FIN)/Ilkka Kivimäki (FIN)	Fiat 131 Abarth	6h 40m 42s
05	Hannu Mikkola (FIN)/Arne Hertz (S)	Ford Escort RS	6h 45m 19s
06	Bjorn Johansson (S)/Ragnar Spjuth (S)	Opel Kadett GT/E	6h 56m 07s
07	Ola Strömberg (S)/Hansjöran Ericson (S)	Saab 99EMS	7h 05m 55s
08	Lars Carlsson (S)/Mats Nordström (S)	Ford Escort RS2000	7h 10m 27s
09	John Haugland (N)/Martin Holmes (GB)	Datsun 160J	7h 11m 25s
10	Sven-Inge Neby (S)/Lars Bäckman (S)	Volvo 142	7h 12m 37s

Stig Blomqvist/Bjorn Cederberg

ROUND 03 – PORTUGAL (6th-11th March)

01	Hannu Mikkola (FIN)/Arne Hertz (S)	Ford Escort RS	9h 13m 52s
02	Bjorn Waldegård (S)/Hans Thorszelius (S)	Ford Escort RS	9h 16m 36s
03	Ove Andersson (S)/Henry Liddon (GB)	Toyota Celica	9h 35m 00s
04	Andy Dawson (GB)/Martin Holmes (GB)	Datsun 160J	10h 01m 37s
05	Carlos Torres (P)/Pedro de Almeida (P)	Ford Escort RS	10h 05m 49s
06	Harald Demuth (D)/Arwed Fischer (D)	Audi 80 GLE	10h 06m 37s
07	Freddy Kottulinsky (S)/Michael Schwägerl (D)	Audi 80 GLE	10h 52m 38s
08	Joaquim Santos (P)/Albino Tristao (P)	Opel Kadett GT/E	11h 32m 10s
09	Jorge Ortigao (P)/Joaquim Bessa (P)	Opel Ascona	11h 44m 58s
10	Marques Baptista (P)/Isabel Baptista (P)	Opel Ascona	11h 58m 12s

Hannu Mikkola/Arne Hertz

ROUND 04 – SAFARI, AFRICA (12th-16th April)

01	Shekhar Mehta (EAK)/Mike Doughty (EAK)	Datsun 160J	6h 27m
02	Hannu Mikkola (FIN)/Arne Hertz (S)	Mercedes 450 SLC 5.0	7h 15m
03	Markku Alén (FIN)/Ilkka Kivimäki (FIN)	Fiat 131 Abarth	7h 20m
04	Andrew Cowan (GB)/Johnstone Syer (EAK)	Mercedes 280E	7h 36m
05	Rauno Aaltonen (FIN)/Lofty Drews (EAK)	Datsun 160J	8h 06m
06	Bjorn Waldegård (S)/Hans Thorszelius (S)	Mercedes 450 SLC 5.0	9h 20m
07	Mike Kirkland (EAK)/Dave Howarth (EAK)	Datsun 160J	9h 34m
08	Walter Röhrl (D)/Christian Geistdorfer (D)	Fiat 131 Abarth	10h 25m
09	Harry Källström (S)/Claes Billstam (S)	Datsun 160J	10h 43m
10	Sandro Munari (I)/Silvio Maiga (I)	Fiat 131 Abarth	11h 33m

Shekhar Mehta/Mike Doughty

ROUND 05 – ACROPOLIS, GREECE (28th-31st May)

01	Bjorn Waldegård (S)/Hans Thorszelius (S)	Ford Escort RS	13h 35m 06s
02	Timo Salonen (FIN)/Seppo Harjanne (FIN)	Datsun 160J	14h 07m 04s
03	Harry Källström (S)/Claes Billstam (S)	Datsun 160J	14h 11m 39s
04	Jean Ragnotti (F)/Jean-Marc André (F)	Renault 5 Alpine	14h 19m 16s
05	'Iaveris' (GR)/Costas Stefanis (GR)	Ford Escort RS	14h 36m 01s
06	Iorgis Moschous (GR)/'Simerta' (GR)	Datsun 160J	14h 54m 27s
07	Evangelos Gallo (GR)/Dimitris Petropoulos (CZ)	Datsun 160J	15h 04m 08s
08	Vaclav Blahna (CZ)/Jiri Motal (CZ)	Skoda 130RS	16h 09m 22s
09	Nikolay Elizarov (URS)/Viktor Moskovski (URS)	Lada 21011	16h 12m 15s
10	Sergey Vukovich (URS)/Anatoli Brum (URS)	Lada 21011	16h 33m 11s

Bjorn Waldegård/Hans Thorszelius

ROUND 06 – NEW ZEALAND (14th-18th July)

01	Hannu Mikkola (FIN)/Arne Hertz (FIN)	Ford Escort RS	8h 05m 46s
02	Blair Robson (NZ)/Chris Porter (NZ)	Ford Escort RS	8h 27m 03s
03	Ari Vatanen (FIN)/David Richards (GB)	Ford Escort RS	8h 29m 40s
04	Paul Adams (NZ)/Mike Franchi (NZ)	Ford Escort RS	8h 29m 54s
05	Shane Murland (NZ)/Peter Parnell (NZ)	Vauxhall Chevette 2300HS	9h 04m 23s
06	David Parkes (NZ)/Stuart Green (NZ)	Ford Escort RS1600	9h 09m 34s
07	Brian Green (NZ)/Robert Orr (NZ)	Ford Escort RS	9h 12m 36s
08	Roger Goss (NZ)/Colin Green (NZ)	Mazda RX3	9h 26m 15s
09	Malcolm Stewart (NZ)/Doug Parkhill (NZ)	Ford Escort Mexico	9h 27m 21s
10	Bob Robb (NZ)/Malcolm Gavin (NZ)	Datsun Violet 710	9h 37m 22

Hannu Mikkola/Arne Hertz

ROUND 07 – 1000 LAKES, FINLAND (24th-28th August)

01	Markku Alén (FIN)/Ilkka Kivimäki (FIN)	Fiat 131 Abarth	4h 01m 11s
02	Ari Vatanen (FIN)/David Richards (GB)	Ford Escort RS	4h 02m 42s
03	Bjorn Waldegård (S)/Claes Billstam (S)	Ford Escort RS	4h 07m 15s
04	Ulf Grönholm (FIN)/Bob Rehnström (S)	Fiat 131 Abarth	4h 10m 41s
05	Timo Salonen (FIN)/Seppo Harjanne (FIN)	Datsun 160J	4h 11m 50s
06	Lasse Lampi (FIN)/Pentti Kuukkala (FIN)	Ford Escort RS	4h 14m 14s
07	Tapio Rainio (FIN)/Erkki Nyman (FIN)	Toyota Celica 2000GT	4h 14m 20s
08	Per Eklund (S)/Hans Sylvan (S)	Triumph TR7 V8	4h 17m 48s
09	Erkki Pitkänen (FIN)/Juhani Paalama (FIN)	Datsun 160J	4h 20m 01s
10	Pekka Vilpponen (FIN)/Rauno Kangasniemi (FIN)	Ford Escort RS	4h 20m 24s

Markku Alén/Ilkka Kivimäki

ROUND 08 – CANADA (13th-16th September)

01	Bjorn Waldegård (S)/Hans Thorszelius (S)	Ford Escort RS	3h 35m 32s
02	Timo Salonen (FIN)/Seppo Harjanne (FIN)	Datsun 160J	3h 36m 10s
03	Ari Vatanen (FIN)/David Richards (GB)	Ford Escort RS	3h 41m 50s
04	Andy Dawson (GB)/Kevin Gormley (GB)	Datsun 160J	3h 50m 55s
05	Taisto Heinonen (CDN)/Erkki Nyman (FIN)	Toyota Celica	3h 56m 21s
06	Hendrick Blok (USA)/Doug Shepherd (USA)	Mitsubishi Mirage	4h 41m 56s
07	Jack Swayze (CDN)/Izim Okerem (CDN)	Datsun 160J	4h 50m 27s
08	Claude Laurent (F)/Jacques Marché (F)	Peugeot 104 ZS	4h 52m 35s
09	Nicole Quimet (CDN)/Yves Fontaine (CDN)	Datsun 510	5h 04m 05s
10	Paul Bourgeois (CDN)/Robert Blouin (CDN)	Mitsubishi Colt	5h 06m 01s

Bjorn Waldegård/Hans Thorszelius

ROUND 09 – SANREMO, ITALY (1st-7th October)

01	'Tony' Fassina (I)/Mauro Mannini (I)	Lancia Stratos	12h 37m 17s
02	Walter Röhrl (D)/Christian Geistdörfer (D)	Fiat 131 Abarth	12h 41m 31s
03	Attilio Bettega (I)/Maurizio Perissinot (I)	Fiat 131 Abarth	12h 55m 59s
04	Tony Pond (GB)/Ian Grindrod (GB)	Talbot Sunbeam	13h 05m 22s
05	Dario Cerrato (I)/Luciano Guizzardi (I)	Opel Ascona	13h 11m 15s
06	Markku Alén (FIN)/Ilkka Kivimäki (FIN)	Fiat 131 Abarth	13h 18m 00s
07	Angelo Presotto (I)/Max Sghedoni (I)	Ford Escort RS2000	13h 26m 14s
08	Antonio Tognana (I)/Luciano Tedeschini (I)	Opel Kadett GT/E	13h 46m 38s
09	'Nico' (I)/Giorgio Barban (I)	Lancia Stratos	14h 06m 56s
10	Paolo Pasutti (I)/Rinaldo Danelutti (I)	Porsche Carrera RS	14h 14m 25s

'Tony' Fassina/Mauro Mannini

ROUND 10 – CORSICA, FRANCE (2nd-4th November)

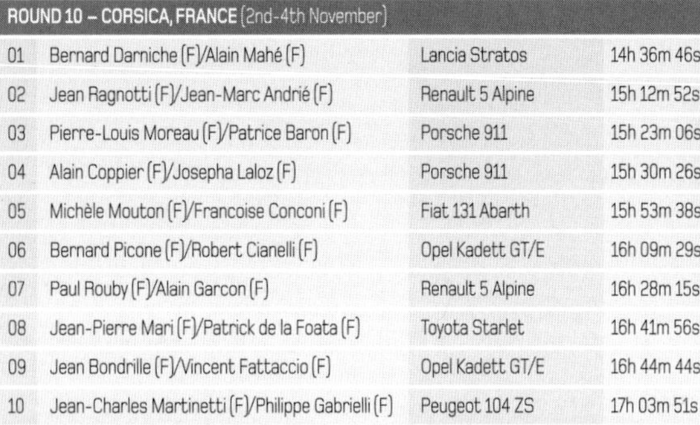

01	Bernard Darniche (F)/Alain Mahé (F)	Lancia Stratos	14h 36m 46s
02	Jean Ragnotti (F)/Jean-Marc André (F)	Renault 5 Alpine	15h 12m 52s
03	Pierre-Louis Moreau (F)/Patrice Baron (F)	Porsche 911	15h 23m 06s
04	Alain Coppier (F)/Josepha Laloz (F)	Porsche 911	15h 30m 26s
05	Michèle Mouton (F)/Francoise Conconi (F)	Fiat 131 Abarth	15h 53m 38s
06	Bernard Picone (F)/Robert Cianelli (F)	Opel Kadett GT/E	16h 09m 29s
07	Paul Rouby (F)/Alain Garcon (F)	Renault 5 Alpine	16h 28m 15s
08	Jean-Pierre Mari (F)/Patrick de la Foata (F)	Toyota Starlet	16h 41m 56s
09	Jean Bondrille (F)/Vincent Fattaccio (F)	Opel Kadett GT/E	16h 44m 44s
10	Jean-Charles Martinetti (F)/Philippe Gabrielli (F)	Peugeot 104 ZS	17h 03m 51s

Bernard Darniche/Alain Mahé

ROUND 11 – RAC, GREAT BRITAIN (18th-21st November)

01	Hannu Mikkola (FIN)/Arne Hertz (S)	Ford Escort RS	8h 03m 38s
02	Russell Brookes (GB)/Paul White (GB)	Ford Escort RS	8h 14m 07s
03	Timo Salonen (FIN)/Stuart Pegg (RSA)	Datsun 160J	8h 16m 22s
04	Ari Vatanen (FIN)/David Richards (GB)	Ford Escort RS	8h 19m 53s
05	Markku Alén (FIN)/Ilkka Kivimäki (FIN)	Lancia Stratos	8h 20m 23s
06	John Taylor (GB)/Phil Short (GB)	Ford Escort RS2000	8h 24m 01s
07	Pentti Airikkala (FIN)/Risto Virtanen (FIN)	Vauxhall Chevette 2300HS	8h 25m 57s
08	Walter Röhrl (D)/Christian Geistdorfer (FIN)	Fiat 131 Abarth	8h 26m 37s
09	Bjorn Waldegård (S)/Hans Thorszelius (S)	Ford Escort RS2000	8h 29m 12s
10	Greg Carr (AUS)/Fred Gocentas (AUS)	Ford Escort RS1800	8h 29m 31s

Hannu Mikkola/Arne Hertz

ROUND 12 – IVORY COAST, AFRICA (9th-14th December)

01	Hannu Mikkola (FIN)/Arne Hertz (S)	Mercedes 450 SLC 5.0	3h 23m
02	Bjorn Waldegård (S)/Hans Thorszelius (S)	Mercedes 450 SLC 5.0	3h 58m
03	Andrew Cowan (GB)/Klaus Kaiser (D)	Mercedes 450 SLC 5.0	4h 10m
04	Vic Preston Jr. (EAK)/Mike Doughty (EAK)	Mercedes 450 SLC 5.0	4h 17m
05	Ove Andersson (S)/Henry Liddon (S)	Toyota Celica Liftback	6h 08m
06	Alain Ambrosino (F)/Robert Schneck (F)	Peugeot 504 V6 Coupe	8h 48m
07	Michel Mitri (F)/Jean-Pierre Fornaro (F)	Datsun 160J	12h 15m
08	Jean-Pierre Paure (F)/Alain Manfredini (F)	Datsun 160J	13h 48m
	Only 8 finishers		

Hannu Mikkola/Arne Hertz

FINAL DRIVERS' CHAMPIONSHIP POSITIONS		
01	Björn Waldegård	112
02	Hannu Mikkola	111
03	Markku Alén	68
04	Timo Salonen	50
05	Ari Vatanen	50
06	Bernard Darniche	40
07	Jean Ragnotti	25
08	Andrew Cowan	22
09	Walter Röhrl	21
10	Stig Blomqvist	20
10 =	Shekhar Mehta/'Tony' Fassina	20

FINAL MANUFACTURERS' CHAMPIONSHIP POSITIONS		
01	Ford	122
02	Datsun	108
03	Fiat	92
04	Lancia	65
05	Toyota	58
06	Opel	49
07	Renault	41
08	Mercedes	35
09	Porsche	32
10	Vauxhall	31

1980

ROUND 01 – MONTE CARLO (19th-25th January)

01	Walter Röhrl (D)/Christian Geistdörfer (D)	Fiat 131 Abarth	8h 42m 20s
02	Bernard Darniche (F)/Alain Mahé (F)	Lancia Stratos HF	8h 52m 58s
03	Björn Waldegård (S)/Hans Thorszelius (S)	Fiat 131 Abarth	8h 53m 48s
04	Anders Kulläng (S)/Bruno Berglund (S)	Opel Ascona 400	8h 54m 24s
05	Per Eklund (S)/Hans Sylvan (S)	Volkswagen Golf GTI	8h 56m 47s
06	Attilio Bettega (I)/Mario Mannucci (I)	Fiat Ritmo 75 Abarth	8h 58m 43s
07	Michèle Mouton (F)/Annie Arrii (F)	Fiat 131 Abarth	9h 06m 13s
08	Jochi Kleint (D)/Gunter Wanger (D)	Opel Ascona 400	9h 07m 50s
09	Alain Coppier (F)/Josépha Laloz (F)	Porsche 911 SC	9h 12m 00s
10	Salvador Servià (E)/Alex Brustenga (E)	Ford Fiesta	9h 12m 00s

Walter Röhrl/Christian Geistdörfer

ROUND 02 – SWEDEN (15th-17th February)

01	Anders Kulläng (S)/Bruno Berglund (S)	Opel Ascona 400	4h 17m 52s
02	Stig Blomqvist (S)/Björn Cederberg (S)	Saab 99 Turbo	4h 19m 22s
03	Björn Waldegård (S)/Hans Thorszelius (S)	Fiat 131 Abarth	4h 21m 39s
04	Hannu Mikkola (FIN)/Arne Hertz (S)	Ford Escort RS	4h 23m 49s
05	Björn Johansson (S)/Ragnar Spjuth (S)	Opel Kadett GT/E	4h 25m 13s
06	Pentti Airikkala (FIN)/Risto Virtanen (FIN)	Vauxhall Chevette 2300HSR	4h 25m 44s
07	Timo Salonen (FIN)/Seppo Harjanne (FIN)	Datsun 160J	4h 28m 01s
08	Per Eklund (S)/Hans Sylvan (S)	Datsun 160J	4h 30m 09s
09	Bengt Nilsson (S)/Lennart Berggren (S)	Opel Kadett GT/E	4h 33m 55s
10	Ingvar Carlsson (S)/Sven-Roine Hasselberg (S)	BMW 320i	4h 33m 58s

Anders Kulläng/Bruno Berglund

ROUND 03 – PORTUGAL (4th-9th March)

01	Walter Röhrl (D)/Christian Geistdörfer (D)	Fiat 131 Abarth	8h 45m 35s
02	Markku Alén (FIN)/Ilkka Kivimäki (FIN)	Fiat 131 Abarth	8h 59m 54s
03	Guy Fréquelin (F)/Jean Todt (F)	Talbot Sunbeam Lotus	9h 16m 04s
04	Björn Waldegård (S)/Hans Thorszelius (S)	Mercedes 450 SLC 5.0	9h 29m 22s
05	Ingvar Carlsson (S)/Claes Billstam (S)	Mercedes 450 SLC 5.0	9h 40m 22s
06	Ove Andersson (S)/Henry Liddon (GB)	Toyota Celica 2000GT	9h 54m 51s
07	Carlos Torres (P)/António Morais (P)	Ford Escort RS2000	10h 08m 13s
08	Jorge Recalde (RA)/Hector Moyana (RA)	Ford Escort RS	10h 49m 39s
09	'Ray' (MC)/Pierre Gandolfo (F)	Ford Escort RS	11h 09m 22s
10	Maciej Stawowiak (PL)/Ryszard Zyszkowski (PL)	FSO Polonez 2000	11h 15m 34s

Walter Röhrl/Christian Geistdörfer

ROUND 04 – SAFARI, AFRICA (3rd-7th April)

01	Shekhar Mehta (EAK)/Mike Doughty (EAK)	Datsun 160J	3h 27m
02	Rauno Aaltonen (FIN)/Lofty Drews (EAK)	Datsun 160J	4h 02m
03	Vic Preston Jr (EAK)/John Lyall (EAK)	Mercedes 450 SLC 5.0	5h 07m
04	Mike Kirkland (EAK)/Dave Haworth (EAK)	Datsun 160J	5h 45m
05	Jean-Pierre Nicolas (F)/Henry Liddon (GB)	Opel Ascona 400	6h 41m
06	Andrew Cowan (GB)/Klaus Kaiser (D)	Mercedes 450 SLC 5.0	7h 03m
07	Yoshio Iwashita (J)/Yoshimasa Nakahara (J)	Datsun Silvia S110	7h 15m
08	Johnny Hellier (EAK)/Chris Bates (EAK)	Datsun 160J	7h 20m
09	Jochi Kleint (D)/Gunter Wanger (D)	Opel Ascona 400	7h 22m
10	Björn Waldegård (S)/Hans Thorszelius (S)	Mercedes 450 SLC 5.0	7h 33m

Shekhar Mehta/Mike Doughty

ROUND 05 – ACROPOLIS, GREECE (26th-29th May)			
01	Ari Vatanen (FIN)/David Richards (GB)	Ford Escort RS1800	12h 55m 44s
02	Timo Salonen (FIN)/Seppo Harjanne (FIN)	Datsun 160J	12h 58m 26s
03	Markku Alén (FIN)/Ilkka Kivimäki (FIN)	Fiat 131 Abarth	13h 02m 48s
04	Anders Kulläng (S)/Bruno Berglund (S)	Opel Ascona 400	13h 06m 47s
05	Walter Röhrl (D)/Christian Geistdörfer (D)	Fiat 131 Abarth	13h 18m 54s
06	Ove Andersson (S)/Henry Liddon (GB)	Toyota Celica 2000GT	13h 18m 54s
07	Harry Källström (S)/Bo Thorszelius (S)	Datsun 160J	13h 18m 56s
08	Attilio Bettega (I)/Arnaldo Bernacchini (I)	Fiat 131 Abarth	13h 20m 37s
09	'Siroco' (GR)/Manólis Makrinos (GR)	Lancia Stratos HF	13h 37m 07s
10	Timo Mäkinen (FIN)/Jean Todt (F)	Peugeot 504 V6 Coupé	13h 39m 49s

Ari Vatanen/David Richards

ROUND 06 – ARGENTINA (19th-24th July)			
01	Walter Röhrl (D)/Christian Geistdörfer (D)	Fiat 131 Abarth	12h 48m 36s
02	Hannu Mikkola (FIN)/Arne Hertz (S)	Mercedes 500 SLC	13h 04m 35s
03	Carlos Reutemann (RA)/Mirko Perissutti (I)	Fiat 131 Abarth	13h 35m 26s
04	Shekhar Mehta (EAK)/Yvonne Mehta (EAK)	Datsun 160J	13h 57m 49s
05	Jean-Claude Lefèbvre (F)/Christian Delferrier (B)	Peugeot 504 V6 Coupé	14h 33m 31s
06	Domingo De Vitta (ROU)/Daniel Muzio (ROU)	Ford Escort 1.6	15h 00m 25
07	Francisco Alcuaz (RA)/Daniel Griwieniec (RA)	Peugeot 504 TN	15h 13m 03s
08	Nestor García Veiga (RA)/Marcelo Tornqvist (RA)	Peugeot 504 TN	15h 38m 04s
09	Federico West (ROU)/Gregorio Assadourian (ROU)	Ford Escort 1.6	15h 58m 04s
10	Jorge Maggi (RA)/Hector Valles (RA)	Peugeot 504 TN	16h 18m 59s

Walter Röhrl/Christian Geistdörfer

ROUND 07 – 1000 LAKES, FINLAND (29th-31st August)			
01	Markku Alén (FIN)/Ilkka Kivimäki (FIN)	Fiat 131 Abarth	4h 24m 11s
02	Ari Vatanen (FIN)/David Richards (GB)	Ford Escort RS1800	4h 25m 07s
03	Per Eklund (S)/Hans Sylvan (S)	Triumph TR7 V8	4h 35m 25s
04	Björn Johansson (S)/Ragnar Spjuth (S)	Opel Ascona 400	4h 36m 43s
05	Lasse Lampi (FIN)/Pentti Kuukkala (FIN)	Ford Escort RS1800	4h 37m 02s
06	Timo Salonen (FIN)/Seppo Harjanne (FIN)	Datsun 160J	4h 39m 00s
07	Tapio Rainio (FIN)/Erkki Nyman (FIN)	Toyota Celica 2000GT	4h 44m 23s
08	Erkki Pitkänen (FIN)/Roman Fehrmann (FIN)	Datsun 160J	4h 47m 43s
09	Heikki Enomaa (FIN)/Jyrki Ahava (FIN)	Talbot Sunbeam Lotus	4h 50m 22s
10	Peter Geitel (FIN)/Rolf Mesterton (FIN)	Datsun 160J	4h 57m 59s

Markku Alén/Ilkka Kivimäki

ROUND 08 – NEW ZEALAND (13th-17th September)			
01	Timo Salonen (FIN)/Seppo Harjanne (FIN)	Datsun 160J	12h 06m 57s
02	Walter Röhrl (D)/Christian Geistdörfer (D)	Fiat 131 Abarth	12h 09m 38s
03	Hannu Mikkola (FIN)/Arne Hertz (S)	Mercedes 500 SLC	12h 29m 22s
04	George Fury (AUS)/Monty Suffern (AUS)	Datsun 160J	12h 34m 10s
05	Björn Waldegård (S)/Hans Thorszelius (S)	Mercedes 500 SLC	12h 42m 38s
06	Paul Adams (NZ)/Jim Scott (NZ)	Vauxhall Chevette 2300HSR	12h 49m 20s
07	Paddy Davidson (NZ)/Paul Greaves (NZ)	Ford Escort RS1600	13h 19m 26s
08	David Parkes (NZ)/Stuart Green (NZ)	Ford Escort RS1600	13h 19m 53s
09	Glenn McIntyre (NZ)/Dennis Roderick (NZ)	Ford Escort RS1600	13h 22m 05s
10	Morrie Chandler (NZ)/Don Campbell (NZ)	Mitsubishi Lancer	13h 30m 50s

Timo Salonen/Seppo Harjanne

ROUND 09 – SANREMO, ITALY (6th-11th October)			
01	Walter Röhrl (D)/Christian Geistdörfer (D)	Fiat 131 Abarth	10h 22m 42s
02	Ari Vatanen (FIN)/David Richards (GB)	Ford Escort RS1800	10h 29m 17s
03	Hannu Mikkola (FIN)/Arne Hertz (S)	Ford Escort RS	10h 36m 52s
04	Guy Fréquelin (F)/Jean Todt (F)	Talbot Sunbeam Lotus	10h 39m 29s
05	Henri Toivonen (FIN)/Antero Lindqvist (FIN)	Talbot Sunbeam Lotus	10h 40m 27s
06	Attilio Bettega (I)/Arnaldo Bernacchini (I)	Fiat 131 Abarth	10h 48m 02s
07	Angelo Presotto (I)/Max Sghedoni (I)	Ford Escort RS2000	11h 14m 50s
08	Antonillo Zordan (I)/Orlando Dalla Benetta (I)	Opel Ascona	11h 54m 34s
09	Giorgio Bernocchi (I)/Federico Scotti (I)	Opel Ascona 400	12h 28m 45s
10	Massimo Paolieri (I)/Giuseppe Agostini (I)	Ford Escort RS2000	12h 40m 52s

Walter Röhrl/Christian Geistdörfer

ROUND 10 – CORSICA, FRANCE (24th-25th October)			
01	Jean-Luc Thérier (F)/Michel Vial (F)	Porsche 911 SC	14h 51m 43s
02	Walter Röhrl (D)/Christian Geistdörfer (D)	Fiat 131 Abarth	15h 02m 06s
03	Alain Coppier (F)/Josépha Laloz (F)	Porsche 911 SC	15h 17m 21s
04	Bruno Saby (F)/'Tilber' (MC)	Renault 5 Turbo	15h 21m 25s
05	Michèle Mouton (F)/Annie Arrii (F)	Fiat 131 Abarth	15h 23m 57s
06	Andy Dawson (GB)/Kevin Gormley (GB)	Datsun 160J	15h 54m 57s
07	Christian Gardavot (F)/Christian Audibert (F)	Porsche 911 SC	16h 26m 37s
08	Paul Rouby (F)/Alain Garçon (F)	Renault 5 Alpine	16h 33m 02s
09	Jean-Felix Farrucci (F)/Albert Gori (F)	Opel Kadett GT/E	16h 43m 11s
10	Jean Bagarry (F)/Alain Bonne (F)	Porsche 911	16h 49m 31s

Jean-Luc Thérier/Michel Vial

ROUND 11 – RAC, GREAT BRITAIN (16th-19th November)			
01	Henri Toivonen (FIN)/Paul White (GB)	Talbot Sunbeam Lotus	8h 17m 33s
02	Hannu Mikkola (FIN)/Arne Hertz (S)	Ford Escort RS1800	8h 22m 09s
03	Guy Fréquelin (F)/Jean Todt (F)	Talbot Sunbeam Lotus	8h 31m 24s
04	Russell Brookes (GB)/Peter Bryant (GB)	Talbot Sunbeam Lotus	8h 32m 16s
05	Anders Kulläng (S)/Bruno Berglund (S)	Opel Ascona 400	8h 33m 47s
06	Timo Mäkinen (F)/Martin Holmes (GB)	Ford Escort RS1800	8h 43m 41s
07	Tony Pond (GB)/Fred Gallagher (GB)	Triumph TR7 V8	8h 46m 43s
08	Andy Dawson (GB)/Kevin Gormley (GB)	Datsun 160J	8h 48m 08s
09	Bror Danielsson (S)/David Booth (GB)	Ford Escort RS1800	8h 55m 58s
10	George Hill (GB)/Ronald Varley (GB)	Vauxhall Chevette 2300HSR	8h 58m 40s

Henri Toivonen/Paul White

ROUND 12 – IVORY COAST, AFRICA (9th-14th December)			
01	Björn Waldegård (S)/Hans Thorszelius (S)	Mercedes 500 SLC	2hrs 36m
02	Jorge Recalde (RA)/Nestor Straimel (RA)	Mercedes 500 SLC	3hrs 47m
03	Alain Ambrosino (F)/Jean-Robert (F)	Peugeot 504 V6 Coupé	5hrs 17m
04	Samir Assef (LEB)/Gilbert Fourcade (F)	Toyota Celica 2000GT	5hrs 38m
05	Vic Preston Jr (EAK)/Claes Billstam (S)	Mercedes 500 SLC	5hrs 43m
06	Sandro Munari (I)/Jacques Jaubert (F)	Fiat 131 Abarth	6hrs 16m
07	Per Eklund (S)/Hans Sylvan (S)	Toyota Celica 2000GT	7hrs 55m
08	Jean-Claude Lefèbvre (F)/Christian Delferrier (B)	Peugeot 504 V6 Coupé	8hrs 25m
09	Jean-François Vincens (F)/Solange Vincens (F)	Mitsubishi Lancer	12hrs 59m
10	Naguib Saad (CI)/François Dromard (CI)	Datsun 160J	14hrs 46m

Björn Waldegård/Hans Thorszelius

FINAL DRIVERS' CHAMPIONSHIP POSITIONS			FINAL MANUFACTURERS' CHAMPIONSHIP POSITIONS		
01	Walter Röhrl	118	01	Fiat	120
02	Hannu Mikkola	64	02	Datsun	93
03	Björn Waldegård	63	03	Ford	90
04	Ari Vatanen	50	04	Mercedes	79
05	Anders Kulläng	48	05	Opel	71
06	Markku Alén	47	06	Talbot	49
07	Timo Salonen	45	07	Toyota	32
08	Guy Fréquelin	34	08	Peugeot	30
09	Shekhar Mehta	30	09	Porsche	28
10	Henri Toivonen	28	10	Lancia	20

1981

ROUND 01 – MONTE CARLO (24th-30th January)

01	Jean Ragnotti (F)/Jean-Marc Andrié (F)	Renault 5 Turbo	9h 55m 55s
02	Guy Fréquelin (F)/Jean Todt (F)	Talbot Sunbeam Lotus	9h 58m 49s
03	Jochi Kleint (D)/Gunther Wanger (D)	Opel Ascona 400	10h 02m 54s
04	Anders Kulläng (S)/Bruno Berglund (S)	Opel Ascona 400	10h 08m 44s
05	Henri Toivonen (FIN)/Fred Gallagher (GB)	Talbot Sunbeam Lotus	10h 11m 42s
06	Bernard Darniche (F)/Alain Mahé (F)	Lancia Stratos HF	10h 13m 02s
07	Markku Alén (FIN)/Ilkka Kivimäki (FIN)	Fiat 131 Abarth	10h 14m 07s
08	Björn Waldegård (S)/Hans Thorszelius (S)	Ford Escort RS1800	10h 21m 52s
09	Jacques Alméras (F)/'Tilber (MC)	Porsche 911 SC	10h 33m 38s
10	Alain Coppier (F)/Josépha Laloz (F)	Renault 5 Turbo	10h 37m 25s

Jean Ragnotti/Jean-Marc Andrié

ROUND 02 – SWEDEN (13th-15th February)

01	Hannu Mikkola (FIN)/Arne Hertz (S)	Audi Quattro	3h 48m 07s
02	Ari Vatanen (FIN)/David Richards (GB)	Ford Escort RS1800	3h 50m 00s
03	Pentti Airikkala (FIN)/Risto Virtanen (FIN)	Ford Escort RS1800	3h 51m 47s
04	Anders Kulläng (S)/Bruno Berglund (S)	Opel Ascona 400	3h 53m 12s
05	Stig Blomqvist (S)/Björn Cederberg (S)	Saab 99 Turbo	3h 53m 37s
06	Björn Johansson (S)/Sven-Erik Andersson (S)	Opel Ascona 400	3h 54m 38s
07	Lasse Lampi (FIN)/Pentti Kuukkala (FIN)	Ford Escort RS1800	3h 57m 26s
08	Ola Strömberg (S)/Hansjöran Ericson (S)	Saab 99 EMS	4h 00m 31s
09	Per Eklund (S)/Ragnar Spjuth (S)	Porsche 911 SC	4h 00m 39s
10	Sören Nilsson (S)/Anders Olsson (S)	Datsun 160J	4h 09m 48s

Hannu Mikkola/Arne Hertz

ROUND 03 – PORTUGAL (4th-7th March)

01	Markku Alén (FIN)/Ilkka Kivimäki (FIN)	Fiat 131 Abarth	8h 27m 26s
02	Henri Toivonen (SF)/Fred Gallagher (GB)	Talbot Sunbeam Lotus	8h 36m 36s
03	Björn Waldegård (S)/Hans Thorszelius (FIN)	Toyota Celica 2000GT	8h 43m 47s
04	Michèle Mouton (F)/Fabrizia Pons (I)	Audi Quattro	8h 49m 57s
05	Tony Pond (GB)/Ian Grindrod (GB)	Datsun 160J	8h 57m 39s
06	Guy Fréquelin (F)/Jean Todt (F)	Talbot Sunbeam Lotus	9h 17m 52s
07	Rafael 'Cid' (E)/Miguel Oliveira (P)	Ford Escort RS	9h 48m 03s
08	'Mêquêpê' (P)/Miguel Vilar (P)	Opel Kadett GT/E	10h 10m 02s
09	Joaquim Moutinho (P)/António Morais (P)	Opel Kadett GT/E	10h 16m 14s
10	Kenjiro Shinozuka (J)/Bryan Harris (GB)	Ford Escort RS1800	10h 22m 04s

Markku Alén/Ilkka Kivimäki

ROUND 04 – SAFARI, AFRICA (16th-20th April)

01	Shekhar Mehta (EAK)/Mike Doughty (EAK)	Datsun Violet GT	3h 39m
02	Rauno Aaltonen (FIN)/Lofty Drews (EAK)	Datsun Violet GT	3h 44m
03	Mike Kirkland (EAK)/Dave Haworth (EAK)	Datsun 160J	4h 51m
04	Timo Salonen (FIN)/Seppo Harjanne (FIN)	Datsun Silvia 200SX	7h 28m
05	Jochi Kleint (D)/Gunter Wanger (D)	Opel Ascona 400	8h 06m
06	Jean-Claude Lefèbvre (F)/Christian Delferrier (B)	Peugeot 504 V6 Coupé	9h 12m
07	Yoshio Iwashita (J)/Yoshimasa Nakahara (J)	Datsun Silvia 200SX	10h 11m
08	Jayant Shah (EAK)/Rishad Ramir (EAK)	Datsun 160J	10h 30m
09	Malcolm Smith (USA)/David Doig (EAK)	Dodge Ramcharger	13h 18m
10	Rod Hall (USA)/Chris Bates (EAK)	Dodge Ramcharger	14h 16m

Shekhar Mehta/Mike Doughty

ROUND 05 – CORSICA, FRANCE (30th April-2nd May)

01	Bernard Darniche (F)/Alain Mahé (F)	Lancia Stratos HF	14h 26m 23s
02	Guy Fréquelin (F)/Jean Todt (F)	Talbot Sunbeam Lotus	14h 42m 25s
03	Tony Pond (GB)/Ian Grindrod (GB)	Datsun Violet GT	14h 45m 29s
04	Jean-Pierre Ballet (F)/Jacky Guinchard (F)	Porsche 911 SC	15h 17m 09s
05	Terry Kaby (GB)/Rob Arthur (GB)	Datsun 160J	15h 22m 06s
06	Per Eklund (S)/Jan-Olof Bohlin (S)	Toyota Celica 2000GT	15h 43m 33s
07	Jean-Michel Tichadou (I)/Jean-Paul Pandolfi (I)	Ford Escort RS	15h 45m 51s
08	Gérard Swaton (F)/Bernard Cordesse (F)	Porsche 911 SC	15h 46m 29s
09	Camille Bartoli (F)/Gilbert Poletti (F)	Renault 5 Turbo	15h 54m 34s
10	Jean-Felix Farrucci (F)/Albert Gori (F)	Opel Ascona	15h 59m 40s

Bernard Darniche/Alain Mahé

ROUND 06 – ACROPOLIS, GREECE (1st-4th June)

01	Ari Vatanen (FIN)/David Richards (GB)	Ford Escort RS1800	13h 17m 25s
02	Markku Alén (FIN)/Ilkka Kivimäki (FIN)	Fiat 131 Abarth	13h 22m 00s
03	Attilio Bettega (I)/Maurizio Perissinot (I)	Fiat 131 Abarth	13h 25m 19s
04	Guy Fréquelin (F)/Jean Todt (F)	Talbot Sunbeam Lotus	13h 50m 44s
05	Shekhar Mehta (EAK)/Yvonne Mehta (EAK)	Datsun 160J	13h 54m 40s
06	Iórgis Moschous (GR)/Alex Konstantakos (GR)	Datsun Violet GT	13h 57m 22s
07	'Carlo' (GR)/Mihalis Kriadis (GR)	Renault 5 Alpine	16h 03m 59s
08	Václav Blahna (CZ)/Pavel Schovánek (CZ)	Skoda 130RS	16h 05m 09s
09	Pavlos Moschoutis (GR)/Stamatis Vellis (GR)	Ford Escort RS	16h 29m 55s
10	Claude Laurent (F)/Jacques Marché (F)	Peugeot 505 SRD	16h 36m 25s

Ari Vatanen/David Richards

ROUND 07 – ARGENTINA (18th-23rd July)

01	Guy Fréquelin (F)/Jean Todt (F)	Talbot Sunbeam Lotus	14h 22m 52s
02	Shekhar Mehta (EAK)/Yvonne Mehta (EAK)	Datsun Violet GT	15h 01m 04s
03	Jorge Recalde (RA)/Jorge del Buono (RA)	Datsun 160J	16h 01m 19s
04	Ernesto Soto (RA)/Carlos Silva (RA)	Renault 12 TS	17h 12m 50s
05	Ricardo Albertengo (RA)/Oscar Alberto (RA)	Peugeot 504	17h 38m 35s
06	Luis Etchegoyen (ROU)/Natalio Horowitz (ROU)	Ford Escort 1.6	17h 45m 30s
07	Federico West (ROU)/Gregorio Assadourian (ROU)	Ford Escort 1.6	18h 04m 32s
08	Luis Romero (RA)/Alberto Sora (RA)	Renault 12 TS	18h 37m 21s
09	Miguel Tubal (RA)/Jorge Guiral (RA)	Datsun 160J	18h 57m 21s
10	Horacio Maglione (RA)/Javier Concepción (RA)	Peugeot 504	19h 11m 59s

Guy Fréquelin/Jean Todt

ROUND 08 – BRAZIL (6th-8th August)

01	Ari Vatanen (FIN)/David Richards (GB)	Ford Escort RS1800	9h 39m 40s
02.	Guy Fréquelin (F)/Jean Todt (F)	Talbot Sunbeam Lotus	9h 48m 11s
03	Domingo De Vitta (ROU)/Daniel Muzio (ROU)	Ford Escort RS	10h 19m 46s
04	Jorge Recalde (RA)/Jorge del Buono (RA)	Datsun 160J	10h 46m 50s
05	Carlos Torres (P)/António Morais (P)	Ford Escort RS2000	11h 10m 45s
06	Gustavo Trelles (ROU)/Luis Caulim (RA)	Fiat 147	12h 06m 35s
07	Horacio Maglione (RA)/Javier Concepción (RA)	Peugeot 504	12h 26m 04s
08	Julio Berges (ROU)/Ricardo Ivetich (ROU)	Fiat 147	12h 35m 15s
09	Maria Carmo Zacarias (BR)/Zilda Zacarias (BR)	Volkswagen Gol 1.6	13h 22m 24s
	Only 9 finishers		

Ari Vatanen/David Richards

ROUND 09 – 1000 LAKES, FINLAND (28th-30th August)

01	Ari Vatanen (FIN)/David Richards (GB)	Ford Escort RS1800	4h 07m 27s
02	Markku Alén (FIN)/Ilkka Kivimäki (FIN)	Fiat 131 Abarth	4h 08m 26s
03	Hannu Mikkola (FIN)/Arne Hertz (S)	Audi Quattro	4h 10m 19s
04	Timo Salonen (FIN)/Seppo Harjanne (FIN)	Datsun Violet GT	4h 13m 26s
05	Pentti Airikkala (FIN)/Risto Virtanen (FIN)	Ford Escort RS1800	4h 15m 40s
06	Björn Johansson (S)/Sven-Erik Andersson (S)	Opel Ascona 400	4h 16m 18s
07	Lasse Lampi (FIN)/Pentti Kuukkala (FIN)	Ford Escort RS1800	4h 16m 41s
08	Stig Blomqvist (S)/Björn Cederberg (S)	Talbot Sunbeam Lotus	4h 19m 09s
09	Björn Waldegård (S)/Hans Thorszelius (S)	Toyota Celica 2000GT	4h 20m 27s
10	Antero Laine (FIN)/Juha Piironen (FIN)	Mitsubishi Lancer Turbo	4h 24m 00s

Ari Vatanen/David Richards

ROUND 10 – SANREMO, ITALY (5th-10th October)

01	Michèle Mouton (F)/Fabrizia Pons (I)	Audi Quattro	8h 05m 50s
02	Henri Toivonen (FIN)/Fred Gallagher (GB)	Talbot Sunbeam Lotus	8h 09m 15s
03	'Tony' Fassina (I)/'Rudy' (I)	Opel Ascona 400	8h 12m 08s
04	Hannu Mikkola (FIN)/Arne Hertz (S)	Audi Quattro	8h 18m 20s
05	'Lucky' (I)/Fabio Penariol (I)	Opel Ascona 400	8h 19m 51s
06	Miki Biasion (I)/Tiziano Siviero (I)	Opel Ascona 400	8h 21m 44s
07	Ari Vatanen (FIN)/David Richards (GB)	Ford Escort RS1800	8h 23m 35s
08	Dario Cerrato (I)/Luciano Guizzardi (I)	Fiat 131 Abarth	8h 25m 33s
09	Markku Alén (FIN)/Ilkka Kivimäki (FIN)	Fiat 131 Abarth	8h 26m 45s
10	Federico Ormezzano (I)/Claudio Berro (I)	Talbot Sunbeam Lotus	8h 33m 47s

Michèle Mouton/Fabrizia Pons

ROUND 11 – IVORY COAST, AFRICA (26th–31st October)

01	Timo Salonen (FIN)/Seppo Harjanne (FIN)	Datsun Violet GT	9h 57m
02	Per Eklund (S)/Ragnar Spjuth (S)	Toyota Celica 2000GT	11h 09m
03	Shekhar Mehta (EAK)/Mike Doughty (EAK)	Datsun Violet GT	11h 22m
04	Michel Mitri (F)/Marcel Copetti (F)	Datsun 160J	12h 29m
05	Guy Fréquelin (F)/Jean Todt (F)	Peugeot 504 V6 Coupé	13h 15m
06	Alain Ambrosino (F)/Daniel Le Saux (F)	Peugeot 504 V6 Coupé	13h 16m
07	Samir Assef (LEB)/Jacques Jaubert (F)	Toyota Celica 2000GT	16h 40m
08	Jacques Durieu (CI)/Pierre Tastet (CI)	Peugeot 504 V6 Coupé	24h 53m
09	Ari Vatanen (FIN)/David Richards (GB)	Ford Escort RS1800	32h 12m

Only 9 finishers

Timo Salonen/Seppo Harjanne

ROUND 12 – RAC, GREAT BRITAIN (22ndh–25th November)

01	Hannu Mikkola (FIN)/Arne Hertz (S)	Audi Quattro	8h 30m 00s
02	Ari Vatanen (FIN)/David Richards (GB)	Ford Escort RS1800	8h 41m 05s
03	Stig Blomqvist (S)/Björn Cederberg (S)	Talbot Sunbeam Lotus	8h 43m 36s
04	Pentti Airikkala (FIN)/Phil Short GB()	Ford Escort RS1800	8h 48m 43s
05	Jean Ragnotti (F)/Martin Holmes (GB)	Renault 5 Turbo	8h 53m 55s
06	Per Eklund (S)/Ragnar Spjuth (S)	Toyota Celica 2000GT	8h 54m 54s
07	Sören Nilsson (S)/Anders Olsson (S)	Datsun 160J	8h 57m 20s
08	Terry Kaby (GB)/Rob Arthur (GB)	Toyota Celica 2000GT	9h 01m 18s
09	Anders Kulläng (S)/Bruno Berglund (S)	Mitsubishi Lancer Turbo	9h 05m 22s
10	Roger Clark (GB)/Chris Searle (GB)	Ford Escort RS1800	9h 08m 24s

Hannu Mikkola/Arne Hertz

FINAL DRIVERS' CHAMPIONSHIP POSITIONS			FINAL MANUFACTURERS' CHAMPIONSHIP POSITIONS		
01	Ari Vatanen	96	01	Talbot	117
02	Guy Fréquelin	89	02	Datsun	106
03	Hannu Mikkola	62	03	Ford	90
04	Markku Alén	56	04	Opel	69
05	Shekhar Mehta	55	05	Audi	63
06	Timo Salonen	40	06	Fiat	63
07	Henri Toivonen	38	07	Renault	61
08	Michèle Mouton	30	08	Toyota	54
09	Pentti Airikkala	30	09	Peugeot	37
10	Per Eklund	29	10	Lancia	28

1982

ROUND 01 – MONTE CARLO (16th–22nd January)

01	Walter Röhrl (D)/Christian Geistdörfer (D)	Opel Ascona 400	8h 20m 33s
02	Hannu Mikkola (FIN)/Arne Hertz (S)	Audi Quattro	8h 24m 22s
03	Jean-Luc Thérier (F)/Michel Vial (F)	Porsche 911 SC	8h 32m 38s
04	Guy Fréquelin (F)/Jean-François Fauchille (F)	Porsche 911 SC	8h 37m 40s
05	Bruno Saby (F)/Françoise Sappey (F)	Renault 5 Turbo	8h 43m 34s
06	Dany Snobeck (F)/Denise Emmanuelli (F)	Renault 5 Turbo	8h 50m 28s
07	Jochi Kleint (D)/Gunther Wanger (D)	Opel Ascona 400	8h 59m 40s
08	Philippe Touren (F)/Jean-Louis Alric (F)	Renault 5 Turbo	9h 06m 34s
09	Jean-Pierre Ballet (F)/'Tilber' (MC)	Porsche 911 SC	9h 09m 00s
10	Jürgen Barth (D)/Roland Kussmaul (D)	Porsche 924 GTS	9h 09m 46s

Walter Röhrl/Christian Geistdörfer

ROUND 02 – SWEDEN (12th–14th February)

01	Stig Blomqvist (S)/Björn Cederberg (S)	Audi Quattro	3h 40m 15s
02	Ari Vatanen (FIN)/Terry Harryman (GB)	Ford Escort RS1800	3h 42m 51s
03	Walter Röhrl (D)/Christian Geistdörfer (D)	Opel Ascona 400	3h 44m 29s
04	Per Eklund (S)/Ragnar Spjuth (S)	Saab 99 Turbo	3h 45m 20s
05	Michèle Mouton (F)/Fabrizia Pons (I)	Audi Quattro	3h 46m 08s
06	Lasse Lampi (FIN)/Pentti Kuukkala (FIN)	Ford Escort RS1800	3h 46m 14s
07	Sören Nilsson (S)/Anders Olsson (S)	Nissan Violet GT	3h 48m 41s
08	Kalle Grundel (S)/Rolf Melleroth (S)	Volkswagen Golf GTI	3h 50m 30s
09	Bengt Thorsell (S)/Jan-Olof Bohlin (S)	Ford Escort RS1800	3h 51m 09s
10	Mikael Ericsson (S)/Jan Sandström (S)	Audi 80 Coupé	3h 52m 48s

Stig Blomqvist/Björn Cederberg

ROUND 03 – PORTUGAL (3rd–6th March)

01	Michèle Mouton (F)/Fabrizia Pons (I)	Audi Quattro	7h 39m 36s
02	Per Eklund (S)/Ragnar Spjuth (S)	Toyota Celica 2000GT	7h 52m 43s
03	Franz Wittmann (A)/Peter Diekmann (D)	Audi Quattro	8h 07m 25s
04	Carlos Torres (P)/Filipe Lopes (P)	Ford Escort RS1800	8h 30m 58s
05	Alain Coppier (F)/Josépha Laloz (F)	Citroën Visa	8h 54m 11s
06	Mário Silva (P)/Rui Bevilacqua (P)	Ford Escort RS1800	9h 01m 12s
07	António Ferreira da Cunha (P)/Carlos Resende (P)	Opel Ascona	9h 29m 09s
08	Christian Dorche (F)/Patricia Trivero (F)	Citroën Visa	9h 35m 39s
09	Olivier Tabatoni (F)/Michel Cadier (F)	Citroën Visa	9h 40m 36s
10	Jorge Fleck (BR)/Silvio Klein (B)	Opel Kadett GT/E	9h 40m 55s

Michèle Mouton/Fabrizia Pons

ROUND 04 – SAFARI, AFRICA (8th–12th April)

01	Shekhar Mehta (EAK)/Mike Doughty (EAK)	Nissan Violet GT	4h 26m
02	Walter Röhrl (D)/Christian Geistdörfer (D)	Opel Ascona 400	5h 07m
03	Mike Kirkland (EAK)/Anton Levitan (EAK)	Nissan Violet GTS	6h 16m
04	Tony Pond (GB)/Terry Harryman (GB)	Nissan Violet GTS	7h 00m
05	Jayant Shah (EAK)/Aslam Khan (EAK)	Nissan 160J	8h 15m
06	Rob Collinge (EAK)/Mike Fraser (EAK)	Range Rover	8h 54m
07	Yoshinobu Takahashi (J)/Mahendra Gohil (EAK)	Subaru Leone 4WD	12h 20m
08	Frank Tundo (EAK)/Quentin Thomson (EAK)	Mitsubishi Colt Lancer	12h 53m
09	Javaid Alam (EAK)/Arshad Khan (EAK)	Subaru Leone 4WD	13h 51m
10	Ramesh Khoda (EAK)/Jasvinder Matharu (EAK)	Subaru Leone 4WD	15h 35m

Shekhar Mehta/Mike Doughty

ROUND 05 – CORSICA, FRANCE (6th–8th May)

01	Jean Ragnotti (F)/Jean-Marc Andrié (F)	Renault 5 Turbo	14h 11m 19s
02	Jean-Claude Andruet (F)/'Biche' (F)	Ferrari 308 GTB	14h 16m 57s
03	Bernard Béguin (F)/Jean-Jacques Lenne (F)	Porsche 911 SC	14h 20m 11s
04	Walter Röhrl (D)/Christian Geistdörfer (D)	Opel Ascona 400	14h 20m 41s
05	Bruno Saby (F)/Françoise Sappey (F)	Renault 5 Turbo	14h 27m 31s
06	Guy Fréquelin (F)/Jean-François Fauchille (F)	Porsche 911 SC	14h 35m 16s
07	Michèle Mouton (F)/Fabrizia Pons (I)	Audi Quattro	14h 43m 48s
08	Francis Vincent (F)/Francis Calvier (F)	Porsche 911 SC	14h 43m 55s
09	Markku Alén (FIN)/Ilkka Kivimäki (FIN)	Lancia Rally 037	14h 53m 18s
10	Robert Simonetti (F)/Jean-Michel Simonetti (F)	Renault 5 Turbo	15h 35m 43s

Jean Ragnotti/Jean-Marc Andrié

ROUND 06 – ACROPOLIS, GREECE (26th–29th June)

01	Michèle Mouton (F)/Fabrizia Pons (I)	Audi Quattro	12h 54m 44s
02	Walter Röhrl (D)/Christian Geistdörfer (D)	Opel Ascona 400	13h 08m 23s
03	Henri Toivonen (FIN)/Fred Gallagher (GB)	Opel Ascona 400	13h 17m 21s
04	Shekhar Mehta (EAK)/Yvonne Mehta (EAK)	Nissan Violet GT	13h 17m 28s
05	Iórgis Moschous (GR)/Alex Konstantakos (GR)	Nissan Violet GTS	13h 36m 44s
06	Jimmy McRae (GB)/Ian Grindrod (GB)	Opel Ascona 400	13h 40m 16s
07	Pavlos Moschoutis (GR)/'Silef' (GR)	Fiat 131 Abarth	14h 21m 48s
08	'Leonidas' (GR)/Sokrátis Kokkinis (GR)	Renault 5 Turbo	14h 37m 28s
09	Anastasios Gemenis (GR)/Ioánnis Kepetzis (GR)	Nissan 160J	16h 06m 10s
10	Fritz Heisler (D)/Walter Blieberger (D)	Ford Escort RS1800	16h 10m 04s

Michèle Mouton/Fabrizia Pons

ROUND 07 – NEW ZEALAND (26th-29th June)			
01	Björn Waldegård (S)/Hans Thorszelius (S)	Toyota Celica 2000GT	10h 28m 08s
02	Per Eklund (S)/Ragnar Spjuth (S)	Toyota Celica 2000GT	10h 31m 21s
03	Walter Röhrl (D)/Christian Geistdörfer (D)	Opel Ascona 400	10h 33m 37s
04	Timo Salonen (FIN)/Seppo Harjanne (FIN)	Nissan Violet GTS	10h 41m 25s
05	Rod Millen (NZ)/John Bellefleur (CDN)	Mazda RX7	10h 54m 54s
06	Tony Teesdale (NZ)/Gary Smith (NZ)	Ford Escort RS1800	11h 30m 17s
07	Jean-Louis Leyraud (F)/Eric Johnston (NZ)	Ford Escort RS1800	11h 37m 22s
08	Malcolm Stewart (NZ)/Doug Parkhill (NZ)	Ford Escort RS	11h 51m 26s
09	Paul Adams (NZ)/Jim Scott (NZ)	Toyota Starlet	11h 55m 06s
10	Reg Cook (NZ)/Wayne Jones (NZ)	Nissan Bluebird Turbo	11h 55m 54s

Björn Waldegård/Hans Thorszelius

ROUND 08 – BRAZIL (11th-14th August)			
01	Michèle Mouton (F)/Fabrizia Pons (I)	Audi Quattro	8h 16m 24s
02	Walter Röhrl (D)/Christian Geistdörfer (D)	Opel Ascona 400	8h 51m 49s
03	Domingo De Vitta (ROU)/Daniel Muzio (ROU)	Ford Escort 1.6	10h 15m 30s
04	Aparecido Rodrigues (BR)/José Mattos (BR)	Volkswagen Passat 1.6	11h 41m 08s
05	Ricardo Costa (BR)/Valter Vieira (BR)	Volkswagen Passat 1.6	12h 07m 32s
	Only 5 finishers		

Michèle Mouton/Fabrizia Pons

ROUND 09 – 1000 LAKES, FINLAND (27th-29th August)			
01	Hannu Mikkola (FIN)/Arne Hertz (S)	Audi Quattro	4h 19m 05s
02	Stig Blomqvist (S)/Björn Cederberg (S)	Audi Quattro	4h 19m 33s
03	Pentti Airikkala (FIN)/Juha Piironen (FIN)	Mitsubishi Lancer Turbo	4h 23m 22s
04	Timo Salonen (FIN)/Seppo Harjanne (FIN)	Nissan Silvia Turbo	4h 25m 02s
05	Antero Laine (FIN)/Risto Virtanen (FIN)	Talbot Sunbeam Lotus	4h 31m 54s
06	Russell Brookes (GB)/Ronan Morgan (GB)	Vauxhall Chevette 2300HSR	4h 37m 10s
07	Harri Uotila (FIN)/Timi Leino (FIN)	Ford Escort RS	4h 48m 10s
08	Jouni Kinnunen (FIN)/Juhani Nieminen (FIN)	Ford Escort RS	4h 51m 03s
09	Seppo Mustonen (FIN)/Erkki Pakkanen (FIN)	Ford Escort RS	4h 53m 47s
10	Henri Palmroos (FIN)/Ilkka Riipinen (FIN)	Ford Escort RS	4h 55m 55s

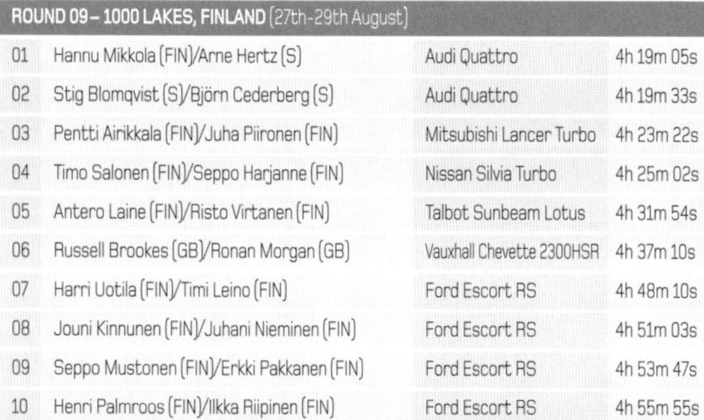

Hannu Mikkola/Arne Hertz

ROUND 10 – SANREMO, ITALY (3rd-8th October)			
01	Stig Blomqvist (S)/Björn Cederberg (S)	Audi Quattro	8h 37m 47s
02	Hannu Mikkola (FIN)/Arne Hertz (S)	Audi Quattro	8h 40m 03s
03	Walter Röhrl (D)/Christian Geistdörfer (D)	Opel Ascona 400	8h 40m 14s
04	Michèle Mouton (F)/Fabrizia Pons (I)	Audi Quattro	8h 40m 59s
05	Henri Toivonen (FIN)/Fred Gallagher (GB)	Opel Ascona 400	8h 41m 43s
06	Michele Cinotto (I)/Emilio Radaelli (I)	Audi Quattro	8h 55m 51s
07	Anders Kulläng (S)/Bruno Berglund (S)	Mitsubishi Lancer Turbo	9h 02m 09s
08	Miki Biasion (I)/Tiziano Siviero (I)	Opel Ascona 400	9h 25m 50s
09	Livio Lupidi (I)/Arles Montenesi (I)	Renault 5 Turbo	9h 40m 03s
10	Vittorio Caneva (I)/Loris Roggia (I)	Citroën Visa	10h 03m 48s

Stig Blomqvist/Björn Cederberg

ROUND 11 – IVORY COAST, AFRICA (27th October-1st November)			
01	Walter Röhrl (D)/Christian Geistdörfer (D)	Opel Ascona 400	8h 43m
02	Per Eklund (S)/Ragnar Spjuth (S)	Toyota Celica 2000GT	10h 17m
03	Björn Waldegård (S)/Hans Thorszelius (S)	Toyota Celica 2000GT	11h 00m
04	Bruno Saby (F)/Daniel Le Saux (F)	Renault 5 Turbo	17h 51m
05	Alain Ambrosino (F)/Jean-François Fauchille (F)	Peugeot 505 V6	19h 43m
06	Eugène Salim (CI)/Clement Konan (CI)	Mitsubishi Colt Lancer	23h 48m
	Only 6 finishers		

Walter Röhrl/Christian Geistdörfer

ROUND 12 – RAC, GREAT BRITAIN (21st-25th November)			
01	Hannu Mikkola (FIN)/Arne Hertz (FIN)	Audi Quattro	8h 01m 46s
02	Michèle Mouton (F)/Fabrizia Pons (F)	Audi Quattro	8h 06m 03s
03	Henri Toivonen (FIN)/Fred Gallagher (FIN)	Opel Ascona 400	8h 06m 12s
04	Markku Alén (FIN)/Ilkka Kivimäki (FIN)	Lancia Rally 037	8h 11m 43s
05	Harald Demuth (D)/John Daniels (D)	Audi Quattro	8h 14m 10s
06	Russell Brookes (GB)/Mike Broad (GB)	Vauxhall Chevette 2300HSR	8h 14m 50s
07	Björn Waldegård (S)/Ragnar Spjuth (S)	Toyota Celica 2000GT	8h 16m 29s
08	Stig Blomqvist (S)/Björn Cederberg (S)	Talbot Sunbeam Lotus	8h 17m 12s
09	Per Eklund (S)/Dave Whittock (S)	Toyota Celica 2000GT	8h 21m 42s
10	Malcolm Wilson (GB)/Mike Greasley (GB)	Audi Quattro	8h 22m 32s

Hannu Mikkola/Arne Hertz

FINAL DRIVERS' CHAMPIONSHIP POSITIONS			FINAL MANUFACTURERS' CHAMPIONSHIP POSITIONS		
01	Walter Röhrl	109	01	Audi	116
02	Michèle Mouton	97	02	Opel	104
03	Hannu Mikkola	70	03	Nissan	57
04	Stig Blomqvist	58	04	Ford	55
05	Per Eklund	57	05	Toyota	41
06	Björn Waldegård	36	06	Renault	34
07	Henri Toivonen	32	07	Porsche	28
08	Shekhar Mehta	30	07=	Mitsubishi	28
09	Bruno Saby	26	09	Lancia	25
10	Jean Ragnotti	20	10	Talbot	24

1983

ROUND 01 – MONTE CARLO (22nd-29th January)			
01	Walter Röhrl (D)/Christian Geistdörfer (D)	Lancia Rally 037	7h 58m 57s
02	Markku Alén (FIN)/Ilkka Kivimäki (FIN)	Lancia Rally 037	8h 05m 59s
03	Stig Blomqvist (S)/Björn Cederberg (S)	Audi Quattro A1	8h 10m 15s
04	Hannu Mikkola (FIN)/Arne Hertz (S)	Audi Quattro A1	8h 13m 02s
05	Ari Vatanen (FIN)/Terry Harryman (GB)	Opel Ascona 400	8h 14m 03s
06	Henri Toivonen (FIN)/Fred Gallagher (GB)	Opel Ascona 400	8h 15m 54s
07	Jean Ragnotti (F)/Jean-Marc Andrié (F)	Renault 5 Turbo	8h 18m 10s
08	Jean-Claude Andruet (F)/'Biche' (F)	Lancia Rally 037	8h 19m 37s
09	Francis Serpaggi (F)/Michel Neri (F)	Lancia Rally 037	8h 32m 40s
10	Salvador Servià (E)/Jorge Sabater (E)	Opel Ascona 400	8h 40m 02s

Walter Röhrl/Christian Geistdörfer

ROUND 02 – SWEDEN (11th-13th February)			
01	Hannu Mikkola (FIN)/Arne Hertz (S)	Audi Quattro A1	4h 28m 47s
02	Stig Blomqvist (S)/Björn Cederberg (S)	Audi 80 Quattro	4h 29m 34s
03	Lasse Lampi (FIN)/Pentti Kuukkala (FIN)	Audi Quattro A1	4h 32m 51s
04	Michèle Mouton (F)/Fabrizia Pons (I)	Audi Quattro A1	4h 33m 56s
05	Kalle Grundel (S)/Rolf Melleroth (S)	Volkswagen Golf GTI	4h 38m 33s
06	Ari Vatanen (FIN)/Terry Harryman (GB)	Opel Ascona 400	4h 40m 38s
07	Sören Nilsson (S)/Anders Olsson (S)	Nissan Bluebird Turbo	4h 41m 48s
08	Mikael Ericsson (S)/Bo Thorszelius (S)	Audi 80 Coupé	4h 41m 55s
09	Lars-Erik Walfridsson (S)/Lars Bäckman (S)	Renault 5 Turbo	4h 44m 16s
10	Ola Strömberg (S)/Bruno Berglund (S)	Saab 99 Turbo	4h 45m 12s

Hannu Mikkola/Arne Hertz

ROUND 03 – PORTUGAL (2nd-5th March)			
01	Hannu Mikkola (FIN)/Arne Hertz (S)	Audi Quattro A1	7h 17m 24s
02	Michèle Mouton (F)/Fabrizia Pons (I)	Audi Quattro A1	7h 18m 19s
03	Walter Röhrl (D)/Christian Geistdörfer (D)	Lancia Rally 037	7h 19m 14s
04	Markku Alén (FIN)/Ilkka Kivimäki (FIN)	Lancia Rally 037	7h 24m 29s
05	Adartico Vudafieri (I)/Maurizio Perissinot (I)	Lancia Rally 037	7h 41m 49s
06	Antonio Zanini (E)/Victor Sabater (E)	Talbot Sunbeam Lotus	7h 50m 29s
07	Franz Wittmann (A)/Peter Diekmann (D)	Audi Quattro A1	7h 53m 56s
08	Terry Kaby (GB)/Rob Arthur (GB)	Nissan 240RS	7h 54m 08s
09	Joaquim Santos (P)/Miguel Oliveira (P)	Ford Escort RS1800	8h 16m 38s
10	Georg Fischer (A)/Michael Weinzierl (A)	Mitsubishi Lancer Turbo	8h 27m 52s

Hannu Mikkola/Arne Hertz

ROUND 04 – SAFARI, AFRICA (30th March-4th April)			
01	Ari Vatanen (FIN)/Terry Harryman (GB)	Opel Ascona 400	396 points
02	Hannu Mikkola (FIN)/Arne Hertz (S)	Audi Quattro A1	402 points
03	Michèle Mouton (F)/Fabrizia Pons (I)	Audi Quattro A1	455 points
04	Jayant Shah (EAK)/Aslam Khan (EAK)	Nissan 240RS	478 points
05	Yoshio Takaoka (J)/Shigeo Sunahara (J)	Subaru Leone 1800	831 points
06	Yasuhiro Iwase (J)/Sudhir Vinayak (EAK)	Nissan 160J	843 points
07	Yoshinobu Takahashi (J)/Peter Pringle (EAK)	Subaru Leone 1800	882 points
08	Johnny Hellier (EAK)/John Hope (EAK)	Peugeot 504 V6 Pick-up	907 points
09	Ian Duncan (EAK)/Gavin Bennett (EAK)	Nissan 1200 Pick-Up	913 points
10	Azar Anwar (EAK)/Tim Davis (EAK)	Nissan 160J	959 points

Ari Vatanen/Terry Harryman

ROUND 05 – CORSICA, FRANCE (5th-7th May)			
01	Markku Alén (FIN)/Ilkka Kivimäki (FIN)	Lancia Rally 037	12h 43m 38s
02	Walter Röhrl (D)/Christian Geistdörfer (D)	Lancia Rally 037	12h 45m 27s
03	Adartico Vudafieri (I)/Luigi Pirollo (I)	Lancia Rally 037	12h 50m 08s
04	Attilio Bettega (I)/Maurizio Perissinot (I)	Lancia Rally 037	12h 57m 27s
05	Bruno Saby (F)/Chris Williams (GB)	Renault 5 Turbo	13h 25m 37s
06	Tony Pond (GB)/Rob Arthur (GB)	Nissan 240RS	13h 44m 51s
07	Ange-Paul Franceschi (F)/Patrick Giudicelli (F)	Renault 5 Turbo	14h 11m 17s
08	Jean-Sébastien Couloumiès (F)/Claudine Causse (F)	Opel Ascona	14h 21m 09s
09	Alain Coppier (F)/Josépha Laloz (F)	Citroën Visa Chrono	14h 28m 21s
10	Jean-Michel Guyot (F)/Jacques Raspaud (F)	Renault 5 Turbo	14h 35m 47s

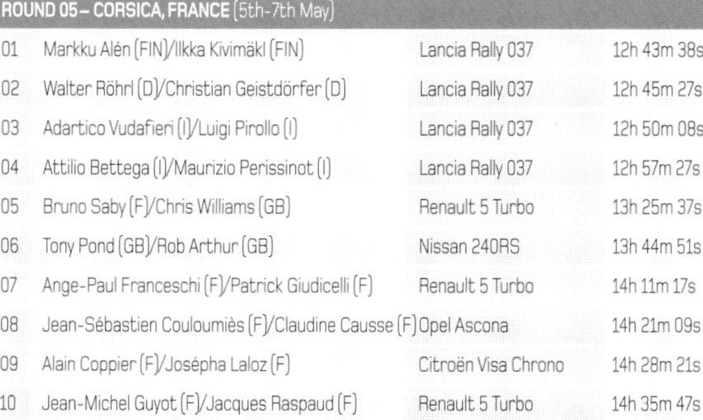

Markku Alén/Ilkka Kivimäki

ROUND 06 – ACROPOLIS, GREECE (30th May-2nd June)			
01	Walter Röhrl (D)/Christian Geistdörfer (D)	Lancia Rally 037	11h 12m 22s
02	Markku Alén (FIN)/Ilkka Kivimäki (FIN)	Lancia Rally 037	11h 18m 42s
03	Stig Blomqvist (S)/Björn Cederberg (S)	Audi Quattro A2	11h 26m 18s
04	Ari Vatanen (FIN)/Terry Harryman (GB)	Opel Manta 400	11h 35m 11s
05	Attilio Bettega (I)/Maurizio Perissinot (I)	Lancia Rally 037	11h 36m 38s
06	Shekhar Mehta (EAK)/Yvonne Mehta (EAK)	Nissan 240RS	11h 45m 41s
07	Franz Wittmann (A)/Kurt Nestinger (A)	Audi Quattro A1	11h 54m 03s
08	Jimmy McRae (GB)/Ian Grindrod (GB)	Opel Manta 400	11h 56m 23s
09	Philippe Wambergue (F)/Vincent Laverne (F)	Citroën Visa Chrono	13h 17m 30s
10	Maurice Chomat (F)/Didier Breton (F)	Citroën Visa Chrono	13h 28m 08s

Walter Röhrl/Christian Geistdörfer

ROUND 07 – NEW ZEALAND (25th-28th June)			
01	Walter Röhrl (D)/Christian Geistdörfer (D)	Lancia Rally 037	12h 10m 13s
02	Timo Salonen (FIN)/Seppo Harjanne (FIN)	Nissan 240RS	12h 26m 11s
03	Attilio Bettega (I)/Maurizio Perissinot (I)	Lancia Rally 037	12h 41m 42s
04	Shekhar Mehta (EAK)/Yvonne Mehta (EAK)	Nissan 240RS	13h 10m 35s
05	Jim Donald (NZ)/Chris Porter (NZ)	Nissan Bluebird Turbo	13h 20m 50s
06	Malcolm Stewart (NZ)/Doug Parkhill (NZ)	Ford Escort RS1800	13h 30m 58s
07	Reg Cook (NZ)/Wayne Jones (NZ)	Nissan 240RS	13h 35m 15s
08	Paul Adams (NZ)/Jim Scott (NZ)	Toyota Starlet	13h 52m 55s
09	Morrie Chandler (NZ)/Don Campbell (NZ)	Mitsubishi Lancer Turbo	14h 05m 45s
10	Kevin Smith (NZ)/Nick Tulitt (NZ)	Toyota Corolla GT	14h 13m 35s

Walter Röhrl/Christian Geistdörfer

ROUND 08 – ARGENTINA (2nd-6th August)			
01	Hannu Mikkola (FIN)/Arne Hertz (S)	Audi Quattro A2	10h 18m 54s
02	Stig Blomqvist (S)/Björn Cederberg (S)	Audi Quattro A2	10h 21m 28s
03	Michèle Mouton (F)/Fabrizia Pons (I)	Audi Quattro A2	10h 25m 35s
04	Shekhar Mehta (EAK)/Yvonne Mehta (EAK)	Audi Quattro A2	10h 40m 02s
05	Markku Alén (FIN)/Ilkka Kivimäki (FIN)	Lancia Rally 037	10h 50m 12s
06	Franz Wurz (A)/Rudi Stohl (A)	Audi 80 Quattro	12h 09m 37s
07	Ernesto Soto (RA)/Mario Stillo (RA)	Renault 18 GTX	12h 40m 48s
08	Jorge Recalde (RA)/Jorge del Buono (RA)	Renault 18 GTX	13h 01m 04s
09	Carlos Celis (RA)/Ernesto Quiróz (RA)	Renault 12 TSA	13h 51m 06s
10	Gerardo Campo (RA)/Omar Carbonari (RA)	Renault 12 TSA	14h 54m 25s

Hannu Mikkola/Arne Hertz

ROUND 09 – 1000 LAKES, FINLAND (26th-28th August)			
01	Hannu Mikkola (FIN)/Arne Hertz ()Swe	Audi Quattro A2	4h 23m 44s
02	Stig Blomqvist (S)/Björn Cederberg (S)	Audi Quattro A2	4h 24m 05s
03	Markku Alén (FIN)/Ilkka Kivimäki (FIN)	Lancia Rally 037	4h 24m 33s
04	Per Eklund (S)/Ragnar Spjuth (S)	Audi Quattro A2	4h 26m 03s
05	Pentti Airikkala (FIN)/Juha Piironen (FIN)	Lancia Rally 037	4h 32m 09s
06	Juha Kankkunen (FIN)/Staffan Pettersson (FIN)	Toyota Celica TCT	4h 34m 49s
07	Lasse Lampi (FIN)/Pentti Kuukkala (FIN)	Audi Quattro A2	4h 35m 36s
08	Timo Salonen (FIN)/Seppo Harjanne (FIN)	Nissan 240RS	4h 37m 54s
09	Erkki Pitkänen (FIN)/Juhani Paalama (FIN)	Nissan 240RS	4h 45m 27s
10	Jari Niemi (FIN)/Erkki Nyman (FIN)	Ford Escort RS2000	4h 50m 24s

Hannu Mikkola/Arne Hertz

ROUND 10 – SANREMO, ITALY (2nd-8th October)			
01	Markku Alén (FIN)/Ilkka Kivimäki (FIN)	Lancia Rally 037	8h 50m 17s
02	Walter Röhrl (D)/Christian Geistdörfer (D)	Lancia Rally 037	8h 52m 26s
03	Attilio Bettega (I)/Maurizio Perissinot (I)	Lancia Rally 037	8h 55m 27s
04	Henri Toivonen (FIN)/Fred Gallagher (GB)	Opel Manta 400	8h 59m 49s
05	Miki Biasion (I)/Tiziano Siviero (I)	Lancia Rally 037	9h 00m 42s
06	Dario Cerrato (I)/Giuseppe Cerri (I)	Opel Manta 400	9h 08m 04s
07	Michèle Mouton (F)/Fabrizia Pons (I)	Audi Quattro A2	9h 14m 20s
08	'Lucky' (I)/'Rudy' (I)	Opel Manta 400	9h 17m 17s
09	Bernard Darniche (F)/Alain Mahé (F)	Audi Quattro A2	9h 28m 35s
10	Gabriele Noberasco (I)/Daniele Cianci (I)	Alfa Romeo GTV6	9h 58m 39s

Markku Alén/Ilkka Kivimäki

ROUND 11 – IVORY COAST, AFRICA (25th-30th October)			
01	Björn Waldegård (S)/Hans Thorszelius (S)	Toyota Celica TCT	5h 18m
02	Hannu Mikkola (FIN)/Arne Hertz (S)	Audi Quattro A2	5h 29m
03	Per Eklund (S)/Ragnar Spjuth (S)	Toyota Celica TCT	6h 58m
04	Samir Assef (LEB)/Solange Barrault (CI)	Toyota Celica 2000GT	12h 09m
05	Alain Ambrosino (F)/Daniel Le Saux (F)	Peugeot 505 V6	14h 22m
06	Eugène Salim (CI)/Clement Konan (CI)	Mitsubishi Lancer Turbo	16h 08m
07	Claude Thibault (CI)/Elizabeth Clave (CI)	Mitsubishi Colt Lancer	23h 02m
08	Michel Molinie (CI)/Marc Molinie (CI)	Nissan 160J	23h 10m

Only 8 finishers

Björn Waldegård/Hans Thorszelius

ROUND 12 – RAC, GREAT BRITAIN (19th-23rd November)			
01	Stig Blomqvist (S)/Björn Cederberg (S)	Audi Quattro A2	8h 50m 28s
02	Hannu Mikkola (FIN)/Arne Hertz (S)	Audi Quattro A2	9h 00m 21s
03	Jimmy McRae (GB)/Ian Grindrod (GB)	Opel Manta 400	9h 12m 19s
04	Lasse Lampi (FIN)/Pentti Kuukkala (FIN)	Audi Quattro A2	9h 16m 57s
05	Russell Brookes (GB)/Mike Broad (GB)	Vauxhall Chevette 2300HSR	9h 19m 01s
06	John Buffum (USA)/Neil Wilson (GB)	Audi Quattro A2	9h 21m 16s
07	Juha Kankkunen (FIN)/Juha Piironen (FIN)	Toyota Celica TCT	9h 31m 49s
08	Kalle Grundel (S)/Reinhard Michel (D)	Volkswagen Golf GTI	9h 38m 20s
09	Mikael Sundström (FIN)/David Orrick (GB)	Opel Ascona	9h 42m 18s
10	Mats Jonsson (S)/Johnny Johansson (S)	Opel Ascona B	9h 45m 07s

Stig Blomqvist/Björn Cederberg

FINAL DRIVERS' CHAMPIONSHIP POSITIONS			FINAL MANUFACTURERS' CHAMPIONSHIP POSITIONS		
01	Hannu Mikkola	125	01	Lancia	118
02	Walter Röhrl	102	02	Audi	116
03	Markku Alén	100	03	Opel	87
04	Stig Blomqvist	89	04	Nissan	52
05	Michèle Mouton	53	05	Renault	27
06	Ari Vatanen	44	06	Toyota	24
07	Attilio Bettega	42	07	Subaru	13
08	Lasse Lampi	26	08	British Leyland	11
09	Shekhar Mehta	26	08=	Volkswagen	11
10	Per Eklund	22	10	Peugeot	10

1984

ROUND 01 – MONTE CARLO (21st-27th January)

01	Walter Röhrl (D)/Christian Geistdörfer (D)	Audi Quattro A2	8h 52m 29s
02	Stig Blomqvist (S)/Björn Cederberg (S)	Audi Quattro A2	8h 53m 42s
03	Hannu Mikkola (FIN)/Arne Hertz (S)	Audi Quattro A2	9h 05m 09s
04	Jean-Luc Thérier (F)/Michel Vial (F)	Renault 5 Turbo	9h 16m 53s
05	Attilio Bettega (I)/Maurizio Perissinot (I)	Lancia Rally 037	9h 21m 41s
06	Miki Biasion (I)/Tiziano Siviero (I)	Lancia Rally 037	9h 29m 49s
07	Bernard Darniche (F)/Alain Mahé (F)	Audi 80 Quattro	9h 32m 39s
08	Markku Alén (FIN)/Ilkka Kivimäki (FIN)	Lancia Rally 037	9h 36m 05s
09	Kalle Grundel (S)/Peter Diekmann (D)	Volkswagen Golf GTI	9h 44m 53s
10	Timo Salonen (FIN)/Seppo Harjanne (FIN)	Nissan 240RS	9h 46m 53s

Walter Röhrl/Christian Geistdörfer

ROUND 02 – SWEDEN (10th-12th February)

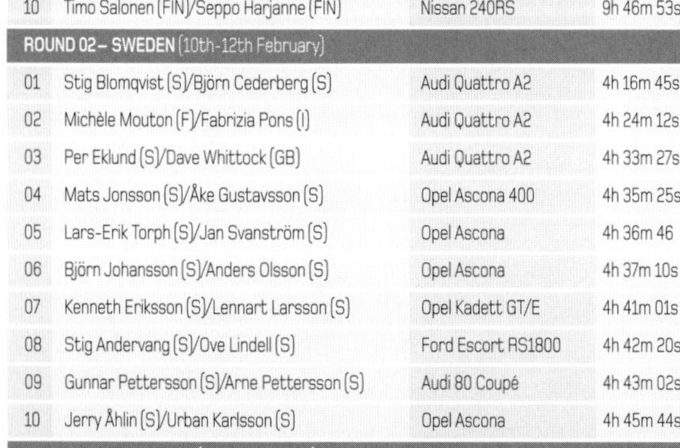

01	Stig Blomqvist (S)/Björn Cederberg (S)	Audi Quattro A2	4h 16m 45s
02	Michèle Mouton (F)/Fabrizia Pons (I)	Audi Quattro A2	4h 24m 12s
03	Per Eklund (S)/Dave Whittock (GB)	Audi Quattro A2	4h 33m 27s
04	Mats Jonsson (S)/Åke Gustavsson (S)	Opel Ascona 400	4h 35m 25s
05	Lars-Erik Torph (S)/Jan Svanström (S)	Opel Ascona	4h 36m 46
06	Björn Johansson (S)/Anders Olsson (S)	Opel Ascona	4h 37m 10s
07	Kenneth Eriksson (S)/Lennart Larsson (S)	Opel Kadett GT/E	4h 41m 01s
08	Stig Andervang (S)/Ove Lindell (S)	Ford Escort RS1800	4h 42m 20s
09	Gunnar Pettersson (S)/Arne Pettersson (S)	Audi 80 Coupé	4h 43m 02s
10	Jerry Åhlin (S)/Urban Karlsson (S)	Opel Ascona	4h 45m 44s

Stig Blomqvist/Björn Cederberg

ROUND 03 – PORTUGAL (6th-11th March)

01	Hannu Mikkola (FIN)/Arne Hertz (S)	Audi Quattro A2	7h 35m 32s
02	Markku Alén (FIN)/Ilkka Kivimäki (FIN)	Lancia Rally 037	7h 35m 59s
03	Attilio Bettega (I)/Maurizio Perissinot (I)	Lancia Rally 037	7h 58m 21s
04	Miki Biasion (I)/Tiziano Siviero (I)	Lancia Rally 037	7h 59m 22s
05	Jean Ragnotti(F)/Pierre Thimonier (F)	Renault 5 Turbo	8h 13m 42s
06	Walter Röhrl (D)/Christian Geistdörfer (D)	Audi Quattro A2	8h 21m 22s
07	Kalle Grundel (S)/Peter Diekmann (D)	Volkswagen Golf GTI	8h 39m 00s
08	Jorge Ortigão (P)/João Batista (P)	Toyota Corolla 16V	9h 19m 44s
09	Christian Dorche (F)/Gilles Thimonier (F)	Citroën Visa Chrono	9h 25m 03s
10	Russell Gooding (GB)/Rodger Jenkins (GB)	Vauxhall Chevette 2300HSR	9h 34m 37s

Hannu Mikkola/Arne Hertz

ROUND 04 – SAFARI, AFRICA (19th-23rd April)

01	Björn Waldegård (S)/Hans Thorszelius (S)	Toyota Celica TCT	2h 02m
02	Rauno Aaltonen (FIN)/Lofty Drews (EAK)	Opel Manta 400	2h 13m
03	Hannu Mikkola (FIN)/Arne Hertz (S)	Audi Quattro A2	2h 25m
04	Markku Alén (FIN)/Ilkka Kivimäki (FIN)	Lancia Rally 037	3h 08m
05	Shekhar Mehta (EAK)/Rob Combes (EAK)	Nissan 240RS	3h 35m
06	Vic Preston, Jr (EAK)/John Lyall (EAK)	Lancia Rally 037	4h 14m
07	Timo Salonen (FIN)/Seppo Harjanne (FIN)	Nissan 240RS	5h 52m
08	Franz Wittmann (A)/Peter Diekmann (D)	Audi Quattro A2	8h 35m
09	Yoshio Iwashita (J)/Yoshimasa Nakahara (J)	Nissan 240RS	8h 56m
10	Basil Criticos (EAK)/John Rose (EAK)	Audi 80 Quattro	9h 53m

Björn Waldegård/Hans Thorszelius

ROUND 05 – CORSICA, FRANCE (3rd-5th May)

01	Markku Alén (FIN)/Ilkka Kivimäki (FIN)	Lancia Rally 037	13h 24m 56s
02	Miki Biasion (I)/Tiziano Siviero (I)	Lancia Rally 037	13h 29m 11s
03	Jean Ragnotti (F)/Pierre Thimonier (F)	Renault 5 Turbo	13h 33m 16s
04	Jean-Pierre Nicolas (F)/Charley Pasquier (F)	Peugeot 205 Turbo 16	13h 44m 50s
05	Stig Blomqvist (S)/Björn Cederberg (S)	Audi Quattro A2	13h 45m 55s
06	Jean-Claude Andruet (F)/Martine Rick (F)	Lancia Rally 037	13h 48m 07s
07	Attilio Bettega (I)/Sergio Cresto (USA)	Lancia Rally 037	13h 55m 40s
08	François Chatriot (F)/Michel Périn (F)	Renault 5 Turbo	13h 57m 24s
09	Guy Fréquelin (F)/'Tilber' (MC)	Opel Manta 400	14h 08m 53s
10	Yves Loubet (F)/Patricia Trivero (F)	Alfa Romeo GTV6	14h 48m 11s

Markku Alén/Ilkka Kivimäki

ROUND 06 – ACROPOLIS, GREECE (26th-31st May)

01	Stig Blomqvist (S)/Björn Cederberg (S)	Audi Quattro A2	10h 41m 51s
02	Hannu Mikkola (FIN)/Arne Hertz (S)	Audi Quattro A2	10h 44m 58s
03	Markku Alén (FIN)/Ilkka Kivimäki (FIN)	Lancia Rally 037	10h 56m 01s
04	Attilio Bettega (I)/Sergio Cresto (USA)	Lancia Rally 037	11h 03m 49s
05	John Buffum (USA)/Fred Gallagher (GB)	Audi Quattro A2	11h 22m 10s
06	Timo Salonen (FIN)/Seppo Harjanne (FIN)	Nissan 240RS	11h 26m 29s
07	Shekhar Mehta (EAK)/Yvonne Mehta (EAK)	Nissan 240RS	11h 33m 57s
08	Iórgis Moschous (GR)/Alex Konstantakos (GR)	Nissan 240RS	11h 47m 45s
09	Achim Warmbold (D)/'Biche' (F)	Mazda RX7	12h 06m 51s
10	Yoshio Iwashita (J)/Yoshimasa Nakahara (J)	Nissan 240RS	12h 36m 26s

Stig Blomqvist/Björn Cederberg

ROUND 07 – NEW ZEALAND (23rd-26th June)

01	Stig Blomqvist (S)/Björn Cederberg (S)	Audi Quattro A2	10h 40m 41s
02	Markku Alén (FIN)/Ilkka Kivimäki (FIN)	Lancia Rally 037	10h 45m 28s
03	Hannu Mikkola (FIN)/Arne Hertz (S)	Audi Quattro A2	10h 48m 10s
04	Timo Salonen (FIN)/Seppo Harjanne (FIN)	Nissan 240RS	11h 05m 29s
05	Björn Waldegård (S)/Hans Thorszelius (S)	Toyota Celica TCT	11h 35m 58s
06	Reg Cook (NZ)/Wayne Jones (NZ)	Nissan 240RS	11h 44m 10s
07	Malcolm Stewart (NZ)/Doug Parkhill (NZ)	Ford Escort RS1800	11h 46m 00s
08	'Possum' Bourne (NZ)/Michael Eggleton (NZ)	Subaru Leone RX Turbo	12h 04m 46s
09	Tony Teesdale (NZ)/Gary Smith (NZ)	Subaru Leone RX Turbo	12h 21m 01s
10	Blair Robson (NZ)/Don Campbell (NZ)	Mitsubishi Lancer Turbo	12h 52m 08s

Stig Blomqvist/Björn Cederberg

ROUND 08 – ARGENTINA (27th July-1st August)

01	Stig Blomqvist (S)/Björn Cederberg (S)	Audi Quattro A2	10h 33m 38s
02	Hannu Mikkola (FIN)/Arne Hertz (S)	Audi Quattro A2	10h 36m 54s
03	Jorge Recalde (RA)/Jorge del Buono (RA)	Audi Quattro A2	10h 38m 48s
04	Mario Stillo (RA)/Daniel Stillo (RA)	Renault 12 TS	12h 12m 20s
05	Yasuhiro Iwase (J)/Surinder Thatthi (EAK)	Opel Ascona 400	12h 18m 24s
06	Miguel Torrás (RA)/Fernando Stella (RA)	Renault 12 TS	12h 20m 57s
07	Carlos Bassi (RA)/Roberto Syriani (RA)	Peugeot 504	12h 56m 23s
08	Hugo Hernándes (RA)/Adolfo Coggiola (RA)	Peugeot 504	13h 09m 12s
09	Omar Del Giovanni (RA)/Rogue Pérez (RA)	Fiat 128	13h 16m 30s
10	Nonnemacher Pérez (RA)/Enrique Marongiu (RA)	Peugeot 504	13h 37m 56s

Stig Blomqvist/Björn Cederberg

ROUND 09 – 1000 LAKES, FINLAND (26th-28th August)

01	Ari Vatanen (FIN)/Terry Harryman (GB)	Peugeot 205 Turbo 16	4h 08m 49s
02	Markku Alén (FIN)/Ilkka Kivimäki (FIN)	Lancia Rally 037	4h 10m 49s
03	Henri Toivonen (FIN)/Juha Piironen (FIN)	Lancia Rally 037	4h 12m 57s
04	Stig Blomqvist (S)/Björn Cederberg (S)	Audi Quattro A2	4h 14m 01s
05	Juha Kankkunen (FIN)/Fred Gallagher (GB)	Toyota Celica TCT	4h 19m 39s
06	Per Eklund (S)/Dave Whittock (GB)	Audi Quattro A2	4h 20m 18s
07	Erkki Pitkänen (FIN)/Rolf Mesterton (FIN)	Nissan 240RS	4h 33m 58s
08	Bruno Saby (F)/Jean-Franc~ois Fauchille (F)	Renault 5 Turbo	4h 35m 26s
09	Jouko Pöysti (FIN)/Reijo Savolin (FIN)	Opel Ascona 400	4h 36m 37s
10	Kalevi Aho (FIN)/Timo Hakala (FIN)	Opel Manta 400	4h 36m 51s

Ari Vatanen/Terry Harryman

ROUND 10 – SANREMO, ITALY (30th September-5th October)

01	Ari Vatanen (FIN)/Terry Harryman (GB)	Peugeot 205 Turbo 16	8h 44m 34s
02	Attilio Bettega (I)/Maurizio Perissinot (I)	Lancia Rally 037	8h 50m 01s
03	Miki Biasion (I)/Tiziano Siviero (I)	Lancia Rally 037	8h 53m 58s
04	Fabrizio Tabaton (I)/Luciano Tedeschini (I)	Lancia Rally 037	9h 07m 53s
05	Jean-Pierre Nicolas (F)/Charley Pasquier (F)	Peugeot 205 Turbo 16	9h 13m 16s
06	Kalle Grundel (S)/Peter Diekmann (D)	Volkswagen Golf GTI	9h 43m 30s
07	Massimo Ercolani (SMR)/Popi Amati (I)	Opel Ascona 400	9h 50m 02s
08	Gerhard Kalnay (A)/Franz Zehetner (A)	Opel Ascona 400	9h 57m 46s
09	Michele Rayneri (I)/Ergy Bartolich (I)	Fiat Ritmo Abarth 130 TC	10h 05m 05s
10	Werner Grissmann (A)/Jörg Pattermann (A)	Audi 80 Quattro	10h 13m 22s

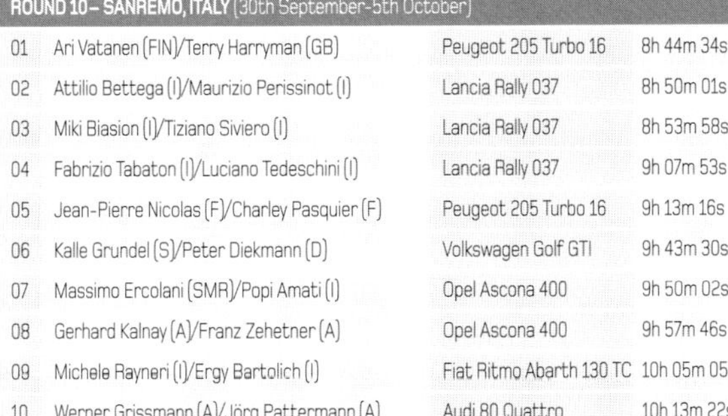

Ari Vatanen/Terry Harryman

ROUND 11 – IVORY COAST, AFRICA (31st October-4 November)

01	Stig Blomqvist (S)/Björn Cederberg (S)	Audi Sport Quattro	5h 24m
02	Hannu Mikkola (FIN)/Arne Hertz (S)	Audi Quattro A2	5h 46m
03	Shekhar Mehta (EAK)/Rob Combes (EAK)	Nissan 240RS	6h 28m
04	Alain Ambrosino (F)/Daniel Le Saux (F)	Opel Manta 400	7h 03m
05	David Horsey (EAK)/David Williamson (EAK)	Peugeot 504 V6 Pick-up	13h 58m
06	Patrick Tauziac (F)/Lois Cournil (CI)	Mitsubishi Colt	24h 13m

Only 6 finishers

Stig Blomqvist/Björn Cederberg

ROUND 12 – RAC, GREAT BRITAIN (25th-29th November)

01	Ari Vatanen (FIN)/Terry Harryman (GB)	Peugeot 205 Turbo 16	9:19.48
02	Hannu Mikkola (FIN)/Arne Hertz (S)	Audi Quattro A2	9:20.29
03	Per Eklund (S)/Dave Whittock (GB)	Toyota Celica TCT	9:37.07
04	Michèle Mouton (F)/Fabrizia Pons (I)	Audi Sport Quattro	9:37.28
05	Russell Brookes (GB)/Mike Broad (GB)	Opel Manta 400	9:48.06
06	Timo Salonen (FIN)/Seppo Harjanne (FIN)	Nissan 240RS	9:49.37
07	Jimmy McRae (GB)/Mike Nicholson (GB)	Opel Manta 400	10:04.20
08	Shekhar Mehta (EAK)/Yvonne Mehta (EAK)	Nissan 240RS	10:07.01
09	Bertie Fisher (GB)/Austin Frazer (GB)	Opel Manta 400	10:14.19
10	Mikael Ericsson (S)/Claes Billstam (S)	Audi 80 Quattro	10:15.03

Ari Vatanen/Terry Harryman

FINAL DRIVERS' CHAMPIONSHIP POSITIONS			FINAL MANUFACTURERS' CHAMPIONSHIP POSITIONS		
01	Stig Blomqvist	125	01	Audi	120
02	Hannu Mikkola	104	02	Lancia	108
03	Markku Alén	90	03	Peugeot	74
04	Ari Vatanen	60	04	Toyota	62
05	Attilio Bettega	49	05	Renault	55
06	Miki Biasion	43	06	Opel	48
07	Per Eklund	30	07	Nissan	46
08	Björn Waldegård	28	08	Volkswagen	34
09	Shekhar Mehta	27	09	Subaru	11
10	Timo Salonen	27	10	Alfa Romeo	9

1985

ROUND 01 – MONTE CARLO (26th January-1st February)

01	Ari Vatanen (FIN)/Terry Harryman (GB)	Peugeot 205 Turbo 16	10h 20m 49s
02	Walter Röhrl (D)/Christian Geistdörfer (D)	Audi Sport Quattro	10h 26m 06s
03	Timo Salonen (FIN)/Seppo Harjanne (FIN)	Peugeot 205 Turbo 16	10h 30m 54s
04	Stig Blomqvist (S)/Björn Cederberg (S)	Audi Sport Quattro	10h 40m 11s
05	Bruno Saby (F)/Jean-François Fauchille (F)	Peugeot 205 Turbo 16	10h 40m 45s
06	Henri Toivonen (FIN)/Juha Piironen (FIN)	Lancia Rally 037	10h 43m 26s
07	Dany Snobeck (F)/Jean-Pierre Béchu (F)	Renault 5 Turbo	11h 09m 05s
08	Jean-Claude Andruet (F)/Annick Peuvergne (F)	Citroën Visa 1000 Pistes	11h 13m 12s
09	Miki Biasion (I)/Tiziano Siviero (I)	Lancia Rally 037	11h 13m 51s
10	Maurice Chomat (F)/Didier Breton (F)	Citroën Visa 1000 Pistes	11h 20m 00s

Ari Vatanen/Terry Harryman

ROUND 02 – SWEDEN (15th-17th February)

01	Ari Vatanen (FIN)/Terry Harryman (GB)	Peugeot 205 Turbo 16	4h 38m 49s
02	Stig Blomqvist (S)/Björn Cederberg (S)	Audi Sport Quattro	4h 40m 38s
03	Timo Salonen (FIN)/Seppo Harjanne (FIN)	Peugeot 205 Turbo 16	4h 42m 15s
04	Hannu Mikkola (FIN)/Arne Hertz (S)	Audi Sport Quattro	4h 50m 32s
05	Per Eklund (S)/Dave Whittock (GB)	Audi Quattro A2	4h 55m 50s
06	Gunnar Pettersson (S)/Arne Pettersson (S)	Audi 80 Quattro	5h 02m 03s
07	Mikael Ericsson (S)/Johnny Johansson (S)	Audi 80 Quattro	5h 03m 16s
08	Ingvar Carlsson (S)/Benny Melander (S)	Mazda RX 7	5h 08m 35s
09	Mats Jonsson (S)/Åke Gustavsson (S)	Opel Ascona 400	5h 09m 07s
10	Kenneth Eriksson (S)/Bo Thorszelius (S)	Opel Kadett GSI	5h 10m 22s

Ari Vatanen/Terry Harryman

ROUND 03 – PORTUGAL (6th-9th March)

01	Timo Salonen (FIN)/Seppo Harjanne (FIN)	Peugeot 205 Turbo 16	8h 07m 25s
02	Miki Biasion (I)/Tiziano Siviero (I)	Lancia Rally 037	8h 12m 12s
03	Walter Röhrl (D)/Christian Geistdörfer (D)	Audi Sport Quattro	8h 13m 23s
04	Stig Blomqvist (S)/Björn Cederberg (S)	Audi Sport Quattro	8h 31m 11s
05	Werner Grissmann (A)/Jörg Pattermann (A)	Audi Quattro A2	9h 13m 20s
06	José Miguel (P)/José Nascimento (P)	Ford Escort RS1800	9h 20m 42s
07	Carlos Bica (P)/João Sena (P)	Ford Escort RS1800	9h 38m 01s
08	Santinho Mendes (P)/Rui Cunha (P)	Nissan 240RS	9h 40m 01s
09	Jorge Ortigão (P)/João Batista (P)	Toyota Corolla GT	9h 52m 25s
10	Pedro Faria (P)/António Manuel (P)	Ford Escort RS1800	10h 13m 16s

Timo Salonen/Seppo Harjanne

ROUND 04 – SAFARI, AFRICA (4th-8th April)

01	Juha Kankkunen (FIN)/Fred Gallagher (GB)	Toyota Celica TCT	5h 18m
02	Björn Waldegård (S)/Hans Thorszelius (S)	Toyota Celica TCT	5h 52m
03	Mike Kirkland (EAK)/Anton Levitan (EAK)	Nissan 240RS	6h 01m
04	Rauno Aaltonen (FIN)/Lofty Drews (EAK)	Opel Manta 400	6h 12m
05	Erwin Weber (D)/Gunther Wanger (D)	Opel Manta 400	6h 36m
06	Alain Ambrosino (F)/Daniel Le Saux (F)	Nissan 240RS	7h 58m
07	Timo Salonen (FIN)/Seppo Harjanne (FIN)	Peugeot 205 Turbo 16	9h 09m
08	Yasuhiro Iwase (J)/Sudhir Vinayak (EAK)	Opel Ascona 400	12h 22m
09	Ashok Patel (EAK)/Dalbir Kandola (EAK)	Nissan 240RS	13h 49m
10	Carlo Vittuli (EAK)/Robin Nixon (EAK)	Subaru RX Turbo	14h 50m

Juha Kankkunen/Fred Gallagher

ROUND 05 – CORSICA, FRANCE (2nd-4th May)			
01	Jean Ragnotti (F)/Pierre Thimonier (F)	Renault 5 Maxi Turbo	12:54.15
02	Bruno Saby (F)/Jean-François Fauchille (F)	Peugeot 205 Turbo 16 E2	13:06.47
03	Bernard Béguin (F)/Jean-Jacques Lenne (F)	Porsche 911 SC RS	13:20.04
04	Billy Coleman (GB)/Ronan Morgan (GB)	Porsche 911 SC RS	13:51.22
05	Yves Loubet (F)/Jean-Bernard Vieu (F)	Alfa Romeo GTV6	14:03.53
06	Bertrand Balas (F)/Eric Lainé (F)	Alfa Romeo GTV6	14:17.53
07	Jean-Claude Bouquet (F)/Christian Morel (F)	Talbot Samba Rallye	14:24.37
08	Camille Bartoli (F)/Bernard Falempin (F)	Renault 5 Turbo	14:26.30
09	Jean-Jacques Paoletti (F)/Claude Santucci (F)	Renault 5 Turbo	14:53.35
10	Patrick Bernardini (F)/José Bernardini (F)	BMW 323i	14:56.22

Jean Ragnotti/Pierre Thimonier

ROUND 06 – ACROPOLIS, GREECE (27th-30th May)			
01	Timo Salonen (FIN)/Seppo Harjanne (FIN)	Peugeot 205 Turbo 16	10h 20m 19
02	Stig Blomqvist (S)/Björn Cederberg (S)	Audi Sport Quattro	10h 24.34
03	Ingvar Carlsson (S)/Benny Melander (S)	Mazda RX 7	11h 08.25
04	Shekhar Mehta (EAK)/Yvonne Mehta (EAK)	Nissan 240RS	11h 10.46
05	Saeed Al-Hajri (QAT)/John Spiller (GB)	Porsche 911 SC RS	11h 21.50
06	Achim Warmbold (D)/'Biche' (F)	Mazda RX 7	11h 25.16
07	Mike Kirkland (EAK)/Anton Levitan (EAK)	Nissan 240RS	11h 27.51
08	Iórgis Moschous (GR)/Dimitris Vazakas (GR)	Nissan 240RS	11h 45.52
09	Franz Wittmann (A)/Max Ogrisek (A)	Volkswagen Golf GTI	12h 07.05
10	'Stratissino' (GR)/Evangelos Sassalos (GR)	Nissan 240RS	13h 15.53

Timo Salonen/Seppo Harjanne

ROUND 07 – NEW ZEALAND (29th June-2nd July)			
01	Timo Salonen (FIN)/Seppo Harjanne (FIN)	Peugeot 205 Turbo 16 E2	8h 29m 16s
02	Ari Vatanen (FIN)/Terry Harryman (GB)	Peugeot 205 Turbo 16 E2	8h 30m 33s
03	Walter Röhrl (D)/Christian Geistdörfer (D)	Audi Sport Quattro	8h 31m 42s
04	Stig Blomqvist (S)/Björn Cederberg (S)	Audi Sport Quattro	8h 35m 22s
05	Malcolm Stewart (NZ)/Doug Parkhill (NZ)	Audi Quattro A2	9h 29m 04s
06	Reg Cook (NZ)/Wayne Jones (NZ)	Nissan 240RS	9h 46m 53s
07	Inky Tulloch (NZ)/John Cowan (NZ)	Ford Escort RS1800	9h 49m 08s
08	'Possum' Bourne (NZ)/Michael Eggleton (NZ)	Subaru Leone RX Turbo	9h 52m 01s
09	Jim Donald (NZ)/Kevin Lancaster (NZ)	Nissan 240RS	10h 01m 35s
10	Tony Teesdale (NZ)/Bob Haldane (NZ)	Subaru Leone RX Turbo	10h 02m 06s

Timo Salonen/Seppo Harjanne

ROUND 08 – ARGENTINA (30th July-3rd August)			
01	Timo Salonen (FIN)/Seppo Harjanne (FIN)	Peugeot 205 Turbo 16 E2	10h 04m 33s
02	Wilfried Wiedner (A)/Franz Zehetner (A)	Audi Quattro A2	10h 18m 29s
03	Carlos Reutemann (RA)/Jean-François Fauchille (F)	Peugeot 205 Turbo 16 E2	10h 35m 47s
04	Shekhar Mehta (EAK)/Yvonne Mehta (EAK)	Nissan 240RS	11h 04m 46s
05	Ernesto Soto (RA)Martin Christie (RA)	Renault 18 GTX	11h 10m 58s
06	Mario Stillo (RA)/Daniel Stillo (RA)	Renault 12 TS	11h 49m 42s
07	Jayant Shah (EAK)/Lofty Drews (EAK)	Nissan 240RS	12h 02m 16s
08	Sady Bordin (BR)/Joaquim Cunha (BR)	Chevrolet Chevette	12h 13m 46s
09	Federico West (ROU)/Gregorio Assadourian (ROU)	Ford Escort 1.6	12h 31m 15
10	Luis Etchegoyen (ROU)/Luis Borrallo (ROU)	Ford Escort 1.6	12h 37m 00s

Timo Salonen/Seppo Harjanne

ROUND 09 – 1000 LAKES, FINLAND (23rd-25th August)			
01	Timo Salonen (FIN)/Seppo Harjanne (FIN)	Peugeot 205 Turbo 16 E2	4h 10m 35s
02	Stig Blomqvist (S)/Björn Cederberg (S)	Audi Sport Quattro E2	4h 11m 23s
03	Markku Alén (FIN)/Ilkka Kivimäki (FIN)	Lancia Rally 037	4h 14m 14s
04	Henri Toivonen (FIN)/Juha Piironen (FIN)	Lancia Rally 037	4h 22m 01s
05	Kalle Grundel (S)/Peter Diekmann (D)	Peugeot 205 Turbo 16 E2	4h 22m 03s
06	Per Eklund (S)/Bruno Berglund (S)	Audi Quattro A2	4h 23m 08s
07	Björn Waldegård (S)/Hans Thorszelius (S)	Toyota Celica TCT	4h 30m 08s
08	Mikael Ericsson (S)/Reinhard Michel (S)	Audi 80 Quattro	4h 37m 51s
09	Lars-Erik Torph (S)/Jan Svanström (S)	Volkswagen Golf GTI	4h 38m 26s
10.	Sebastian Lindholm (FIN)/Staffan Pettersson (FIN)	Audi 80 Quattro	4h 46m 51s

Timo Salonen/Seppo Harjanne

ROUND 10 – SANREMO, ITALY (29th September-4th October)			
01	Walter Röhrl (D)/Christian Geistdörfer (D)	Audi Sport Quattro E2	7h 10m 10s
02	Timo Salonen (FIN)/Seppo Harjanne (FIN)	Peugeot 205 Turbo 16 E2	7h 16m 39s
03	Henri Toivonen (FIN)/Juha Piironen (FIN)	Lancia Rally 037	7h 18m 02s
04	Markku Alén (FIN)/Ilkka Kivimäki (FIN)	Lancia Rally 037	7h 18m 43s
05	Dario Cerrato (I)/Giuseppe Cerri (I)	Lancia Rally 037	7h 25m 35s
06	Miki Biasion (I)/Tiziano Siviero (I)	Lancia Rally 037	7h 33m 33s
07	Giovanni Del Zoppo (I)/Betty Tognana (I)	Peugeot 205 Turbo 16 E2	7h 58m 02s
08	Werner Grissmann (A)/Jörg Pattermann (A)	Audi Quattro A2	8h 15m 16s
09	Franz Wittmann (A)/Matthias Feltz (D)	Volkswagen Golf GTI	8h 15m 47s
10	'Tchine' (MC)/Pierre Gandolfo (F)	Opel Manta 400	8h 28m 56s

Walter Röhrl/Christian Geistdörfer

ROUND 11 – IVORY COAST, AFRICA (30 October-2nd November)			
01	Juha Kankkunen (FIN)/Fred Gallagher (GB)	Toyota Celica TCT	4h 46m
02	Björn Waldegård (S)/Hans Thorszelius (S)	Toyota Celica TCT	4h 46m
03	Alain Ambrosino (F)/Daniel Le Saux (F)	Nissan 240RS	6h 19m
04	Mike Kirkland (EAK)/Rob Combes (EAK)	Nissan 240RS	8h 36m
05	Eugène Salim (CI)/Clement Konan (CI)	Mitsubishi Lancer Turbo	16h 36m
06	Alessandro Molino (I)/Christian Masséla (F)	Subaru Leone RX Turbo	19h 53m
07	Gilles Petit de Granville (CI)/Denis Carrascosa (CI)	Toyota Celica GT	22h 34m
08	Doïc Dieval (CI)/Lois Cournil (CI)	Mitsubishi Lancer	25h 24m
	Only 8 finishers		

Juha Kankkunen/Fred Gallagher

ROUND 12 RAC, GREAT BRITIAN (24th-28th November)			
01	Henri Toivonen (FIN)/Neil Wilson (GB)	Lancia Delta S4	9h 32m 05s
02	Markku Alén (FIN)/Ilkka Kivimäki (FIN)	Lancia Delta S4	9h 33m 01s
03	Tony Pond (GB)/Rob Arthur (GB)	MG Metro 6R4	9h 34m 32s
04	Per Eklund (S)/Björn Cederberg (S)	Audi Quattro A2	9h 58m 35s
05	Juha Kankkunen (FIN)Fred Gallagher (GB)	Toyota Celica TCT	10h 10m 53s
06	Jimmy McRae (GB)/Ian Grindrod (GB)	Opel Manta 400	10h 16m 01s
07	Terry Kaby (GB)/Kevin Gormley (GB)	Nissan 240RS	10h 24m 08s
08	Russell Brookes (GB)/Mike Broad (GB)	Opel Manta 400	10h 25m 50s
09	Rod Millen (NZ)/Brian Rainbow (GB)	Mazda RX 7	10h 29m 39s
10	Ingvar Carlsson (S)/Benny Melander (S)	Mazda RX 7	10h 29m 57s

Henri Toivonen/Neil Wilson

FINAL DRIVERS' CHAMPIONSHIP POSITIONS		
01	Timo Salonen	127
02	Stig Blomqvist	75
03	Walter Röhrl	59
04	Ari Vatanen	55
05	Juha Kankkunen	48
06	Henri Toivonen	48
07	Markku Alén	37
08	Björn Waldegård	34
09	Mike Kirkland	26
10	Per Eklund	24

FINAL MANUFACTURERS' CHAMPIONSHIP POSITIONS		
01	Peugeot	142
02	Audi	126
03	Lancia	70
04	Nissan	56
05	Toyota	44
06	Renault	38
07	Volkswagen	29
08	Opel	25
09	Porsche	24
10	Mazda	22

1986

ROUND 01 – MONTE CARLO (18th-24th January)

01	Henri Toivonen (FIN)/Sergio Cresto (USA)	Lancia Delta S4	10h 11m 24s
02	Timo Salonen (FIN)/Seppo Harjanne (FIN)	Peugeot 205 Turbo 16 E2	10h 15m 28s
03	Hannu Mikkola (FIN)/Arne Hertz (S)	Audi Sport Quattro E2	10h 18m 46s
04	Walter Röhrl (D)/Christian Geistdörfer (D)	Audi Sport Quattro E2	10h 20m 59s
05	Juha Kankkunen (FIN)/Juha Piironen (FIN)	Peugeot 205 Turbo 16 E2	10h 39m 47s
06	Bruno Saby (F)/Jean-François Fauchille (F)	Peugeot 205 Turbo 16 E2	10h 45m 54s
07	Salvador Servià (E)/Jorge Sabater (E)	Lancia Rally 037	10h 58m 32s
08	Alain Oreille (F)/Sylvie Oreille (F)	Renault 11 Turbo	11h 23m 47s
09	Kenneth Eriksson (S)/Peter Diekmann (D)	Volkswagen Golf GTI 16V	11h 26m 56s
10	Franz Wittmann (A)/Matthias Feltz (D)	Volkswagen Golf GTI 16V	11h 32m 08s

Henri Toivonen/Sergio Cresto

ROUND 02 – SWEDEN (14th-16th February)

01	Juha Kankkunen (FIN)/Juha Piironen (FIN)	Peugeot 205 Turbo 16 E2	5h 09m 19s
02	Markku Alén (FIN)/Ilkka Kivimäki (FIN)	Lancia Delta S4	5h 11m 13s
03	Kalle Grundel (S)/Benny Melander (S)	Ford RS200	5h 15m 35s
04	Mikael Ericsson (S)/Reinhard Michel (D)	Audi 90 Quattro	5h 24m 39s
05	Gunnar Pettersson (S)/Arne Pettersson (S)	Audi Coupé Quattro	5h 24m 57s
06	Jean-Claude Andruet (F)/Annick Peuvergne (F)	Citroën BX4TC	5h 33m 05s
07	Kenneth Eriksson (S)/Peter Diekmann (D)	Volkswagen Golf GTI 16V	5h 34m 30s
08	Roger Ericsson (S)/Per Rosendahl (S)	Subaru RXTurbo	5h 38m 01s
09	Björn Johansson (S)/Anders Olsson (S)	Opel Kadett GSI	5h 41m 22s
10	Sören Nilsson (S)/Åke Gustavsson (S)	Audi 90 Quattro	5h 42m 51s

Juha Kankkunen/Juha Piironen

ROUND 03 – PORTUGAL (5th-8th March)

01	Joaquim Moutinho (P)/Edgar Fortes (P)	Renault 5 Turbo	7h 50m 44s
02	Carlos Bica (P)/Cândido Júnior (P)	Lancia Rally 037	8h 04m 11s
03	Giovanni Del Zoppo (I)/Loris Roggia (I)	Fiat Uno Turbo	8h 07m 36s
04	Jorge Ortigão (P)/Pedro Perez (P)	Toyota Corolla GT	8h 10m 26s
05	'Tchine' (MC)/Gilles Thimonier (F)	Opel Manta 400	8h 13m 04s
06	Jean-Sébastien Couloumiès (F)/Claudine Causse (F)	Peugeot 205 GTI	8h 36m 27s
07	Ramiro Fernandes (P)/António Monteiro (P)	Fiat Ritmo Abarth 130 TC	8h 40m 26s
08	Giovanni Recordati (I)/Freddy Delorme (F)	Opel Manta 400	8h 47m 31s
09	António Segurado (P)/Fernando Prata (P)	Renault 11 Turbo	8h 49m 18s
10	António Coutinho (P)/António Manuel (P)	Toyota Corolla GT	8h 50m 44s

Joaquim Moutinho/Edgar Fortes

ROUND 04 – SAFARI, AFRICA (29th March-2 April)

01	Björn Waldegård (S)/Fred Gallagher (GB)	Toyota Celica TCT	5h 06m
02	Lars-Erik Torph (S)/Bo Thorszelius (S)	Toyota Celica TCT	5h 34m
03	Markku Alén (FIN)/Ilkka Kivimäki (FIN)	Lancia Rally 037	6h 12m
04	Erwin Weber (D)/Gunter Wanger (D)	Toyota Celica TCT	6h 20m
05	Juha Kankkunen (FIN)/Juha Piironen (FIN)	Peugeot 205 Turbo 16 E2	7h 12m
06	Mike Kirkland (EAK)/Robin Nixon (EAK)	Subaru RX Turbo	7h 37m
07	Frank Tundo (EAK)/Quentin Thomson (EAK)	Subaru RX Turbo	8h 11m
08	Shekhar Mehta (EAK)/Rob Combes (EAK)	Peugeot 205 Turbo 16 E2	8h 12m
09	Greg Criticos (EAK)/Marzio Kravos (EAK)	Lancia Rally 037	9h 05m
10	Johnny Hellier (EAK)/David Williamson (EAK)	Lancia Rally 037	9h 11m

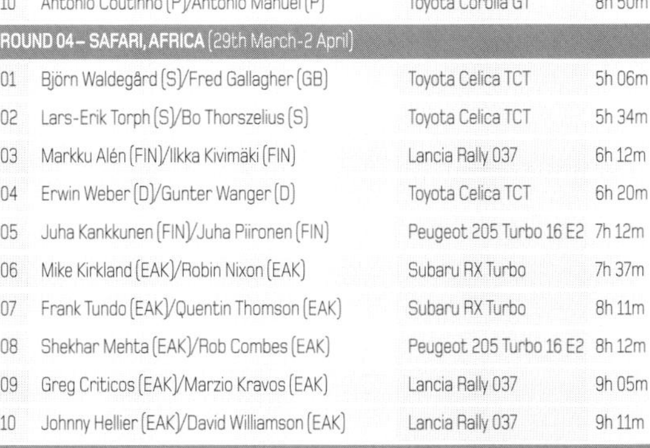

Björn Waldegård/Fred Gallagher

ROUND 05 – CORSICA, FRANCE (1st-3rd May)

01	Bruno Saby (F)/Jean-François Fauchille (F)	Peugeot 205 Turbo 16 E2	11h 52m 44s
02	François Chatriot (F)/Michel Périn (F)	Renault 5 Maxi Turbo	12h 06m 32s
03	Yves Loubet (F)/Jean-Marc Andrié (F)	Alfa Romeo GTV6	12h 45m 59s
04	Jean Ragnotti (F)/Pierre Thimonier (F)	Renault 11 Turbo	12h 56m 12s
05	Jean-Claude Torre (F)/Patrick De La Foata (F)	Renault 5 Turbo	13h 02m 33s
06	Paul Rouby (F)/Jean-Louis Martin (F)	Renault 5 Turbo	13h 03m 48s
07	Michel Neri (F)/Rocky Demedardi (F)	Renault 5 Turbo	13h 08m 00s
08	Kenneth Eriksson (S)/Peter Diekmann (D)	Volkswagen Golf GTI 16V	13h 21m 21s
09	Gilbert Casanova (F)/Philippe Martini (F)	Talbot Samba Rallye	13h 21m 32s
10	Christian Gardavot (F)/Rémy Levivier (F)	Porsche 911 SC	13h 27m 40s

Bruno Saby/Jean-François Fauchille

ROUND 06 – ACROPOLIS, GREECE (2nd-4th June)

01	Juha Kankkunen (FIN)/Juha Piironen (FIN)	Peugeot 205 Turbo 16 E2	7h 20m 01s
02	Miki Biasion (I)/Tiziano Siviero (I)	Lancia Delta S4	7h 21m 38s
03	Bruno Saby (F)/Jean-François Fauchille (F)	Peugeot 205 Turbo 16 E2	7h 29m 55s
04	Saeed Al-Hajri (QAT)/John Spiller (GB)	Porsche 911 SC RS	8h 11m 11s
05	'Stratissino' (GR)/Kóstas Fertakis (GR)	Nissan 240RS	8h 20m 51s
06	Rudi Stohl (A)/Reinhard Kaufmann (A)	Audi Coupé Quattro	8h 24m 44s
07	Kenneth Eriksson (S)/Peter Diekmann (D)	Volkswagen Golf GTI 16V	8h 27m 25s
08	Iórgis Moschous (GR)/Dimitris Vazakas (GR)	Nissan 240RS	8h 28m 34s
09	Franz Wittmann (A)/Matthias Feltz (D)	Volkswagen Golf GTI 16V	8h 34m 22s
10	Michele Rayneri (I)/Stefano Cassina (I)	Fiat Uno Turbo	8h 40m 00s

Juha Kankkunen/Juha Piironen

ROUND 07 – NEW ZEALAND (5th-8th July)

01	Juha Kankkunen (FIN)/Juha Piironen (FIN)	Peugeot 205 Turbo 16 E2	5h 43m 45s
02	Markku Alén (FIN)/Ilkka Kivimäki (FIN)	Lancia Delta S4	5h 45m 25s
03	Miki Biasion (I)/Tiziano Siviero (I)	Lancia Delta S4	5h 53m 36s
04	Mikael Ericsson (S)/Claes Billstam (S)	Lancia Delta S4	5h 56m 37s
05	Timo Salonen (FIN)/Seppo Harjanne (FIN)	Peugeot 205 Turbo 16 E2	6h 16m 36s
06	Neil Allport (NZ)/Rodger Freeth (NZ)	Mazda RX 7	6h 27m 27s
07	Kenneth Eriksson (S)/Peter Diekmann (D)	Volkswagen Golf GTI 16V	6h 34m 15s
08	Paddy Davidson (NZ)/Mike Carmichael (NZ)	Nissan 240RS	6h 36m 18s
09	Reg Cook (NZ)/Wayne Jones (NZ)	Nissan 240RS	6h 38m 12s
10	Rod Millen (NZ)/John Bellefleur (CDN)	Mazda Familia 4WD	6h 40m 03s

Juha Kankkunen/Juha Piironen

ROUND 08 – ARGENTINA (6th-9th August)

01	Miki Biasion (I)/Tiziano Siviero (I)	Lancia Delta S4	6h 36m 26s
02	Markku Alén (FIN)/Ilkka Kivimäki (FIN)	Lancia Delta S4	6h 36m 50s
03	Stig Blomqvist (S)/Bruno Berglund (S)	Peugeot 205 Turbo 16 E2	6h 40m 42s
04	Jorge Recalde (RA)/Jorge del Buono (RA)	Lancia Delta S4	6h 41m 33s
05	Kenneth Eriksson (S)/Peter Diekmann (D)	Volkswagen Golf GTI 16V	7h 22m 17s
06	Rudi Stohl (A)/Reinhard Kaufmann (A)	Audi Coupé Quattro	7h 30m 05s
07	Franz Wittmann (A)/Matthias Feltz (D)	Volkswagen Golf GTI 16V	7h 36m 30s
08	José Celsi (CHI)/Elvio Olave (CHI)	Subaru RX Turbo	7h 48m 44s
09	Ernesto Soto (RA)/Martin Christie (RA)	Renault 18 GTX	7h 51m 43s
10	Basil Criticos (EAK)/Surinder Thatthi (EAK)	Opel Manta 400	8h 02m 44s

Miki Biasion/Tiziano Siviero

ROUND 09 – 1000 LAKES, FINLAND (5th-7th September)

01	Timo Salonen (FIN)/Seppo Harjanne (FIN)	Peugeot 205 Turbo 16 E2	3h 32m 45s
02	Juha Kankkunen (FIN)/Juha Piironen (FIN)	Peugeot 205 Turbo 16 E2	3h 33m 09s
03	Markku Alén (FIN)/Ilkka Kivimäki (FIN)	Lancia Delta S4	3h 34m 30s
04	Stig Blomqvist (S)/Bruno Berglund (S)	Peugeot 205 Turbo 16 E2	3h 35m 22s
05	Mikael Ericsson (S)/Claes Billstam (S)	Lancia Delta S4	3h 41m 11s
06	Kalle Grundel (S)/Benny Melander (S)	Lancia Delta S4	3h 42m 35s
07	Per Eklund (S)/Dave Whittock (GB)	MG Metro 6R4	3h 43m 43s
08	Harri Toivonen (FIN)/Cedric Wrede (FIN)	MG Metro 6R4	3h 52m 19s
09	Lasse Lampi (FIN)/Pentti Kuukkala (FIN)	Audi Coupé Quattro	3h 54m 25s
10	Malcolm Wilson (GB)/Nigel Harris (GB)	MG Metro 6R4	3h 56m 02s

Timo Salonen/Seppo Harjanne

ROUND 10 – IVORY COAST (24th-27th September)

01	Björn Waldegård (S)/Fred Gallagher (GB)	Toyota Celica TCT	1h 29m
02	Lars-Erik Torph (S)/Bo Thorszelius (S)	Toyota Celica TCT	1h 37m
03	Erwin Weber (D)/Gunther Wanger (D)	Toyota Celica TCT	2h 27m
04	Robin Ulyate (EAK)/Ian Street (EAK)	Toyota Celica TCT	3h 05m
05	Samir Assef (LIB)/Christian Boy (F)	Opel Manta 400	3h 25m
06	Wilfried Wiedner (A)/Franz Zehetner (A)	Audi Quattro A2	3h 30m
07	Rudi Stohl (A)/Reinhard Kaufmann (A)	Audi 80 Quattro	5h 20m
08	Alain Ambrosino (F)/Daniel Le Saux (F)	Nissan 240RS	5h 31m
09	Patrick Copetti (F)/Jean-Michel Dionneau (F)	Toyota Corolla GT	10h 39m
10	Martial Yace (CI)/Jean-Paul Yace (CI)	Mitsubishi Lancer Turbo	14h 28m

Björn Waldegård/Fred Gallagher

ROUND 1 – RAC, GREAT BRITAIN (16th-19th November)			
01	Timo Salonen (FIN)/Seppo Harjanne (FIN)	Peugeot 205 Turbo 16 E2	5h 21m 11s
02	Markku Alén (FIN)/Ilkka Kivimäki (FIN)	Lancia Delta S4	5h 22m 33s
03	Juha Kankkunen (FIN)/Juha Piironen (FIN)	Peugeot 205 Turbo 16 E2	5h 27m 16s
04	Mikael Sundström (FIN)/Voitto Silander (FIN)	Peugeot 205 Turbo 16 E2	5h 27m 42s
05	Kalle Grundel (S)/Benny Melander (S)	Ford RS200	5h 29m 32s
06	Tony Pond (GB)/Rob Arthur (GB)	MG Metro 6R4	5h 30m 14s
07	Per Eklund (S)/Dave Whittock (GB)	MG Metro 6R4	5h 33m 12s
08	Jimmy McRae (GB)/Ian Grindrod (GB)	MG Metro 6R4	5h 35m 08s
09	David Llewellin (GB)/Phil Short (GB)	MG Metro 6R4	5h 40m 38s
10	Ingvar Carlsson (S)/Jan-Olof Bohlin (S)	Mazda Familia 4WD	6h 00m 33s

Timo Salonen/Seppo Harjanne

ROUND 12 – OLYMPUS, UNITED STATES (4th-7th December)			
01	Markku Alén (FIN)/Ilkka Kivimäki (FIN)	Lancia Delta S4	5h 26m 10s
02	Juha Kankkunen (FIN)/Juha Piironen (FIN)	Peugeot 205 Turbo 16 E2	5h 29m 36s
03	John Buffum (USA)/Neil Wilson (GB)	Audi Sport Quattro	5h 50m 24s
04	Lars-Erik Torph (S)/Bo Thorszelius (S)	Toyota Celica TCT	5h 56m 29s
05	Björn Waldegård (S)/Fred Gallagher (GB)	Toyota Celica TCT	5h 58m 32s
06	Paolo Alessandrini (I)/Alex Alessandrini (I)	Lancia Delta S4	6h 01m 55s
07	Rod Millen (NZ)/John Bellefleur (CDN)	Mazda Familia 4WD	6h 12m 56s
08	'Possum' Bourne (NZ)/Jim Scott (NZ)	Subaru RX Turbo	6h 20m 27s
09	Clive Smith (NZ)/Harry Ward III (USA)	Toyota Corolla GT	6h 32m 13s
10	Paul Choiniere (USA)/Tom Grimshaw (USA)	Audi 80 Quattro	6h 45m 28s

Markku Alén/Ilkka Kivimäki

FINAL DRIVERS' CHAMPIONSHIP POSITIONS		
01	Juha Kankkunen	118
02	Markku Alén	104
03	Timo Salonen	63
04	Björn Waldegård	48
05	Miki Biasion	47
06	Lars-Erik Torph	40
07	Bruno Saby	38
08	Mikael Ericsson	28
09	Kalle Grundel	26
10	Kenneth Eriksson	25

FINAL MANUFACTURERS' CHAMPIONSHIP POSITIONS		
01	Peugeot	137
02	Lancia	122
03	Volkswagen	65
04	Audi	29
05	Ford	24
06	Toyota	20
07	Renault	14
08	Subaru	13
09	Austin Rover	12
10	Citroën	10

1987

ROUND 01 – MONTE CARLO (17th-22nd January)			
01	Miki Biasion (I)/Tiziano Siviero (I)	Lancia Delta HF 4WD	7h 39m 50s
02	Juha Kankkunen (FIN)/Juha Piironen (FIN)	Lancia Delta HF 4WD	7h 40m 49s
03	Walter Röhrl (D)/Christian Geistdörfer (D)	Audi 200 Quattro	7h 44m 00s
04	Ingvar Carlsson (S)/Per Carlsson (S)	Mazda 323 4WD	7h 55m 45s
05	Kenneth Eriksson (S)/Peter Diekmann (D)	Volkswagen Golf GTI 16V	8h 08m 09s
06	Jean-Pierre Ballet (F)/Marie-Christine Lallement (F)	Citroën Visa 1000 Pistes	8h 09m 58s
07	Christian Dorche (F)/Didier Breton (F)	Citroën Visa 1000 Pistes	8h 11m 44s
08	Jean Ragnotti (F)/Pierre Thimonier (F)	Renault 11 Turbo	8h 13m 26s
09	Erwin Weber (D)/Matthias Feltz (D)	Volkswagen Golf GTI 16V	8h 15m 57s
10	François Chatriot (F)/Michel Périn (F)	Renault 11 Turbo	8h 17m 04s

Miki Biasion/Tiziano Siviero

ROUND 02 – SWEDEN (13th-14th February)			
01	Timo Salonen (FIN)/Seppo Harjanne (FIN)	Mazda 323 4WD	4h 11m 00s
02	Mikael Ericsson (S)/Claes Billstam (S)	Lancia Delta HF 4WD	4h 11m 23s
03	Juha Kankkunen (Fin)/Juha Piironen (FIN)	Lancia Delta HF 4WD	4h 12m 46s
04	Ingvar Carlsson (S)/Per Carlsson (S)	Mazda 323 4WD	4h 13m 01s
05.	Markku Alén (FIN)/Ilkka Kivimäki (FIN)	Lancia Delta HF 4WD	4h 14m 26s
06	Stig Blomqvist (S)/Bruno Berglund (S)	Ford Sierra XR 4x4	4h 14m 30s
07	Per Eklund (S)/Dave Whittock (GB)	Audi Coupé Quattro	4h 14m 48s
08	Kenneth Eriksson (S)/Peter Diekmann (D)	Volkswagen Golf GTI 16V	4h 15m 25s
09	Bror Danielsson (S)/Anders Eklind (S)	Audi Coupé Quattro	4h 17m 47s
10	Erik Johansson (S)/Jan Ostensson (S)	Audi Coupé Quattro	4h 18m 08s

Timo Salonen/Seppo Harjanne

ROUND 03 – PORTUGAL (11th-14th March)			
01	Markku Alén (FIN)/Ilkka Kivimäki (FIN)	Lancia Delta HF 4WD	7h 09m 39s
02	Jean Ragnotti (F)/Pierre Thimonier (F)	Renault 11 Turbo	7h 12m 32s
03	Kenneth Eriksson (S)/Peter Diekmann (D)	Volkswagen Golf GTI 16V	7h 14m 37s
04	Juha Kankkunen (FIN)/Juha Piironen (FIN)	Lancia Delta HF 4WD	7h 20m 46s
05	François Chatriot (F)/Michel Périn (F)	Renault 11 Turbo	7h 25m 14s
06	Georg Fischer (A)/Thomas Zeltner (A)	Audi Coupé Quattro	7h 29m 07s
07	Rudi Stohl (A)/Ernst Röhringer (A)	Audi Coupé Quattro	7h 38m 18s
08	Miki Biasion (I)/Tiziano Siviero (I)	Lancia Delta HF 4WD	7h 44m 05s
09	Joaquim Santos (P)/Miguel Oliveira (P)	Ford Sierra RS Cosworth	7h 52m 59s
10	Jorge Recalde (RA)/Jorge del Buono (RA)	Fiat Uno Turbo	7h 55m 09s

Markku Alén/Ilkka Kivimäki

ROUND 04 – SAFARI, AFRICA (16th-20th April)			
01	Hannu Mikkola (FIN)/Arne Hertz (S)	Audi 200 Quattro	3h 39m 44s
02	Walter Röhrl (D)/Christian Geistdörfer (D)	Audi 200 Quattro	3h 56m 59s
03	Lars-Erik Torph (S)/Benny Melander (S)	Toyota Supra 3.0i	4h 31m 09s
04	Erwin Weber (D)/Matthias Feltz (D)	Volkswagen Golf GTI 16V	5h 47m 27s
05	Per Eklund (S)/Dave Whittock (D)	Subaru RX Turbo	6h 00m 42s
06	Robin Ulyate (EAK)/Ian Street (EAK)	Toyota Supra 3.0i	6h 33m 07s
07	Rudi Stohl (A)/Jürgen Bertl (D)	Audi Coupé Quattro	6h 45m 27s
08	Mike Kirkland (EAK)/Robin Nixon (EAK)	Nissan 200SX	7h 14m 04s
09	Rauno Aaltonen (FIN)/Lofty Drews (EAK)	Opel Kadett GSI	8h 08m 10s
10	Ari Vatanen (FIN)/'Tilber' (MC)	Subaru RX Turbo	9h 06m 17s

Hannu Mikkola/Arne Hertz

ROUND 05 – CORSICA, FRANCE (7th-9th May)			
01	Bernard Béguin (F)/Jean-Jacques Lenne (F)	BMW M3	7h 22m 30s
02	Yves Loubet (F)/Jean-Bernard Vieu (F)	Lancia Delta HF 4WD	7h 24m 38s
03	Miki Biasion (I)/Tiziano Siviero (I)	Lancia Delta HF 4WD	7h 24m 58s
04	Jean Ragnotti (F)/Pierre Thimonier (F)	Renault 11 Turbo	7h 25m 11s
05	François Chatriot (F)/Michel Périn (F)	Renault 11 Turbo	7h 27m 05s
06	Marc Duez (B)/Georges Biar (B)	BMW M3	7h 37m 58s
07	Carlos Sainz (E)/António Boto (E)	Ford Sierra RS Cosworth	7h 41m 16s
08	Didier Auriol (F)/Bernard Occelli (F)	Ford Sierra RS Cosworth	7h 44m 16s
09	Alain Oreille (F)/Sylvie Oreille (F)	Renault 11 Turbo	7h 50m 08s
10	Laurent Poggi (F)/Jean-Paul Chiaroni (F)	Volkswagen Golf GTI 16V	7h 52m 52s

Bernard Béguin/Jean-Jacques Lenne

ROUND 06 – ACROPOLIS, GREECE (31st May-3rd June)			
01	Markku Alén (FIN)/Ilkka Kivimäki (FIN)	Lancia Delta HF 4WD	7h 25m 57s
02	Juha Kankkunen (FIN)/Juha Piironen (FIN)	Lancia Delta HF 4WD	7h 26m 45s
03	Hannu Mikkola (FIN)/Arne Hertz (S)	Audi 200 Quattro	7h 31m 21s
04	Jorge Recalde (RA)/Jorge del Buono (RA)	Audi Coupé Quattro	7h 32m 29s
05	Jean Ragnotti (F)/Pierre Thimonier (F)	Renault 11 Turbo	7h 34m 27s
06	Erwin Weber (D)/Matthias Feltz (D)	Volkswagen Golf GTI 16V	7h 36m 53s
07	Miki Biasion (I)/Tiziano Siviero (I)	Lancia Delta HF 4WD	7h 53m 54s
08	François Chatriot (F)/Michel Périn (F)	Renault 11 Turbo	7h 58m 07s
09	Rudi Stohl (A)/Ernst Röhringer (A)	Audi Coupé Quattro	8h 04m 04s
10	Mike Kirkland (EAK)/Robin Nixon (EAK)	Nissan 200SX	8h 07m 46s

Markku Alén/Ilkka Kivimäki

ROUND 07 – OLYMPUS, UNITED STATES (26th-29th June)

01	Juha Kankkunen (FIN)/Juha Piironen (FIN)	Lancia Delta HF 4WD	5h 59m 24s
02	Miki Biasion (I)/Tiziano Siviero (I)	Lancia Delta HF 4WD	5h 59m 36s
03	Markku Alén (FIN)/Ilkka Kivimäki (FIN)	Lancia Delta HF 4WD	6h 00m 06s
04	Rod Millen (NZ)/John Bellefleur (CDN)	Mazda 323 4WD	6h 11m 12s
05	Paolo Alessandrini (I)/Alex Alessandrini (I)	Lancia Delta HF 4WD	6h 14m 05s
06	Björn Waldegård (S)/Fred Gallagher (GB)	Toyota Supra 3.0i	6h 17m 26s
07	Jorge Recalde (RA)/Jorge del Buono (RA)	Lancia Delta HF 4WD	6h 23m 07s
08	Shekhar Mehta (EAK)/Yvonne Mehta (EAK)	Nissan 200SX	6h 24m 46s
09	Per Eklund (S)/Dave Whittock (GB)	Nissan 200SX	6h 25m 03s
10	Clive Smith (NZ)/Harry Ward III (USA)	Toyota Corolla GT	6h 35m 06s

Juha Kankkunen/Juha Piironen

ROUND 08 – NEW ZEALAND (11th-14th July)

01	Franz Wittmann (A)/Jörg Pattermann (A)	Lancia Delta HF 4WD	6h 56m 00s
02	Kenneth Eriksson (S)/Peter Diekmann (D)	Volkswagen Golf GTI 16V	6h 56m 47s
03	'Possum' Bourne (NZ)/Michael Eggleton (NZ)	Subaru RX Turbo	7h 04m 25s
04	Tony Teesdale (NZ)/Greg Horne (NZ)	Mazda 323 4WD	7h 18m 31s
05	David Officer (AUS)/Kate Officer (AUS)	Mitsubishi Starion Turbo	7h 35m 12s
06	Ken Adamson (NZ)/Greg Adamson (NZ)	Toyota Corolla GT	7h 40m 17s
07	Stuart Weeber (NZ)/John Kennard (GB)	Toyota Starlet	8h 00m 50s
08	Simon Davies (NZ)/Simon Curry (NZ)	Subaru RX Turbo	8h 05m 41s
09	Kouichi Hazu (J)/Hakaru Ichino (J)	Isuzu Gemini	8h 09m 58s
10	Grant Goile (NZ)/Tony Morrison (NZ)	Toyota Starlet	8h 12m 41s

Franz Wittmann/Jörg Pattermann

ROUND 09 – ARGENTINA (4th-8th August)

01	Miki Biasion (I)/Tiziano Siviero (I)	Lancia Delta HF 4WD	7h 10m 27s
02	Jorge Recalde (RA)/Jorge del Buono (RA)	Lancia Delta HF 4WD	7h 11m 28s
03	Erwin Weber (D)/Matthias Feltz (D)	Volkswagen Golf GTI 16V	7h 37m 11s
04	Kenneth Eriksson (S)/Peter Diekmann (D)	Volkswagen Golf GTI 16V	7h 59m 16s
05	Gabriel Raies (RA)/Raúl Campana (RA)	Renault 18 GTX	8h 02m 43s
06	Paulo Lemos (BR)/Artur Cezar (BR)	Volkswagen Gol 1.6	8h 08m 42
07	Jorge Fleck (BR)/Silvio Klein (BR)	Volkswagen Gol 1.6	8h 13m 12s
08	Jorge Bescham (RA)/José Garcia (RA)	Fiat Regata 85	8h 31m 28s
09	Ernesto Soto (RA)/Martin Christie (RA)	Renault 18 GTX	8h 35m 48s
10	Alejandro Schmauk (CHI)/Felipe Horta (CHI)	Alfa Romeo 33 4x4	8h 39m 12s

Miki Biasion/Tiziano Siviero

ROUND 10 – 1000 LAKES, FINLAND (27th-30th August)

01	Markku Alén (FIN)/Ilkka Kivimäki (FIN)	Lancia Delta HF 4WD	5h 12m 22s
02	Ari Vatanen (FIN)/Terry Harryman (GB)	Ford Sierra RS Cosworth	5h 17m 54s
03	Stig Blomqvist (S)/Bruno Berglund (S)	Ford Sierra RS Cosworth	5h 18m 51s
04	Per Eklund (S)/Dave Whittock (GB)	Audi Coupé Quattro	5h 21m 00s
05	Juha Kankkunen (FIN)/Juha Piironen (FIN)	Lancia Delta HF 4WD	5h 21m 34s
06	Thorbjörn Edling (S)/Hans Andersson (S)	Mazda 323 4WD	5h 23m 47s
07	Sebastian Lindholm (FIN)/Staffan Pettersson (FIN)	Audi Coupé Quattro	5h 26m 45s
08	Tomi Palmqvist (FIN)/Arto Juselius (FIN)	Audi Coupé Quattro	5h 28m 28s
09	Erik Johansson (S)/Johnny Johansson (S)	Audi Coupé Quattro	5h 30m 47s
10	Timo Heinonen (FIN)/Tapio Eirtovaara (FIN)	Audi Coupé Quattro	5h 41m 07s

Markku Alén/Ilkka Kivimäki

ROUND 11 – IVORY COAST, AFRICA (22nd-26th September)

01	Kenneth Eriksson (S)/Peter Diekmann (D)	Volkswagen Golf GTI 16V	48m 57s
02	Shekhar Mehta (EAK)/Rob Combes (EAK)	Nissan 200SX	1h 09m 18s
03	Erwin Weber (D)/Matthias Feltz (D)	Volkswagen Golf GTI 16V	2h 05m 56s
04	Patrick Tauziac (F)/Claude Papin (F)	Mitsubishi Starion Turbo	5h 38m 53s
05	Patrick Copetti (F)/Jean-Michel Dionneau (F)	Toyota Corolla GT	6h 53m 38s
06	Adolphe Choteau (CI)/Jean-Pierre Van de Wauwer (B)	Toyota Corolla GT	7h 57m 16s
07	Martial Yace (CI)/Jean-Paul Yace (CI)	Mitsubishi Starion Turbo	11h 01m 43s
08	Alessandro Molino (I)/Nicola Albanese (I)	Lancia Delta HF 4WD	15h 21m 19s
09	Fredrik Donner (FIN)/Cedric Wrede (FIN)	Subaru RX Turbo	15h 35m 39s
10	Lambert Kouame (CI)/Koffy Kouame (CI)	Toyota Celica GT	21h 43m 04s

Kenneth Eriksson/Peter Diekmann

ROUND 12 – SANREMO, ITALY (12th-15th October)

01	Miki Biasion (I)/Tiziano Siviero (I)	Lancia Delta HF 4WD	6h 09m 19s
02	Bruno Saby (F)/Jean-François Fauchille (F)	Lancia Delta HF 4WD	6h 14m 30s
03	Jean Ragnotti (F)/Pierre Thimonier (F)	Renault 11 Turbo	6h 16m 55s
04	Didier Auriol (F)/Bernard Occelli (F)	Ford Sierra RS Cosworth	6h 18m 13s
05	Fabrizio Tabaton (I)/Luciano Tedeschini (I)	Lancia Delta HF 4WD	6h 20m 05s
06	Guy Fréquelin (F)/Didier Breton (F)	Opel Kadett GSI	6h 20m 37s
07	Alex Fiorio (I)/Luigi Pirollo (I)	Lancia Delta HF 4WD	6h 22m 15s
08	Mikael Ericsson (S)/Claes Billstam (S)	Lancia Delta HF 4WD	6h 24m 00s
09	Paolo Alessandrini (I)/Alex Alessandrini (I)	Lancia Delta HF 4WD	6h 29m 53s
10	Sepp Haider (A)/Jörg Pattermann (A)	Opel Kadett GSI	6h 33m 36s

Miki Biasion/Tiziano Siviero

ROUND 13 – RAC, GREAT BRITAIN (22nd-25th November)

01	Juha Kankkunen (FIN)/Juha Piironen (FIN)	Lancia Delta HF 4WD	5h 26m 36s
02	Stig Blomqvist (S)/Bruno Berglund (S)	Ford Sierra RS Cosworth	5h 30m 16s
03	Jimmy McRae (GB)/Ian Grindrod (GB)	Ford Sierra RS Cosworth	5h 33m 15s
04	Mikael Ericsson (S)/Claes Billstam (S)	Lancia Delta HF 4WD	5h 35m 11s
05	Markku Alén (FIN)/Ilkka Kivimäki (FIN)	Lancia Delta HF 4WD	5h 35m 26s
06	David Llewellin (GB)Phil Short (GB)	Audi Coupé Quattro	5h 45m 41s
07	Mats Jonsson (S)/Johnny Johansson (S)	Opel Kadett GSI	5h 48m 36s
08	Carlos Sainz (E)/António Boto (E)	Ford Sierra RS Cosworth	5h 49m 16s
09	Kenneth Eriksson (S)/Peter Diekmann (D)	Volkswagen Golf GTI 16V	5h 51m 20s
10	Roger Ericsson (S)/Per Rosendahl (S)	Subaru RX Turbo	5h 58m 36s

Juha Kankkunen/Juha Piironen

FINAL DRIVERS' CHAMPIONSHIP POSITIONS			FINAL MANUFACTURERS' CHAMPIONSHIP POSITIONS		
01	Juha Kankkunen	100	01	Lancia	140
02	Miki Biasion	94	02	Audi	82
03	Markku Alén	88	03	Renault	71
04	Kenneth Eriksson	70	04	Volkswagen	64
05	Jean Ragnotti	51	05	Ford	62
06	Erwin Weber	44	06	Mazda	52
07	Stig Blomqvist	33	07	Toyota	22
08	Hannu Mikkola	32	08	BMW	20
09	Jorge Recalde	30	09	Opel	16
10	Mikael Ericsson	28	10	Subaru	12

1988

ROUND 01 – MONTE CARLO (16th-21st January)

01	Bruno Saby (F)/Jean-François Fauchille (F)	Lancia Delta HF 4WD	7h 19m 11s
02	Alex Fiorio (I)/Luigi Pirollo (I)	Lancia Delta HF 4WD	7h 30m 01s
03	Jean-Pierre Ballet (F)/Marie-Christine Lallement (F)	Peugeot 205 GTI	7h 42m 46s
04	Alain Oreille (F)/Jean-Marc André (F)	Renault 11 Turbo	7h 51m 56s
05	Timo Salonen (FIN)/Seppo Harjanne (FIN)	Mazda 323 4WD	7h 56m 08s
06	François Chauche (F)/Thierry Barjou (F)	BMW 325iX	7h 56m 22s
07	Christophe Spiliotis (MC)/Isabelle Spiliotis (MC)	Audi Coupé Quattro	7h 58m 16s
08	Giovanni Del Zoppo (I)/Pierangelo Scalvini (I)	Lancia Delta HF 4WD	7h 59m 56s
09	Pierre Bos (F)/Jean-Claude Leuvrey (F)	Audi Coupé Quattro	8h 03m 01s
10	Richard Frau (F)/Philippe David (F)	Renault 5 GT Turbo	8h 03m 37s

Bruno Saby/Jean-François Fauchille

ROUND 02 – SWEDEN (4th-6th February)

01	Markku Alén (FIN)/Ilkka Kivimäki (FIN)	Lancia Delta HF 4WD	5h 02m 31s
02	Stig Blomqvist (S)/Benny Melander (S)	Ford Sierra XR4x4	5h 04m 08s
03	Lars-Erik Torph (S)/Tina Thörner (S)	Audi Coupé Quattro	5h 10m 03s
04	Erik Johansson (S)/Johnny Johansson (S)	Audi Coupé Quattro	5h 12m 27s
05	Håkan Eriksson (S)/Jan Svanström (S)	Opel Kadett GSI 16V	5h 14m 08s
06	Björn Johansson (S)/Anders Olsson (S)	Audi Coupé Quattro	5h 14m 17s
07	Bror Danielsson (S)/Anders Eklind (S)	Audi Coupé Quattro	5h 14m 47s
08	Malcolm Wilson (GB)/Ian Grindrod (GB)	Opel Kadett GSI 16V	5h 16m 18s
09	Sebastian Lindholm (FIN)/Staffan Pettersson (FIN)	Audi Coupé Quattro	5h 16m 40s
10	Tomas Jansson (S)/Ingemar Algerstedt (S)	Audi 80 Quattro	5h 18m 39s

Markku Alén/Ilkka Kivimäki

ROUND 03 – PORTUGAL (1st–6th March)			
01	Miki Biasion (I)/Carlo Cassina (I)	Lancia Delta Integrale	6h 44m 01s
02	Alex Fiorio (I)/Luigi Pirollo (I)	Lancia Delta HF 4WD	6h 52m 47s
03	Yves Loubet (F)/Jean-Bernard Vieu (F)	Lancia Delta HF 4WD	6h 53m 23s
04	Hannu Mikkola (FIN)/Christian Geistdörfer (D)	Mazda 323 4WD	6h 54m 45s
05	Stig Blomqvist (S)/Benny Melander (S)	Ford Sierra RS Cosworth	6h 55m 39s
06	Markku Alén (FIN)/Ilkka Kivimäki (FIN)	Lancia Delta Integrale	6h 56m 09s
07	Erwin Weber (D)/Matthias Feltz (D)	Volkswagen Golf GTI 16V	7h 07m 45s
08	Inverno Amaral (P)/Joaquim Neto (P)	Renault 11 Turbo	7h 11m 41s
09	Carlos Bica (P)/Fernando Prata (P)	Lancia Delta HF 4WD	7h 17m 55s
10	Jorge Recalde (RA)/Jorge del Buono (RA)	Lancia Delta Integrale	7h 19m 56s

Miki Biasion/Carlo Cassina

ROUND 04 – SAFARI, AFRICA (31st March–4th April)			
01	Miki Biasion (I)/Tiziano Siviero (I)	Lancia Delta Integrale	2h 51m 04s
02	Mike Kirkland (EAK)/Robin Nixon (EAK)	Nissan 200SX	3h 03m 57s
03	Per Eklund (S)/Dave Whittock (GB)	Nissan 200SX	3h 38m 26s
04	Kenneth Eriksson (S)/Peter Diekmann (D)	Toyota Supra Turbo	3h 53m 46s
05	Juha Kankkunen (FIN)/Juha Piironen (FIN)	Toyota Supra Turbo	4h 16m 22s
06	Ian Duncan (EAK)/Ian Munro (EAK)	Subaru RX Turbo	4h 28m 34s
07	Björn Waldegård (S)/Fred Gallagher (GB)	Toyota Supra Turbo	4h 29m 31s
08	Rudi Stohl (A)/Reinhard Kaufmann (A)	Audi Coupé Quattro	4h 50m 09s
09	'Possum' Bourne (NZ)/Rodger Freeth (NZ)	Subaru RX Turbo	7h 23m 50s
10	Jim Heather-Hayes (EAK)/Anton Levitan (EAK)	Nissan March Turbo	9h 25m 42s

Miki Biasion/Tiziano Siviero

ROUND 05 – CORSICA, FRANCE (3rd–6th May)			
01	Didier Auriol (F)/Bernard Occelli (F)	Ford Sierra RS Cosworth	7h 12m 04s
02	Yves Loubet (F)/Jean-Bernard Vieu (F)	Lancia Delta Integrale	7h 15m 09s
03	Bruno Saby (F)/Jean-François Fauchille (F)	Lancia Delta Integrale	7h 16m 53s
04	François Chatriot (F)/Michel Périn (F)	BMW M3	7h 23m 28s
05	Carlos Sainz (E)/Luis Moya (E)	Ford Sierra RS Cosworth	7h 26m 09s
06	Kenneth Eriksson (S)/Peter Diekmann (D)	Toyota Celica GT-Four	7h 29m 24s
07	Bernard Béguin (F)/Jean-Jacques Lenne (F)	BMW M3	7h 35m 08s
08	Paul Rouby (F)/Jean-Louis Martin (F)	Alfa Romeo 75 V6 3.0	7h 44m 59s
09	César Baroni (F)/Michel Rousseau (F)	Ford Sierra RS Cosworth	7h 45m 17s
10	Alain Oreille (F)/Sylvie Oreille (F)	Renault 5 GT Turbo	7h 46m 02s

Didier Auriol/Bernard Occelli

ROUND 06 – ACROPOLIS, GREECE (29th May–1st June)			
01	Miki Biasion (I)/Tiziano Siviero (I)	Lancia Delta Integrale	7h 03m 00
02	Mikael Ericsson (S)/Claes Billstam (S)	Lancia Delta Integrale	7h 04m 43
03	Alex Fiorio (I)/Luigi Pirollo (I)	Lancia Delta Integrale	7h 10m 40
04	Markku Alén (FIN)/Ilkka Kivimäki (FIN)	Lancia Delta Integrale	7h 13m 46
05	Rudi Stohl (A)/Ernst Röhringer (A)	Audi Coupé Quattro	7h 33m 49
06	'Jigger' (GR)/Kóstas Stefanis (GR)	Lancia Delta Integrale	7h 37m 14
07	'Stratissino' (GR)/Kóstas Fertakis (GR)	Nissan 200SX	7h 42m 38
08	Kóstas Apostolou (GR)/Mihalis Kriadis (GR)	Volkswagen Golf GTI	7h 58m 03
09	Flory Roothaert (B)/Christian Wauters (B)	Nissan 200SX	8h 05m 25
10	Pascal Gaban (B)/Willy Lux (B)	Mazda 323 4WD	8h 21m 23

Miki Biasion/Tiziano Siviero

ROUND 07 – OLYMPUS, UNITED STATES (23rd–26th June)			
01	Miki Biasion (I)/Tiziano Siviero (I)	Lancia Delta Integrale	5h 28m 44s
02	Alex Fiorio (I)/Luigi Pirollo (I)	Lancia Delta Integrale	5h 34m 07s
03	John Buffum (USA)/John Bellefleur (CDN)	Audi Coupé Quattro	5h 44m 59s
04	Georg Fischer (A)/Thomas Zeltner (A)	Audi 200 Quattro	5h 47m 08s
05	Giovanni Del Zoppo (I)/Pierangelo Scalvini (I)	Lancia Delta Integrale	5h 48m 56s
06	Jorge Recalde (RA)/Jorge del Buono (RA)	Lancia Delta Integrale	5h 51m 38s
07	Nobuhiro Tajima (JAP)/Kenzo Sudo (JAP)	Suzuki Cultus GTI	6h 07m 24s
08	Rod Millen (NZ)/Harry Ward III (USA)	Mazda 323 4WD	6h 15m 11s
09	Alan Carter (NZ)/Martin Headland (CDN)	Suzuki Cultus GTI	6h 17m 05s
10	Michael Lieu (HK)/Geoff Case (USA)	Mitsubishi Galant VR-4	6h 21m 56s

Miki Biasion/Tiziano Siviero

ROUND 08 – NEW ZEALAND (9th–12th July)			
01	Sepp Haider (A)/Ferdi Hinterleitner (A)	Opel Kadett GSI 16V	7h 38m 39s
02	Ray Wilson (NZ)/Stuart Lewis (NZ)	Mazda 323 4WD	7h 57m 16s
03	Malcolm Stewart (NZ)/John Kennard (GB)	Audi Coupé Quattro	8h 02m 25s
04	David Officer (AUS)/Kate Officer (AUS)	Mitsubishi Starion Turbo	8h 04m 20s
05	Ross Meekings (NZ)/Steve March (NZ)	Toyota Corolla 16V	8h 05m 06s
06	Marty Roestenburg (NZ)/Pat Norris (NZ)	Toyota Starlet	8h 21m 02s
07	Joe McAndrew (NZ)/Mike Wilkin (NZ)	Toyota Starlet	8h 29m 18s
08	Tetsuo Sano (J)/Takeo Henmi (J)	Toyota Celica GT-Four	8h 29m 54s
09	Dave Strong (NZ)/Jeff Grove (NZ)	Daihatsu Charade GTI	8h 38m 08s
10	Murray Walker (NZ)/Neil Harris (NZ)	Suzuki Swift GTI	8h 38m 35s

Sepp Haider/Ferdi Hinterleitner

ROUND 09 – ARGENTINA (2nd–6th August)			
01	Jorge Recalde (RA)/Jorge del Buono (RA)	Lancia Delta Integrale	7h 05m 16s
02	Miki Biasion (I)/Tiziano Siviero (I)	Lancia Delta Integrale	7h 08m 51s
03	Franz Wittmann (A)/Jörg Pattermann (A)	Lancia Delta Integrale	7h 34m 13s
04	Rudi Stohl (A)/Ernst Röhringer (A)	Audi 90 Quattro	7h 51m 39s
05	José Celsi (CHI)/Elvio Olave (CHI)	Subaru RX Turbo	8h 10m 57s
06	Juan Maria Traverso (RA)/Rubén Valentini (RA)	Renault 18 GTX	8h 27m 33s
07	Marcelo Raies (RA)/Sigfrido Schroeder (RA)	Renault 18 GTX	8h 30m 12s
08	Claudio Israel (CHI)/Manuel Jaurena (CHI)	Toyota Corolla GT	8h 35m 24s
09	José Luis Grasso (RA)/José Volta (RA)	Fiat Regata 85	8h 37m 26s
10	Norberto Gianre (RA)/Geronimo Giaccone (RA)	Fiat 147	8h 40m 42s

Jorge Recalde/Jorge del Buono

ROUND 10 – 1000 LAKES, FINLAND (26th–28th August)			
01	Markku Alén (FIN)/Ilkka Kivimäki (FIN)	Lancia Delta Integrale	4h 35m 29s
02	Mikael Ericsson (S)/Claes Billstam (S)	Lancia Delta Integrale	4h 38m 24s
03	Didier Auriol (F)/Bernard Occelli (F)	Ford Sierra RS Cosworth	4h 45m 15s
04	Timo Salonen (FIN)/Seppo Harjanne (FIN)	Mazda 323 4WD	4h 45m 50s
05	Stig Blomqvist (S)/Benny Melander (S)	Ford Sierra RS Cosworth	4h 46m 32s
06	Carlos Sainz (E)/Luis Moya (E)	Ford Sierra RS Cosworth	4h 46m 41s
07	Alex Fiorio (I)/Luigi Pirollo (I)	Lancia Delta Integrale	4h 53m 14s
08	Harry Joki (S)/Per Carlsson (S)	Lancia Delta Integrale	4h 55m 11s
09	Tomas Jansson (S)/Ingemar Algerstedt (S)	Audi 80 Quattro	4h 55m 32s
10	Mats Jonsson (S)/Lars Bäckman (S)	Opel Kadett GSI 16V	4h 56m 48s

Markku Alén/Ilkka Kivimäki

ROUND 11 – IVORY COAST, AFRICA (20th–24th September)			
01	Alain Ambrosino (F)/Daniel Le Saux (F)	Nissan 200SX	3h 34m 51s
02	Pascal Gaban (B)/Willy Lux (B)	Mazda 323 4WD	5h 06m 33s
03	Patrick Tauziac (F)/Claude Papin (F)	Mitsubishi Starion Turbo	7h 20m 20s
04	Alain Oudit (F)/Patrice Lemarie (F)	Volkswagen Golf GTI 16V	7h 53m 08s
05	Adolphe Choteau (CI)/Jean-Pierre Claverie (F)	Toyota Corolla GT	7h 53m 48s
06	Didier Monin (B)/Eddy Chevaillier (B)	Mazda 323 4WD	8h 08m 16s
07	Roberto Ambrosoli (I)/Renzo Veronelli (I)	Mazda 323 4WD	9h 49m 02s
08	Soumare Mafall (CI)/Angelberg Kady (CI)	Toyota Corolla GT	11h 26m 02s
09	Michel Molinie (CI)/Marc Molinie (CI)	Volkswagen Golf GTI	11h 54m 08s
10	Samir Assef (LEB)/Kouamo Assale (LEB)	Toyota Corolla GT	12h 42m 03s

Alain Ambrosino/Daniel Le Saux

ROUND 12 – SANREMO, ITALY (10th–14th October)			
01	Miki Biasion (I)/Tiziano Siviero (I)	Lancia Delta Integrale	6h 06m 41s
02	Alex Fiorio (I)/Luigi Pirollo (I)	Lancia Delta Integrale	6h 07m 34s
03	Dario Cerrato (I)/Giuseppe Cerri (I)	Lancia Delta Integrale	6h 08m 35s
04	Markku Alén (FIN)/Ilkka Kivimäki (FIN)	Lancia Delta Integrale	6h 08m 55s
05	Carlos Sainz (E)/Luis Moya (E)	Ford Sierra RS Cosworth	6h 12m 59s
06	Kenneth Eriksson (S)/Peter Diekmann (D)	Toyota Celica GT-Four	6h 16m 36s
07	Stig Blomqvist (S)/Benny Melander (S)	Ford Sierra RS Cosworth	6h 29m 58s
08	Raimund Baumschlager (A)/Andreas Wolf (A)	Volkswagen Golf GTI 16V	6h 36m 20s
09	Paola De Martini (I)/Umberta Gibellini (I)	Audi 90 Quattro	6h 37m 07s
10	Paolo Alessandrini (I)/Alex Alessandrini (I)	Lancia Delta Integrale	6h 37m 45s

Miki Biasion/Tiziano Siviero

ROUND 13 – RAC, GREAT BRITAIN (20th-24th November)			
01	Markku Alén (FIN)/Ilkka Kivimäki (FIN)	Lancia Delta Integrale	7h 15m 37s
02	Timo Salonen (FIN)/Voitto Silander (FIN)	Mazda 323 4WD	7h 19m 43s
03	Björn Waldegård (S)/Fred Gallagher (GB)	Toyota Celica GT-Four	7h 22m 16s
04	Pentti Airikkala (FIN)/Brian Murphy (GB)	Lancia Delta Integrale	7h 25m 06s
05	Armin Schwarz (D)/Arne Hertz (S)	Audi 200 Quattro	7h 26m 43s
06	Stig Blomqvist (S)/Benny Melander (S)	Ford Sierra RS Cosworth	7h 34m 22s
07	Carlos Sainz (E)/Luis Moya (E)	Ford Sierra RS Cosworth	7h 36m 53s
08	Stig-Olov Walfridsson (S)/Gunnar Barth (S)	Audi 80 Quattro	7h 41m 06s
09	Mats Jonsson (S)/Lars Bäckman (S)	Opel Kadett GSI 16V	7h 48m 56s
10	Kalle Grundel (S)/Johnny Johansson (S)	Peugeot 309 GTI	7h 49m 38s

Markku Alén/Ilkka Kivimäki

FINAL DRIVERS' CHAMPIONSHIP POSITIONS			FINAL MANUFACTURERS' CHAMPIONSHIP POSITIONS		
01	Miki Biasion	115	01	Lancia	140
02	Markku Alén	86	02	Ford	79
03	Alex Fiorio	76	03	Audi	71
04	Stig Blomqvist	41	04	Mazda	66
05	Timo Salonen	33	05	Toyota	46
06	Bruno Saby	32	06	Renault	32
06=	Didier Auriol	32	07	BMW	25
08	Mikael Ericsson	30	08	Nissan	23
09	Jorge Recalde	27	09	Subaru	18

1989

ROUND 01 – SWEDEN (6th-8th January)			
01	Ingvar Carlsson (S)/Per Carlsson (S)	Mazda 323 4WD	4h 58m 15s
02	Per Eklund (S)/Dave Whittock (GB)	Lancia Delta Integrale	4h 59m 18s
03	Kenneth Eriksson (S)/Staffan Parmander (S)	Toyota Celica GT-Four	4h 59m 57s
04	Mikael Ericsson (S)/Claes Billstam (S)	Lancia Delta Integrale	5h 01m 58s
05	Stig Blomqvist (S)/Benny Melander (S)	Audi 200 Quattro	5h 02m 52s
06	Sebastian Lindholm (FIN)/Pentti Kuukkala (FIN)	Lancia Delta Integrale	5h 03m 00s
07	Leif Asterhag (S)/Ragnar Spjuth (S)	Toyota Celica GT-Four	5h 03m 17s
08	Stig-Olov Walfridsson (S)/Gunnar Barth (S)	Audi 80 Quattro	5h 07m 45s
09	Björn Johansson (S)/Anders Olsson (S)	Opel Kadett GSI 16V	5h 07m 57s
10	Håkan Eriksson (S)/Jan Svanström (S)	Opel Kadett GSI 16V	5h 14m 07s

Ingvar Carlsson/Per Carlsson

ROUND 02 – MONTE CARLO (21st-26th January)			
01	Miki Biasion (I)/Tiziano Siviero (I)	Lancia Delta Integrale	7h 13m 27s
02	Didier Auriol (F)/Bernard Occelli (F)	Lancia Delta Integrale	7h 19m 54s
03	Bruno Saby (F)/Jean-François Fauchille (F)	Lancia Delta Integrale	7h 21m 08s
04	Hannu Mikkola (FIN)/Christian Geistdörfer (D)	Mazda 323 4WD	7h 25m 41s
05	Juha Kankkunen (FIN)/Juha Piironen (FIN)	Toyota Celica GT-Four	7h 28m 16s
06	Patrick Snijers (B)/Dany Colebunders (B)	Toyota Celica GT-Four	7h 31m 38s
07	Dario Cerrato (I)/Gianni Vasino (I)	Lancia Delta Integrale	7h 44m 21s
08	Marc Duez (B)/Alain Lopes (B)	BMW M3	7h 47m 29s
09	Paola De Martini (I)/Umberta Gibellini (I)	Audi 90 Quattro	7h 58m 33s
10	Alain Oreille (F)/Gilles Thimonier (F)	Renault 5 GT Turbo	7h 59m 30s

Miki Biasion/Tiziano Siviero

ROUND 03 – PORTUGAL (28th February-4th March)			
01	Miki Biasion (I)/Tiziano Siviero (I)	Lancia Delta Integrale	6h 47m 01s
02	Markku Alén (FIN)/Ilkka Kivimäki (FIN)	Lancia Delta Integrale	6h 57m 19s
03	Alex Fiorio (I)/Luigi Pirollo (I)	Lancia Delta Integrale	7h 10m 19s
04	Georg Fischer (A)/Thomas Zeltner (A)	Audi 200 Quattro	7h 21m 56s
05	Marc Duez (B)/Alain Lopes (B)	BMW M3	7h 26m 29s
06	Carlos Bica (P)/Fernando Prata (P)	Lancia Delta HF 4WD	7h 29m 59s
07	Grégoire De Mévius (B)/Willy Lux (B)	Mazda 323 4WD	7h 33m 44s
08	Paolo Andreucci (I)/Carlo Cassina (I)	Lancia Delta Integrale	7h 37m 48s
09	Fredrik Skoghag (S)/Peter Diekmann (D)	Lancia Delta Integrale	7h 41m 20s
10	Gustavo Trelles (ROU)/Ricardo Ivetich (ROU)	Lancia Delta Integrale	7h 49m 06s

Miki Biasion/Tiziano Siviero

ROUND 04 – SAFARI, AFRICA (23rd-27th March)			
01	Miki Biasion (I)/Tiziano Siviero (I)	Lancia Delta Integrale	6h 55m 27s
02	Mike Kirkland (EAK)/Robin Nixon (EAK)	Nissan 200SX	8h 16m 11s
03	Stig Blomqvist (S)/Björn Cederberg (S)	Volkswagen Golf GTI 16V	9h 17m 39s
04	Björn Waldegård (S)/Fred Gallagher (GB)	Toyota Supra Turbo	9h 46m 23s
05	Ian Duncan (EAK)/Ian Munro (EAK)	Toyota Supra Turbo	9h 57m 28s
06	Vic Preston, Jr (EAK)/John Lyall (EAK)	Nissan 200SX	10h 35m 21s
07	'Possum' Bourne (NZ)/Rodger Freeth (NZ)	Subaru RX Turbo	10h 38m 45s
08	Erwin Weber (D)/Matthias Feltz (D)	Volkswagen Golf GTI 16V	11h 04m 10s
09	Jim Heather-Hayes (EAK)/Anton Levitan (EAK)	Subaru RX Turbo	11h 08m 07s
10	Alex Fiorio (I)/Giacomo Luchi (I)	Lancia Delta Integrale	12h 26m 12s

Miki Biasion/Tiziano Siviero

ROUND 05 – CORSICA, FRANCE (23rd-26th April)			
01	Didier Auriol (F)/Bernard Occelli (F)	Lancia Delta Integrale	7h 12m 39s
02	François Chatriot (F)/Michel Périn (F)	BMW M3	7h 14m 36s
03	Juha Kankkunen (FIN)/Juha Piironen (FIN)	Toyota Celica GT-Four	7h 16m 29s
04	Yves Loubet (F)/Jean-Marc André (F)	Lancia Delta Integrale	7h 17m 28s
05	Bernard Béguin (F)/Jean-Bernard Vieu (F)	BMW M3	7h 20m 51s
06	Marc Duez (B)/Alain Lopes (B)	BMW M3	7h 26m 53s
07	Gianfranco Cunico (I)/Max Sghedoni (I)	Ford Sierra RS Cosworth	7h 34m 20s
08	Alain Oreille (I)/Gilles Thimonier (F)	Renault 5 GT Turbo	7h 51m 14s
09	Paola De Martini (I)/Umberta Gibellini (I)	Audi 90 Quattro	7h 53m 43s
10	Claude Balesi (F)/Jean-Paul Cirindini (F)	Renault 5 GT Turbo	7h 56m 07s

Didier Auriol/Bernard Occelli

ROUND 06 – ACROPOLIS, GREECE (27th May-1st June)			
01	Miki Biasion (I)/Tiziano Siviero (I)	Lancia Delta Integrale	7h 31m 43s
02	Didier Auriol (F)/Bernard Occelli (F)	Lancia Delta Integrale	7h 33m 41s
03	Alex Fiorio (I)/Luigi Pirollo (I)	Lancia Delta Integrale	7h 35m 14s
04	Jimmy McRae (GB)/Rob Arthur (GB)	Mitsubishi Galant VR-4	7h 43m 58s
05	Jorge Recalde (RA)/Jorge del Buono (RA)	Lancia Delta Integrale	7h 57m 20s
06	Rudi Stohl (A)/Ernst Röhringer (A)	Audi 90 Quattro	8h 27m 24s
07	Kenjiro Shinozuka (J)/John Meadows (GB)	Mitsubishi Galant VR-4	8h 29m 36s
08	Armin Schwarz (D)/Klaus Wicha (D)	Audi 200 Quattro	8h 29m 57s
09	'Jigger' (GR)/Kóstas Stefanis (GR)	Lancia Delta Integrale	8h 42m 25s
10	Per Eklund (S)/Dave Whittock (GB)	Nissan March Super Turbo	8h 47m 43s

Miki Biasion/Tiziano Siviero

ROUND 07 – NEW ZEALAND (15th-18th July)			
01	Ingvar Carlsson (S)/Per Carlsson (S)	Mazda 323 4WD	6h 59m 55s
02	Rod Millen (NZ)/Tony Sircombe (NZ)	Mazda 323 4WD	7h 02m 37s
03	Malcolm Wilson (GB)/Ian Grindrod (GB)	Vauxhall Astra GTE	7h 03m 24s
04	Mats Jonsson (S)/Lars Bäckman (S)	Opel Kadett GSI 16V	7h 04m 06s
05	Colin McRae (GB)/Derek Ringer (GB)	Ford Sierra RS Cosworth	7h 11m 35s
06	Kenjiro Shinozuka (J)/Fred Gocentas (AUS)	Mitsubishi Galant VR-4	7h 22m 16s
07	Ray Wilson (NZ)/Stuart Lewis (NZ)	Mazda 323 4WD	7h 23m 13s
08	Saeed Al-Hajri (QAT)/Steve Bond (GB)	Ford Sierra RS Cosworth	7h 28m 09s
09	Ross Dunkerton (AUS)/Steve McKimmie (AUS)	Mitsubishi Galant VR-4	7h 30m 08s
10	Ken Adamson (NZ)/Greg Adamson (NZ)	Mazda 323 4WD	7h 33m 03s

Ingvar Carlsson/Per Carlsson

ROUND 08 – ARGENTINA (1st-5th August)			
01	Mikael Ericsson (S)/Claes Billstam (S)	Lancia Delta Integrale	7h 06m 00s
02	Alex Fiorio (I)/Luigi Pirollo (I)	Lancia Delta Integrale	7h 08m 26s
03	Jorge Recalde (RA)/Jorge del Buono (RA)	Lancia Delta Integrale	7h 19m 42s
04	Georg Fischer (A)/Thomas Zeltner (A)	Audi 200 Quattro	7h 42m 10s
05	Ernesto Soto (RA)/Martin Christie (RA)	Renault 18 GTX	7h 48m 15s
06	Fernando Stella (RA)/Edgardo Gait (RA)	Renault 18 GTX	7h 56m 42s
07	Gustavo Trelles (ROU)/Ricardo Ivetich (ROU)	Lancia Delta Integrale	7h 59m 01s
08	Juan Maria Traverso (RA)/Rubén Valentini (RA)	Renault 18 GTX	7h 59m 55s
09	Jorge Bescham (RA)/José Garcia (RA)	Fiat Regata 85	8h 11m 28
10	Edio Fuchter (BR)/Ricardo Costa (RA)	Volkswagen Gol 1.6	8h 21m 22s

Mikael Ericsson/Claes Billstam

ROUND 09 – 1000 LAKES, FINLAND (25th-27th August)

01	Mikael Ericsson (S)/Claes Billstam (S)	Mitsubishi Galant VR-4	4h 42m 03s
02	Timo Salonen (FIN)/Voitto Silander (FIN)	Mazda 323 4WD	4h 43m 44s
03	Carlos Sainz (E)/Luís Moya (E)	Toyota Celica GT-Four	4h 44m 38s
04	Kenneth Eriksson (S)/Staffan Parmander (S)	Toyota Celica GT-Four	4h 47m 49s
05	Thorbjörn Edling (S)/Kent Nilsson (S)	Mazda 323 4WD	4h 50m 01s
06	Miki Biasion (I)/Tiziano Siviero (I)	Lancia Delta Integrale	4h 53m 01s
07	Armin Schwarz (D)/Klaus Wicha (D)	Audi 200 Quattro	4h 53m 57s
08	Stig-Olov Walfridsson (S)/Anders Dawidsson (S)	Audi 80 Quattro	5h 00m 10s
09	Risto Buri (FIN)/Jyrki Stenroos (FIN)	Audi 200 Quattro	5h 02m 27s
10	Esa Saarenpää (FIN)/Olli Männistö (FIN)	Audi 90 Quattro	5h 03m 57s

Mikael Ericsson/Claes Billstam

ROUND 10 – AUSTRALIA (14th-17th September)

01	Juha Kankkunen (FIN)/Juha Piironen (FIN)	Toyota Celica GT-Four	5h 32m 09s
02	Kenneth Eriksson (S)/Staffan Parmander (S)	Toyota Celica GT-Four	5h 33m 16s
03	Markku Alén (FIN)/Ilkka Kivimäki (FIN)	Lancia Delta Integrale	5h 34m 22s
04	Alex Fiorio (I)/Luigi Pirollo (I)	Lancia Delta Integrale	5h 37m 10s
05	Rod Millen (NZ)/Tony Sircombe (NZ)	Mazda 323 4WD	5h 52m 22s
06	Malcolm Wilson (GB)/Ian Grindrod (GB)	Vauxhall Astra GTE	5h 53m 00s
07	Kenjiro Shinozuka (J)/Fred Gocentas (AUS)	Mitsubishi Galant VR-4	6h 09m 11s
08	Wayne Bell (AUS)/David Boddy (AUS)	Mazda 323 4WD	6h 11m 01s
09	Ed Ordynski (AUS)/Lyndon Wilson (AUS)	Mitsubishi Galant VR-4	6h 11m 42s
10	'Possum' Bourne (NZ)/Rodger Freeth (NZ)	Subaru RX Turbo	6h 15m 19s

Juha Kankkunen/Juha Piironen

ROUND 11 – SANREMO, ITALY (8th-12th October)

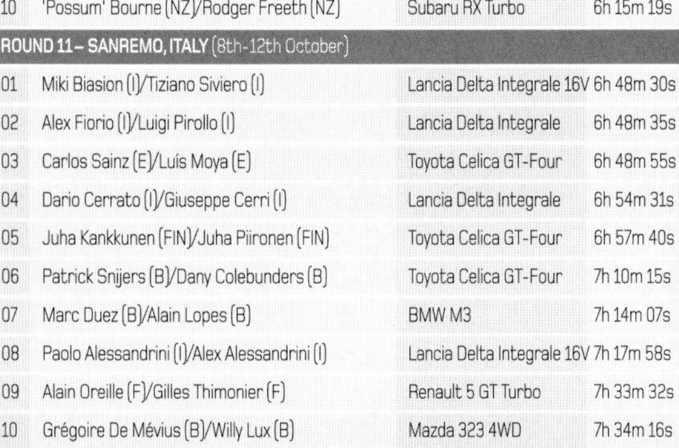

01	Miki Biasion (I)/Tiziano Siviero (I)	Lancia Delta Integrale 16V	6h 48m 30s
02	Alex Fiorio (I)/Luigi Pirollo (I)	Lancia Delta Integrale	6h 48m 35s
03	Carlos Sainz (E)/Luís Moya (E)	Toyota Celica GT-Four	6h 48m 55s
04	Dario Cerrato (I)/Giuseppe Cerri (I)	Lancia Delta Integrale	6h 54m 31s
05	Juha Kankkunen (FIN)/Juha Piironen (FIN)	Toyota Celica GT-Four	6h 57m 40s
06	Patrick Snijers (B)/Dany Colebunders (B)	Toyota Celica GT-Four	7h 10m 15s
07	Marc Duez (B)/Alain Lopes (B)	BMW M3	7h 14m 07s
08	Paolo Alessandrini (I)/Alex Alessandrini (I)	Lancia Delta Integrale 16V	7h 17m 58s
09	Alain Oreille (F)/Gilles Thimonier (F)	Renault 5 GT Turbo	7h 33m 32s
10	Grégoire De Mévius (B)/Willy Lux (B)	Mazda 323 4WD	7h 34m 16s

Miki Biasion/Tiziano Siviero

ROUND 12 – IVORY COAST, AFRICA (29th October-2 November)

01	Alain Oreille (F)/Gilles Thimonier (F)	Renault 5 GT Turbo	8h 32m 54s
02	Patrick Tauziac (F)/Claude Papin (F)	Mitsubishi Starion Turbo	11h 36m 50s
03	Adolphe Choteau (CI)/Jean-Pierre Claverie (F)	Toyota Corolla GT	13h 41m 07s
04	André Segolen (F)/Yvan Aimon (F)	Toyota Corolla 16V	14h 20m 48s
05	Patrice Servant (F)/David Charbonnel (F)	Toyota Corolla 16V	15h 24m 04s
06	José Graziani (F)/Denis Occelli (CI)	Toyota Corolla 16V	15h 27m 47s
07	Benoît Antoine (F)/Christian Raymond (F)	Peugeot 205 GTI	16h 01m 52s
	Only 7 finishers		

Alain Oreille/Gilles Thimonier

ROUND 13 – RAC, GREAT BRITAIN (19th-23rd November)

01	Pentti Airikkala (FIN)/Ronan McNamee (GB)	Mitsubishi Galant VR-4	6h 19m 22s
02	Carlos Sainz (E)/Luís Moya (E)	Toyota Celica GT-Four	6h 20m 50s
03	Juha Kankkunen (FIN)/Juha Piironen (FIN)	Toyota Celica GT-Four	6h 23m 11s
04	Kenneth Eriksson (S)/Staffan Parmander (S)	Toyota Celica GT-Four	6h 25m 30s
05	Ari Vatanen (FIN)/Bruno Berglund (S)	Mitsubishi Galant VR-4	6h 27m 44s
06	Timo Salonen (FIN)/Voitto Silander (FIN)	Mazda 323 4WD	6h 28m 19s
07	Mikael Sundström (FIN)/Juha Repo (FIN)	Mazda 323 4WD	6h 30m 56s
08	Ingvar Carlsson (S)/Per Carlsson (S)	Mazda 323 4WD	6h 32m 54s
09	Hannu Mikkola (FIN)/Arne Hertz (S)	Mazda 323 4WD	6h 35m 52s
10	Malcolm Wilson (GB)/Ian Grindrod (GB)	Vauxhall Astra GTE	6h 40m 11s

Pentti Airikkala/Ronan McNamee

FINAL DRIVERS' CHAMPIONSHIP POSITIONS			FINAL MANUFACTURERS' CHAMPIONSHIP POSITIONS		
01	Miki Biasion	106	01	Lancia	140
02	Alex Fiorio	65	02	Toyota	101
03	Juha Kankkunen	60	03	Mazda	67
04	Mikael Ericsson	50	04	Mitsubishi	58
05	Didier Auriol	50	05	Audi	43
06	Kenneth Eriksson	47	06	BMW	37
07	Ingvar Carlsson	43	07	Renault	30
08	Carlos Sainz	39	08	Nissan	18
09	Markku Alén	27	09	Volkswagen	14
10	Alain Oreille	26	10	Renault	10

1990

ROUND 01 – MONTE CARLO (19th-25th January)

01	Didier Auriol (F)/Bernard Occelli (F)	Lancia Delta Integrale 16V	5h 56m 52s
02	Carlos Sainz (E)/Luís Moya (E)	Toyota Celica GT-Four	5h 57m 44s
03	Miki Biasion (I)/Tiziano Siviero (I)	Lancia Delta Integrale 16V	6h 00m 31s
04	Dario Cerrato (I)/Giuseppe Cerri (I)	Lancia Delta Integrale 16V	6h 04m 43s
05	Armin Schwarz (D)/Klaus Wicha (D)	Toyota Celica GT-Four	6h 06m 04s
06	Bruno Saby (F)/Daniel Grataloup (F)	Lancia Delta Integrale 16V	6h 10m 09s
07	Mikael Ericsson (S)/Claes Billstam (S)	Toyota Celica GT-Four	6h 16m 33s
08	Timo Salonen (FIN)/Voitto Silander (FIN)	Mazda 323 4WD	6h 18m 33s
09	François Delecour (F)/'Tilber' (MC)	Peugeot 309 GTI	6h 18m 45s
10	Bertrand Balas (F)/Eric Lainé (F)	Lancia Delta Integrale 16V	6h 38m 52s

Didier Auriol/Bernard Occelli

ROUND 02 – PORTUGAL (6th-10th March)

01	Miki Biasion (I)/Tiziano Siviero (I)	Lancia Delta Integrale 16V	6h 17m 57s
02	Didier Auriol (F)/Bernard Occelli (F)	Lancia Delta Integrale 16V	6h 20m 33s
03	Juha Kankkunen (FIN)/Juha Piironen (FIN)	Lancia Delta Integrale 16V	6h 23m 08s
04	Dario Cerrato (I)/Giuseppe Cerri (I)	Lancia Delta Integrale 16V	6h 34m 23s
05	Carlos Bica (P)/Fernando Prata (P)	Lancia Delta Integrale 16V	6h 45m 24s
06	Hannu Mikkola (FIN)/Arne Hertz (S)	Mazda 323 4WD	6h 48m 21s
07	Jorge Recalde (RA)/Martin Christie (RA)	Lancia Delta Integrale 16V	6h 53m 01s
08	Marc Duez (B)/Alain Lopes (B)	Ford Sierra RS Cosworth	6h 54m 11s
09	Joaquim Santos (P)/Miguel Oliveira (P)	Ford Sierra RS Cosworth	6h 55m 14s
10	Ronald Holzer (D)/Klaus Wendel (D)	Lancia Delta Integrale	6h 59m 57s

Miki Biasion/Tiziano Siviero

ROUND 03 – SAFARI, AFRICA (11th-16th April)

01	Björn Waldegård (S)/Fred Gallagher (GB)	Toyota Celica GT-Four	8h 39m 11s
02	Juha Kankkunen (FIN)/Juha Piironen (FIN)	Lancia Delta Integrale	9h 17m 23s
03	Mikael Ericsson (S)/Claes Billstam (S)	Toyota Celica GT-Four	11h 26m 58s
04	Carlos Sainz (E)/Luís Moya (E)	Toyota Celica GT-Four	12h 58m 42s
05	Kenjiro Shinozuka (J)/John Meadows (GB)	Mitsubishi Galant VR-4	15h 11m 31s
06	Jim Heather-Hayes (EAK)/Anton Levitan (EAK)	Subaru Legacy RS	15h 12m 40s
07	Rudi Stohl (A)/Reinhard Kaufmann (A)	Audi 90 Quattro	17h 49m 58s
08	Patrick Njiru (EAK)/David Williamson (EAK)	Subaru Legacy RS	18h 04m 51s
09	Ashok Pattni (EAK)/Bob Khan (EAK)	Daihatsu Charade 1.3i	28h 54m 51s
10	Steve Anthony (EAK)/Phil Valentine (EAK)	Daihatsu Charade 1.3i	30h 49m 30s

Björn Waldegård/Fred Gallagher

ROUND 04 – CORSICA, FRANCE (6th-9th May)

01	Didier Auriol (F)/Bernard Occelli (F)	Lancia Delta Integrale 16V	6h 45m 16s
02	Carlos Sainz (E)/Luís Moya (E)	Toyota Celica GT-Four	6h 45m 52s
03	François Chatriot (F)/Michel Périn (F)	BMW M3	6h 49m 05s
04	Bruno Saby (F)/Daniel Grataloup (F)	Lancia Delta Integrale 16V	6h 51m 12s
05	Raimund Baumschlager (A)/Ruben Zeltner (A)	Volkswagen Golf GTI 16V	7h 21m 26s
06	Laurent Poggi (F)/Edouard Buresi (F)	Citroën AX Sport	7h 23m 30s
07	Claude Balesi (F)/Jean-Paul Cirindini (F)	Renault 5 GT Turbo	7h 24m 05s
08	Alain Oreille (F)/Michel Roissard (F)	Renault 5 GT Turbo	7h 25m 37s
09	Paola De Martini (I)/Umberta Gibellini (I)	Audi 90 Quattro	7h 31m 20s
10	Sylvain Polo (F)/Hervé Sauvage (F)	Renault 5 GT Turbo	7h 31m 56s

Didier Auriol/Bernard Occelli

ROUND 05 – ACROPOLIS, GREECE (3rd-6th June)			
01	Carlos Sainz (E)/Luís Moya (E)	Toyota Celica GT-Four	7h 34m 44s
02	Juha Kankkunen (FIN)/Juha Piironen (FIN)	Lancia Delta Integrale 16V	7h 35m 30s
03	Miki Biasion (I)/Tiziano Siviero (I)	Lancia Delta Integrale 16V	7h 37m 42s
04	Mikael Ericsson (S)/Claes Billstam (S)	Toyota Celica GT-Four	7h 49m 40s
05	Alex Fiorio (I)/Luigi Pirollo (I)	Lancia Delta Integrale 16V	8h 02m 07s
06	Michele Rayneri (I)/Loris Roggia (I)	Lancia Delta Integrale 16V	8h 22m 08s
07	'Jigger' (GR)/Kóstas Stefanis (GR)	Lancia Delta Integrale 16V	8h 36m 57s
08	Ian Duncan (EAK)/Yvonne Mehta (EAK)	Subaru Legacy RS	8h 52m 39s
09	Gustavo Trelles (ROU)/Daniel Muzio (ROU)	Lancia Delta Integrale 16V	8h 59m 10s
10	Pavlos Moschoutis (GR)/Efthiminios Sassalos (GR)	Nissan 200SX	9h 02m 05s

Carlos Sainz/Luís Moya

ROUND 06 – NEW ZEALAND (30th June-3rd July)			
01	Carlos Sainz (E)/Luís Moya (E)	Toyota Celica GT-Four	6h 48m 26s
02	Ingvar Carlsson (S)/Per Carlsson (S)	Mazda 323 4WD	6h 49m 57s
03	Erwin Weber (D)/Matthias Feltz (D)	Volkswagen Golf Rallye G60	6h 56m 24s
04	Ross Dunkerton (AUS)/Fred Gocentas (AUS)	Mitsubishi Galant VR-4	7h 00m 28s
05	'Possum' Bourne (NZ)/Rodger Freeth (NZ)	Subaru Legacy RS	7h 05m 48s
06	Tommi Mäkinen (FIN)/Seppo Harjanne (FIN)	Mitsubishi Galant VR-4	7h 09m 13s
07	Gustavo Trelles (ROU)/Daniel Muzio (ROU)	Lancia Delta Integrale 16V	7h 11m 14s
08	Jorge Recalde (RA)/Martin Christie (RA)	Lancia Delta Integrale 16V	7h 17m 17s
09	Gilberto Pianezzola (I)/Lucio Baggio (I)	Toyota Celica GT-Four	7h 23m 58s
10	Alain Oreille (F)/Michel Roissard (F)	Renault 5 GT Turbo	7h 25m 35s

Carlos Sainz/Luís Moya

ROUND 07 – ARGENTINA (24th-28th July)			
01	Miki Biasion (I)/Tiziano Siviero (I)	Lancia Delta Integrale 16V	6h 51m 27s
02	Carlos Sainz (E)/Luís Moya (E)	Toyota Celica GT-Four	6h 59m 29s
03	Didier Auriol (F)/Bernard Occelli (F)	Lancia Delta Integrale 16V	7h 26m 22s
04	Rudi Stohl (A)/Reinhard Kaufmann (A)	Audi 90 Quattro	7h 50m 48s
05	Ernesto Soto (RA)/Jorge del Buono (RA)	Lancia Delta Integrale 16V	7h 53m 19s
06	Alain Oreille (F)/Michel Roissard (F)	Renault 5 GT Turbo	7h 56m 35s
07	Marcelo Raies (RA)/Jorge Gonzales (RA)	Renault 18 GTX	8h 33m 10s
08	Gabriel Martin (RA)/José Volta (RA)	Fiat Regata 85	8h 39m 23s
09	Oscar Maccari (RA)/Carlos Ostaschinsky (RA)	Renault 18 GTX	8h 43m 16s
10	Fernando Marino (RA)/Rudolfo Ghilini (RA)	Fiat Regata 85	9h 04m 12s

Miki Biasion/Tiziano Siviero

ROUND 08 – 1000 LAKES, FINLAND (23rd-26th August)			
01	Carlos Sainz (E)/Luís Moya (E)	Toyota Celica GT-Four	4h 40m 55s
02	Ari Vatanen (FIN)/Bruno Berglund (S)	Mitsubishi Galant VR-4	4h 41m 14s
03	Kenneth Eriksson (S)/Staffan Parmander (S)	Mitsubishi Galant VR-4	4h 45m 53s
04	Markku Alén (FIN)/Ilkka Kivimäki (FIN)	Subaru Legacy RS	4h 46m 47s
05	Juha Kankkunen (FIN)/Juha Piironen (FIN)	Lancia Delta Integrale 16V	4h 47m 10s
06	Timo Salonen (FIN)/Voitto Silander (FIN)	Mazda 323 GTX	4h 49m 02s
07	Lasse Lampi (FIN)/Pentti Kuukkala (FIN)	Mitsubishi Galant VR-4	4h 50m 14s
08	Sebastian Lindholm (FIN)/Timo Hantunen (FIN)	Lancia Delta Integrale 16V	4h 50m 51s
09	Esa Saarenpää (FIN)/Olli Männistö (FIN)	Audi 90 Quattro	5h 04m 26s
10	Risto Buri (FIN)/Jyrki Stenroos (FIN)	Audi 200 Quattro	5h 05m 06s

Carlos Sainz/Luís Moya

ROUND 09 – AUSTRALIA (20th-23rd September)			
01	Juha Kankkunen (FIN)/Juha Piironen (FIN)	Lancia Delta Integrale 16V	5h 43m 48s
02	Carlos Sainz (E)/Luís Moya (E)	Toyota Celica GT-Four	5h 45m 28s
03	Alex Fiorio (I)/Luigi Pirollo (I)	Lancia Delta Integrale 16V	5h 49m 28s
04	'Possum' Bourne (NZ)/Rodger Freeth (NZ)	Subaru Legacy RS	5h 57m 45s
05	Ingvar Carlsson (S)/Per Carlsson (S)	Mazda 323 4WD	6h 00m 49s
06	Grégoire De Mévius (B)/Arne Hertz (S)	Mazda 323 4WD	6h 04m 57s
07	Tommi Mäkinen (FIN)/Seppo Harjanne (FIN)	Mitsubishi Galant VR-4	6h 09m 44s
08	Gustavo Trelles (ROU)/Daniel Muzio (ROU)	Lancia Delta Integrale 16V	6h 16m 26s
09	Kiyoshi Inoue (J)/Satoshi Hayashi (J)	Mitsubishi Galant VR-4	6h 20m 00s
10	Ed Ordynski (AUS)/Jeremy Browne (AUS)	Mitsubishi Galant VR-4	6h 20m 31s

Juha Kankkunen/Juha Piironen

ROUND 10 – SANREMO, ITALY (14th-18th October)			
01	Didier Auriol (F)/Bernard Occelli (F)	Lancia Delta Integrale 16V	7h 30m 38s
02	Juha Kankkunen (FIN)/Juha Piironen (FIN)	Lancia Delta Integrale 16V	7h 31m 23s
03	Carlos Sainz (E)/Luís Moya (E)	Toyota Celica GT-Four	7h 32m 23s
04	Dario Cerrato (I)/Giuseppe Cerri (I)	Lancia Delta Integrale 16V	7h 33m 25s
05	Piero Liatti (I)/Luciano Tedeschini (I)	Lancia Delta Integrale 16V	7h 33m 25s
06	Mikael Ericsson (S)/Claes Billstam (S)	Toyota Celica GT-Four	7h 37m 12s
07	Piergiorgio Deila (I)/Pierangelo Scalvini (I)	Lancia Delta Integrale 16V	7h 37m 49s
08	Alex Fiorio (I)/Luigi Pirollo (I)	Lancia Delta Integrale 16V	7h 38m 23s
09	Giuseppe Grossi (I)/Alex Mari (I)	Lancia Delta Integrale 16V	7h 56m 57s
10	Alex Fassina (I)/Max Chiapponi (I)	Ford Sierra RS Cosworth 4x4	h 58m 13s

Didier Auriol/Bernard Occelli

ROUND 11 – IVORY COAST, AFRICA (28th October-1st November)			
01	Patrick Tauziac (F)/Claude Papin (F)	Mitsubishi Galant VR-4	4h 54m
02	Rudi Stohl (A)/Ernst Röhringer (A)	Audi 90 Quattro	5h 56m
03	Alain Oreille (F)/Michel Roissard (F)	Renault 5 GT Turbo	6h 52m
04	Alain Ambrosino (F)/Daniel Le Saux (F)	Nissan March Super Turbo	8h 09m
05	Patrice Servant (F)/David Charbonnel (F)	Toyota Corolla 16V	8h 25m
06	Michel Molinie (CI)/Patrice Lemarie (F)	Toyota Corolla 16V	9h 35m
07	Jean-Philippe Bernier (F)/Yves Malus (F)	Toyota Corolla 16V	10h 35m
08	Viviane Fvina (CMR)/Nathalie Chastagnol (F)	Toyota Corolla FX 16V	11h 27m
09	Jean-Michel Dionneau (F)/Thierry Brion (F)	Toyota Celica GT-Four	11h 53m
10	Adolphe Choteau (CI)/Jean-Pierre Claverie (F)	Toyota Corolla 16V	12h 42m

Patrick Tauziac/Claude Papin

ROUND 12 – RAC, GREAT BRITAIN (25th-28th November)			
01	Carlos Sainz (E)/Luís Moya (E)	Toyota Celica GT-Four	5h 43m 16s
02	Kenneth Eriksson (S)/Staffan Parmander (S)	Mitsubishi Galant VR-4	5h 44m 58s
03	Miki Biasion (I)/Tiziano Siviero (I)	Lancia Delta Integrale 16V	5h 47m 22s
04	Mats Jonsson (S)/Lars Bäckman (S)	Toyota Celica GT-Four	5h 49m 40s
05	Didier Auriol (F)/Bernard Occelli (F)	Lancia Delta Integrale 16V	5h 51m 02s
06	Colin McRae (GB)/Derek Ringer (GB)	Ford Sierra RS Cosworth 4x4	5h 53m 17s
07	Armin Schwarz (D)/Arne Hertz (S)	Toyota Celica GT-Four	5h 54m 56s
08	David Llewellin (GB)/Phil Short (GB)	Toyota Celica GT-Four	5h 56m 43s
09	Alex Fiorio (I)/Luigi Pirollo (I)	Ford Sierra RS Cosworth 4x4	5h 59m 22s
10	Robert Droogmans (B)/Ronny Joosten (B)	Lancia Delta Integrale 16V	6h 05m 31s

Carlos Sainz/Luís Moya

FINAL DRIVERS' CHAMPIONSHIP POSITIONS			FINAL MANUFACTURERS' CHAMPIONSHIP POSITIONS		
01	Carlos Sainz	140	01	Lancia	137
02	Didier Auriol	95	02	Toyota	131
03	Juha Kankkunen	85	03	Mitsubishi	56
04	Miki Biasion	76	04	Subaru	43
05	Mikael Ericsson	32	05	Mazda	30
06	Dario Cerrato	30	06	Renault	24
07	Rudi Stohl	29	07	Audi	24
08	Kenneth Eriksson	27	08	Ford	22
09	Alex Fiorio	25	09	BMW	14
10	Ingvar Carlsson	23	10	Volkswagen	10

1991

ROUND 01 – MONTE CARLO (24th–30th January)

01	Carlos Sainz (E)/Luis Moya (E)	Toyota Celica GT-Four	6h 57m 21s
02	Miki Biasion (I)/Tiziano Siviero (I)	Lancia Delta Integrale 16V	7h 02m 20s
03	François Delecour (F)/Anne-Chantal Pauwels (F)	Ford Sierra RS Cosworth 4x4	7h 02m 33s
04	Armin Schwarz (D)/Arne Hertz (S)	Toyota Celica GT-Four	7h 03m 52s
05	Juha Kankkunen (FIN)/Juha Piironen (FIN)	Lancia Delta Integrale 16V	7h 05m 07s
06	Bruno Saby (F)/Daniel Grataloup (F)	Lancia Delta Integrale 16V	7h 06m 34s
07	Malcolm Wilson (GB)/Nicky Grist (GB)	Ford Sierra RS Cosworth 4x4	7h 08m 36s
08	Timo Salonen (FIN)/Voitto Silander (FIN)	Mitsubishi Galant VR-4	7h 08m 43s
09	Yves Loubet (F)/Jean-Paul Chiaroni (F)	Lancia Delta Integrale 16V	7h 10m 00s
10	Alex Fiorio (I)/Luigi Pirollo (I)	Ford Sierra RS Cosworth 4x4	7h 21m 03s

Carlos Sainz/Luís Moya

ROUND 02 – SWEDEN (16th–18th February)

01	Kenneth Eriksson (S)/Staffan Parmander (S)	Mitsubishi Galant VR-4	4h 56m 16s
02	Mats Jonsson (S)/Lars Bäckman (S)	Toyota Celica GT-Four	4h 56m 36s
03	Markku Alén (FIN)/Ilkka Kivimäki (FIN)	Subaru Legacy RS	4h 57m 20s
04	Ingvar Carlsson (S)/Per Carlsson (S)	Mazda 323 GTX	5h 01m 55s
05	Lasse Lampi (FIN)/Pentti Kuukkala (FIN)	Mitsubishi Galant VR-4	5h 02m 57s
06	Björn Johansson (S)/Anders Olsson (S)	Mazda 323 GTX	5h 05m 36s
07	Hannu Mikkola (FIN)/Johnny Johansson (S)	Mazda 323 GTX	5h 06m 10s
08	Per Eklund (S)/Jan-Olof Bohlin (S)	Lancia Delta Integrale 16V	5h 06m 58s
09	Didier Auriol (F)/Bernard Occelli (F)	Lancia Delta Integrale 16V	5h 08m 59s
10	Leif Asterhag (S)/Claes Billstam (S)	Toyota Celica GT-Four	5h 10m 25s

Kenneth Eriksson/Staffan Parmander

ROUND 03 – PORTUGAL (5th–9th March)

01	Carlos Sainz (E)/Luis Moya (E)	Toyota Celica GT-Four	6h 06m 36s
02	Didier Auriol (F)/Bernard Occelli (F)	Lancia Delta Integrale 16V	6h 07m 23s
03	Miki Biasion (I)/Tiziano Siviero (I)	Lancia Delta Integrale 16V	6h 08m 41s
04	Juha Kankkunen (FIN)/Juha Piironen (FIN)	Lancia Delta Integrale 16V	6h 13m 57s
05	Markku Alén (FIN)/Ilkka Kivimäki (FIN)	Subaru Legacy RS	6h 34m 12s
06	François Chatriot (F)/Michel Périn (F)	Subaru Legacy RS	6h 35m 34s
07	Jesús Puras (E)/José Arrarte (E)	Mazda 323 GTX	6h 50m 17s
08	Grégoire De Mévius (B)/Hervé Sauvage (F)	Mazda 323 GTX	6h 55m 38s
09	Ernst Harrach (A)/Michael Uhl (D)	Lancia Delta Integrale 16V	7h 09m 18s
10	Carlos Bica (P)/Fernando Prata (P)	Lancia Delta Integrale 16V	7h 10m 44s

Carlos Sainz/Luís Moya

ROUND 04 – SAFARI, AFRICA (27th March–1st April)

01	Juha Kankkunen (FIN)/Juha Piironen (FIN)	Lancia Delta Integrale 16V	2h 07m 10s
02	Mikael Ericsson (S)/Claes Billstam (S)	Toyota Celica GT-Four	2h 33m 34s
03	Jorge Recalde (RA)/Martin Christie (RA)	Lancia Delta Integrale 16V	2h 46m 13s
04	Björn Waldegård (S)/Fred Gallagher (GB)	Toyota Celica GT-Four	3h 56m 08s
05	Stig Blomqvist (S)/Benny Melander (S)	Nissan Sunny GTI-R	5h 17m 24s
06	Ian Duncan (EAK)/David Williamson (EAK)	Subaru Legacy RS	5h 47m 32s
07	Mike Kirkland (EAK)/Surinder Thatthi (EAK)	Nissan Sunny GTI-R	6h 04m 35s
08	Kenjiro Shinozuka (J)/John Meadows (GB)	Mitsubishi Galant VR-4	7h 42m 35s
09	Guy Jack (EAK)/Des Page-Morris (EAK)	Daihatsu Charade GTXX	9h 57m 34s
10	Steve Anthony (EAK)/Phil Valentine (EAK)	Daihatsu Charade 1.3i	10h 22m 20s

Juha Kankkunen/Juha Piironen

ROUND 05 – CORSICA, FRANCE (28 April–1st May)

01	Carlos Sainz (E)/Luis Moya (E)	Toyota Celica GT-Four	7h 05m 29s
02	Didier Auriol (F)/Bernard Occelli (F)	Lancia Delta Integrale 16V	7h 06m 34s
03	Gianfranco Cunico (I)/Stefano Evangelisti (I)	Ford Sierra RS Cosworth 4x4	7h 11m 39s
04	Marc Duez (B)/Klaus Wicha (D)	Toyota Celica GT-Four	7h 13m 12s
05	Malcolm Wilson (GB)/Nicky Grist (GB)	Ford Sierra RS Cosworth 4x4	7h 17m 19s
06	Yves Loubet (F)/Jean-Paul Chiaroni (F)	Lancia Delta Integrale 16V	7h 24m 12s
07	Patrick Bernardini (F)/Philippe Dran (F)	BMW M3	7h 24m 25s
08	Philippe Bugalski (F)/Denis Giraudet (F)	Renault Clio 16S	7h 24m 52s
09	François Chatriot (F)/Michel Périn (F)	Subaru Legacy RS	7h 36m 56s
10	Jean-Pierre Manzagol (F)/Georges Monti (F)	Renault 5 GT Turbo	7h 54m 54s

Carlos Sainz/Luís Moya

ROUND 06 – ACROPOLIS, GREECE (2nd–5th June)

01	Juha Kankkunen (FIN)/Juha Piironen (FIN)	Lancia Delta Integrale 16V	7h 20m 05s
02	Carlos Sainz (E)/Luis Moya (E)	Toyota Celica GT-Four	7h 21m 06s
03	Miki Biasion (I)/Tiziano Siviero (I)	Lancia Delta Integrale 16V	7h 23m 35s
04	Didier Auriol (F)/Bernard Occelli (F)	Lancia Delta Integrale 16V	7h 24m 47s
05	Armin Schwarz (D)/Arne Hertz (S)	Toyota Celica GT-Four	7h 25m 40s
06	Mikael Ericsson (S)/Claes Billstam (S)	Toyota Celica GT-Four	7h 30m 00s
07	Kenneth Eriksson (S)/Staffan Parmander (S)	Mitsubishi Galant VR-4	7h 36m 05s
08	Hannu Mikkola (FIN)/Johnny Johansson (S)	Mazda 323 GTX	7h 36m 54s
09	David Llewellin (GB)/Peter Diekmann (D)	Nissan Sunny GTI-R	7h 50m 45s
10	'Jigger' (GR)/Kóstas Stefanis (GR)	Lancia Delta Integrale 16V	8h 15m 48s

Juha Kankkunen/Juha Piironen

ROUND 07 – NEW ZEALAND (26th–30th June)

01	Carlos Sainz (E)/Luis Moya (E)	Toyota Celica GT-Four	6h 57m 18s
02	Juha Kankkunen (FIN)/Juha Piironen (FIN)	Lancia Delta Integrale 16V	6h 58m 33s
03	Didier Auriol (F)/Bernard Occelli (F)	Lancia Delta Integrale 16V	6h 59m 36s
04	Markku Alén (FIN)/Ilkka Kivimäki (FIN)	Subaru Legacy RS	7h 03m 02s
05	Neil Allport (NZ)/Jim Robb (NZ)	Mazda 323 GTX	7h 28m 19s
06	Rod Millen (NZ)/Tony Sircombe (NZ)	Mazda 323 GTX	7h 30m 51s
07	Brian Stokes (NZ)/Jeff Judd (NZ)	Ford Sierra RS Cosworth 4x4	7h 31m 40s
08	Ingvar Carlsson (S)/Per Carlsson (S)	Mazda 323 GTX	7h 42m 38s
09	Ross Meekings (NZ)/Steve March (NZ)	Toyota Celica GT-Four	7h 46m 43s
10	Brian Watkin (NZ)/Stuart Roberts (NZ)	Subaru Legacy RS	7h 47m 17s

Carlos Sainz/Luís Moya

ROUND 08 – ARGENTINA (23rd–27th July)

01	Carlos Sainz (E)/Luis Moya (E)	Toyota Celica GT-Four	6h 37m 31s
02	Miki Biasion (I)/Tiziano Siviero (I)	Lancia Delta Integrale 16V	6h 37m 39s
03	Didier Auriol (F)/Bernard Occelli (F)	Lancia Delta Integrale 16V	6h 38m 36s
04	Juha Kankkunen (FIN)/Juha Piironen (FIN)	Lancia Delta Integrale 16V	6h 43m 24s
05	Jorge Recalde (RA)/Martin Christie (RA)	Lancia Delta Integrale 16V	6h 49m 30s
06	Mikael Ericsson (S)/Claes Billstam (S)	Toyota Celica GT-Four	6h 50m 13s
07	Mohammed Bin Sulayem (UAE)/Ronan Morgan (GB)	Toyota Celica GT-Four	7h 11m 09s
08	Gustavo Trelles (ROU)/Ricardo Ivetich (ROU)	Lancia Delta Integrale 16V	7h 14m 02s
09	Grégoire De Mévius (B)/Hervé Sauvage (F)	Mazda 323 GTX	7h 35m 19s
10	Minna Sillankorva (FIN)/Michela Marangoni (I)	Lancia Delta Integrale 16V	7h 36m 24s

Carlos Sainz/Luís Moya

ROUND 09 – 1000 LAKES, FINLAND (22nd–25th August)

01	Juha Kankkunen (FIN)/Juha Piironen (FIN)	Lancia Delta Integrale 16V	4h 36m 52s
02	Didier Auriol (F)/Bernard Occelli (F)	Lancia Delta Integrale 16V	4h 37m 48s
03	Kenneth Eriksson (S)/Staffan Parmander (S)	Mitsubishi Galant VR-4	4h 39m 15s
04	Carlos Sainz (E)/Luis Moya (E)	Toyota Celica GT-Four	4h 39m 47s
05	Tommi Mäkinen (FIN)/Seppo Harjanne (FIN)	Mazda 323 GTX	4h 40m 55s
06	Mats Jonsson (S)/Lars Bäckman (S)	Toyota Celica GT-Four	4h 41m 37s
07	Ari Vatanen (FIN)/Bruno Berglund (S)	Ford Sierra RS Cosworth 4x4	4h 41m 52s
08	Stig Blomqvist (S)/Benny Melander (S)	Nissan Sunny GTI-R	4h 44m 16s
09	Armin Schwarz (D)/Arne Hertz (S)	Toyota Celica GT-Four	4h 45m 04s
10	David Llewellin (GB)/Peter Diekmann (D)	Nissan Sunny GTI-R	4h 50m 13s

Juha Kankkunen/Juha Piironen

ROUND 10 – AUSTRALIA (20th–24th September)

01	Juha Kankkunen (FIN)/Juha Piironen (FIN)	Lancia Delta Integrale 16V	5h 48m 48s
02	Kenneth Eriksson (S)/Staffan Parmander (S)	Mitsubishi Galant VR-4	5h 50m 01s
03	Armin Schwarz (D)/Arne Hertz (S)	Toyota Celica GT-Four	5h 54m 42s
04	Markku Alén (FIN)/Ilkka Kivimäki (FIN)	Subaru Legacy RS	5h 58m 15s
05	Timo Salonen (FIN)/Voitto Silander (FIN)	Mitsubishi Galant VR-4	6h 00m 54s
06	Rod Millen (NZ)/Tony Sircombe (NZ)	Mazda 323 GTX	6h 04m 37s
07	Ross Dunkerton (AUS)/Fred Gocentas (AUS)	Mitsubishi Galant VR-4	6h 05m 24s
08	Jorge Recalde (RA)/Martin Christie (RA)	Lancia Delta Integrale 16V	6h 09m 21s
09	Neal Bates (AUS)/David Jorgensen (AUS)	Toyota Celica GT-Four	6h 20m 04s
10	Ed Ordynski (AUS)/Harry Mansson (AUS)	Mitsubishi Galant VR-4	6h 34m 00s

Juha Kankkunen/Juha Piironen

ROUND 11 – SANREMO, ITALY (13th-17th October)			
01	Didier Auriol (F)/Bernard Occelli (F)	Lancia Delta Integrale 16V	6h 34m 26s
02	Miki Biasion (I)/Tiziano Siviero (I)	Lancia Delta Integrale 16V	6h 37m 16s
03	Dario Cerrato (I)/Giuseppe Cerri (I)	Lancia Delta Integrale 16V	6h 41m 07s
04	François Delecour (F)/Anne-Chantal Pauwels (F)	Ford Sierra RS Cosworth 4x4	6h 44m 41s
05	Andrea Aghini (I)/Sauro Farnocchia (I)	Lancia Delta Integrale 16V	6h 47m 12s
06	Carlos Sainz (E)/Luís Moya (E)	Toyota Celica GT-Four	6h 47m 33
07	Piero Liatti (I)/Luciano Tedeschini (I)	Lancia Delta Integrale 16V	6h 48m 12s
08	Armin Schwarz (D)/Arne Hertz (S)	Toyota Celica GT-Four	6h 48m 26s
09	Alex Fiorio (I)/Luigi Pirollo (I)	Ford Sierra RS Cosworth 4x4	6h 50m 12s
10	Malcolm Wilson (GB)/Nicky Grist (GB)	Ford Sierra RS Cosworth 4x4	6h 55m 18s

Didier Auriol/Bernard Occelli

ROUND 12 – IVORY COAST, AFRICA (27th-31st October)			
01	Kenjiro Shinozuka (J)/John Meadows (GB)	Mitsubishi Galant VR-4	3h 30m 16s
02	Patrick Tauziac (F)/Claude Papin (F)	Mitsubishi Galant VR-4	5h 39m 04s
03	Rudi Stohl (A)/Reinhard Kaufmann (A)	Audi 90 Quattro	8h 08m 01s
04	Patrice Servant (F)/Thierry Pansolin (F)	Audi 90 Quattro	9h 29m 19s
05	Adolphe Choteau (CI)/Jean-Pierre Claverie (F)	Toyota Corolla 16V	9h 47m 26s
06	Philippe Doué (F)/Laurent Urlique (F)	Renault Clio 16S	10h 08m 35s
07	Damien Chaballe (B)/Jacky Delvaux (B)	Suzuki Cultus GTI	11h 54m 57s
08	Nicolas Min (B)/Joseph Lambert (B)	Mazda 323 GTX	12h 34m 54s
09	Jean-Claude Dupuis (SUI)/Nathalie Chastagnol (F)	Toyota Corolla 16V	13h 09m 50s
	Only 9 finishers		

Kenjiro Shinozuka/John Meadows

ROUND 13 – CATALUNYA, SPAIN (10th-13th November)			
01	Armin Schwarz (D)/Arne Hertz (S)	Toyota Celica GT-Four	6h 44m 42s
02	Juha Kankkunen (FIN)/Juha Piironen (FIN)	Lancia Delta Integrale 16V	6h 46m 15s
03	François Delecour (F)/Daniel Grataloup (F)	Ford Sierra RS Cosworth 4x4	6h 46m 20s
04	Mia Bardolet (E)/Antonio Rodríguez (E)	Ford Sierra RS Cosworth 4x4	6h 50m 22s
05	Andrea Aghini (I)/Sauro Farnocchia (I)	Lancia Delta Integrale 16V	6h 51m 44s
06	Jorge Recalde (RA)/Martin Christie (RA)	Lancia Delta Integrale 16V	7h 03m 42s
07	Luís Monzón (E)/Alex Romaní (E)	Lancia Delta Integrale 16V	7h 09m 08s
08	Fernando Capdevila (E)/Alfredo Rodríguez (E)	Ford Sierra RS Cosworth 4x4	7h 37m 51s
09	Joaquim Casasayas (E)/Manuel Dalmases (E)	Peugeot 309 GTI	7h 50m 24s
10	José Maria Ponce (E)/José Carlos Déniz (E)	BMW 325iX	7h 50m 33s

Armin Schwarz/Arne Hertz

ROUND 14 – RAC, GREAT BRITIAN (24th-28th November)			
01	Juha Kankkunen (FIN)/Juha Piironen (FIN)	Lancia Delta Integrale 16V	5h 46m 43s
02	Kenneth Eriksson (S)/Staffan Parmander (S)	Mitsubishi Galant VR-4	5h 49m 35s
03	Carlos Sainz (E)/Luís Moya (E)	Toyota Celica GT-Four	5h 52m 43s
04	Timo Salonen (FIN)/Voitto Silander (FIN)	Mitsubishi Galant VR-4	5h 55m 34s
05	Ari Vatanen (FIN)/Bruno Berglund (S)	Subaru Legacy RS	5h 56m 50s
06	François Delecour (F)/Daniel Grataloup (F)	Ford Sierra RS Cosworth 4x4	6h 02m 04s
07	Hannu Mikkola (FIN)/Johnny Johansson (S)	Mazda 323 GTX	6h 02m 41s
08	Marc Duez (B)/Klaus Wicha (D)	Toyota Celica GT-Four	6h 08m 44s
09	Bruno Saby (F)/Jean-François Fauchille (F)	Lancia Delta Integrale 16V	6h 10m 42s
10	Louise Aitken-Walker (GB)/Tina Thorner (S)	Ford Sierra RS Cosworth 4x4	6h 23m 29s

Juha Kankkunen/Juha Piironen

FINAL DRIVERS' CHAMPIONSHIP POSITIONS			FINAL MANUFACTURERS' CHAMPIONSHIP POSITIONS		
01	Juha Kankkunen	150	01	Lancia	137
02	Carlos Sainz	143	02	Toyota	128
03	Didier Auriol	101	03	Mitsubishi	62
04	Miki Biasion	69	04	Ford	54
05	Kenneth Eriksson	66	05	Mazda	44
06	Armin Schwarz	55	06	Subaru	42
07	François Delecour	40	07	Nissan	16
08	Markku Alén	40	08	BMW	6
09	Jorge Recalde	29	09	Renault	4
10	Mikael Ericsson	27	10	Daihatsu	2

1992

ROUND 01 – MONTE CARLO (23rd-28th January)			
01	Didier Auriol (F)/Bernard Occelli (F)	Lancia Delta HF Integrale	6h 54m 20s
02	Carlos Sainz (E)/Luís Moya (E)	Toyota Celica Turbo 4WD	6h 56m 25s
03	Juha Kankkunen (FIN)/Juha Piironen (FIN)	Lancia Delta HF Integrale	6h 57m 17s
04	François Delecour (F)/Daniel Grataloup (F)	Ford Sierra RS Cosworth 4x4	6h 59m 02s
05	Philippe Bugalski (F)/Denis Giraudet (F)	Lancia Delta HF Integrale	7h 04m 32s
06	Timo Salonen (FIN)/Voitto Silander (FIN)	Mitsubishi Galant VR-4	7h 05m 21s
07	François Chatriot (F)/Michel Périn (F)	Nissan Sunny GTI-R	7h 10m 47s
08	Miki Biasion (I)/Tiziano Siviero (I)	Ford Sierra RS Cosworth 4x4	7h 11m 18s
09	Tommi Mäkinen (FIN)/Seppo Harjanne (FIN)	Nissan Sunny GTI-R	7h 12m 58s
10	Christophe Spiliotis (MC)/Isabelle Spiliotis (MC)	Ford Sierra RS Cosworth 4x4	7h 42m 41s

Didier Auriol/Bernard Occelli

ROUND 02 – SWEDEN (13th-16th February)			
01	Mats Jonsson (S)/Lars Bäckman (S)	Toyota Celica GT-Four	5h 24m 37s
02	Colin McRae (GB)/Derek Ringer (GB)	Subaru Legacy RS	5h 25m 16s
03	Stig Blomqvist (S)/Benny Melander (S)	Nissan Sunny GTI-R	5h 26m 09s
04	Markku Alén (FIN)/Ilkka Kivimäki (FIN)	Toyota Celica GT-Four	5h 26m 25s
05	Leif Asterhag (S)/Tina Thörner (S)	Toyota Celica GT-Four	5h 30m 53s
06	Per Eklund (S)/Johnny Johansson (S)	Subaru Legacy RS	5h 35m 12s
07	Björn Johansson (S)/Anders Olsson (S)	Mazda 323 GTX	5h 38m 58s
08	Lasse Lampi (FIN)/Pentti Kuukkala (FIN)	Mitsubishi Galant VR-4	5h 41m 51s
09	Sören Nilsson (S)/Per-Ove Persson (S)	Mitsubishi Galant VR-4	5h 43m 22s
10	Jarmo Kytölehto (FIN)/Kari Jokinen (FIN)	Mitsubishi Galant VR-4	5h 49m 29s

Mats Jonsson/Lars Bäckman

ROUND 03 – PORTUGAL (3rd-7th March)			
01	Juha Kankkunen (FIN)/Juha Piironen (FIN)	Lancia Delta HF Integrale	6h 24m 37s
02	Miki Biasion (I)/Tiziano Siviero (I)	Ford Sierra RS Cosworth 4x4	6h 26m 10s
03	Carlos Sainz (E)/Luís Moya (E)	Toyota Celica Turbo 4WD	6h 29m 36s
04	Markku Alén (FIN)/Ilkka Kivimäki (FIN)	Toyota Celica Turbo 4WD	6h 30m 09s
05	Timo Salonen (FIN)/Voitto Silander (FIN)	Mitsubishi Galant VR-4	6h 31m 16s
06	François Chatriot (F)/Michel Périn (F)	Nissan Sunny GTI-R	6h 45m 41s
07	Mia Bardolet (E)/Josep Autet (E)	Ford Sierra RS Cosworth 4x4	6h 53m 55s
08	Joaquim Santos (P)/Carlos Magalhães (P)	Toyota Celica GT-Four	7h 01m 20s
09	Carlos Menem Jr (RA)/Victor Zucchini (PAR)	Lancia Delta HF Integrale	7h 02m 47s
10	José Miguel (P)/Luís Lisboa (P)	Ford Sierra RS Cosworth 4x4	7h 13m 08s

Juha Kankkunen/Juha Piironen

ROUND 04 – SAFARI, AFRICA (27th March-1st April)			
01	Carlos Sainz (E)/Luís Moya (E)	Toyota Celica Turbo 4WD	2h 35m
02	Juha Kankkunen (FIN)/Juha Piironen (FIN)	Lancia Delta HF Integrale	3h 27m
03	Jorge Recalde (RA)/Martin Christie (RA)	Lancia Delta HF Integrale	3h 34m
04	Mikael Ericsson (S)/Nicky Grist (GB)	Toyota Celica Turbo 4WD	4h 13m
05	Markku Alén (FIN)/Ilkka Kivimäki (FIN)	Toyota Celica Turbo 4WD	5h 40m
06	Ian Duncan (EAK)/David Williamson (EAK)	Toyota Celica GT-Four	6h 38m
07	Sarbi Rai (EAK)/Supee Soin (EAK)	Toyota Celica GT-Four	8h 29m
08	Patrick Njiru (EAK)/Ian Munro (EAK)	Subaru Legacy RS	8h 54m
09	Per Eklund (S)/Johnny Johansson (S)	Subaru Legacy RS	9h 41m
10	Kenjiro Shinozuka (J)/John Meadows (GB)	Mitsubishi Galant VR-4	10h 30m

Carlos Sainz/Luís Moya

ROUND 05 – CORSICA, FRANCE (3rd-6th May)

01	Didier Auriol (F)/Bernard Occelli (F)	Lancia Delta HF Integrale	5h 34m 49s
02	François Delecour (F)/Daniel Grataloup (F)	Ford Sierra RS Cosworth 4x4	5h 36m 15s
03	Philippe Bugalski (F)/Denis Giraudet (F)	Lancia Delta HF Integrale	5h 38m 04s
04	Carlos Sainz (E)/Luís Moya (E)	Toyota Celica Turbo 4WD	5h 39m 22s
05	Armin Schwarz (D)/Arne Hertz (S)	Toyota Celica Turbo 4WD	5h 40m 42s
06	Andrea Aghini (I)/Sauro Farnocchia (I)	Lancia Delta HF Integrale	5h 42m 19s
07	Miki Biasion (I)/Tiziano Siviero (I)	Ford Sierra RS Cosworth 4x4	5h 42m 21s
08	Piero Liatti (I)/Luciano Tedeschini (I)	Lancia Delta HF Integrale	5h 48m 42s
09	Jean Ragnotti (F)/Gilles Thimonier (F)	Renault Clio 16S	5h 55m 09s
10	Alain Oreille (F)/Jean-Marc André (F)	Renault Clio 16S	6h 01m 03s

Didier Auriol/Bernard Occelli

ROUND 06 – ACROPOLIS, GREECE (31st May-3rd June)

01	Didier Auriol (F)/Bernard Occelli (F)	Lancia Delta HF Integrale	7h 12m 08s
02	Juha Kankkunen (FIN)/Juha Piironen (FIN)	Lancia Delta HF Integrale	7h 13m 37s
03	Miki Biasion (I)/Tiziano Siviero (I)	Ford Sierra RS Cosworth 4x4	7h 14m 33s
04	Colin McRae (GB)/Derek Ringer (GB)	Subaru Legacy RS	7h 16m 02s
05	François Delecour (F)/Daniel Grataloup (F)	Ford Sierra RS Cosworth 4x4	7h 27m 22s
06	Jorge Recalde (RA)/Martin Christie (RA)	Lancia Delta HF Integrale	7h 31m 58s
07	Alex Fiorio (I)/Vittorio Brambilla (I)	Lancia Delta HF Integrale	7h 44m 53s
08	'Jigger' (GR)/Kóstas Stefanis (GR)	Toyota Celica GT-Four	8h 00m 35s
09	Grégoire De Mévius (B)/Willy Lux (B)	Nissan Sunny GTI-R	8h 05m 11s
10	Fernando Capdevila (E)/Alfredo Rodríguez (E)	Ford Sierra RS Cosworth 4x4	8h 07m 40s

Didier Auriol/Bernard Occelli

ROUND 07 – NEW ZEALAND (25th-29th June)

01	Carlos Sainz (E)/Luís Moya (E)	Toyota Celica Turbo 4WD	6h 36m 10s
02	Piero Liatti (I)/Luciano Tedeschini (I)	Lancia Delta HF Integrale	6h 40m 40s
03	Ross Dunkerton (AUS)/Fred Gocentas (AUS)	Mitsubishi Galant VR-4	6h 46m 22s
04	Mikael Sundström (FIN)/Jakke Honkanen (FIN)	Lancia Delta Integrale 16V	7h 03m 12s
05	Ed Ordynski (AUS)/Harry Mansson (AUS)	Mitsubishi Galant VR-4	7h 06m 04s
06	Yoshio Fujimoto (J)/Hakaru Ichino (J)	Nissan Pulsar GTI-R	7h 08m 36s
07	Will Orr (NZ)/Heather Orr (NZ)	Subaru Legacy RS	7h 12m 39s
08	Seiichiro Taguchi (J)/Ceris Clarke (NZ)	Mitsubishi Galant VR-4	7h 13m 31s
09	Barry Sexton (NZ)/Neil Cathcart (NZ)	Mazda 323 GTX	7h 14m 12s
10	Craig Stallard (AUS)/Graeme Jesse (AUS)	Mitsubishi Galant VR-4	7h 15m 16s

Carlos Sainz/Luís Moya

ROUND 08 – ARGENTINA (22nd-25th July)

01	Didier Auriol (F)/Bernard Occelli (F)	Lancia Delta HF Integrale	4h 47m 26s
02	Carlos Sainz (E)/Luís Moya (E)	Toyota Celica Turbo 4WD	4h 49m 44s
03	Gustavo Trelles (ROU)/Jorge del Buono (RA)	Lancia Delta HF Integrale	5h 01m 31s
04	Alex Fiorio (I)/Vittorio Brambilla (I)	Lancia Delta HF Integrale	5h 15m 19s
05	Rudi Stohl (A)/Peter Diekmann (D)	Audi 90 Quattro	5h 34m 33s
06	Carlos Menem Jr (RA)/Victor Zucchini (PAR)	Lancia Delta HF Integrale	5h 34m 39s
07	Gabriel Raies (RA)/José Volta (RA)	Renault 18 GTX	5h 42m 24s
08	Miguel Torrás (RA)/Luís Maciel (RA)	Renault 18 GTX	5h 43m 22s
09	Hiroshi Nishiyama (J)/Yoichi Yamazaki (J)	Nissan Pulsar GTI-R	5h 56m 32s
10	Walter d'Agostini (RA)/Juan Turra (RA)	Renault 18 GTX	5h 57m 35s

Didier Auriol/Bernard Occelli

ROUND 09 – 1000 LAKES, FINLAND (27th-30th August)

01	Didier Auriol (F)/Bernard Occelli (F)	Lancia Delta HF Integrale	4h 32m 45s
02	Juha Kankkunen (FIN)/Juha Piironen (FIN)	Lancia Delta HF Integrale	4h 33m 25s
03	Markku Alén (FIN)/Ilkka Kivimäki (FIN)	Toyota Celica Turbo 4WD	4h 34m 44s
04	Ari Vatanen (FIN)/Bruno Berglund (S)	Subaru Legacy RS	4h 35m 17s
05	Miki Biasion (I)/Tiziano Siviero (I)	Ford Sierra RS Cosworth 4x4	4h 41m 46s
06	Lasse Lampi (FIN)/Pentti Kuukkala (FIN)	Mitsubishi Galant VR-4	4h 42m 41s
07	Sebastian Lindholm (FIN)/Timo Hantunen (FIN)	Ford Sierra RS Cosworth 4x4	4h 43m 58s
08	Colin McRae (GB)/Derek Ringer (GB)	Subaru Legacy RS	4h 48m 30s
09	Philippe Bugalski (F)/Denis Giraudet (F)	Lancia Delta HF Integrale	4h 49m 40s
10	Jarmo Kytölehto (FIN)/Arto Kapanen (FIN)	Mitsubishi Galant VR-4	4h 57m 14s

Didier Auriol/Bernard Occelli

ROUND 10 – AUSTRALIA (19th-22nd September)

01	Didier Auriol (F)/Bernard Occelli (F)	Lancia Delta HF Integrale	5h 13m 12s
02	Juha Kankkunen (FIN)/Juha Piironen (FIN)	Lancia Delta HF Integrale	5h 14m 53s
03	Carlos Sainz (E)/Luís Moya (E)	Toyota Celica Turbo 4WD	5h 15m 16s
04	Jorge Recalde (RA)/Martin Christie (RA)	Lancia Delta HF Integrale	5h 32m 05s
05	Ross Dunkerton (AUS)/Fred Gocentas (AUS)	Mitsubishi Galant VR-4	5h 35m 15s
06	'Possum' Bourne (NZ)/Rodger Freeth (NZ)	Subaru Legacy RS	5h 46m 52s
07	Ed Ordynski (AUS)/Mark Stacey (AUS)	Mitsubishi Galant VR-4	5h 51m 39s
08	Tolley Challis (AUS)/Rod Vanderstraaten (AUS)	Mitsubishi Galant VR-4	5h 54m 26s
09	Kiyoshi Inoue (J)/Yoshimasa Nakahara (J)	Mitsubishi Galant VR-4	5h 54m 38s
10.	Craig Stallard (AUS)/Graeme Jesse (AUS)	Mitsubishi Galant VR-4	6h 06m 37s

Didier Auriol/Bernard Occelli

ROUND 11 – SANREMO, ITALY (12th-14th October)

01	Andrea Aghini (I)/Sauro Farnocchia (I)	Lancia Delta HF Integrale	5h 52m 11s
02	Juha Kankkunen (FIN)/Juha Piironen (FIN)	Lancia Delta HF Integrale	5h 52m 51s
03	François Delecour (F)/Daniel Grataloup (F)	Ford Sierra RS Cosworth 4x4	5h 53m 53s
04	Miki Biasion (I)/Tiziano Siviero (I)	Ford Sierra RS Cosworth 4x4	5h 54m 06s
05	Alex Fiorio (I)/Vittorio Brambilla (I)	Lancia Delta HF Integrale	6h 00m 58s
06	Gilberto Pianezzola (I)/Loris Roggia (I)	Lancia Delta HF Integrale	6h 08m 20s
07	Piero Liatti (I)/Luciano Tedeschini (I)	Lancia Delta HF Integrale	6h 13m 28s
08	César Baroni (F)/Philippe David (F)	Lancia Delta HF Integrale	6h 15m 50s
09	Bruno Thiry (B)/Stéphane Prévot (B)	Opel Calibra 16V	6h 37m 39s
10	Giovanni Manfrinato (I)/Claudio Condotta (I)	Ford Sierra RS Cosworth 4x4	6h 42m 18s

Andrea Aghini/Sauro Farnocchia

ROUND 12 – IVORY COAST, AFRICA (31st October-2 November)

01	Kenjiro Shinozuka (J)/John Meadows (GB)	Mitsubishi Galant VR-4	4h 09m 41s
02	Bruno Thiry (B)/Stéphane Prévot (B)	Opel Kadett GSI 16V	5h 32m 59s
03	Patrice Servant (F)/Thierry Brion (F)	Audi 90 Quattro	5h 38m 02s
04	Hiroshi Nishiyama (J)/Hisashi Yamaguchi (J)	Nissan Pulsar GTI-R	6h 24m 07s
05	Samir Assef (LEB)/Clement Konan (CI)	Toyota Celica GT-Four	7h 42m 27s
06	Alain Oudit (F)/Frédéric Spaak (F)	Nissan Sunny GTI-R	7h 46m 36s
07	Manfred Stohl (A)/Kay Gerlach (D)	Audi 90 Quattro	8h 14m 19s
08	Denis Occelli (CI)/Frank Michel (F)	Toyota Corolla 16V	8h 44m 44s
09	Jean-Claude Dupuis (CH)/Nathalie Copetti (F)	Toyota Corolla 16V	9h 04m 49s
10	Guy Colsoul (B)/Edy Paquay (B)	Mitsubishi Galant VR-4	10h 42m 25s

Kenjiro Shinozuka/John Meadows

ROUND 13 – CATALUNYA, SPAIN (9th-11th November)

01	Carlos Sainz (E)/Luís Moya (E)	Toyota Celica Turbo 4WD	6h 21m 13s
02	Juha Kankkunen (FIN)/Juha Piironen (FIN)	Lancia Delta HF Integrale	6h 21m 49s
03	Andrea Aghini (I)/Sauro Farnocchia (I)	Lancia Delta HF Integrale	6h 22m 45s
04	Alex Fiorio (I)/Vittorio Brambilla (I)	Lancia Delta HF Integrale	6h 27m 39s
05	Armin Schwarz (D)/Arne Hertz (S)	Toyota Celica Turbo 4WD	6h 29m 43s
06	Jesús Puras (E)/Alex Romaní (E)	Lancia Delta HF Integrale	6h 29m 43s
07	Gustavo Trelles (ROU)/Jorge del Buono (RA)	Lancia Delta HF Integrale	6h 31m 30s
08	Pedro Diego (E)/Iciar Muguerza (E)	Lancia Delta HF Integrale	6h 43m 30s
09	Mohammed Bin Sulayem (UAE)/Ronan Morgan (GB)	Ford Sierra RS Cosworth 4x4	7h 02m 13s
10	Didier Auriol (F)/Bernard Occelli (F)	Lancia Delta HF Integrale	7h 12m 12s

Carlos Sainz/Luís Moya

ROUND 14 – RAC, GREAT BRITAIN (22nd-25th November)

01	Carlos Sainz (E)/Luís Moya (E)	Toyota Celica Turbo 4WD	5h 23m 06s
02	Ari Vatanen (FIN)/Bruno Berglund (S)	Subaru Legacy RS	5h 25m 22s
03	Juha Kankkunen (FIN)/Juha Piironen (FIN)	Lancia Delta HF Integrale	5h 25m 51s
04	Markku Alén (FIN)/Ilkka Kivimäki (FIN)	Toyota Celica Turbo 4WD	5h 26m 35s
05	Miki Biasion (I)/Tiziano Siviero (I)	Ford Sierra RS Cosworth 4x4	5h 26m 47s
06	Colin McRae (GB)/Derek Ringer (GB)	Subaru Legacy RS	5h 31m 41s
07	Kenneth Eriksson (S)/Staffan Parmander (S)	Mitsubishi Galant VR-4	5h 33m 26s
08	Tommi Mäkinen (FIN)/Seppo Harjanne (FIN)	Nissan Sunny GTI-R	5h 35m 07s
09	Malcolm Wilson (GB)/Bryan Thomas (GB)	Ford Sierra RS Cosworth 4x4	5h 35m 26s
10	Andrea Aghini (I)/Sauro Farnocchia (I)	Lancia Delta HF Integrale	5h 37m 58s

Carlos Sainz/Luís Moya

FINAL DRIVERS' CHAMPIONSHIP POSITIONS		
01	Carlos Sainz	144
02	Juha Kankkunen	134
03	Didier Auriol	121
04	Miki Biasion	60
05	Markku Alén	50
06	François Delecour	45
07	Andrea Aghini	39
08	Colin McRae	34
09	Alex Fiorio	32
10	Jorge Recalde	28

FINAL MANUFACTURERS' CHAMPIONSHIP POSITIONS		
01	Lancia	140
02	Toyota	116
03	Ford	94
04	Subaru	60
05	Mitsubishi	44
06	Nissan	37
07	Audi	10
08	Renault	9
09	Opel	2

1993

ROUND 01 – MONTE CARLO (21st-27th January)

01	Didier Auriol (F)/Bernard Occelli (F)	Toyota Celica Turbo 4WD	6h 13m 43s
02	François Delecour (F)/Daniel Grataloup (F)	Ford Escort RS Cosworth	6h 13m 58s
03	Miki Biasion (I)/Tiziano Siviero (I)	Ford Escort RS Cosworth	6h 16m 59s
04	Kenneth Eriksson (S)/Staffan Parmander (S)	Mitsubishi Lancer RS	6h 31m 30s
05	Juha Kankkunen (FIN)/Juha Piironen (FIN)	Toyota Celica Turbo 4WD	6h 32m 43s
06	Armin Schwarz (D)/Nicky Grist (GB)	Mitsubishi Lancer RS	6h 39m 45s
07	Olivier Burri (CH)/Christophe Hofmann (CH)	Ford Sierra RS Cosworth 4x4	6h 51m 03s
08	Bruno Thiry (B)/Stéphane Prévot (B)	Opel Astra GSI 16V	6h 54m 08s
09	Christophe Spiliotis (MC)/Hervé Thibaud (F)	Lancia Delta HF Integrale	6h 56m 24s
10	Jean-Baptiste Serpaggi (F)/Francis Serpaggi (F)	Ford Escort RS Cosworth	6h 57m 58s

Didier Auriol/Bernard Occelli

ROUND 02 – SWEDEN (12th-14th February)

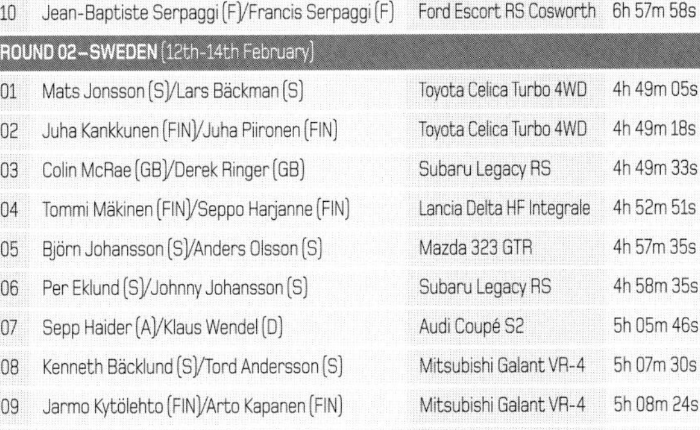

01	Mats Jonsson (S)/Lars Bäckman (S)	Toyota Celica Turbo 4WD	4h 49m 05s
02	Juha Kankkunen (FIN)/Juha Piironen (FIN)	Toyota Celica Turbo 4WD	4h 49m 18s
03	Colin McRae (GB)/Derek Ringer (GB)	Subaru Legacy RS	4h 49m 33s
04	Tommi Mäkinen (FIN)/Seppo Harjanne (FIN)	Lancia Delta HF Integrale	4h 52m 51s
05	Björn Johansson (S)/Anders Olsson (S)	Mazda 323 GTR	4h 57m 35s
06	Per Eklund (S)/Johnny Johansson (S)	Subaru Legacy RS	4h 58m 35s
07	Sepp Haider (A)/Klaus Wendel (D)	Audi Coupé S2	5h 05m 46s
08	Kenneth Bäcklund (S)/Tord Andersson (S)	Mitsubishi Galant VR-4	5h 07m 30s
09	Jarmo Kytölehto (FIN)/Arto Kapanen (FIN)	Mitsubishi Galant VR-4	5h 08m 24s
10	Per Svan (S)/Johan Olsson (S)	Opel Astra GSI 16V	5h 12m 05s

Mats Jonsson/Lars Bäckman

ROUND 03 – PORTUGAL (3rd-6th March)

01	François Delecour (F)/Daniel Grataloup (F)	Ford Escort RS Cosworth	6h 20m 37s
02	Miki Biasion (I)/Tiziano Siviero (I)	Ford Escort RS Cosworth	6h 21m 32s
03	Andrea Aghini (I)/Sauro Farnocchia (I)	Lancia Delta HF Integrale	6h 23m 17s
04	Markku Alén (FIN)/Ilkka Kivimäki (FIN)	Subaru Legacy RS	6h 24m 23s
05	Kenneth Eriksson (S)/Staffan Parmander (S)	Mitsubishi Lancer RS	6h 25m 28s
06	Alex Fiorio (I)/Vittorio Brambilla (I)	Lancia Delta HF Integrale	6h 26m 18s
07	Colin McRae (GB)/Derek Ringer (GB)	Subaru Legacy RS	6h 37m 25s
08	Jorge Bica (P)/Joaquim Capelo (P)	Lancia Delta HF Integrale	6h 51m 42s
09	Alex Fassina (I)/Luigi Pirollo (I)	Mazda 323 GTR	7h 11m 46s
10	Bruno Thiry (B)/Stéphane Prévot (B)	Opel Astra GSI 16V	7h 12m 18s

François Delecour/Daniel Grataloup

ROUND 04 – SAFARI, AFRICA (8th-12th April)

01	Juha Kankkunen (FIN)/Juha Piironen (FIN)	Toyota Celica Turbo 4WD	3h 54m
02	Markku Alén (FIN)/Ilkka Kivimäki (FIN)	Toyota Celica Turbo 4WD	4h 03m
03	Ian Duncan (EAK)/Ian Munro (EAK)	Toyota Celica Turbo 4WD	5h 24m
04	Yasuhiro Iwase (J)/Sudhir Vinayak (EAK)	Toyota Celica Turbo 4WD	5h 35m
05	Guy Jack (EAK)/Des Page-Morris (EAK)	Daihatsu Charade GTXX	7h 44m
06	Ashok Pattni (EAK)/Zahid Mogul (EAK)	Daihatsu Charade GTXX	8h 39m
07	Marco Brighetti (EAK)/Abdul Sidi (EAK)	Daihatsu Charade GTXX	8h 57m
08	Rudi Stohl (A)/Peter Diekmann (D)	Audi Coupé S2	9h 14m
09	Basmat Shamji (EAK)/Peter Stone (EAK)	Subaru Legacy RS	10h 07m
10	Manfred Stohl (A)/Kay Gerlach (D)	Audi 90 Quattro	10h 43m

Juha Kankkunen/Juha Piironen

ROUND 05 – CORSICA, FRANCE (2nd-4th May)

01	François Delecour (F)/Daniel Grataloup (F)	Ford Escort RS Cosworth	6h 14m 41s
02	Didier Auriol (F)/Bernard Occelli (F)	Toyota Celica Turbo 4WD	6h 15m 43s
03	François Chatriot (F)/Denis Giraudet (F)	Toyota Celica Turbo 4WD	6h 17m 23s
04	Carlos Sainz (E)/Luís Moya (E)	Lancia Delta HF Integrale	6h 18m 29s
05	Colin McRae (GB)/Derek Ringer (GB)	Subaru Legacy RS	6h 23m 44s
06	Bernard Béguin (F)/Jean-Paul Chiaroni (F)	Ford Escort RS Cosworth	6h 31m 12s
07	Miki Biasion (I)/Tiziano Siviero (I)	Ford Escort RS Cosworth	6h 33m 39s
08	Jean Ragnotti (F)/Gilles Thimonier (F)	Renault Clio Williams	6h 36m 11s
09	Alain Oreille (F)/Jean-Marc André (F)	Renault Clio Williams	6h 38m 48s
10	Giovanni Manfrinato (I)/Claudio Condotta (I)	Ford Escort RS Cosworth	6h 55m 30s

François Delecour/Daniel Grataloup

ROUND 06 – ACROPOLIS, GREECE (30th May-1st June)

01	Miki Biasion (I)/Tiziano Siviero (I)	Ford Escort RS Cosworth	6h 54m 35s
02	Carlos Sainz (E)/Luís Moya (E)	Lancia Delta HF Integrale	6h 55m 48s
03	Armin Schwarz (D)/Nicky Grist (GB)	Mitsubishi Lancer RS	6h 57m 19s
04	Andrea Aghini (I)/Sauro Farnocchia (I)	Lancia Delta HF Integrale	7h 00m 15s
05	Gustavo Trelles (ROU)/Jorge del Buono (RA)	Lancia Delta HF Integrale	7h 02m 39s
06	Tommi Mäkinen (FIN)/Seppo Harjanne (FIN)	Lancia Delta HF Integrale	7h 02m 44s
07	Alex Fiorio (I)/Vittorio Brambilla (I)	Lancia Delta HF Integrale	7h 23m 44s
08	Kóstas Apostolou (GR)/Mihalis Kriadis (GR)	Lancia Delta HF Integrale	7h 39m 00s
09	Nikos Tsadaris (GR)/Elias Kafaoglou (GR)	Lancia Delta HF Integrale	7h 39m 45s
10	Alex Fassina (I)/Luigi Pirollo (I)	Mazda 323 GTR	8h 08m 04s

Miki Biasion/Tiziano Siviero

ROUND 07 – ARGENTINA (14th-17th July)

01	Juha Kankkunen (FIN)/Nicky Grist (GB)	Toyota Celica Turbo 4WD	5h 32m 31s
02	Miki Biasion (I)/Tiziano Siviero (I)	Ford Escort RS Cosworth	5h 34m 25s
03	Didier Auriol (F)/Bernard Occelli (F)	Toyota Celica Turbo 4WD	5h 49m 29s
04	Gustavo Trelles (ROU)/Jorge del Buono (RA)	Lancia Delta HF Integrale	6h 00m 36s
05	Carlos Menem Jr (RA)/Victor Zucchini (PAR)	Ford Escort RS Cosworth	6h 04m 05s
06	Mohammed Bin Sulayem (UAE)/Ronan Morgan (GB)	Ford Escort RS Cosworth	6h 09m 42s
07	Rudi Stohl (A)/Peter Diekmann (D)	Audi Coupé S2	6h 21m 53s
08	António Coutinho (P)/Paulo Brandão (P)	Ford Escort RS Cosworth	6h 30m 53s
09	Gabriel Raies (RA)/José Volta (RA)	Renault 18 GTX	6h 33m 01s
10	José Ceccheto (RA)/Justo Carrera (RA)	Fiat Regata 2000	6h 43m 37s

Juha Kankkunen/Nicky Grist

ROUND 08 – NEW ZEALAND (5th-8th August)

01	Colin McRae (GB)/Derek Ringer (GB)	Subaru Legacy RS	6h 12m 31s
02	François Delecour (F)/Daniel Grataloup (F)	Ford Escort RS Cosworth	6h 12m 58s
03	Didier Auriol (F)/Bernard Occelli (F)	Toyota Celica Turbo 4WD	6h 13m 00s
04	Carlos Sainz (E)/Luís Moya (E)	Lancia Delta HF Integrale	6h 14m 38s
05	Juha Kankkunen (FIN)/Nicky Grist (GB)	Toyota Celica Turbo 4WD	6h 15m 26s
06	'Possum' Bourne (NZ)/Rodger Freeth (NZ)	Subaru Legacy RS	6h 20m 46s
07	Gustavo Trelles (ROU)/Jorge del Buono (RA)	Lancia Delta HF Integrale	6h 23m 48s
08	Neil Allport (NZ)/Jim Robb (NZ)	Mazda 323 GTR	6h 36m 58s
09	Joe McAndrew (NZ)/Bob Haldane (NZ)	Subaru Legacy RS	6h 43m 29s
10	Yoshio Fujimoto (J)/Hakaru Ichino (J)	Mitsubishi Lancer RS	6h 43m 58s

Colin McRae/Derek Ringer

ROUND 09 – 1000 LAKES, FINLAND (27th-29th August)			
01	Juha Kankkunen (FIN)/Denis Giraudet (F)	Toyota Celica Turbo 4WD	4h 23m 51s
02	Ari Vatanen (FIN)/Bruno Berglund (S)	Subaru Impreza 555	4h 24m 38s
03	Didier Auriol (F)/Bernard Occelli (F)	Toyota Celica Turbo 4WD	4h 26m 01s
04	Tommi Mäkinen (FIN)/Seppo Harjanne (FIN)	Lancia Delta HF Integrale	4h 28m 26s
05	Kenneth Eriksson (S)/Staffan Parmander (S)	Mitsubishi Lancer RS	4h 29m 32s
06	Sebastian Lindholm (FIN)/Timo Hantunen (FIN)	Ford Escort RS Cosworth	4h 31m 34s
07	Hannu Mikkola (FIN)/Arne Hertz (S)	Toyota Celica Turbo 4WD	4h 32m 33s
08	Lasse Lampi (FIN)/Pentti Kuukkala (FIN)	Mitsubishi Galant VR-4	4h 33m 18s
09	Armin Schwarz (D)/Nicky Grist (GB)	Mitsubishi Lancer RS	4h 34m 06s
10	Marcus Grönholm (FIN)/Voitto Silander (FIN)	Toyota Celica Turbo 4WD	4h 40m 20s

Juha Kankkunen/Denis Giraudet

ROUND 10 – AUSTRALIA (18th-21st September)			
01	Juha Kankkunen (FIN)/Nicky Grist (GB)	Toyota Celica Turbo 4WD	5h 19m 58s
02	Ari Vatanen (FIN)/Bruno Berglund (S)	Subaru Legacy RS	5h 25m 50s
03	François Delecour (F)/Daniel Grataloup (F)	Ford Escort RS Cosworth	5h 43m 42s
04	Ross Dunkerton (AUS)/Fred Gocentas (AUS)	Mitsubishi Lancer RS	5h 46m 18s
05	Sepp Haider (A)/Klaus Wendel (D)	Audi Coupé S2	5h 49m 08s
06	Colin McRae (GB)/Derek Ringer (GB)	Subaru Legacy RS	5h 56m 33s
07	Ed Ordynski (AUS)/Mark Stacey (AUS)	Mitsubishi Lancer RS	5h 58m 42s
08	Neal Bates (AUS)/Coral Taylor (AUS)	Toyota Celica Turbo 4WD	6h 04m 50s
09	Kiyoshi Inoue (J)/Satoshi Hayashi (J)	Mitsubishi Lancer RS	6h 09m 04s
10	David Officer (AUS)/Kate Officer (AUS)	Mitsubishi Lancer RS	6h 11m 43s

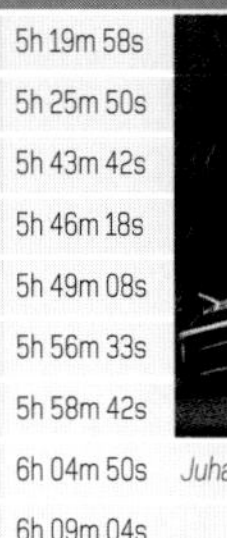
Juha Kankkunen/Nicky Grist

ROUND 11 – SANREMO, ITALY (11th-13th October)			
01	Gianfranco Cunico (I)/Stefano Evangelisti (I)	Ford Escort RS Cosworth	6h 19m 40s
02	Patrick Snijers (B)/Dany Colebunders (B)	Ford Escort RS Cosworth	6h 30m 08s
03	Gilberto Pianezzola (I)/Loris Roggia (I)	Lancia Delta HF Integrale	6h 38m 03s
04	Piero Liatti (I)/Alex Alessandrini (I)	Subaru Legacy RS	6h 44m 47s
05	Bruno Thiry (B)/Stéphane Prévot (B)	Opel Astra GSI 16V	6h 46m 27s
06	Renato Travaglia (I)/Alex Mari (I)	Ford Escort RS Cosworth	6h 58m 21s
07	Andrea Dallavilla (I)/Danilo Fappani (I)	Ford Escort RS Cosworth	6h 58m 31s
08	Angelo Medeghini (I)/Paolo Cecchini (I)	Peugeot 106 XSI	6h 58m 38s
09	Freddy Loix (B)/Johnny Vranken (B)	Opel Astra GSI 16V	7h 04m 55s
10	Alex Fassina (I)/Luigi Pirollo (I)	Mazda 323 GTR	7h 08m 02s

Gianfranco Cunico/Stefano Evangelisti

ROUND 12 – CATALUNYA, SPAIN (2nd-4th November)			
01	François Delecour (F)/Daniel Grataloup (F)	Ford Escort RS Cosworth	5h 36m 19s
02	Didier Auriol (F)/Bernard Occelli (F)	Toyota Celica Turbo 4WD	5h 37m 19s
03	Juha Kankkunen (FIN)/Nicky Grist (GB)	Toyota Celica Turbo 4WD	5h 40m 28s
04	Miki Biasion (I)/Tiziano Siviero (I)	Ford Escort RS Cosworth	5h 42m 57s
05	Alex Fiorio (I)/Vittorio Brambilla (I)	Lancia Delta HF Integrale	5h 44m 07s
06	Gustavo Trelles (ROU)/Jorge del Buono (RA)	Lancia Delta HF Integrale	5h 46m 27s
07	Bruno Thiry (B)/Stéphane Prévot (B)	Opel Astra GSI 16V	6h 03m 47s
08	Luís Climent (E)/José Muñoz (E)	Opel Astra GSI 16V	6h 07m 37s
09	Mia Bardolet (E)/Joaquim Muntada (E)	Opel Astra GSI 16V	6h 08m 02s
10	Oriol Gómez (E)/Marc Martí (E)	Peugeot 106 XSI	6h 18m 19s

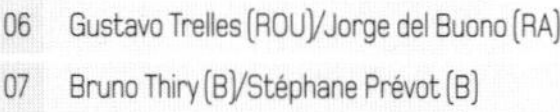
François Delecour/Daniel Grataloup

ROUND 13 – RAC, GREAT BRITAIN (21st-24th November)			
01	Juha Kankkunen (FIN)/Nicky Grist (GB)	Toyota Celica Turbo 4WD	6h 25m 48s
02	Kenneth Eriksson (S)/Staffan Parmander (S)	Mitsubishi Lancer RS	6h 27m 32s
03	Malcolm Wilson (GB)/Bryan Thomas (GB)	Ford Escort RS Cosworth	6h 30m 51s
04	François Delecour (F)/Daniel Grataloup (F)	Ford Escort RS Cosworth	6h 32m 57s
05	Ari Vatanen (FIN)/Bruno Berglund (S)	Subaru Impreza 555	6h 33m 59s
06	Didier Auriol (F)/Bernard Occelli (F)	Toyota Celica Turbo 4WD	6h 39m 39s
07	Richard Burns (GB)/Robert Reid (GB)	Subaru Legacy RS	6h 47m 25s
08	Armin Schwarz (D)/Peter Thul (D)	Mitsubishi Lancer RS	6h 51m 02s
09	Mats Jonsson (S)/Lars Bäckman (S)	Toyota Celica Turbo 4WD	7h 00m 48s
10	Alister McRae (GB)/David Senior (GB)	Subaru Legacy RS	7h 02m 12s

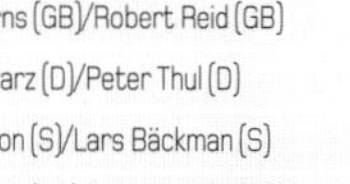

Juha Kankkunen/Nicky Grist

FINAL DRIVERS' CHAMPIONSHIP POSITIONS		
01	Juha Kankkunen	135
02	François Delecour	112
03	Didier Auriol	92
04	Miki Biasion	76
05	Colin McRae	50
06	Kenneth Eriksson	41
07	Ari Vatanen	38
08	Carlos Sainz	35
09	Gustavo Trelles	28
10	Tommi Mäkinen	26

FINAL MANUFACTURERS' CHAMPIONSHIP POSITIONS		
01	Toyota	157
02	Ford	145
03	Subaru	112
04	Mitsubishi	86
05	Lancia	75

1994

ROUND 01 – MONTE CARLO (22nd-27th January)			
01	François Delecour (F)/Daniel Grataloup (F)	Ford Escort RS Cosworth	6h 12m 20s
02	Juha Kankkunen (FIN)/Nicky Grist (GB)	Toyota Celica Turbo 4WD	6h 13m 25s
03	Carlos Sainz (E)/Luís Moya (E)	Subaru Impreza 555	6h 14m 07s
04	Miki Biasion (I)/Tiziano Siviero (I)	Ford Escort RS Cosworth	6h 16m 56s
05	Kenneth Eriksson (S)/Staffan Parmander (S)	Mitsubishi Lancer RS	6h 19m 17s
06	Bruno Thiry (B)/Stéphane Prévot (B)	Ford Escort RS Cosworth	6h 19m 18s
07	Armin Schwarz (D)/Klaus Wicha (D)	Mitsubishi Lancer RS	6h 29m 19s
08	Pierre-Manuel Jenot (F)/'Slo' (F)	Ford Escort RS Cosworth	6h 49m 16s
09	Jesús Puras (E)/Alex Romani (E)	Ford Escort RS Cosworth	6h 54m 49s
10	Colin McRae (GB)/Derek Ringer (GB)	Subaru Impreza 555	7h 01m 30s

François Delecour/Daniel Grataloup

ROUND 02 – PORTUGAL (1st-4th March)			
01	Juha Kankkunen (FIN)/Nicky Grist (GB)	Toyota Celica Turbo 4WD	6h 20m 59
02	Didier Auriol (F)/Bernard Occelli (F)	Toyota Celica Turbo 4WD	6h 21m 39
03	Miki Biasion (I)/Tiziano Siviero (I)	Ford Escort RS Cosworth	6h 21m 49
04	Carlos Sainz (E)/Luís Moya (E)	Subaru Impreza 555	6h 23m 15
05	Fernando Peres (P)/Ricardo Caldeira (P)	Ford Escort RS Cosworth	6h 49m 39
06	José Carlos Macedo (P)/Miguel Borges (P)	Renault Clio Williams	7h 05m 52
07	Raphael Sperrer (A)/Ernst Loidl (A)	Audi Coupé S2	7h 11m 49
08	Jesús Puras (E)/Carlos del Barrio (E)	Ford Escort RS Cosworth	7h 16m 17
09	Rui Madeira (P)/Nuno da Silva (P)	Ford Sierra RS Cosworth 4x4	7h 25m 37
10	Pavel Sibera (CZ)/Petr Gross (CZ)	Skoda Favorit 136L	7h 29m 22

Juha Kankkunen/Nicky Grist

ROUND 03 – SAFARI, AFRICA (31st March-3rd April)			
01	Ian Duncan (EAK)/David Williamson (EAK)	Toyota Celica Turbo 4WD	20h 49
02	Kenjiro Shinozuka (J)/Pentti Kuukkala (FIN)	Mitsubishi Lancer Evo 2	21h 14m
03	Didier Auriol (F)/Bernard Occelli (F)	Toyota Celica Turbo 4WD	21h 59m
04	Patrick Njiru (EAK)/Abdul Sidi (EAK)	Subaru Impreza WRX	23h 30m
05	Richard Burns (GB)/Robert Reid (GB)	Subaru Impreza WRX	23h 40m
06	Rudi Stohl (A)/Jürgen Bertl (D)	Audi Coupé S2	26h 30m
07	Karim Hirji (UGA)/Frank Nekusa (UGA)	Toyota Celica Turbo 4WD	26h 36m
08	Sammy Aslam (EAK)/Joey Ghose (EAK)	Volkswagen Golf GTI 16V	27h 03m
09	Rob Hellier (EAK)/Phil Valentine (EAK)	Mitsubishi Galant VR-4	28h 04m
10	Azar Anwar (EAK)/Shailen Shah (EAK)	Subaru Legacy Estate	29h 54m

Ian Duncan/David Williamson

ROUND 04 – CORSICA, FRANCE (5th-7th May)			
01	Didier Auriol (F)/Bernard Occelli (F)	Toyota Celica Turbo 4WD	5h 57m 46s
02	Carlos Sainz (E)/Luís Moya (E)	Subaru Impreza 555	5h 58m 47s
03	Andrea Aghini (I)/Sauro Farnocchia (I)	Toyota Celica Turbo 4WD	5h 59m 57s
04	Juha Kankkunen (FIN)/Nicky Grist (GB)	Toyota Celica Turbo 4WD	6h 00m 29s
05	Miki Biasion (I)/Tiziano Siviero (I)	Ford Escort RS Cosworth	6h 02m 33s
06	Bruno Thiry (B)/Stéphane Prévot (B)	Ford Escort RS Cosworth	6h 02m 45s
07	Patrick Bernardini (F)/Rocky Demedardi (F)	Ford Escort RS Cosworth	6h 13m 33s
08	Jean Ragnotti (F)/Gilles Thimonier (F)	Renault Clio Williams	6h 17m 30s
09	Serge Jordan (F)/Jack Boyère (F)	Renault Clio Williams	6h 20m 47s
10	Marc Massarotto (F)/Jean-Pierre Gordon (F)	BMW M3	6h 25m 06s

Didier Auriol/Bernard Occelli

ROUND 05 – ACROPOLIS, GREECE (29th-31st May)

Pos	Driver/Co-driver	Car	Time
01	Carlos Sainz (E)/Luís Moya (E)	Subaru Impreza 555	6h 36m 38s
02	Armin Schwarz (D)/Klaus Wicha (D)	Mitsubishi Lancer Evo 2	6h 40m 39s
03	Juha Kankkunen (FIN)/Nicky Grist (GB)	Toyota Celica Turbo 4WD	6h 42m 31s
04	Alex Fiorio (I)/Vittorio Brambilla (I)	Lancia Delta HF Integrale	6h 50m 58s
05	Ari Vatanen (FIN)/Fabrizia Pons (I)	Ford Escort RS Cosworth	6h 52m 03s
06	Malcolm Wilson (GB)/Bryan Thomas (GB)	Ford Escort RS Cosworth	6h 59m 25s
07	Yoshio Fujimoto (J)/Arne Hertz (S)	Toyota Celica Turbo 4WD	7h 09m 30s
08	Aris Vovos (GR)/Kóstas Fertakis (GR)	Lancia Delta HF Integrale	7h 19m 15s
09	Emil Triner (CZ)/Jiri Klima (CZ)	Skoda Favorit 136L	7h 37m 02s
10	Pavel Sibera (CZ)/Petr Gross (CZ)	Skoda Favorit 136L	7h 37m 46s

Carlos Sainz/Luís Moya

ROUND 06 – ARGENTINA (30th June-2nd July)

Pos	Driver/Co-driver	Car	Time
01	Didier Auriol (F)/Bernard Occelli (F)	Toyota Celica Turbo 4WD	5h 50m 42s
02	Carlos Sainz (E)/Luís Moya (E)	Subaru Impreza 555	5h 50m 48s
03	Ari Vatanen (FIN)/Fabrizia Pons (I)	Ford Escort RS Cosworth	5h 57m 22s
04	Bruno Thiry (B)/Stéphane Prévot (B)	Ford Escort RS Cosworth	6h 01m 49s
05	Jorge Recalde (RA)/Martin Christie (RA)	Mitsubishi Lancer Evo 2	6h 27m 04s
06	Jorge Bescham (RA)/José García (RA)	Ford Escort RS Cosworth	6h 33m 59s
07	Rudi Stohl (A)/Peter Diekmann (D)	Audi Coupé S2	6h 47m 38s
08	Isolde Holderied (D)/Tina Thörner (S)	Mitsubishi Lancer RS	6h 51m 31s
09	Gabriel Raies (RA)/José Volta (RA)	Renault 18 GTX	7h 02m 51s
10	Gustavo Ramonda (RA)/Horacio Berra (RA)	Mitsubishi Galant VR-4	7h 11m 28s

Didier Auriol/Bernard Occelli

ROUND 07 – NEW ZEALAND (29th-31st July)

Pos	Driver/Co-driver	Car	Time
01	Colin McRae (GB)/Derek Ringer (GB)	Subaru Impreza 555	5h 39m 56s
02	Juha Kankkunen (FIN)/Nicky Grist (GB)	Toyota Celica Turbo 4WD	5h 42m 10s
03	Armin Schwarz (D)/Klaus Wicha (D)	Mitsubishi Lancer Evo 2	5h 45m 27s
04	Kenneth Eriksson (S)/Staffan Parmander (S)	Mitsubishi Lancer Evo 2	5h 49m 38s
05	Didier Auriol (F)/Bernard Occelli (F)	Toyota Celica Turbo 4WD	5h 51m 52s
06	Joe McAndrew (NZ)/Bob Haldane (NZ)	Subaru Legacy RS	5h 59m 40s
07	Yoshio Fujimoto (J)/Arne Hertz (S)	Toyota Celica Turbo 4WD	6h 05m 11s
08	Brian Stokes (NZ)/Jeff Judd (NZ)	Ford Escort RS Cosworth	6h 06m 05s
09	Ed Ordynski (AUS)/Mark Stacey (AUS)	Mitsubishi Lancer RS	6h 08m 50s
10	Kiyoshi Inoue (J)/Yoshimasa Nakahara (J)	Mitsubishi Lancer Evo 2	6h 11m 55s

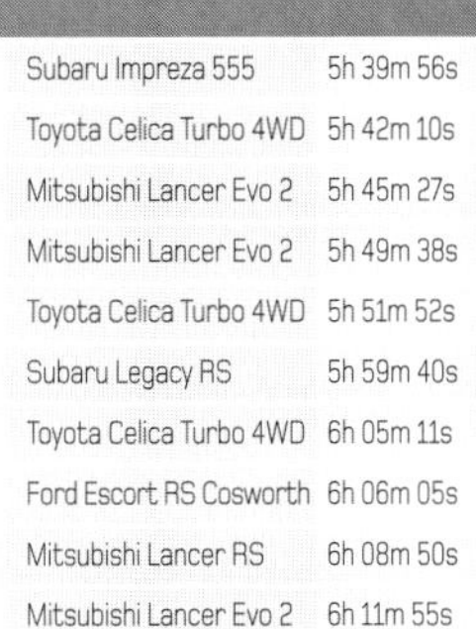

Colin McRae/Derek Ringer

ROUND 08 – 1000 LAKES, FINLAND (26th-28th August)

Pos	Driver/Co-driver	Car	Time
01	Tommi Mäkinen (FIN)/Seppo Harjanne (FIN)	Ford Escort RS Cosworth	4h 33m 44s
02	Didier Auriol (F)/Bernard Occelli (F)	Toyota Celica Turbo 4WD	4h 34m 06s
03	Carlos Sainz (E)/Luís Moya (E)	Subaru Impreza 555	4h 34m 48s
04	François Delecour (F)/Daniel Grataloup (F)	Ford Escort RS Cosworth	4h 39m 22s
05	Marcus Grönholm (FIN)/Voitto Silander (FIN)	Toyota Celica Turbo 4WD	4h 40m 55s
06	Lasse Lampi (FIN)/Pentti Kuukkala (FIN)	Mitsubishi Galant VR-4	4h 45m 47s
07	Thomas Rådström (S)/Lars Bäckman (S)	Toyota Celica Turbo 4WD	4h 50m 09s
08	Jarmo Kytölehto (FIN)/Arto Kapanen (FIN)	Mitsubishi Lancer RS	4h 51m 55s
09	Juha Kankkunen (FIN)/Nicky Grist (GB)	Toyota Celica Turbo 4WD	4h 53m 29s
10	Olli Harkki (FIN)/Antti Virjula (FIN)	Mitsubishi Lancer RS	4h 58m 37s

Tommi Mäkinen/Seppo Harjanne

ROUND 09 – SANREMO, ITALY (9th-12 October)

Pos	Driver/Co-driver	Car	Time
01	Didier Auriol (F)/Bernard Occelli (F)	Toyota Celica Turbo 4WD	5h 56m 40s
02	Carlos Sainz (E)/Luís Moya (E)	Subaru Impreza 555	5h 57m 01s
03	Miki Biasion (I)/Tiziano Siviero (I)	Ford Escort RS Cosworth	5h 57m 27s
04	Bruno Thiry (B)/Stéphane Prévot (B)	Ford Escort RS Cosworth	5h 57m 57s
05	Colin McRae (GB)/Derek Ringer (GB)	Subaru Impreza 555	5h 58m 16s
06	Gianfranco Cunico (I)/Stefano Evangelisti (I)	Ford Escort RS Cosworth	5h 58m 31s
07	Juha Kankkunen (FIN)/Nicky Grist (GB)	Toyota Celica GT-Four	6h 00m 58s
08	Piero Longhi (I)/Flavio Zanella (I)	Toyota Celica Turbo 4WD	6h 05m 49s
09	Malcolm Wilson (GB)/Bryan Thomas (GB)	Ford Escort RS Cosworth	6h 07m 42s
10	Jorge Bica (P)/Joaquim Capelo (P)	Lancia Delta HF Integrale	6h 27m 06s

Didier Auriol/Bernard Occelli

ROUND 10 – RAC, GREAT BRITAIN (20th-23rd November)

Pos	Driver/Co-driver	Car	Time
01	Colin McRae (GB)/Derek Ringer (GB)	Subaru Impreza 555	5h 17m 25s
02	Juha Kankkunen (FIN)/Nicky Grist (GB)	Toyota Celica GT-Four	5h 20m 58s
03	Bruno Thiry (B)/Stéphane Prévot (B)	Ford Escort RS Cosworth	5h 27m 37s
04	Stig Blomqvist (S)/Benny Melander (S)	Ford Escort RS Cosworth	5h 30m 13s
05	Ari Vatanen (FIN)/Fabrizia Pons (I)	Ford Escort RS Cosworth	5h 34m 25s
06	Didier Auriol (F)/Bernard Occelli (F)	Toyota Celica Turbo 4WD	5h 47m 57s
07	Gwyndaf Evans (GB)/Howard Davies (GB)	Ford Escort RS 2000	5h 52m 24s
08	Jan Habig (RSA)/Douglas Judd (RSA)	Ford Escort RS Cosworth	5h 53m 16s
09	Tommi Mäkinen (FIN)/Seppo Harjanne (FIN)	Nissan Sunny GTI	5h 53m 20s
10	Grégoire De Mévius (B)/Willy Lux (B)	Opel Astra GSI 16V	5h 53m 54s

Colin McRae/Derek Ringer

FINAL DRIVERS' CHAMPIONSHIP POSITIONS

Pos	Driver	Points
01	Didier Auriol	116
02	Carlos Sainz	99
03	Juha Kankkunen	93
04	Colin McRae	49
05	Bruno Thiry	44
06	Miki Biasion	42
07	Armin Schwarz	31
08	François Delecour	30
09	Ari Vatanen	28
10	Tommi Mäkinen	22

FINAL MANUFACTURERS' CHAMPIONSHIP POSITIONS

Pos	Manufacturer	Points
01	Toyota	151
02	Subaru	140
03	Ford	116
NC	Mitsubishi	41

1995

ROUND 01 – MONTE CARLO (22nd-26th January)

Pos	Driver/Co-driver	Car	Time
01	Carlos Sainz (E)/Luís Moya (E)	Subaru Impreza 555	6h 32m 31s
02	François Delecour (F)/Catherine François (F)	Ford Escort RS Cosworth	6h 34m 56s
03	Juha Kankkunen (FIN)/Nicky Grist (GB)	Toyota Celica GT-Four	6h 36m 28s
04	Tommi Mäkinen (FIN)/Seppo Harjanne (FIN)	Mitsubishi Lancer Evo 2	6h 37m 12s
05	Bruno Thiry (B)/Stéphane Prévot (B)	Ford Escort RS Cosworth	6h 39m 18s
06	Andrea Aghini (I)/Sauro Farnocchia (I)	Mitsubishi Lancer Evo 2	6h 43m 17s
07	Jean Ragnotti (F)/Gilles Thimonier (F)	Renault Clio Maxi	7h 04m 26s
08	Piero Liatti (I)/Alex Alessandrini (I)	Subaru Impreza 555	7h 09m 54s
09	Philippe Camandona (CH)/Georges Crausaz (CH)	Ford Escort RS Cosworth	7h 13m 01s
10	Isolde Holderied (D)/Tina Thörner (S)	Mitsubishi Lancer Evo 2	7h 13m 34s

Carlos Sainz/Luís Moya

ROUND 02 – SWEDEN (10th-12th February)

Pos	Driver/Co-driver	Car	Time
01	Kenneth Eriksson (S)/Staffan Parmander (S)	Mitsubishi Lancer Evo 2	4h 51m 27s
02	Tommi Mäkinen (FIN)/Seppo Harjanne (FIN)	Mitsubishi Lancer Evo 2	4h 51m 39s
03	Thomas Rådström (S)/Lars Bäckman (S)	Toyota Celica GT-Four	4h 52m 34s
04	Juha Kankkunen (FIN)/Nicky Grist (GB)	Toyota Celica GT-Four	4h 53m 45s
05	Didier Auriol (F)/Bernard Occelli (F)	Toyota Celica GT-Four	4h 53m 47s
06	Bruno Thiry (B)/Stéphane Prévot (B)	Ford Escort RS Cosworth	4h 56m 58s
07	Stig Blomqvist (S)/Benny Melander (S)	Ford Escort RS Cosworth	4h 58m 16s
08	Tomas Jansson (S)/Ingemar Algerstedt (S)	Toyota Celica GT-Four	4h 59m 29s
09	Armin Schwarz (D)/Klaus Wicha (D)	Toyota Celica GT-Four	5h 01m 12s
10	Kenneth Bäcklund (S)/Tord Andersson (S)	Mitsubishi Lancer Evo 2	5h 04m 11s

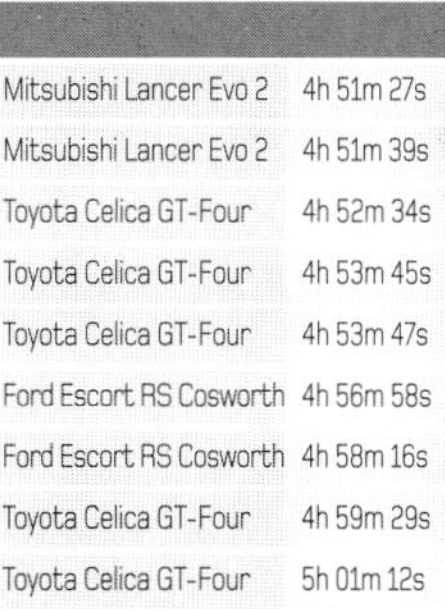

Kenneth Eriksson/Staffan Parmander

ROUND 03 – PORTUGAL (8th-10th March)			
01	Carlos Sainz (E)/Luís Moya (E)	Subaru Impreza 555	5h 32m 37s
02	Juha Kankkunen (FIN)/Nicky Grist (GB)	Toyota Celica GT-Four	5h 32m 49s
03	Colin McRae (GB)/Derek Ringer (GB)	Subaru Impreza 555	5h 35m 51s
04	Armin Schwarz (D)/Klaus Wicha (D)	Toyota Celica GT-Four	5h 37m 36s
05	Didier Auriol (F)/Bernard Occelli (F)	Toyota Celica GT-Four	5h 38m 50s
06	Bruno Thiry (B)/Stéphane Prévot (B)	Ford Escort RS Cosworth	5h 41m 23s
07	Richard Burns (GB)/Robert Reid (GB)	Subaru Impreza 555	5h 46m 58s
08	Alex Fiorio (I)/Vittorio Brambilla (I)	Ford Escort RS Cosworth	5h 58m 44s
09	Rui Madeira (P)/Nuno da Silva (P)	Mitsubishi Lancer Evo 2	6h 03m 36s
10	Jorge Recalde (RA)/Martin Christie (RA)	Mitsubishi Lancer Evo 2	6h 07m 22s

Carlos Sainz/Luís Moya

ROUND 04 – CORSICA, FRANCE (3rd-5th May)			
01	Didier Auriol (F)/Denis Giraudet (F)	Toyota Celica GT-Four	5h 14m 49s
02	François Delecour (F)/Catherine François (F)	Ford Escort RS Cosworth	5h 15m 04s
03	Andrea Aghini (I)/Sauro Farnocchia (I)	Mitsubishi Lancer Evo 3	5h 15m 46s
04	Carlos Sainz (E)/Luís Moya (E)	Subaru Impreza 555	5h 16m 07s
05	Colin McRae (GB)/Derek Ringer (GB)	Subaru Impreza 555	5h 16m 32s
06	Piero Liatti (I)/Alex Alessandrini (I)	Subaru Impreza 555	5h 17m 16s
07	Patrick Bernardini (F)/Jean-Marc André (F)	Ford Escort RS Cosworth	5h 17m 54s
08	Tommi Mäkinen (FIN)/Seppo Harjanne (FIN)	Mitsubishi Lancer Evo 3	5h 19m 39s
09	Philippe Bugalski (F)/Jean-Paul Chiaroni (F)	Renault Clio Maxi	5h 20m 25s
10	Juha Kankkunen (FIN)/Nicky Grist (GB)	Toyota Celica GT-Four	5h 24m 50s

Didier Auriol/Denis Giraudet

ROUND 05 – NEW ZEALAND (27th-30th July)			
01	Colin McRae (GB)/Derek Ringer (GB)	Subaru Impreza 555	5h 33m 06s
02	Didier Auriol (F)/Denis Giraudet (F)	Toyota Celica GT-Four	5h 33m 50s
03	Juha Kankkunen (FIN)/Nicky Grist (GB)	Toyota Celica GT-Four	5h 34m 15s
04	Armin Schwarz (D)/Klaus Wicha (D)	Toyota Celica GT-Four	5h 34m 51s
05	Kenneth Eriksson (S)/Staffan Parmander (S)	Mitsubishi Lancer Evo 3	5h 35m 38s
06	François Delecour (F)/Catherine François (F)	Ford Escort RS Cosworth	5h 37m 30s
07	'Possum' Bourne (NZ)/Tony Sircombe (NZ)	Subaru Impreza 555	5h 42m 01s
08	Neil Allport (NZ)/Craig Vincent (NZ)	Ford Escort RS Cosworth	5h 54m 47s
09	Jorge Recalde (RA)/Martin Christie (RA)	Mitsubishi Lancer Evo 2	5h 57m 45s
10	Rui Madeira (P)/Nuno da Silva (P)	Mitsubishi Lancer Evo 2	5h 58m 16s

Colin McRae/Derek Ringer

ROUND 06 – AUSTRALIA (15th-18th September)			
01	Kenneth Eriksson (S)/Staffan Parmander (S)	Mitsubishi Lancer Evo 3	4h 53m 59s
02	Colin McRae (GB)/Derek Ringer (GB)	Subaru Impreza 555	4h 54m 18s
03	Juha Kankkunen (FIN)/Nicky Grist (GB)	Toyota Celica GT-Four	4h 55m 54s
04	Tommi Mäkinen (FIN)/Seppo Harjanne (FIN)	Mitsubishi Lancer Evo 3	4h 57m 26s
05	Armin Schwarz (D)/Klaus Wicha (D)	Toyota Celica GT-Four	4h 58m 10s
06	Bruno Thiry (B)/Stéphane Prévot (B)	Ford Escort RS Cosworth	5h 10m 51s
07	Yoshio Fujimoto (J)/Arne Hertz (S)	Toyota Celica GT-Four	5h 16m 36s
08	Ed Ordynski (AUS)/Mark Stacey (AUS)	Mitsubishi Lancer Evo 3	5h 21m 05s
09	Neal Bates (AUS)/Coral Taylor (AUS)	Toyota Celica GT-Four	5h 24m 41s
10	Jorge Recalde (RA)/Martin Christie (RA)	Mitsubishi Lancer Evo 2	5h 25m 53s

Kenneth Eriksson/Staffan Parmander

ROUND 07 – CATALUNYA, SPAIN (23rd-25th October)			
01	Carlos Sainz (E)/Luís Moya (E)	Subaru Impreza 555	5h 05m 58s
02	Colin McRae (GB)/Derek Ringer (GB)	Subaru Impreza 555	5h 06m 49s
03	Piero Liatti (I)/Alex Alessandrini (I)	Subaru Impreza 555	5h 07m 56s
04	François Delecour (F)/Catherine François (F)	Ford Escort RS Cosworth	5h 08m 38s
05	Andrea Aghini (I)/Sauro Farnocchia (I)	Mitsubishi Lancer Evo 3	5h 08m 52s
06	Gustavo Trelles (ROU)/Jorge del Buono (RA)	Toyota Celica GT-Four	5h 11m 54s
07	Oriol Gómez (E)/Marc Martí (E)	Renault Clio Williams	5h 18m 01s
08	Andrea Navarra (I)/Renzo Casazza (I)	Toyota Celica GT-Four	5h 18m 20s
09	Josep Bassas (E)/Antonio Rodriguez (E)	BMW M3	5h 28m 06s
10	Yvan Postel (F)/Olivier Peyret (F)	Subaru Impreza 555	5h 32m 38s

Carlos Sainz/Luís Moya

ROUND 08 – RAC, GREAT BRITAIN (19th-22nd November)			
01	Colin McRae (GB)/Derek Ringer (GB)	Subaru Impreza 555	5h 09m 19s
02	Carlos Sainz (E)/Luís Moya (E)	Subaru Impreza 555	5h 09m 55s
03	Richard Burns (GB)/Robert Reid (GB)	Subaru Impreza 555	5h 15m 58s
04	Alister McRae (GB)/Chris Wood (GB)	Ford Escort RS Cosworth	5h 20m 34s
05	Bruno Thiry (B)/Stéphane Prévot (B)	Ford Escort RS Cosworth	5h 21m 11s
06	Gwyndaf Evans (GB)/Howard Davies (GB)	Ford Escort RS 2000	5h 42m 07s
07	Rui Madeira (P)/Nuno da Silva (P)	Mitsubishi Lancer Evo 2	5h 44m 04s
08	Jarmo Kytölehto (FIN)/Arto Kapanen (FIN)	Nissan Sunny GTI	5h 45m 19s
09	Masao Kamioka (J)/Kevin Gormley (GB)	Subaru Impreza WRX	5h 50m 21s
10	Alain Oreille (F)/Jack Boyère (F)	Renault Clio Maxi	5h 50m 40s

Colin McRae/Derek Ringer

FINAL DRIVERS' CHAMPIONSHIP POSITIONS		
01	Colin McRae	90
02	Carlos Sainz	85
DQ	Juha Kankkunen	62
DQ	Didier Auriol	51
03	Kenneth Eriksson	48
04	François Delecour	46
05	Tommi Mäkinen	38
06	Bruno Thiry	34
DQ	Armin Schwarz	30
07	Andrea Aghini	26
08	Piero Liatti	21
09	Richard Burns	16
DQ	Thomas Rådström	12
10	Alister McRae	10

FINAL MANUFACTURERS' CHAMPIONSHIP POSITIONS		
01	Subaru	350
02	Mitsubishi	307
DQ	Toyota	260
03	Ford	244

1996

ROUND 01 – SWEDEN (9th-11th February)			
01	Tommi Mäkinen (FIN)/Seppo Harjanne (FIN)	Mitsubishi Lancer Evo 3	4h 37m 10s
02	Carlos Sainz (E)/Luís Moya (E)	Ford Escort RS Cosworth	4h 37m 33s
03	Colin McRae (GB)/Derek Ringer (GB)	Subaru Impreza 555	4h 38m 15s
04	Juha Kankkunen (FIN)/Nicky Grist (GB)	Toyota Celica GT-Four	4h 38m 38s
05	Kenneth Eriksson (S)/Staffan Parmander (S)	Subaru Impreza 555	4h 39m 36s
06	Thomas Rådström (S)/Lars Bäckman (S)	Toyota Celica GT-Four	4h 40m 00s
07	Marcus Grönholm (FIN)/Timo Rautiainen (FIN)	Toyota Celica Turbo 4WD	4h 41m 58s
08	Stig Blomqvist (S)/Benny Melander (S)	Ford Escort RS Cosworth	4h 42m 56s
09	Tomas Jansson (S)/Ingemar Algerstedt (S)	Toyota Celica GT-Four	4h 43m 54s
10	Didier Auriol (F)/Bernard Occelli (F)	Subaru Impreza 555	4h 43m 56s

Tommi Mäkinen/Seppo Harjanne

ROUND 02 – SAFARI, AFRICA (5th-7th April)			
01	Tommi Mäkinen (FIN)/Seppo Harjanne (FIN)	Mitsubishi Lancer Evo 3	12h 41m 24s
02	Kenneth Eriksson (S)/Staffan Parmander (S)	Subaru Impreza 555	12h 55m 40s
03	Ian Duncan (EAK)/David Williamson (EAK)	Toyota Celica GT-Four	13h 23m 24s
04	Colin McRae (GB)/Derek Ringer (GB)	Subaru Impreza 555	13h 48m 28s
05	Piero Liatti (I)/Mario Ferfoglia (I)	Subaru Impreza 555	14h 06m 54s
06	Kenjiro Shinozuka (J)/Pentti Kuukkala (FIN)	Mitsubishi Lancer Evo 3	14h 44m 39s
07	Stig Blomqvist (S)/Benny Melander (S)	Ford Escort RS Cosworth	15h 09m 27s
08	Hideaki Miyoshi (J)/Tinu Khan (EAK)	Subaru Impreza Estate	15h 50m 20s
09	Patrick Njiru (EAK)/Rick Mathews (EAK)	Subaru Impreza Estate	15h 58m 44s
10	Jonathan Toroitich (EAK)/Ibrahim Choge (EAK)	Toyota Celica Turbo 4WD	17h 08m 41s

Tommi Mäkinen/Seppo Harjanne

ROUND 03 – INDONESIA (10th-12th May)

01	Carlos Sainz (E)/Luís Moya (E)	Ford Escort RS Cosworth	5h 30m 00s
02	Piero Liatti (I)/Fabrizia Pons (I)	Subaru Impreza 555	5h 30m 23s
03	Juha Kankkunen (FIN)/Nicky Grist (GB)	Toyota Celica GT-Four	5h 31m 02s
04	Yoshio Fujimoto (J)/Arne Hertz (S)	Toyota Celica Turbo 4WD	5h 49m 44s
05	Reza Pribadi (RI)/Denis Giraudet (F)	Toyota Celica GT-Four	6h 05m 17s
06	Michael Lieu (HKG)/Yoshimasa Nakahara (J)	Subaru Impreza WRX	6h 07m 22s
07	Shigeyuki Konishi (J)/Hakaru Ichino (J)	Subaru Impreza WRX	6h 15m 08s
08	Irvan Gading (RI)/Karel Harilatu (RI)	Subaru Impreza 555	6h 15m 55s
09	Chandra Alim (RI)/Prihatin Kasiman (RI)	Mitsubishi Lancer Evo 3	6h 21m 41s
10	Bambang Hartono (RI)/Agung Baskoro (RI)	Mitsubishi Lancer Evo 3	6h 22m 10s

Carlos Sainz/Luís Moya

ROUND 04 – ACROPOLIS, GREECE (2nd-4th June)

01	Colin McRae (GB)/Derek Ringer (GB)	Subaru Impreza 555	5h 33m 12s
02	Tommi Mäkinen (FIN)/Seppo Harjanne (FIN)	Mitsubishi Lancer Evo 3	5h 34m 02s
03	Carlos Sainz (E)/Luís Moya (E)	Ford Escort RS Cosworth	5h 36m 33s
04	Piero Liatti (I)/Fabrizia Pons (I)	Subaru Impreza 555	5h 38m 02s
05	Kenneth Eriksson (S)/Staffan Parmander (S)	Subaru Impreza 555	5h 40m 17s
06	Bruno Thiry (B)/Stéphane Prévot (B)	Ford Escort RS Cosworth	5h 41m 18s
07	Freddy Loix (B)/Sven Smeets (B)	Toyota Celica GT-Four	5h 43m 13s
08	Gilberto Pianezzola (I)/Loris Roggia (I)	Toyota Celica GT-Four	5h 48m 46s
09	Patrick Bernardini (F)/Bernard Occelli (F)	Ford Escort RS Cosworth	5h 54m 33s
10	Jean-Pierre Richelmi (MC)/Thierry Barjou (F)	Toyota Celica Turbo 4WD	5h 58m 36s

Colin McRae/Derek Ringer

ROUND 05 – ARGENTINA (4th-6th July)

01	Tommi Mäkinen (FIN)/Seppo Harjanne (FIN)	Mitsubishi Lancer Evo 3	5h 48m 42s
02	Carlos Sainz (E)/Luís Moya (E)	Ford Escort RS Cosworth	5h 50m 17s
03	Kenneth Eriksson (S)/Staffan Parmander (S)	Subaru Impreza 555	5h 53m 21s
04	Richard Burns (GB)/Robert Reid (GB)	Mitsubishi Lancer Evo 3	5h 56m 43s
05	Bruno Thiry (B)/Stéphane Prévot (B)	Ford Escort RS Cosworth	5h 57m 07s
06	Gilberto Pianezzola (I)/Loris Roggia (I)	Toyota Celica GT-Four	6h 02m 59s
07	Piero Liatti (I)/Fabrizia Pons (I)	Subaru Impreza 555	6h 04m 03s
08	Rui Madeira (P)/Nuno da Silva (P)	Toyota Celica GT-Four	6h 05m 09s
09	Patrick Bernardini (F)/Catherine François (F)	Ford Escort RS Cosworth	6h 09m 20s
10	Uwe Nittel (D)/Tina Thörner (S)	Mitsubishi Lancer Evo 3	6h 14m 26s

Tommi Mäkinen/Seppo Harjanne

ROUND 06 – 1000 LAKES, FINLAND (23rd-26th August)

01	Tommi Mäkinen (FIN)/Seppo Harjanne (FIN)	Mitsubishi Lancer Evo 3	4h 04m 13s
02	Juha Kankkunen (FIN)/Nicky Grist (GB)	Toyota Celica GT-Four	4h 04m 59s
03	Jarmo Kytölehto (FIN)/Arto Kapanen (FIN)	Ford Escort RS Cosworth	4h 06m 50s
04	Marcus Grönholm (FIN)/Timo Rautiainen (FIN)	Toyota Celica GT-Four	4h 06m 55s
05	Kenneth Eriksson (S)/Staffan Parmander (S)	Subaru Impreza 555	4h 07m 35s
06	Thomas Rådström (S)/Lars Bäckman (S)	Toyota Celica GT-Four	4h 08m 22s
07	Sebastian Lindholm (FIN)/Timo Hantunen (FIN)	Ford Escort RS Cosworth	4h 09m 30s
08	Lasse Lampi (FIN)/Jyrki Stenroos (FIN)	Mitsubishi Lancer Evo 3	4h 16m 14s
09	Rui Madeira (P)/Nuno da Silva (P)	Toyota Celica GT-Four	4h 20m 47s
10	Angelo Medeghini (I)/Barbara Medeghini (I)	Subaru Impreza 555	4h 22m 41s

Tommi Mäkinen/Seppo Harjanne

ROUND 07 – AUSTRALIA (13th-16th September)

01	Tommi Mäkinen (FIN)/Seppo Harjanne (FIN)	Mitsubishi Lancer Evo 3	4h 08m 50s
02	Kenneth Eriksson (S)/Staffan Parmander (S)	Subaru Impreza 555	4h 10m 07s
03	Carlos Sainz (E)/Luís Moya (E)	Ford Escort RS Cosworth	4h 10m 11s
04	Colin McRae (GB)/Derek Ringer (GB)	Subaru Impreza 555	4h 12m 01s
05	Richard Burns (GB)/Robert Reid (GB)	Mitsubishi Lancer Evo 3	4h 12m 15s
06	Bruno Thiry (B)/Stéphane Prévot (B)	Ford Escort RS Cosworth	4h 17m 38s
07	Piero Liatti (I)/Fabrizia Pons (I)	Subaru Impreza 555	4h 20m 21s
08	'Possum' Bourne (NZ)/Craig Vincent (NZ)	Subaru Impreza 555	4h 20m 57s
09	Yoshio Fujimoto (J)/Arne Hertz (S)	Toyota Celica GT-Four	4h 36m 42s
10	Ed Ordynski (AUS)/Mark Stacey (AUS)	Mitsubishi Lancer Evo 3	4h 37m 37s

Tommi Mäkinen/Seppo Harjanne

ROUND 08 – SANREMO, ITALY (13th-15th October)

01	Colin McRae (GB)/Derek Ringer (GB)	Subaru Impreza 555	4h 26m 57s
02	Carlos Sainz (E)/Luís Moya (E)	Ford Escort RS Cosworth	4h 27m 19s
03	Bruno Thiry (B)/Stéphane Prévot (B)	Ford Escort RS Cosworth	4h 29m 06s
04	Freddy Loix (B)/Sven Smeets (B)	Toyota Celica GT-Four	4h 29m 54s
05	Kenneth Eriksson (S)/Staffan Parmander (S)	Subaru Impreza 555	4h 29m 57s
06	Gianfranco Cunico (I)/Pierangelo Scalvini (I)	Ford Escort RS Cosworth	4h 30m 41s
07	Gilberto Pianezzola (I)/Loris Roggia (I)	Toyota Celica GT-Four	4h 30m 58s
08	Didier Auriol (F)/Denis Giraudet (F)	Mitsubishi Lancer Evo 3	4h 31m 50s
09	Angelo Medeghini (I)/Barbara Medeghini (I)	Subaru Impreza 555	4h 34m 59s
10	Patrick Bernardini (F)/Dominique Savignoni (F)	Ford Escort RS Cosworth	4h 34m 59s

Colin McRae/Derek Ringer

ROUND 09 – CATALUNYA, SPAIN (4th-6th November)

01	Colin McRae (GB)/Derek Ringer (GB)	Subaru Impreza 555	4h 14m 20s
02	Piero Liatti (I)/Fabrizia Pons (I)	Subaru Impreza 555	4h 14m 27s
03	Bruno Thiry (B)/Stéphane Prévot (B)	Ford Escort RS Cosworth	4h 15m 38s
04	Freddy Loix (B)/Sven Smeets (B)	Toyota Celica GT-Four	4h 15m 55s
05	Tommi Mäkinen (FIN)/Juha Repo (FIN)	Mitsubishi Lancer Evo 3	4h 16m 12s
06	Patrick Bernardini (F)/Dominique Savignoni (F)	Ford Escort RS Cosworth	4h 17m 30s
07	Kenneth Eriksson (S)/Staffan Parmander (S)	Subaru Impreza 555	4h 18m 01s
08	Oriol Gómez (E)/Marc Martí (E)	Renault Mégane Maxi	4h 18m 22s
09	Rui Madeira (P)/Nuno da Silva (P)	Toyota Celica GT-Four	4h 19m 19s
10	Angelo Medeghini (I)/Barbara Medeghini (I)	Subaru Impreza 555	4h 21m 58s

Colin McRae/Derek Ringer

FINAL DRIVERS' CHAMPIONSHIP POSITIONS

01	Tommi Mäkinen	123
02	Colin McRae	92
03	Carlos Sainz	89
04	Kenneth Eriksson	78
05	Piero Liatti	56
06	Bruno Thiry	44
07	Juha Kankkunen	37
08	Freddy Loix	24
09	Richard Burns	18
10	Marcus Grönholm	14

FINAL MANUFACTURERS' CHAMPIONSHIP POSITIONS

01	Subaru	401
02	Mitsubishi	322
03	Ford	299

1997

ROUND 01 – MONTE CARLO (19th-22nd January)

01	Piero Liatti (I)/Fabrizia Pons (I)	Subaru Impreza WRC	4h 26m 58s
02	Carlos Sainz (E)/Luís Moya (E)	Ford Escort WRC	4h 27m 53s
03	Tommi Mäkinen (FIN)/Seppo Harjanne (FIN)	Mitsubishi Lancer Evo 4	4h 29m 29s
04	Armin Schwarz (D)/Denis Giraudet (F)	Ford Escort WRC	4h 32m 03s
05	Uwe Nittel (D)/Tina Thörner (S)	Mitsubishi Lancer Evo 3	4h 42m 42s
06	Henrik Lundgaard (DEN)/Freddy Pedersen (DEN)	Toyota Celica GT-Four	4h 45m 26s
07	Olivier Burri (CH)/Christophe Hofmann (CH)	Subaru Impreza 555	4h 45m 35s
08	Isolde Holderied (D)/Catherine François (F)	Toyota Celica GT-Four	4h 50m 39s
09	Gustavo Trelles (ROU)/Jorge del Buono (RA)	Mitsubishi Lancer Evo 3	4h 51m 59s
10	Armin Kremer (D)/Sven Behling (D)	Mitsubishi Lancer Evo 3	4h 52m 51s

Piero Liatti/Fabrizia Pons

ROUND 02 – SWEDEN (7th-10th February)

01	Kenneth Eriksson (S)/Staffan Parmander (S)	Subaru Impreza WRC	3h 51m 49s
02	Carlos Sainz (E)/Luís Moya (E)	Ford Escort WRC	3h 52m 05s
03	Tommi Mäkinen (FIN)/Seppo Harjanne (FIN)	Mitsubishi Lancer Evo 4	3h 52m 15s
04	Colin McRae (GB)/Nicky Grist (GB)	Subaru Impreza WRC	3h 52m 20s
05	Thomas Rådström (S)/Lars Bäckman (S)	Toyota Celica GT-Four	3h 54m 47s
06	Armin Schwarz (D)/Denis Giraudet (F)	Ford Escort WRC	3h 55m 45s
07	Tomas Jansson (S)/Per-Ola Svensson (S)	Toyota Celica GT-Four	3h 55m 47s
08	Marcus Grönholm (FIN)/Timo Rautiainen (FIN)	Toyota Celica GT-Four	3h 56m 04s
09	Mats Jonsson (S)/Johnny Johansson (S)	Ford Escort RS Cosworth	3h 57m 02s
10	Stig Blomqvist (S)/Benny Melander (S)	Ford Escort RS Cosworth	3h 58m 35s

Kenneth Eriksson/Staffan Parmander

ROUND 03 – SAFARI, AFRICA (1st-3rd March)			
01	Colin McRae (GB)/Nicky Grist (GB)	Subaru Impreza WRC	11h 29m 00s
02	Richard Burns (GB)/Robert Reid (GB)	Mitsubishi Carisma GT Evo 4	11h 36m 04s
03	Ian Duncan (EAK)/David Williamson (EAK)	Toyota Celica GT-Four	11h 40m 18s
04	Armin Schwarz (D)/Denis Giraudet (F)	Ford Escort WRC	13h 07m 23s
05	Jonathan Toroitich (EAK)/Ibrahim Choge (EAK)	Toyota Celica Turbo 4WD	13h 51m 32s
06	Frédéric Dor (F)/Kevin Gormley (GB)	Subaru Impreza 555	15h 13m 52s
07	Emmanuel Katto (UGA)/James Opoka (UGA)	Toyota Celica Turbo 4WD	15h 30m 05s
08	Rudi Stohl (A)/Jürgen Bertl (D)	Audi Coupé S2	15h 48m 17s
09	Johnny Hellier (EAK)/Stefano Rocca (I)	Subaru Impreza WRX	15h 48m 44s
10	Karim Hirji (UGA)/Frank Nekusa (UGA)	Toyota Celica GT-Four	16h 31m 37s

Colin McRae/Nicky Grist

ROUND 04 – PORTUGAL (23rd-26th March)			
01	Tommi Mäkinen (FIN)/Seppo Harjanne (FIN)	Mitsubishi Lancer Evo 4	4h 53m 01s
02	Freddy Loix (B)/Sven Smeets (B)	Toyota Celica GT-Four	4h 57m 06s
03	Armin Schwarz (D)/Denis Giraudet (F)	Ford Escort WRC	4h 59m 34s
04	Grégoire De Mévius (B)/Jean-Marc Fortin (B)	Ford Escort WRC	5h 05m 29s
05	Jean-Pierre Richelmi (MC)/Thierry Barjou (F)	Ford Escort RS Cosworth	5h 10m 17s
06	Masao Kamioka (J)/Kevin Gormley (GB)	Subaru Impreza 555	5h 10m 40s
07	Gustavo Trelles (ROU)/Jorge del Buono (RA)	Mitsubishi Lancer Evo 3	5h 10m 54s
08	Manfred Stohl (A)/Peter Müller (A)	Mitsubishi Lancer Evo 3	5h 11m 04s
09	Alister McRae (GB)/David Senior (GB)	Volkswagen Golf Kit Car	5h 12m 54s
10	Adruzilo Lopes (P)/Luís Lisboa (P)	Peugeot 306 Maxi	5h 13m 42s

Tommi Mäkinen/Seppo Harjanne

ROUND 05 – CATALUNYA, SPAIN (14th-16th April)			
01	Tommi Mäkinen (FIN)/Seppo Harjanne (FIN)	Mitsubishi Lancer Evo 4	4h 08m 46s
02	Piero Liatti (I)/Fabrizia Pons (I)	Subaru Impreza WRC	4h 08m 53s
03	Gilles Panizzi (F)/Hervé Panizzi (F)	Peugeot 306 Maxi	4h 11m 55s
04	Colin McRae (GB)/Nicky Grist (GB)	Subaru Impreza WRC	4h 12m 20s
05	Angelo Medeghini (I)/Barbara Medeghini (ITA	Subaru Impreza WRX	4h 13m 51s
06	Rui Madeira (P)/Nuno da Silva (P)	Subaru Impreza 555	4h 15m 12s
07	Jaime Azcona (E)/Julius Billmaier (D)	Peugeot 306 Maxi	4h 16m 28s
08	Uwe Nittel (D)/Tina Thörner (S)	Mitsubishi Lancer Evo 3	4h 17m 25s
09	Raphael Sperrer (A)/Per Carlsson (S)	Renault Mégane Maxi	4h 18m 32s
10	Carlos Sainz (E)/Luís Moya (E)	Ford Escort WRC	4h 18m 43s

Tommi Mäkinen/Seppo Harjanne

ROUND 06 – CORSICA, FRANCE (5th-7th May)			
01	Colin McRae (GB)/Nicky Grist (GB)	Subaru Impreza WRC	4h 31m 08s
02	Carlos Sainz (E)/Luís Moya (E)	Ford Escort WRC	4h 31m 16s
03	Gilles Panizzi (F)/Hervé Panizzi (F)	Peugeot 306 Maxi	4h 31m 46s
04	François Delecour (F)/Daniel Grataloup (F)	Peugeot 306 Maxi	4h 32m 03s
05	Piero Liatti (I)/Fabrizia Pons (I)	Subaru Impreza WRC	4h 33m 07s
06	Philippe Bugalski (F)/Jean-Paul Chiaroni (F)	Renault Mégane Maxi	4h 37m 48s
07	Serge Jordan (F)/Jack Boyère (F)	Renault Mégane Maxi	4h 39m 36s
08	Uwe Nittel (D)/Tina Thörner (S)	Mitsubishi Lancer Evo 3	4h 40m 48s
09	Armin Schwarz (D)/Phil Mills (GB)	Ford Escort WRC	4h 41m 43s
10	Francis Mariani (F)/Gilles Thimonier (F)	Subaru Impreza 555	4h 44m 55s

Colin McRae/Nicky Grist

ROUND 07 – ARGENTINA (22nd-24th May)			
01	Tommi Mäkinen (FIN)/Seppo Harjanne (FIN)	Mitsubishi Lancer Evo 4	4h 25m 38s
02	Colin McRae (GB)/Nicky Grist (GB)	Subaru Impreza WRC	4h 26m 39s
03	Kenneth Eriksson (S)/Staffan Parmander (S)	Subaru Impreza WRC	4h 30m 06s
04	Marcus Grönholm (FIN)/Timo Rautiainen (FIN)	Toyota Celica GT-Four	4h 35m 16s
05	Didier Auriol (F)/Denis Giraudet (F)	Toyota Celica GT-Four	4h 40m 13s
06	Gustavo Trelles (ROU)/Jorge del Buono (RA)	Mitsubishi Lancer Evo 3	4h 49m 38s
07	Raúl Sufan (RA)/Martin Christie (RA)	Toyota Celica GT-Four	4h 49m 51s
08	Harri Rovanperä (FIN)/Voitto Silander (FIN)	Seat Ibiza GTI 16V	4h 55m 21s
09	Oriol Gómez (E)/Marc Martí (E)	Seat Ibiza GTI 16V	4h 58m 44s
10	Pavel Sibera (CZ)/Petr Gross (CZ)	Skoda Felicia Kit Car	4h 59m 45s

Tommi Mäkinen/Seppo Harjanne

ROUND 08 – ACROPOLIS, GREECE (8th-10th June)			
01	Carlos Sainz (E)/Luís Moya (E)	Ford Escort WRC	4h 56m 24s
02	Juha Kankkunen (FIN)/Juha Repo (FIN)	Ford Escort WRC	4h 56m 41s
03	Tommi Mäkinen (FIN)/Seppo Harjanne (FIN)	Mitsubishi Lancer Evo 4	5h 01m 27s
04	Richard Burns (GB)/Robert Reid (GB)	Mitsubishi Carisma GT Evo 4	5h 01m 31s
05	Thomas Rådström (S)/Denis Giraudet (F)	Toyota Celica GT-Four	5h 04m 11s
06	Uwe Nittel (D)/Tina Thörner (S)	Mitsubishi Lancer Evo 3	5h 06m 26s
07	Grégoire De Mévius (B)/Jean-Marc Fortin (B)	Ford Escort WRC	5h 07m 49s
08	Yukihiko Sakurai (J)/Ronan Morgan (GB)	Subaru Impreza 555	5h 11m 15s
09	Aris Vovos (GR)/Ioánnis Alvanos (GR)	Subaru Impreza 555	5h 12m 05s
10	Leonídas Kyrkos (GR)/Níkos Panou (GR)	Ford Escort WRC	5h 14m 33s

Carlos Sainz/Luís Moya

ROUND 09 – NEW ZEALAND (2nd-5th August)			
01	Kenneth Eriksson (S)/Staffan Parmander (S)	Subaru Impreza WRC	4h 14m 11s
02	Carlos Sainz (E)/Luís Moya (E)	Ford Escort WRC	4h 14m 24s
03	Juha Kankkunen (FIN)/Juha Repo (FIN)	Ford Escort WRC	4h 14m 30s
04	Richard Burns (GB)/Robert Reid (GB)	Mitsubishi Carisma GT Evo 4	4h 15m 29s
05	'Possum' Bourne (NZ)/Craig Vincent (NZ)	Subaru Impreza 555	4h 20m 05s
06	Neal Bates (AUS)/Coral Taylor (AUS)	Toyota Celica GT-Four	4h 25m 53s
07	Gustavo Trelles (ROU)/Jorge del Buono (RA)	Mitsubishi Lancer Evo 3	4h 27m 55s
08	Raúl Sufan (RA)/Martin Christie (RA)	Toyota Celica GT-Four	4h 29m 23s
09	Brian Stokes (NZ)/Garry Cowan (NZ)	Ford Escort RS Cosworth	4h 29m 38s
10	Reece Jones (NZ)/Leo Bult (NZ)	Mitsubishi Lancer Evo 4	4h 29m 57s

Kenneth Eriksson/Staffan Parmander

ROUND 10 – FINLAND (29th-31st August)			
01	Tommi Mäkinen (FIN)/Seppo Harjanne (FIN)	Mitsubishi Lancer Evo 4	3h 16m 18s
02	Juha Kankkunen (FIN)/Juha Repo (FIN)	Ford Escort WRC	3h 16m 25s
03	Jarmo Kytölehto (FIN)/Arto Kapanen (FIN)	Ford Escort WRC	3h 18m 18s
04	Sebastian Lindholm (FIN)/Timo Hantunen (FIN)	Ford Escort WRC	3h 18m 53s
05	Tomas Jansson (S)/Per-Ola Svensson (S)	Toyota Celica GT-Four	3h 21m 12s
06	Pasi Hagström (FIN)/Tero Gardemeister (FIN)	Toyota Celica GT-Four	3h 22m 48s
07	Uwe Nittel (D)/Tina Thörner (S)	Mitsubishi Lancer Evo 4	3h 25m 15s
08	Didier Auriol (F)/Denis Giraudet (F)	Toyota Corolla WRC	3h 26m 57s
09	Jouko Puhakka (FIN)/Keijo Eerola (FIN)	Mitsubishi Carisma GT Evo 4	3h 27m 59s
10	Harri Rovanperä (FIN)/Voitto Silander (FIN)	Seat Ibiza GTI 16V	3h 28m 21s

Tommi Mäkinen/Seppo Harjanne

ROUND 11 – INDONESIA (19th-21st September)			
01	Carlos Sainz (E)/Luís Moya (E)	Ford Escort WRC	4h 37m 30s
02	Juha Kankkunen (FIN)/Juha Repo FIN)	Ford Escort WRC	4h 37m 46s
03	Kenneth Eriksson (S)/Staffan Parmander (S)	Subaru Impreza WRC	4h 38m 49s
04	Richard Burns (GB)/Robert Reid (GB)	Mitsubishi Carisma GT Evo 4	4h 39m 24s
05	Yoshio Fujimoto (J)/Arne Hertz (S)	Toyota Celica GT-Four	4h 58m 34s
06	Karamjit Singh (MAL)/Allen Oh (MAL)	Proton Wira 4WD	5h 03m 02s
07	Harri Rovanperä (FIN)/Voitto Silander (FIN)	Seat Ibiza GTI 16V	5h 06m 36s
08	Shigeyuki Konishi (J)/Tony Sircombe (NZ)	Subaru Impreza 555	5h 09m 21s
09	Erwin Weber (D)/Manfred Hiemer (D)	Seat Ibiza GTI 16V	5h 10m 07s
10	Reza Pribadi (RI)/Klaus Wicha (D)	Subaru Impreza 555	5h 11m 27s

Carlos Sainz/Luís Moya

ROUND 12 – SANREMO, ITALY (13th-15th October)			
01	Colin McRae (GB)/Nicky Grist (GB)	Subaru Impreza WRC	4h 08m 25s
02	Piero Liatti (I)/Fabrizia Pons (I)	Subaru Impreza WRC	4h 08m 31s
03	Tommi Mäkinen (FIN)/Seppo Harjanne (FIN)	Mitsubishi Lancer Evo 4	4h 08m 37s
04	Carlos Sainz (E)/Luís Moya (E)	Ford Escort WRC	4h 08m 39s
05	Freddy Loix (B)/Sven Smeets (B)	Toyota Corolla WRC	4h 09m 15s
06	Juha Kankkunen (FIN)/Juha Repo (FIN)	Ford Escort WRC	4h 09m 18s
07	Andrea Aghini (I)/Loris Roggia (I)	Toyota Celica GT-Four	4h 11m 13s
08	Didier Auriol (F)/Denis Giraudet (F)	Toyota Corolla WRC	4h 11m 58s
09	Diego Oldrati (I)/Paolo Lizzi (I)	Subaru Impreza 555	4h 17m 44s
10	Harri Rovanperä (FIN)/Voitto Silander (FIN)	Seat Ibiza GTI 16V	4h 21m 57s

Colin McRae/Nicky Grist

ROUND 13 – AUSTRALIA (30th October-2 November)			
01	Colin McRae (GB)/Nicky Grist (GB)	Subaru Impreza WRC	4h 05m 31s
02	Tommi Mäkinen (FIN)/Seppo Harjanne (FIN)	Mitsubishi Lancer Evo 4	4h 05m 37s
03	Didier Auriol (F)/Denis Giraudet (F)	Toyota Corolla WRC	4h 05m 52s
04	Richard Burns (GB)/Robert Reid (GB)	Mitsubishi Carisma GT Evo 4	4h 06m 10s
05	'Possum' Bourne (NZ)/Craig Vincent (NZ)	Subaru Impreza 555	4h 13m 23s
06	Ed Ordynski (AUS)/Mark Stacey (AUS)	Mitsubishi Lancer Evo 3	4h 14m 55s
07	Freddy Loix (B)/Sven Smeets (B)	Toyota Celica GT-Four	4h 15m 26s
08	Neal Bates (AUS)/Coral Taylor (AUS)	Toyota Corolla WRC	4h 16m 39s
09	Raül Sufan (RA)/Martin Christie (RA)	Toyota Celica GT-Four	4h 24m 34s
10	Harri Rovanperä (FIN)/Voitto Silander (FIN)	Seat Ibiza GTI 16V	4h 30m 27s

Colin McRae/Nicky Grist

ROUND 14 – RAC, GREAT BRITAIN (23rd-25th November)			
01	Colin McRae (GB)/Nicky Grist (GB)	Subaru Impreza WRC	3h 54m 31s
02	Juha Kankkunen (FIN)/Juha Repo (FIN)	Ford Escort WRC	3h 57m 18s
03	Carlos Sainz (E)/Luís Moya (E)	Ford Escort WRC	3h 58m 24s
04	Richard Burns (GB)/Robert Reid (GB)	Mitsubishi Carisma GT Evo 4	3h 59m 30s
05	Marcus Grönholm (FIN)/Timo Rautiainen (FIN)	Toyota Corolla WRC	4h 00m 43s
06	Tommi Mäkinen (FIN)/Seppo Harjanne (FIN)	Mitsubishi Lancer Evo 4	4h 01m 31s
07	Piero Liatti (I)/Fabrizia Pons (I)	Subaru Impreza WRC	4h 03m 11s
08	Ari Vatanen (FIN)/Roger Freeman (GB)	Ford Escort WRC	4h 11m 59s
09	Harri Rovanperä (FIN)/Voitto Silander (FIN)	Seat Ibiza GTI 16V	4h 17m 34s
10	Angelo Medeghini (I)/Barbara Medeghini (I)	Ford Escort WRC	4h 18m 06s

Colin McRae/Nicky Grist

FINAL DRIVERS' CHAMPIONSHIP POSITIONS		
01	Tommi Mäkinen	63
02	Colin McRae	62
03	Carlos Sainz	51
04	Juha Kankkunen	29
05	Kenneth Eriksson	28
06	Piero Liatti	24
07	Richard Burns	21
08	Armin Schwarz	11
09	Freddy Loix	8
10	Gilles Panizzi	8

FINAL MANUFACTURERS' CHAMPIONSHIP POSITIONS		
01	Subaru	114
02	Ford	90
03	Mitsubishi	86

1998

ROUND 01 – MONTE CARLO (19th-21st January)			
01	Carlos Sainz (E)/Luís Moya (E)	Toyota Corolla WRC	4h 28m 00s
02	Juha Kankkunen (FIN)/Juha Repo (FIN)	Ford Escort WRC	4h 28m 41s
03	Colin McRae (GB)/Nicky Grist (GB)	Subaru Impreza WRC	4h 29m 01s
04	Piero Liatti (I)/Fabrizia Pons (I)	Subaru Impreza WRC	4h 29m 13s
05	Richard Burns (GB)/Robert Reid (GB)	Mitsubishi Carisma GT Evo 4	4h 29m 23s
06	Bruno Thiry (B)/Stéphane Prévot (B)	Ford Escort WRC	4h 30m 20s
07	Uwe Nittel (D)/Tina Thörner (S)	Mitsubishi Carisma GT Evo 4	4h 34m 21s
08	Armin Kremer (D)/Klaus Wicha (D)	Subaru Impreza WRC	4h 37m 40s
09	Gilles Panizzi (F)/Hervé Panizzi (F)	Peugeot 306 Maxi	4h 39m 24s
10	François Delecour (F)/Daniel Grataloup (F)	Peugeot 306 Maxi	4h 40m 02s

Carlos Sainz/Luís Moya

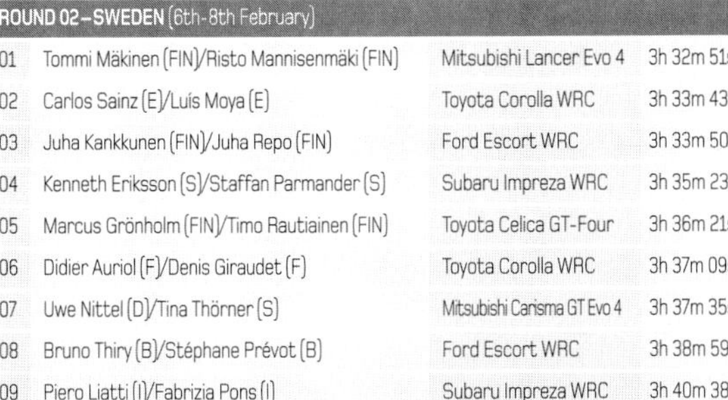

ROUND 02 – SWEDEN (6th-8th February)			
01	Tommi Mäkinen (FIN)/Risto Mannisenmäki (FIN)	Mitsubishi Lancer Evo 4	3h 32m 51s
02	Carlos Sainz (E)/Luís Moya (E)	Toyota Corolla WRC	3h 33m 43s
03	Juha Kankkunen (FIN)/Juha Repo (FIN)	Ford Escort WRC	3h 33m 50s
04	Kenneth Eriksson (S)/Staffan Parmander (S)	Subaru Impreza WRC	3h 35m 23s
05	Marcus Grönholm (FIN)/Timo Rautiainen (FIN)	Toyota Celica GT-Four	3h 36m 21s
06	Didier Auriol (F)/Denis Giraudet (F)	Toyota Corolla WRC	3h 37m 09s
07	Uwe Nittel (D)/Tina Thörner (S)	Mitsubishi Carisma GT Evo 4	3h 37m 35s
08	Bruno Thiry (B)/Stéphane Prévot (B)	Ford Escort WRC	3h 38m 59s
09	Piero Liatti (I)/Fabrizia Pons (I)	Subaru Impreza WRC	3h 40m 38s
10	Mats Jonsson (S)/Johnny Johansson (S)	Ford Escort RS Cosworth	3h 41m 05s

Tommi Mäkinen/Risto Mannisenmäki

ROUND 03 – SAFARI, AFRICA (28th February-2nd March)			
01	Richard Burns (GB)/Robert Reid (GB)	Mitsubishi Carisma GT Evo 4	8h 57m 34s
02	Juha Kankkunen (FIN)/Juha Repo (FIN)	Ford Escort WRC	9h 07m 01s
03	Ari Vatanen (FIN)/Fred Gallagher (GB)	Ford Escort WRC	9h 07m 26s
04	Didier Auriol (F)/Denis Giraudet (F)	Toyota Corolla WRC	9h 12m 00s
05	Harri Rovanperä (FIN)/Voitto Silander (FIN)	Seat Ibiza GTI 16V Evo 2	11h 03m 12s
06	Raimund Baumschlager (A)/Klaus Wicha (D)	Volkswagen Golf Kit Car	11h 17m 35s
07	Luís Climent (E)/Alex Romaní (E)	Mitsubishi Lancer Evo 3	11h 25m 37s
08	Kris Rosenberger (A)/Per Carlsson (S)	Volkswagen Golf Kit Car	11h 43m 21s
09	Marco Brighetti (EAK)/Abdul Sidi (EAK)	Subaru Impreza 555	11h 53m 35s
10	Karim Hirji (UGA)/Frank Nekusa (UGA)	Toyota Celica GT-Four	12h 01m 03s

Richard Burns/Robert Reid

ROUND 04 – PORTUGAL (22nd-26th March)			
01	Colin McRae (GB)/Nicky Grist (GB)	Subaru Impreza WRC	4h 20m 58s
02	Carlos Sainz (E)/Luís Moya (E)	Toyota Corolla WRC	4h 21m 00s
03	Freddy Loix (B)/Sven Smeets (B)	Toyota Corolla WRC	4h 21m 43s
04	Richard Burns (GB)/Robert Reid (GB)	Mitsubishi Carisma GT Evo 4	4h 21m 51s
05	Ari Vatanen (FIN)/Fred Gallagher (GB)	Ford Escort WRC	4h 24m 18s
06	Piero Liatti (I)/Fabrizia Pons (I)	Subaru Impreza WRC	4h 24m 22s
07	Juha Kankkunen (FIN)/Juha Repo (FIN)	Ford Escort WRC	4h 24m 35s
08	Grégoire De Mévius (B)/Jean-Marc Fortin (B)	Subaru Impreza WRC	4h 27m 57s
09	Rui Madeira (P)/Nuno da Silva (P)	Toyota Celica GT-Four	4h 31m 22s
10	Krzysztof Holowczyc (PL)/Maciej Wislawski (PL)	Subaru Impreza WRC	4h 32m 56s

Colin McRae/Nicky Grist

ROUND 05 – CATALUNYA, SPAIN (20th-22nd April)			
01	Didier Auriol (F)/Denis Giraudet (F)	Toyota Corolla WRC	4h 18m 36s
02	Freddy Loix (B)/Sven Smeets (B)	Toyota Corolla WRC	4h 19m 30s
03	Tommi Mäkinen (FIN)/Risto Mannisenmäki (FIN)	Mitsubishi Lancer Evo 5	4h 19m 46s
04	Richard Burns (GB)/Robert Reid (GB)	Mitsubishi Carisma GT Evo 5	4h 20m 10s
05	Philippe Bugalski (F)/Jean-Paul Chiaroni (F)	Citroën Xsara Kit Car	4h 20m 28s
06	Gilles Panizzi (F)/Hervé Panizzi (F)	Peugeot 306 Maxi	4h 20m 44s
07	Carlos Sainz (E)/Luís Moya (E)	Toyota Corolla WRC	4h 21m 05s
08	François Delecour (F)/Daniel Grataloup (F)	Peugeot 306 Maxi	4h 21m 24s
09	Uwe Nittel (D)/Tina Thörner (S)	Mitsubishi Carisma GT Evo 4	4h 22m 45s
10	Rui Madeira (P)/Nuno da Silva (P)	Toyota Corolla WRC	4h 25m 24s

Didier Auriol/Denis Giraudet

ROUND 06 – CORSICA, FRANCE (4th-6th May)			
01	Colin McRae (GB)/Nicky Grist (GB)	Subaru Impreza WRC	4h 02m 46s
02	François Delecour (F)/Daniel Grataloup (F)	Peugeot 306 Maxi	4h 03m 14s
03	Piero Liatti (I)/Fabrizia Pons (I)	Subaru Impreza WRC	4h 03m 16s
04	Gilles Panizzi (F)/Hervé Panizzi (F)	Peugeot 306 Maxi	4h 03m 23s
05	Bruno Thiry (B)/Stéphane Prévot (B)	Ford Escort WRC	4h 03m 32s
06	Didier Auriol (F)/Denis Giraudet (F)	Toyota Corolla WRC	4h 05m 26s
07	Fabien Doenlen (F)/Jean-Marc André (F)	Citroën Xsara Kit Car	4h 06m 48s
08	Carlos Sainz (E)/Luís Moya (E)	Toyota Corolla WRC	4h 06m 50s
09	Juha Kankkunen (FIN)/Juha Repo (FIN)	Ford Escort WRC	4h 07m 34s
10	Patrick Magaud (F)/Michel Périn (F)	Citroën Xsara Kit Car	4h 10m 59s

Colin McRae/Nicky Grist

ROUND 07 – ARGENTINA (20th–23rd May)

01	Tommi Mäkinen (FIN)/Risto Mannisenmäki (FIN)	Mitsubishi Lancer Evo 5	4h 22m 07s
02	Carlos Sainz (E)/Luis Moya (E)	Toyota Corolla WRC	4h 22m 34s
03	Juha Kankkunen (FIN)/Juha Repo (FIN)	Ford Escort WRC	4h 22m 34s
04	Richard Burns (GB)/Robert Reid (GB)	Mitsubishi Carisma GT Evo 5	4h 23m 02s
05	Colin McRae (GB)/Nicky Grist (GB)	Subaru Impreza WRC	4h 23m 25s
06	Piero Liatti (I)/Fabrizia Pons (I)	Subaru Impreza WRC	4h 27m 14s
07	Krzysztof Holowczyc (PL)/Maciej Wislawski (PL)	Subaru Impreza WRC	4h 33m 46s
08	Marco Galanti (PAR)/Victor Zucchini (PAR)	Toyota Corolla WRC	4h 44m 23s
09	Gustavo Trelles (ROU)/Martin Christie (RA)	Mitsubishi Lancer Evo 5	4h 46m 52s
10	Oriol Gómez (E)/Marc Martí (E)	Seat Ibiza GTI 16V Evo 2	4h 47m 48s

Tommi Mäkinen/Risto Mannisenmäki

ROUND 08 – ACROPOLIS, GREECE (7th–9th June)

01	Colin McRae (GB)/Nicky Grist (GB)	Subaru Impreza WRC	4h 26m 31s
02	Didier Auriol (F)/Denis Giraudet (F)	Toyota Corolla WRC	4h 26m 51s
03	Juha Kankkunen (FIN)/Juha Repo (FIN)	Ford Escort WRC	4h 27m 15s
04	Carlos Sainz (E)/Luis Moya (E)	Toyota Corolla WRC	4h 28m 09s
05	Freddy Loix (B)/Sven Smeets (B)	Toyota Corolla WRC	4h 29m 20s
06	Piero Liatti (I)/Fabrizia Pons (I)	Subaru Impreza WRC	4h 37m 18s
07	Rui Madeira (P)/Nuno da Silva (P)	Toyota Corolla WRC	4h 39m 01s
08	Leonidas Kyrkos (GR)/Ioánnis Stavropoulos (GR)	Ford Escort WRC	4h 40m 33s
09	Jean-Pierre Richelmi (MC)/Freddy Delorme (F)	Subaru Impreza 555	4h 41m 52s
10	Volkan Isik (TUR)/Ilham Dökümcü (TUR)	Toyota Celica GT-Four	4h 43m 38s

Colin McRae/Nicky Grist

ROUND 09 – NEW ZEALAND (24th–27th July)

01	Carlos Sainz (E)/Luis Moya (E)	Toyota Corolla WRC	3h 54m 57s
02	Didier Auriol (F)/Denis Giraudet (F)	Toyota Corolla WRC	3h 55m 01s
03	Tommi Mäkinen (FIN)/Risto Mannisenmäki (FIN)	Mitsubishi Lancer Evo 5	3h 56m 40s
04	Juha Kankkunen (FIN)/Juha Repo (FIN)	Ford Escort WRC	3h 57m 03s
05	Colin McRae (GB)/Nicky Grist (GB)	Subaru Impreza WRC	3h 58m 47s
06	Piero Liatti (I)/Fabrizia Pons (I)	Subaru Impreza WRC	3h 59m 25s
07	Thomas Rådström (S)/Lars Bäckman (S)	Toyota Corolla WRC	4h 02m 28s
08	Yoshihiro Kataoka (J)/Satoshi Hayashi (J)	Mitsubishi Lancer Evo 3	4h 10m 11s
09	Richard Burns (GB)/Robert Reid (GB)	Mitsubishi Carisma GT Evo 5	4h 10m 26s
10	Yoshio Fujimoto (J)/Tony Sircombe (NZ)	Toyota Corolla WRC	4h 10m 27s

Carlos Sainz/Luis Moya

ROUND 10 – FINLAND (21st–23rd August)

01	Tommi Mäkinen (FIN)/Risto Mannisenmäki (FIN)	Mitsubishi Lancer Evo 5	3h 16m 56s
02	Carlos Sainz (E)/Luis Moya (E)	Toyota Corolla WRC	3h 17m 31s
03	Juha Kankkunen (FIN)/Juha Repo (FIN)	Ford Escort WRC	3h 17m 41s
04	Didier Auriol (F)/Denis Giraudet (F)	Toyota Corolla WRC	3h 19m 25s
05	Richard Burns (GB)/Robert Reid (GB)	Mitsubishi Carisma GT Evo 5	3h 19m 52s
06	Thomas Rådström (S)/Gunnar Barth (S)	Toyota Corolla WRC	3h 20m 07s
07	Marcus Grönholm (FIN)/Timo Rautiainen (FIN)	Toyota Corolla WRC	3h 21m 02s
08	Jarmo Kytölehto (FIN)/Arto Kapanen (FIN)	Subaru Impreza WRC	3h 23m 46s
09	Pasi Hagström (FIN)/Tero Gardemeister (FIN)	Toyota Celica GT-Four	3h 28m 11s
10	Bruno Thiry (B)/Stéphane Prévot (B)	Ford Escort WRC	3h 30m 05s

Tommi Mäkinen/Risto Mannisenmäki

ROUND 11 – SANREMO, ITALY (12th–14th October)

01	Tommi Mäkinen (FIN)/Risto Mannisenmäki (FIN)	Mitsubishi Lancer Evo 5	4h 34m 34s
02	Piero Liatti (I)/Fabrizia Pons (I)	Subaru Impreza WRC	4h 34m 50s
03	Colin McRae (GB)/Nicky Grist (GB)	Subaru Impreza WRC	4h 36m 04s
04	Carlos Sainz (E)/Luis Moya (E)	Toyota Corolla WRC	4h 36m 06s
05	Gilles Panizzi (F)/Hervé Panizzi (F)	Peugeot 306 Maxi	4h 37m 55s
06	Bruno Thiry (B)/Stéphane Prévot (B)	Ford Escort WRC	4h 38m 21s
07	Richard Burns (GB)/Robert Reid (GB)	Mitsubishi Carisma GT Evo 5	4h 39m 15s
08	Andrea Dallavilla (I)/Danilo Fappani (I)	Subaru Impreza WRC	4h 39m 39s
09	Andrea Aghini (I)/Loris Roggia (I)	Toyota Corolla WRC	4h 40m 10s
10	Andrea Navarra (I)/Renzo Casazza (I)	Subaru Impreza WRC	4h 40m 28s

Tommi Mäkinen/Risto Mannisenmäki

ROUND 12 – AUSTRALIA (5th–8th November)

01	Tommi Mäkinen (FIN)/Risto Mannisenmäki (FIN)	Mitsubishi Lancer Evo 5	3h 52m 48s
02	Carlos Sainz (E)/Luis Moya (E)	Toyota Corolla WRC	3h 53m 05s
03	Didier Auriol (F)/Denis Giraudet (F)	Toyota Corolla WRC	3h 53m 13s
04	Colin McRae (GB)/Nicky Grist (GB)	Subaru Impreza WRC	3h 53m 20s
05	Juha Kankkunen (FIN)/Juha Repo (FIN)	Ford Escort WRC	3h 53m 44s
06	Freddy Loix (B)/Sven Smeets (B)	Toyota Corolla WRC	3h 56m 42s
07	Bruno Thiry (B)/Stéphane Prévot (B)	Ford Escort WRC	3h 57m 03s
08	'Possum' Bourne (NZ)/Craig Vincent (NZ)	Subaru Impreza 555	3h 59m 30s
09	Sebastian Lindholm (FIN)/Jukka Aho (FIN)	Ford Escort WRC	4h 02m 50s
10	Ed Ordynski (AUS)/Mark Stacey (AUS)	Mitsubishi Lancer Evo 3	4h 04m 15s

Tommi Mäkinen/Risto Mannisenmäki

ROUND 13 – GREAT BRITAIN (22nd–24th November)

01	Richard Burns (GB)/Robert Reid (GB)	Mitsubishi Carisma GT Evo 5	3h 50m 30s
02	Juha Kankkunen (FIN)/Juha Repo (FIN)	Ford Escort WRC	3h 54m 17s
03	Bruno Thiry (B)/Stéphane Prévot (B)	Ford Escort WRC	3h 55m 58s
04	Grégoire De Mévius (B)/Jean-Marc Fortin (B)	Subaru Impreza WRC	3h 58m 25s
05	Sebastian Lindholm (FIN)/Jukka Aho (FIN)	Ford Escort WRC	3h 58m 46s
06	Harri Rovanperä (FIN)/Risto Pietiläinen (FIN)	Seat Córdoba WRC	4h 01m 03s
07	Armin Schwarz (D)/Manfred Hiemer (D)	Ford Escort WRC	4h 02m 47s
08	Krzysztof Holowczyc (PL)/Maciej Wislawski (PL)	Subaru Impreza WRC	4h 03m 37s
09	Markko Märtin (EE)/Toomas Kitsing (EE)	Toyota Celica GT-Four	4h 07m 41s
10	Manfred Stohl (A)/Peter Müller (A)	Mitsubishi Lancer Evo 5	4h 09m 37s

Richard Burns/Robert Reid

FINAL DRIVERS' CHAMPIONSHIP POSITIONS

01	Tommi Mäkinen	58
02	Carlos Sainz	56
03	Colin McRae	45
04	Juha Kankkunen	39
05	Didier Auriol	34
06	Richard Burns	33
07	Piero Liatti	17
08	Freddy Loix	13
09	Bruno Thiry	8
10	François Delecour	6

FINAL MANUFACTURERS' CHAMPIONSHIP POSITIONS

01	Mitsubishi	91
02	Toyota	85
03	Subaru	65
04	Ford	53
05	Seat	1

1999

ROUND 01 – MONTE CARLO (17th–20th January)

01	Tommi Mäkinen (FIN)/Risto Mannisenmäki (FIN)	Mitsubishi Lancer Evo 6	5h 16m 50s
02	Juha Kankkunen (FIN)/Juha Repo (FIN)	Subaru Impreza WRC	5h 18m 35s
03	Didier Auriol (F)/Denis Giraudet (F)	Toyota Corolla WRC	5h 20m 43s
04	François Delecour (F)/Dominique Savignoni (F)	Ford Escort WRC	5h 20m 51s
05	Bruno Thiry (B)/Stéphane Prévot (B)	Subaru Impreza WRC	5h 20m 53s
06	Piero Liatti (I)/Carlo Cassina (I)	SEAT Córdoba WRC	5h 23m 48s
07	Harri Rovanperä (FIN)/Risto Pietiläinen (FIN)	SEAT Córdoba WRC	5h 23m 52s
08	Richard Burns (GB)/Robert Reid (GB)	Subaru Impreza WRC	5h 26m 15s
09	Henrik Lundgaard (DEN)/Freddy Pedersen (DEN)	Toyota Corolla WRC	5h 30m 56s
10	Marc Duez (B)/Philippe Dupuy (F)	Mitsubishi Carisma GT Evo 5	5h 43m 31s

Tommi Mäkinen/Risto Mannisenmäki

ROUND 02 – SWEDEN (12th–14th February)

01	Tommi Mäkinen (FIN)/Risto Mannisenmäki (FIN)	Mitsubishi Lancer Evo 5	3h 29m 15s
02	Carlos Sainz (E)/Luis Moya (E)	Toyota Corolla WRC	3h 29m 33s
03	Thomas Rådström (S)/Fred Gallagher (GB)	Ford Focus WRC	3h 29m 53s
04	Didier Auriol (F)/Denis Giraudet (F)	Toyota Corolla WRC	3h 29m 55s
05	Richard Burns (GB)/Robert Reid (GB)	Subaru Impreza WRC	3h 35m 04s
06	Juha Kankkunen (FIN)/Juha Repo (FIN)	Subaru Impreza WRC	3h 35m 10s
07	Pasi Hagström (FIN)/Tero Gardemeister (FIN)	Toyota Corolla WRC	3h 37m 39s
08	Markko Märtin (EE)/Toomas Kitsing (EE)	Ford Escort WRC	3h 38m 57s
09	Freddy Loix (B)/Sven Smeets (B)	Mitsubishi Carisma GT Evo 5	3h 39m 21s
10	Bruno Thiry (B)/Stéphane Prévot (B)	Subaru Impreza WRC	3h 39m 48s

Tommi Mäkinen/Risto Mannisenmäki

ROUND 03 – SAFARI, AFRICA (26th-28th February)

Pos	Crew	Car	Time
01	Colin McRae (GB)/Nicky Grist (GB)	Ford Focus WRC	8h 41m 39s
02	Didier Auriol (F)/Denis Giraudet (F)	Toyota Corolla WRC	8h 56m 05s
03	Carlos Sainz (E)/Luís Moya (E)	Toyota Corolla WRC	8h 59m 46s
04	Ian Duncan (EAK)/David Williamson (EAK)	Toyota Corolla WRC	9h 05m 35s
05	Petter Solberg (N)/Fred Gallagher (GB)	Ford Focus WRC	9h 26m 28s
06	Harri Rovanperä (FIN)/Risto Pietiläinen (FIN)	SEAT Córdoba WRC	9h 40m 08s
07	Frédéric Dor (F)/Kevin Gormley (GB)	Subaru Impreza WRC	9h 41m 38s
08	Hamed Al-Wahaibi (OMA)/Tony Sircombe (NZ)	Mitsubishi Carisma GT Evo 5I	0h 05m 09s
09	Luís Climent (E)/Alex Romaní (E)	Mitsubishi Lancer Evo 3	10h 08m 24s
10	Hideaki Miyoshi (J)/Eido Osawa (J)	Subaru Impreza 555	10h 42m 00s

Colin McRae/Nicky Grist

ROUND 04 – PORTUGAL (21st-24th March)

Pos	Crew	Car	Time
01	Colin McRae (GB)/Nicky Grist (GB)	Ford Focus WRC	4h 05m 41s
02	Carlos Sainz (E)/Luís Moya (E)	Toyota Corolla WRC	4h 05m 54s
03	Didier Auriol (F)/Denis Giraudet (F)	Toyota Corolla WRC	4h 05m 58s
04	Richard Burns (GB)/Robert Reid (GB)	Subaru Impreza WRC	4h 06m 37s
05	Tommi Mäkinen (FIN)/Risto Mannisenmäki (FIN)	Mitsubishi Lancer Evo 5	4h 06m 46s
06	Bruno Thiry (B)/Stéphane Prévot (B)	Subaru Impreza WRC	4h 13m 11s
07	Volkan Isik (TUR)/Erkan Bodur (TUR)	Toyota Corolla WRC	4h 15m 07s
08	Matthias Kahle (D)/Dieter Schneppenheim (D)	Toyota Corolla WRC	4h 15m 15s
09	Rui Madeira (P)/Nuno da Silva (P)	Subaru Impreza WRC	4h 15m 51s
10	Luís Climent (E)/Alex Romaní (E)	Subaru Impreza WRC	4h 17m 10s

Colin McRae/Nicky Grist

ROUND 05 – CATALUNYA, SPAIN (19th-21st April)

Pos	Crew	Car	Time
01	Philippe Bugalski (F)/Jean-Paul Chiaroni (F)	Citroën Xsara Kit Car	4h 13m 45s
02	Didier Auriol (F)/Denis Giraudet (F)	Toyota Corolla WRC	4h 14m 17s
03	Tommi Mäkinen (FIN)/Risto Mannisenmäki (FIN)	Mitsubishi Lancer Evo 5	4h 16m 06s
04	Freddy Loix (B)/Sven Smeets (B)	Mitsubishi Carisma GT Evo 5	4h 16m 21s
05	Richard Burns (GB)/Robert Reid (GB)	Subaru Impreza WRC	4h 17m 47s
06	Juha Kankkunen (FIN)/Juha Repo (FIN)	Subaru Impreza WRC	4h 18m 32s
07	Bruno Thiry (B)/Stéphane Prévot (B)	Subaru Impreza WRC	4h 18m 46s
08	Oriol Gómez (E)/Oriol Julià (E)	Renault Mégane Maxi	4h 19m 34s
09	Luís Climent (E)/Alex Romaní (E)	Subaru Impreza WRC	4h 20m 14s
10	Piero Liatti (I)/Carlo Cassina (I)	SEAT Córdoba WRC	4h 20m 53s

Philippe Bugalski/Jean-Paul Chiaroni

ROUND 06 – CORSICA, FRANCE (7th-9th May)

Pos	Crew	Car	Time
01	Philippe Bugalski (F)/Jean-Paul Chiaroni (F)	Citroën Xsara Kit Car	3h 44m 35s
02	Jesús Puras (E)/Marc Martí (E)	Citroën Xsara Kit Car	3h 45m 10s
03	Carlos Sainz (E)/Luís Moya (E)	Toyota Corolla WRC	3h 45m 45s
04	Colin McRae (GB)/Nicky Grist (GB)	Ford Focus WRC	3h 45m 53s
05	Didier Auriol (F)/Denis Giraudet (F)	Toyota Corolla WRC	3h 46m 08s
06	Tommi Mäkinen (FIN)/Risto Mannisenmäki (FIN)	Mitsubishi Lancer Evo 5	3h 47m 26s
07	Richard Burns (GB)/Robert Reid (GB)	Subaru Impreza WRC	3h 47m 42s
08	Freddy Loix (B)/Sven Smeets (B)	Mitsubishi Carisma GT Evo 5	3h 50m 27s
09	Piero Liatti (I)/Carlo Cassina (I)	SEAT Córdoba WRC	3h 51m 41s
10	Tapio Laukkanen (FIN)/Kaj Lindström (FIN)	Renault Mégane Maxi	3h 54m 32s

Philippe Bugalski/Jean-Paul Chiaroni

ROUND 07 – ARGENTINA (22nd-25th May)

Pos	Crew	Car	Time
01	Juha Kankkunen (FIN)/Juha Repo (FIN)	Subaru Impreza WRC	4h 17m 15s
02	Richard Burns (GB)/Robert Reid (GB)	Subaru Impreza WRC	4h 17m 17s
03	Didier Auriol (F)/Denis Giraudet (F)	Toyota Corolla WRC	4h 17m 55s
04	Tommi Mäkinen (FIN)/Risto Mannisenmäki (FIN)	Mitsubishi Lancer Evo 5	4h 18m 40s
05	Carlos Sainz (E)/Luís Moya (E)	Toyota Corolla WRC	4h 19m 43s
06	Thomas Rådström (S)/Fred Gallagher (GB)	Ford Focus WRC	4h 22m 07s
07	Gustavo Trelles (ROU)/Martin Christie (RA)	Mitsubishi Lancer Evo 5	4h 39m 46s
08	Jorge Recalde (RA)/José García (RA)	Mitsubishi Lancer Evo 5	4h 41m 09s
09	Claudio Menzi (RA)/Rodolfo Ortiz (RA)	Subaru Impreza WRX	4h 41m 33s
10	Frédéric Dor (F)/Kevin Gormley (GB)	Subaru Impreza WRC	4h 45m 18s

Juha Kankkunen/Juha Repo

ROUND 08 – ACROPOLIS, GREECE (6th-9th June)

Pos	Crew	Car	Time
01	Richard Burns (GB)/Robert Reid (GB)	Subaru Impreza WRC	4h 21m 21s
02	Carlos Sainz (E)/Luís Moya (E)	Toyota Corolla WRC	4h 22m 22s
03	Tommi Mäkinen (FIN)/Risto Mannisenmäki (FIN)	Mitsubishi Lancer Evo 5	4h 24m 01s
04	Freddy Loix B)/Sven Smeets (B)	Mitsubishi Carisma GT Evo 5	4h 25m 33s
05	Markko Märtin (EE)/Toomas Kitsing (EE)	Toyota Corolla WRC	4h 30m 02s
06	Leonidas Kyrkos (GR)/Ioánnis Stavropoulos (GR)	Ford Escort WRC	4h 35m 17s
07	Luís Climent (E)/Alex Romaní (E)	Subaru Impreza WRC	4h 35m 25s
08	Abdullah Bakhashab (KSA)/Michael Park (GB)	Toyota Corolla WRC	4h 36m 18s
09	Toshi Arai (J)/Roger Freeman (GB)	Subaru Impreza WRC	4h 37m 05s
10	Frédéric Dor (F)/Didier Breton (F)	Subaru Impreza WRC	4h 39m 16s

Richard Burns/Robert Reid

ROUND 09 – NEW ZEALAND (15th-18th July)

Pos	Crew	Car	Time
01	Tommi Mäkinen (FIN)/Risto Mannisenmäki (FIN)	Mitsubishi Lancer Evo 6	4h 11m 07s
02	Juha Kankkunen (FIN)/Juha Repo (FIN)	Subaru Impreza WRC	4h 12m 44s
03	Toni Gardemeister (FIN)/Paavo Lukander (FIN)	SEAT Córdoba WRC	4h 13m 56s
04	Didier Auriol (F)/Denis Giraudet (F)	Toyota Corolla WRC	4h 17m 22s
05	'Possum' Bourne (NZ)/Craig Vincent (NZ)	Subaru Impreza WRC	4h 17m 55s
06	Carlos Sainz (E)/Luís Moya (E)	Toyota Corolla WRC	4h 19m 23s
07	Matthias Kahle (D)/Dieter Schneppenheim (D)	Toyota Corolla WRC	4h 25m 44s
08	Freddy Loix (B)/Sven Smeets (B)	Mitsubishi Carisma GT Evo 6	4h 26m 34s
09	Gustavo Trelles (ROU)/Martin Christie (RA)	Mitsubishi Lancer Evo 6	4h 20m 32s
10	Hamed Al-Wahaibi (OMA)/Tony Sircombe (NZ)	Mitsubishi Lancer Evo 5	4h 30m 21s

Tommi Mäkinen/Risto Mannisenmäki

ROUND 10 – FINLAND (20th-22nd August)

Pos	Crew	Car	Time
01	Juha Kankkunen (FIN)/Juha Repo (FIN)	Subaru Impreza WRC	3h 08m 54s
02	Richard Burns (GB)/Robert Reid (GB)	Subaru Impreza WRC	3h 09m 04s
03	Carlos Sainz (E)/Luís Moya (E)	Toyota Corolla WRC	3h 09m 12s
04	Marcus Grönholm (FIN)/Timo Rautiainen (FIN)	Peugeot 206 WRC	3h 10m 26s
05	Harri Rovanperä (FIN)/Risto Pietiläinen (FIN)	SEAT Córdoba WRC E2	3h 11m 04s
06	Toni Gardemeister (FIN)/Paavo Lukander (FIN)	SEAT Córdoba WRC E2	3h 12m 04s
07	Sebastian Lindholm (FIN)/Jukka Aho (FIN)	Ford Escort WRC	3h 12m 59s
08	Janne Tuohino (FIN)/Miika Anttila (FIN)	Ford Escort WRC	3h 17m 59s
09	François Delecour (F)/Daniel Grataloup (F)	Peugeot 206 WRC	3h 18m 48s
10	Freddy Loix (B)/Sven Smeets (B)	Mitsubishi Carisma GT Evo 6	3h 19m 43s

Juha Kankkunen/Juha Repo

ROUND 11 – CHINA (17th-19th September)

Pos	Crew	Car	Time
01	Didier Auriol (F)/Denis Giraudet (F)	Toyota Corolla WRC	3h 38m 36s
02	Richard Burns (GB)/Robert Reid (GB)	Subaru Impreza WRC	3h 39m 32s
03	Carlos Sainz (E)/Luís Moya (E)	Toyota Corolla WRC	3h 40m 56s
04	Juha Kankkunen (FIN)/Juha Repo (FIN)	Subaru Impreza WRC	3h 43m 54s
05	Harri Rovanperä (FIN)/Risto Pietiläinen (FIN)	SEAT Córdoba WRC E2	3h 47m 52s
06	Volkan Isik (TR)/Erkan Bodur (TR)	Toyota Corolla WRC	3h 54m 42s
07	Toshi Arai (J)/Roger Freeman (GB)	Subaru Impreza WRX	3h 58m 32s
08	Gustavo Trelles (ROU)/Martin Christie (RA)	Mitsubishi Lancer Evo 5	4h 06m 33s
09	Katsuhiko Taguchi (J)/Ron Teoh (MAL)	Mitsubishi Lancer Evo 6	4h 09m 46s
10	Alister McRae (GB)/David Senior (GB)	Hyundai Coupé Evo 2	4h 11m 51s

Didier Auriol/Denis Giraudet

ROUND 12 – SANREMO, ITALY (11th-13th October)

Pos	Crew	Car	Time
01	Tommi Mäkinen (FIN)/Risto Mannisenmäki (FIN)	Mitsubishi Lancer Evo 6	4h 26m 45s
02	Gilles Panizzi (F)/Hervé Panizzi (F)	Peugeot 206 WRC	4h 27m 03s
03	Didier Auriol (F)/Denis Giraudet (F)	Toyota Corolla WRC	4h 27m 27s
04	Freddy Loix (B)/Sven Smeets (B)	Mitsubishi Carisma GT Evo 6	4h 29m 58s
05	Andrea Aghini (I)/Loris Roggia (I)	Toyota Corolla WRC	4h 30m 35s
06	Juha Kankkunen (FIN)/Juha Repo (FIN)	Subaru Impreza WRC	4h 30m 45s
07	Simon Jean-Joseph (F)/Fred Gallagher (GB)	Ford Focus WRC	4h 30m 59s
08	Marcus Grönholm (FIN)/Timo Rautiainen (FIN)	Peugeot 206 WRC	4h 31m 25s
09	Gianfranco Cunico (I)/Luigi Pirollo (I)	Subaru Impreza WRC	4h 32m 35s
10	Andrea Navarra (I)/Simona Fideli (I)	Ford Escort WRC	4h 34m 47s

Tommi Mäkinen/Risto Mannisenmäki

ROUND 13 – AUSTRALIA (4th-7th November)			
01	Richard Burns (GB)/Robert Reid (GB)	Subaru Impreza WRC	3h 44m 31s
02	Carlos Sainz (E)/Luís Moya (E)	Toyota Corolla WRC	3h 44m 43s
03	Tommi Mäkinen (FIN)/Risto Mannisenmäki (FIN)	Mitsubishi Lancer Evo 6	3h 49m 02s
04	Freddy Loix (B)/Sven Smeets (B)	Mitsubishi Carisma GT Evo 6	3h 52m 04s
05	Marcus Grönholm (FIN)/Timo Rautiainen (FIN)	Peugeot 206 WRC	3h 52m 33s
06	Harri Rovanperä (FIN)/Risto Pietiläinen (FIN)	SEAT Córdoba WRC E2	3h 52m 44s
07	Thomas Rådström (S)/Fred Gallagher (GB)	Ford Focus WRC	3h 53m 01s
08	Toshi Arai (J)/Roger Freeman (GB)	Subaru Impreza 555	4h 05m 49s
09	Kenneth Eriksson (S)/Staffan Parmander (S)	Hyundai Coupé Evo 2	4h 05m 58s
10	Martin Rowe (GB)/Derek Ringer (GB)	Renault Mégane Maxi	4h 06m 29s

Richard Burns/Robert Reid

ROUND 14 – GREAT BRITAIN (21st-23rd November)			
01	Richard Burns (GB)/Robert Reid (GB)	Subaru Impreza WRC	3h 53m 44s
02	Juha Kankkunen (FIN)/Juha Repo (FIN)	Subaru Impreza WRC	3h 55m 31s
03	Harri Rovanperä (FIN)/Risto Pietiläinen (FIN)	SEAT Córdoba WRC E2	3h 58m 39s
04	Bruno Thiry (B)/Stéphane Prévot (B)	Skoda Octavia WRC	4h 02m 11s
05	Freddy Loix (B)/Sven Smeets (B)	Mitsubishi Carisma GT Evo 6	4h 03m 19s
06	Thomas Rådström (S)/Gunnar Barth (S)	Ford Focus WRC	4h 03m 47s
07	Gilles Panizzi (F)/Hervé Panizzi (F)	Peugeot 206 WRC	4h 04m 17s
08	Markko Märtin (EE)/Toomas Kitsing (EE)	Toyota Corolla WRC	4h 05m 21s
09	Petter Solberg (N)/Phil Mills (GB)	Ford Focus WRC	4h 06m 54s
10	Matthias Kahle (D)/Dieter Schneppenheim (D)	Toyota Corolla WRC	4h 08m 48s

Richard Burns/Robert Reid

FINAL DRIVERS' CHAMPIONSHIP POSITIONS		
01	Tommi Mäkinen	62
02	Richard Burns	55
03	Didier Auriol	52
04	Juha Kankkunen	44
05	Carlos Sainz	44
06	Colin McRae	23
07	Philippe Bugalski	20
08	Freddy Loix	14
09	Harri Rovanperä	10
10	Jesús Puras	

FINAL MANUFACTURERS' CHAMPIONSHIP POSITIONS		
01	Toyota	109
02	Subaru	105
03	Mitsubishi	83
04	Ford	37
05	SEAT	23
06	Peugeot	11
07	Skoda	6

2000

ROUND 01 – MONTE CARLO (21st-23rd January)			
01	Tommi Mäkinen (FIN)/Risto Mannisenmäki (FIN)	Mitsubishi Lancer Evo 6	4h 23m 35s
02	Carlos Sainz (E)/Luís Moya (E)	Ford Focus WRC	4h 25m 00s
03	Juha Kankkunen (FIN)/Juha Repo (FIN)	Subaru Impreza WRC3	4h 26m 57s
04	Toni Gardemeister (FIN)/Paavo Lukander (FIN)	Seat Córdoba WRC E2	4h 27m 20s
05	Bruno Thiry (B)/Stéphane Prévot (B)	Toyota Corolla WRC	4h 28m 24s
06	Freddy Loix (B)/Sven Smeets (B)	Mitsubishi Carisma GT Evo 6	4h 30m 39s
07	Armin Schwarz (D)/Manfred Hiemer (D)	Skoda Octavia WRC	4h 33m 24s
08	Olivier Burri (CH)/Christophe Hofmann (CH)	Toyota Corolla WRC	4h 34m 17s
09	Manfred Stohl (A)/Peter Müller (A)	Mitsubishi Lancer Evo 6	4h 44m 17s
10	Luís Climent (E)/Alex Romaní (E)	Skoda Octavia WRC	4h 44m 25s

Tommi Mäkinen/Risto Mannisenmäki

ROUND 02 – SWEDEN (11th-13th February)			
01	Marcus Grönholm (FIN)/Timo Rautiainen (FIN)	Peugeot 206 WRC	3h 20m 33s
02	Tommi Mäkinen (FIN)/Risto Mannisenmäki (FIN)	Mitsubishi Lancer Evo 6	3h 20m 40s
03	Colin McRae (GB)/Nicky Grist (GB)	Ford Focus WRC	3h 20m 47s
04	Thomas Rådström (S)/Tina Thörner (S)	Toyota Corolla WRC	3h 20m 48s
05	Richard Burns (GB)/Robert Reid (GB)	Subaru Impreza WRC	3h 21m 08s
06	Juha Kankkunen (FIN)/Juha Repo (FIN)	Subaru Impreza WRC	3h 23m 20s
07	François Delecour (F)/Daniel Grataloup (F)	Peugeot 206 WRC	3h 25m 05s
08	Freddy Loix (B)/Sven Smeets (B)	Mitsubishi Carisma GT Evo 6	3h 25m 41s
09	Markko Märtin (EE)/Michael Park (GB)	Toyota Corolla WRC	3h 25m 47s
10	Didier Auriol (F)/Denis Giraudet (F)	Seat Córdoba WRC E2	3h 25m 49s

Marcus Grönholm/Timo Rautiainen

ROUND 03 – SAFARI, AFRICA (25th-27th February)			
01	Richard Burns (GB)/Robert Reid (GB)	Subaru Impreza WRC	8h 33m 13s
02	Juha Kankkunen (FIN)/Juha Repo (FIN)	Subaru Impreza WRC	8h 37m 50s
03	Didier Auriol (F)/Denis Giraudet (F)	Seat Córdoba WRC E2	8h 55m 57s
04	Carlos Sainz (E)/Luís Moya (E)	Ford Focus WRC	9h 01m 31s
05	Petter Solberg (N)/Phil Mills (GB)	Ford Focus WRC	9h 04m 40s
06	Toshi Arai (J)/Roger Freeman (GB)	Subaru Impreza WRC	9h 19m 16s
07	Armin Schwarz (D)/Manfred Hiemer (D)	Skoda Octavia WRC	9h 32m 11s
08	Luís Climent (E)/Alex Romaní (E)	Skoda Octavia WRC	9h 51m 13s
09	Claudio Menzi (RA)/Edgardo Galindo (RA)	Mitsubishi Lancer Evo 6	10h 39m 07s
10	Roberto Sánchez (RA)/Jorge del Buono (RA)	Subaru Impreza WRX	10h 57m 05s

Richard Burns/Robert Reid

ROUND 04 – PORTUGAL (16th-19th March)			
01	Richard Burns (GB)/Robert Reid (GB)	Subaru Impreza WRC	4h 34m 00s
02	Marcus Grönholm (FIN)/Timo Rautiainen (FIN)	Peugeot 206 WRC	4h 34m 06s
03	Carlos Sainz (E)/Luís Moya (E)	Ford Focus WRC	4h 36m 09s
04	Harri Rovanperä (FIN)/Risto Pietiläinen (FIN)	Toyota Corolla WRC	4h 37m 18s
05	François Delecour (F)/Daniel Grataloup (F)	Peugeot 206 WRC	4h 38m 06s
06	Freddy Loix (B)/Sven Smeets (B)	Mitsubishi Carisma GT Evo 6	4h 41m 28s
07	Markko Märtin (EE)/Michael Park (GB)	Toyota Corolla WRC	4h 41m 41s
08	Armin Schwarz (D)/Manfred Hiemer (D)	Skoda Octavia WRC	4h 41m 47s
09	Toni Gardemeister (FIN)/Paavo Lukander (FIN)	Seat Córdoba WRC E2	4h 42m 24s
10	Didier Auriol (F)/Denis Giraudet (F)	Seat Córdoba WRC E2	4h 46m 38s

Richard Burns/Robert Reid

ROUND 05 – CATALUNYA, SPAIN (31st March-2nd April)			
01	Colin McRae (GB)/Nicky Grist (GB)	Ford Focus WRC	4h 07m 13s
02	Richard Burns (GB)/Robert Reid (GB)	Subaru Impreza WRC	4h 07m 18s
03	Carlos Sainz (E)/Luís Moya (E)	Ford Focus WRC	4h 07m 24s
04	Tommi Mäkinen (FIN)/Risto Mannisenmäki (FIN)	Mitsubishi Lancer Evo 6	4h 07m 53s
05	Marcus Grönholm (FIN)/Timo Rautiainen (FIN)	Peugeot 206 WRC	4h 09m 04s
06	Gilles Panizzi (F)/Hervé Panizzi (F)	Peugeot 206 WRC	4h 09m 23s
07	François Delecour (F)/Daniel Grataloup (F)	Peugeot 206 WRC	4h 10m 49s
08	Freddy Loix (B)/Sven Smeets (B)	Mitsubishi Carisma GT Evo 6	4h 11m 25s
09	Andrea Navarra (I)/Simona Fedeli (I)	Toyota Corolla WRC	4h 12m 18s
10	Markko Märtin (EE)/Michael Park (GB)	Toyota Corolla WRC	4h 12m 42s

Colin McRae/Nicky Grist

ROUND 06 – ARGENTINA (11th-14th May)			
01	Richard Burns (GB)/Robert Reid (GB)	Subaru Impreza WRC	4h 10m 20s
02	Marcus Grönholm (FIN)/Timo Rautiainen (FIN)	Peugeot 206 WRC	4h 11m 28s
03	Tommi Mäkinen (FIN)/Risto Mannisenmäki (FIN)	Mitsubishi Lancer Evo 6	4h 11m 52s
04	Juha Kankkunen (FIN)/Juha Repo (FIN)	Subaru Impreza WRC	4h 12m 43s
05	Freddy Loix (B)/Sven Smeets (B)	Mitsubishi Carisma GT Evo 6	4h 18m 54s
06	Petter Solberg (N)/Phil Mills (GB)	Ford Focus WRC	4h 21m 20s
07	Alister McRae (GB)/David Senior (GB)	Hyundai Accent WRC	4h 23m 38s
08	Kenneth Eriksson (S)/Staffan Parmander (S)	Hyundai Accent WRC	4h 30m 55s
09	Gustavo Trelles (ROU)/Jorge del Buono (RA)	Mitsubishi Lancer Evo 6	4h 32m 00s
10	Gabriel Pozzo (RA)/Rodolfo Ortíz (RA)	Mitsubishi Lancer Evo 6	4h 33m 01s

Richard Burns/Robert Reid

ROUND 07 – ACROPOLIS, GREECE (9th-11th June)			
01	Colin McRae (GB)/Nicky Grist (GB)	Ford Focus WRC	4h 56m 54s
02	Carlos Sainz (E)/Luis Moya (E)	Ford Focus WRC	4h 57m 17s
03	Juha Kankkunen (FIN)/Juha Repo (FIN)	Subaru Impreza WRC	5h 03m 33s
04	Toshi Arai (J)/Roger Freeman (GB)	Subaru Impreza WRC	5h 04m 35s
05	Armin Schwarz (D)/Manfred Hiemer (D)	Skoda Octavia WRC	5h 06m 05s
06	Abdullah Bakhashab (KSA)/Bobby Willis (GB)	Toyota Corolla WRC	5h 09m 49s
07	Jean-Pierre Richelmi (MC)/Thierry Barjou (F)	Subaru Impreza WRC	5h 10m 28s
08	Frédéric Dor (F)/Didier Breton (F)	Subaru Impreza WRC	5h 10m 54s
09	François Delecour (F)/Daniel Grataloup (F)	Peugeot 206 WRC	5h 12m 07s
10	Ioánnis Papadimitriou (GR)/Nikos Petrópoulos (GR)	Subaru Impreza WRC	5h 13m 16s

Colin McRae/Nicky Grist

ROUND 08 – NEW ZEALAND (13th-16th July)			
01	Marcus Grönholm (FIN)/Timo Rautiainen (FIN)	Peugeot 206 WRC	3h 45m 13s
02	Colin McRae (GB)/Nicky Grist (GB)	Ford Focus WRC	3h 45m 27s
03	Carlos Sainz (E)/Luis Moya (E)	Ford Focus WRC	3h 46m 31s
04	Petter Solberg (N)/Phil Mills (GB)	Ford Focus WRC	3h 48m 14s
05	Kenneth Eriksson (S)/Staffan Parmander (S)	Hyundai Accent WRC	3h 48m 26s
06	'Possum' Bourne (NZ)/Craig Vincent (NZ)	Subaru Impreza WRC	3h 52m 08s
07	Manfred Stohl (A)/Peter Müller (A)	Mitsubishi Lancer Evo 6	3h 57m 05s
08	Geof Argyle (NZ)/Paul Fallon (NZ)	Mitsubishi Lancer Evo 6	3h 58m 00s
09	Gustavo Trelles (ROU)/Jorge del Buono (RA)	Mitsubishi Lancer Evo 6	3h 58m 51s
10	Reece Jones (NZ)/Leo Bult (NZ)	Mitsubishi Lancer Evo 6	3h 59m 26s

Marcus Grönholm/Timo Rautiainen

ROUND 09 – FINLAND (18th-20th August)			
01	Marcus Grönholm (FIN)/Timo Rautiainen (FIN)	Peugeot 206 WRC	3h 22m 37s
02	Colin McRae (GB)/Nicky Grist (GB)	Ford Focus WRC	3h 23m 43s
03	Harri Rovanperä (FIN)/Risto Pietiläinen (FIN)	Toyota Corolla WRC	3h 23m 46s
04	Tommi Mäkinen (FIN)/Risto Mannisenmäki (FIN)	Mitsubishi Lancer Evo 6	3h 24m 15s
05	Sebastian Lindholm (FIN)/Jukka Aho (FIN)	Peugeot 206 WRC	3h 25m 43s
06	François Delecour (F)/Daniel Grataloup (F)	Peugeot 206 WRC	3h 27m 42s
07	Pasi Hagström (FIN)/Tero Gardemeister (FIN)	Toyota Corolla WRC	3h 27m 53s
08	Juha Kankkunen (FIN)/Juha Repo (FIN)	Subaru Impreza WRC	3h 28m 30s
09	Alister McRae (GB)/David Senior (GB)	Hyundai Accent WRC	3h 28m 46s
10	Markko Märtin (EE)/Michael Park (GB)	Toyota Corolla WRC	3h 29m 27s

Marcus Grönholm/Timo Rautiainen

ROUND 10 – CYPRUS (8th-10th September)			
01	Carlos Sainz (E)/Luis Moya (E)	Ford Focus WRC	5h 26m 04s
02	Colin McRae (GB)/Nicky Grist (GB)	Ford Focus WRC	5h 26m 42s
03	François Delecour (F)/Daniel Grataloup (F)	Peugeot 206 WRC	5h 27m 35s
04	Richard Burns (GB)/Robert Reid (GB)	Subaru Impreza WRC	5h 28m 09s
05	Tommi Mäkinen (FIN)/Risto Mannisenmäki (FIN)	Mitsubishi Lancer Evo 6	5h 29m 03s
06	Markko Märtin (EE)/Michael Park (GB)	Toyota Corolla WRC	5h 29m 50s
07	Juha Kankkunen (FIN)/Juha Repo (FIN)	Subaru Impreza WRC	5h 33m 06s
08	Freddy Loix (B)/Sven Smeets (B)	Mitsubishi Carisma GT Evo 6	5h 34m 10s
09	Toshi Arai (J)/Roger Freeman (GB)	Subaru Impreza WRC	5h 35m 20s
10	Simon Jean-Joseph (F)/Jack Boyère (F)	Subaru Impreza WRC	5h 48m 21s

Carlos Sainz/Luis Moya

ROUND 11 – CORSICA, FRANCE (29th September-1st October)			
01	Gilles Panizzi (F)/Hervé Panizzi (F)	Peugeot 206 WRC	4h 02m 14s
02	François Delecour (F)/Daniel Grataloup (F)	Peugeot 206 WRC	4h 02m 47s
03	Carlos Sainz (E)/Luis Moya (E)	Ford Focus WRC	4h 03m 26s
04	Richard Burns (GB)/Robert Reid (GB)	Subaru Impreza WRC	4h 03m 45s
05	Marcus Grönholm (FIN)/Timo Rautiainen (FIN)	Peugeot 206 WRC	4h 04m 11s
06	Piero Liatti (I)/Carlo Cassina (I)	Ford Focus WRC	4h 05m 08s
07	Simon Jean-Joseph (F)/Jack Boyère (F)	Subaru Impreza WRC	4h 05m 23s
08	Didier Auriol (F)/Denis Giraudet (F)	Seat Córdoba WRC E3	4h 05m 44s
09	Sébastien Loeb (F)/Daniel Elena (MC)	Toyota Corolla WRC	4h 09m 07s
10	Fabrice Morel (F)/David Marty (F)	Peugeot 206 WRC	4h 09m 34s

Gilles Panizzi/Hervé Panizzi

ROUND 12 – SANREMO, ITALY (20th-22nd October)			
01	Gilles Panizzi (F)/Hervé Panizzi (F)	Peugeot 206 WRC	3h 52m 07s
02	François Delecour (F)/Daniel Grataloup (F)	Peugeot 206 WRC	3h 52m 24s
03	Tommi Mäkinen (FIN)/Risto Mannisenmäki (FIN)	Mitsubishi Lancer Evo 6	3h 53m 00s
04	Marcus Grönholm (FIN)/Timo Rautiainen (FIN)	Peugeot 206 WRC	3h 53m 09s
05	Carlos Sainz (E)/Luis Moya (E)	Ford Focus WRC	3h 53m 18s
06	Colin McRae (GB)/Nicky Grist (GB)	Ford Focus WRC	3h 53m 47s
07	Simon Jean-Joseph (F)/Jack Boyère (F)	Subaru Impreza WRC	3h 54m 04s
08	Freddy Loix (B)/Sven Smeets (B)	Mitsubishi Carisma GT Evo 6	3h 54m 30s
09	Petter Solberg (N)/Phil Mills (GB)	Subaru Impreza WRC	3h 54m 39s
10	Sébastien Loeb (F)/Daniel Elena (F)	Toyota Corolla WRC	3h 55m 41s

Gilles Panizzi/Hervé Panizzi

ROUND 13 – AUSTRALIA (9th-12th November)			
01	Marcus Grönholm (FIN)/Timo Rautiainen (FIN)	Peugeot 206 WRC	3h 43m 57s
02	Richard Burns (GB)/Robert Reid (GB)	Subaru Impreza WRC	3h 43m 59s
03	François Delecour (F)/Daniel Grataloup (F)	Peugeot 206 WRC	3h 45m 10s
04	Kenneth Eriksson (S)/Staffan Parmander (S)	Hyundai Accent WRC	3h 45m 17s
05	Tapio Laukkanen (FIN)/Kaj Lindström (FIN)	Ford Focus WRC	3h 46m 28s
06	Toni Gardemeister (FIN)/Paavo Lukander (FIN)	Seat Córdoba WRC E3	3h 46m 46s
07	'Possum' Bourne (NZ)/Craig Vincent (NZ)	Subaru Impreza WRC	3h 48m 30s
08	Didier Auriol (F)/Denis Giraudet (F)	Seat Córdoba WRC E3	3h 51m 51s
09	Neal Bates (AUS)/Coral Taylor (AUS)	Toyota Corolla WRC	3h 53m 04s
10	Katsuhiko Taguchi (J)/Bobby Willis (GB)	Mitsubishi Lancer Evo 6	3h 57m 43s

Marcus Grönholm/Timo Rautiainen

ROUND 14 – GREAT BRITAIN (23rd-26th November)			
01	Richard Burns (GB)/Robert Reid (GB)	Subaru Impreza WRC	3h 43m 01s
02	Marcus Grönholm (FIN)/Timo Rautiainen (FIN)	Peugeot 206 WRC	3h 44m 07s
03	Tommi Mäkinen (FIN)/Risto Mannisenmäki (FIN)	Mitsubishi Lancer Evo 6	3h 44m 16s
04	Carlos Sainz (E)/Luis Moya (E)	Ford Focus WRC	3h 44m 35s
05	Juha Kankkunen (FIN)/Juha Repo (FIN)	Subaru Impreza WRC	3h 44m 48s
06	François Delecour (F)/Daniel Grataloup (F)	Peugeot 206 WRC	3h 44m 50s
07	Markko Märtin (EE)/Michael Park (GB)	Toyota Corolla WRC	3h 46m 26s
08	Gilles Panizzi (F)/Hervé Panizzi (F)	Peugeot 206 WRC	3h 46m 37s
09	Didier Auriol (F)/Denis Giraudet (F)	Seat Córdoba WRC E3	3h 47m 29s
10	Harri Rovanperä (FIN)/Risto Pietiläinen (FIN)	Seat Córdoba WRC E3	3h 48m 12s

Richard Burns/Robert Reid

FINAL DRIVERS' CHAMPIONSHIP POSITIONS		
01	Marcus Grönholm	65
02	Richard Burns	60
03	Carlos Sainz	46
04	Colin McRae	43
05	Tommi Mäkinen	36
06	François Delecour	24
07	Gilles Panizzi	21
08	Juha Kankkunen	20
09	Harri Rovanperä	7
10	Petter Solberg	6

FINAL MANUFACTURERS' CHAMPIONSHIP POSITIONS		
01	Peugeot	111
02	Ford	91
03	Subaru	88
04	Mitsubishi	43
05	Seat	11
06	Hyundai	8
06=	Skoda	8

2001

ROUND 01 – MONTE CARLO (19th-21st January)			
01	Tommi Mäkinen (FIN)/Risto Mannisenmäki (FIN)	Mitsubishi Lancer Evo 6	4h 38m 04s
02	Carlos Sainz (E)/Luís Moya (E)	Ford Focus WRC	4h 9m 05s
03	François Delecour (F)/Daniel Grataloup (F)	Ford Focus WRC	4h 40m 09s
04	Armin Schwarz (D)/Manfred Hiemer (D)	Skoda Octavia WRC	4h 40m 30s
05	Toni Gardemeister (FIN)/Paavo Lukander (FIN)	Peugeot 206 WRC	4h 43m 56s
06	Freddy Loix (B)/Sven Smeets (B)	Mitsubishi Carisma GT Evo 6	4h 44m 30s
07	Alister McRae (GB)/David Senior (GB)	Hyundai Accent WRC	4h 47m 08s
08	Bruno Thiry (B)/Stéphane Prévot (B)	Skoda Octavia WRC	4h 51m 59s
09	Olivier Gillet (CH)/Freddy Delorme (F)	Mitsubishi Lancer Evo 6	4h 54m 28s
10	Manfred Stohl (A)/Ilka Petrasko (A)	Mitsubishi Lancer Evo 6	4h 55m 54s

Tommi Mäkinen/Risto Mannisenmäki

ROUND 02 – SWEDEN (9th-11th February)			
01	Harri Rovanperä (FIN)/Risto Pietiläinen (FIN)	Peugeot 206 WRC	3h 27m 01s
02	Thomas Rådström (S)/Tina Thörner (S)	Mitsubishi Carisma GT Evo 6	3h 27m 29s
03	Carlos Sainz (E)/Luís Moya (E)	Ford Focus WRC	3h 27m 38s
04	Toni Gardemeister (FIN)/Paavo Lukander (FIN)	Peugeot 206 WRC	3h 29m 06s
05	François Delecour (F)/Daniel Grataloup (F)	Ford Focus WRC	3h 29m 26s
06	Petter Solberg (N)/Phil Mills (GB)	Subaru Impreza WRC	3h 29m 49s
07	Daniel Carlsson (S)/Benny Melander (S)	Toyota Corolla WRC	3h 30m 19s
08	Kenneth Eriksson (S)/Staffan Parmander (S)	Hyundai Accent WRC	3h 30m 36s
09	Colin McRae (GB)/Nicky Grist (GB)	Ford Focus WRC	3h 31m 29s
10	Bruno Thiry (B)/Stéphane Prévot (B)	Skoda Octavia WRC	3h 32m 24s

Harri Rovanperä/Risto Pietiläinen

ROUND 03 – PORTUGAL (8th-11th March)			
01	Tommi Mäkinen (FIN)/Risto Mannisenmäki (FIN)	Mitsubishi Lancer Evo 6	3h 46m 42s
02	Carlos Sainz (E)/Luís Moya (E)	Ford Focus WRC	3h 46m 50s
03	Marcus Grönholm (FIN)/Timo Rautiainen (FIN)	Peugeot 206 WRC	3h 49m 37s
04	Richard Burns (GB)/Robert Reid (GB)	Subaru Impreza WRC	3h 50m 06s
05	François Delecour (F)/Daniel Grataloup (F)	Ford Focus WRC	3h 56m 48s
06	Alister McRae (GB)/David Senior (GB)	Hyundai Accent WRC	3h 58m 50s
07	Kenneth Eriksson (S)/Staffan Parmander (S)	Hyundai Accent WRC	4h 00m 14s
08	Didier Auriol (F)/Denis Giraudet (F)	Peugeot 206 WRC	4h 02m 50s
09	Tapio Laukkanen (FIN)/Kaj Lindström (FIN)	Toyota Corolla WRC	4h 03m 18s
10	Pasi Hagström (FIN)/Tero Gardemeister (FIN)	Toyota Corolla WRC	4h 06m 14s

Tommi Mäkinen/Risto Mannisenmäki

ROUND 04 – CATALUNYA, SPAIN (23rd-25th March)			
01	Didier Auriol (F)/Denis Giraudet (F)	Peugeot 206 WRC	3h 40m 54s
02	Gilles Panizzi (F)/Hervé Panizzi (F)	Peugeot 206 WRC	3h 41m 17s
03	Tommi Mäkinen (FIN)/Risto Mannisenmäki (FIN)	Mitsubishi Lancer Evo 6	3h 41m 56s
04	Freddy Loix (B)/Sven Smeets (B)	Mitsubishi Carisma GT Evo 6	3h 43m 11s
05	Carlos Sainz (E)/Luís Moya (E)	Ford Focus WRC	3h 43m 30s
06	François Delecour (F)/Daniel Grataloup (F)	Ford Focus WRC	3h 43m 38s
07	Richard Burns (GB)/Robert Reid (GB)	Subaru Impreza WRC	3h 43m 57s
08	Philippe Bugalski (F)/Jean-Paul Chiaroni (F)	Citroën Xsara WRC	3h 44m 20s
09	Simon Jean-Joseph (F)/Jack Boyère (F)	Peugeot 206 WRC	3h 45m 54s
10	Bruno Thiry (B)/Stéphane Prévot (B)	Skoda Octavia WRC	3h 46m 58s

Didier Auriol/Denis Giraudet

ROUND 05 – ARGENTINA (3rd-6th May)			
01	Colin McRae (GB)/Nicky Grist (GB)	Ford Focus WRC	4h 18m 25s
02	Richard Burns (GB)/Robert Reid (GB)	Subaru Impreza WRC	4h 18m 52s
03	Carlos Sainz (E)/Luís Moya (E)	Ford Focus WRC	4h 20m 11s
04	Tommi Mäkinen (FIN)/Risto Mannisenmäki (FIN)	Mitsubishi Lancer Evo 6	4h 21m 37s
05	Petter Solberg (N)/Phil Mills (GB)	Subaru Impreza WRC	4h 22m 12s
06	Freddy Loix (B)/Sven Smeets (B)	Mitsubishi Carisma GT Evo 6	4h 24m 05s
07	François Delecour (F)/Daniel Grataloup (F)	Ford Focus WRC	4h 24m 36s
08	Toshi Arai (J)/Glenn MacNeall (AUS)	Subaru Impreza WRC	4h 29m 21s
09	Alister McRae (GB)/David Senior (GB)	Hyundai Accent WRC	4h 32m 24s
10	Gabriel Pozzo (RA)/Daniel Stillo (RA)	Mitsubishi Lancer Evo 6	4h 38m 40s

Colin McRae/Nicky Grist

ROUND 06 – CYPRUS (1st-3rd June)			
01	Colin McRae (GB)/Nicky Grist (GB)	Ford Focus WRC	5h 07m 32s
02	Richard Burns (GB)/Robert Reid (GB)	Subaru Impreza WRC	5h 07m 49s
03	Carlos Sainz (E)/Luís Moya (E)	Ford Focus WRC	5h 07m 59s
04	Toshi Arai (J)/Glenn MacNeall (AUS)	Subaru Impreza WRC	5h 13m 11s
05	Freddy Loix (B)/Sven Smeets (B)	Mitsubishi Carisma GT Evo 6	5h 13m 42s
06	Pasi Hagström (FIN)/Tero Gardemeister (FIN)	Toyota Corolla WRC	5h 17m 05s
07	Alister McRae (GB)/David Senior (GB)	Hyundai Accent WRC	5h 18m 08s
08	Bruno Thiry (B)/Stéphane Prévot (B)	Skoda Octavia WRC	5h 19m 10s
09	Armin Schwarz (D)/Manfred Hiemer (D)	Skoda Octavia WRC	5h 20m 20s
10	Abdullah Bakhashab (KSA)/Bobby Willis (GB)	Toyota Corolla WRC	5h 29m 44s

Colin McRae/Nicky Grist

ROUND 07 – ACROPOLIS, GREECE (15th-17th June)			
01	Colin McRae (GB)/Nicky Grist (GB)	Ford Focus WRC	4h 19m 01s
02	Petter Solberg (N)/Phil Mills (GB)	Subaru Impreza WRC	4h 19m 50s
03	Harri Rovanperä (FIN)/Risto Pietiläinen (FIN)	Peugeot 206 WRC	4h 20m 37s
04	Tommi Mäkinen (FIN)/Risto Mannisenmäki (FIN)	Mitsubishi Lancer Evo 6	4h 21m 17s
05	François Delecour (F)/Daniel Grataloup (F)	Ford Focus WRC	4h 21m 37s
06	Philippe Bugalski (F)/Jean-Paul Chiaroni (F)	Citroën Xsara WRC	4h 23m 02s
07	Armin Schwarz (D)/Manfred Hiemer (D)	Skoda Octavia WRC	4h 24m 58s
08	Simon Jean-Joseph (F)/Jack Boyère (F)	Peugeot 206 WRC	4h 26m 29s
09	Freddy Loix (B)/Sven Smeets (B)	Mitsubishi Carisma GT Evo 6	4h 27m 02s
10	Bruno Thiry (B)/Stéphane Prévot (B)	Skoda Octavia WRC	4h 27m 37s

Colin McRae/Nicky Grist

ROUND 08 – SAFARI, AFRICA (20th-22nd July)			
01	Tommi Mäkinen (FIN)/Risto Mannisenmäki (FIN)	Mitsubishi Lancer Evo 6	8h 58m 37s
02	Harri Rovanperä (FIN)/Risto Pietiläinen (FIN)	Peugeot 206 WRC	9h 11m 14s
03	Armin Schwarz (D)/Manfred Hiemer (D)	Skoda Octavia WRC	9h 16m 12s
04	François Delecour (F)/Daniel Grataloup (F)	Ford Focus WRC	9h 19m 13s
05	Freddy Loix (B)/Sven Smeets (B)	Mitsubishi Carisma GT Evo 6	10h 42m 39s
06	Gabriel Pozzo (RA)/Daniel Stillo (RA)	Mitsubishi Lancer Evo 6	11h 05m 23s
07	Marcos Ligato (RA)/Rubén García (RA)	Mitsubishi Lancer Evo 6	11h 06m 47s
08	Rory Green (EAK)/Orson Taylor (EAK)	Subaru Impreza 555	11h 54m 33s
09	Azar Anwar (EAK)/Tom Muriuki (EAK)	Mitsubishi Lancer Evo	12h 12m 30s
10	Rudi Stohl (A)/Peter Müller (A)	Mitsubishi Lancer Evo 6	13h 40m 00

Tommi Mäkinen/Risto Mannisenmäki

ROUND 09 – FINLAND (24th-26th August)			
01	Marcus Grönholm (FIN)/Timo Rautiainen (FIN)	Peugeot 206 WRC	3h 23m 12s
02	Richard Burns (GB)/Robert Reid (GB)	Subaru Impreza WRC	3h 23m 37s
03	Colin McRae (GB)/Nicky Grist (GB)	Ford Focus WRC	3h 23m 45s
04	Harri Rovanperä (FIN)/Risto Pietiläinen (FIN)	Peugeot 206 WRC	3h 23m 46s
05	Markko Märtin (EE)/Michael Park (GB)	Subaru Impreza WRC	3h 24m 30s
06	Carlos Sainz (E)/Luís Moya (E)	Ford Focus WRC	3h 24m 53s
07	Petter Solberg (N)/Phil Mills (GB)	Subaru Impreza WRC	3h 25m 52s
08	Sebastian Lindholm (FIN)/Timo Hantunen (FIN)	Peugeot 206 WRC	3h 25m 57s
09	Pasi Hagström (FIN)/Tero Gardemeister (FIN)	Toyota Corolla WRC	3h 28m 14
10	Freddy Loix (B)/Sven Smeets (B)	Mitsubishi Carisma GT Evo 6	3h 28m 18s

Marcus Grönholm/Timo Rautiainen

ROUND 10 – NEW ZEALAND (21st-23rd September)			
01	Richard Burns (GB)/Robert Reid (GB)	Subaru Impreza WRC	3h 47m 28s
02	Colin McRae (GB)/Nicky Grist (GB)	Ford Focus WRC	3h 48m 12s
03	Harri Rovanperä (FIN)/Risto Pietiläinen (FIN)	Peugeot 206 WRC	3h 48m 18s
04	Carlos Sainz (E)/Luís Moya (E)	Ford Focus WRC	3h 48m 20s
05	Marcus Grönholm (FIN)/Timo Rautiainen (FIN)	Peugeot 206 WRC	3h 48m 23s
06	Didier Auriol (F)/Denis Giraudet (F)	Peugeot 206 WRC	3h 48m 39s
07	Petter Solberg (N)/Phil Mills (GB)	Subaru Impreza WRC	3h 49m 43s
08	Tommi Mäkinen (FIN)/Risto Mannisenmäki (FIN)	Mitsubishi Lancer Evo 6	3h 49m 49s
09	Alister McRae (GB)/David Senior (GB)	Hyundai Accent WRC	3h 51m 01s
10	Kenneth Eriksson (S)/Staffan Parmander (S)	Hyundai Accent WRC	3h 51m 49s

Richard Burns/Robert Reid

ROUND 11 – SANREMO, ITALY (4th-7th October)

01	Gilles Panizzi (F)/Hervé Panizzi (F)	Peugeot 206 WRC	4h 05m 49s
02	Sébastien Loeb (F)/Daniel Elena (F)	Citroën Xsara WRC	4h 06m 00s
03	Didier Auriol (F)/Denis Giraudet (F)	Peugeot 206 WRC	4h 06m 44s
04	Carlos Sainz (E)/Luis Moya (E)	Ford Focus WRC	4h 07m 01s
05	Renato Travaglia (I)/Flavio Zanella (I)	Peugeot 206 WRC	4h 07m 21s
06	François Delecour (F)/Daniel Grataloup (F)	Ford Focus WRC	4h 08m 18s
07	Marcus Grönholm (FIN)/Timo Rautiainen (FIN)	Peugeot 206 WRC	4h 08m 36s
08	Colin McRae (GB)/Nicky Grist (GB)	Ford Focus WRC	4h 09m 43s
09	Petter Solberg (N)/Phil Mills (GB)	Subaru Impreza WRC	4h 09m 49s
10	Simon Jean-Joseph (F)/Jack Boyère (F)	Peugeot 206 WRC	4h 09m 51s

Gilles Panizzi/Hervé Panizzi

ROUND 12 – CORSICA, FRANCE (19th-21st October)

01	Jesús Puras (E)/Marc Martí (E)	Citroën Xsara WRC	3h 58m 35s
02	Gilles Panizzi (F)/Hervé Panizzi (F)	Peugeot 206 WRC	3h 58m 53s
03	Didier Auriol (F)/Denis Giraudet (F)	Peugeot 206 WRC	3h 59m 47s
04	Richard Burns (GB)/Robert Reid (GB)	Subaru Impreza WRC	4h 03m 28s
05	Petter Solberg (N)/Phil Mills (GB)	Subaru Impreza WRC	4h 03m 29s
06	Markko Märtin (EE)/Michael Park (GB)	Subaru Impreza WRC	4h 03m 57s
07	Harri Rovanperä (FIN)/Risto Pietiläinen (FIN)	Peugeot 206 WRC	4h 06m 02s
08	Piero Liatti (I)/Carlo Cassina (I)	Hyundai Accent WRC	4h 06m 44s
09	Alister McRae (GB)/David Senior (GB)	Hyundai Accent WRC	4h 07m 28s
10	François Delecour (F)/Daniel Grataloup (F)	Ford Focus WRC	4h 08m 41s

Jesús Puras/Marc Martí

ROUND 13 – AUSTRALIA (1st-4th November)

01	Marcus Grönholm (FIN)/Timo Rautiainen (FIN)	Peugeot 206 WRC	3h 17m 01s
02	Richard Burns (GB)/Robert Reid (GB)	Subaru Impreza WRC	3h 17m 41s
03	Didier Auriol (F)/Denis Giraudet (F)	Peugeot 206 WRC	3h 18m 21s
04	Harri Rovanperä (FIN)/Risto Pietiläinen (FIN)	Peugeot 206 WRC	3h 18m 32s
05	Colin McRae (GB)/Nicky Grist (GB)	Ford Focus WRC	3h 18m 41s
06	Tommi Mäkinen (FIN)/Timo Hantunen (FIN)	Mitsubishi Lancer WRC	3h 20m 04s
07	Petter Solberg (N)/Phil Mills (GB)	Subaru Impreza WRC	3h 20m 42s
08	Carlos Sainz (E)/Luis Moya (E)	Ford Focus WRC	3h 22m 00s
09	Gilles Panizzi (F)/Hervé Panizzi (F)	Peugeot 206 WRC	3h 22m 10s
10	Alister McRae (GB)/David Senior (GB)	Hyundai Accent WRC	3h 24m 33s

Marcus Grönholm/Timo Rautiainen

ROUND 14 – GREAT BRITAIN (23rd-25th November)

01	Marcus Grönholm (FIN)/Timo Rautiainen (FIN)	Peugeot 206 WRC	3h 23m 44s
02	Harri Rovanperä (FIN)/Risto Pietiläinen (FIN)	Peugeot 206 WRC	3h 26m 11s
03	Richard Burns (GB)/Robert Reid (GB)	Subaru Impreza WRC	3h 27m 00s
04	Alister McRae (GB)/David Senior (GB)	Hyundai Accent WRC	3h 30m 33s
05	Armin Schwarz (D)/Manfred Hiemer (D)	Skoda Octavia WRC	3h 31m 16s
06	Kenneth Eriksson (S)/Staffan Parmander (S)	Hyundai Accent WRC	3h 31m 55s
07	Didier Auriol (F)/Denis Giraudet (F)	Peugeot 206 WRC	3h 32m 05s
08	Bruno Thiry (B)/Stéphane Prévot (B)	Skoda Octavia WRC	3h 34m 40s
09	Grégoire De Mévius (B)/Jack Boyère (F)	Peugeot 206 WRC	3h 38m 02s
10	Toshi Arai (J)/Tony Sircombe (J)	Subaru Impreza WRC	3h 38m 51s

Marcus Grönholm/Timo Rautiainen

FINAL DRIVERS' CHAMPIONSHIP POSITIONS

01	Richard Burns	44
02	Colin McRae	42
03	Tommi Mäkinen	41
04	Marcus Grönholm	36
05	Harri Rovanperä	36
06	Carlos Sainz	33
07	Didier Auriol	23
08	Gilles Panizzi	22
09	François Delecour	15
10	Petter Solberg	11

FINAL MANUFACTURERS' CHAMPIONSHIP POSITIONS

01	Peugeot	106
02	Ford	86
03	Mitsubishi	69
04	Subaru	66
05	Skoda	17
06=	Hyundai	17

2002

ROUND 01 – MONTE CARLO (18th-20th January)

01	Tommi Mäkinen (FIN)/Kaj Lindström (FIN)	Subaru Impreza WRC	3h 59m 30s
02	Sébastien Loeb (F)/Daniel Elena (F)	Citroën Xsara WRC	4h 00m 44s
03	Carlos Sainz (E)/Luis Moya (E)	Ford Focus WRC	4h 00m 46s
04	Colin McRae (GB)/Nicky Grist (GB)	Ford Focus WRC	4h 01m 28s
05	Marcus Grönholm (FIN)/Timo Rautiainen (FIN)	Peugeot 206 WRC	4h 01m 38s
06	Petter Solberg (N)/Phil Mills (GB)	Subaru Impreza WRC	4h 02m 00s
07	Gilles Panizzi (F)/Hervé Panizzi (F)	Peugeot 206 WRC	4h 02m 50s
08	Richard Burns (GB)/Robert Reid (GB)	Peugeot 206 WRC	4h 03m 47s
09	François Delecour (F)/Daniel Grataloup (F)	Mitsubishi Lancer WRC	4h 05m 06s
10	Toni Gardemeister (FIN)/Paavo Lukander (FIN)	Skoda Octavia WRC	4h 06m 13s

Tommi Mäkinen/Kaj Lindström

ROUND 02 – SWEDEN (1st-3rd February)

01	Marcus Grönholm (FIN)/Timo Rautiainen (FIN)	Peugeot 206 WRC	3h 07m 28s
02	Harri Rovanperä (FIN)/Risto Pietiläinen (FIN)	Peugeot 206 WRC	3h 08m 53s
03	Carlos Sainz (E)/Luis Moya (E)	Ford Focus WRC	3h 09m 54s
04	Richard Burns (GB)/Robert Reid (GB)	Peugeot 206 WRC	3h 10m 02s
05	Alister McRae (GB)/David Senior (GB)	Mitsubishi Lancer WRC	3h 11m 43s
06	Colin McRae (GB)/Nicky Grist (GB)	Ford Focus WRC	3h 11m 43s
07	Janne Tuohino (FIN)/Petri Vihavainen (FIN)	Ford Focus WRC	3h 11m 52s
08	Juha Kankkunen (FIN)/Juha Repo (FIN)	Hyundai Accent WRC	3h 12m 05s
09	Sebastian Lindholm (FIN)/Timo Hantunen (FIN)	Peugeot 206 WRC	3h 12m 25s
10	François Duval (B)/Jean-Marc Fortin (B)	Ford Focus WRC	3h 14m 01s

Marcus Grönholm/Timo Rautiainen

ROUND 03 – CORSICA, FRANCE (8th-10th March)

01	Gilles Panizzi (F)/Hervé Panizzi (F)	Peugeot 206 WRC	3h 54m 40s
02	Marcus Grönholm (FIN)/Timo Rautiainen (FIN)	Peugeot 206 WRC	3h 55m 20s
03	Richard Burns (GB)/Robert Reid (GB)	Peugeot 206 WRC	3h 55m 32s
04	Philippe Bugalski (F)/Jean-Paul Chiaroni (F)	Citroën Xsara WRC	3h 56m 42s
05	Petter Solberg (N)/Phil Mills (GB)	Subaru Impreza WRC	3h 57m 08s
06	Carlos Sainz (E)/Luis Moya (E)	Ford Focus WRC	3h 57m 13s
07	François Delecour (F)/Daniel Grataloup (F)	Mitsubishi Lancer WRC	3h 59m 48s
08	Markko Märtin (EE)/Michael Park (GB)	Ford Focus WRC	4h 00m 00s
09	Freddy Loix (B)/Sven Smeets (B)	Hyundai Accent WRC	4h 00m 54s
10	Alister McRae (GB)/David Senior (GB)	Mitsubishi Lancer WRC	4h 01m 12s

Gilles Panizzi/Hervé Panizzi

ROUND 04 – CATALUNYA, SPAIN (22nd-24th March)

01	Gilles Panizzi (F)/Hervé Panizzi (F)	Peugeot 206 WRC	3h 34m 09s
02	Richard Burns (GB)/Robert Reid (GB)	Peugeot 206 WRC	3h 34m 46s
03	Philippe Bugalski (F)/Jean-Paul Chiaroni (F)	Citroën Xsara WRC	3h 35m 22s
04	Marcus Grönholm (FIN)/Timo Rautiainen (FIN)	Peugeot 206 WRC	3h 35m 51s
05	Petter Solberg (N)/Phil Mills (GB)	Subaru Impreza WRC	3h 36m 10s
06	Colin McRae (GB)/Nicky Grist (GB)	Ford Focus WRC	3h 37m 36s
07	Harri Rovanperä (FIN)/Risto Pietiläinen (FIN)	Peugeot 206 WRC	3h 37m 49s
08	Markko Märtin (EE)/Michael Park (GB)	Ford Focus WRC	3h 37m 52s
09	François Delecour (F)/Daniel Grataloup (F)	Mitsubishi Lancer WRC	3h 39m 37s
10	Freddy Loix (B)/Sven Smeets (B)	Hyundai Accent WRC	3h 39m 39s

Gilles Panizzi/Hervé Panizzi

ROUND 05 – CYPRUS (19th-21st April)			
01	Marcus Grönholm (FIN)/Timo Rautiainen (FIN)	Peugeot 206 WRC	4h 21m 25s
02	Richard Burns (GB)/Robert Reid (GB)	Peugeot 206 WRC	4h 22m 22s
03	Tommi Mäkinen (FIN)/Kaj Lindström (FIN)	Subaru Impreza WRC	4h 22m 24s
04	Harri Rovanperä (FIN)/Risto Pietiläinen (FIN)	Peugeot 206 WRC	4h 22m 44s
05	Petter Solberg (N)/Phil Mills (GB)	Subaru Impreza WRC	4h 23m 43s
06	Colin McRae (GB)/Nicky Grist (GB)	Ford Focus WRC	4h 24m 11s
07	Armin Schwarz (D)/Manfred Hiemer (D)	Hyundai Accent WRC	4h 24m 13s
08	Markko Märtin (EE)/Michael Park (GB)	Ford Focus WRC	4h 25m 48s
09	Kenneth Eriksson (S)/Tina Thörner (S)	Skoda Octavia WRC	4h 28m 43s
10	Gilles Panizzi (F)/Hervé Panizzi (F)	Peugeot 206 WRC	4h 29m 37s

Marcus Grönholm/Timo Rautiainen

ROUND 06 – ARGENTINA (16th-19th March)			
01	Carlos Sainz (E)/Luis Moya (E)	Ford Focus WRC	4h 08m 09s
02	Petter Solberg (N)/Phil Mills (GB)	Subaru Impreza WRC	4h 08m 13s
03	Colin McRae (GB)/Nicky Grist (GB)	Ford Focus WRC	4h 10m 28s
04	Markko Märtin (EE)/Michael Park (GB)	Ford Focus WRC	4h 11m 01s
05	Toni Gardemeister (FIN)/Paavo Lukander (FIN)	Skoda Octavia WRC	4h 13m 27s
06	Kenneth Eriksson (S)/Tina Thörner (S)	Skoda Octavia WRC	4h 14m 25s
07	Juha Kankkunen (FIN)/Juha Repo (FIN)	Hyundai Accent WRC	4h 16m 12s
08	Alister McRae (GB)/David Senior (GB)	Mitsubishi Lancer WRC	4h 16m 58s
09	Gabriel Pozzo (RA)/Daniel Stillo (RA)	Skoda Octavia WRC	4h 22m 08s
10	Ramón Ferreyros (PER)/Diego Vallejo (E)	Mitsubishi Lancer Evo 7	4h 32m 27s

Carlos Sainz/Luís Moya

ROUND 07 – ACROPOLIS, GREECE (13th-16th June)			
01	Colin McRae (GB)/Nicky Grist (GB)	Ford Focus WRC	4h 27m 43s
02	Marcus Grönholm (FIN)/Timo Rautiainen (FIN)	Peugeot 206 WRC	4h 28m 08s
03	Carlos Sainz (E)/Luís Moya (E)	Ford Focus WRC	4h 29m 29s
04	Harri Rovanperä (FIN)/Risto Pietiläinen (FIN)	Peugeot 206 WRC	4h 29m 41s
05	Petter Solberg (N)/Phil Mills (GB)	Subaru Impreza WRC	4h 29m 42s
06	Markko Märtin (EE)/Michael Park (GB)	Ford Focus WRC	4h 30m 23s
07	Sébastien Loeb (F)/Daniel Elena (F)	Citroën Xsara WRC	4h 31m 29s
08	Thomas Rådström (S)/Denis Giraudet (F)	Citroën Xsara WRC	4h 32m 52s
09	Armin Schwarz (D)/Manfred Hiemer (D)	Hyundai Accent WRC	4h 33m 04s
10	Toni Gardemeister (FIN)/Paavo Lukander (FIN)	Skoda Octavia WRC	4h 35m 01s

Colin McRae/Nicky Grist

ROUND 08 – SAFARI, AFRICA (12th-14th July)			
01	Colin McRae (GB)/Nicky Grist (GB)	Ford Focus WRC	7h 58m 28s
02	Harri Rovanperä (FIN)/Risto Pietiläinen (FIN)	Peugeot 206 WRC	8h 01m 18s
03	Thomas Rådström (S)/Denis Giraudet (F)	Citroën Xsara WRC	8h 17m 06s
04	Markko Märtin (EE)/Michael Park (GB)	Ford Focus WRC	8h 19m 56s
05	Sébastien Loeb (F)/Daniel Elena (F)	Citroën Xsara WRC	8h 20m 16s
06	Gilles Panizzi (F)/Hervé Panizzi (F)	Peugeot 206 WRC	8h 33m 09s
07	Roman Kresta (CZ)/Jan Tománek (CZ)	Skoda Octavia WRC	8h 53m 06s
08	Juha Kankkunen (FIN)/Juha Repo (FIN)	Hyundai Accent WRC	9h 09m 59s
09	Alister McRae (GB)/David Senior (GB)	Mitsubishi Lancer WRC	9h 15m 41s
10	Karamjit Singh (MAL)/Allen Oh (MAL)	Proton Pert	10h 27m 55s

Colin McRae/Nicky Grist

ROUND 09 – FINLAND (8th-11th August)			
01	Marcus Grönholm (FIN)/Timo Rautiainen (FIN)	Peugeot 206 WRC	3h 17m 52s
02	Richard Burns (GB)/Robert Reid (GB)	Peugeot 206 WRC	3h 19m 19s
03	Petter Solberg (N)/Phil Mills (GB)	Subaru Impreza WRC	3h 20m 42s
04	Carlos Sainz (E)/Luís Moya (E)	Ford Focus WRC	3h 20m 46s
05	Markko Märtin (EE)/Michael Park (GB)	Ford Focus WRC	3h 21m 02s
06	Tommi Mäkinen (FIN)/Kaj Lindström (FIN)	Subaru Impreza WRC	3h 22m 26s
07	Sebastian Lindholm (FIN)/Timo Hantunen (FIN)	Peugeot 206 WRC	3h 23m 28s
08	Jani Paasonen (FIN)/Arto Kapanen (FIN)	Mitsubishi Lancer WRC	3h 23m 47s
09	Freddy Loix (B)/Sven Smeets (B)	Hyundai Accent WRC	3h 24m 00s
10	Sébastien Loeb (F)/Daniel Elena (F)	Citroën Xsara WRC	3h 24m 06s

Marcus Grönholm/Timo Rautiainen

ROUND 10 – GERMANY (22th-25th August)			
01	Sébastien Loeb (F)/Daniel Elena (F)	Citroën Xsara WRC	3h 47m 17s
02	Richard Burns (GB)/Robert Reid (GB)	Peugeot 206 WRC	3h 47m 31s
03	Marcus Grönholm (FIN)/Timo Rautiainen (FIN)	Peugeot 206 WRC	3h 48m 36s
04	Colin McRae (GB)/Nicky Grist (GB)	Ford Focus WRC	3h 51m 02s
05	Bruno Thiry (B)/Stéphane Prévot (B)	Peugeot 206 WRC	3h 52m 36s
06	Markko Märtin (EE)/Michael Park (GB)	Ford Focus WRC	3h 52m 50s
07	Tommi Mäkinen (FIN)/Kaj Lindström (FIN)	Subaru Impreza WRC	3h 52m 56s
08	Carlos Sainz (E)/Luís Moya (E)	Ford Focus WRC	3h 53m 34s
09	François Delecour (F)/Daniel Grataloup (F)	Mitsubishi Lancer WRC	3h 53m 53s
10	Kenneth Eriksson (S)/Tina Thörner (S)	Skoda Octavia WRC	4h 00m 51s

Sébastien Loeb/Daniel Elena

ROUND 11 – SANREMO, ITALY (19th-22nd September)			
01	Gilles Panizzi (F)/Hervé Panizzi (F)	Peugeot 206 WRC	4h 10m 15s
02	Marcus Grönholm (FIN)/Timo Rautiainen (FIN)	Peugeot 206 WRC	4h 10m 36s
03	Petter Solberg (N)/Phil Mills (GB)	Subaru Impreza WRC	4h 11m 22s
04	Richard Burns (GB)/Robert Reid (GB)	Peugeot 206 WRC	4h 11m 34s
05	Markko Märtin (EE)/Michael Park (GB)	Ford Focus WRC	4h 12m 10s
06	Jesús Puras (E)/Carlos del Barrio (E)	Citroën Xsara WRC	4h 12m 54s
07	Cédric Robert (F)/Gérald Bedon (F)	Peugeot 206 WRC	4h 13m 16s
08	Colin McRae (GB)/Nicky Grist (GB)	Ford Focus WRC	4h 15m 33s
09	Harri Rovanperä (FIN)/Voitto Silander (FIN)	Peugeot 206 WRC	4h 16m 34s
10	François Delecour (F)/Daniel Grataloup (F)	Mitsubishi Lancer WRC	4h 17m 40s

Gilles Panizzi/Hervé Panizzi

ROUND 12 – NEW ZEALAND (2nd-5th October)			
01	Marcus Grönholm (FIN)/Timo Rautiainen (FIN)	Peugeot 206 WRC	3h 58m 45s
02	Harri Rovanperä (FIN)/Voitto Silander (FIN)	Peugeot 206 WRC	4h 02m 33s
03	Tommi Mäkinen (FIN)/Kaj Lindström (FIN)	Subaru Impreza WRC	4h 03m 11s
04	Carlos Sainz (E)/Luís Moya (E)	Ford Focus WRC	4h 04m 34s
05	Juha Kankkunen (FIN)/Juha Repo (FIN)	Hyundai Accent WRC	4h 05m 55s
06	Freddy Loix (B)/Sven Smeets (B)	Hyundai Accent WRC	4h 06m 37s
07	Gilles Panizzi (F)/Hervé Panizzi (F)	Peugeot 206 WRC	4h 07m 09s
08	Toni Gardemeister (FIN)/Paavo Lukander (FIN)	Skoda Octavia WRC	4h 07m 41s
09	François Delecour (F)/Daniel Grataloup (F)	Mitsubishi Lancer WRC	4h 09m 29s
10	Armin Schwarz (D)/Manfred Hiemer (D)	Hyundai Accent WRC	4h 10m 20s

Marcus Grönholm/Timo Rautiainen

ROUND 13 – AUSTRALIA (10th-13th November)			
01	Marcus Grönholm (FIN)/Timo Rautiainen (FIN)	Peugeot 206 WRC	3h 35m 56s
02	Harri Rovanperä (FIN)/Voitto Silander (FIN)	Peugeot 206 WRC	3h 36m 53s
03	Petter Solberg (N)/Phil Mills (GB)	Subaru Impreza WRC	3h 37m 25s
04	Carlos Sainz (E)/Luís Moya (E)	Ford Focus WRC	3h 39m 05s
05	Markko Märtin (EE)/Michael Park (GB)	Ford Focus WRC	3h 42m 18s
06	Toni Gardemeister (FIN)/Paavo Lukander (FIN)	Skoda Octavia WRC	3h 43m 08s
07	Sébastien Loeb (F)/Daniel Elena (F)	Citroën Xsara WRC	3h 45m 02s
08	Kenneth Eriksson (S)/Tina Thörner (S)	Skoda Octavia WRC	3h 48m 42s
09	Jani Paasonen (FIN)/Arto Kapanen (FIN)	Mitsubishi Lancer WRC	3h 49m 22s
10	Manfred Stohl (A)/Ilka Petrasko (A)	Mitsubishi Lancer Evo 6	3h 55m 17s

Marcus Grönholm/Timo Rautiainen

ROUND 14 – GREAT BRITAIN (14th-17th November)			
01	Petter Solberg (GB)/Phil Mills (GB)	Subaru Impreza WRC	3hrs 30m 36s
02	Markko Märtin (EE)/Michael Park (GB)	Ford Focus WRC	3h 31m 00s
03	Carlos Sainz (E)/Luís Moya (E)	Ford Focus WRC	3h 32m 12s
04	Tommi Mäkinen (FIN)/Kaj Lindström (FIN)	Subaru Impreza WRC	3h 33m 13s
05	Colin McRae (GB)/Derek Ringer (GB)	Ford Focus WRC	3h 33m 37s
06	Mark Higgins (GB)/Bryan Thomas (GB)	Ford Focus WRC	3h 35m 38s
07	Harri Rovanperä (FIN)/Voitto Silander (FIN)	Peugeot 206 WRC	3h 35m 52s
08	Freddy Loix (B)/Sven Smeets (B)	Hyundai Accent WRC	3h 35m 52s
09	Juha Kankkunen (FIN)/Juha Repo (FIN)	Hyundai Accent WRC	3h 36m 05s
10	Toni Gardemeister (FIN)/Paavo Lukander (FIN)	Skoda Octavia WRC	3h 36m 39s

Petter Solberg/Phil Mills

FINAL DRIVERS' CHAMPIONSHIP POSITIONS			FINAL MANUFACTURERS' CHAMPIONSHIP POSITIONS		
01	Marcus Grönholm	77	01	Peugeot	165
02	Petter Solberg	37	02	Ford	104
03	Carlos Sainz	36	03	Subaru	67
04	Colin McRae	35	04	Hyundai	10
05	Richard Burns	34	05	Skoda	9
06	Gilles Panizzi	31	06	Mitsubishi	9
07	Harri Rovanperä	30			
08	Tommi Mäkinen	22			
09	Markko Märtin	20			
10	Sébastien Loeb	18			

2003

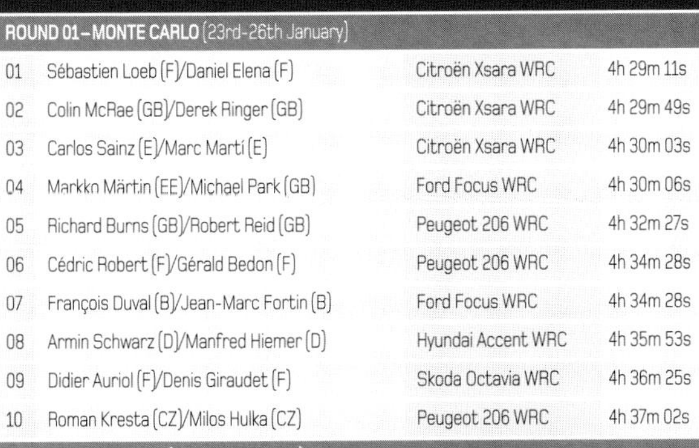

ROUND 01 – MONTE CARLO (23rd-26th January)

01	Sébastien Loeb (F)/Daniel Elena (F)	Citroën Xsara WRC	4h 29m 11s
02	Colin McRae (GB)/Derek Ringer (GB)	Citroën Xsara WRC	4h 29m 49s
03	Carlos Sainz (E)/Marc Marti (E)	Citroën Xsara WRC	4h 30m 03s
04	Markko Märtin (EE)/Michael Park (GB)	Ford Focus WRC	4h 30m 06s
05	Richard Burns (GB)/Robert Reid (GB)	Peugeot 206 WRC	4h 32m 27s
06	Cédric Robert (F)/Gérald Bedon (F)	Peugeot 206 WRC	4h 34m 28s
07	François Duval (B)/Jean-Marc Fortin (B)	Ford Focus WRC	4h 34m 28s
08	Armin Schwarz (D)/Manfred Hiemer (D)	Hyundai Accent WRC	4h 35m 53s
09	Didier Auriol (F)/Denis Giraudet (F)	Skoda Octavia WRC	4h 36m 25s
10	Roman Kresta (CZ)/Milos Hulka (CZ)	Peugeot 206 WRC	4h 37m 02s

Sébastien Loeb/Daniel Elena

ROUND 02 – SWEDEN (6th-9th February)

01	Marcus Grönholm (FIN)/Timo Rautiainen (FIN)	Peugeot 206 WRC	3h 03m 28s
02	Tommi Mäkinen (FIN)/Kaj Lindström (FIN)	Subaru Impreza WRC	3h 04m 18s
03	Richard Burns (GB)/Robert Reid (GB)	Peugeot 206 WRC	3h 04m 46s
04	Markko Märtin (EE)/Michael Park (GB)	Ford Focus WRC	3h 05m 13s
05	Colin McRae (GB)/Derek Ringer (GB)	Citroën Xsara WRC	3h 05m 43s
06	Petter Solberg (N)/Phil Mills (GB)	Subaru Impreza WRC	3h 05m 47s
07	Sébastien Loeb (F)/Daniel Elena (F)	Citroën Xsara WRC	3h 06m 42s
08	Toni Gardemeister (FIN)/Paavo Lukander (FIN)	Skoda Octavia WRC	3h 06m 47s
09	Carlos Sainz (E)/Marc Marti (E)	Citroen Xsara WRC	3h 06m 52s
10	Freddy Loix (B)/Sven Smeets (B)	Hyundai Accent WRC	3h 07m 04s

Marcus Grönholm/Timo Rautiainen

ROUND 03 – TURKEY (27th February-2nd March)

01	Carlos Sainz (E)/Marc Marti (E)	Citroën Xsara WRC	4h 32m 14s
02	Richard Burns (GB)/Robert Reid (GB)	Peugeot 206 WRC	4h 33m 02s
03	François Duval (B)/Jean-Marc Fortin (B)	Ford Focus WRC	4h 34m 00s
04	Colin McRae (GB)/Derek Ringer (GB)	Citroën Xsara WRC	4h 34m 23s
05	Gilles Panizzi (F)/Hervé Panizzi (F)	Peugeot 206 WRC	4h 34m 55s
06	Markko Märtin (EE)/Michael Park (GB)	Ford Focus WRC	4h 35m 39s
07	Toni Gardemeister (FIN)/Paavo Lukander (FIN)	Skoda Octavia WRC	4h 37m 27s
08	Tommi Mäkinen (FIN)/Kaj Lindström (FIN)	Subaru Impreza WRC	4h 39m 32s
09	Marcus Grönholm (FIN)/Timo Rautiainen (FIN)	Peugeot 206 WRC	4h 43m 06s
10	Freddy Loix (B)/Sven Smeets (B)	Hyundai Accent WRC	4h 43m 54s

Carlos Sainz/Marc Marti

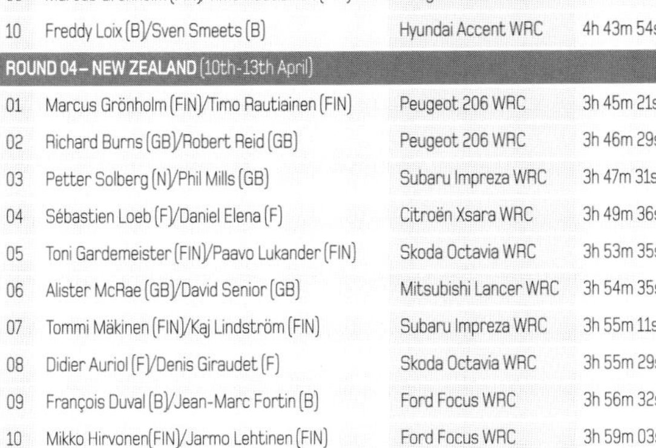

ROUND 04 – NEW ZEALAND (10th-13th April)

01	Marcus Grönholm (FIN)/Timo Rautiainen (FIN)	Peugeot 206 WRC	3h 45m 21s
02	Richard Burns (GB)/Robert Reid (GB)	Peugeot 206 WRC	3h 46m 29s
03	Petter Solberg (N)/Phil Mills (GB)	Subaru Impreza WRC	3h 47m 31s
04	Sébastien Loeb (F)/Daniel Elena (F)	Citroën Xsara WRC	3h 49m 36s
05	Toni Gardemeister (FIN)/Paavo Lukander (FIN)	Skoda Octavia WRC	3h 53m 35s
06	Alister McRae (GB)/David Senior (GB)	Mitsubishi Lancer WRC	3h 54m 35s
07	Tommi Mäkinen (FIN)/Kaj Lindström (FIN)	Subaru Impreza WRC	3h 55m 11s
08	Didier Auriol (F)/Denis Giraudet (F)	Skoda Octavia WRC	3h 55m 29s
09	François Duval (B)/Jean-Marc Fortin (B)	Ford Focus WRC	3h 56m 32s
10	Mikko Hirvonen (FIN)/Jarmo Lehtinen (FIN)	Ford Focus WRC	3h 59m 03s

Marcus Grönholm/Timo Rautiainen

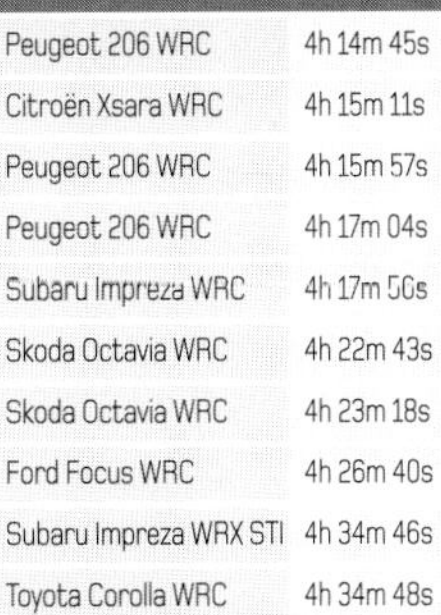

ROUND 05 – ARGENTINA (8th-11th May)

01	Marcus Grönholm (FIN)/Timo Rautiainen (FIN)	Peugeot 206 WRC	4h 14m 45s
02	Carlos Sainz (E)/Marc Marti (E)	Citroën Xsara WRC	4h 15m 11s
03	Richard Burns (GB)/Robert Reid (GB)	Peugeot 206 WRC	4h 15m 57s
04	Harri Rovanperä (FIN)/Risto Pietiläinen (FIN)	Peugeot 206 WRC	4h 17m 04s
05	Petter Solberg (N)/Phil Mills (GB)	Subaru Impreza WRC	4h 17m 56s
06	Didier Auriol (F)/Denis Giraudet (F)	Skoda Octavia WRC	4h 22m 43s
07	Toni Gardemeister (FIN)/Paavo Lukander (FIN)	Skoda Octavia WRC	4h 23m 18s
08	François Duval (B)/Jean-Marc Fortin (B)	Ford Focus WRC	4h 26m 40s
09	Toshi Arai (J)/Tony Sircombe (NZ)	Subaru Impreza WRX STI	4h 34m 46s
10	Gabriel Raies (RA)/Jorge Pérez (RA)	Toyota Corolla WRC	4h 34m 48s

Marcus Grönholm/Timo Rautiainen

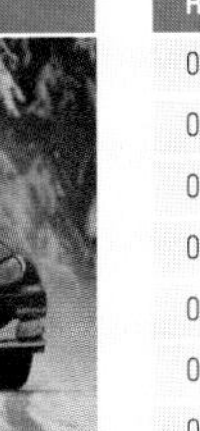

ROUND 06 – ACROPOLIS, GREECE (5th-8th June)

01	Markko Märtin (EE)/Michael Park (GB)	Ford Focus WRC	4h 53m 40s
02	Carlos Sainz (E)/Marc Marti (E)	Citroën Xsara WRC	4h 54m 26s
03	Petter Solberg (N)/Phil Mills (GB)	Subaru Impreza WRC	4h 54m 33s
04	Richard Burns (GB)/Robert Reid (GB)	Peugeot 206 WRC	4h 55m 47s
05	Tommi Mäkinen (FIN)/Kaj Lindström (FIN)	Subaru Impreza WRC	4h 55m 52s
06	Harri Rovanperä (FIN)/Risto Pietiläinen (FIN)	Peugeot 206 WRC	4h 57m 25s
07	Gilles Panizzi (F)/Hervé Panizzi (F)	Peugeot 206 WRC	4h 57m 34s
08	Colin McRae (GB)/Derek Ringer (GB)	Citroën Xsara WRC	4h 57m 45s
09	Didier Auriol (F)/Denis Giraudet (F)	Skoda Octavia WRC	5h 00m 07s
10	Jari-Matti Latvala (FIN)/Carl Williamson (GB)	Ford Focus WRC	5h 05m 13s

Markko Märtin/Michael Park

ROUND 07 – CYPRUS (19th-22nd June)

01	Petter Solberg (N)/Phil Mills (GB)	Subaru Impreza WRC	5h 09m 12s
02	Harri Rovanperä (FIN)/Risto Pietiläinen (FIN)	Peugeot 206 WRC	5h 13m 26s
03	Sébastien Loeb (F)/Daniel Elena (F)	Citroën Xsara WRC	5h 13m 29s
04	Colin McRae (GB)/Derek Ringer (GB)	Citroën Xsara WRC	5h 13m 57s
05	Carlos Sainz (E)/Marc Marti (E)	Citroën Xsara WRC	5h 14m 54s
06	Mikko Hirvonen (FIN)/Jarmo Lehtinen (FIN)	Ford Focus WRC	5h 18m 11s
07	Armin Schwarz (D)/Manfred Hiemer (D)	Hyundai Accent WRC	5h 22m 41s
08	Alistair Ginley (GB)/Rory Kennedy (GB)	Ford Focus WRC	5h 33m 09s
09	Toshi Arai (J)/Tony Sircombe (NZ)	Subaru Impreza WRX STI	5h 39m 13s
10	Martin Rowe (GB)/Trevor Agnew (GB)	Subaru Impreza WRX STI	5h 42m 56s

Petter Solberg/Phil Mills

ROUND 08 – GERMANY (24th-27th July)

01	Sébastien Loeb (F)/Daniel Elena (F)	Citroën Xsara WRC	3h 46m 50s
02	Marcus Grönholm (FIN)/Timo Rautiainen (FIN)	Peugeot 206 WRC	3h 46m 54s
03	Richard Burns (GB)/Robert Reid (GB)	Peugeot 206 WRC	3h 47m 10s
04	Colin McRae (GB)/Derek Ringer (GB)	Citroën Xsara WRC	3h 47m 21s
05	Markko Märtin (EE)/Michael Park (GB)	Ford Focus WRC	3h 47m 48s
06	Carlos Sainz (E)/Marc Marti (E)	Citroën Xsara WRC	3h 48m 29s
07	François Duval (B)/Stéphane Prévot (B)	Ford Focus WRC	3h 48m 38s
08	Petter Solberg (N)/Phil Mills (GB)	Subaru Impreza WRC	3h 49m 20s
09	Cédric Robert (F)/Gérald Bedon (F)	Peugeot 206 WRC	3h 50m 03s
10	Gilles Panizzi (F)/Hervé Panizzi (F)	Peugeot 206 WRC	3h 50m 30s

Sébastien Loeb/Daniel Elena

ROUND 09 – FINLAND (7th-10th August)

01	Markko Märtin (EE)/Michael Park (GB)	Ford Focus WRC	3h 21m 51s
02	Petter Solberg (N)/Phil Mills (GB)	Subaru Impreza WRC	3h 22m 50s
03	Richard Burns (GB)/Robert Reid (GB)	Peugeot 206 WRC	3h 22m 51s
04	Carlos Sainz (E)/Marc Martí (E)	Citroën Xsara WRC	3h 23m 50s
05	Sébastien Loeb (F)/Daniel Elena (F)	Citroën Xsara WRC	3h 24m 40s
06	Tommi Mäkinen (FIN)/Kaj Lindström (FIN)	Subaru Impreza WRC	3h 25m 16s
07	Janne Tuohino (FIN)/Jukka Aho (FIN)	Ford Focus WRC	3h 26m 14
08	Sebastian Lindholm (FIN)/Timo Hantunen (FIN)	Peugeot 206 WRC	3h 26m 31s
09	Juuso Pykälistö (FIN)/Esko Mertsalmi (FIN)	Peugeot 206 WRC	3h 28m 15s
10	Freddy Loix (B)/Sven Smeets (B)	Hyundai Accent WRC	3h 30m 11s

Markko Märtin/Michael Park

ROUND 10 – AUSTRALIA (4th-7th September)

01	Petter Solberg (N)/Phil Mills (GB)	Subaru Impreza WRC	3h 32m 07s
02	Sébastien Loeb (F)/Daniel Elena (F)	Citroën Xsara WRC	3h 32m 33s
03	Richard Burns (GB)/Robert Reid (GB)	Peugeot 206 WRC	3h 34m 00s
04	Colin McRae (GB)/Derek Ringer (GB)	Citroën Xsara WRC	3h 34m 37s
05	Carlos Sainz (E)/Marc Martí (E)	Citroën Xsara WRC	3h 34m 44s
06	Tommi Mäkinen (FIN)/Kaj Lindström (FIN)	Subaru Impreza WRC	3h 35m 08s
07	Harri Rovanperä (FIN)/Risto Pietiläinen (FIN)	Peugeot 206 WRC	3h 36m 11s
08	Freddy Loix (B)/Sven Smeets (B)	Hyundai Accent WRC	3h 39m 07s
09	Mikko Hirvonen (FIN)/Jarmo Lehtinen (FIN)	Ford Focus WRC	3h 39m 17s
10	François Duval (B)/Stéphane Prévot (B)	Ford Focus WRC	3h 39m 53s

Petter Solberg/Phil Mills

ROUND 11 – SANREMO, ITALY (2nd-5th October)

01	Sébastien Loeb (F)/Daniel Elena (F)	Citroën Xsara WRC	4h 16m 33s
02	Gilles Panizzi (F)/Hervé Panizzi (F)	Peugeot 206 WRC	4h 17m 02s
03	Markko Märtin (EE)/Michael Park (GB)	Ford Focus WRC	4h 17m 28s
04	Carlos Sainz (E)/Marc Martí (E)	Citroën Xsara WRC	4h 19m 06s
05	François Duval (B)/Stéphane Prévot (B)	Ford Focus WRC	4h 20m 32s
06	Colin McRae (GB)/Derek Ringer (GB)	Citroën Xsara WRC	4h 20m 57s
07	Richard Burns (GB)/Robert Reid (GB)	Peugeot 206 WRC	4h 23m 43s
08	Philippe Bugalski (F)/Jean-Paul Chiaroni (F)	Citroën Xsara WRC	4h 23m 46s
09	Cédric Robert (F)/Gérald Bedon (F)	Peugeot 206 WRC	4h 23m 59s
10	Tommi Mäkinen (FIN)/Kaj Lindström (FIN)	Subaru Impreza WRC	4h 24m 05s

Sébastien Loeb/Daniel Elena

ROUND 12 – CORSICA, FRANCE (16th-19th October)

01	Petter Solberg (N)/Phil Mills (GB)	Subaru Impreza WRC	4h 20m 15s
02	Carlos Sainz (E)/Marc Martí (E)	Citroën Xsara WRC	4h 20m 51s
03	François Duval (B)/Stéphane Prévot (B)	Ford Focus WRC	4h 20m 57s
04	Marcus Grönholm (FIN)/Timo Rautiainen (FIN)	Peugeot 206 WRC	4h 21m 24s
05	Colin McRae (GB)/Derek Ringer (GB)	Citroën Xsara WRC	4h 21m 41s
06	Gilles Panizzi (F)/Hervé Panizzi (F)	Peugeot 206 WRC	4h 22m 14s
07	Tommi Mäkinen (FIN)/Kaj Lindström (FIN)	Subaru Impreza WRC	4h 22m 41s
08	Richard Burns (GB)/Robert Reid (GB)	Peugeot 206 WRC	4h 22m 52s
09	Philippe Bugalski (F)/Jean-Paul Chiaroni (F)	Citroën Xsara WRC	4h 23m 02s
10	Mikko Hirvonen (FIN)/Jarmo Lehtinen (FIN)	Ford Focus WRC	4h 24m 10s

Petter Solberg/Phil Mills

ROUND 13 – CATALUNYA, SPAIN (23rd-26th October)

01	Gilles Panizzi (F)/Hervé Panizzi (F)	Peugeot 206 WRC	3h 55m 09s
02	Sébastien Loeb (F)/Daniel Elena (F)	Citroën Xsara WRC	2h 55m 22s
03	Markko Märtin (EE)/Michael Park (GB)	Ford Focus WRC	3h 55m 23s
04	François Duval (B)/Stéphane Prévot (B)	Ford Focus WRC	3h 56m 04s
05	Petter Solberg (N)/Phil Mills (GB)	Subaru Impreza WRC	3h 56m 20s
06	Marcus Grönholm (FIN)/Timo Rautiainen (FIN)	Peugeot 206 WRC	3h 56m 38s
07	Carlos Sainz (E)/Marc Martí (E)	Citroën Xsara WRC	3h 56m 52s
08	Tommi Mäkinen (FIN)/Kaj Lindström (FIN)	Subaru Impreza WRC	3h 57m 04s
09	Colin McRae (GB)/Derek Ringer (GB)	Citroën Xsara WRC	3h 58m 24s
10	Philippe Bugalski (F)/Jean-Paul Chiaroni (F)	Citroën Xsara WRC	4h 00m 23s

Gilles Panizzi/Hervé Panizzi

ROUND 14 – GREAT BRITAIN (6th-9th November)

01	Petter Solberg (N)/Phil Mills (GB)	Subaru Impreza WRC	3h 28m 58s
02	Sébastien Loeb (F)/Daniel Elena (F)	Citroën Xsara WRC	3h 29m 41s
03	Tommi Mäkinen (FIN)/Kaj Lindström (FIN)	Subaru Impreza WRC	3h 31m 56s
04	Colin McRae (GB)/Derek Ringer (GB)	Citroën Xsara WRC	3h 34m 26s
05	François Duval (B)/Stéphane Prévot (B)	Ford Focus WRC	3h 36m 14s
06	Freddy Loix (B)/Sven Smeets (B)	Peugeot 206 WRC	3h 37m 04s
07	Manfred Stohl (A)/Ilka Minor (A)	Peugeot 206 WRC	3h 37m 46s
08	Roman Kresta (CZ)/Jan Tomanek (CZ)	Peugeot 206 WRC	3h 38m 00s
09	Juuso Pykalisto (FIN)/Risto Mannisenmaki (FIN)	Peugeot 206 WRC	3h 38m 51s
10	Jari-Matti Latvala (FIN)/Mika Antilla (FIN)	Ford Focus WRC	3h 41m 23s

Petter Solberg/Phil Mills

FINAL DRIVERS' CHAMPIONSHIP POSITIONS

01	Petter Solberg	72
02	Sebastien Loeb	71
03	Carlos Sainz	63
04	Richard Burns	58
05	Markko Martin	49
06	Marcus Gronholm	46
07	Colin McRae	45
08	François Duval	30
08=	Tommi Makinen	30
10	Gilles Panizzi	27

FINAL MANUFACTURERS' CHAMPIONSHIP POSITIONS

01	Citroen	160
02	Peugeot	145
03	Subaru	109
04	Ford	93
05	Skoda	23
06	Hyundai	12

Thanks to Kathy Ager, Tim Clarke, John Davenport, Martin Holmes, Reinhard Klein, Bob McCaffrey, Colin McMaster, Keith Oswin, Maurice Selden, Alistair Staley, Jon Tingle, Tjeerd van der Zee (www.rallybase.com), Kevin Wood, Tim Wright